PRODUCING RESULTS WITH THE MANAGEMENT PROCESS

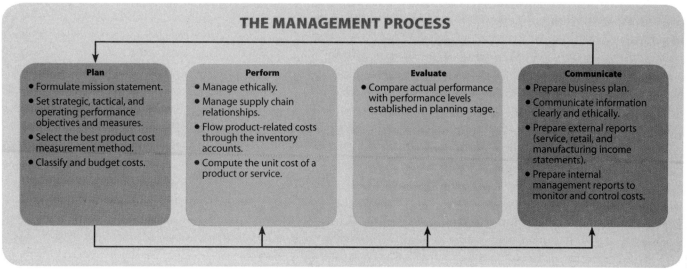

THE MANAGEMENT PROCESS

Plan
- Formulate mission statement.
- Set strategic, tactical, and operating performance objectives and measures.
- Select the best product cost measurement method.
- Classify and budget costs.

Perform
- Manage ethically.
- Manage supply chain relationships.
- Flow product-related costs through the inventory accounts.
- Compute the unit cost of a product or service.

Evaluate
- Compare actual performance with performance levels established in planning stage.

Communicate
- Prepare business plan.
- Communicate information clearly and ethically.
- Prepare external reports (service, retail, and manufacturing income statements).
- Prepare internal management reports to monitor and control costs.

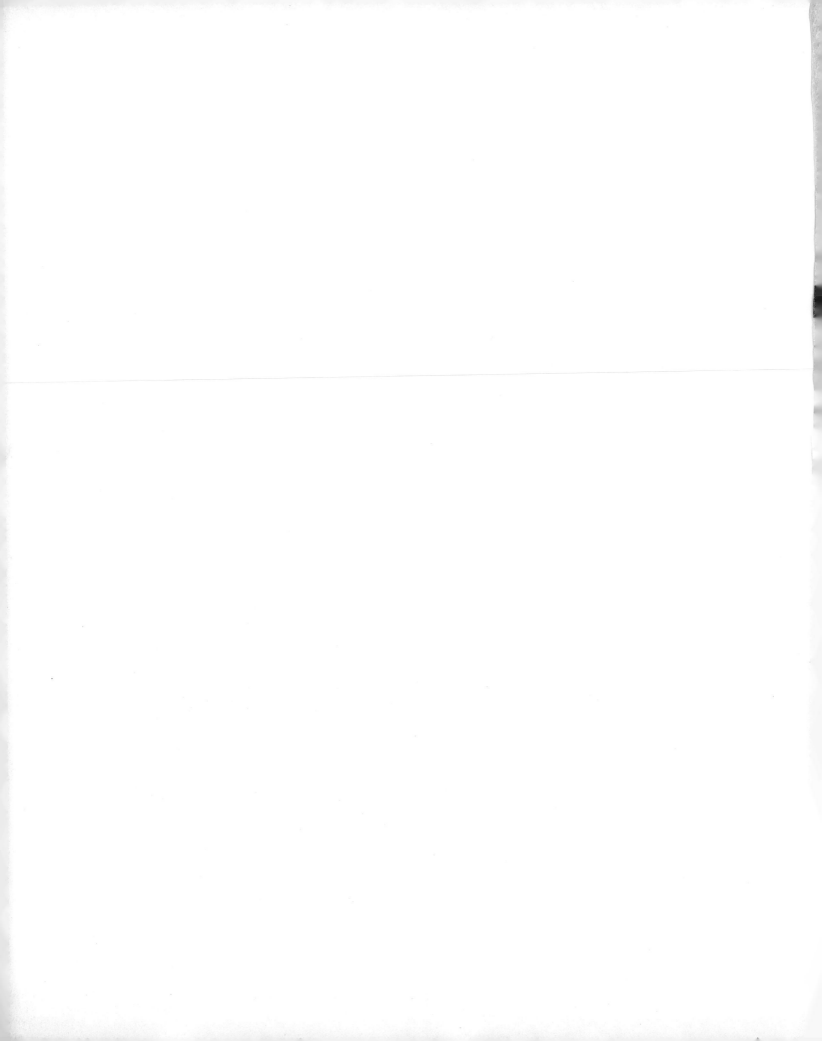

Managerial Accounting

TENTH EDITION

Susan V. Crosson, M.S. Accounting, C.P.A.

Emory University

Belverd E. Needles, Jr., Ph.D., C.P.A., C.M.A.

DePaul University

SOUTH-WESTERN
CENGAGE Learning·

Australia · Brazil · Japan · Korea · Mexico · Singapore · Spain · United Kingdom · United States

SOUTH-WESTERN
CENGAGE Learning·

Managerial Accounting, 10e

Susan Crosson and Belverd Needles

Senior Vice President, LRS/Acquisitions &
    Solutions Planning: Jack W. Calhoun

Editorial Director, Business & Economics:
    Erin Joyner

Editor-in-Chief: Rob Dewey

Executive Editor: Sharon Oblinger

Development Editor: Krista Kellman

Editorial Assistant: A.J. Smiley

Sr. Brand Manager: Kristen Hurd

Sr. Market Development Manager:
    Natalie Livingston

Sr. Marketing Communications Manager:
    Sarah Greber

Marketing Coordinator: Eileen Corcoran

Sr. Content Project Manager: Scott Dillon

Media Editor: Lysa Kosins

Manufacturing Planner: Doug Wilke

Production Service: Cenveo Publisher Services

Sr. Art Director: Stacy Jenkins Shirley

Internal and Cover Designer: Craig Ramsdell

Cover Image: © Martin Marraud/Getty Images

Rights Acquisition Director: Audrey Pettengill

Exam*View*® is a registered trademark of eInstruction Corp.

The financial statements are included for illustrative and education purposes only.
Nothing herein should be construed as financial advice.

Except where otherwise noted, all content in this title is © Cengage Learning.

Library of Congress Control Number: 2012956556

ISBN-13: 978-1-133-94059-3
ISBN-10: 1-133-94059-5

South-Western
5191 Natorp Boulevard
Mason, OH 45040
USA

Cengage Learning is a leading provider of customized learning solutions with office
locations around the globe, including Singapore, the United Kingdom, Australia,
Mexico, Brazil, and Japan. Locate your local office at: **www.cengage.com/global**

Cengage Learning products are represented in Canada by Nelson Education, Ltd.

For your course and learning solutions, visit **www.cengage.com**
Purchase any of our products at your local college store or at our
preferred online store **www.cengagebrain.com**

Printed in the United States of America
2 3 4 5 6 7 18 17 16

BRIEF CONTENTS

CONTENTS

CHAPTER 6 **The Budgeting Process** 199

CHAPTER 7 **Flexible Budgets and Performance Analysis** 247

We talked to over 150 instructors and discovered that current textbooks did not effectively:

- Help students logically process information
- Build on what students already know in a carefully guided sequence
- Reinforce core accounting concepts throughout the chapters
- Help students see how the pieces of accounting fit together

Crosson/Needles addresses these challenges by creating a better solution for you. This includes new features and a brand new structure for enhanced learning.

We have worked hard to create a textbook that mirrors the way you learn!

A LOGICAL METHODOLOGY TO BUILDING KNOWLEDGE:
THE THREE SECTION APPROACH

Crosson/Needles continuously evolves to meet the needs of today's learner. As a result of our research, the chapters have been organized into a **Three Section Approach**, which helps students more easily digest the content.

ThreeSection
APPROACH

❶ The first section is **Concepts** and focuses on the overarching accounting concepts that require consistent reiteration throughout the course.

❷ With a clear understanding of the concepts, you can proceed to the second section, **Accounting Applications**. Here, you can practice the application of accounting procedures with features like "Apply It!".

❸ Finally, move to section three, **Business Applications**. This section illustrates how the concepts and procedures are used to make business decisions. Real company examples are used throughout the chapter to show the relevance of accounting.

"I think this new chapter structure would be much easier for students to read and comprehend."

Shannon Ogden
Black River Technical College

TriLevel
PROBLEM

TriLevel Problems within CengageNOW mirror the Three Section Approach and connect the sections—Concepts, Accounting Applications, and Business Applications. In this way, the problems teach you to think holistically about an accounting issue.

Breaking Down the Three Section Approach

SECTION 1: CONCEPTS ➡

In Section 1, students experience the **Concepts** related to each chapter. In this case, *concepts* are the overarching accounting concepts that need to be reinforced throughout the accounting course, such as measurement, recognition, the matching rule, and classification.

Every chapter's Section 1 reinforces these key concepts so that once students understand the concepts, they can apply them to every aspect of the management process—from planning to performing to evaluating to communicating information about a business. This is a clear and logical way to present accounting.

SECTION 1   CONCEPTS

CONCEPTS
- Comparability
- Understandability

RELEVANT LEARNING OBJECTIVE

LO 1 Define *budgeting* and describe how it relates to the concepts of comparability and understandability.

LO 1 Concepts Underlying the Budgeting Process

Budgeting is the process of identifying, gathering, summarizing, and communicating financial and nonfinancial information about an organization's future activities. The budgeting process provides managers of all types of organizations the opportunity to match their organizational goals with the resources necessary to accomplish those goals. Budgeting empowers all in the organization to understand organizational goals in terms of their responsibilities and be held accountable for budget plans and results since they can be compared. Budgeting is synonymous with managing an organization. **Budgets** are plans of action based on forecasted transactions, activities, and events.

The concepts of *understandability* and *comparability* underlie the power of budgeting. Budgeting enhances *understandability*, since managers and employees will understand their organizational roles and responsibilities based on how the budget links the organization's strategic plans to its annual plans. Because the budget expresses these plans and objectives in concrete monetary terms, managers and employees are able to understand and act in ways that will achieve them. Budgeting enhances *comparability*,

"It does a very good job in explaining each concept and reinforcing each one by giving specific examples."

Paul Jaijairam
Bronx Community College

SECTION 2: ACCOUNTING APPLICATIONS

In Section 2, students learn the accounting procedures and the technical **application** of concepts. Students can apply the fundamental concepts they have already learned in Section 1. Section 2 includes things like building budgets and creating schedules and reports.

SECTION 2

ACCOUNTING APPLICATIONS

- Prepare operating budgets
  - Sales budget
  - Production budget
  - Direct materials purchases budget
  - Direct labor budget
  - Overhead budget
  - Selling and administrative expenses budget
  - Cost of goods manufactured budget
- Prepare financial budgets
  - Budgeted income statement
  - Cash budget
  - Budgeted balance sheet

RELEVANT LEARNING OBJECTIVES

LO2 Identify the elements of a master budget in different types of organizations and the guidelines for preparing budgets.

ACCOUNTING APPLICATIONS

LO2 Preparation of a Master Budget

Exhibits 1, 2, and 3 display the elements of a master budget for a manufacturing organization, a retail organization, and a service organization, respectively. As these illustrations indicate, the process of preparing a master budget is similar in all three types of organizations in that each prepares a set of operating budgets that serve as the basis for preparing the financial budgets. The sales budget (or, in service organizations, the service revenue budget) is prepared first because it is used to estimate sales volume and revenues. Once managers know the quantity of products or services to be sold and how many sales dollars to expect, they can develop other budgets that will enable them to manage their resources so that they generate profits on those sales.

Exhibit 1
Preparation of a Master Budget for a Manufacturing Organization

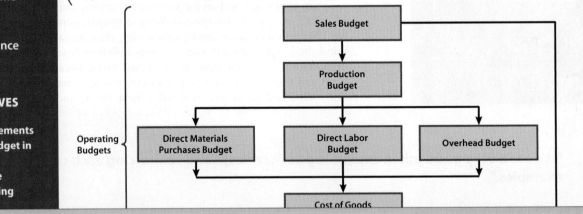

"Section 2 walks through the accounting procedures very well. I like the use of a visual plus the narrative to explain the procedures."

Gerald Childs
Waukesha County Technical College

SECTION 3: BUSINESS APPLICATIONS

With a solid foundation of the fundamental accounting concepts as well as how to apply these concepts when performing accounting procedures, students are now ready for Section 3: **Business Applications**. This section teaches students how managerial accounting information is used to make business decisions.

SECTION 3   BUSINESS APPLICATIONS

BUSINESS APPLICATIONS
- Planning
- Performing
- Evaluating
- Communicating

RELEVANT LEARNING OBJECTIVE

LO 5 Explain why budgeting is essential to the management process.

LO 5   Budgeting and the Management Process

Budgets are essential to accomplishing an organization's strategic plan. They are used to communicate understandable information, coordinate activities and resource usage, motivate employees, and provide comparative information to evaluate performance. For example, a board of directors may use budgets to determine managers' areas of responsibility and to measure managers' performance in those areas. Budgets are also used to manage and account for cash.

Advantages of Budgeting

Budgeting is advantageous for organizations, because budgets:

- foster organizational communication
- ensure a focus both on future events and on resolving day-to-day issues
- assign resources and the responsibility to use them wisely to managers who are held accountable for their results
- can identify potential constraints before they become problems
- facilitate congruence between organizational and personal goals
- define organizational goals and objectives numerically, against which actual performance results can be evaluated

Budgeting and Goals

Budgeting helps managers achieve both long-term and short-term goals.

Long-Term Goals   **Strategic planning** is the process by which management establishes an organization's long-term goals. These goals define the direction that an organization will take and are the basis for making annual operating plans and preparing budgets. Long-term goals cannot be vague. They must set specific tactical targets and timetables and assign responsibility to specific personnel. For example, a long-term goal for a company that currently holds only 4 percent of its product's market share might specify that the vice president of marketing is to develop strategies to ensure that the company controls 10 percent of the market in five years and 15 percent by the end of ten years.

"This is a nice and useful touch to help students tie everything together. The theory can be dry at times, so this recap helps engage the students' attention again."

Dennis Mullen
City College of San Francisco

EXAMPLES, ACTIVITIES, AND PRACTICE

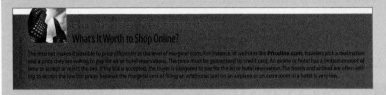

What's It Worth to Shop Online?

The Internet makes it possible to price efficiently at the level of marginal costs. For instance, at websites like **Priceline.com**, travelers pick a destination and a price they are willing to pay for air or hotel reservations. The price must be guaranteed by credit card. An airline or hotel has a limited amount of time to accept or reject the bid. If the bid is accepted, the buyer is obligated to pay for the air or hotel reservation. The hotels and airlines are often willing to accept the low bid prices because the marginal cost of filling an additional seat on an airplane or an extra room in a hotel is very low.

◀ **Business Perspective**

Throughout the chapter, **Business Perspective** features keep students engaged by providing real business context and examples from well-known companies, including **Google**, **CVS**, **Boeing**, **Ford Motor Company**, **Microsoft**, **L.L. Bean**, and **The Walt Disney Company**.

BUSINESS INSIGHT
Framerica Corporation

Framerica Corporation is one of the leading manufacturers of picture frames in North America. Because the company believes its work force is its most valuable asset, one of its priorities is to help employees attain their personal goals. One highly effective way of achieving congruence between a company's goals and its employees' personal aspirations is through a participatory budgeting process—an ongoing dialogue that involves personnel at all levels of the company in making budgeting decisions. This ongoing dialogue provides both managers and lower-level employees with insight into the company's current activities and future direction and motivates them to improve their performance, which, in turn, improves the company's performance.

1. CONCEPT ▶ *What concepts underlie the usefulness of the budgeting process?*

2. ACCOUNTING APPLICATION ▶ *How does the budgeting process translate long-term goals into operating objectives?*

3. BUSINESS APPLICATION ▶ *Why are budgets an essential part of planning, controlling, evaluating, and reporting on business?*

TriLevel Problem

Framerica Corporation

The beginning of this chapter focused on **Framerica Corporation**. One of Framerica's priorities is to help employees attain personal goals. A participatory budgeting process is a highly effective way to achieve goal congruence between a company's goals and objectives and employee personal aspirations. Complete the following requirements in order to answer the questions posed at the beginning of the chapter.

Section 1: Concepts
What concepts underlie the usefulness of the budgeting process?

Section 2: Accounting Applications
How does the budgeting process translate long-term goals into operating objectives?
     Assume Framerica has an Information Processing Division that provides database management services for the professional photographers and artists who buy its frames. Suppose the division uses state-of-the-art equipment and employs five information specialists. Each specialist works an average of 160 hours a month. Assume the division's controller has compiled the following information:

Business Insight and TriLevel Problems ▲

Each chapter opens with a **Business Insight** that shows how a small company would use accounting information to make decisions. The Business Insight poses three questions—each of which will be answered in one of the three sections of the chapter. At the end of each chapter, the **TriLevel Problem** revisits the Business Insight company to tie the three sections together.

Apply It! and Try It! ▶

Apply It! activities throughout the chapter illustrate and solve a short exercise and then reference end-of-chapter assignments where students can go to **Try It!** This provides students with an example to reference as they are working to complete homework, making getting started less intimidating.

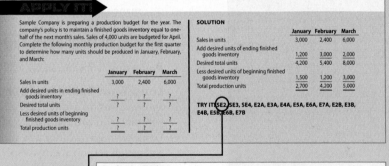

APPLY IT!

Sample Company is preparing a production budget for the year. The company's policy is to maintain a finished goods inventory equal to one-half of the next month's sales. Sales of 4,000 units are budgeted for April. Complete the following monthly production budget for the first quarter to determine how many units should be produced in January, February, and March:

	January	February	March
Sales in units	3,000	2,400	6,000
Add desired units in ending finished goods inventory	?	?	?
Desired total units	?	?	?
Less desired units of beginning finished goods inventory	?	?	?
Total production units	?	?	?

SOLUTION

	January	February	March
Sales in units	3,000	2,400	6,000
Add desired units of ending finished goods inventory	1,200	3,000	2,000
Desired total units	4,200	5,400	8,000
Less desired units of beginning finished goods inventory	1,500	1,200	3,000
Total production units	2,700	4,200	5,000

TRY IT! SE2, SE3, SE4, E2A, E3A, E4A, E5A, E6A, E7A, E2B, E3B, E4B, E5B, E6B, E7B

Production Budget

SE2. Windsor Lock Company's controller is preparing a production budget for the year. The company's policy is to maintain a finished goods inventory equal to one-half of the following month's sales. Sales of 5,000 locks are budgeted for April. Complete the monthly production budget for the first quarter:

TriLevel

PROBLEM

NEW TriLevel Problems within CengageNOW follow the same Three Section Approach the book employs by including *Concepts, Accounting Applications,* and *Business Applications*. The problems reinforce and apply overarching concepts while also tying the three sections together to give students a complete understanding.

Transaction Analysis

The process of assigning business transactions to accounts is called [Select ▾].

One of the most important classification issues in accounting is the difference between an asset and their cost is classified as an [Select ▾]. If the items will be used in the future, they are classified as

Travis Services is an office cleaning company. Consider Travis Services' transactions during its first mo

(a)	Received cash from Stanley Travis, in exchange for stock, $18,680.
(b)	Performed services for a client on account, $6,530.
(c)	Purchased equipment with cash, $12,920.
(d)	Performed services for a customer who paid cash, $7,150.
(e)	Purchased supplies with cash, $3,480.

Use the following T accounts to record these transactions. You will need to record the transactions in bottom) on the debit or credit side of the T account, whichever is appropriate.

Cash	Accounts Receivable	Supplies

Equipment	Fees Earned	Common Stock

As supplies are used, Travis Services debits Supplies Expense and credits Supplies.

Stanley Travis would like to charge Supplies Expense when the supplies are purchased. He wants to

  a. "Great idea. By increasing expenses Travis Services income is lowered and that translates to lo
  b. "Accounting rules dictate that purchases that are consumed in future periods be classified as a
    purposes."

© Cengage Learning 2014

"Any time the students are engaged in the learning process and have to actively participate, I think they enhance their retention of the material. The ability to relate this to an actual company (whether real or not) allows students to see this information in practice."

Chuck Smith
Iowa Western Community College

96% of instructors surveyed said that the TriLevel Problem adequately coached students through thinking about an issue.

"The [TriLevel Problem] links procedure to the creation and use of information, and closes that loop between what students are doing and why it is useful."

Andy Williams
Edmonds Community College

"It reviews everything students have learned in a format they will find useful, and it links the three areas together. I love this. Each one ending with a business application."

Joan Ryan
Clackamas Community College

NEW Blueprint Problems ▶

In CengageNOW, these problems cover primary learning objectives and help students understand the fundamental accounting concepts and their associated building blocks—not just memorize the formulas required for a single concept. *Blueprint Problems* include rich feedback and explanations, providing students with an excellent learning resource.

Blueprint Problem: Predetermined, overapplied, and underapplied overhead

The Nature of Overhead

Recall that unit costs include direct materials, direct labor, and overhead. The costs for direct materials and dir...
production or sales, and some overhead costs are unknown until the end of the period or early in the next per...
to determine unit costs, because overhead costs are not always directly related to units produced. Therefore,...
the beginning of the year, and applied to production throughout the year. This requires three steps:

1. Calculate the predetermined overhead rate.
2. Apply the overhead throughout the year.
3. Reconcile the applied and actual overhead at the end of the year.

Predetermined Overhead Rate

The overhead costs are allocated to jobs using a common measure related to each job. This measure is called...
should reflect the consumption or use of the overhead costs. There are basically three types of drivers (or acti...

To calculate the predetermined overhead rate, you must first estimate the overhead costs for the year, as wel...

Match the type of driver with its cause.

Driver	Cause
1. Volume:	Select ⌄
2. Time:	Select ⌄
3. Cost:	Select ⌄

Disposal of Fixed Assets

When a fixed asset is being disposed of (sold or discarded), an entry to record depreciation will most likely be necessary before recording the disposal of the asset,
since the last depreciation entry for the asset, unless the amount of time is insignificant, such as a few days.

An entry for depreciation will:

- Select ⌄ total expenses for the current period.
- Select ⌄ the book value of the asset.
- Select ⌄ the gain/loss calculation for the asset disposal.

After depreciation has been recorded (if necessary), any gain or loss is calculated and then the journal entry
2007. The purchase price was $50,000, the residual value was determined to be $5,000 and the useful life w
company disposed of the asset on July 1, 2009. Depreciation of $4,500 was recorded on that day, resulting i
independent scenarios. The gain/loss calculation and journal entry to record the disposal under each scenari

Cash received: $0 $24,750 $27,500 $30,000

        Scenario A   Scenario B   Scenario C   Scenario D

Scenario A: Gain/loss calculation:

Original cost, January 1, 2007	$50,000
Less: Accumulated depreciation (as of July 1, 2009)	22,500
Book value, July 1, 2009	$27,500
Cash received	0
Loss on disposal of asset	$27,500

Asset disposal entry on July 1, 2009:

Accumulated Depreciation–Machine	22,500	
Loss on Disposal of Asset	27,500	
Machine		50,000

© Cengage Learning 2014

NEW Blueprint Connections ▲

Blueprint Connections in CengageNOW build upon concepts covered and introduced within the *Blueprint Problems*. These scenario-based exercises help reinforce students' knowledge of the concept.

NEW Animated Activities ▶

Animated Activities in CengageNOW are videos that guide students through selected core topics using a realistic company example to illustrate how the concepts relate to the everyday activities of a business.

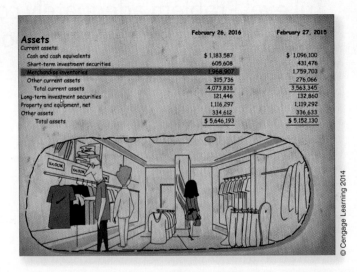

Assets	February 26, 2016	February 27, 2015
Current assets:		
Cash and cash equivalents	$ 1,183,587	$ 1,096,100
Short-term investment securities	605,608	431,476
Merchandise inventories	1,968,907	1,759,703
Other current assets	315,736	276,066
Total current assets	4,073,838	3,563,345
Long-term investment securities	121,446	132,860
Property and equipment, net	1,116,297	1,119,292
Other assets	334,612	336,633
Total assets	$ 5,646,193	$ 5,152,130

© Cengage Learning 2014

NEW Check My Work Feedback ▼

Written feedback is now available when students click on "Check My Work" in CengageNOW to provide students with valuable guidance as they work through homework items.

Incorrect

▼ Additional Feedback

Rework the formula above to solve for Fixed Costs:

Fixed Costs = Sales - Variable Costs - Operating Income

Now consider what happens to this formula when Operating Income is equal to zero.

© Cengage Learning 2014

NEW Post-submission Feedback ▼

After students have submitted their assignments for a grade in CengageNOW, they can go back and see the correct answers to better understand where they might have gotten off track.

▼ Hide Feedback   ×

Incorrect

▼ Additional Feedback
a. Sales minus sales returns and allowances and minus sales discounts equals net sales.
b. Net sales minus the cost of merchandise sold equals gross profit.
c. Gross profit minus operating expenses minus other revenue and expenses equals net income.

▼ Solution
Correct Response

[ ] eBook

Exercise 6-3
Income Statement for Merchandiser

For the fiscal year, **sales** were $6,750,000, **sales discounts** were $120,000, **sales returns and allowances** were $90,000, and the **cost of merchandise sold** was $4,000,000.

a. What was the amount of **net sales**?
$ 6540000

b. What was the amount of **gross profit**?
$ 2540000

c. If total operating expenses were $1,200,000, could you determine net income?
No, there could be separately reported "other income" and "other expense" items [▼]

© Cengage Learning 2014

NEW Apply It Demos
These demonstration videos in CengageNOW will help students complete end-of-chapter questions from Section 2.

ACKNOWLEDGMENTS

In developing and refining the tenth edition of *Managerial Accounting*, we wanted to ensure that we were creating a textbook that truly reflected the way we teach accounting. To do so, we asked for feedback from over 150 professors, other professional colleagues, and students. We want to recognize those who made special contributions to our efforts in preparing this edition through their reviews, suggestions, and participation in surveys, interviews, and focus groups. We cannot begin to say how grateful we are for the feedback from the many instructors who have generously shared their responses and teaching experiences with us.

John G. Ahmad, *Northern Virginia Community College*
Robert Almon, *South Texas College*
Elizabeth Ammann, *Lindenwood University*
Paul Andrew, *SUNY, Morrisville*
Ryan Andrew, *Columbia College Chicago*
Sidney Askew, *Borough of Manhattan Community College*
Joe Atallah, *Irvine Valley College*
Shele Bannon, *Queensborough Community College*
Michael Barendse, *Grossmont College*
Beverly R. Beatty, *Anne Arundel Community College*
Robert Beebe, *Morrisville State College*
Teri Bernstein, *Santa Monica College*
Cynthia Bird, *Tidewater Community College*
David B. Bojarsky, *California State University*
Linda Bolduc, *Mount Wachusett Community College*
John Bongorno, *Cuyahoga Community College*
Anna Boulware, *St. Charles Community College*
Amy Bourne, *Oregon State University*
Thomas Branton, *Alvin Community College*
Billy Brewster, *University of Texas at Arlington*
Nina E. Brown, *Tarrant County College*
Tracy L. Bundy, *University of Louisiana at Lafayette*
Jacqueline Burke, *Hofstra University*
Marci L. Butterfield, *University of Utah*
Charles Caliendo, *University of Minnesota*
Gerald Childs, *Waukesha County Technical College*
James J. Chimenti, *Jamestown Community College*
Alice Chu, *Golden West College*
Sandra Cohen, *Columbia College*
Lisa Cole, *Johnson County Community College*
Debora Constable, *Georgia Perimeter College*
Barry Cooper, *Borough of Manhattan Community College*
Cheryl Copeland, *California State University, Fresno*
Susan Cordes, *Johnson County Community College*

Meg Costello, *Oakland Community College*
Richard Culp, *Ball State University*
Sue Cunningham, *Rowan Cabarrus Community College*
Robin D'Agati, *Palm Beach State College*
Emmanuel Danso, *Palm Beach State College*
Robert Derstine, *Kutztown University*
Michael Dole, *Marquette University*
Jap Efendi, *University of Texas at Arlington*
Dustin Emhart, *North Georgia Technical College*
Denise M. English, *Boise State University*
Michael Farina, *Cerritos College*
J. Thomas Franco, *Wayne County Community College*
Dean Gray, *Reedley College*
Timothy Green, *North Georgia Technical College*
Timothy Griffin, *Hillsborough Community College*
Teri Grimmer, *Portland Community College*
Michael J. Gurevitz, *Montgomery College*
Qian Hao, *Wilkes University*
Sara Harris, *Arapahoe Community College*
Syed Hasan, *George Mason University*
Wendy Heltzer, *DePaul University*
Merrily Hoffman, *San Jacinto College*
Shanelle Hopkins, *Carroll Community College*
David Hossain, *California State University, Los Angeles*
Phillip Imel, *NOVA Community College, Annadale*
ThankGod O. Imo, *Tompkins Cortland Community College*
Paul Jaijairam, *Bronx Community College*
Gene Johnson, *Clark College*
Howard A. Kanter, *DePaul University*
Irene Kim, *George Washington University*
Christopher Kinney, *Mount Wachusett Community College*
Gordon Klein, *University of California, Los Angeles*
Shirly A. Kleiner, *Johnson County Community College*
Leon Korte, *University of South Dakota*

Lynn Krausse, *Bakersfield College*

Les Kren, *University of Wisconsin, Milwaukee*

Donnie Kristof-Nelson, *Edmonds Community College*

Christopher Kwak, *De Anza College*

Richard Lau, *California State University, Los Angeles*

Suzanne R. Laudadio, *Durham Technical Community College*

George Leonard, *St. Petersburg College*

Lydia Leporte, *Tidewater Community College*

Hui Lin, *DePaul University*

Joseph Lipari, *Montclair State*

Xiang Liu, *California State University, San Bernardino*

Angelo Luciano, *Columbia College*

Susan Lueders, *DePaul University*

Cathy Lumbattis, *Southern Illinois University*

Sakthi Mahenthiran, *Butler University*

Eileen Marutzky, *DePaul University*

Robert Maxwell, *College of the Canyons*

Mark McCarthy, *DePaul University*

Clarice McCoy, *Brookhaven College*

Terra McGhee, *University of Texas at Arlington*

Florence McGovern, *Bergen Community College*

Cheryl McKay, *Monroe County Community College*

John McQuilkin, *Roger Williams University*

Jeanette Milius, *Iowa Western Community College*

Jeanne K. Miller, *Cypress College*

Rita Mintz, *Calhoun Community College*

Jill Mitchell, *Northern Virginia Community College, Annandale*

Odell Moon, *Victor Valley College*

Kathleen Moreno, *Abraham Baldwin Agricultural College*

Walter Moss, *Cuyahoga Community College*

Dennis Mullen, *City College of San Francisco*

Elizabeth A. Murphy, *DePaul University*

Penny Nunn, *Henderson Community College*

Christopher O'Byrne, *Cuyamaca College*

Shannon Ogden, *Black River Technical College*

Glenn Pate, *Palm Beach State College*

Sy Pearlman, *California State University, Long Beach*

Rama Ramamurthy, *College of William & Mary*

Lawrence A. Roman, *Cuyahoga Community College*

Gregg Romans, *Ivy Tech Community College*

Joan Ryan, *Clackamas Community College*

Donna B. Sanders, *Guilford Technical Community College*

Regina Schultz, *Mount Wachusett Community College*

Jay Semmel, *Broward College*

Andreas Simon, *California Polytechnic State University*

Jaye Simpson, *Tarrant County College*

Alice Sineath, *Forsyth Technical Community College*

Kimberly Sipes, *Kentucky State University*

Chuck Smith, *Iowa Western Community College*

Robert K. Smolin, *Citrus College*

Jennifer Sneed, *Arkansas State University, Newport*

Lyle Stelter, *Dakota County Technical College*

Rhonda Stone, *Black River Technical College*

Gracelyn Stuart-Tuggle, *Palm Beach State College – Boca Raton*

Linda Tarrago, *Hillsborough Community College*

Steve Teeter, *Utah Valley University*

Don Trippeer, *SUNY Oneonta*

Robert Urell, *Irvine Valley College*

La Vonda Ramey, *Schoolcraft College*

Patricia Walczak, *Lansing Community College*

Scott Wandler, *University of New Orleans*

Chris Widmer, *Tidewater Community College*

Andy Williams, *Edmonds Community College*

Wanda Wong, *Chabot College*

Ronald Zhao, *Monmouth University*

Teri Zuccaro, *Clarke University*

We also wish to express deep appreciation to colleagues at Santa Fe Community College, Emory University, and DePaul University, who have been extremely supportive and encouraging.

Finally, very important to the quality of this book are our Developmental Editor, Krista Kellman; Executive Editor, Sharon Oblinger; and Senior Brand Manager, Kristen Hurd.

Susan V. Crosson received her B.B.A. degree in economics and accounting from Southern Methodist University and her M.S. degree in accounting from Texas Tech University. She is currently teaching in the Goizueta Business School at Emory University in Atlanta, Georgia. Until recently, she was the Accounting Faculty Lead and Professor at Santa Fe College in Gainesville, Florida. She has also been on the faculty of the University of Florida; Washington University in St. Louis; University of Oklahoma; Johnson County Community College in Kansas; and Kansas City Kansas Community College. She is internationally known for her YouTube accounting videos as an innovative application of pedagogical strategies. In recognition of her professional and academic activities, she was a recipient of the Outstanding Service Award from the American Accounting Association (AAA), an Institute of Management Accountants' Faculty Development Grant to blend technology into the classroom, the Florida Association of Community Colleges Professor of the Year Award for Instructional Excellence, and the University of Oklahoma's Halliburton Education Award for Excellence. Currently, she serves as President of the Teaching, Learning, and Curriculum section of the AAA. Recently, she served as a Supply Chain Leader for The Commission on Accounting Higher Education, which published *"Pathways to a Profession," Charting a National Strategy for the Next Generation of Accountants*. She has also served on various committees for the AICPA, Florida Institute of CPAs, and the Florida Association of Accounting Educators.

Belverd E. Needles, Jr., received B.B.A. and M.B.A. degrees from Texas Tech University and his Ph.D. degree from the University of Illinois at Urbana-Champaign. He teaches financial accounting, managerial accounting, and auditing at DePaul University, where he is an internationally recognized expert in international accounting and education. He has published in leading journals and is the author or editor of more than 20 books and monographs. His current research relates to international financial reporting, performance measurement, and corporate governance of high-performance companies in the United States, Europe, India, and Australia. His textbooks are used throughout the world and have received many awards, including (in 2008) the McGuffey Award from the Text and Academic Authors Association. Active in many academic and professional organizations, he is immediate past Vice-President-Education of the American Accounting Association. He has received the Distinguished Alumni Award from Texas Tech University, the Illinois CPA Society Outstanding Educator Award and its Life-Time Achievement Award, the Joseph A. Silvoso Faculty Award of Merit from the Federation of Schools of Accountancy, the Ledger & Quill Award of Merit, and the Ledger & Quill Teaching Excellence Award. He was named Educator of the Year by the American Institute of CPAs, Accountant of the Year for Education by the national honorary society Beta Alpha Psi, and Outstanding International Accounting Educator by the American Accounting Association. He has received the Excellence in Teaching Award from DePaul University.

CHAPTER 1
Managerial Accounting and Cost Concepts

BUSINESS INSIGHT
The Hershey Company

With net sales in the billions, **The Hershey Company** does indeed fulfill its mission statement of "bringing sweet moments of Hershey happiness to the world every day." To continue achieving business results, Hershey's managers must know a lot about the costs of producing and selling its Reese's, KitKat, Twizzlers, Kisses, Jolly Rancher, Ice Breakers, and other products and be familiar with the managerial accounting concepts discussed in this chapter. Go to Hershey's website (www.hersheys.com) to have a tour of the world's largest chocolate factory and to view how various candy bar brands are made.

1. **CONCEPT** ▶ *How does managerial accounting recognize and define costs?*

2. **ACCOUNTING APPLICATION** ▶ *How do companies like Hershey determine the cost of a candy bar?*

3. **BUSINESS APPLICATION** ▶ *How does managerial accounting facilitate the management process as managers plan, organize, and control costs?*

LEARNING OBJECTIVES

LO 1 Distinguish managerial accounting from financial accounting.

LO 2 Explain how managers recognize costs and how they define product or service unit cost.

LO 3 Describe the flow of costs through a manufacturer's inventory accounts.

LO 4 Compare how service, retail, and manufacturing organizations report costs on their financial statements and how they account for inventories.

LO 5 Compute the unit cost of a product or service.

LO 6 Explain how managerial accounting supports the management process to produce business results.

LO 7 Identify the standards of ethical conduct for management accountants.

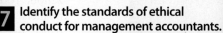

Jurchyks/Shutterstock

CONCEPTS
- Measurement
- Recognition
- Classification

RELEVANT LEARNING OBJECTIVES

LO 1 Distinguish managerial accounting from financial accounting.

LO 2 Explain how managers recognize costs and how they define product or service unit cost.

LO 1 The Role of Managerial Accounting

Both financial and managerial accounting reports adhere to the fundamental concepts of *cost measurement* and *recognition* when providing past, present, and future information about an organization's performance. Financial accounting reports follow strict guidelines defined by generally accepted accounting principles when reporting on past operations to external users. In contrast, to plan, control, and measure an organization's current and future operations and to make decisions about products or services, managers and other internal users rely on the information managerial accounting provides. The role of managerial accounting is to enable managers and people throughout an organization to:

- make informed decisions
- be more effective at their jobs
- improve the organization's performance

The Institute of Management Accountants (IMA) defines **managerial accounting** (or *management accounting*) as follows:

> *Management accounting is a profession that involves partnering in management decision making, devising planning and performance management systems, and providing expertise in financial reporting and control to assist management in the formulation and implementation of an organization's strategy.*[1]

This definition recognizes that regulation, globalization, and technology changes have redefined the management accountant's role to be a strategic partner within an organization. Today, managerial accounting information includes nonfinancial data as well as financial data in performance management, planning and budgeting, corporate governance, risk management, and internal controls.

Managerial Accounting and Financial Accounting: A Comparison

Both managerial accounting and financial accounting assist decision makers by identifying, measuring, processing, and communicating relevant information. Both provide managers with key measures of a company's performance and with cost information for valuing inventories on the balance sheet. However, managerial accounting and financial accounting differ in a number of ways, as summarized in Exhibit 1. Note that managerial accounting is not a subordinate activity to financial accounting. Rather, it is a process that includes financial accounting, tax accounting, information analysis, and other accounting activities.

The primary users of managerial accounting information are people inside the organization, whereas financial accounting prepares financial statements for parties outside the organization (owners or stockholders, lenders, customers, and governmental agencies). Although these reports are prepared primarily for external use, managers also rely on them in evaluating an organization's performance.

Because managerial accounting reports are for internal use, their format is driven by the user's needs. They may report either historical or future-oriented information without any formal guidelines or restrictions. That means that managerial accounting can use innovative analyses and presentation techniques to enhance the usefulness of information to people within the company. In contrast, financial accounting reports, which focus on past performance, must follow generally accepted accounting principles as specified by the Securities and Exchange Commission (SEC).

The information in managerial accounting reports may be objective and verifiable, expressed in monetary terms or in physical measures of time or objects; or they may be more subjective and based on estimates. In contrast, the statements that financial

Exhibit 1
Comparison of Managerial Accounting and Financial Accounting

Areas of Comparison	Managerial Accounting	Financial Accounting
Primary users	Managers, employees, supply-chain partners	Owners or stockholders, lenders, customers, governmental agencies
Report format	Flexible, driven by user's needs	Based on generally accepted accounting principles
Purpose of reports	Provide information for planning, control, performance measurement, and decision making	Provide information on past performance
Nature of information	Objective and verifiable for decision making; more subjective for planning (relies on estimates); confidential and private	Objective and verifiable; publicly available
Units of measure	Monetary at historical or current market or projected values; physical measures of time or number of objects	Monetary at historical or current market values
Frequency of reports	Prepared as needed; may or may not be on a periodic basis	Prepared on a periodic basis

© Cengage Learning 2014

accounting provides must be based on objective and verifiable information, which is generally historical and measured in monetary terms. Managerial accounting reports are prepared annually, quarterly, monthly, or even daily. Financial statements, on the other hand, are usually prepared and distributed on a quarterly and annual basis.

APPLY IT!

Indicate whether each of the characteristics that follows relates to managerial accounting (MA) or financial accounting (FA). (*Hint:* More than one answer may apply.)

a. Focuses on various segments of the business entity

b. Demands objectivity

c. Relies on the criterion of usefulness rather than formal guidelines in reporting information

d. Measures units in historical dollars

e. Reports information on a regular basis

f. Uses only monetary measures for reports

g. Adheres to generally accepted accounting principles

h. Prepares reports whenever needed

SOLUTION
a. MA; b. FA; c. MA; d. FA and MA; e. FA; f. FA; g. FA; h. MA

TRY IT! SE1

LO2 Concepts Underlying Costs

A key question for managers is "How much does it cost?" We begin by looking at how managers in different organizations *recognize* and *classify* information about costs.

Cost Recognition

In addition to *recognizing* costs for financial reporting, a single cost can be *classified* and used in several ways, depending on the purpose of the analysis. Exhibit 2 provides an overview of commonly used cost recognition classifications. These classifications enable managers to do the following:

■ Control costs by determining which are traceable to a particular cost object, such as a service or product.

■ Calculate the number of units that must be sold to achieve a certain level of profit (cost behavior).

Exhibit 2
Overview of Cost Recognition Classifications

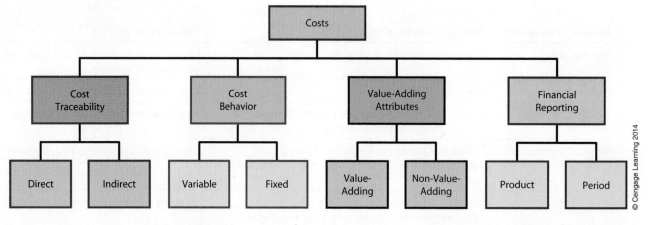

■ Identify the costs of activities that do and do not add value to a product or service.
■ Recognize and measure costs for the preparation of financial statements.

Managers in manufacturing, retail, and service organizations use cost information to prepare budgets, make pricing and other decisions, calculate variances between estimated and actual costs, and communicate results.

Cost Measurement

Managers *measure* costs by tracing them to cost objects, such as products or services, sales territories, departments, or operating activities.

■ **Direct costs** are costs that can be measured conveniently and economically by tracing them to a cost object. For example, the wages of workers who make candy bars can be conveniently traced to a particular batch because of time cards and payroll records. Similarly, the cost of chocolate's main ingredients—chocolate liquor, cocoa butter, sugar, and milk—can be easily traced.

■ **Indirect costs** are costs that cannot be measured conveniently and economically by tracing them to a cost object. Some examples include the nails used in furniture, the salt used in candy, and the rivets used in airplanes. For the sake of accuracy, however, these indirect costs must be included in the cost of a product or service. Because they are difficult to trace or an insignificant amount, management uses a formula to assign them to cost objects.

> Cost classification involves identifying costs and sorting them into direct or indirect, variable or fixed, value-adding or non-value-adding, or product or period, depending on the purpose of the analysis.

The examples that follow illustrate cost objects and their direct and indirect costs in service, retail, and manufacturing organizations.

■ **Service organization:** In organizations such as an accounting firm, costs can be traced to a specific service, such as preparation of tax returns. Direct costs for such a service include the costs of computer usage and the accountant's labor. Indirect costs include the costs of supplies, office rental, utilities, secretarial labor, telephone usage, and depreciation of office furniture.

■ **Retail organization:** Costs for retailers can be traced to a department. For example, the direct costs of a grocery store's produce department include the costs of fruits and vegetables and the wages of employees in that department. Indirect costs include the costs of utilities to cool the produce displays and the storage and handling of the produce.

- **Manufacturing organization:** Costs for organizations such as **The Hershey Company** can be traced to the product. Direct costs include the costs of the materials and labor needed to make the candy. Indirect costs include the costs of utilities, depreciation of plant and equipment, insurance, property taxes, inspection, supervision, maintenance of machinery, storage, and handling.

Financial Reporting

In order for managers to make good decisions, they need managerial accounting information about the costs involved in making a product or providing a service. Managers *recognize* and *measure* costs as period costs or product costs.

- **Period costs** (or *noninventoriable costs*) are costs of resources that are not assigned to products. They are *recognized* as operating expenses on the income statement. Selling, administrative, and general expenses are examples of period costs.
- **Product costs** (or *inventoriable costs*) include direct materials, direct labor, and overhead (indirect costs). Product costs are *recognized* on the income statement as cost of goods sold and on the balance sheet as inventory. Product costs can be further *classified* as being either direct costs or indirect costs.

> **STUDY NOTE:** Period costs and product costs can be explained by using the matching rule (accrual accounting). Period costs are charged against the revenue of the current period, and product costs must be charged to the period in which the product generates revenue.

Product unit cost is the cost of manufacturing a single unit of a product. It is made up of the costs of direct materials, direct labor, and overhead. These three cost elements are accumulated as a batch of products is produced. When the batch is completed, the total costs are divided by the units produced to determine product unit cost. **Service unit cost** is the cost to perform one service. The direct materials element does not apply, so only direct labor and overhead would be totaled and divided by the number of services performed. The three elements of product or service cost are defined as follows.

- **Direct materials costs:** The costs of materials that can be conveniently and economically measured when making specific units of the product. Some examples of direct materials are the meat and bun in hamburgers, the oil and additives in a gallon of gasoline, and the sugar used in making candy. Direct materials may also include parts that a company purchases from another manufacturer, e.g., a battery and windshield for an automobile.
- **Direct labor costs:** The costs of the hands-on labor needed to make a product or service that can be measured when making specific units. For example, the wages of production-line workers are direct labor costs.
- **Overhead costs** (or *service overhead, factory overhead, factory burden, manufacturing overhead,* or *indirect production costs*): The costs that cannot be practically or conveniently measured directly to an end product or service. They include **indirect materials costs**, such as the costs of nails, rivets, lubricants, and small tools, and **indirect labor costs**, such as the costs of labor for maintenance, inspection, engineering design, supervision, and materials handling. Other indirect manufacturing costs include the costs of building maintenance, property taxes, property insurance, depreciation on plant and equipment, rent, and utilities.*

To illustrate product costs and the manufacturing process, we'll refer to Choice Candy Company, which has identified the following elements of the product cost of one candy bar:

- **Direct materials costs:** costs of sugar, chocolate, and wrapper
- **Direct labor costs:** costs of labor used in making the candy bar
- **Overhead costs:** indirect materials costs, including the costs of salt and flavorings; indirect labor costs, including the costs of labor to move materials to the production area and to inspect the candy bars during production; and other indirect overhead costs, including depreciation on the building and equipment, utilities, property taxes, and insurance

---

*Overhead costs are allocated to a product's cost using either traditional or activity-based costing methods, which we discuss in the next chapter.

Business Perspective
Has Technology Shifted the Elements of Product Costs?

New technology and manufacturing processes have created new patterns of product costs. The three elements of product costs are still direct materials, direct labor, and overhead, but the percentage that each contributes to the total cost of a product has changed. From the 1950s through the 1970s, direct material and labor costs accounted for 75 percent of total product cost. Improved production technology caused a dramatic shift in the three product cost elements. Machines replaced people, significantly reducing direct labor costs. Today, only 50 percent of the cost of a product is directly traceable to the product. The other 50 percent is overhead, an indirect cost.

Prime Costs and Conversion Costs The three elements of product cost can be also grouped into prime costs and conversion costs.

- **Prime costs:** The primary costs of production. They are the sum of the direct materials costs and direct labor costs.
- **Conversion costs:** The costs of converting or processing direct materials into a finished product. They are the sum of direct labor costs and overhead costs.

These *classifications* are important for understanding the costing methods discussed in later chapters. Exhibit 3 summarizes the relationships among the product cost recognition classifications presented so far.

Exhibit 3
Relationships Among Product Cost Recognition Classifications

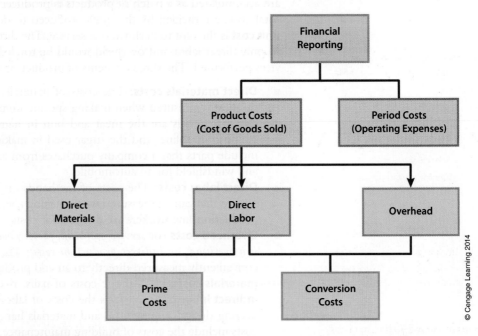

© Cengage Learning 2014

Cost Behavior

Managers are also interested in the way costs respond to changes in volume or activity. By analyzing those variable and fixed patterns of behavior, they gain information to make better management decisions.

- A **variable cost** is a cost that changes in direct proportion to a change in productive output (or some other measure of volume).
- A **fixed cost** is a cost that remains constant within a defined range of activity or time period.

All types of organizations have variable and fixed costs.

- **Service organization:** Because the number of passengers drives the consumption of food and beverages on a flight, the cost of peanuts and beverages is a variable cost for **Southwest Airlines**. Fixed costs include the depreciation on the plane and the salaries and benefits of the flight and ground crews.

■ **Retail organization:** The variable costs of a grocery store like **Kroger** or **Trader Joe's** include the cost of groceries sold and any sales commissions. Fixed costs include the costs of building and lot rental, depreciation on store equipment, and the manager's salary.

■ **Manufacturing organization:** The variable costs of a manufacturer like **The Hershey Company** or Choice Candy include the costs of direct materials (e.g., sugar, cocoa), direct labor, indirect materials (e.g., salt), and indirect labor (e.g., inspection and maintenance labor). Fixed costs include the costs of supervisors' salaries and depreciation on buildings.

Value-Adding versus Non-Value-Adding Costs

Costs can also be *classified* as value-adding or non-value-adding.

■ A **value-adding cost** is the cost of an activity that increases the market value of a product or service.

■ A **non-value-adding cost** is the cost of an activity that adds cost to a product or service but does not increase its market value.

Managers examine the value-adding attributes of their company's operating activities and, wherever possible, reduce or eliminate activities that do not directly add value to the company's products or services. For example, the costs of administrative activities, such as accounting and human resource management, are non-value-adding costs. Because they are necessary for the operation of the business, they are monitored closely but cannot be eliminated.

Exhibit 4 shows how some costs of a manufacturer like Choice Candy can be *recognized* in terms of traceability, behavior, value attribute, and financial reporting.

Exhibit 4
Examples of Cost Recognition Classifications for a Candy Manufacturer

Cost Examples	Traceability to Product	Cost Behavior	Value Attribute	Financial Reporting
Sugar for candy	Direct	Variable	Value-adding	Product (direct materials)
Labor for mixing	Direct	Variable	Value-adding	Product (direct labor)
Labor for supervision	Indirect	Fixed	Non-value-adding	Product (overhead)
Depreciation on mixing machine	Indirect	Fixed	Value-adding	Product (overhead)
Sales commission	—*	Variable	Value-adding**	Period
Accountant's salary	—*	Fixed	Non-value-adding	Period

*Sales commissions and accountants' salaries cannot be directly or indirectly traced to a cost object; they are not product costs.

**Sales commissions can be value-adding because customers' perceptions of the salesperson and the selling experience can strongly affect their perceptions of the product's market value.

APPLY IT!

Indicate whether each of the following costs for a gourmet chocolate candy maker is recognized as a product or a period cost, a variable or a fixed cost, a value-adding or a non-value-adding cost, and, if it is a product cost, a direct or an indirect candy cost:

a. Chocolate

b. Office rent

c. Candy chef wages

d. Dishwasher wages

e. Pinch of salt

f. Utilities to run mixer

SOLUTION

	Cost Recognition Classification			
	Product or Period	**Variable or Fixed**	**Value-Adding or Non-Value-Adding**	**Direct or Indirect**
a. Chocolate	Product	Variable	Value-adding	Direct
b. Office rent	Period	Fixed	Non-value-adding	—
c. Candy chef	Product	Variable	Value-adding	Direct
d. Dishwasher	Product	Variable	Value-adding	Indirect
e. Pinch of salt	Product	Variable	Value-adding	Indirect
f. Utilities to run mixer	Product	Variable	Value-adding	Indirect

TRY IT! SE2, SE3, E1A, E2A, E3A, E1B, E2B, E3B

SECTION 2   ACCOUNTING APPLICATIONS

LO 3 Inventory Accounts in Manufacturing Organizations

Transforming materials into finished products requires a number of production and production-related activities. A manufacturing organization's accounting system tracks these activities as product costs flowing through the Materials Inventory, Work in Process Inventory, and Finished Goods Inventory accounts.

Document Flows and Cost Flows Through the Inventory Accounts

Managers accumulate and report manufacturing costs based on documents pertaining to production and production-related activities. Exhibit 5 summarizes the typical relationships among the production activities, the documents for each of the three cost elements, and the inventory accounts affected by the activities. Looking at these relationships provides insight into how costs flow through the three inventory accounts and when an activity must be recorded in the accounting records. To illustrate document flow and changes in inventory balances for production activities in Exhibit 5, we continue with our example of Choice Candy Company, a typical manufacturing business.

Purchase of Materials

■ **Step 1. Acquiring the materials.** The purchasing process starts with a *purchase request* submitted for specific quantities of materials needed. A qualified manager approves the request. Based on the information in the purchase request, the Purchasing Department prepares a *purchase order* and sends it to a supplier.

■ **Step 2. Receiving the materials.** When the materials arrive, an employee on the receiving dock examines the materials and enters the information into the company database as a *receiving report*. The system matches the information on the receiving report with the descriptions and quantities listed on the purchase order. A materials handler moves the newly arrived materials from the receiving area to the materials storeroom.

■ **Step 3. Paying for the materials.** Choice Candy's accounting department receives a *vendor's invoice* from the supplier requesting payment for the materials. The cost of those materials increases the balance of the Materials Inventory account and an account payable is recognized. If all documents match, payment is authorized.

Production of Goods

■ **Step 4. Preparing the materials for production.** When candy bars are scheduled for production, the storeroom clerk receives a *materials request form*. In addition to showing authorization, it describes the types and quantities of materials that the storeroom clerk is to send to the production area, and it authorizes the release of those materials from the materials inventory into production.

■ **Step 5. Sending the materials into production.** If all is in order, the storeroom clerk has the materials handler move the materials to the production floor.

■ **Step 6. Producing goods.** Each of the production employees who make the candy bars prepares a *time card* to record the number of hours he or she has worked on this and other orders each day. A *job order cost card* can be used to record all direct materials, direct labor, and overhead costs incurred as the products move through production.

Exhibit 5
Activities, Documents, and Cost Flows Through the Inventory Accounts of a Manufacturing Organization

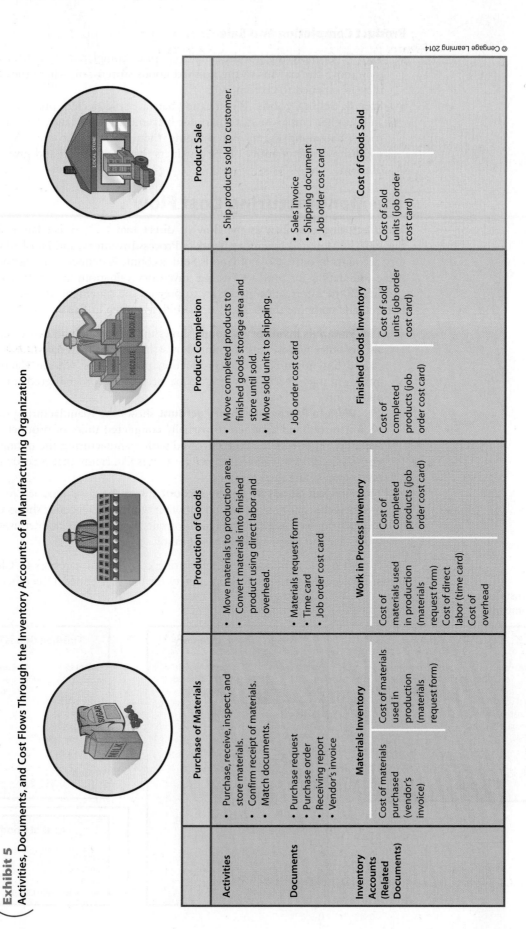

	Purchase of Materials	Production of Goods	Product Completion	Product Sale
Activities	• Purchase, receive, inspect, and store materials. • Confirm receipt of materials. • Match documents.	• Move materials to production area. • Convert materials into finished product using direct labor and overhead.	• Move completed products to finished goods storage area and store until sold. • Move sold units to shipping.	• Ship products sold to customer.
Documents	• Purchase request • Purchase order • Receiving report • Vendor's invoice	• Materials request form • Time card • Job order cost card	• Job order cost card	• Sales invoice • Shipping document • Job order cost card
Inventory Accounts (Related Documents)	**Materials Inventory** Cost of materials purchased (vendor's invoice) | Cost of materials used in production (materials request form)	**Work in Process Inventory** Cost of materials used in production (materials request form) Cost of direct labor (time card) Cost of overhead | Cost of completed products (job order cost card)	**Finished Goods Inventory** Cost of completed products (job order cost card) | Cost of sold units (job order cost card)	**Cost of Goods Sold** Cost of sold units (job order cost card)

Product Completion and Sale

- **Step 7. Completing goods.** Employees place completed candy bars in cartons and then move the cartons to the finished goods storeroom, where they are kept until they are shipped to customers.
- **Step 8. Selling goods.** When candy bars are sold, a clerk prepares a *sales invoice*, and another employee fills the order by removing the candy bars from the storeroom, packaging them, and shipping them to the customer. A *shipping document* shows the quantity of the products that are shipped and gives a description of them.

The Manufacturing Cost Flow

Manufacturing cost flow is the flow of direct materials, direct labor, and overhead through the Materials Inventory, Work in Process Inventory, and Finished Goods Inventory accounts into the Cost of Goods Sold account. A defined manufacturing cost flow is the foundation for product costing, inventory valuation, and financial reporting. It supplies all the information necessary to prepare the statement of cost of goods manufactured and compute the cost of goods sold, as shown in Exhibit 8.

- The **Materials Inventory account** shows the balance of the cost of unused materials. In other words, this account shows the cost of materials that have been purchased but not used in the production process. For Choice Candy, this might include things like milk, sugar, cocoa beans, and other ingredients necessary to make candy.
- The **Work in Process Inventory account** shows the manufacturing costs that have been incurred and assigned to partially completed units of product. This account therefore represents the costs involved with manufacturing the unfinished product. For Choice Candy, this might include things like candy that is ready to eat but has not yet been packaged for sale.
- The **Finished Goods Inventory account** shows the costs assigned to all completed products that have not been sold. In other words, this account shows the cost of the product that is complete and ready for sale. For Choice Candy, this would include things like the wrapped packages of candy.

Exhibit 6 summarizes the manufacturing cost flow as it relates to Choice Candy's inventory accounts and production activity for the year ended December 31. To show

Exhibit 6
Manufacturing Cost Flow: Choice Candy Company

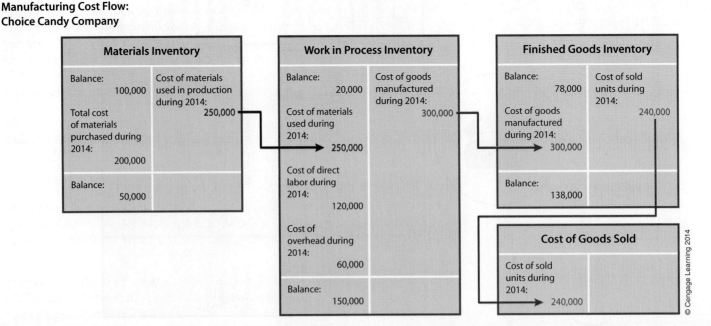

the basic flows in this example, we assume that all materials are direct materials to the candy bars produced.

Materials Inventory The Materials Inventory account holds the balance of the cost of materials that have been purchased, but have not yet been used in the production process.

The Materials Inventory Account

Transactions Choice Candy began the period with $100,000 in Beginning Materials Inventory. During the period, Choice Candy purchased $200,000 of direct materials and used $250,000 of direct materials.

Analysis Because there are no indirect materials in this case, the Materials Inventory account shows the balance of unused direct materials.

▲ The cost of direct materials purchased *increases* the balance of the *Materials Inventory* account.

▼ The cost of direct materials used by the Production Department *decreases* the *Materials Inventory* account as it flows into the Work in Process Inventory account.

Application of Double Entry

Materials Inventory			
Balance	100,000	Cost of materials used in production during 2014	250,000
Total cost of materials purchased during 2014	200,000		
Balance	50,000		

Comment If indirect materials had been used, the cost of the indirect materials transferred would

▲ *increase* the balance of the *Overhead* account

▼ *decrease* the balance of the *Materials Inventory* account

We discuss overhead in more detail in the next chapter.

STUDY NOTE: *When costs are transferred from one inventory account to another in a manufacturing company, they remain assets. They are on the balance sheet and are not expensed on the income statement until the finished goods are sold.*

Work in Process Inventory The Work in Process Inventory account records the balance of partially completed units of the product. As direct materials and direct labor enter the production process, their costs are added to the Work in Process Inventory account. The cost of overhead for the current period is also added. The total costs of direct materials, direct labor, and overhead incurred and transferred to the Work in Process Inventory account during a period are called **total manufacturing costs** (or *current manufacturing costs*).

Exhibit 6 recaps the inflows of direct materials, direct labor, and overhead into the Work in Process Inventory T account and the resulting outflow of completed product costs.

The Work in Process Inventory Account

Transactions Choice Candy began the period with $20,000 in beginning Work in Process Inventory. Choice Candy used $250,000 of direct materials, $120,000 of direct labor, and $60,000 of overhead during the period to manufacture $300,000 of goods.

Analysis

▲ The costs of the direct materials used to manufacture the candy bars *increase* the balance of the *Work in Process Inventory* account as the costs flow out of the Material Inventory account and into Work in Process Inventory (see previous transaction).

▲ The costs of the direct labor used to manufacture the candy bars *increase* the balance of the *Work in Process Inventory* account.

▲ The costs of overhead used to support the manufacture of the candy bars *increase* the balance of the *Work in Process Inventory* account.

Application of Double Entry

Work in Process Inventory			
Balance	20,000	Cost of goods manufactured during 2014	300,000
Cost of materials used during 2014	250,000		
Cost of direct labor during 2014	120,000		
Cost of overhead during 2014	60,000		
Balance	150,000		

Comment The cost of all units completed and moved to Finished Goods Inventory during a period is the **cost of goods manufactured**.

▼ The cost of goods manufactured *decreases* the balance of the *Work in Process Inventory* account as these costs flow into the Finished Goods Inventory account.

Finished Goods Inventory The Finished Goods Inventory account holds the balance of costs assigned to all completed products that a manufacturing company has not yet sold.

The Finished Goods Inventory Account

Transactions Choice Candy began the period with $78,000 in beginning Finished Goods Inventory. During the period, Choice Candy manufactured $300,000 of goods and sold $240,000 units.

Analysis

▲ The cost of goods manufactured *increases* the balance in the *Finished Goods Inventory* account when the goods are completed and flow out of the Work in Process Inventory account and into the Finished Goods account.

▼ The cost of goods sold *decreases* the balance in the *Finished Goods* account.

Application of Double Entry

Finished Goods Inventory			
Balance	78,000	Cost of sold units during 2014	240,000
Cost of goods manufactured during 2014	300,000		
Balance	138,000		

Cost of Goods Sold		
Cost of sold units during 2014	240,000	

Comment The cost of all units sold during a period that move out of Finished Goods Inventory is called the **cost of goods sold**.

APPLY IT! ▶

Given the following information, use T accounts to compute the ending balances of the Materials Inventory, Work in Process Inventory, and Finished Goods Inventory accounts:

Materials Inventory, beginning balance	$ 230
Work in Process Inventory, beginning balance	250
Finished Goods Inventory, beginning balance	380
Direct materials purchased	850
Direct materials (DM) used	740
Direct labor (DL) costs	970
Overhead (OH) costs	350
Cost of goods manufactured (COGM)	1,230
Cost of goods sold (COGS)	935

SOLUTION

Materials Inventory			
Beg. bal.	230	Used	740
Purchased	850		
End. bal.	340		

Work in Process Inventory			
Beg. bal.	250	COGM	1,230
DM	740		
DL	970		
OH	350		
End. bal.	1,080		

Finished Goods Inventory			
Beg. bal.	380	COGS	935
COGM	1,230		
End. bal.	675		

TRY IT! SE4, SE5

LO 4 Financial Statements and the Reporting of Costs

Managers prepare financial statements at least once a year to communicate the results of their activities. The key to preparing an income statement or a balance sheet in any kind of organization is *recognizing* and *measuring* its cost of goods or services sold and the value of its inventories, if any.

Income Statement and Accounting for Inventories

All organizations—service, retail, and manufacturing—use the following income statement format:

$$\text{Sales} - \frac{\text{Cost of Sales or}}{\text{Cost of Goods Sold}} = \text{Gross Margin} - \frac{\text{Operating}}{\text{Expenses}} = \frac{\text{Operating}}{\text{Income}}$$

How the cost of sales or cost of goods sold is computed, however, varies depending on the organization.

Service organizations like **Southwest Airlines** and **United Parcel Service (UPS)** sell services and not products. They maintain no inventories and they have no inventory accounts. Instead, service organizations use cost of sales. For example, suppose that UPS delivers packages of chocolate to Choice Candy. The cost of sales for UPS would include the wages and salaries of personnel plus the expense of the trucks, planes, supplies, and anything else used to deliver packages for Choice Candy.

In contrast, retail organizations, such as **Wal-Mart** and **The Gap**, which purchase products ready for resale, maintain just one inventory account on the balance sheet. This

Merchandise Inventory account reflects the costs of goods held for resale. Suppose a retailer had a balance of $3,000 in its Merchandise Inventory account at the beginning of the year. During the year, its purchases of products totaled $23,000 (adjusted for purchase discounts, returns and allowances, and freight-in). At year-end, its Merchandise Inventory balance was $4,500. As illustrated in Exhibit 7, the cost of goods sold was thus $21,500 ($3,000 + $23,000 = $26,000 − $4,500 = $21,500).

On the other hand, manufacturing organizations like **The Hershey Company**, **Godiva Chocolatier, Inc.**, or Choice Candy, which make products for sale, maintain three inventory accounts on the balance sheet: Materials Inventory, Work in Process Inventory, and Finished Goods Inventory. Suppose that Choice Candy had a balance of $52,000 in its Finished Goods Inventory account at the beginning of the year. During the year, the cost of the products that the company manufactured totaled $144,000. At year end, its Finished Goods Inventory balance was $78,000. As illustrated in Exhibit 7, the cost of goods sold would be $118,000 ($52,000 + $144,000 = $196,000 − $78,000 = $118,000).

Exhibit 7 compares the financial statements of service, retail, and manufacturing organizations. Note the differences in inventory accounts and cost of goods sold.

Exhibit 7
Financial Statements of Service, Retail, and Manufacturing Organizations

	Service Company	Retail Company	Manufacturing Company
Income Statement	Sales − Cost of sales = Gross margin − Operating expenses = Operating income	Sales − Cost of goods sold* = Gross margin − Operating expenses = Operating income *Cost of goods sold: 　Beginning merchandise inventory + Net cost of purchases = Cost of goods available for sale − Ending merchandise inventory = Cost of goods sold	Sales − Cost of goods sold† = Gross margin − Operating expenses = Operating income †Cost of goods sold: 　Beginning finished goods inventory + Cost of goods manufactured = Cost of goods available for sale − Ending finished goods inventory = Cost of goods sold
Balance Sheet (Current Assets Section)	No inventory accounts	One inventory account: 　Merchandise Inventory 　(finished product ready for sale)	Three inventory accounts: 　Materials Inventory 　(unused materials) 　Work in Process Inventory 　(unfinished product) 　Finished Goods Inventory 　(finished product ready for sale)
Example With Numbers		Income Statement: 　Beg. merchandise inventory　$ 3,000 + Net cost of purchases　　　　23,000 = Cost of goods available for sale　$26,000 − End. merchandise inventory　4,500 = Cost of goods sold　　　　$21,500 Balance Sheet: 　Merchandise inventory, ending　$ 4,500	Income Statement: 　Beg. finished goods inventory　$ 52,000 + Cost of goods manufactured　144,000 = Cost of goods available for sale　$196,000 − End. finished goods inventory　78,000 = Cost of goods sold　　　　$118,000 Balance Sheet:* 　Finished goods inventory, ending　$ 78,000 　*The balance sheet would also disclose 　the following: 　Materials inventory, ending 　Work in process inventory, ending

© Cengage Learning 2014

Statement of Cost of Goods Manufactured

As illustrated in Exhibit 7, for manufacturing companies, the cost of goods manufactured needs to be determined before cost of goods sold can be computed. The cost of goods manufactured is calculated in the **statement of cost of goods manufactured**, which summarizes the flow of all manufacturing costs incurred during the period. Exhibit 8 shows Choice Candy's statement of cost of goods manufactured for the year.

Exhibit 8
Statement of Cost of Goods Manufactured and Partial Income Statement for a Manufacturing Organization

Choice Candy Company
Statement of Cost of Goods Manufactured
For the Year

Direct materials used:		
Beginning materials inventory	$100,000	
Direct materials purchased	200,000	
Cost of direct materials available for use	$300,000	
Less ending materials inventory	50,000	
Step 1: Cost of direct materials used		$250,000
Direct labor		120,000
Overhead		60,000
Step 2: Total manufacturing costs		$430,000
Add beginning work in process inventory		20,000
Total cost of work in process during the year		$450,000
Less ending work in process inventory		150,000
Step 3: Cost of goods manufactured		$300,000

Choice Candy Company
Income Statement
For the Year

Sales		$500,000
Cost of goods sold:		
Beginning finished goods inventory	$ 78,000	
Cost of goods manufactured	300,000	
Cost of goods available for sale	$378,000	
Less ending finished goods inventory	138,000	
Cost of goods sold		240,000
Gross margin		$260,000
Selling and administrative expenses		160,000
Operating income		$100,000

The statement of cost of goods manufactured is developed in three steps.

- **Step 1. Compute the cost of direct materials used during the accounting period.** As shown in Exhibit 8, for Choice Candy, this would be computed as follows.

Beginning Materials Inventory	+	Direct Materials Purchased	=	Direct Materials Available for Use
$100,000	+	$200,000	=	$300,000

Direct Materials Available for Use	−	Ending Materials Inventory	=	Direct Materials Used
$300,000	−	$50,000	=	$250,000

■ **Step 2. Calculate total manufacturing costs for the period.** As shown in Exhibit 8, for Choice Candy this would be computed as follows.

Direct Materials	+	Direct Labor	+	Overhead	=	Total Manufacturing Costs
$250,000	+	$120,000	+	$60,000	=	$430,000

■ **Step 3. Determine total cost of goods manufactured for the period.** As shown in Exhibit 8, for Choice Candy this would be computed as follows.

Beginning Work in Process Inventory	+	Total Manufacturing Costs	−	Ending Work in Process Inventory	=	Cost of Goods Manufactured
$20,000	+	$430,000	−	$150,000	=	$300,000

Cost of Goods Sold and a Manufacturer's Income Statement

Exhibit 8 shows the relationship between Choice Candy's income statement and its statement of cost of goods manufactured. The total amount of the cost of goods manufactured is carried over to the income statement, where it is used to compute the cost of goods sold. The cost of goods sold is considered an expense in the period in which the goods are sold.

Beginning Finished Goods Inventory	+	Cost of Goods Manufactured	=	Cost of Goods Available for Sale
$78,000	+	$300,000	=	$378,000

Cost of Goods Available for Sale (what was available for sale)	−	Ending Finished Goods Inventory (what was not sold)	=	Cost of Goods Sold
$378,000	−	$138,000	=	$240,000

APPLY IT!

Given the following information, compute the ending balances of the Materials Inventory, Work in Process Inventory, and Finished Goods Inventory accounts:

Materials inventory, beginning balance	$ 230
Work in process inventory, beginning balance	250
Finished goods inventory, beginning balance	380
Direct materials purchased	850
Direct materials used	740
Direct labor costs	970
Overhead costs	350
Cost of goods completed	1,230
Cost of goods sold	935

SOLUTION

Materials Inventory, ending balance:

Materials Inventory, beginning balance	$ 230
Direct materials purchased	850
Direct materials used	(740)
Materials Inventory, ending balance	$ 340

Work in Process Inventory, ending balance:

Work in Process Inventory, beginning balance	$ 250
Direct materials used	740
Direct labor costs	970
Overhead costs	350
Cost of goods completed	(1,230)
Work in Process Inventory, ending balance	$ 1,080

Finished Goods Inventory, ending balance:

Finished Goods Inventory, beginning balance	$ 380
Cost of goods completed	1,230
Cost of goods sold	(935)
Finished Goods Inventory, ending balance	$ 675

TRY IT! SE6, E4A, E5A, E6A, E7A, E4B, E5B, E6B, E7B

LO 5 Measurement of Product Costs

Making or delivering products, selling insurance policies, or preparing a client's income taxes are all examples of a product or service that can be produced and sold, but how much does a single unit cost?

Computing Product Unit Cost

Product unit cost is the cost of manufacturing a single unit of a product. It is made up of the cost of goods manufactured costs of direct materials, direct labor, and overhead. These three cost elements are accumulated as a batch of products is being produced. When the batch has been completed, the product unit cost is computed.

$$\text{Product Unit Cost} = \frac{\text{Direct Materials Cost} + \text{Direct Labor Cost} + \text{Overhead Cost}}{\text{Number of Units Produced}}$$

or

$$\text{Product Unit Cost} = \text{Direct Materials Cost per Unit} + \text{Direct Labor Cost per Unit} + \text{Overhead Cost per Unit}$$

Product Cost Measurement Methods

How products flow physically and how costs are incurred does not always match. For example, Choice Candy physically produces candy bars 24 hours a day, 7 days a week, but the accounting department only does accounting 8 hours a day, 5 days a week. Because product cost data must be available 24/7, managers may use estimates or predetermined standards to compute product costs during the period. At the end of the period, these estimates are reconciled with the actual product costs so actual product costs appear in the financial statements. The three methods managers and accountants can use to calculate product unit cost include:

- Actual costing
- Normal costing
- Standard costing

Exhibit 9 summarizes how these three methods use actual and estimated costs.

Exhibit 9
Three Product Cost-Measurement Methods: Actual and Estimated Costs

© Cengage Learning 2014

Product Cost Elements	Actual Costing	Normal Costing	Standard Costing
Direct materials	Actual costs	Actual costs	Estimated costs
Direct labor	Actual costs	Actual costs	Estimated costs
Overhead	Actual costs	Estimated costs	Estimated costs

Actual Costing Method The **actual costing method** uses the actual costs of direct materials, direct labor, and overhead to calculate the product unit cost. These costs, however, may not be known until the end of the period. In the following example, assume the product unit cost is computed after the job is completed and all cost information is known.

Choice Candy produced 3,000 candy bars for a customer. The company accountant calculated the actual costs for the order as follows: direct materials, $540; direct labor, $420; and overhead, $240. The actual product unit cost for the order was $0.40, calculated as follows.

Actual direct materials ($540 ÷ 3,000 candy bars)	$0.18
Actual direct labor ($420 ÷ 3,000 candy bars)	0.14
Actual overhead ($240 ÷ 3,000 candy bars)	0.08
Actual product cost per candy bar ($1,200 ÷ 3,000 candy bars)	$0.40

Normal Costing Method The **normal costing method** combines the easy-to-track actual direct costs of materials and labor with estimated overhead costs to determine a product unit cost. The normal costing method is simple and allows a smooth assignment of overhead costs to production during a period. At the end of the period, any difference between the estimated and actual costs must be identified and removed so that the financial statements show only the actual product costs.

For Choice Candy, assume the company accountant used normal costing to price the order for 3,000 candy bars and that overhead was applied to the product's cost using an estimated rate of 50 percent of direct labor costs. In this case, the costs for the order would include the actual direct materials cost of $540, the actual direct labor cost of $420, and an estimated overhead cost of $210 ($420 × 50%). The product unit cost would be $0.39:

Actual direct materials ($540 ÷ 3,000 candy bars)	$0.18
Actual direct labor ($420 ÷ 3,000 candy bars)	0.14
Estimated overhead ($210 ÷ 3,000 candy bars)	0.07
Normal product cost per candy bar ($1,170 ÷ 3,000 candy bars)	$0.39

Standard Costing Method Managers sometimes need product cost information before the accounting period begins so that they can control the cost of operating activities or price a proposed product for a customer. In such situations, product unit costs must be estimated, and the standard costing method can be helpful. The **standard costing method** uses estimated or standard costs of direct materials, direct labor, and overhead to calculate the product unit cost. Standard costing is very useful in performance management and evaluation because a manager can compare actual and standard costs to compute the variances.*

Assume that Choice Candy is placing a bid to manufacture 2,000 candy bars for a new customer. From standard cost information developed at the beginning of the period, the company accountant estimates the following costs: $0.20 per unit for direct materials, $0.15 per unit for direct labor, and $0.09 per unit for overhead (assuming a standard overhead rate of 60 percent of direct labor cost). The standard cost per unit would be $0.44:

Standard direct materials	$0.20
Standard direct labor	0.15
Standard overhead ($0.15 × 60%)	0.09
Standard product cost per candy bar	$0.44

Computing Service Unit Cost

Delivering products, representing people in courts of law, selling insurance policies, and computing people's income taxes are typical of the services performed in service organizations. Like other services, these are labor-intensive processes supported by indirect materials or supplies, indirect labor, and other overhead costs. The most important cost in a service organization is the direct cost of labor that can be traceable to the service rendered. The indirect costs incurred in performing a service are similar to those incurred in manufacturing a product. They are *classified* as overhead. These service costs appear on service organizations' income statements as cost of sales.

APPLY IT!

Fickle Picking Services provides inexpensive, high-quality labor for farmers growing vegetable and fruit crops. In September, Fickle Picking paid laborers $4,000 to harvest 500 acres of apples. The company incurred overhead costs of $2,400 for apple-picking services in September. This amount included the costs of transporting the laborers to the orchards; of providing facilities, food, and beverages for the laborers; and of scheduling, billing, and collecting from the farmers. Of this amount, 50 percent was related to picking apples. Compute the cost per acre to pick apples.

SOLUTION

Total cost to pick apples: $4,000 + (0.50 × $2,400) = $5,200

Cost per acre to pick apples: $5,200 ÷ 500 acres = $10.40 per acre

TRY IT! SE7, E8A, E9A, E8B, E9B

---

*This is covered in more detail in the chapter on standard costing and variance analysis.

BUSINESS APPLICATIONS
■ Planning
■ Performing
■ Evaluating
■ Communicating
■ Ethics

RELEVANT LEARNING OBJECTIVES

LO 6 Explain how managerial accounting supports the management process to produce business results.

LO 7 Identify the standards of ethical conduct for management accountants.

LO 6 Managerial Accounting and the Management Process

The fundamentals of managing an organization include planning and forecasting operations, organizing and coordinating resources and data, and commanding and controlling resources. Managers use managerial accounting principles to guide their actions and decisions in the management process. Although management actions differ from organization to organization, they generally follow a four-stage management process:

■ planning
■ performing
■ evaluating
■ communicating

Managerial accounting is essential in each stage of the process.

Planning Exhibit 10 shows the overall framework in which planning takes place. The overriding **goal/vision** of a business is to increase the value of the stakeholders' interest in the business. The fundamental way in which the company will achieve this goal/

Exhibit 10
Overview of the Planning Framework

Goal/Vision: To increase the value of stakeholders' interest in the business

↓

Mission Statement: Fundamental way in which the company will achieve the goal of increasing stakeholders' value

↓

Strategic Objectives: Broad, long-term goals that determine the fundamental nature and direction of the business and that serve as a guide for decision making

↓

Tactical Objectives: Mid-term goals for positioning the business to achieve its long-term strategies

↓

Operating Objectives: Short-term goals that outline expectations for performance of day-to-day operations

↓

Business Plan: A comprehensive statement of how the company will achieve its objectives

↓

Budgets: Expressions of the business plan in financial terms

© Cengage Learning 2014

Business Perspective
What's Going on in the Grocery Business?

Sales at large supermarket chains, such as **Kroger**, **Safeway**, and **Albertson's**, have been flat and profits weak because both ends of their customer market are being squeezed. Large-scale retailers like **Wal-Mart** and **Costco** are attracting cost-conscious grocery shoppers, and upscale grocery customers are being lured by quality to specialty grocers like **Trader Joe's** and **Whole Foods Market**. Other grocery chains are reconsidering their company's mission and strategic options by adding new products and services, such as walk-in medical clinics, closing stores and downsizing, or entering new geographic markets.[2]

vision is described in its **mission statement.** This statement also expresses the company's identity and unique character. For example, **Wal-Mart**'s mission statement says that the company wants "to give ordinary folk the chance to buy the same things as rich people." **The Hershey Company**'s mission is "bringing sweet moments of Hershey happiness to the world every day."

The mission statement is essential to the planning process, which must consider how to add value through strategic, tactical, and operating objectives.

- **Strategic objectives**: Broad, long-term goals that determine the fundamental nature and direction of a business and that serve as a guide for decision making. Strategic objectives involve such basic issues as what a company's main products or services will be, who its primary customers will be, and where it will operate. They stake out a company's strategic position—whether it will be a cost leader, quality leader, or niche satisfier.
- **Tactical objectives**: Mid-term goals that position an organization to achieve its long-term strategies. These objectives, which usually cover a three- to five-year period, lay the groundwork for attaining the company's strategic objectives.
- **Operating objectives**: Short-term goals that outline expectations for the performance of day-to-day operations. Operating objectives link to performance targets and specify how success will be measured.

A **business plan** is a comprehensive statement of how a company will achieve its strategic, tactical, and operating objectives. It is usually expressed in financial terms in the form of budgets, and it often includes performance goals for individuals, teams, products, or services. A business plan provides a full description of the business, including a complete operating budget for the first two years of operations. The **budget** must include a forecasted income statement, a forecasted statement of cash flows, and a forecasted balance sheet.

Performing Planning alone does not guarantee satisfactory operating results. Management must implement the business plan in ways that make optimal use of available resources in an ethical manner.

Critical to managing any retail business is a thorough understanding of the supply chain. As Exhibit 11 shows, the **supply chain** (or *supply network*) is the path that leads from the suppliers to the final consumer. In the supply chain for a company that produces and sells candy, materials and resources flow from growers and suppliers to the company (manufacturer) and then on to candy distributors to retailers to consumers. Managers' knowledge of their supply chain allows them to coordinate deliveries from local growers and international suppliers so that they can meet the demands of customers without having too much or too little inventory on hand.

Exhibit 11
The Supply Chain

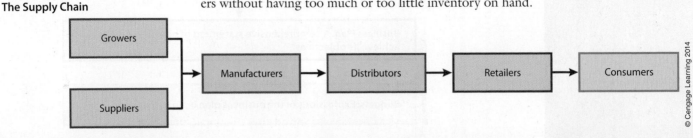

Business Perspective
What Do You Do to Cure a Bottleneck Headache?

A single seat belt can have as many as 50 parts, and getting the parts from suppliers was once a big problem for **Autoliv, Inc.**, a Swedish maker of auto safety devices. Autoliv's plant in Indianapolis was encountering constant bottlenecks in dealing with 125 different suppliers. To keep the production lines going required high-priced, rush shipments on a daily basis. To solve the problem, the company began using supply-chain management, keeping in touch with suppliers through the Internet rather than through faxes and phone calls. This system allowed suppliers to monitor the inventory at Autoliv and thus to anticipate problems. It also provided information on quantity and time of recent shipments, as well as continuously updated forecasts of parts that would be needed in the next 12 weeks. With supply-chain management, Autoliv reduced inventory by 75 percent and rush freight costs by 95 percent.[3]

Evaluating

Managers evaluate operating results by comparing the organization's actual performance with the performance levels established in the planning stage. They earmark any significant variations for further analysis so that they can correct the problems. If the problems are the result of a change in the organization's operating environment, the managers may revise their original estimates and/or objectives.

Communicating

Whether accounting reports are prepared for internal or external use, they must provide accurate information and clearly communicate this information. Inaccurate or confusing internal reports can have a negative effect on a company's operations. Full disclosure and transparency in financial statements issued to external parties is a basic concept of generally accepted accounting principles, and violation of this principle can result in stiff penalties. After several scandals, Congress passed legislation that requires the top management of companies to certify that financial statements filed with the SEC are accurate. The penalty for issuing false public reports can be loss of compensation, fines, and jail time.

The key to producing accurate and useful internal and external reports is to apply the four *w's:*

- **Why?** Know the purpose of the report. Focus on it as you write.
- **Who?** Identify the audience for your report. Communicate at a level that matches your readers' understanding of the issue and their familiarity with accounting information. A detailed, informal report may be appropriate for your manager, but a more concise summary may be necessary for other audiences, such as the president or board of directors of your organization.
- **What?** What information is needed, and what method of presentation is best? Select relevant information from reliable sources. You may draw information from pertinent documents or from interviews with knowledgeable managers and employees. The information should be not only relevant but also easy to read and understand. You may need to include visual aids, such as bar charts or graphs, to present the information clearly.
- **When?** Know the due date for the report. Strive to prepare an accurate report on a timely basis. If the report is urgently needed, you may have to sacrifice some accuracy in the interest of timeliness.

In summary, managerial accounting can provide a constant stream of relevant information to the management process. Managers start with a business plan, implement the plan, and evaluate and report the results. Accounting information helps managers develop their business plan, communicate that plan to their employees or their bank, evaluate their operating performance, and report the results of operations. As you can see in Exhibit 12, accounting plays a critical role in managing the operations of any organization.

Exhibit 12
Producing Results with the Management Process

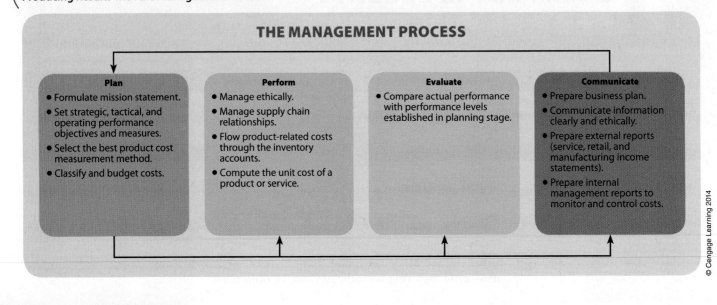

THE MANAGEMENT PROCESS

Plan
- Formulate mission statement.
- Set strategic, tactical, and operating performance objectives and measures.
- Select the best product cost measurement method.
- Classify and budget costs.

Perform
- Manage ethically.
- Manage supply chain relationships.
- Flow product-related costs through the inventory accounts.
- Compute the unit cost of a product or service.

Evaluate
- Compare actual performance with performance levels established in planning stage.

Communicate
- Prepare business plan.
- Communicate information clearly and ethically.
- Prepare external reports (service, retail, and manufacturing income statements).
- Prepare internal management reports to monitor and control costs.

© Cengage Learning 2014

APPLY IT!

Indicate whether each of the following activities takes place during the planning (PL), performing (PE), evaluating (E), or communicating (C) stage of the management process.

a. Changing regular price to clearance price
b. Reporting results to appropriate personnel
c. Preparing budgets of operating costs
d. Comparing estimated and actual costs to determine variances

SOLUTION

a. PE,   b. C,   c. PL,   d. E

TRY IT! SE8, SE9, E10A, E11A, E10B, E11B

LO 7 Standards of Ethical Conduct

Managers consider the interests of external parties (e.g., customers, owners, suppliers, governmental agencies, and the local community) when they make decisions about the proper use of organizational resources and the financial reporting of their actions. When ethical conflicts arise, management accountants have a responsibility to help managers balance those interests.

To be viewed credibly by the various parties who rely on the information they provide, management accountants must adhere to the highest standards of performance. To provide guidance, the Institute of Management Accountants has issued standards of ethical conduct for practitioners of managerial accounting and financial management. Those standards, presented in Exhibit 13, emphasize that management accountants have responsibilities in the following areas:

- competence
- confidentiality
- integrity
- credibility

Exhibit 13
Statement of Ethical Professional Practice

Members of IMA shall behave ethically. A commitment to ethical professional practice includes: overarching principles that express our values, and standards that guide our conduct.

PRINCIPLES

IMA's overarching ethical principles include: Honesty, Fairness, Objectivity, and Responsibility. Members shall act in accordance with these principles and shall encourage others within their organizations to adhere to them.

STANDARDS

A member's failure to comply with the following standards may result in disciplinary action.

I. COMPETENCE

Each member has a responsibility to:

1. Maintain an appropriate level of professional expertise by continually developing knowledge and skills.
2. Perform professional duties in accordance with relevant laws, regulations, and technical standards.
3. Provide decision support information and recommendations that are accurate, clear, concise, and timely.
4. Recognize and communicate professional limitations or other constraints that would preclude responsible judgment or successful performance of an activity.

II. CONFIDENTIALITY

Each member has a responsibility to:

1. Keep information confidential except when disclosure is authorized or legally required.
2. Inform all relevant parties regarding appropriate use of confidential information. Monitor subordinates' activities to ensure compliance.
3. Refrain from using confidential information for unethical or illegal advantage.

III. INTEGRITY

Each member has a responsibility to:

1. Mitigate actual conflicts of interest. Regularly communicate with business associates to avoid apparent conflicts of interest. Advise all parties of any potential conflicts.
2. Refrain from engaging in any conduct that would prejudice carrying out duties ethically.
3. Abstain from engaging in or supporting any activity that might discredit the profession.

IV. CREDIBILITY

Each member has a responsibility to:

1. Communicate information fairly and objectively.
2. Disclose all relevant information that could reasonably be expected to influence an intended user's understanding of the reports, analyses, or recommendations.
3. Disclose delays or deficiencies in information, timeliness, processing, or internal controls in conformance with organization policy and/or applicable law.

RESOLUTION OF ETHICAL CONFLICT

In applying the Standards of Ethical Professional Practice, you may encounter problems identifying unethical behavior or resolving an ethical conflict. When faced with ethical issues, you should follow your organization's established policies on the resolution of such conflict. If these policies do not resolve the ethical conflict, you should consider the following courses of action:

Discuss the issue with your immediate supervisor except when it appears that the supervisor is involved. In that case, present the issue to the next level. If you cannot achieve a satisfactory resolution, submit the issue to the next management level. If your immediate superior is the chief executive officer or equivalent, the acceptable reviewing authority may be a group such as the audit committee, executive committee, board of directors, board of trustees, or owners. Contact with levels above the immediate superior should be initiated only with your superior's knowledge, assuming he or she is not involved. Communication of such problems to authorities or individuals not employed or engaged by the organization is not considered appropriate, unless you believe there is a clear violation of the law.

Clarify relevant ethical issues by initiating a confidential discussion with an IMA Ethics Counselor or other impartial advisor to obtain a better understanding of possible courses of action.

Consult your own attorney as to legal obligations and rights concerning the ethical conflict.

Source: *IMA Statement of Ethical Professional Practice*, Institute of Management Accountants, www.imanet.org. Reprinted by permission.

Business Perspective
How to Blow the Whistle on Fraud

According to **PricewaterhouseCoopers**'s fourth biennial survey of more than 5,400 companies in 40 countries, eradicating fraud is extremely difficult. Despite increased attention to fraud detection systems and stronger internal controls, half of the companies interviewed had fallen victim to some type of fraud in the previous two years. The average cost of the fraud was about $3.2 million per company. Fraud appeared most likely to happen in Africa, North America, and Central-Eastern Europe.

The Sarbanes-Oxley Act of 2002 requires that all publicly traded companies have an anonymous incident reporting system. Such a system can help prevent fraud, as can hotlines that provide guidance on ethical dilemmas involved in reporting fraud. An example of such an ethics hotline is the one that the Institute of Management Accountants instituted in 2002. However, PricewaterhouseCoopers's study found that the best fraud deterrents were a company-wide risk management system with a continuous proactive fraud-monitoring component and a strong ethical culture to which all employees subscribe.[4]

APPLY IT!

Rank in order of importance the management accountant's four areas of responsibility: competence, confidentiality, integrity, and credibility. Explain the reasons for your ranking.

SOLUTION

Rankings will vary depending on the reasoning used concerning the four areas of responsibility. Ranking differences among individuals also reinforces the fact that we approach ethical behavior in a variety of ways and why a code of ethics is necessary.

TRY IT! SE10, E12A, E13A, E12B, E13B

TriLevel Problem

The Hershey Company

The beginning of this chapter focused on **The Hershey Company**, a well-known company that manufactures and sells quality chocolate bars and other candies. Complete the following requirements in order to answer the questions posed at the beginning of the chapter.

Section 1: Concepts
How does managerial accounting recognize and define costs?

In this chapter, we learned that how managers recognize and define costs depends on how the cost information is used for decision making. Based on what you learned, match this chapter's cost classifications and uses.

Cost Classifications	Use of Cost Analysis
a. Direct costs; indirect costs	1. Classify costs for the preparation of financial statements.
b. Product costs; period costs	
c. Variable costs; fixed costs	2. Calculate the number of units that must be sold to achieve a certain level of profit (cost behavior).
d. Value-adding costs; non-value-adding costs	3. Identify the costs of activities that do and do not add value to a product or service.
	4. Control costs by tracking them to a particular cost object, such as a service or product.

1. Discuss the three elements of product or service cost.
2. Define product or service unit cost.

Section 2: Accounting Applications

How do companies like Hershey determine the cost of a candy bar?

Assume that one of Hershey's factories produces 50-pound blocks of dark chocolate and that it needs to prepare a year-end balance sheet and income statement, as well as a statement of cost of goods manufactured, and compute its product's actual unit cost. During the year, the factory purchased $361,920 of direct materials. The factory's direct labor costs for the year were $99,085 (10,430 hours at $9.50 per hour); its indirect labor costs totaled $126,750 (20,280 hours at $6.25 per hour). Account balances for the year were as follows.

Account	Balance
Plant Supervision	$ 42,500
Factory Insurance	8,100
Utilities, Factory	29,220
Depreciation, Factory Building	46,200
Depreciation, Factory Equipment	62,800
Factory Security	9,460
Factory Repair and Maintenance	14,980
Selling and Administrative Expenses	76,480
Materials Inventory, beginning	26,490
Work in Process Inventory, beginning	101,640
Finished Goods Inventory, beginning	148,290
Materials Inventory, ending	24,910
Work in Process Inventory, ending	100,400
Finished Goods Inventory, ending	141,100

1. Compute the cost of materials used during the year.
2. From the cost of materials used, compute the total manufacturing costs for the year.
3. From the total manufacturing costs for the year, compute the cost of goods manufactured during the year.
4. If 13,397 units (1 unit = 50-pound block of dark chocolate) were manufactured during the year, what was the actual product unit cost? (Round to two decimal places.)

Section 3: Business Applications

How does managerial accounting facilitate the management process as managers plan, organize, and control costs?

To answer this question, match this chapter's management responsibilities with when they occur within the management process.

a. Plan
b. Perform
c. Evaluate
d. Communicate

1. Track the flow of product costs
2. Compare actual and planned results
3. Prepare financial statements
4. Manage ethically
5. Classify costs
6. Prepare internal management reports
7. Communicate clearly and ethically
8. Select the best product cost measurement method
9. Formulate mission statement
10. Set strategic, tactical, and operating performance objectives and measures
11. Prepare business plan
12. Compute the unit cost of a product or service

SOLUTION

Concepts

1. 1. b; 2. c; 3. d; 4. a

2. Managers must analyze the elements of a product or service unit cost, which may include the traceable costs of direct materials and direct labor, and the indirect costs known as overhead.

3. Product unit cost is defined as the cost of manufacturing a single unit of product. Service unit cost is defined as the cost of performing a single service.

Accounting Applications

1. Cost of materials used:

Materials inventory, beginning	$ 26,490
Direct materials purchased	361,920
Cost of materials available for use	$388,410
Less materials inventory, ending	24,910
Cost of materials used	$363,500

2. Total manufacturing costs:

Cost of materials used		$363,500
Direct labor costs		99,085
Overhead costs:		
Indirect labor	$126,750	
Plant supervision	42,500	
Factory insurance	8,100	
Utilities, factory	29,220	
Depreciation, factory building	46,200	
Depreciation, factory equipment	62,800	
Factory security	9,460	
Factory repair and maintenance	14,980	
Total overhead costs		340,010
Total manufacturing costs		$802,595

3. Cost of goods manufactured:

Total manufacturing costs	$802,595
Add work in process inventory, beginning	101,640
Total cost of work in process during the year	$904,235
Less work in process inventory, ending	100,400
Cost of goods manufactured	$803,835

4. Actual product unit cost:

$$\frac{\text{Cost of Goods Manufactured}}{\text{Number of Units Manufactured}} = \frac{\$803,835}{13,397 \text{ units}} = \$60.00^*$$

*Rounded

Section 3: Business Applications

1. b	7. d
2. c	8. a
3. d	9. a
4. b	10. a
5. a	11. d
6. d	12. b

Chapter Review

Distinguish managerial accounting from financial accounting. **LO 1**

Managerial accounting involves partnering with management in decision making, devising planning and performance management systems to assist management in the formulation and implementation of an organization's strategy. Managerial accounting reports provide information for planning, control, performance measurement, and decision making to managers and employees. These reports have a flexible format; they can present either historical or future-oriented information expressed in dollar amounts or physical measures. In contrast, financial accounting reports provide information about an organization's past performance to owners, lenders, customers, and governmental agencies on a periodic basis. Financial accounting reports follow strict guidelines defined by generally accepted accounting principles.

Explain how managers recognize costs and how they define product or service unit cost. **LO 2**

A single cost can be recognized as a direct or an indirect cost, a variable or a fixed cost, a value-adding or a non-value-adding cost, and a product or a period cost. The three measured elements of product costs are direct materials, direct labor, and overhead. Direct materials costs are the costs of materials measured when making a product that can be traced to specific product units. Direct labor costs include all labor costs that can be traced to specific product units. All other production-related costs are measured and recognized as overhead costs. Such costs cannot be easily traced to end products or services, so a cost allocation method is used to assign them to products or services. When a batch of products has been completed, the product unit cost is computed by dividing the total cost of direct materials, direct labor, and overhead by the total number of units produced.

These cost classifications enable managers to control costs by tracing them to cost objects, to calculate the number of units that must be sold to obtain a certain level of profit, to identify the costs of activities that do and do not add value to a product or service, and to prepare financial statements for parties outside the organization. Managers in manufacturing, retail, and service organizations use information about operating costs and product or service unit costs to prepare budgets, make pricing and other decisions, calculate variances between estimated and actual costs, and communicate results.

Describe the flow of costs through a manufacturer's inventory accounts. **LO 3**

The flow of costs through the inventory accounts begins when costs for direct materials, direct labor, and overhead are incurred. Materials costs flow first into the Materials Inventory account, which is used to record the costs of materials when they are received and again when they are issued for use in a production process. All manufacturing-related costs—direct materials, direct labor, and overhead—are recorded in the Work in Process Inventory account. When products are completed, their costs are transferred from the Work in Process Inventory account to the Finished Goods Inventory account. When the products are sold, these costs are transferred to the Cost of Goods Sold account.

Compare how service, retail, and manufacturing organizations report costs on their financial statements and how they account for inventories. **LO 4**

Because the operations of service, retail, and manufacturing organizations differ, their financial statements differ as well. A service organization maintains no inventory accounts on its balance sheet. The cost of sales on its income statement reflects the net cost of the services sold. A retail organization, which purchases products ready for resale, maintains only a Merchandise Inventory account. The cost of goods sold is simply the difference between the cost of goods available for sale and the ending merchandise inventory. A manufacturing organization maintains three inventory accounts: Materials Inventory, Work in Process Inventory, and Finished Goods Inventory. Manufacturing costs flow through all three inventory accounts. During the accounting period, the cost of completed products is transferred to the Finished Goods Inventory account, and the cost of units that have been manufactured and sold is transferred to the Cost of Goods Sold account.

Compute the unit cost of a product or service. **LO 5**

The product unit cost is computed by dividing the cost of goods manufactured by the total number of units produced. The product unit cost can be calculated using the actual, normal, or standard costing method. Under actual costing, the actual costs are used to compute the product unit cost. Under normal costing, the actual costs of direct materials and direct labor are combined with the estimated cost of overhead to determine the product unit cost. Under standard costing, the estimated costs are used to calculate the product unit cost. The components of product cost may be classified as prime costs or conversion costs. Prime costs are the primary costs of production--the sum of direct materials costs and direct labor costs. Conversion costs are the costs of converting direct materials into finished product—the sum of direct labor costs and overhead costs.

Service organizations have no materials costs; but they do have both direct labor costs and overhead costs. To determine the cost of performing a service, professional labor and service-related overhead costs are included in the analysis.

Explain how managerial accounting supports the management process to produce business results. **LO 6**

Managerial accounting supports each stage of the management process. When managers plan, they work with managerial accounting to establish strategic, tactical, and operating objectives that reflect their company's mission and to formulate a business plan for achieving those objectives. The plan is usually expressed in the form of budgets. When managers implement the plan, they use the information provided in the budgets to manage the business in the context of its supply chain. In evaluating performance, managers compare actual performance with planned performance and take steps to correct any problems. Reports reflect the results of planning, executing, and evaluating operations and may be prepared for external or internal use.

Identify the standards of ethical conduct for management accountants. **LO 7**

The Statement of Ethical Professional Practice emphasizes the Institute of Management Accounting members' responsibilities in the areas of competence, confidentiality, integrity, and credibility. These standards of conduct help management accountants recognize and avoid situations that could compromise their ability to supply management with accurate and relevant information.

Key Terms

actual costing method 17 (LO5)
budget 20 (LO6)
business plan 20 (LO6)
conversion costs 6 (LO2)
cost of goods manufactured 12 (LO3)
cost of goods sold 12 (LO3)
direct costs 4 (LO2)
direct labor costs 5 (LO2)
direct materials costs 5 (LO2)
Finished Goods Inventory account 10 (LO3)
fixed cost 6 (LO2)
goal/vision 19 (LO6)

indirect costs 4 (LO2)
indirect labor costs 5 (LO2)
indirect materials costs 5 (LO2)
managerial accounting 2 (LO1)
manufacturing cost flow 10 (LO3)
Materials Inventory account 10 (LO3)
mission statement 20 (LO6)
non-value-adding cost 7 (LO2)
normal costing method 18 (LO5)
operating objectives 20 (LO6)
overhead costs 5 (LO2)
period costs 5 (LO2)
prime costs 6 (LO2)

product costs 5 (LO2)
product unit cost 5 (LO2)
service unit cost 5 (LO2)
standard costing method 18 (LO5)
statement of cost of goods manufactured 15 (LO4)
strategic objectives 20 (LO6)
supply chain 20 (LO6)
tactical objectives 20 (LO6)
total manufacturing costs 11 (LO3)
value-adding cost 7 (LO2)
variable cost 6 (LO2)
Work in Process Inventory account 10 (LO3)

Chapter Assignments

DISCUSSION QUESTIONS

LO 1   **DQ1. CONCEPT ▶ BUSINESS APPLICATION ▶** How do the concepts of cost measurement and cost recognition underlie management accountants partnering with managers?

LO 1   **DQ2. CONCEPT ▶** Explain how this statement: "Managerial accounting and financial accounting work is interrelated and the accountants must work together closely" relates to accounting concepts.

LO 1   **DQ3.** In 1982, the IMA defined management accounting as follows.

> *The process of identification, measurement, accumulation, analysis, preparation, interpretation, and communication of financial information used by management to plan, evaluate, and control within the organization and to assure appropriate use of and accountability for its resources.*[5]

Compare this definition with the updated one that appears in LO1. Has the role of a management accountant changed?

LO 5   **DQ4. CONCEPT ▶** Describe the three cost measurement methods that can be used to compute the unit cost of a product or service.

LO 6   **DQ5. CONCEPT ▶ BUSINESS APPLICATION ▶** How do managers in various organizations use cost information in the management process to measure and recognize costs during a period?

SHORT EXERCISES

LO 1   **Managerial Accounting versus Financial Accounting**

SE1. Indicate whether each of the following characteristics relates to managerial accounting (MA) or financial accounting (FA):

a. Forward looking
b. Publicly reported
c. Complies with accounting standards
d. Usually confidential
e. Reports past performance
f. Uses physical measures as well as monetary ones for reports
g. Driven by user needs
h. Focuses on business decision making

LO 2   **Elements of Manufacturing Costs**

SE2. CONCEPT ▶ Stoney Saure, accountant for Votives, Inc., must group the costs of manufacturing tealights. Indicate whether each of the following items should be classified as direct materials (DM), direct labor (DL), overhead (O), or none of these (N). Also indicate whether each is a prime cost (PC), a conversion cost (CC), or neither (N). (*Hint:* More than one answer per category may apply.)

a. Cost of wax
b. Depreciation of the cost of vats to hold melted wax
c. Cost of Gigi's time to dip the wicks into the wax
d. Rent on the factory where candles are made
e. Cost of coloring for candles
f. Steve's commission to sell candles to Brightlights, Inc.
g. Cost of Ramos's time to design candles for Halloween

LO 2 **Cost Recognition**

SE3. CONCEPT ▶ Indicate whether each of the following is a direct cost (D), an indirect cost (ID), or neither (N) and whether it is a variable (V) or a fixed (F) cost. Also indicate whether each adds value (VA) or does not add value (NVA) to the product and whether each is a product cost (PD) or a period cost (PER).

a. Production foreman's salary
b. Straight-line depreciation on office equipment
c. Wages of a production-line worker

LO 3 **Cost Flow in a Manufacturing Organization**

SE4. Given the following information, compute the ending balances of the Materials Inventory, Work in Process Inventory, and Finished Goods Inventory accounts:

Materials Inventory, beginning balance	$ 25,000
Work in Process Inventory, beginning balance	5,750
Finished Goods Inventory, beginning balance	38,000
Direct materials purchased	85,000
Direct materials used	74,000
Direct labor costs	70,000
Overhead costs	35,000
Cost of goods manufactured	133,000
Cost of goods sold	103,375

LO 3 **Document Flows in a Manufacturing Organization**

SE5. Identify the document needed to support each of the following activities in a manufacturing organization:

a. Recording direct labor time at the beginning and end of each work shift
b. Placing an order for direct materials with a supplier
c. Receiving direct materials at the shipping dock
d. Recording the costs of a specific job's direct materials, direct labor, and overhead
e. Issuing direct materials into production
f. Fulfilling a Production Department request for the purchase of direct materials
g. Billing the customer for a completed order

LO 4 **Income Statement for a Manufacturing Organization**

SE6. Using the following information from Nathan Company, prepare an income statement through operating income for the year:

Sales	$900,000
Finished goods inventory, beginning	45,000
Cost of goods manufactured	575,000
Finished goods inventory, ending	80,000
Operating expenses	300,000

LO 5 **Computation of Product Unit Cost**

SE7. What is the product unit cost for Job SZ, which consists of 600 units and has total manufacturing costs of direct materials, $4,800; direct labor, $7,200; and overhead, $3,600? What are the prime costs and conversion costs per unit?

LO **6** **The Management Process**

SE8. BUSINESS APPLICATION ▶ Indicate whether each of the following management activities in a department store is part of planning (PL), performing (PE), evaluating (E), or communicating (C):

a. Completing a balance sheet and income statement at the end of the year
b. Meeting with sales managers to develop performance measures for sales personnel
c. Training a clerk to complete a cash sale
d. Renting a local warehouse to store excess inventory of clothing
e. Preparing an annual sales budget for each department and the entire store
f. Evaluating the performance of the shoe department by examining the significant differences between its actual and planned expenses for the month

LO **6** **Strategic Positioning**

SE9. BUSINESS APPLICATION ▶ Organizations stake out different strategic positions to add value and achieve success. Some strive to be low-cost leaders like **Wal-Mart**, while others become the high-end quality leaders like **Whole Foods Market**. Identify which of the following organizations are low-cost leaders (C) and which are quality leaders (Q):

a. Tiffany & Co.
b. Yale University
c. Local community college
d. Lexus
e. All-you-can-eat restaurant
f. Rent-a-Wreck
g. Apple Computers
h. Coca-Cola
i. Store-brand soda

LO **7** **Ethical Conduct**

SE10. BUSINESS APPLICATION ▶ ABC Cosmetics Company's managerial accountant has lunch every day with his friend who is a managerial accountant for XYZ Cosmetics, Inc., a competitor of ABC. Last week, ABC's accountant couldn't decide how to treat some information in a report he was preparing, so he discussed it with his friend. Is ABC's accountant adhering to the ethical standards of management accountants? Defend your answer.

EXERCISES: SET A

LO **2** **Cost Recognition**

E1A. CONCEPT ▶ Indicate whether each of the following costs for a moped manufacturer is a product or a period cost, a variable or a fixed cost, a value-adding or a non-value-adding cost, and, if it is a product cost, a direct or an indirect cost of the moped:

Item	Cost Recognition Classifications			
	Product or Period	**Variable or Fixed**	**Value-Adding or Non-Value-Adding**	**Direct or Indirect**
Example: Motor	Product	Variable	Value-adding	Direct

a. Office rent
b. Labor to assemble moped
c. Labor to inspect moped
d. Accountant's salary
e. Lubricant for brakes

LO 4   **Comparison of Income Statement Formats**

E2A. Indicate whether each of these equations applies to a service organization (SER), a retail organization (RET), or a manufacturing organization (MANF):

a. Cost of Sales = Net Cost of Services Sold

b. Cost of Goods Sold = Beginning Merchandise Inventory + Net Cost of Purchases − Ending Merchandise Inventory

c. Cost of Goods Sold = Beginning Finished Goods Inventory + Cost of Goods Manufactured − Ending Finished Goods Inventory

LO 4   **Characteristics of Organizations**

E3A. Indicate whether each of the following is typical of a service organization (SER), a retail organization (RET), or a manufacturing organization (MANF):

a. Purchases products ready for resale

b. Maintains no balance sheet inventory accounts

c. Maintains only one balance sheet inventory account

d. Maintains three balance sheet inventory accounts

e. Designs and makes products for sale

f. Sells services

g. Includes the net cost of purchases in calculating cost of goods sold

h. Determines the net cost of services sold

i. Includes the cost of goods manufactured in calculating cost of goods sold

LO 4   **Statement of Cost of Goods Manufactured**

E4A. During June, Agron, Inc., purchases of direct materials totaled $119,000; direct labor for the month was 3,400 hours at $10.00 per hour. Agron also incurred the following overhead costs: utilities, $5,870; supervision, $17,300; indirect materials, $6,750; depreciation, $6,200; insurance, $1,830; and miscellaneous, $1,100.

Beginning inventory accounts were as follows: Materials Inventory, $48,600; Work in Process Inventory, $55,250; and Finished Goods Inventory, $38,500. Ending inventory accounts were as follows: Materials Inventory, $55,100; Work in Process Inventory, $48,400; and Finished Goods Inventory, $37,450.

Prepare a statement of cost of goods manufactured.

LO 4   **Statement of Cost of Goods Manufactured and Cost of Goods Sold**

E5A. FruTee Corp. makes irrigation sprinkler systems for fruit tree nurseries. FruTee's new controller can find only the following partial information for the past year:

	Lime Division	Lemon Division	Orange Division	Fig Division
Direct materials used	$ 4	$ 7	$ (g)	$ 8
Total manufacturing costs	11	(d)	(h)	17
Overhead	5	3	3	(j)
Direct labor	(a)	9	4	4
Ending work in process inventory	(b)	3	2	5
Cost of goods manufactured	12	23	15	(l)
Beginning work in process inventory	2	(e)	5	(k)
Ending finished goods inventory	2	6	(i)	9
Beginning finished goods inventory	3	(f)	5	7
Cost of goods sold	(c)	21	16	12

Compute the unknown values. List the accounts in the proper order, and show subtotals and totals as appropriate.

LO **4**

Missing Amounts—Manufacturing

E6A. Incomplete inventory and income statement data for Gator Corporation follow. Determine the missing amounts.

	Cost of Goods Sold	Cost of Goods Manufactured	Beginning Finished Goods Inventory	Ending Finished Goods Inventory
a.	$ 15,000	$20,000	$ 1,000	?
b.	$140,000	?	$55,000	$60,000
c.	?	$99,000	$23,000	$29,000

LO **4**

Inventories, Cost of Goods Sold, and Net Income

E7A. The data that follow are for a retail organization and a manufacturing organization.

1. Fill in the missing data for the retail organization:

	First Quarter	Second Quarter	Third Quarter	Fourth Quarter
Sales	$10	$(e)	$15	$(k)
Gross margin	(a)	4	5	(l)
Ending merchandise inventory	5	(f)	5	(m)
Beginning merchandise inventory	4	(g)	(h)	5
Net cost of purchases	(b)	7	11	(n)
Operating income	3	2	(i)	2
Operating expenses	(c)	2	1	4
Cost of goods sold	5	8	(j)	12
Cost of goods available for sale	(d)	12	15	15

2. Fill in the missing data for the manufacturing organization:

	First Quarter	Second Quarter	Third Quarter	Fourth Quarter
Ending finished goods inventory	$(a)	$3	$(h)	$ 6
Cost of goods sold	6	3	5	(l)
Operating income	2	3	2	(m)
Cost of goods available for sale	8	(d)	10	13
Cost of goods manufactured	5	(e)	(i)	8
Gross margin	4	(f)	(j)	7
Operating expenses	2	(g)	4	5
Beginning finished goods inventory	(b)	2	3	(n)
Sales	(c)	10	(k)	14

LO **5**

Unit Cost Determination

E8A. Anderson Winery produces a red wine called Old Vines. Recently, management has become concerned about the increasing cost of making Old Vines and needs to determine if the current selling price of $10 per bottle is adequate. The winery wants to achieve a 25 percent gross profit on the sale of each bottle. The following information is given to you for analysis:

Batch size	6,264 bottles
Costs:	
Total direct materials costs	$25,056
Total direct labor costs	12,528
Total overhead costs	21,924
Total production costs	$59,508

(Continued)

1. Compute the unit cost per bottle for materials, labor, and overhead.
2. **ACCOUNTING CONNECTION** ▶ How would you advise management regarding the price per bottle of wine? (Round to the nearest cent.)
3. Compute the prime costs per unit and the conversion costs per unit.

LO 5   **Unit Costs in a Service Business**

E9A. Roll in the Hay, Inc., provides harvesting services. In June, the business earned $3,600 by cutting, turning, and baling 6,000 bales. During the month, the following costs were incurred: gas, $900; tractor maintenance, $360; and labor, $1,200. Annual tractor depreciation is $3,000. What was the company's cost per bale? (Round to the nearest cent.) What was its revenue per bale? Should the price per bale be increased?

LO 6   **The Management Process**

E10A. BUSINESS APPLICATION ▶ Indicate whether each of the following management activities of a chain of retail stores is part of planning (PL), performing (PE), evaluating (E), or communicating (C):

a. Leasing five delivery trucks for the current year
b. Comparing the actual number with the planned number of customers for the year
c. Developing a strategic plan for a new store
d. Preparing a report showing the past performance of a retail store
e. Developing standards, or expectations, for performance of sales staff for next year
f. Preparing the chain's balance sheet and income statement and distributing them to the board of directors
g. Maintaining an inventory of a variety of merchandise
h. Formulating a corporate policy for the treatment and disposition of recyclables
i. Preparing a report on the types and amounts of recyclables removed from each store in the last three months
j. Recording the time taken to deliver online orders to customers

LO 6   **The Planning Framework**

E11A. BUSINESS APPLICATION ▶ Yuan Xi has just opened a company that imports fine ceramic gifts from China and sells them over the Internet. In planning his business, Xi did the following:

1. Listed his expected expenses and revenues for the first year of operations
2. Determined that he would keep his expenses low and generate enough revenues during the first four months of operations so that he would have a positive cash flow by the fifth month
3. Decided that he wanted the company to provide him with income for a good lifestyle and funds for retirement
4. Developed a complete list of goals, objectives, procedures, and policies relating to how he would find, buy, store, sell, and ship goods and collect payment
5. Decided to focus his business on providing customers with the finest Chinese ceramics at a favorable price
6. Decided to expand his website to include ceramics from other Far Eastern countries over the next five years
7. Decided to solely rely on the Internet to market the products

Match each of Xi's actions to the components of the planning framework: goal, mission, strategic objectives, tactical objectives, operating objectives, business plan, and budget.

LO 7   **Ethical Conduct**

E12A. BUSINESS APPLICATION ▶ Dula Gibbon was recently promoted to accounting manager and now has a new boss, Tim Paine, the corporate controller. Last week, they went to a two-day workshop on accounting security. During the first hour of the first day's program, Paine disappeared. The same thing happened on the second day. During the trip home, Gibbon asked Paine about the conference. Paine replied, "I haven't sat in on one of those workshops in years. This is my R&R time. Those sessions are for the new people. My experience is enough to keep me current. Plus, I have excellent people, like you, to help me."

Does Dula Gibbon have an ethical dilemma? If so, what is it? What are her options? How would you solve her problem? Be prepared to defend your answer.

LO 7 **Corporate Ethics**

E13A. BUSINESS APPLICATION ▶ To answer the following questions, conduct a search of several companies' websites: (1) Does the company have an ethics statement? (2) Does it express a commitment to environmental or social issues? (3) In your opinion, is the company ethically responsible? Select one of the companies you researched and write a brief description of your findings.

EXERCISES: SET B

Visit the textbook companion website at www.cengagebrain.com to access Exercise Set B for this chapter.

PROBLEMS

LO 4 **A Manufacturing Organization's Balance Sheet**

✔ 2d: Cost of goods manufactured: $312,100

P1. The information that follows is from Manufacturing Company's trial balance.

	Debits	Credits
Cash	34,000	
Accounts Receivable	27,000	
Materials Inventory, ending	31,000	
Work in Process Inventory, ending	47,900	
Finished Goods Inventory, ending	54,800	
Factory Supplies	5,700	
Small Tools	9,330	
Land	160,000	
Factory Building	575,000	
Accumulated Depreciation—Factory Building		199,000
Factory Equipment	310,000	
Accumulated Depreciation—Factory Equipment		137,000
Patents	33,500	
Accounts Payable		26,900
Insurance Premiums Payable		6,700
Income Taxes Payable		41,500
Mortgage Payable		343,000
Common Stock		200,000
Retained Earnings		334,130
	1,288,230	1,288,230

REQUIRED

1. Manufacturing organizations use asset accounts that are not needed by retail organizations.
   a. List the titles of the asset accounts that are specifically related to manufacturing organizations.
   b. List the titles of the asset, liability, and equity accounts that you would see on the balance sheets of both manufacturing and retail organizations.

2. Assuming that the following information reflects the results of operations for the year, calculate the (a) gross margin, (b) cost of goods sold, (c) cost of goods available for sale, and (d) cost of goods manufactured:

Operating income	$138,130
Operating expenses	53,670
Sales	500,000
Finished goods inventory, beginning	50,900
Finished goods inventory, ending	54,800

Statement of Cost of Goods Manufactured

P2. Jackplum Vineyards, whose fiscal year begins on November 1, has just completed a record-breaking year producing and selling wine. Its inventory account balances on October 31 of this year were Materials Inventory, $83,800; Work in Process Inventory, $2,700,500; and Finished Goods Inventory, $1,800,200. At the beginning of the year, the inventory account balances were Materials Inventory, $56,200; Work in Process Inventory, $3,300,000; and Finished Goods Inventory, $1,596,400.

During the fiscal year, the company's purchases of direct materials totaled $750,000. Direct labor hours totaled 140,000, and the average labor rate was $11.00 per hour. The following overhead costs were incurred during the year: depreciation—plant and equipment, $85,600; indirect labor, $207,300; property tax—plant and equipment, $96,000; plant maintenance, $80,000; small tools, $42,400; utilities, $96,500; and employee benefits, $176,100.

REQUIRED

Prepare a statement of cost of goods manufactured for the year ended October 31.

Computation of Unit Cost

P3. Keep Cool Industries, Inc., manufactures fans for personal use. Department 70 is responsible for assembling the fan. Department 71 packages them for shipment. Keep Cool recently produced 10,000 fans for a national retailer. In fulfilling this order, the departments incurred the following costs:

	Department	
	70	**71**
Direct materials used	$30,000	$4,000
Direct labor	8,000	2,000
Overhead	5,000	3,000

1. Compute the unit cost for each department.
2. Compute the total unit cost for the national retailer order.
3. **ACCOUNTING CONNECTION** ▶ The selling price for this order was $10 per unit. Was the selling price adequate? List the assumptions and/or computations upon which you based your answer. What suggestions would you make to Keep Cool's management about the pricing of future orders?
4. Compute the prime costs and conversion costs per unit for each department.

Unit Costs in a Service Business

P4. Sunny Day Nursing Home relies heavily on cost data to keep its pricing structures in line with those of its competitors. The facility provides a wide range of services, including assisted living and skilled nursing. The facilities' controller is concerned about the profits generated by the 30-bed memory unit, so she is reviewing current billing procedures for that unit. The focus of her analysis is the unit's billing per patient day. This billing equals the per diem cost of the memory unit plus a 40 percent markup to cover other operating costs and generate a profit. Memory unit patient costs include the following:

Memory aids	$30 per patient day (average)
Doctors' care	1 hour per day @ $200 per hour (actual)
Memory therapy care	3 hours per day @ $90 per hour (actual)
Regular nursing care	24 hours per day @ $30 per hour (average)
Medications	$250 per day (average)
Daily living supplies	$80 per day (average)
Room rental	$400 per day (average)
Food services	$50 per day (average)

The nursing home director has asked the controller to compare the current billing procedure with one that uses industry averages to determine the billing per patient day.

REQUIRED

1. Compute the cost per patient per day.
2. Compute the billing per patient day using the memory unit's existing markup rate.
3. Compute the billing per patient day using the following industry averages for markup rates:

Memory aids	30%	Medications	50%
Doctors' care	50	Daily living supplies	50
Memory therapy care	50	Room rental	30
Regular nursing care	50	Food services	20

4. **ACCOUNTING CONNECTION ▶** Based on your findings in requirements 2 and 3, which billing procedure would you recommend? Why?

LO 7   **Professional Ethics**

P5. BUSINESS APPLICATION ▶ Ted Thalia is Tops Corporation's controller. He has been with the company for 20 years and is being considered for the job of chief financial officer. His boss, who is the current chief financial officer and former company controller, will be Tops's new president. Thalia has just discussed the year-end closing with his boss, who made the following statement during their conversation: "Ted, why are you being so inflexible? I'm only asking you to postpone the $5,000,000 write-off of obsolete inventory for 10 days so that it won't appear on this year's financial statements. Ten days! Do it. Your promotion is coming up, you know. Make sure you keep all the possible outcomes in mind as you complete your year-end work. Oh, and keep this conversation confidential—just between you and me. Okay?"

REQUIRED

1. Identify the ethical issue or issues involved.
2. What do you believe is the appropriate solution to the problem? Be prepared to defend your answer.

ALTERNATE PROBLEMS

LO 4   **A Manufacturing Organization's Balance Sheet**

✔ 2d: Cost of goods manufactured: $352,000

P6. The information that follows is from Miles Production Company's trial balance.

	Debits	Credits
Cash	40,000	
Accounts Receivable	30,000	
Materials Inventory, ending	41,000	
Work in Process Inventory, ending	37,000	
Finished Goods Inventory, ending	70,000	
Production Supplies	5,000	
Small Tools	3,000	
Land	200,000	
Factory Building	600,000	
Accumulated Depreciation—Factory Building		300,000
Production Equipment	210,000	
Accumulated Depreciation—Production Equipment		100,000
Patents	20,000	
Accounts Payable		40,000
Insurance Premiums Payable		6,000
Income Taxes Payable		40,000
Mortgage Payable		400,000
Common Stock		300,000
Retained Earnings		70,000
	1,256,000	1,256,000

(Continued)

REQUIRED

1. Manufacturing organizations use asset accounts that are not needed by retail organizations.
   a. List the titles of the asset accounts that are specifically related to manufacturing organizations.
   b. List the titles of the asset, liability, and equity accounts that you would see on the balance sheets of both manufacturing and retail organizations.
2. Assuming that the following information reflects the results of operations for the year, calculate the (a) gross margin, (b) cost of goods sold, (c) cost of goods available for sale, and (d) cost of goods manufactured:

Operating income	$ 68,000
Operating expenses	40,000
Sales	450,000
Finished goods inventory, beginning	60,000

LO 4

SPREADSHEET

✔ Cost of goods manufactured: $10,163,200

Statement of Cost of Goods Manufactured

P7. Reggi Vineyards produces a full line of varietal wines. The company, whose fiscal year begins on November 1, has just completed a record-breaking year. Its inventory account balances on October 31 of this year were Materials Inventory, $1,803,800; Work in Process Inventory, $2,764,500; and Finished Goods Inventory, $1,883,200. At the beginning of the year, the inventory account balances were Materials Inventory, $2,156,200; Work in Process Inventory, $3,371,000; and Finished Goods Inventory, $1,596,400.

During the fiscal year, the company's purchases of direct materials totaled $6,750,000. Direct labor hours totaled 142,500, and the average labor rate was $8.20 per hour. The following overhead costs were incurred during the year: depreciation—plant and equipment, $685,600; indirect labor, $207,300; property tax—plant and equipment, $94,200; plant maintenance, $83,700; small tools, $42,400; utilities, $96,500; and employee benefits, $76,100.

REQUIRED

Prepare a statement of cost of goods manufactured for the fiscal year ended October 31.

LO 5

SPREADSHEET

✔ 2: Total unit cost: $13.72
✔ 4: Dept. 60 prime costs: $9.06
✔ 4: Dept. 60 conversion costs: $3.54

Computation of Unit Cost

P8. Disco Industries, Inc., manufactures discs for several of the leading recording studios in the United States and Europe. Department 60 is responsible for pressing each disc. Department 61 then packages them for shipment. Disco recently produced 4,000 discs for Vintage Records Company. In fulfilling this order, the departments incurred the following costs:

	Department	
	60	**61**
Direct materials used	$29,440	$3,920
Direct labor	6,800	2,560
Overhead	7,360	4,800

1. Compute the unit cost for each department.
2. Compute the total unit cost for the Vintage Records Company order.
3. **ACCOUNTING CONNECTION** ▶ The selling price for this order was $14 per unit. Was the selling price adequate? List the assumptions and/or computations upon which you based your answer. What suggestions would you make to Disco's management about the pricing of future orders?
4. Compute the prime costs and conversion costs per unit for each department.

LO 5

✔ 1: Total cost per patient day: $2,792
✔ 3: Total cost per patient day using industry average: $4,013

Unit Costs in a Service Business

P9. Everymans Hospital relies heavily on cost data to keep its pricing structures in line with those of its competitors. The hospital provides a wide range of services, including intensive care, intermediate care, and a neonatal nursery. The hospital's controller is concerned about the profits generated by the 30-bed intensive care unit (ICU), so she is reviewing current billing procedures for that unit. The focus of her analysis is the hospital's billing per ICU patient day. This billing equals the per diem cost of intensive care plus a 40 percent markup to cover other operating costs and generate a profit. ICU patient costs include the following:

Equipment usage	$180 per day (average)
Doctors' care	2 hours per day @ $360 per hour (actual)
Special nursing care	4 hours per day @ $85 per hour (actual)
Regular nursing care	24 hours per day @ $28 per hour (average)
Medications	$240 per day (average)
Medical supplies	$150 per day (average)
Room rental	$350 per day (average)
Food and services	$140 per day (average)

The hospital director has asked the controller to compare the current billing procedure with one that uses industry averages to determine the billing per patient day.

REQUIRED

1. Compute the cost per patient per day.
2. Compute the billing per patient day using the hospital's existing markup rate. (Round to the nearest dollar.)
3. Compute the billing per patient day using the following industry averages for markup rates:

Equipment	30%	Medications	50%
Doctors' care	50	Medical supplies	50
Special nursing care	40	Room rental	30
Regular nursing care	50	Food and services	25

4. **ACCOUNTING CONNECTION ▶** Based on your findings in requirements 2 and 3, which billing procedure would you recommend? Why?

LO 7 **Professional Ethics**

P10. BUSINESS APPLICATION ▶ For almost a year, OK Company has been changing its manufacturing processes. Management has asked for employees' assistance in the transition and has offered bonuses for suggestions that cut time from the production operation. Jim Han and Jerome Smith each identified a time-saving opportunity and turned in their suggestions to their boss.

The boss sent the suggestions to the committee charged with reviewing employees' suggestions, which inadvertently identified them as being the boss's own. The committee decided that the two suggestions were worthy of reward and voted a large bonus for the boss. When notified of this, the boss could not bring himself to identify the true authors of the suggestions.

When Han and Smith heard about their boss's bonus, they confronted him and expressed their grievances. He told them that he needed the recognition to be eligible for an upcoming promotion and promised that if they kept quiet about the matter, he would make sure that they both received significant raises.

REQUIRED

1. Should Han and Smith keep quiet? What other options are open to them?
2. How should their boss have dealt with Han's and Smith's complaints?

CASES

LO 2 **Conceptual Understanding: Cost Recognition**

C1. CONCEPT ▶ Visit a local fast-food restaurant. Observe all aspects of the operation and take notes on the entire process. Describe the procedures used to take, process, and fill an order and deliver the food to the customer. Based on your observations, make a list of the costs incurred by the restaurant. Then create a table similar to Exhibit 4 in the

(Continued)

text, in which you recognize the costs you have identified by their traceability (direct or indirect), cost behavior (variable or fixed), value attribute (value-adding or non-value-adding), and implications for financial reporting (product or period costs). Bring your notes and your table to class and be prepared to discuss your findings.

LO **2, 6**

Business Communication: Management Decision about a Supporting Service Function

C2. As the manager of grounds maintenance for a large insurance company in Missouri, you are responsible for maintaining the grounds surrounding the company's three buildings, the six entrances to the property, and the recreational facilities, which include a golf course, a soccer field, jogging and bike paths, and tennis, basketball, and volleyball courts. Maintenance includes gardening (watering, planting, mowing, trimming, removing debris, and so on) and land improvements (e.g., repairing or replacing damaged or worn concrete and gravel areas).

Early in January, you receive a memo from the company president requesting information about the cost of operating your department for the last 12 months. She has received a bid from Outsource Landscapes, Inc., to perform the gardening activities you now perform. You are to prepare a cost report that will help her decide whether to keep gardening activities within the company or to outsource the work.

1. **BUSINESS APPLICATION** ▶ Before preparing your report, answer the following questions:
   a. What kinds of information do you need about your department?
   b. Why is this information relevant?
   c. Where would you go to obtain this information (sources)?
   d. When would you want to obtain this information?

2. Draft a report showing only headings and line items that best communicate the costs of your department. How would you change your report if the president asked you to reduce the costs of operating your department?

3. **CONCEPT** ▶ One of your department's cost accounts is the Maintenance Expense—Garden Equipment account.
   a. Is this a direct or an indirect cost?
   b. Is it a product or a period cost?
   c. Is it a variable or a fixed cost?
   d. Does the activity add value to the company business of insurance services?
   e. Is it a budgeted or an actual cost in your report?

LO **4, 6**

Conceptual Understanding: Management Information Needs

C3. H&Y Drug Corporation manufactures most of its three pharmaceutical products in India. Inventory balances for March and April follow.

	March 31	April 30
Materials Inventory	$258,400	$228,100
Work in Process Inventory	138,800	127,200
Finished Goods Inventory	111,700	114,100

During April, purchases of direct materials, which include natural materials, basic organic compounds, catalysts, and suspension agents, totaled $612,600. Direct labor costs were $160,000, and actual overhead costs were $303,500. Sales of the company's three products for April totaled $2,188,400. General and administrative expenses were $362,000.

1. Prepare a statement of cost of goods manufactured and an income statement through operating income for the month ended April 30.
2. Why is it that the total manufacturing costs do not equal the cost of goods manufactured?
3. What additional information would you need to determine the profitability of each of the three product lines?
4. **CONCEPT** ▶ Indicate whether each of the following is a product cost or a period cost:
   a. Import duties for indirect materials
   b. Shipping expenses to deliver manufactured products to the United States

    c. Rent for manufacturing facilities in India

    d. Salary of the American manager working at the Indian manufacturing facilities

    e. Training costs for an Indian accountant

LO **6**   **Interpreting Managerial Reports: Financial Performance Measures**

C4. Shape It Manufacturing Company makes sheet metal products. For the past several years, the company's income has been declining. Its statements of cost of goods manufactured and income statements for the last two years are shown here. Review and comment on why the ratios for Shape It's profitability have deteriorated.

Shape It Manufacturing Company
Statements of Cost of Goods Manufactured
For the Years Ended December 31

	This Year		Last Year	
Direct materials used:				
Materials inventory, beginning	$ 91,240		$ 93,560	
Direct materials purchased (net)	987,640		959,940	
Cost of direct materials available for use	$1,078,880		$1,053,500	
Less materials inventory, ending	95,020		91,240	
Cost of direct materials used		$ 983,860		$ 962,260
Direct labor		571,410		579,720
Total overhead		482,880		452,110
Total manufacturing costs		$2,038,150		$1,994,090
Add work in process inventory, beginning		148,875		152,275
Total cost of work in process during the period		$2,187,025		$2,146,365
Less work in process inventory, ending		146,750		148,875
Cost of goods manufactured		$2,040,275		$1,997,490

Shape It Manufacturing Company
Income Statements
For the Years Ended December 31

	This Year		Last Year	
Sales		$2,942,960		$3,096,220
Cost of goods sold	$ 142,640		$ 184,820	
Cost of goods manufactured	2,040,275		1,997,490	
Cost of goods available for sale	$2,182,915		$2,182,310	
Less finished goods inventory, ending	186,630		142,640	
Total		1,996,285		2,039,670
Gross margin		$ 946,675		$1,056,550
Selling and administrative expenses:				
Sales salaries and commissions	$ 394,840		$ 329,480	
Advertising expense	116,110		194,290	
Other selling expenses	82,680		72,930	
Administrative expenses	242,600		195,530	
Total selling and administrative expenses		836,230		792,230
Income from operations		$ 110,445		$ 264,320
Other revenues and expenses:				
Interest expense		54,160		56,815
Income before income taxes		$ 56,285		$ 207,505
Income tax expense		19,137		87,586
Net income		$ 37,148		$ 119,919

(Continued)

1. In preparing your comments, compute the following ratios for each year:
   a. Ratios of cost of direct materials used to total manufacturing costs, direct labor to total manufacturing costs, and total overhead to total manufacturing costs. (Round to one decimal place.)
   b. Ratios of sales salaries and commission expense, advertising expense, other selling expenses, administrative expenses, and total selling and administrative expenses to sales. (Round to one decimal place.)
   c. Ratios of gross margin to sales and net income to sales. (Round to one decimal place.)
2. From your evaluation of the ratios computed in **1,** state the probable causes of the decline in net income.
3. What other factors or ratios do you believe should be considered in determining the cause of the company's decreased income?

LO **6, 7**   ### Ethical Dilemma: Preventing Pollution and the Costs of Waste Disposal

C5. BUSINESS APPLICATION ▶ Lake Waburg Power Plant provides power to a metropolitan area of 4 million people. The plant's controller, Sunny Hope, has just returned from a conference on the Environmental Protection Agency's regulations concerning pollution prevention. She is meeting with the company's president, Guy Poe, to discuss the impact of the EPA's regulations on the plant.

"Guy, I'm really concerned. We haven't been monitoring the disposal of the radioactive material we send to the Willis Disposal Plant. If Willis is disposing of our waste material improperly, we could be sued," said Sunny. "We also haven't been recording the costs of the waste as part of our product cost. Ignoring those costs will have a negative impact on our decision about the next rate hike."

"Sunny, don't worry. I don't think we need to concern ourselves with the waste we send to Willis. We pay the company to dispose of it. The company takes it off our hands, and it's their responsibility to manage its disposal. As for the cost of waste disposal, I think we would have a hard time justifying a rate increase based on a requirement to record the full cost of waste as a cost of producing power. Let's just forget about waste and its disposal as a component of our power cost. We can get our rate increase without mentioning waste disposal," replied Guy.

What responsibility for monitoring the waste disposal practices at the Willis Disposal Plant does Lake Waburg Power Plant have? Should Sunny take Guy's advice to ignore waste disposal costs in calculating the cost of power? Be prepared to discuss your response.

Continuing Case: Cookie Company

C6. BUSINESS APPLICATION ▶ Each of the rest of the chapters in this text includes a "cookie company" case that allows you to explore operating your own cookie business. For this chapter, you will form a company team and assign roles to team members. As a team, you will prepare a mission statement; set strategic, tactical, and operating objectives; decide on a company name; set cookie specifications, decide on a cookie recipe, and answer some questions about product costs.

REQUIRED

1. Join with 4 or 5 other students in the class to form a company team. (Your instructor may assign groups or allow students to organize their own teams.)
2. In researching how to start and run a cookie business, your team found the following three examples of cookie company mission statements:
   ■ To provide cheap cookies that taste great with fast and courteous service!
   ■ To make the best chocolate chip cookies that anyone has ever tasted!
   ■ To handmake the best in custom cookie creations!

   a. Consider which of the mission statements most closely expresses what you want your company's identity and unique character to be. Why?
   b. Will your business focus on cost, quality, or satisfying a specific need?
   c. Write your company's mission statement.

3. Based on your mission statement, describe your company's broad long-term strategic objectives:
   a. What will be your main products?
   b. Who will be your primary customers?
   c. Where will you operate your business?

4. Your team made the following decisions about your business:
   - To list expected expenses and revenues for the first six months of operations
   - To keep expenses low and generate enough revenues during the first two months of operations to have a positive cash flow by the third month
   - To develop a complete list of goals, objectives, procedures, and policies relating to how to find, buy, store, sell, and ship goods and collect payment
   - To rely solely on the Internet to market products
   - To expand the e-commerce website to include 20 varieties of cookies over the next five years

   Match each of the above to the following components of the planning framework: strategic objectives, tactical objectives, operating objectives, business plan, and budget.

5. As a team:
   - Determine the name of your cookie company.
   - Determine team members' tasks, and make team assignments (e.g., mixer, baker, quality controller, materials purchaser, accountant, marketing manager).
   - Assign each task an hourly pay rate or monthly salary based on your team's perception of the job market for the task involved.
   - Give the plan compiled thus far to your instructor and all team members in writing.

6. As a team, determine cookie specifications: quality, size, appearance, and special features (such as types of chips or nuts), as well as quantity and packaging.

7. As a team, select a cookie recipe that best fits the company's mission.

8. As a team, answer the following questions and submit the answers to your instructor:
   - Will your company use actual or normal costing when computing the cost per cookie? Explain your answer.
   - List the types of costs that your company will recognize as overhead.

CHAPTER 2
Costing Systems: Job Order Costing

Club Car is the world's largest manufacturer of electric vehicles. Its product portfolio includes golf carts, commercial utility vehicles, multi-passenger shuttle vehicles, and rough-terrain and off-road utility vehicles. When Club Car builds made-to-order golf carts, its customers can choose the type of wheels and windshield the golf cart should have, the cart's interior and exterior trim, the upholstery fabric, and a dashboard with or without oversized cup holders. They can also specify whether they want the cart to have a music system, a global positioning system, and a propane heater. They can even specify the sound of the golf cart's horn. In this chapter, we focus on the job order costing system—the type of system that makers of special-order products, such as a customized golf cart, use to account for costs and to make informed product decisions.

1. **CONCEPT** ▶ *Why is a job order costing system appropriate for Club Car to measure and recognize costs?*

2. **ACCOUNTING APPLICATION** ▶ *How does a product costing system account for costs when made-to-order products or services are produced?*

3. **BUSINESS APPLICATION** ▶ *How does a job order costing system help managers organize and control costs and facilitate management decisions?*

LEARNING OBJECTIVES

LO 1 Distinguish between the two basic types of product costing systems, and identify the information that each provides.

LO 2 Explain the cost flow in a manufacturer's job order costing system.

LO 3 Prepare a job order cost card, and compute a job order's product or service unit cost.

LO 4 Explain cost allocation, and describe how allocating overhead costs figures into calculating product or service unit cost.

LO 5 Explain why unit cost measurement is important to the management process in producing business results.

SECTION 1 — CONCEPTS

CONCEPTS

■ Cost measurement

■ Cost recognition

■ Matching rule
(accrual accounting)

**RELEVANT
LEARNING OBJECTIVE**

LO 1 Distinguish between
the two basic types of
product costing systems, and
identify the information that
each provides.

LO 1 Concepts Underlying Product Costing Systems

A **product costing system** is used to account for an organization's product costs and to provide timely and accurate unit cost information for pricing, cost planning and control, inventory valuation, and financial statement preparation.

■ The product costing system enables managers to measure and recognize costs throughout the management process.

■ It provides a measurement and recognition structure for *matching* the recording of the revenues earned from product or service sales to their related cost flows.

Job Order and Process Costing Systems

Two basic types of product costing systems have been developed: job order costing systems and process costing systems.

A **job order costing system** is used by companies that make unique or special-order products, such as custom-tailored suits. A job order costing system *measures* and *recognizes* the costs of direct materials, direct labor, and overhead to a specific batch of products or a specific **job order** (i.e., a customer order for a specific number of specially designed, made-to-order products) by using job order cost cards. A **job order cost card** is usually an electronic or paper document on which all costs incurred in the production of a particular job order—a completed unit—are recorded and *matched* with the job's revenues. In other words, in a job order costing system, the specific job or batch of a product (not a department or work cell) is the focus of *cost measurement* and *recognition*.

A **process costing system** is used by companies that produce large amounts of similar products or liquid products or that have long, continuous production runs of identical products. Makers of soft drinks, candy, bricks, and paper would use such a system. It first traces the costs of direct materials, direct labor, and overhead to processes, departments, or work cells and then assigns the costs to the products manufactured by those processes, departments, or work cells during a specific period using a process cost report. A **process cost report** is usually an electronic or paper document prepared every period for each process, department, or work cell and is explained fully in the next chapter.

The typical product costing system combines parts of job order costing and process costing to create a hybrid system known as an **operations costing system**.

Exhibit 1 summarizes the characteristics of both costing systems.

Exhibit 1

Characteristics of Job Order Costing and Process Costing Systems

Job Order Costing System	Process Costing System
Traces production costs to a specific job order	Traces production costs to processes, departments, or work cells and then assigns the costs to products manufactured
Measures the cost of each completed unit	Measures costs in terms of units completed during a specific period
Uses a single Work in Process Inventory account	Uses several Work in Process Inventory accounts
Measures the cost of all job orders using one inventory account	Measures costs of each process, department, or work cell, using an inventory account for each
Typically used by companies that make unique or special-order products, such as customized publications, built-in cabinets, or made-to-order draperies	Typically used by companies that make large amounts of similar products or liquid products or that have long, continuous production runs of identical products, such as paint, soft drinks, candy, bricks, and paper

© Cengage Learning 2014

APPLY IT!

State whether a job order costing system or a process costing system would typically be used to account for the costs of the following:

a. Manufacturing golf tees

b. Manufacturing custom-designed fencing for a specific golf course

c. Providing pet grooming

d. Manufacturing golf balls

e. Manufacturing dog food

f. Providing private golf lessons

SOLUTION

a. process;   b. job order;
c. job order;   d. process;
e. process;   f. job order

TRY IT! SE1, E1A, E2A, E3A, E1B, E2B, E3B

SECTION 2

ACCOUNTING APPLICATIONS

ACCOUNTING APPLICATIONS

- Prepare a job order cost card
- Compute a job order's product or service unit cost

RELEVANT LEARNING OBJECTIVES

LO 2 Explain the cost flow in a manufacturer's job order costing system.

LO 3 Prepare a job order cost card, and compute a job order's product or service unit cost.

LO 4 Explain cost allocation, and describe how allocating overhead costs figures into calculating product or service unit cost.

LO 2 Job Order Costing in a Manufacturing Company

The basic parts of a job order costing system are the cost measurement and recognition procedures, electronic documents, and accounts that a company uses when it incurs costs for direct materials, direct labor, and overhead. Job order cost cards and cost flows through the inventory accounts form the core of a job order costing system.

Let's take a hypothetical company, Custom Golf Carts, which builds both customized and general-purpose golf carts. To study these cost flows, let's look at how Custom operates.

- Direct materials costs include the costs of a cart frame, wheels, upholstered seats, a windshield, a motor, and a rechargeable battery.
- Direct labor costs include the wages of the two production workers who assemble the golf carts.
- Overhead costs include indirect materials costs for upholstery zippers; cloth straps to hold equipment in place; wheel lubricants, screws and fasteners; silicon to attach the windshield; indirect labor costs for moving materials to the production area and inspecting a golf cart during its construction; depreciation on the manufacturing plant and equipment used to make the golf carts; and utilities, insurance, and property taxes related to the manufacturing plant.

Exhibit 2 shows the flow of each of these costs. The beginning balance in the Materials Inventory account means that there are already direct and indirect materials in the materials storeroom. The beginning balance in Work in Process Inventory means that Job CC is in production (with specifics given in the job order cost card). The zero beginning balance in Finished Goods Inventory means that all previously completed golf carts have been shipped.

Materials

The purchasing process begins with a request for specific quantities of direct and indirect materials that are needed for a sales order but are not currently available in the materials storeroom. When the new materials arrive, the Accounting Department records the materials purchased. It is helpful to understand the process of tracking production costs as they flow through the three inventory accounts and the entries that are triggered by the organization's source documents. The entries that track product cost flows are provided as background.

Purchase of Materials

Transactions 1 and 2 During the month, Custom made two purchases on credit. In transaction **1**, the company purchased cart frames costing $572 and wheels costing $340 for a total of $912. In transaction **2**, the company purchased indirect materials costing $82.

Analysis The journal entry to record these purchases

▲ *increases* the *Materials Inventory* account with a debit

▲ *increases* the *Accounts Payable* account with a credit

Journal Entries

	Dr.	Cr.
Materials Inventory	912	
Accounts Payable		912
Materials Inventory	82	
Accounts Payable		82

Comment Cost of direct and indirect materials are *recognized* when purchased.

Exhibit 2
The Job Order Costing System—Custom Golf Carts, Inc.

Materials Inventory			
Beg. bal.	1,230	(3)	1,880
(1)	912	(3)	96
(2)	82		
End. bal.	**248**		

Payroll Payable			
		(4)	1,640
		(5)	760
		End. bal.	**2,400**

Overhead			
(3)	96	(8)	1,394
(5)	760		
(6)	295		
(7)	240		
	1,391		*1,394*
(11)	3		
End. bal.	**—**		

Cash			
		(6)	295
		End. bal.	**295**

Accounts Receivable			
(10)	3,000		
End. bal.	**3,000**		

Accumulated Depreciation			
		(7)	240
		End. bal.	**240**

Work in Process Inventory			
Beg. bal.	400	(9)	3,880
(3)	1,880		
(4)	1,640		
(8)	1,394		
End. bal.	**1,434**		

Finished Goods Inventory			
Beg. bal.	—	(10)	1,940
(9)	3,880		
End. bal.	**1,940**		

Cost of Goods Sold			
(10)	1,940	(11)	3
End. bal.	**1,937**		

Accounts Payable			
		(1)	912
		(2)	82
		End. bal.	**994**

Sales			
		(10)	3,000
		End. bal.	**3,000**

Transfer of Direct Materials to Production

Transaction 3—Direct Materials When golf carts are scheduled for production, requested materials are sent to the production area. Custom requested $1,880 of direct materials for the production of two jobs. These costs are also recorded on the corresponding job order cost cards. Job CC, a batch run of two general-purpose golf carts already in production, required $1,038 of the additional direct materials. Job JB, a customized golf cart made to the specifications of an individual customer, Alex Special, required $842 of the direct materials.

Analysis The journal entry to record the transfer of direct materials to production

    ▲ *increases* the *Work in Process Inventory* account with a debit (and also *increases* the charges to the corresponding job order cost cards)

    ▼ *decreases* the *Materials Inventory* account with a credit

Journal Entry

	Dr.	Cr.
Work in Process Inventory—Job CC	1,038	
Work in Process Inventory—Job JB	842	
Materials Inventory		1,880

Comment Custom processes requests for direct materials through journal entries to track cost flows and *measure* the cost of each job order.

Transfer of Indirect Materials to Production

Transaction 3—Indirect Materials Custom also requests indirect materials. When indirect materials are requested and sent to production, the indirect materials cost flows from the Materials Inventory account into the Overhead account.

Analysis The journal entry to record the transfer of indirect materials to production

▲ *increases* the *Overhead* account with a debit

▼ *decreases* the *Materials Inventory* account with a credit

Journal Entry

	Dr.	Cr.
Overhead	96	
Materials Inventory		96

Comment Custom processes requests for indirect materials through journal entries to track cost flows and *measure* the actual cost of overhead.

Labor

In general, the payroll costs include salaries and wages for direct and indirect production labor as well as for nonproduction-related employees. Custom's two production employees assemble the golf carts. Several other employees support production by moving materials and inspecting the products.

Payroll Costs Incurred for Production Labor

Transactions 4 and 5 Transactions **4** and **5** show the total production-related wages earned by employees during the period. Custom incurred $1,640 of direct labor costs—$1,320 for Job CC and $320 for Job JB—(transaction **4**) and $760 indirect labor costs (transaction **5**).

Analysis The journal entry to record the direct labor costs

▲ *increases* the *Work in Process Inventory* account with a debit

▲ *increases* the *Payroll Payable* account with a credit

The journal entry to record the indirect labor costs

▲ *increases* the *Overhead* account with a debit

▲ *increases* the *Payroll Payable* account with a credit

Journal Entry

	Dr.	Cr.
Work in Process Inventory—Job CC	1,320	
Work in Process Inventory—Job JB	320	
Payroll Payable		1,640
Overhead (indirect labor costs)	760	
Payroll Payable		760

Comment Custom *recognizes* labor costs through journal entries to *measure* the direct labor cost of each job order and to measure the actual cost of indirect labor and other nonproduction-related labor cost flows into overhead.

Overhead

Thus far, indirect materials and indirect labor have been the only costs debited to the Overhead account. Other actual indirect production costs, such as utilities, property taxes, insurance, and depreciation, are also charged to the Overhead account as they are incurred during the period.

Other Overhead Costs Incurred for Production

Transactions 6 and 7 Transaction **6** shows that other indirect costs amounting to $295 were paid. Transaction **7** records the $240 of production-related depreciation.

Analysis The journal entry to record incurring actual overhead costs

▲ *increases* the *Overhead* account with a debit

▼ *decreases* the *Cash* and *Accumulated Depreciation* accounts with a credit

Journal Entry

	Dr.	Cr.
Overhead	295	
Cash		295
Overhead	240	
Accumulated Depreciation		240

Comment Custom *recognizes* actual overhead costs on the debit side of the Overhead account so it can *measure* them against the overhead costs estimated for job orders.

During the period, to *recognize* all product-related costs for a job, an overhead cost estimate is applied to a job using a predetermined rate since the business uses a normal costing method to *measure* product costs. Based on its budget and past experience, Custom currently uses a predetermined overhead rate of 85 percent of direct labor costs.

Estimate of Overhead Costs

Transaction 8 In transaction **8**, Custom estimates the overhead incurred by each job to date by charging each job order in process with a percentage of its labor cost incurred. Total overhead of $1,394 is applied to the job orders, with $1,122 going to Job CC (85 percent of $1,320) and $272 going to Job JB (85 percent of $320).

Analysis The journal entry to record applying overhead using a predetermined rate

▲ *increases* the *Work in Process Inventory* account with a debit for $1,394 (85 percent of $1,640; see transaction **4**)

▼ *decreases* the *Overhead* account with a credit for the applied overhead of $1,394

Journal Entry

	Dr.	Cr.
Work in Process Inventory—Job CC	1,122	
Work in Process Inventory—Job JB	272	
Overhead		1,394

Comment Custom compares the actual (debit side of the Overhead account) and applied (credit side of the Overhead account) overhead amounts at the end of the period to determine the accuracy of job order overhead *cost recognition*.

Completed Units

When a custom job or a batch of general-purpose golf carts is completed and ready for sale, the products are moved from the manufacturing area to the finished goods storeroom.

Transfer of Completed Production to Finished Goods

Transaction 9 In transaction **9**, a job order is completed and transferred to the Finished Goods Inventory account since it is ready for sale. Custom's Job CC is completed and its cost of $3,880 is transferred from the Work in Process Inventory account to the Finished Goods Inventory account. The $3,880 includes the beginning balance of $400, materials of $1,038, labor of $1,320, and overhead of $1,122. Thus, the cost to produce one golf cart is $1,940 ($3,880 ÷ 2).

Analysis The journal entry to record completing a job order

- ▲ *increases* the *Finished Goods Inventory* account with a debit
- ▼ *decreases* the *Work in Process Inventory* account with a credit

Journal Entry

	Dr.	Cr.
Finished Goods Inventory	3,880	
Work in Process Inventory—Job CC		3,880

Comment When a job order is complete, its job order cost card has *measured* and *recognized* all the costs associated with its production. The job's cost of goods manufactured and product unit cost can be computed. The card is also transferred to the finished goods file.

Sold Units

When a company uses a perpetual inventory system, as Custom does, two accounting entries are made when products are sold. One is prompted by the sales invoice and records the quantity and selling price of the products sold. The other entry, prompted by the delivery of products to a customer, records the quantity and cost of the products shipped.

Sales and the Transfer of Production Costs to Cost of Goods Sold

Transaction 10 In transaction **10**, a golf cart is sold to a customer and its cost of the goods sold is recognized. The $3,000 sales price of the one general-purpose golf cart sold on account by Custom is recorded. As was explained in Transaction **9**, the sold golf cart's related cost is $1,940. This cost is now transferred from the Finished Goods Inventory account to the Cost of Goods Sold account.

Analysis The journal entry to record a product's sales price and associated costs

- ▲ *increases* the *Accounts Receivable* account
- ▲ *increases* the *Sales* account
- ▲ *increases* the *Cost of Goods Sold* account
- ▼ *decreases* the *Finished Goods Inventory* account

Journal Entries

	Dr.	Cr.
Accounts Receivable (sales price of 1 unit sold)	3,000	
Sales (sales price of 1 unit sold)		3,000
Cost of Goods Sold (unit cost)	1,940	
Finished Goods Inventory (unit cost)		1,940

Comment When a job or product is sold, its revenues are *matched* with its costs. Since the job or product's revenue and costs have been *measured* and *recognized*, profitability can be analyzed. Notice the Finished Goods Inventory account has an ending balance of $1,940 for the one remaining unsold car from Job CC.

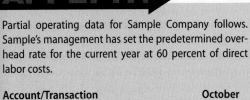

Partial operating data for Sample Company follows. Sample's management has set the predetermined overhead rate for the current year at 60 percent of direct labor costs.

SOLUTION

Materials Inventory

Beg. bal.	4,000	Used		16,000
(a) Purchases	15,000			
End. bal.	**3,000**			

Account/Transaction	October
Beginning Materials Inventory	$ 4,000
Beginning Work in Process Inventory	6,000
Beginning Finished Goods Inventory	2,000
Direct materials used	16,000
Direct materials purchased	(a)
Direct labor costs	24,000
Overhead applied	(b)
Cost of units completed	(c)
Cost of Goods Sold	50,000
Ending Materials Inventory	3,000
Ending Work in Process Inventory	10,000
Ending Finished Goods Inventory	(d)

Work in Process Inventory

Beg. bal.	6,000	(c) Completed during period	50,400
Direct materials used	16,000		
Direct labor	24,000		
(b) Overhead applied	14,400*		
End. bal.	**10,000**		

Using T accounts, compute the unknown values. Show all your computations.

Finished Goods Inventory

Beg. bal.	2,000	Cost of goods sold	50,000
(c) Completed during period	50,400		
(d) **End. bal.**	**2,400**		

*$24,000 × 60% = $14,400

TRY IT! SE2, SE3, SE4, E4A, E5A, E6A, E7A, E8A, E4B, E5B, E6B, E7B, E8B

LO 3 A Job Order Cost Card and the Computation of Unit Cost

STUDY NOTE: *Traditionally, job order cost cards were paper, but today, most cards reside electronically in a computer system.*

In a job order costing system, each job in production has a job order cost card. As costs are incurred, they are classified by job and recorded on the appropriate card.

A Manufacturer's Job Order Cost Card

A manufacturer's job order cost card typically has space for direct materials, direct labor, and overhead costs, as shown in Exhibit 3. It also includes the job order number, product specifications, customer name, date of the order, projected completion date, and a cost summary. As a job incurs direct materials and direct labor costs, its job order cost card is updated. Overhead is also posted to the job order cost card at the predetermined rate.

Job order cost cards for incomplete jobs make up the subsidiary ledger for the Work in Process Inventory account. To ensure correctness, the ending balance in the Work in Process Inventory account is compared with the total of the costs shown on the job order cost cards.

Computation of Unit Cost

A job order costing system simplifies the calculation of product unit costs. When a job is finished, the costs of direct materials, direct labor, and overhead that have been recorded on its job order cost card are totaled. The product unit cost is then computed and entered on the job order cost card. It will be used to value items in inventory. The job

JOB ORDER COST CARD *
Custom Golf Carts, Inc.
Spring Hill, Florida

Job Order: ____CC____

Customer: __Stock__   Batch: ___X___   Custom: _____

Specifications: __Two general-purpose golf carts__

Date of Order: __2/26/14__

Date of Completion: __3/6/14__

Costs Charged to Job	Previous Months	Current Month	Total Cost
Direct materials	$165	$1,038	$1,203
Direct labor	127	1,320	1,447
Overhead (85% of direct labor cost)	108*	1,122	1,230*
Totals	$400	$3,480	$3,880
Units completed			÷ 2
Product unit cost			$1,940

*Rounded to nearest dollar

© Cengage Learning 2014

order cost card in Exhibit 3 shows the costs for completed Job CC. The product unit cost is computed as follows.

Product Unit Cost = Total Costs for Job ÷ Number of Good (Salable) Units Produced
= $3,880 ÷ 2
= $1,940

Job Order Costing in a Service Organization

Many service organizations use a job order costing system to compute the cost of rendering services. The most important cost for a service organization is labor, which is accounted for through the use of time cards. The cost flow of services is similar to the cost flow of manufactured products. Job order cost cards are used to keep track of the labor, materials and supplies, and service overhead incurred for each job.

To cover these costs and earn a profit, many service organizations base jobs on **cost-plus contracts**. Such contracts require the customer to pay all costs incurred in performing the job plus a predetermined amount of profit, which is based on the amount of costs incurred. When the job is complete, the costs on the completed job order cost card become the cost of services.

To illustrate how a service organization uses a job order costing system, assume that Dream Golf Retreats earns its revenue by designing and selling golf retreat packages to corporate clients. Exhibit 4 shows Dream Golf Retreats' job order cost card for Work Corporation. Costs have been categorized into three separate activities: planning, golf activities, and nongolf activities.

STUDY NOTE: Job order cost cards for service businesses record costs by activities done for the job. The activity costs may include supplies, labor, and overhead.

Exhibit 4
Job Order Cost Card for a Service Organization

Job Order: 2011-A7

JOB ORDER COST CARD
Dream Golf Retreats

Customer: Work Corporation	**Batch:** _____	**Custom:** X

Specifications: Golf retreat for 45 executives

Date of Order: 3/24/14   **Date of Completion:** 4/8/14

Costs Charged to Job	Previous Months	Current Month	Total Cost
Planning:			
Supplies	$ 100	$ —	$ 100
Labor	850		850
Overhead (40% of planning labor costs)	340	—	340
Totals	$1,290	$ 0	$1,290
Golf activities:			
Supplies	$ 970	$1,200	$2,170
Labor	400	620	1,020
Overhead (50% of on-site labor costs)	200	310	510
Totals	$1,570	$2,130	$3,700
Nongolf activities:			
Cost of outsourcing	$ 90	$ 320	$ 410
Totals	$ 90	$ 320	$ 410

Cost Summary to Date	Total Cost
Planning	$1,290
Golf activities	3,700
Nongolf activities	410
Total	$5,400
Profit margin (15% of total cost)	810
Job revenue	$6,210

As Exhibit 4 illustrates, the service overhead cost for planning is 40 percent of planning labor cost ($850 × 0.40 = $340) and the service overhead cost for golf activities is 50 percent of on-site labor cost ($1,020 × 0.50 = $510). Total costs incurred for this job were $5,400. Dream Golf Retreats' cost-plus contract with Work Corporation has a 15 percent profit guarantee. Therefore, $810 of profit margin ($5,400 × 0.15 = $810) is added to the total cost to arrive at the total contract revenue ($5,400 + $810 = $6,210), which is billed to Work Corporation.

APPLY IT!

Complete the following job order cost card for six handcrafted sets of golf clubs:

Job Order <u>16</u>

JOB ORDER COST CARD
Craftsman Golf Clubs
World of Golf, FL

Customer: Kalpesh Patel   Batch: ___   Custom: X

Specifications: 6 sets of clubs

Date of Order: 5/4/14   Date of Completion: 6/8/14

Costs Charged to Job	Previous Months	Current Month	Total Cost
Direct materials	$3,500	$2,800	$?
Direct labor	2,300	1,600	?
Overhead applied	1,150	800	?
Totals	$?	$?	$?
Units completed			÷ ?
Product unit cost			$?

SOLUTION

Job Order <u>16</u>

JOB ORDER COST CARD
Craftsman Golf Clubs
World of Golf, FL

Customer: Kalpesh Patel   Batch: ___   Custom: X

Specifications: 6 sets of clubs

Date of Order: 5/4/14   Date of Completion: 6/8/14

Costs Charged to Job	Previous Months	Current Month	Total Cost
Direct materials	$3,500	$2,800	$ 6,300
Direct labor	2,300	1,600	3,900
Overhead applied	1,150	800	1,950
Totals	$6,950	$5,200	$12,150
Units completed			÷ 6
Product unit cost			$ 2,025

TRY IT! SE5, SE6, SE7, E6A, E7A, E8A, E9A, E10A, E11A, E12A, E13A, E6B, E7B, E8B, E9B, E10B, E11B, E12B, E13B

LO 4 Cost Allocation

The costs of direct materials and direct labor can be easily traced to a product or service, but overhead costs are indirect costs that must be collected and allocated in some manner since their physical flow and how these costs are incurred do not always match. For example, utilities are used daily, but the utility bill comes once a month.

■   **Cost allocation** is the process of assigning a collection of indirect costs, such as overhead, to a specific **cost object**, such as a product or service, a department, or an operating activity, using an allocation base known as a cost driver.

■   A **cost driver** might be direct labor hours, direct labor costs, units produced, or another activity base that has a cause-and-effect relationship with the cost.

■   As the cost driver increases in volume, it causes the **cost pool**—the collection of indirect costs assigned to a cost object—to increase in amount.

AfriPics.com/Alamy

Cost allocation is the process of assigning costs to a specific cost object using a cost driver. This ties the cost to an identifiable and measurable activity base.

Allocating the Costs of Overhead

Allocating overhead costs to products or services is a four-step process.

Step 1. Planning the Overhead Rate Before a period begins, managers determine cost pools and cost drivers and calculate a **predetermined overhead rate** as follows.

$$\frac{\text{Predetermined}}{\text{Overhead Rate}} = \frac{\text{Estimated Overhead Costs}}{\text{Estimated Cost Driver Activity}}$$

For example, earlier in this chapter, Custom Golf Carts used a predetermined overhead rate of 85 percent of direct labor costs.

Step 2. Applying the Overhead Rate As units of the product or service are produced during the period, the estimated overhead costs are assigned to the product or service using the predetermined overhead rate as follows.

$$\text{Overhead Applied} = \text{Predetermined Overhead Rate} \times \text{Actual Cost Driver Activity}$$

The purpose of this calculation is to assign a consistent overhead cost to each unit produced during the period.

Custom used a predetermined overhead rate of 85 percent of direct labor costs to apply overhead of $1,394, with $1,122 going to Job CC (85% of $1,320 direct labor costs) and $272 going to Job JB (85% of $320 direct labor costs) as shown in Transaction **8** in Exhibit 2.

Step 3. Recording Actual Overhead Costs The actual overhead costs are recorded as they are incurred during the period. These costs include the actual costs of indirect materials, indirect labor, depreciation, property taxes, and other production costs. The entry for the actual overhead costs debits the Overhead account and credits the asset, contra-asset, or liability account(s) affected.

For example, Custom incurred actual overhead costs for indirect materials, indirect labor, other indirect costs, and production-related depreciation by debiting Overhead and crediting the appropriate accounts, as shown in Transactions **3**, **5**, **6**, and **7** in Exhibit 2.

Step 4. Reconciling the Applied and Actual Overhead Amounts At the end of the period, the difference between the applied and actual overhead costs is calculated and reconciled.

For example, Custom incurred actual overhead costs of $1,391 and applied overhead of $1,394, as shown in the Overhead account in Exhibit 2.

STUDY NOTE: Why do financial statements require the reconciliation of overhead costs? Financial statements report actual cost information; therefore, estimated overhead costs applied during the accounting period must be adjusted to reflect actual overhead costs.

Overhead			
(3)	96	(8)	1,394
(5)	760		
(6)	295		
(7)	240		
		Bal. (overapplied)	3

Overapplied Overhead If the overhead costs applied to production during the period are greater than the actual overhead costs, the difference in the amounts represents **overapplied overhead costs**. If this difference is immaterial, the Overhead account is debited or increased and the Cost of Goods Sold or Cost of Sales account is credited or decreased by the difference. If the difference is material for the products produced, adjustments are made to the accounts affected—that is, the Work in Process Inventory, Finished Goods Inventory, and Cost of Goods Sold accounts.

For example, Custom determined that actual overhead cost for the period ($1,391) is less than the overhead applied during the period ($1,394), resulting in the $3 credit balance. This $3 overapplied balance must be closed to the Cost of Goods Sold account, as shown in Transaction 11 in Exhibit 2.

Closing the Overhead Account

Transaction 11 In transaction 11, Custom closes the Overhead account balance to Cost of Goods Sold at the end of a period so the Cost of Goods Sold account will contain the actual costs of direct materials, direct labor, and overhead. Overhead has a $3 credit balance so Custom has overapplied overhead costs to the jobs produced.

Analysis The journal entry to close immaterial overapplied overhead

▲ *increases* the *Overhead* account with a debit

▼ *decreases* the *Cost of Goods Sold* account with a credit

Journal Entry

	Dr.	Cr.
Overhead	3	
Cost of Goods Sold		3

Comment Custom compares the actual (debit side of the Overhead account) and applied (Credit side of the Overhead account) overhead amounts at the end of the period and closes the difference to improve the accuracy of *cost measurement* of products produced and sold.

Underapplied Overhead If the overhead costs applied to production during the period are less than the actual overhead costs, the difference represents **underapplied overhead costs**. If the difference is immaterial, the Cost of Goods Sold or Cost of Sales account is debited or increased and the Overhead account is credited or decreased by this difference. If the difference is material for the products produced, adjustments are made to the accounts affected—that is, the Work in Process Inventory, Finished Goods Inventory, and Cost of Goods Sold accounts.

If the actual overhead debit balance exceeds the applied overhead credit balance, then the Overhead account is said to be underapplied and the debit balance must be closed to the Cost of Goods Sold account. The journal entry would be as follows.

	Dr.	Cr.
Cost of Goods Sold	XX	
Overhead		XX

Actual Cost of Goods Sold or Cost of Sales

The adjustment for overapplied or underapplied overhead costs is necessary to reflect the actual overhead costs on the income statement. For example, Custom Golf Carts determined Cost of Goods Sold ending balance was actually $1,937 after the overapplied amount of $3 reduced Cost of Goods Sold, as shown in Exhibit 2.

Exhibit 5 summarizes the four steps involved in allocating overhead costs to products or services in terms of their timing, the procedures involved, and the entries required. It also shows how the cost flows in the various steps affect the accounting records.

Exhibit 5
Allocating Overhead Cost: A Four-Step Process

Year 1 ──► Year 2 ──────────────────────►
                        January 1   December 31

	Step 1: Planning the Overhead Rate	Step 2: Applying the Overhead Rate	Step 3: Recording Actual Overhead Costs	Step 4: Reconciling Applied and Actual Overhead Costs
Timing and Procedure	Before the accounting period begins, determine cost pools and cost drivers. Calculate the overhead rate by dividing the cost pool of total estimated overhead costs by the total estimated cost driver level.	During the accounting period, as units are produced, apply overhead costs to products by multiplying the predetermined overhead rate for each cost pool by the actual cost driver level for that pool. Record costs.	Record actual overhead costs as they are incurred during the accounting period.	At the end of the accounting period, calculate and reconcile the difference between applied and actual overhead costs.

Entry	None	Increase Work in Process Inventory account and decrease Overhead account:
		 Dr. Work in Process Inventory XX
		    Cr. Overhead XX
			Increase Overhead account and decrease asset accounts or increase contra-asset or liability accounts:
			 Dr. Overhead XX
			    Cr. Various Accounts XX
				Entry will vary depending on how costs have been applied. If overapplied, increase Overhead and decrease Cost of Goods Sold. If underapplied, increase Cost of Goods Sold and decrease Overhead.

Cost Flow Through the Accounts		Overhead 	Overhead Actual overhead costs recorded	**Overapplied:** Overhead

Cost Flow Through the Accounts — Step 2:

Overhead
	Overhead applied using predetermined rate

Work in Process Inventory
Overhead applied using predetermined rate	

Cost Flow Through the Accounts — Step 3:

Overhead
Actual overhead costs recorded	

Various Asset and Liability Accounts
	Actual overhead costs recorded

Cost Flow Through the Accounts — Step 4:

Overapplied:
Overhead
Actual overhead costs recorded	Overhead applied using predetermined rate
	Overapplied
Bal. $0	

Cost of Goods Sold
Bal.	Overapplied
Actual Bal.	

Underapplied:
Overhead
Actual overhead costs recorded	Overhead applied using predetermined rate
	Underapplied
Bal. $0	

Cost of Goods Sold
Bal.	
Underapplied	
Actual Bal.	

Allocating Overhead: The Traditional Approach

The traditional approach to applying overhead costs to a product or service is to use a single plantwide overhead rate. This approach is especially useful when companies manufacture only one product or a few very similar products that require the same production processes and production-related activities, such as setup, inspection, and materials handling. The total overhead costs constitute one cost pool, and a traditional activity base—such as direct labor hours, direct labor costs, machine hours, or units of production—is the cost driver.

Allocating Overhead: The ABC Approach

Activity-based costing (ABC) is a more accurate method of assigning overhead costs to products or services. It categorizes all indirect costs by activity, traces the indirect costs to those activities, and assigns activity costs to products or services using a cost driver related to the cause of the cost. A company that uses ABC identifies production-related activities or tasks and the events that cause, or drive, those activities, such as number of inspections or maintenance hours. As a result, many smaller activity pools are created from the single overhead cost pool used in the traditional method. This means that managers will calculate many rates. There will be an activity cost rate for each activity pool, which must be applied to products or services produced. Managers must select an appropriate number of activity pools instead of the traditional plantwide rate for overhead.

More careful cost allocation means that managers will have better information for decision making. The ABC approach to allocating overhead will be covered in a later chapter.

APPLY IT!

1. Compute the predetermined overhead rate for Sample Service Company if its estimated overhead costs for the coming year will be $15,000 and 5,000 direct labor hours will be worked.
2. Calculate the amount of overhead costs applied by Sample Company to one of its jobs if the job required 10 direct labor hours to complete.
3. Compute the total cost of the job if prime (direct material and direct labor) costs incurred by Sample Company to complete it were $60. If the job contained 5 units of service, what is the unit cost?
4. Using the traditional overhead rate computed in Step 1, determine the total amount of overhead applied to operations during the year if Sample Company compiles a total of 4,900 labor hours worked.
5. If Sample Company's actual overhead costs for the year are $14,800, compute the amount of under- or overapplied overhead for the year. Will the Cost of Goods Sold account be increased or decreased to correct the under- or overapplication of overhead?

SOLUTION

1. $$\text{Predetermined Overhead Rate} = \frac{\text{Estimated Overhead Costs}}{\text{Estimated Direct Labor Hours (DLH)}}$$

$$= \frac{\$15,000}{5,000 \text{ DLH}} = \$3 \text{ per DLH}$$

2. Overhead Costs Applied = Predetermined Overhead Rate × Actual Hours Worked
   = $3 per DLH × 10 Actual Direct Labor Hours Worked
   = $30

3. Total Cost = Prime Costs + Applied Overhead Cost
   = $60 + $30
   = $90

$$\text{Unit Cost} = \frac{\text{Total Cost of Job}}{\text{Units Produced}}$$

$$= \frac{\$90}{5 \text{ units}}$$

= $18 per unit

4. Overhead Costs Applied = Predetermined Overhead Rate × Actual Hours Worked
   = $3 per DLH × 4,900 Actual Hours Worked
   = $14,700

5. Overhead Costs Applied = $14,700
   Actual Overhead Costs = 14,800
   Underapplied Overhead = $ 100, which will increase the Cost of Goods Sold account

TRY IT! SE8, SE9, SE10, E9A, E10A, E11A, E12A, E13A, E14A, E15A, E9B, E10B, E11B, E12B, E13B, E14B, E15B

**BUSINESS
APPLICATIONS**
■ Planning
■ Performing
■ Evaluating
■ Communicating

**RELEVANT
LEARNING OBJECTIVE**

LO 5   Explain why unit cost
measurement is
important to the
management process in
producing business results.

LO 5 Product Unit Cost Information and the Management Process

Managers depend on relevant and reliable information about costs to manage their organizations. Although they vary in their approaches, managers share the same basic concerns as they move through the management process.

Planning

Managers' unit cost knowledge helps them set reasonable selling prices and estimate the cost of their products or services.

■ In manufacturing companies, such as **Club Car**, **LLC**, **Toyota**, and **Levi Strauss & Co.**, managers use unit cost information to develop budgets, establish product prices, and plan production volumes.
■ In service organizations, such as **Google**, **H&R Block**, and **UPS**, managers use cost information to develop budgets, establish prices, set sales goals, and determine human resource needs.

Performing

Managers make decisions every day about controlling costs, managing the company's activity volume, ensuring quality, and negotiating prices. They use timely cost and volume information and actual unit costs to support their decisions.

■ In manufacturing companies, managers use cost information to decide whether to drop a product line, add a production shift, outsource the manufacture of a subassembly to another company, bid on a special order, or negotiate a selling price.
■ In service organizations, managers use cost information to make decisions about bidding on jobs, dropping a current service, outsourcing a task to an independent contractor, adding staff, or negotiating a price.

Evaluating

When managers evaluate results, they watch for changes in cost and quality. They compare actual and targeted total and unit costs, assess relevant price and volume information, and then adjust their planning and decision-making strategies. For example, if a service business's unit cost has risen, managers may break the unit cost down into its many components to analyze where costs can be cut or how the service can be performed more efficiently.

Communicating

Internal and external users analyze the data in the performance evaluation reports to determine whether the business is achieving cost goals. When managers report to stakeholders, they prepare financial statements.

■ In manufacturing companies, managers use product unit costs to determine inventory balances and the cost of goods sold.
■ In service organizations, managers use unit costs of services to determine the cost of sales.

When managers prepare internal performance evaluation reports, they compare actual unit costs with targeted costs, as well as actual and targeted nonfinancial measures of performance.

Supporting the Management Process

Exhibit 6 shows how managers use unit cost information throughout the management process to fulfill the management concepts of planning and forecasting operations, organizing and coordinating resources and data, and commanding and controlling the organization's resources.

Exhibit 6
Job Order Costing and the Management Process

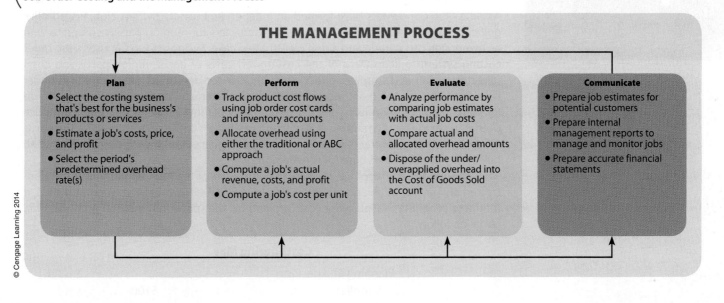

THE MANAGEMENT PROCESS

Plan
- Select the costing system that's best for the business's products or services
- Estimate a job's costs, price, and profit
- Select the period's predetermined overhead rate(s)

Perform
- Track product cost flows using job order cost cards and inventory accounts
- Allocate overhead using either the traditional or ABC approach
- Compute a job's actual revenue, costs, and profit
- Compute a job's cost per unit

Evaluate
- Analyze performance by comparing job estimates with actual job costs
- Compare actual and allocated overhead amounts
- Dispose of the under/overapplied overhead into the Cost of Goods Sold account

Communicate
- Prepare job estimates for potential customers
- Prepare internal management reports to manage and monitor jobs
- Prepare accurate financial statements

© Cengage Learning 2014

APPLY IT!

Shelley's Kennel provides pet boarding. Shelley, the owner, must make several business decisions soon. Write *yes* or *no* to indicate whether knowing the cost to board one animal for one day (i.e., the service unit cost) can help Shelley answer these questions.

a. Is the daily boarding fee high enough to cover the kennel's costs?

b. How much profit will the kennel make if it boards an average of 10 dogs per day for 50 weeks?

c. What costs can be reduced to make the kennel's boarding fee competitive with other kennels?

SOLUTION

a. yes; b. yes; c. yes

TRY IT! SE11

TriLevel Problem

Club Car

Digital Vision/Jupiter Images

The beginning of this chapter focused on **Club Car**, a company that makes both general-purpose and customized golf carts. Complete the following requirements in order to answer the questions posed at the beginning of the chapter.

Section 1: Concepts

Why is a job order costing system appropriate for Club Car to measure and recognize costs?

Section 2: Accounting Applications

How does a product costing system account for costs when made-to-order products or services are produced?

Assume Club Car owners have formed an independent loyalty owners club. Periodically, golf cart owners gather at the company headquarters for reunion parties complete with an owner golf cart parade and a golf cart–shaped cake. Suppose Club Car uses a job order costing system to keep track of the customized costs of each reunion party. Job costs (direct materials and supplies, direct labor, and service overhead) are categorized under three activities: planning and design, reunion, and cleanup. The service overhead charge for planning and design is 30 percent of the party planner's labor costs, and the service overhead charge for the reunion is 50 percent of the cost of the cake created for the party. Assume a cost-plus contract with a 20 percent profit guarantee for each party is used when billing the loyalty owners club for the reunions.

Suppose one manager has tracked all of the costs of the reunion party that was contracted on May 28, 2014, and scheduled for June 5, 2014. Now that the work is finished, it is time to complete the job order cost card and bill the sponsor. The costs for the reunion party job follow.

Costs during May	
Planning and design:	
Supplies	$100
Party planner labor	250
Costs during June	
Reunion:	
Cake creation	500
Direct labor	160
Cleanup:	
Janitorial service cost	400

1. Create the job order cost card for the reunion party job.

2. What amount will the manager bill for the job?

3. Using the format of the Work in Process Inventory account in Exhibit 2, reconstruct the beginning balance and costs for the current month. What is the ending balance for the account?

Section 3: Business Applications

How does a job order costing system help managers organize and control costs and facilitate management decisions? To answer this question, match this chapter's manager responsibilities with when they occur within the management process.

a. Plan
b. Perform
c. Evaluate
d. Communicate

1. Compute a job's cost per unit
2. Select the best product costing system
3. Compare actual and allocated overhead amounts
4. Compute a job's actual costs, price, and profit
5. Estimate a job's costs, price, and profit
6. Prepare accurate financial statements
7. Compare actual job costs with job estimates
8. Compute the predetermined overhead rate(s)
9. Track the flow of product costs
10. Prepare job estimates for potential customers
11. Prepare internal management reports
12. Dispose of under/overapplied overhead to Cost of Goods Sold
13. Allocate overhead using either the traditional or ABC approach

SOLUTION

Concepts

Whether a product costing system is appropriate to *measure* and *recognize* costs depends on the nature of the production process. Because the production of custom-made items and the production of mass-produced items involve different processes, they require different costing systems to measure and recognize product costs. When a product is made to order like the customized golf cart, it is possible to use a job order costing system, which recognizes and collects the costs of each order and *matches* them against the revenue generated by the order. When a product is mass produced, like the general-purpose golf cart, the costs of a specific unit cannot be recognized because there is a continuous flow of similar products. For this reason, a process costing system is used to collect and match a period's costs and revenues for the products sold.

Accounting Applications

1.

JOB ORDER COST CARD

Customer: Loyalty Owners Club   Batch: ___   Custom: X

Specifications: Reunion party

Date of Order: 5/28/2014   Date of Completion: 6/5/2014

Cost Charged to Job	Previous Month	Current Month	Total Costs
Planning and design:			
Supplies	$100	$ —	$ 100
Party planner labor	250	—	250
Overhead (30% of planning labor costs)	75	—	75
Totals	$425	$ —	$ 425
Reunion:			
Cake creation	$ —	$ 500	$ 500
Direct labor	—	160	160
Overhead (50% of cake creation cost)	—	250	250
Totals	$ —	$ 910	$ 910
Cleanup:			
Janitorial service costs		$ 400	$ 400
Total		$ 400	$ 400
Cost Summary to Date			
Planning			$ 425
Reunion			910
Cleanup			400
Total			$1,735
Profit margin (20% of total cost)			347
Job revenue			$2,082

2. The manager will bill $2,082.00 for this job.

3.

Work in Process Inventory

Beg. bal.	0	Completed and transferred to Cost of Sales	1,735
Planning and design:			
Supplies	100		
Party planner labor	250		
Overhead	75		
Party:			
Cake creation	500		
Direct labor	160		
Overhead	250		
Cleanup:			
Janitorial service costs	400		
End. bal.	—		

Section 3: Business Applications

1. b	8. a
2. a	9. d
3. c	10. d
4. b	11. d
5. a	12. c
6. d	13. b
7. c	

Chapter Review

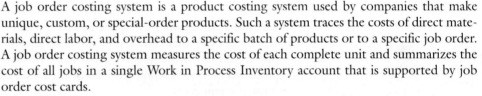

Distinguish between the two basic types of product costing systems, and identify the information that each provides. LO 1

A job order costing system is a product costing system used by companies that make unique, custom, or special-order products. Such a system traces the costs of direct materials, direct labor, and overhead to a specific batch of products or to a specific job order. A job order costing system measures the cost of each complete unit and summarizes the cost of all jobs in a single Work in Process Inventory account that is supported by job order cost cards.

A process costing system is a product costing system used by companies that produce large amounts of similar products or liquid products or that have long, continuous production runs of identical products. Such a system first traces the costs of direct materials, direct labor, and overhead to processes, departments, or work cells and then assigns the costs to the products manufactured by those processes, departments, or work cells. A process costing system uses several Work in Process Inventory accounts, one for each department, process, or work cell.

Explain the cost flow in a manufacturer's job order costing system. LO 2

In a manufacturer's job order costing system, the costs of materials are first charged to the Materials Inventory account. The actual overhead costs are debited to the Overhead account. As products are manufactured, the costs of direct materials and direct labor are debited to the Work in Process Inventory account and are recorded on each job's job order cost card. Overhead costs are applied and debited to the Work in Process Inventory account and credited to the Overhead account using a predetermined overhead rate. They too are recorded on the job order cost card. When products and jobs are completed, their costs are transferred to the Finished Goods Inventory account. Then, when the products are sold and shipped, their costs are transferred to the Cost of Goods Sold account.

Prepare a job order cost card, and compute a job order's product or service unit cost. LO 3

All costs of direct materials, direct labor, and overhead for a particular job are accumulated on a job order cost card. When the job has been completed, those costs are totaled. The total is then divided by the number of good units produced to find the product unit cost. The product unit cost is entered on the job order cost card and will be used to value items in inventory.

Many service organizations use a job order costing system to track the costs of labor, materials and supplies, and service overhead to specific customer jobs. Labor is an important cost for service organizations. To cover their costs and earn a profit, service organizations often base jobs on cost-plus contracts, which require the customer to pay all costs incurred plus a predetermined amount of profit.

Explain cost allocation, LO 4 and describe how allocating overhead costs figures into calculating product or service unit cost.

Cost allocation is the process of assigning indirect costs to a specific cost object using an allocation base known as a cost driver. The allocation of overhead costs requires the pooling of overhead costs that are affected by a common activity and the selection of a cost driver whose activity level causes a change in the cost pool. A cost pool is the collection of overhead costs assigned to a cost object. A cost driver is an activity base that causes the cost pool to increase in amount as the volume of activity increases.

Allocating overhead is a four-step process that involves planning a rate at which overhead costs will be assigned to products or services, assigning overhead costs at this predetermined rate to products or services during production, recording actual overhead costs as they are incurred, and reconciling the difference between the actual and applied overhead costs. The Cost of Goods Sold or Cost of Sales account is corrected for an amount of over- or underapplied overhead costs assigned to the products or services. In manufacturing companies, if the difference is material, adjustments are made to the Work in Process Inventory, Finished Goods Inventory, and Cost of Goods Sold accounts.

The traditional method applies overhead costs by estimating one predetermined overhead rate and multiplying that rate by the actual cost driver level. When the ABC method is used, overhead costs are grouped into a number of cost pools related to specific activities. For each activity pool, cost drivers are identified, and cost driver levels are estimated. Overhead is applied to the product or service by multiplying the various activity rates by their actual cost driver level. The product or service unit cost is computed either by dividing the total product or service cost by the total number of units produced or by determining the cost per unit for each element of the cost and summing those per-unit costs.

Explain why unit cost LO 5 measurement is important to the management process in producing business results.

When managers plan, information about costs helps them develop budgets, establish prices, set sales goals, plan production volumes, estimate product or service unit costs, and determine human resource needs. Daily, managers use cost information to make decisions about controlling costs, managing the company's volume of activity, ensuring quality, and negotiating prices. When managers evaluate results, they analyze actual and targeted information to evaluate performance and make any necessary adjustments to their planning and decision-making strategies. When managers communicate with stakeholders, they use unit costs to determine inventory balances and the cost of goods or services sold for the financial statements. They also use internal reports that compare the organization's measures of actual and targeted unit costs to determine whether the cost goals for products or services are being achieved. Reports may also contain nonfinancial measures of performance.

Key Terms

activity-based costing
  (ABC) 59 (LO4)
cost allocation 55 (LO4)
cost driver 55 (LO4)
cost object 55 (LO4)
cost-plus contracts 53 (LO3)
cost pool 55 (LO4)

job order 46 (LO1)
job order cost card 46 (LO1)
job order costing system 46 (LO1)
operations costing
  system 46 (LO1)
overapplied overhead
  costs 56 (LO4)

predetermined overhead
  rate 56 (LO4)
process cost report 46 (LO1)
process costing system 46 (LO1)
product costing system 46 (LO1)
underapplied overhead
  costs 57 (LO4)

Chapter Assignments

DISCUSSION QUESTIONS

LO 1   **DQ1. CONCEPT** ▶ Describe the accounting concepts that focus on determining the amount of cost, when costs should be recorded, and to what costs should be compared.

LO 1   **DQ2. CONCEPT** ▶ What are some of the cost measurement and cost recognition differences between the two basic types of product costing systems?

LO 2   **DQ3. CONCEPT** ▶ Why does the concept of matching underlie the cost flows in a job order costing system?

LO 4   **DQ4. CONCEPT** ▶ Why do the concepts of cost recognition and cost measurement underlie the four steps necessary to allocate overhead costs?

LO 5   **DQ5. BUSINESS APPLICATION** ▶ Why is the determination of unit cost information using job order costing important in the management process?

SHORT EXERCISES

LO 1   **Job Order Versus Process Costing Systems**

SE1. State whether a job order costing system or a process costing system would typically be used to account for the costs of the following:

a. Manufacturing bottles
b. Manufacturing custom-designed swimming pools
c. Manufacturing one-size-fits-all robes
d. Providing babysitting
e. Manufacturing canned food
f. Providing accounting services

LO 2   **Transactions in a Manufacturer's Job Order Costing System**

SE2. For each of the following transactions, state which account(s) would be debited and credited in a job order costing system:

a. Purchased materials on account, $12,000.
b. Charged direct labor to production, $3,000.
c. Requested direct materials for production, $6,000.
d. Applied overhead to jobs in process, $4,000.

LO 2   **Transactions in a Manufacturer's Job Order Costing System**

SE3. Enter the following transactions into T accounts:

a. Incurred $34,000 of direct labor and $18,000 of indirect labor.
b. Applied overhead based on 12,680 labor hours @ $6 per labor hour.

LO 2   **Accounts for Job Order Costing**

SE4. Identify the accounts in which each of the following transactions for Oak Leaf Furniture, a custom manufacturer of oak tables and chairs, would be debited and credited:

1. Issued oak materials into production for Job ABC.
2. Recorded direct labor time for the first week in February for Job ABC.
3. Purchased indirect materials from a vendor on account.
4. Received a production-related electricity bill.
5. Applied overhead to Job ABC.
6. Completed but did not yet sell Job ABC.

LO 3   **Job Order Cost Card**

SE5. Complete the following job order cost card for five custom-built computer systems:

Job Order 16

JOB ORDER COST CARD
Custom Computers
Kowloon, Hong Kong

Customer: L. Kim   Batch: ___   Custom: X

Specifications: 5 Computer Systems

Date of Order: 4/4/2014   Date of Completion: 6/8/2014

Costs Charged to Job	Previous Months	Current Month	Total Cost
Direct materials	$540	$820	$?
Direct labor	340	620	?
Overhead applied	880	550	?
Totals	$?	$?	$?
Units completed			÷ ?
Product unit cost			$?

LO 3   **Job Order Costing in a Service Organization**

SE6. A desert landscaping business is doing custom landscape work for J. Abbott. For each of the following transactions, state which account(s) would be debited and credited by the landscape business:

a. Sent J. Abbott a bill for landscape design.
b. Purchased gravel on credit, which was delivered to J. Abbott's yard.
c. Paid three employees to prepare soil for gravel.
d. Paid for cactus plants and planted them in J. Abbott's yard.

LO 3   **Job Order Costing with Cost-Plus Contracts**

SE7. Complete the following job order cost card for an individual tax return:

Job Order A7

JOB ORDER COST CARD
Doremus Tax Service
Puyallup, Washington

Customer: Arthur Farnsworth   Batch: ___   Custom: X

Specifications: Annual Individual Tax Return

Date of Order: 3/24/2014   Date of Completion: 4/8/2014

Costs Charged to Job	Previous Months	Current Month	Total Cost
Client interview:			
Supplies	$ 10	$ —	$?
Labor	50	60	?
Overhead (40% of interview labor costs)	20	24	?
Totals	$?	$?	$?
Preparation of return:			
Supplies	$ —	$ 16	$?
Computer time	—	12	?
Labor	—	240	?
Overhead (50% of preparation labor costs)	—	120	?
Totals	$ —	$?	$?
Delivery:			
Postage	$ —	$ 8	$?
Total	$ —	$?	$?

Cost Summary to Date	Total Cost
Client interview	$?
Preparation of return	?
Delivery	?
Total	$?
Profit margin (20% of total cost)	?
Job revenue	$?

LO 4   **Calculation of Underapplied or Overapplied Overhead**

SE8. At year end, records show that actual overhead costs incurred were $25,870 and the amount of overhead costs applied to production was $27,000. Identify the amount of under- or overapplied overhead, and indicate whether the Cost of Goods Sold account should be increased or decreased to reflect actual overhead costs.

LO 4   **Computation of Overhead Rate**

SE9. Compute the overhead rate per service request for the Maintenance Department if estimated overhead costs are $18,290 and the number of estimated service requests is 3,100.

LO 4   **Allocation of Overhead to Production**

SE10. Calculate the amount of overhead costs applied to production if the predetermined overhead rate is $4 per direct labor hour and 1,200 direct labor hours were worked.

LO 5   **Uses of Unit Cost Information**

SE11. ACCOUNTING CONNECTION ▶ Doug, the owner of a miniature golf course with 36 holes of miniature golf, must make several business decisions soon. Write *yes* or *no* to indicate whether knowing the cost to provide one golf game (i.e., the service unit cost) can help Doug answer these questions:

a. Is the fee for playing a golf game high enough to cover the related cost?
b. How much profit will Miniature Golf make if it sells an average of 100 games per day for 50 weeks?
c. What costs can be reduced to make the fee more competitive?

EXERCISES: SET A

LO 1   **Product Costing**

E1A. Custom Publishers Company specializes in print-on-demand books. The company needs information to budget next year's activities. Write *yes* or *no* to indicate whether each of the following costs is likely to be available in the company's product costing system:

a. cost of paper
b. advertising costs
c. printing machine setup costs
d. depreciation of printing machinery
e. repair costs for printing machinery

f. costs to deliver books to customers
g. office supplies costs
h. sales commissions
i. costs to design a book cover
j. cost of ink

LO 1   **Costing Systems: Industry Linkage**

E2A. Which of the following products would typically be accounted for using a job order costing system? Which would typically be accounted for using a process costing system?

a. glue
b. toothpicks
c. restaurant meal
d. clothing repair by a tailor
e. birthday cake

f. liquid soap
g. propane gas canisters used to barbeque
h. standard compressed-gas cylinders used by scuba divers

LO 1   **Costing Systems: Industry Linkage**

E3A. Which of the following products would typically be accounted for using a job order costing system? Which would typically be accounted for using a process costing system?

a. standard shirt buttons   e. flea collars for cats
b. printed graduation announcements   f. oatmeal cereal
c. everyday glassware   g. personal weight loss program
d. a limited edition sculpture   h. an original painting

LO 2   **Job Order Cost Flow**

E4A. ACCOUNTING CONNECTION ▶ The three product cost elements—direct materials, direct labor, and overhead—flow through a job order costing system in a structured, orderly fashion. Specific accounts and subsidiary ledgers are used to verify and record cost information. Write a paragraph describing the cost flow in a job order costing system.

LO 2   **Work in Process Inventory: T Account Analysis**

E5A. On July 1, Tin Hau Company's Work in Process Inventory account showed a beginning balance of $9,000. The Materials Inventory account showed a beginning balance of $40,000. Production activity for July was as follows: (a) Direct materials costing $28,800 were requested for production; (b) total production-related payroll was $10,600, of which $2,600 was used to pay for indirect labor; (c) indirect materials costing $8,400 were purchased and used; and (d) overhead was applied at a rate of 120 percent of direct labor costs.

1. Record Tin Hau's materials, labor, and overhead costs for July in T accounts.

2. Compute the ending balance in the Work in Process Inventory account. Assume a transfer of $45,000 to the Finished Goods Inventory account during the period.

LO 2, 3   **T Account Analysis with Unknowns**

E6A. Partial operating data for Census Company follow. Management has set the predetermined overhead rate for the current year at 125 percent of direct labor costs.

Account/Transaction	June	July
Beginning Materials Inventory	$ (a)	$ (e)
Beginning Work in Process Inventory	8,605	(f)
Beginning Finished Goods Inventory	7,764	6,660
Direct materials requested	5,025	(g)
Materials purchased	5,100	6,216
Direct labor costs	4,760	5,540
Overhead applied	(b)	(h)
Cost of units completed	(c)	21,861
Cost of Goods Sold	16,805	(i)
Ending Materials Inventory	3,014	2,628
Ending Work in Process Inventory	(d)	(j)
Ending Finished Goods Inventory	6,660	3,515

Using T accounts, compute the unknown values. Show all your computations.

LO 2, 3   **T Account Analysis with Unknowns**

E7A. Partial operating data for Brent Cross Company follow. Management has set the predetermined overhead rate for the current year at 90 percent of direct labor costs.

Account/Transaction	December
Beginning Materials Inventory	$142,000
Beginning Work in Process Inventory	66,000
Beginning Finished Goods Inventory	129,000
Direct materials used	256,000
Direct materials purchased	(a)
Direct labor costs	390,000
Overhead applied	(b)
Cost of units completed	(c)
Cost of Goods Sold	953,400
Ending Materials Inventory	50,000
Ending Work in Process Inventory	138,600
Ending Finished Goods Inventory	(d)

Using T accounts and the data provided, compute the unknown values. Show all your computations.

LO **2, 3**   **Job Order Costing: T Account Analysis**

E8A. Custom Floral, Inc., produces special-order artificial flower arrangements, so it uses a job order costing system. Overhead is applied at the rate of 80 percent of direct labor cost. The following is a list of transactions for June:

June   1   Purchased direct materials on account, $300.
       2   Purchased indirect materials on account, $50.
      4   Requested direct materials costing $250 ($200 used on Job AX and $50 used on Job BY) and indirect materials costing $40 for production.
    10   Paid the following overhead costs: utilities, $40; manufacturing rent, $300; and maintenance charges, $10.
    15   Recorded the following gross wages and salaries for employees: direct labor, $1,000 ($700 for Job AX and $300 for Job BY); indirect labor, $300.
    15   Applied overhead to production.
    16   Completed and transferred Job AX and Job BY to finished goods inventory; total cost of both jobs was $2,050.
    20   Delivered Job AX to the customer; total production cost was $1,460 and billed customer for the sales price $2,000.
    30   Recorded these overhead costs (adjusting entries): prepaid insurance expired, $30; and depreciation—machinery, $150.

REQUIRED

1. Record the entries for all transactions in June using T accounts for the following: Materials Inventory, Work in Process Inventory, Finished Goods Inventory, Overhead, Cash, Accounts Receivable, Prepaid Insurance, Accumulated Depreciation—Machinery, Accounts Payable, Payroll Payable, Sales, and Cost of Goods Sold. Determine the partial account balances. Assume no beginning inventory balances. Also assume that when the payroll was recorded, entries were made to the Payroll Payable account.

2. Compute the amount of underapplied or overapplied overhead as of June 30 and transfer it to the Cost of Goods Sold account.

LO **3, 4**   **Job Order Cost Card and Computation of Product Unit Cost**

E9A. In February 2014, Storage Company worked on five job orders for specialty cedar storage cabinets. It began Job Z-6 for Cedar Safe, Inc., on February 10 and completed it on February 24. Partial data for Job Z-6 are as follows.

(Continued)

	Costs	Machine Hours Used
Direct materials:		
Cedar	$8,000	
Pine	6,000	
Hardware	2,000	
Assembly supplies	1,000	
Direct labor:		
Sawing	3,000	120
Shaping	2,000	210
Finishing	2,500	150
Assembly	3,000	50

Storage Company produced a total of 50 cabinets for Job Z-6. Its current predetermined overhead rate is $20 per machine hour. From the information given, prepare a job order cost card and compute the job order's product unit cost.

LO 3, 4   **Computation of Product Unit Cost**

E10A. MS Company uses job order costing to determine the product unit cost of one of its products based on the following costs incurred during March: liability insurance, manufacturing, $3,500; rent, sales office, $3,000; depreciation, manufacturing equipment, $5,000; direct materials, $34,000; indirect labor, manufacturing, $3,600; indirect materials, $2,000; heat, light, and power, manufacturing, $2,500; fire insurance, manufacturing, $2,400; depreciation, sales equipment, $5,000; rent, manufacturing, $4,000; direct labor, $20,000; manager's salary, manufacturing, $4,800; president's salary, $6,000; sales commissions, $8,000; and advertising expenses, $3,000. The Inspection Department reported that 40,900 good units were produced during March. Determine the unit product cost.

LO 3, 4   **Computation of Product Unit Cost**

E11A. China Trade, Inc., manufactures custom-made stuffed animals. Last month the company produced 500 stuffed pandas for the local zoo to sell at a fund-raising event. Using job order costing, determine the product unit cost of a stuffed panda based on the following costs incurred during the month: manufacturing utilities, $200; depreciation on manufacturing equipment, $250; indirect materials, $150; direct materials, $1,000; indirect labor, $400; direct labor, $1,200; sales commissions, $3,000; president's salary, $4,000; insurance on manufacturing plant, $300; advertising expense, $500; rent on manufacturing plant, $2,500; rent on sales office, $4,000; and legal expense, $250.

LO 3, 4   **Computation of Product Unit Cost**

E12A. Dude Corporation manufactures specialty lines of men's apparel. During February, the company worked on three special orders: B-2, B-3, and B-4. Cost and production data for each order are as follows.

	Job B-2	Job B-3	Job B-4
Direct materials:			
Fabric Q	$1,000	$1,800	$17,600
Fabric Z	2,000	2,200	13,400
Fabric YB	5,000	6,000	2,000
Direct labor:			
Garment maker	4,500	8,000	10,200
Layout	2,500	7,000	9,800
Packaging	3,000	5,000	5,000
Overhead:			
(150% of direct labor costs)	?	?	?
Number of units produced	500	1,200	500

1. Compute the total cost associated with each job. Show the subtotals for each cost category.
2. Compute the product unit cost for each job.

LO **3, 4**   **Job Order Costing in a Service Organization**

E13A. A job order cost card for Cloud Storage Services follows. Complete the missing information. The profit factor in the organization's cost-plus contract is 60 percent of total cost.

JOB ORDER COST CARD
Cloud Storage Services

Customer:	Jayson Holiday
Job Order No.:	XXYQ
Contract Type:	Cost-Plus
Type of Service:	Annual Internet Storage
Date of Completion:	November 6, 2014

Costs Charged to Job	Total Cost
Software installation services:	
Installation labor	$30
Service overhead (?% of installation labor costs)	?
Total	$60
Internet services:	
Internet storage	$10
Service overhead (200% of Internet storage costs)	20
Total	$?

Cost Summary to Date	Total Cost
Software installation services	$?
Internet services	?
Total	$?
Profit margin (60% of total cost)	?
Contract revenue	$?

LO **4**   **Computation of Overhead Rate**

E14A. The overhead costs that Sife Industries, Inc., used to compute its overhead rate for the past year are as follows.

Indirect materials and supplies, repair and maintenance, outside service contracts, indirect labor, factory supervision, factory insurance, heat, light, and power costs	$222,000
Property taxes and miscellaneous overhead costs	13,000
Depreciation, machinery	85,000
Total overhead costs	$320,000

The allocation base for the past year was 40,000 total machine hours. For the next year, all overhead costs except depreciation, property taxes, and miscellaneous overhead are expected to increase by 10 percent. Depreciation should increase by 12 percent, and property taxes and miscellaneous overhead are expected to increase by 20 percent. Plant capacity in terms of machine hours used will increase by 10,000 hours.

1. Compute the past year's overhead rate.
2. Compute the overhead rate for next year.

LO 4

Computation and Application of Overhead Rate

E15A. For Road Patch Company, labor is the highest single expense, totaling $693,000 for 75,000 hours of work last year. Overhead costs for last year were $900,000 and were applied to specific jobs on the basis of labor hours worked. This year, the company anticipates a 25 percent increase in overhead costs. Labor costs will increase by $130,000, and the number of hours worked is expected to increase by 20 percent.

1. Determine the total amount of overhead anticipated this year.
2. Compute the overhead rate for this year.
3. At the end of this year, Road Patch had compiled a total of 89,920 labor hours worked. The actual overhead incurred was $1,143,400.
   a. Using the overhead rate computed in 2, determine the total amount of overhead applied to operations during the year.
   b. Compute the amount of under/overapplied overhead for the year.
   c. **ACCOUNTING CONNECTION ▶** Will the Cost of Goods Sold account be increased or decreased to correct the under/overapplication of overhead?

EXERCISES: SET B

Visit the textbook companion web site at www.cengagebrain.com to access Exercise Set B for this chapter.

PROBLEMS

LO 2

T Account Analysis with Unknowns

✔ d: May ending work in process inventory: $45,770
✔ i: June overhead applied: $57,800

P1. Patriotic Enterprises makes flags. The company's new controller can find only the following partial information for the past two months:

Account/Transaction	May	June
Beginning Materials Inventory	$ 36,240	$ (e)
Beginning Work in Process Inventory	56,480	(f)
Beginning Finished Goods Inventory	44,260	(g)
Materials purchased	(a)	96,120
Direct materials requested	82,320	(h)
Direct labor costs	(b)	72,250
Overhead applied	53,200	(i)
Cost of units completed	(c)	221,400
Cost of Goods Sold	209,050	(j)
Ending Materials Inventory	38,910	41,950
Ending Work in Process Inventory	(d)	(k)
Ending Finished Goods Inventory	47,940	51,180

The current year's predetermined overhead rate is 80 percent of direct labor cost.

REQUIRED

Using T accounts, compute the unknown values.

LO 2, 3, 4

Job Order Costing: T Account Analysis

✔ 2: $260 underapplied overhead

P2. Eagle Carts, Inc., produces special-order golf carts, so Eagle Carts uses a job order costing system. Overhead is applied at the rate of 90 percent of direct labor cost. A list of transactions for January follows.

Jan.　1　Purchased direct materials on account, $215,400.
　　　2　Purchased indirect materials on account, $49,500.
　　　4　Requested direct materials costing $193,200 (all used on Job X) and indirect materials costing $38,100 for production.
　　　10　Paid the following overhead costs: utilities, $4,400; manufacturing rent, $3,800; and maintenance charges, $3,900.

Jan. 15 Recorded the following gross wages and salaries for employees: direct labor, $120,000 (all for Job X); indirect labor, $60,620.

15 Applied overhead to production.

19 Purchased indirect materials costing $27,550 and direct materials costing $190,450 on account.

21 Requested direct materials costing $214,750 (Job X, $178,170; Job Y, $18,170; and Job Z, $18,410) and indirect materials costing $31,400 for production.

31 Recorded the following gross wages and salaries for employees: direct labor, $132,000 (Job X, $118,500; Job Y, $7,000; Job Z, $6,500); indirect labor, $62,240.

31 Applied overhead to production.

31 Completed and transferred Job X (375 carts) and Job Y (10 carts) to finished goods inventory; total cost was $855,990.

31 Shipped Job X to the customer; total production cost was $824,520 and sales price was $996,800.

31 Recorded these overhead costs (adjusting entries): prepaid insurance expired, $3,700; property taxes (payable at year end), $3,400; and depreciation—machinery, $15,500.

REQUIRED

1. Record the entries for all transactions in January using T accounts for the following: Materials Inventory, Work in Process Inventory, Finished Goods Inventory, Overhead, Cash, Accounts Receivable, Prepaid Insurance, Accumulated Depreciation—Machinery, Accounts Payable, Payroll Payable, Property Taxes Payable, Sales, and Cost of Goods Sold. Prepare job order cost cards for Job X, Job Y, and Job Z. (Round product unit cost to two decimal places.) Determine the partial account balances. Assume no beginning inventory balances. Also assume that when the payroll was recorded, entries were made to the Payroll Payable account.

2. Compute the amount of underapplied or overapplied overhead as of January 31 and transfer it to the Cost of Goods Sold account.

3. **ACCOUNTING CONNECTION ▶** Why should the Overhead account's underapplied or overapplied overhead be transferred to the Cost of Goods Sold account?

LO **2, 3, 4**

SPREADSHEET

✔ 2: Cost of units completed during the month: $185,073

Job Order Cost Flow

P3. On May 31, the inventory balances of Tog Designs, a manufacturer of high-quality children's clothing, were as follows: Materials Inventory, $21,360; Work in Process Inventory, $15,112; and Finished Goods Inventory, $17,120. Job order cost cards for jobs in process as of June 30 had the following totals:

Job No.	Direct Materials	Direct Labor	Overhead
24-A	$1,593	$1,290	$1,677
24-B	1,492	1,380	1,794
24-C	1,987	1,760	2,288
24-D	1,608	1,540	2,002

The predetermined overhead rate is 130 percent of direct labor costs. Materials purchased and received in June were as follows.

June 4	$33,120
June 16	28,600
June 22	31,920

Direct labor costs for June were as follows.

June 15 payroll	$23,680
June 29 payroll	25,960

(Continued)

Direct materials requested by production during June were as follows.

June 6	$37,240
June 23	38,960

On June 30, Tog Designs sold on account finished goods with a cost of $183,000 for $320,000.

REQUIRED

1. Using T accounts for Materials Inventory, Work in Process Inventory, Finished Goods Inventory, Overhead, Accounts Receivable, Payroll Payable, Sales, and Cost of Goods Sold, reconstruct the transactions in June, including applying overhead to production.
2. Compute the cost of units completed during the month.
3. Determine the ending inventory balances.
4. Jobs 24-A and 24-C were completed during the first week of July. No additional materials costs were incurred, but Job 24-A required $960 more of direct labor, and Job 24-C needed an additional $1,610 of direct labor. Job 24-A was composed of 1,800 pairs of trousers; Job 24-C, of 900 shirts. Compute the product unit cost for each job.

LO **4**

Allocation of Overhead

✔ 1: Predetermined overhead rate for this year: $2.40 per machine hour
✔ 3: Overapplied overhead: $475

P4. Nature Cosmetics Company applies overhead costs on the basis of machine hours. The overhead rate is computed by analyzing data from the previous year to determine the percentage change in costs. Thus, this year's overhead rate will be based on the percentage change multiplied by last year's costs.

	Last Year
Machine hours	55,360
Overhead costs:	
Indirect labor	$ 23,500
Employee benefits	28,600
Manufacturing supervision	18,500
Utilities	15,000
Factory insurance	7,800
Janitorial services	12,100
Depreciation, factory and machinery	21,300
Miscellaneous overhead	6,000
Total overhead	$132,800

This year the cost of utilities is expected to increase by 40 percent over the previous year; the cost of indirect labor, employee benefits, and miscellaneous overhead is expected to increase by 30 percent over the previous year; the cost of insurance and depreciation is expected to increase by 20 percent over the previous year; and the cost of supervision and janitorial services is expected to increase by 10 percent over the previous year. Machine hours are expected to total 68,786.

REQUIRED

1. Compute the projected costs, and use those costs to calculate the overhead rate for this year. (Round the rate to two decimal places.)
2. Jobs completed during this year and the machine hours used were as follows.

Job No.	Machine Hours
2214	12,300
2215	14,200
2216	9,800
2217	13,600
2218	11,300
2219	8,100

Determine the amount of overhead to be applied to each job and to total production during this year.

3. Actual overhead costs for this year were $165,845. Was overhead underapplied or overapplied? By how much? Should the Cost of Goods Sold account be increased or decreased to reflect actual overhead costs?

4. **ACCOUNTING CONNECTION** ▶ At what point during this year was the overhead rate computed? When was it applied? Finally, when was underapplied or overapplied overhead determined and the Cost of Goods Sold account adjusted to reflect actual costs?

LO 4 **Allocation of Overhead**

✔ Total costs assigned to order: $71,074

P5. Byte Computer Company, a manufacturing organization, has just completed an order that Grater, Ltd., placed for 80 computers. Direct materials, purchased parts, and direct labor costs for the Grater order are as follows.

Cost of direct materials	$36,750
Cost of purchased parts	$21,300
Direct labor hours	220
Average direct labor pay rate	$16

Overhead costs were applied at a single, plantwide overhead rate of 270 percent of direct labor dollars.

REQUIRED

Compute the total cost of the Grater order.

ALTERNATE PROBLEMS

LO 2 **T Account Analysis with Unknowns**

✔ d: July ending work in process
inventory: $38,564
✔ i: August overhead applied: $48,400

P6. Core Enterprises makes peripheral equipment for computers. The company's new controller only has the following partial information for the past two months:

Account/Transaction	July	August
Beginning Materials Inventory	$52,000	$ (e)
Beginning Work in Process Inventory	24,000	(f)
Beginning Finished Goods Inventory	36,000	(g)
Materials purchased	(a)	31,000
Direct materials requested	77,000	(h)
Direct labor costs	(b)	44,000
Overhead applied	53,200	(i)
Cost of units completed	(c)	167,000
Cost of Goods Sold	188,000	(j)
Ending Materials Inventory	27,000	8,000
Ending Work in Process Inventory	(d)	(k)
Ending Finished Goods Inventory	12,000	19,000

The current year's predetermined overhead rate is 110 percent of direct labor cost.

REQUIRED

Using T accounts, compute the unknown values. (Round to the nearest dollar.)

LO 2, 3, 4 **Job Order Costing: T Account Analysis**

✔ 2: $4,581 underapplied overhead

P7. Rhile Industries, Inc., produces colorful and stylish uniforms to order. During September 2014, Rhile completed the following transactions:

Sept. 1 Purchased direct materials on account, $59,400.
3 Requested direct materials costing $26,850 for production (all for Job A).
4 Purchased indirect materials for cash, $22,830.
8 Issued checks for the following overhead costs: utilities, $4,310; manufacturing insurance, $1,925; and repairs, $4,640.

(Continued)

Sept. 10   Requested direct materials costing $29,510 (all used on Job A) and indirect materials costing $6,480 for production.

15   Recorded the following gross wages and salaries for employees: direct labor, $62,900 (all for Job A); indirect labor, $31,610; manufacturing supervision, $26,900; and sales commissions, $32,980.

15   Applied overhead to production at a rate of 120 percent of direct labor cost.

22   Paid the following overhead costs: utilities, $4,270; maintenance, $3,380; and rent, $3,250.

23   Recorded the purchase on account and receipt of $31,940 of direct materials and $9,260 of indirect materials.

27   Requested $28,870 of direct materials (Job A, $2,660; Job B, $8,400; Job C, $17,810) and $7,640 of indirect materials for production.

30   Recorded the following gross wages and salaries for employees: direct labor, $64,220 (Job A, $44,000; Job B, $9,000; Job C, $11,220); indirect labor, $30,290; manufacturing supervision, $28,520; and sales commissions, $36,200.

30   Applied overhead to production at a rate of 120 percent of direct labor cost.

30   Completed and transferred Job A (58,840 units) and Job B (3,525 units) to finished goods inventory; total cost was $322,400.

30   Shipped Job A to the customer; total production cost was $294,200, and sales price was $418,240.

30   Recorded the following adjusting entries: $2,680 for depreciation—manufacturing equipment; and $1,230 for property taxes, manufacturing, payable at month end.

REQUIRED

1. Record the entries for all Rhile's transactions in September using T accounts for the following: Materials Inventory, Work in Process Inventory, Finished Goods Inventory, Overhead, Cash, Accounts Receivable, Accumulated Depreciation—Manufacturing Equipment, Accounts Payable, Payroll Payable, Property Taxes Payable, Sales, Cost of Goods Sold, and Selling and Administrative Expenses. Prepare job order cost cards for Job A, Job B, and Job C. Determine the partial account balances. Assume no beginning inventory balances. Assume also that when payroll was recorded, entries were made to the Payroll Payable account.

2. Compute the amount of underapplied or overapplied overhead for September and transfer it to the Cost of Goods Sold account.

3. **ACCOUNTING CONNECTION ▶** Why should the Overhead account's underapplied or overapplied overhead be transferred to the Cost of Goods Sold account?

LO **2, 3, 4**   ## Job Order Cost Flow

✔ 2: Cost of units completed during the month: $76,470

P8. Tottham Industries is a company that makes special-order sound systems. The chief financial officer has records for February that reveal the following information:

Beginning inventory balances:

Materials Inventory	$27,450
Work in Process Inventory	22,900
Finished Goods Inventory	19,200

Direct materials purchased and received:

February 6	$ 7,200
February 12	8,110
February 24	5,890

Direct labor costs:

February 14	$13,750
February 28	13,230

Direct materials requested for production:

February 4	$9,080
February 13	5,940
February 25	7,600

Job order cost cards for jobs in process on February 28 had the following totals:

Job No.	Direct Materials	Direct Labor	Overhead
AJ-10	$3,220	$1,810	$2,534
AJ-14	3,880	2,110	2,954
AJ-15	2,980	1,640	2,296
AJ-16	4,690	2,370	3,318

The predetermined overhead rate for the month was 140 percent of direct labor costs. Sales for February totaled $152,400, the cost of production for the goods sold was $89,000.

REQUIRED

1. Using T accounts for Materials Inventory, Work in Process Inventory, Finished Goods Inventory, Overhead, Accounts Receivable, Payroll Payable, Sales, and Cost of Goods Sold, reconstruct the transactions in February, including applying overhead to production.
2. Compute the cost of units completed during the month.
3. Determine the ending balances in the inventory accounts.
4. During the first week of March, Jobs AJ-10 and AJ-14 were completed. No additional direct materials costs were incurred, but Job AJ-10 needed $720 more of direct labor, and Job AJ-14 needed an additional $1,140 of direct labor. Job AJ-10 was 40 units; Job AJ-14, 50 units. Compute the product unit cost for each completed job.

LO **4**

✔ 1: Predetermined overhead rate for this year: $5.00 per machine hour
✔ 3: Underapplied overhead: $750

Allocation of Overhead

P9. Gyllstrom Products, Inc., uses a predetermined overhead rate in its production, assembly, and testing departments. One rate is used for the entire company; it is based on machine hours. The rate is determined by analyzing data from the previous year to determine the percentage change in costs. Thus this year's overhead rate will be based on the percentage change multiplied by last year's costs. The following data are available:

	Last Year's Costs
Machine hours	38,000
Overhead costs	
Indirect materials	$ 58,000
Indirect labor	25,000
Supervision	41,000
Utilities	11,200
Labor-related costs	9,000
Depreciation, factory	10,500
Depreciation, machinery	27,000
Property taxes	3,000
Insurance	2,000
Miscellaneous overhead	5,000
Total overhead	$191,700

This year the cost of indirect materials is expected to increase by 30 percent over the previous year. The cost of indirect labor, utilities, machinery depreciation, property taxes, and insurance is expected to increase by 20 percent over the previous year. All other expenses are expected to increase by 10 percent over the previous year. Machine hours for this year are estimated at 45,858.

(Continued)

REQUIRED

1. Compute the projected costs, and use those costs to calculate the overhead rate for this year.
2. During this year, the company completed the following jobs using the machine hours shown:

Job No.	Machine Hours	Job No.	Machine Hours
H–142	7,840	H–201	10,680
H–164	5,260	H–218	12,310
H–175	8,100	H–304	2,460

Determine the amount of overhead applied to each job. What was the total overhead applied during this year?

3. Actual overhead costs for this year were $234,000. Was overhead underapplied or overapplied this year? By how much? Should the Cost of Goods Sold account be increased or decreased to reflect actual overhead costs?
4. **ACCOUNTING CONNECTION** ▶ At what point during this year was the overhead rate computed? When was it applied? Finally, when was underapplied or overapplied overhead determined and the Cost of Goods Sold account adjusted to reflect actual costs?

LO 4   **Allocation of Overhead**

P10. Fraser Products, Inc., which produces copy machines, has just completed packaging an order from Kent Company for 150 machines. Direct materials, purchased parts, and direct labor costs for the Kent order are as follows.

Cost of direct materials	$17,450
Cost of purchased parts	$14,800
Direct labor hours	140
Average direct labor pay rate	$16.50

Overhead costs were applied at a single, plantwide overhead rate of 240 percent of direct labor dollars.

REQUIRED

Compute the total cost of the Kent order.

CASES

LO 1, 5   **Business Communication: Product Costing Systems**

C1. BUSINESS APPLICATION ▶ Hawk Manufacturing manufactures engine parts for motorcycles. Jordan Smith, Hawk Manufacturing's president, wants to improve the quality of the company's operations and products. She believes waste exists in the design and manufacture of standard engine parts. To begin the improvement process, she has asked you to (1) identify the sources of such waste, (2) develop performance measures to account for the waste, and (3) estimate the current costs associated with the waste. She has asked you to submit a memo of your findings within two weeks so that she can begin strategic planning to revise the price at which Hawk sells engine parts to motorcycle manufacturers.

    You have identified two sources of costly waste. The Production Department is redoing work that was not done correctly the first time, and the Engineering Design Department is redesigning products that were not initially designed to customer specifications. Having improper designs has caused the company to buy parts that are not used in production. You have also obtained the following information from the product costing system:

Direct labor costs	$673,402
Engineering design costs	124,709
Indirect labor costs	67,200
Depreciation on production equipment	84,300
Supervisors' salaries	98,340
Direct materials costs	432,223
Indirect materials costs	44,332

1. In preparation for writing your memo, answer the following questions:
   a. For whom are you preparing the memo? What is the appropriate length of the memo?
   b. Why are you preparing the memo?
   c. What information is needed for the memo? Where can you get this information? What performance measure would you suggest for each activity? Is the accounting information sufficient for your memo?
   d. When is the memo due? What can be done to provide accurate and timely information?
2. Prepare an outline of the sections you would want to include in your memo.

LO **2, 5** **Group Activity: Job Order Costing**

C2. Many businesses accumulate costs for each job performed. Examples of businesses that use a job order costing system include print shops, car repair shops, health clinics, and kennels.

Visit a local business that uses job order costing, and interview the owner, manager, or accountant about the job order process and the documents the business uses to accumulate product costs. Write a paper that summarizes the information you obtained. Include the following in your summary:

1. The name of the business and the type of operations performed
2. The name and position of the individual you interviewed
3. A description of the process of starting and completing a job
4. A description of the accounting process and the documents used to track a job
5. Your responses to these questions:
   a. Did the person you interviewed know the actual amount of direct materials, direct labor, and overhead charged to a particular job? If the job includes some estimated costs, how are the estimates calculated? Do the costs affect the determination of the selling price of the product or service?
   b. Compare the documents discussed in this chapter with the documents used by the company you visited. How are they similar, and how are they different?
   c. In your opinion, does the business record and accumulate its product costs effectively? Explain.

LO **3, 5** **Ethical Dilemma: Costing Procedures and Ethics**

C3. Roger Parker, the production manager of Products Company, entered the office of controller Harris Johnson and asked, "Harris, what gives here? I was charged for 330 direct labor hours on Job AD22, and my records show that we spent only 290 hours on that job. That 40-hour difference caused the total cost of direct labor and overhead for the job to increase by over $5,500. Are my records wrong, or was there an error in the direct labor assigned to the job?"

Harris replied, "Don't worry about it, Roger. This job won't be used in your quarterly performance evaluation. Job AD22 was a federal government job, a cost-plus contract, so the more costs we assign to it, the more profit we make. We decided to add a few hours to the job in case there is some follow-up work to do. You know how fussy the feds are." What should Roger Parker do? Discuss Harris Johnson's costing procedure.

LO 3, 5   Conceptual Understanding: Role of Cost Information in Software Development

C4. Software development companies frequently have a problem: When is "good enough" good enough? How many hours should be devoted to developing a new product? The industry's rule of thumb is that developing and shipping new software takes six to nine months. To be the first to market, a company must develop and ship products much more quickly than the industry norm. One performance measure that is used to answer the "good enough" question is a calculation based on the economic value (not cost) of what a company's developers create. The computation takes the estimated current market valuation of a firm and divides it by the number of product developers in the firm, to arrive at the market value created per developer. Some companies refine this calculation further to determine the value that each developer creates per workday. One company has estimated this value to be $10,000. Thus, for one software development company, "good enough" focuses on whether a new product's potential justifies an investment of time by someone who is worth $10,000 per day.

The salary cost of the company's developers is *not* used in the "good enough" calculation. Why is that cost not relevant?

LO 5   Interpreting Management Reports: Nonfinancial Data

C5. BUSINESS APPLICATION ▶ Hawk Manufacturing supplies engine parts to Cherokee Cycle Company, a major U.S. manufacturer of motorcycles. Like all of Cherokee's suppliers, Hawk has always added a healthy profit margin to its cost when quoting selling prices to Cherokee. Recently, however, several companies have offered to supply engine parts to Cherokee for lower prices than Hawk has been charging.

Because Hawk wants to keep Cherokee's business, a team of Hawk's managers analyzed their company's product costs and decided to make minor changes in the company's manufacturing process. No new equipment was purchased, and no additional labor was required. Instead, the machines were rearranged, and some of the work was reassigned.

To monitor the effectiveness of the changes, Hawk introduced three new performance measures to its information system: inventory levels, lead time (total time required for a part to move through the production process), and productivity (number of parts manufactured per person per day). Hawk's goal was to reduce the quantities of the first two performance measures and to increase the quantity of the third.

A section of a recent management report, shown below, summarizes the quantities for each performance measure before and after the changes in the manufacturing process were made.

Measure	Before	After	Improvement
Inventory in dollars	$21,444	$10,772	50%
Lead time in minutes	17	11	35%
Productivity (parts per person per day)	515	1,152	124%

1. Do you believe that Hawk improved the quality of its manufacturing process and the quality of its engine parts? Explain your answer.
2. Can Hawk lower its selling price to Cherokee? Explain your answer.
3. Did the introduction of the new measures affect the design of the product costing system? Explain your answer.
4. Do you believe that the new measures caused a change in Hawk's cost per engine part? If so, how did they cause the change?

Continuing Case: Cookie Company

C6. In the Cookie Company case in the last chapter, your team selected a cookie recipe for your company. In this chapter, your team will use that recipe to bake a batch of cookies, collect cost and time performance data related to the baking, create a marketing display for your company, and vote for the class's favorite cookie during an in-class cookie taste test. The goal of the taste test is to have your team's product voted the "best in class." One rule of the contest is that you may not vote for your own team's product.

1. Design a job measurement document that includes at least the following measures: cost per cookie; number of cookies produced (= number meeting specs + number rejected + number sampled for quality control + unexplained differences); size of cookies before baking; size of cookies after baking; and total throughput time (= mix time + [bake time for one cookie sheet × number of cookie sheets processed] + packaging time + downtime + cleanup time).

2. Design a job order cost card for your company that resembles one of those displayed in this chapter.

3. Using the recipe your team selected and assigning duties as described in the last chapter, bake a batch of cookies, and complete the job measurement document and job order cost card.
   ■ Assume an overhead rate of $2 for every $1 of direct material cost.
   ■ Assign direct labor cost for each production task based on the hourly rate or a monthly salary previously determined by your team.

4. Create a marketing display for your cookie product and bring it to class on the day of the taste test. The marketing display should include 20 cookies on a plate or napkin and a poster that displays your company's name and mission statement, cookie recipe, job measurement document, and job order cost card.

5. During class, each student should look at all of the marketing displays, taste 2 or 3 cookies and, on a ballot provided by your instructor, rank taste test results by giving 1 to the best cookie tasted, 2 to the next best, and so on. Students must sign their ballots before they turn them in to the instructor. (Remember, you cannot cast a vote for your own team's entry.) Your instructor will tabulate the ballots and announce the winning team.

6. Finally, write a review of your team members' efforts and give it to your instructor.

CHAPTER 3
Costing Systems: Process Costing

BUSINESS INSIGHT
Dean Foods

Dean Foods is the largest milk producer and distributor of milk and other dairy products in the United States. Its products are made in over 100 plants under such popular brands as Meadow Gold, Land O'Lakes, Pet, Garelick Farms, Silk, and Horizon Organic. In this chapter, we explain why a company like Dean Foods should use a process costing system and how this system provides the information that managers need to make sound product decisions.

1. CONCEPT ▶ *Why is a process costing system appropriate for Dean Foods to measure and recognize costs?*

2. ACCOUNTING APPLICATION ▶ *How does a product costing system account for costs when identical products or services are produced?*

3. BUSINESS APPLICATION ▶ *How does a process costing system help managers organize and control costs and facilitate management decisions?*

LEARNING OBJECTIVES

 LO 1 Describe a process costing system.

 LO 2 Relate the patterns of product flows to the cost flow methods in a process costing environment, and explain the role of the Work in Process Inventory accounts.

 LO 3 Describe equivalent production, and compute equivalent units.

 LO 4 Prepare a process cost report using the FIFO costing method.

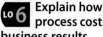 **LO 5** Prepare a process cost report using the average costing method.

LO 6 Explain how managers use a process costing system to produce business results.

SECTION 1

CONCEPTS
- Cost measurement
- Cost recognition
- Matching principle

RELEVANT LEARNING OBJECTIVE

LO 1 Describe a process costing system.

CONCEPTS

LO 1 Concepts Underlying the Process Costing System

Since it is impossible to identify an individual unit of some products until they have been completed (such as a container of milk, a package of jelly beans, or a gallon of ice cream), process costing is used to track and control costs while products are being made. A **process costing system** first *measures* the costs of direct materials, direct labor, and overhead for each process, department, or work cell and then assigns those costs to the products produced during a particular period. Reports prepared at the end of each period *recognize* the costs assigned to products completed and transferred out or to the products remaining in the process, department, or work cell. It provides the cost information for product revenues to be *matched* with the expenses required to generate them. A product costing system, like process costing, provides managers with unit cost information, cost data for management decisions, and ending values for the Materials Inventory, Work in Process Inventory, and Finished Goods Inventory accounts.

Such a system is used for *cost measurement* by companies that make large amounts of similar products or liquid products or that have continuous production runs of identical products. For example, companies that produce paint or chemicals (like **Dow Chemicals**), beverages (like **Coors** and **Coca-Cola**), foods (like **Kellogg Company**), computer chips (like **Apple Computer**), and gallon containers of ice cream are typical users of a process costing system.

In the previous chapter, we focused on job order costing. It's important to note that the difference between job order costing and process costing is that, in process costing, costs are *measured* and *recognized* by production *processes*, such as the Work in Process Inventory account of the Mixing Department, whereas in job order costing, costs are measured and recognized by *jobs* through the job order cost card.

APPLY IT!

Indicate whether the manufacturer of each of the following products should use a job order costing system or a process costing system to accumulate product costs.

a. baby bottles
b. chocolate milk
c. nuclear submarines
d. generic drugs

SOLUTION

a. Process
b. Process
c. Job order
d. Process

TRY IT! SE1, SE2, E1A, E1B

SECTION 2 — ACCOUNTING APPLICATIONS

LO 2 Patterns of Product Flows and Cost Flow Methods

In a process costing environment, products flow in a first-in, first-out (FIFO) fashion through several processes, departments, or work cells and may undergo many different operations. Exhibit 1 illustrates the simple linear production flow of how milk is produced in a series of three processing steps, or departments. Each department has its own Work in Process Inventory account to accumulate the direct materials, direct labor, and overhead costs associated with it.

■ **Homogenization Department:** Raw milk from the cow must be mixed to evenly distribute the butterfat. The homogenized milk and its associated cost then become the direct materials for the next department.

■ **Pasteurization Department:** The homogenized milk is heated to 145 degrees to kill the bacteria found in raw milk. The homogenized, pasteurized milk and all associated costs are then transferred on to the next department.

■ **Packaging Department:** The milk is put into bottles and transferred to Finished Goods Inventory since it is ready for sale.

The product unit cost of a bottle of milk is the sum of the cost elements in all three departments divided by the number of bottles of milk produced.

Exhibit 1
Product Flows in a Process Costing Environment

© Cengage Learning 2014

Even in simple process costing environments, production generally involves a number of separate manufacturing processes, departments, or work cells. For example, the separate processes involved in manufacturing cookies include mixing, baking, and packaging.

To *measure* and *recognize* product costs using process costing requires the preparation of a **process cost report** for each process, department, or work cell as product-related costs flow through the production process. Managers assign these costs to the units that have transferred out of the process and to the units that are still a part of the work in process. They use a cost allocation method, such as the FIFO costing method or the average costing method.

■ In the **first-in, first-out (FIFO) costing method**, the cost flow follows the logical physical flow of production—that is, the costs assigned to the first materials processed are the first costs transferred out when those materials flow to the next process, department, or work cell. Thus, in Exhibit 1, the costs assigned to the homogenized milk would be the first costs transferred to the Pasteurization Department.

- In contrast, the **average costing method** assigns an average cost to all products made during a period. This method thus uses total cost averages and does not try to match cost flow with the physical flow of production.

Cost Flows Through the Work in Process Inventory Accounts

As discussed in the previous chapter, a job order costing system uses a single Work in Process Inventory account, whereas a process costing system has a separate Work in Process Inventory account for each process, department, or work cell. As shown in Exhibit 1, these accounts are the focal point of process costing. As products move from one process, department, or work cell to the next, the costs of the direct materials, direct labor, and overhead associated with them flow to the next Work in Process Inventory account. The journal entry to record the transfer of costs from one process, department, or work cell to another is:

	Dr.	Cr.
Work in Process Inventory (next department)	XX	
Work in Process Inventory (this department)		XX

Once the products are completed, packaged, and ready for sale, their costs are transferred to the Finished Goods Inventory account. The journal entry to record this transfer out of Work in Process Inventory into Finished Goods Inventory is:

	Dr.	Cr.
Finished Goods Inventory	XX	
Work in Process Inventory (last department)		XX

As you will learn later in this chapter, the costs associated with these entries are calculated in a process cost report for the process, department, or work cell.

APPLY IT!

Milk Smoothies, Inc., uses an automated mixing machine in its Mixing Department to combine three raw materials into a product called Strawberry Smoothie Mix. Total costs charged to the Mixing Department's Work in Process Inventory account during the month were $210,000. There were no units in beginning or ending work in process inventory. Prepare the journal entry to transfer the units completed to Finished Goods Inventory.

SOLUTION

Finished Goods Inventory	210,000	
Work in Process Inventory		210,000

TRY IT! SE3, E2A, E3A, E2B, E3B

LO3 Computing Equivalent Production

A process costing system does not associate costs with particular job orders. Instead, it assigns the costs incurred in a process, department, or work cell to the units in production during a period by computing an average cost per unit of effort. Unit cost for the period is computed as follows.

(Direct Materials + Direct Labor + Overhead) ÷ Number of Units = Unit Cost

The number of units in production during the period is a critical question. Do we count only units started and completed during the period? Or should we include partially

While direct materials are usually added to production at the beginning of the process, they can be added at other stages. For example, chocolate chips are added at the end of the mixing process for cookie dough.

completed units in the beginning work in process inventory? And what about incomplete products in the ending work in process inventory?

These questions relate to the concept of equivalent production. **Equivalent production** (or *equivalent units*) applies a percentage-of-completion factor to partially completed units to calculate the equivalent number of whole units produced during a period for each type of input (i.e., direct materials, direct labor, and overhead). The number of equivalent units produced is (1) the sum of total units started and completed during the period and (2) an amount representing the work done on partially completed products in both the beginning and the ending work in process inventories. Equivalent production must be computed separately for each type of input because of differences in the ways in which costs are incurred.

- Direct materials are usually added to production at the beginning of the process.
- The costs of direct labor and overhead are often incurred uniformly throughout the production process. Thus, it is convenient to combine direct labor and overhead when calculating equivalent units. These combined costs are called **conversion costs** (or *processing costs*).

For example, Milk Products Company makes a pint-sized, bottled milk drink. As shown in Exhibit 2, the company started Week 2 with one half-completed unit in process. During Week 2, it started and completed three units, and at the end of Week 2, it had one unit that was three-quarters completed.

Exhibit 2
Computation of Equivalent Production

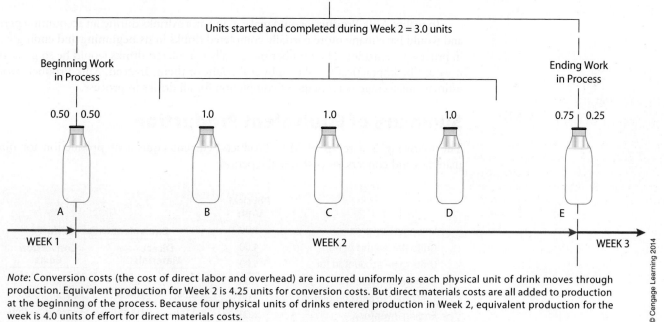

Equivalent production for conversion costs for Week 2 = 4.25 units of bottled product

Units started and completed during Week 2 = 3.0 units

Beginning Work in Process

Ending Work in Process

| 0.50 | 0.50 | 1.0 | 1.0 | 1.0 | 0.75 | 0.25 |

A   B   C   D   E

WEEK 1   WEEK 2   WEEK 3

© Cengage Learning 2014

Note: Conversion costs (the cost of direct labor and overhead) are incurred uniformly as each physical unit of drink moves through production. Equivalent production for Week 2 is 4.25 units for conversion costs. But direct materials costs are all added to production at the beginning of the process. Because four physical units of drinks entered production in Week 2, equivalent production for the week is 4.0 units of effort for direct materials costs.

Equivalent Production for Direct Materials

At Milk Products, all direct materials, including liquids and bottles, are added at the beginning of production. Thus, the unit that was half-completed at the beginning of Week 2 had had all its direct materials added during the previous week. No direct materials costs for this unit are included in the computation of Week 2's equivalent units for the beginning inventory units.

During Week 2, work began on four new units—the three units that were completed and the unit that was three-quarters completed at week's end. Because all direct materials are added at the beginning of the production process, all four units were 100 percent complete with regard to direct materials at the end of Week 2. Thus, for Week 2, the equivalent production for direct materials was 4.0 units. This figure includes direct materials for both the 3.0 units that were started and completed and the 1.0 unit that was three-quarters completed.

Equivalent Production for Conversion Costs

Because conversion costs at Milk Products are incurred uniformly throughout the production process, the equivalent production for conversion costs during Week 2 consists of the following three components:

- the cost to finish the half-completed unit in beginning work in process inventory (0.50)
- the cost to begin and finish three completed units (3.0)
- the cost to begin work on the three-quarters-completed unit in ending work in process inventory (0.75)

Thus, For Week 2, the total equivalent production for conversion costs in units is computed as follows.

$$
\begin{array}{ccccc}
\text{Total Equivalent Units} & = & \text{Beginning} & + & \text{Started and} & + & \text{Ending} \\
\text{for Conversion Costs} & & \text{Inventory} & & \text{Completed} & & \text{Inventory} \\
& = & 0.50 \text{ unit} & + & 3.0 \text{ units} & + & 0.75 \text{ unit} \\
& = & 4.25 \text{ units}
\end{array}
$$

In reality, Milk Products would make many more drinks during an accounting period and would have many more partially completed drinks in its beginning and ending work in process inventories. The number of partially completed drinks would be so great that it would be impractical to take a physical count of them. Instead, Milk Products would estimate an average percentage of completion for all drinks in process.

Summary of Equivalent Production

The following is a recap of Milk Products' current equivalent production for direct materials and conversion costs for the period:

	Physical Units	Equivalent Units of Effort			
		Direct Materials		Conversion Costs	
Beginning inventory	1.00				
Units started this period	4.00				
Units to be accounted for	5.00				
Beginning inventory	1.00	—	0%	0.50	50%
Units started and completed	3.00	3.00	100%	3.00	100%
Ending inventory	1.00	1.00	100%	0.75	75%
Units accounted for	5.00	4.00		4.25	

APPLY IT!

Milk Smoothies, Inc., adds direct materials when it starts its drink mix production process and adds conversion costs uniformly throughout this process. Given the following information from July, compute the current period's equivalent units of production:

- Units in beginning inventory: 2,000
- Units started during the period: 13,000
- Units partially completed: 500
- Percentage of completion of beginning inventory: 100% for direct materials; 40% for conversion costs in previous period
- Percentage of completion of ending work in process inventory: 100% for direct materials; 70% for conversion costs

SOLUTION

Milk Smoothies, Inc.
For the Month Ended July 31

	Physical Units	Direct Materials		Conversion Costs	
		Equivalent Units of Effort			
Beginning inventory	2,000				
Units started this period	13,000				
Units to be accounted for	15,000				
Beginning inventory	2,000	—	0%	1,200	60%
Units started and completed	12,500	12,500	100%	12,500	100%
Ending inventory	500	500	100%	350	70%
Units accounted for	15,000	13,000		14,050	

TRY IT! SE4, E4A, E5A, E6A, E4B, E5B, E6B

LO 4 Preparing a Process Cost Report Using the FIFO Costing Method

STUDY NOTE: *The FIFO method focuses on the work done in the current period only.*

As mentioned earlier, a *process cost report* is a report that managers use to track and analyze costs for a process, department, or work cell in a process costing system. In a process cost report that uses the FIFO costing method, the cost flow follows the logical physical flow of production—that is, the costs assigned to the first products processed are the first costs transferred out when those products flow to the next process, department, or work cell.

To continue with the Milk Products example, assume the following for February:

■ The beginning work in process inventory consists of 6,200 partially completed units (60% processed in the previous period). Beginning inventory cost of $41,540 consisted of materials cost of $20,150 and conversion cost of $21,390.

■ During the period, the 6,200 units in beginning inventory were completed, and 57,500 units were started into production. Current period cost of $510,238 consisted of material cost of $189,750 and conversion cost of $320,488.

■ Of the 57,500 units started during the period, 52,500 units were completed. The other 5,000 units remain in ending work in process inventory and are 45% complete.

Exhibit 3 presents a process cost report for Milk Products.

Exhibit 3
Process Cost Report: FIFO Costing Method

		Physical Units	Direct Materials	% Incurred During Period	Conversion Costs	% Incurred During Period
Step 1: *Account for physical units.*	Beginning inventory (units started last period)	6,200				
	Units started this period	57,500	**Current Equivalent Units of Effort**			
	Units to be accounted for	63,700				
Step 2: *Account for equivalent units.*	Beginning inventory (units completed this period)	6,200	0	0%	2,480	40%
	Units started and completed this period	52,500	52,500	100%	52,500	100%
	Ending inventory (units started but not completed this period)	5,000	5,000	100%	2,250	45%
	Units accounted for	63,700	57,500		57,230	

		Total Costs			
Step 3: *Account for costs.*	Beginning inventory	$ 41,540	=	$ 20,150	+	$ 21,390
	Current costs	510,238	=	189,750	+	320,488
	Total costs	$551,778			

Step 4: *Compute cost per equivalent unit.*	Current Costs		$189,750		$320,488
	Equivalent Units		57,500		57,230
	Cost per equivalent unit	$8.90 =	$3.30	+	$5.60

Step 5: *Assign costs to cost of goods manufactured and ending inventory.*	Cost of goods manufactured and transferred out:				
	From beginning inventory	$ 41,540			
	Current costs to complete	13,888	=	$0	+	(2,480 × $5.60)
	Units started and completed this period	467,250	=	(52,500 × $3.30) +	(52,500 × $5.60)
	Cost of goods manufactured	$522,678		*(No rounding necessary)*	
	Ending inventory	29,100	=	(5,000 × $3.30) +	(2,250 × $5.60)
	Total costs	$551,778			

Work in Process Inventory Account: Cost Recap

Beg. bal.	41,540	Cost of goods	522,678
Direct materials	189,750	manufactured	
Conversion costs	320,488	and transferred out	
End. bal.	**29,100**		

Work in Process Inventory Account: Unit Recap

Beg. bal.	6,200	FIFO units transferred out (from the 6,200 in beginning inventory plus the 52,500 started and completed)	58,700
Units started	57,500		
End. bal.	**5,000**		

© Cengage Learning 2014

As shown in Exhibit 3, the preparation of a process cost report involves five steps. The first two steps account for the units of product being processed. The next two steps account for the costs of the direct materials, direct labor, and overhead being incurred. The final step assigns costs to products being transferred out of the area and to those remaining behind in ending work in process inventory.

Accounting for Units

Managers must account for the physical flow of products through their areas (Step 1) before they can compute equivalent production for the accounting period (Step 2). To continue with the Milk Products example, assume the following for February:

- The beginning work in process inventory consists of 6,200 partially completed units (60 percent processed in the previous period).
- During the period, the 6,200 units in beginning inventory were completed, and 57,500 units were started into production.
- Of the 57,500 units started during the period, 52,500 units were completed. The other 5,000 units remain in ending work in process inventory and are 45 percent complete.

Step 1: Account for Physical Units In Step 1 in Exhibit 3, Milk Products' department manager computes the total units to be accounted for by adding the 6,200 units in beginning inventory to the 57,500 units started into production during this period. These 63,700 units are the actual physical units that the manager is responsible for during the period.

Step 1 continues accounting for physical units. As shown in Exhibit 3, the 6,200 units in beginning inventory that were completed during the period, the 52,500 units that were started and finished in the period, and the 5,000 units remaining in the department at the end of the period are summed, and the total is listed as "units accounted for." (Note that the "units accounted for" must equal the "units to be accounted for" in Step 1.)

Step 2: Account for Equivalent Units The units accounted for in Step 1 are used to compute equivalent production for the department's direct materials and conversion costs for the month in Step 2.

Beginning Inventory. Because all direct materials are added at the beginning of the production process, the 6,200 partially completed units that began February as work in process were already 100 percent complete in regard to direct materials. They were 60 percent complete in regard to conversion costs on February 1. The remaining 40 percent of their conversion costs were incurred as they were completed during the month. Thus, as shown in the "Conversion Costs" column of Exhibit 3, the current equivalent production for their conversion costs is computed as follows.

$$6{,}200 \text{ units} \times 40\% = 2{,}480 \text{ units}$$

Units Started and Completed During the Period. All the costs of the 52,500 units started and completed during February were incurred during this period. Thus, the full amount of 52,500 is entered as the equivalent units for both direct materials costs and conversion costs since 100% of the work was completed during the current period.

Ending Inventory. Because the materials for the 5,000 drinks still in process at the end of February were added when the drinks went into production during the month, the full amount of 5,000 is entered as the equivalent units for direct materials costs. However, these drinks are only 45 percent complete in terms of conversion costs. Thus, as shown in the Conversion Costs column of Exhibit 3, the equivalent production for their conversion costs is computed as follows.

$$5{,}000 \text{ units} \times 45\% = 2{,}250 \text{ units}$$

Totals. Step 2 is completed by summing all the physical units to be accounted for, all equivalent units for direct materials costs, and all equivalent units for conversion costs. Exhibit 3 shows that for February, Milk Products accounted for 63,700 units. Equivalent units for direct materials costs totaled 57,500, and equivalent units for conversion costs totaled 57,230. Once Milk Products knows February's equivalent unit amounts, it can complete the remaining three steps in the preparation of a process cost report.

STUDY NOTE: Units in beginning work in process inventory represent work accomplished in the previous period that has already been assigned a certain portion of its total cost. Those units must be completed in the current period, incurring additional costs. Under FIFO, the amount of effort required to complete beginning work in process inventory is the relevant percentage.

Accounting for Costs

Thus far, we have focused on accounting for units of productive output—in our example, bottled milk drinks. We now turn our focus to the cost information portion of preparing a process cost report.

- In Step 3, all costs charged to the Work in Process Inventory account of each production process, department, or work cell are accumulated and analyzed.
- In Step 4, the cost per equivalent unit for direct materials costs and conversion costs is computed.

To continue with the Milk Products example, assume the following for February:

Work in Process Inventory		
Costs from beginning inventory:		
Direct materials costs	20,150	
Conversion costs	21,390	
Current period costs:		
Direct materials costs	189,750	
Conversion costs	320,488	

STUDY NOTE: *The cost per equivalent unit using the FIFO method measures the current cost divided by current effort. Notice in Exhibit 3 that the cost of beginning work in process inventory is omitted.*

Step 3: Account for Costs As shown in Exhibit 3, all costs for the period are accumulated in the Total Costs column.

Beginning Material Inventory Cost + Conversion Cost = Total Beginning Inventory Cost

$$\$20{,}150 + \$21{,}390 = \$41{,}540$$

Current Period Material Cost + Conversion Cost = Total Current Period Cost

$$\$189{,}750 + \$320{,}488 = \$510{,}238$$

Beginning Inventory Cost + Current Period Cost = Total Cost

$$\$41{,}540 + \$510{,}238 = \$551{,}778$$

Notice that only the Total Costs column is totaled. Because only the current period costs for direct materials and conversion are used in Step 4, there is no need to find the total costs of the direct materials and conversion costs columns in Step 3.

Step 4: Compute Cost per Equivalent Unit Exhibit 3 shows the computation of the current cost per current equivalent unit for direct materials and for conversion costs.

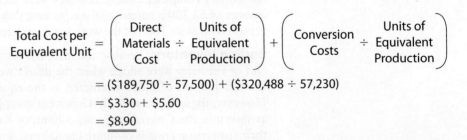

$$= (\$189{,}750 \div 57{,}500) + (\$320{,}488 \div 57{,}230)$$
$$= \$3.30 + \$5.60$$
$$= \underline{\$8.90}$$

Note that the equivalent units are taken from Step 2 of Exhibit 3. Prior period costs attached to units in beginning inventory are not included in these computations because the FIFO costing method uses a separate costing analysis for each accounting period. (The FIFO method treats the costs of beginning inventory separately, in Step 5.)

Assigning Costs

We have focused on accounting for units of productive output, analyzed the costs accumulated in the production process, department, or work cell, and computed the cost per equivalent unit for direct material costs and conversion costs. We now turn to the final step, which is to recognize the costs that are transferred out either to the next production process, department, or work cell or to the Finished Goods Inventory account (i.e., the cost of goods manufactured), as well as the costs that remain in the Work in Process Inventory account.

Step 5: Assign Costs to Cost of Goods Manufactured and Ending Inventory

Step 5 in the preparation of a process costing report uses information from Steps 2 and 4 to assign costs, as shown in Exhibit 3. This final step determines the costs that are transferred out or remain in the Work in Process Inventory account. The total costs assigned to units completed and transferred out and to ending inventory must equal the total costs in Step 3.

STUDY NOTE: *The process cost report is developed for the purpose of assigning a value to one transaction: the transfer of goods from one department to another or to finished goods inventory. The ending balance in the Work in Process Inventory account represents the costs that remain after this transfer.*

Cost of Goods Manufactured and Transferred Out. Step 5 in Exhibit 3 shows that the costs transferred to the Finished Goods Inventory account include the $41,540 in direct materials and conversion costs for completing the 6,200 units in beginning inventory. Step 2 shows that 2,480 equivalent units of conversion costs were required to complete these 6,200 units. Because the equivalent unit conversion cost for February is $5.60, the cost to complete the units carried over from January is computed as follows.

$$2,480 \text{ units} \times \$5.60 = \$13,888$$

Each of the 52,500 units started and completed in February cost $8.90 to produce.

$$52,500 \text{ units} \times \$8.90 = \$467,250$$

To recap the cost assigned to the work completed during the period and transferred to Finished Goods:

$$\$41,540 + \$13,888 + \$467,250 = \$522,678$$

The entry resulting from doing the process cost report for February is:

	Dr.	Cr.
Finished Goods Inventory	522,678	
Work in Process Inventory		522,678

Ending Inventory. All costs remaining in Milk Products' Work in Process Inventory account after the cost of goods manufactured has been transferred out represent the costs of the drinks still in production at the end of February. As shown in Step 5 of Exhibit 3, the balance in the ending Work in Process Inventory is computed as follows.

STUDY NOTE: *All costs must be accounted for, including both costs from beginning inventory and costs incurred during the current period. All costs must be assigned to either ending inventory or the goods transferred out.*

$$(5,000 \text{ units} \times \$3.30 \text{ per unit}) + (2,250 \times \$5.60 \text{ per unit}) = \$29,100$$

Rounding Differences. As you perform Step 5 in any process cost report, remember that the total costs in Steps 3 and 5 must always be the same number. In Exhibit 3, for example, they are both $551,778.

- If the total costs in Steps 3 and 5 are not the same, first check for omission of any costs and for calculation errors.
- If that does not solve the problem, check whether any rounding was necessary in computing the costs per equivalent unit in Step 4. If rounding was done in Step 4, rounding differences will occur when assigning costs in Step 5. In that case, adjust the total costs transferred out for any rounding difference so that the total costs in Step 5 equal the total costs in Step 3.

STUDY NOTE: *Rounding product unit costs to even dollars may lead to a significant difference in total costs, giving the impression that costs have been miscalculated. Round product unit costs to two decimal places where appropriate.*

Recap of Work in Process Inventory Account When the process cost report is complete, an account recap will show the effects of the report on the Work in Process Inventory account for the period. Two recaps of Milk Products' Work in Process Inventory account for February—one for costs and one for units—appear at the end of Exhibit 3.

Process Costing for Two or More Production Departments

In this example, Milk Products has only one production department for making milk drinks, so it needs only one Work in Process Inventory account. However, a company that has more than one production process or department must have a Work in Process Inventory account for each process or department.

For instance, a milk producer like Milk Products has a production department for homogenization, another for pasteurization, and another for packaging needs—three Work in Process Inventory accounts.

■ When products flow from the Homogenization Department to the Pasteurization Department, their costs flow from the Homogenization Department's Work in Process Inventory account to the Pasteurization Department's Work in Process Inventory account.

■ The costs transferred into the Pasteurization Department's Work in Process Inventory account are treated in the same way as the cost of direct materials added at the beginning of the production process.

■ When production flows to the Packaging Department, the accumulated costs (incurred in the two previous departments) are transferred to that department's Work in Process Inventory account.

■ At the end of the period, a separate process cost report is prepared for each department.

APPLY IT!

Pop Chewing Gum Company produces bubble gum. Direct materials are blended at the beginning of the manufacturing process. No materials are lost in the process, so one kilogram of materials input produces one kilogram of bubble gum. Direct labor and overhead costs are incurred uniformly throughout the blending process.

• On June 30, 16,000 units were in process. All direct materials had been added, but the units were only 70 percent complete in regard to conversion costs in the prior period. Direct materials costs of $8,100 and conversion costs of $11,800 were attached to the beginning inventory.

• During July, 405,000 kilograms of materials were used at a cost of $202,500. Direct labor charges were $299,200, and overhead costs applied during July were $284,000.

• The ending work in process inventory was 21,600 kilograms. All direct materials have been added to those units, and 25 percent of the conversion costs have been assigned. Output from the Blending Department is transferred to the Packaging Department.

Required

1. Prepare a process cost report using the FIFO costing method for the Blending Department for July.

2. Identify the amount that should be transferred out of the Work in Process Inventory account, state where those dollars should be transferred, and prepare the appropriate journal entry.

SOLUTION

1.

Pop Chewing Gum Company
Blending Department
Process Cost Report: FIFO Method
For the Month Ended July 31

		Physical Units					

Step 1:
Account for physical units.

	Physical Units
Beginning inventory (units started last period)	16,000
Units started this period	405,000
Units to be accounted for	421,000

Current Equivalent Units of Effort

	Physical Units	Direct Materials	% Incurred During Period	Conversion Costs	% Incurred During Period

Step 2:
Account for equivalent units.

	Physical Units	Direct Materials	% Incurred During Period	Conversion Costs	% Incurred During Period
Beginning inventory (units completed this period)	16,000	0	0%	4,800	30%
Units started and completed this period	383,400	383,400	100%	383,400	100%
Ending inventory (units started but not completed this period)	21,600	21,600	100%	5,400	25%
Units accounted for	421,000	405,000		393,600	

Step 3:
Account for costs.

	Total Costs		Direct Materials		Conversion Costs
Beginning inventory	$ 19,900	=	$ 8,100	+	$ 11,800
Current costs	785,700	=	202,500	+	583,200
Total costs	$805,600				

Step 4:
Compute cost per equivalent unit.

	Total Costs		Direct Materials		Conversion Costs
Current Costs			$202,500		$583,200
Equivalent Units			405,000		393,600
Cost per equivalent unit	$1.98	=	$0.50	+	$1.48*

*Rounded to nearest cent

Step 5:
Assign costs to cost of goods manufactured and ending inventory.

	Total Costs		Direct Materials		Conversion Costs
Cost of goods manufactured and transferred out:					
From beginning inventory	$ 19,900				
Current costs to complete	7,104	=	$0	+	(4,800 × $1.48)
Units started and completed this period	759,132	=	(383,400 × $0.50)	+	(383,400 × $1.48)
Cost of goods manufactured	$786,808				

[Cost of goods manufactured must be $786,808 (add rounding of $672) since Total costs = Ending inventory + Cost of goods manufactured]

	Total Costs		Direct Materials		Conversion Costs
Ending inventory	18,792	=	(21,600 × $0.50)	+	(5,400 × $1.48)
Total costs	$805,600				

Work in Process Inventory Account: Cost Recap

Beg. bal.	19,900	Cost of goods	786,808
Direct materials	202,500	manufactured	
Conversion costs	583,200	and transferred out	
End. bal.	**18,792**		

Work in Process Inventory Account: Unit Recap

Beg. bal.	16,000	FIFO units transferred	399,400
Units started	405,000	out (from the 16,000 in	
		beginning inventory plus the	
		383,400 started and completed)	
End. bal.	**21,600**		

(Continued)

2. The amount of $786,808 should be transferred to the Work in Process Inventory account of the Packaging Department.

    Work in Process Inventory (Packaging Department)   786,808
        Work in Process Inventory (Blending Department)   786,808

TRY IT! SE5, SE6, E7A, E8A, E9A, E10A, E7B, E8B, E9B, E10B

LO 5 Preparing a Process Cost Report Using the Average Costing Method

When a process cost report uses the average costing method, like the one shown in Exhibit 4, cost flows do not follow the logical physical flow of production as they do when the FIFO method is used. Instead, the costs in beginning inventory are combined with current period costs to compute an average product unit cost. Preparing a process cost report using the average costing method involves the same five steps as using the FIFO method, but the procedures for completing the steps differ. Assume that Milk Products uses the average costing method of process costing.

Accounting for Units

The process cost report accounts for the physical units in a production process, department, or work cell during a period. Managers must account for the physical flow of products through their areas (Step 1) before they can compute equivalent production for the accounting period (Step 2). Units to be accounted for equals the physical units in beginning inventory plus the physical units started during the period.

STUDY NOTE: *Step 1 (accounting for physical units) is identical for the average costing and FIFO costing methods.*

Step 1: Account for Physical Units Step 1 of a process cost report accounts for the physical units in a production process, department, or work cell during a period. Units to be accounted for equals the physical units in beginning inventory plus the physical units started during the period. In Step 1 of Exhibit 4, Milk Product's department manager computes the total units to be accounted for as follows.

$$6,200 \text{ units} + 57,500 \text{ units} = 63,700$$

Step 2: Account for Equivalent Units Step 2 also accounts for production during the period in terms of units. After the number of units completed and transferred to finished goods inventory and the number of units in ending inventory have been added to arrive at "units accounted for," the equivalent units in terms of direct materials costs and conversion costs are computed.

STUDY NOTE: *In contrast, as shown in Exhibit 3, the FIFO costing method disregards the previous period costs of units started in the last period and calculates only the equivalent units required in the current period to complete the units in beginning inventory.*

Units Completed and Transferred Out. In Exhibit 4, the average costing method treats both the direct materials costs and the conversion costs of the 58,700 units completed in February (6,200 units from beginning inventory + 52,500 started this period) as if they were incurred in the current period. Thus, the full amount of 58,700 is entered as the equivalent units for these costs.

STUDY NOTE: *The average costing method treats ending inventory in exactly the same way as the FIFO costing method.*

Ending Inventory. Because all direct materials are added at the beginning of the production process, the full amount of 5,000 is entered as the equivalent units for direct materials cost. Because the 5,000 units in ending inventory are only 45 percent complete in terms of conversion costs, the amount of equivalent units is computed as follows.

$$5,000 \text{ units} \times 45\% = 2,250 \text{ units}$$

Totals. When the average costing method is used, Step 2 in a process cost report is completed by summing all the physical units to be accounted for, all equivalent units for direct

Exhibit 4
Process Cost Report: Average Costing Method

		Physical Units					
Step 1:							
Account for physical units.	Beginning inventory (units started last period)	6,200					
	Units started this period	57,500					
	Units to be accounted for	63,700					

Total Equivalent Units of Effort

		Physical Units	Direct Materials	% Incurred During Period	Conversion Costs	% Incurred During Period
Step 2:						
Account for equivalent units.	Units completed and transferred out	58,700	58,700	100%	58,700	100%
	Ending inventory (units started but not completed this period)	5,000	5,000	100%	2,250	45%
	Units accounted for	63,700	63,700		60,950	

		Total Costs		Direct Materials		Conversion Costs
Step 3:						
Account for costs.	Beginning inventory	$ 41,540	=	$ 20,150	+	$ 21,390
	Current costs	510,238	=	189,750	+	320,488
	Total costs	$551,778		$209,900		$341,878

				Direct Materials		Conversion Costs
Step 4:						
Compute cost per equivalent unit.	Total Costs			$209,900		$341,878
	Equivalent Units			63,700		60,950
	Cost per equivalent unit	$8.91	=	$3.30*	+	$5.61*
				*Rounded to nearest cent		

Step 5:

Assign costs to cost of goods manufactured and ending inventory.

Cost of goods manufactured and transferred out $522,655 = (58,700 × $3.30) + (58,700 × $5.61)

(Cost of goods manufactured must be $522,655 (less rounding of $362) since Total costs = Ending inventory + Cost of goods manufactured)

Ending inventory   29,123* = (5,000 × $3.30) + (2,250 × $5.61)

*Rounded to nearest whole dollar

Total costs $551,778

Work in Process Inventory Account: Cost Recap

Beg. bal.	41,540	Cost of goods manufactured and transferred out	522,655
Direct materials	189,750		
Conversion costs	320,488		
End. bal.	**29,123**		

Work in Process Inventory Account: Unit Cost Recap

Beg. bal.	6,200	Units transferred out	58,700
Units started	57,500		
End. bal.	**5,000**		

materials costs, and all equivalent units for conversion costs. Exhibit 4 shows that for February, Milk Products accounted for 63,700 physical units. Equivalent units for direct materials costs totaled 63,700, and equivalent units for conversion costs totaled 60,950.

Accounting for Costs

Step 3 of the report accumulates and analyzes all costs in the Work in Process Inventory account, and Step 4 computes the cost per equivalent unit for direct materials costs and conversion costs. The costs of Milk Products' beginning inventory were $20,150 for direct materials and $21,390 for conversion. Current period costs were $189,750 for direct materials and $320,488 for conversion.

Step 3: Account for Costs All direct materials costs and conversion costs for beginning inventory and the current period are accumulated in the Total Costs column. The total of $551,778 consists of $209,900 in direct materials costs and $341,878 in conversion costs.

Step 4: Compute Cost per Equivalent Unit Step 4 computes the cost per equivalent unit as follows.

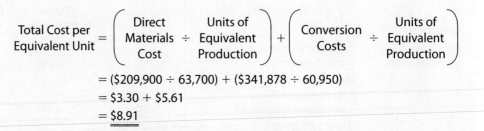

$$= (\$209{,}900 \div 63{,}700) + (\$341{,}878 \div 60{,}950)$$
$$= \$3.30 + \$5.61$$
$$= \underline{\$8.91}$$

- Notice that the cost per equivalent unit for both direct materials and conversion costs has been rounded to the nearest cent. In this text, any rounding differences are assigned to the units transferred out in Step 5.
- Notice also that the average costing and FIFO costing methods use different numerators and denominators in Step 4. Average costing divides *total* cost by *total* equivalent units, whereas FIFO divides *current* costs by *current* equivalent units.

Assigning Costs

We have focused on accounting for units of productive output, analyzed the costs accumulated in the production process, department, or work cell, and computed the cost per equivalent unit for direct material costs and conversion costs. We now turn to the final step, which is to recognize the costs that are transferred out either to the next production process, department, or work cell or to the Finished Goods Inventory account (i.e., the cost of goods manufactured), as well as the costs that remain in the Work in Process Inventory account.

Step 5: Assign Costs to Cost of Goods Manufactured and Ending Inventory

Using information from Steps 2 and 4, Step 5 of a process cost report assigns direct materials and conversion costs to the units transferred out and to the units still in process at the end of the period. As noted, any rounding issues that arise in completing Step 5 are included in units completed and transferred out. Milk Products completes Step 5 as described next.

Cost of Goods Manufactured and Transferred Out. As shown in Exhibit 4, the costs of the units completed and transferred out are assigned by multiplying the equivalent units for direct materials and conversion costs (accounted for in Step 2) by their respective cost per equivalent unit (computed in Step 4) and then totaling these assigned values.

$$\text{Cost of Goods Transferred Out} = (58{,}700 \times \$3.30) + (58{,}700 \times \$5.61) - \$362$$
$$= \$193{,}710 + \$329{,}307 - \$362$$
$$= \underline{\$522{,}655}$$

In this case, because the costs per equivalent unit were rounded in Step 4, a rounding difference of $362 has been deducted from the total cost. The $522,655 of transferred costs will go to the Finished Goods Inventory account, since the goods are ready for sale. The entry resulting from doing the process cost report for February is:

	Dr.	Cr.
Finished Goods Inventory	522,655	
Work in Process Inventory		522,655

Ending Inventory. The costs of the units in ending work in process inventory are assigned in the same way as the costs of cost of goods manufactured and transferred out. In Exhibit 4, the total of costs assigned to ending inventory is computed as follows.

$$(5{,}000 \times \$3.30) + (2{,}250 \times \$5.61) = \$29{,}123$$

The $29,123 (rounded) will appear as the ending balance in the Work in Process Inventory account.

Recap of Work in Process Inventory Account As noted earlier, when a process cost report is complete, an account recap shows the effects of the report on the Work in Process Inventory account for the period. Exhibit 4 includes a cost recap and a unit recap of Milk Products' Work in Process Inventory account for February.

Pop Chewing Gum Company produces several flavors of bubble gum. Direct materials are blended at the beginning of the manufacturing process. No materials are lost in the process, so one kilogram of materials input produces one kilogram of bubble gum. Direct labor and overhead costs are incurred uniformly throughout the blending process.

- On June 30, 16,000 units (kilograms) were in process. All direct materials had been added, but the units were only 70 percent complete in regard to conversion costs in the prior period. Direct materials costs of $8,100 and conversion costs of $11,800 were attached to the beginning inventory.
- During July, 405,000 kilograms of materials were used at a cost of $202,500. Direct labor charges were $299,200, and overhead costs applied during July were $284,000.
- The ending work in process inventory was 21,600 kilograms. All direct materials have been added to those units, and 25 percent of the conversion costs have been assigned. Output from the Blending Department is transferred to the Packaging Department.

Required
1. Prepare a process cost report using the average costing method for the Blending Department for July.
2. Identify the amount that should be transferred out of the Work in Process Inventory account, state where those dollars should be transferred, and prepare the appropriate journal entry.

(Continued)

SOLUTION

1.

Pop Chewing Gum Company
Blending Department
Process Cost Report: Average Costing Method
For the Month Ended July 31

		Physical Units				
Step 1:						
Account for physical units.	Beginning inventory (units started last period)	16,000				
	Units started this period	405,000				
	Units to be accounted for	421,000				

		Physical Units	Direct Materials Costs	% Incurred During Period	Conversion Costs	% Incurred During Period
			Total Equivalent Units of Effort			
Step 2:						
Account for equivalent units.	Units completed and transferred out	399,400	399,400	100%	399,400	100%
	Ending inventory (units started but not completed this period)	21,600	21,600	100%	5,400	25%
	Units accounted for	421,000	421,000		404,800	

		Total Costs				
Step 3:						
Account for costs.	Beginning inventory	$ 19,900	= $ 8,100	+	$ 11,800	
	Current costs	785,700	= 202,500	+	583,200	
	Total costs	$805,600	$210,600		$595,000	

Step 4:						
Compute cost per equivalent unit.	Total Costs		$210,600		$595,000	
	Equivalent Units		421,000		404,800	
	Cost per equivalent unit	$1.97	= $0.50*	+	$1.47*	

*Rounded to nearest cent

Step 5:					
Assign costs to cost of goods manufactured and ending inventory.	Cost of goods manufactured and transferred out (Add rounding of $44)	$786,862	= (399,400 × $0.50) +	(399,400 × $1.47)	
	Ending inventory	18,738	= (21,600 × $0.50) +	(5,400 × $1.47)	
	Total costs	$805,600			

Work in Process Inventory Account: Cost Recap

Beg. bal.	19,900	Cost of	786,862
Direct materials	202,500	goods manufactured	
Conversion costs	583,200	and transferred out	
End. bal.	**18,738**		

Work in Process Inventory Account: Unit Recap

Beg. bal.	16,000	Units	399,400
Units started	405,000	transferred out	
End. bal.	**21,600**		

2. The amount of $786,862 should be transferred to the Work in Process Inventory account of the Packaging Department.

Work in Process Inventory (Packaging Department)	786,862	
Work in Process Inventory (Blending Department)		786,862

TRY IT! SE7, SE8, SE9, SE10, E11A, E12A, E13A, E14A, E15A, E11B, E12B, E13B, E14B, E15B

SECTION 3

BUSINESS APPLICATIONS

BUSINESS APPLICATIONS
- Planning
- Performing
- Evaluating
- Communicating

RELEVANT LEARNING OBJECTIVE

LO 6 Explain how managers use a process costing system to produce business results.

LO 6 The Management Process and the Process Costing System

As noted in the previous chapter, a product costing system provides managers with unit cost information, cost data for management decisions, and ending values for the Materials Inventory, Work in Process Inventory, and Finished Goods Inventory accounts. In this chapter, we focused on a process costing system, the product costing system used by managers at companies that make large amounts of similar products or liquid products. To use process costing, managers must understand product and cost flow patterns, equivalent production, and the preparation of process cost reports. Managers use process costing information in every stage of the management process.

- **Planning:** Managers use information about past and projected product costing and customer preferences to decide what a product should cost. After they have determined a target number of units to be sold, all product-related costs for that targeted number of units can be computed and used in the budget.
- **Performing:** During the period, managers control costs by tracking product and cost flows through their departments or processes and prepare process cost reports to assign production costs to the products manufactured.
- **Evaluating:** Managers evaluate performance by comparing targeted costs with actual costs. If costs have exceeded expectations, managers analyze why this has occurred and adjust their planning and decision-making strategies.
- **Communicating:** Managers use actual units and costs to value inventory on the balance sheet and cost of goods sold on the income statement. Managers are also interested in whether goals for product costs are being achieved.

Notice how managers use process costing throughout the management process to fulfill the management process of planning and forecasting operations, organizing and coordinating resources and data, and commanding and controlling the organization's resources, as illustrated in Exhibit 5.

Exhibit 5
The Management Process and the Process Costing System

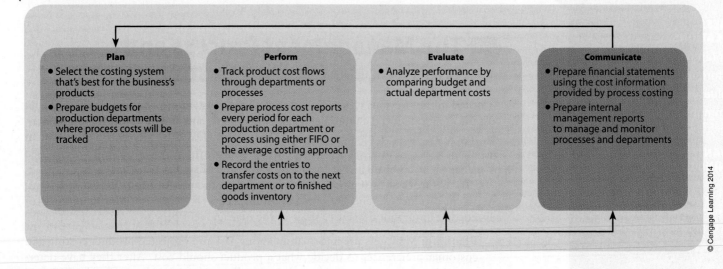

Plan	Perform	Evaluate	Communicate
• Select the costing system that's best for the business's products • Prepare budgets for production departments where process costs will be tracked	• Track product cost flows through departments or processes • Prepare process cost reports every period for each production department or process using either FIFO or the average costing approach • Record the entries to transfer costs on to the next department or to finished goods inventory	• Analyze performance by comparing budget and actual department costs	• Prepare financial statements using the cost information provided by process costing • Prepare internal management reports to manage and monitor processes and departments

© Cengage Learning 2014

Match the activities that follow with one of the stages in the management process.

a. Planning
b. Performing
c. Evaluating
d. Reporting

1. Track the flow of product costs
2. Prepare process cost reports
3. Record entries to transfer costs on to the next department or finished goods inventory
4. Select either the FIFO or weighted average method for process costing

SOLUTION

1. b
2. b
3. b
4. a

TriLevel Problem

Dean Foods

The beginning of this chapter focused on **Dean Foods**, a company known as a leader in the field of milk products. Complete the following requirements in order to answer the questions posed at the beginning of the chapter.

Section 1: Concepts
Why is a process costing system appropriate for Dean Foods to measure and recognize costs?

Section 2: Accounting Applications
How does a product costing system account for costs when identical products or services are produced?

A company like Dean Foods produces several flavors of milk, including chocolate milk. Assume that one of its plants produces chocolate milk. Two basic direct materials, milk and chocolate syrup, are combined by the Mixing Department to make gallons of chocolate milk. No materials are lost in the process, so one gallon of material input produces one gallon of chocolate milk. Direct labor and overhead costs are incurred uniformly throughout the mixing process. How does a product costing system account for costs when identical products like chocolate milk are produced?

Lasse Kristensen/Shutterstock.com

Assume that 15,000 units of chocolate milk were in process at the beginning of the month. All direct materials had been added, but the units were only two-thirds complete in regard to conversion costs. Direct materials costs of $19,200 and conversion costs of $14,400 were attached to the beginning inventory.

During the month, 435,000 gallons of materials were used at a cost of $426,300. Direct labor charges were $100,000, and overhead costs applied during the month were $312,000. The ending work in process inventory was 50,000 gallons. All direct materials have now been added to those units, and 20 percent of the conversion costs have been assigned. Output from the Mixing Department has been transferred to the Packaging Department.

1. Using the FIFO costing method, prepare a process cost report for the Mixing Department for the month.

2. What amount should be transferred out of the Work in Process Inventory account, and to where should those dollars be transferred? Prepare the appropriate journal entry.

3. Using the average costing method, repeat requirement **1**.

4. Answer the questions in requirement **2** as they apply to the process cost report that you prepared in requirement **3**.

Section 3: Business Applications

How does a process costing system help managers organize and control costs and facilitate management decisions? To answer this question, match this chapter's manager responsibilities with when they occur within the management process.

a. Plan	1. Track the flow of product costs
b. Perform	2. Compare actual and budgeted departmental costs
c. Evaluate	3. Prepare financial statements
d. Communicate	4. Prepare process cost reports
	5. Prepare budgets
	6. Prepare internal management reports
	7. Record entries to transfer costs on to the next department or finished goods inventory
	8. Select the best product costing system

SOLUTION

Section 1: Concepts

Because the processing of milk and the production of dairy products involve a continuous flow of similar products, the process costing system is the most appropriate for a company like Dean Foods. Such a system *measures* costs by process, department, or work cell and assigns them to products as they pass through. Companies like Dean Foods can use either the FIFO method or the average costing method of process costing. The process cost report prepared at the end of each period *recognizes* the costs assigned to products completed and transferred out and to the products remaining in the process, department, or work cell. It provides the cost information for product revenues to be *matched* with the expenses required to generate them. A product costing system, like process costing, provides managers with unit cost information, cost data for management decisions, and ending values for the Materials Inventory, Work in Process, and Finished Goods Inventory accounts.

Section 2: Accounting Applications

1.

Mixing Department
Process Cost Report—FIFO Costing Method
For the Month

	Physical Units				
Beginning inventory	15,000				
Units started this period	435,000				
Units to be accounted for	450,000				

		Current Equivalent Units of Effort			
		Direct Materials Costs	% Incurred During Period	Conversion Costs	% Incurred During Period
Beginning inventory	15,000	—	0%	5,000	33%
Units started and completed	385,000	385,000	100%	385,000	100%
Ending inventory	50,000	50,000	100%	10,000	20%
Units accounted for	450,000	435,000		400,000	

	Total Costs				
Beginning inventory	$ 33,600	=	$ 19,200	+	$ 14,400
Current costs	838,300	=	426,300	+	412,000
Total costs	$871,900				
Current Costs			$426,300		$412,000
Equivalent Units			435,000		400,000
Cost per equivalent unit	$2.01	=	$0.98	+	$1.03

Cost of goods manufactured and transferred out:

From beginning inventory	$ 33,600				
Current costs to complete	5,150	=	$0		(5,000 × $1.03)
Units started and completed	773,850	=	(385,000 × $0.98)	+	(385,000 × $1.03)
Cost of goods manufactured	$812,600				
Ending inventory	59,300	=	(50,000 × $0.98)	+	(10,000 × $1.03)
Total costs	$871,900				

2. The amount of $812,600 should be transferred to the Work in Process Inventory account of the Packaging Department.

Work in Process (Packaging Inventory Department)	812,600	
Work in Process (Mixing Inventory Department)		812,600

3.

Mixing Department
Process Cost Report—Average Costing Method
For the Month

	Physical Units	Total Equivalent Units of Effort			
		Direct Materials Costs	% Incurred During Period	Conversion Costs	% Incurred During Period
Beginning inventory	15,000				
Units started this period	435,000				
Units to be accounted for	450,000				
Units completed and transferred out	400,000	400,000	100%	400,000	100%
Ending inventory	50,000	50,000	100%	10,000	20%
Units accounted for	450,000	450,000		410,000	

	Total Costs				
Beginning inventory	$ 33,600	=	$ 19,200	+	$ 14,400
Current costs	838,300	=	426,300	+	412,000
Total costs	$871,900		$445,500		$426,400
Total Costs			$445,500		$426,400
Equivalent Units			450,000		410,000
Cost per equivalent unit	$2.03	=	$0.99	+	$1.04
Cost of goods manufactured and transferred out	$812,000	=	(400,000 × $0.99)	+	(400,000 × $1.04)
Ending inventory	59,900	=	(50,000 × $0.99)	+	(10,000 × $1.04)
Total costs	$871,900				

4. The amount of $812,000 should be transferred to the Work in Process Inventory account of the Packaging Department.

Work in Process (Packaging Inventory Department)	812,000	
Work in Process (Mixing Inventory Department)		812,000

Section 3: Business Applications

1. b   5. a

2. c   6. d

3. d   7. b

4. b   8. a

Chapter Review

Describe a process costing system.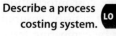
LO 1

A process costing system is used by companies that produce large amounts of similar products or liquid products or that have long, continuous production runs of identical products. Because these companies have a continuous production flow, it would be impractical for them to use a job order costing system, which tracks costs to a specific batch of products or a specific job order. A process costing system accumulates the costs of direct materials, direct labor, and overhead for each process, department, or work cell and assigns those costs to the products as they are produced during a particular period.

Relate the patterns of product flows to the cost flow methods in a process costing environment, and explain the role of the Work in Process Inventory accounts.

During production in a process costing environment, products flow in a first-in, first-out (FIFO) fashion through several processes, departments, or work cells. The process costing system accumulates their costs and passes them on to the next process, department, or work cell. A process cost report may assign costs by using the FIFO costing method, in which the costs assigned to the first products processed are the first costs transferred out, or the average costing method, which assigns an average cost to all products made during a period.

The Work in Process Inventory accounts are the focal point of a process costing system. Each production process, department, or work cell has its own Work in Process Inventory account to which costs are charged. A process cost report assigns the costs that have accumulated during the period to the units that have flowed out of the process, department, or work cell (the cost of goods transferred out) and to the units that are still in process (the cost of ending inventory).

Describe equivalent production, and compute equivalent units.

Equivalent production measures the equivalent number of whole units produced in an accounting period for each type of input. Equivalent units are computed from (1) units in the beginning work in process inventory and their percentage of completion, (2) units started and completed during the period, and (3) units in the ending work in process inventory and their percentage of completion. The computation of equivalent units differs depending on whether the FIFO method or the average costing method is used.

Prepare a process cost report using the FIFO costing method.

In a process cost report that uses the FIFO costing method, the costs assigned to the first products processed are the first costs transferred out. Preparing a process cost report involves five steps. Steps 1 and 2 account for the physical flow of products and compute the equivalent units of production. In Step 3, all direct materials costs and conversion costs for the current period are added to arrive at total costs. In Step 4, the cost per equivalent unit for both direct materials costs and conversion costs is found by dividing those costs by their respective equivalent units. In Step 5, costs are assigned to the units completed and transferred out during the period, as well as to the ending work in process inventory. These costs include the costs incurred in the preceding period and the conversion costs that were needed to complete those units during the current period. That amount is added to the total cost of producing all units started and completed during the period. The result is the total cost transferred out for the units completed during the period. Step 5 also assigns costs to units still in process at the end of the period by multiplying their direct materials costs and conversion costs by their respective equivalent units. The total equals the balance in the Work in Process Inventory account at the end of the period.

Prepare a process cost report using the average costing method.

The average costing method is an alternative method of accounting for production costs. A process costing report that uses the average costing method does not differentiate when work was done on inventory. The costs in the beginning inventory are averaged with the current period costs to compute the product unit costs. These unit costs are used to value the ending balance in Work in Process Inventory and the goods completed and transferred out of the process.

Explain how managers use a process costing system to produce business results.

The product costs provided by a process costing system play a key role in the management process. Managers use past and projected information about product costs to set selling prices and prepare budgets. Each day, managers use cost information to make decisions about controlling costs, the company's volume of activity, ensuring quality, and negotiating prices. They evaluate performance results by comparing targeted costs with actual costs. They use actual units produced and costs incurred to value inventory and the cost of goods sold. They also analyze internal reports that compare the organization's measures of actual and targeted performance to determine whether cost goals for products or services are being achieved.

Key Terms

average costing method 88 (LO2)

conversion costs 89 (LO3)

equivalent production 89 (LO3)

first-in, first-out (FIFO) costing method 87 (LO2)

process cost report 87 (LO2)

process costing system 86 (LO1)

Chapter Assignments

DISCUSSION QUESTIONS

LO **2, 3**   **DQ1. CONCEPT** ▶ Explain why equivalent units are a measure of production effort instead of a physical unit measure of performance.

LO **2, 4, 5**   **DQ2. CONCEPT** ▶ Does the concept of cost recognition underlie why a process cost report is prepared every period for each production department?

LO **4, 5**   **DQ3. CONCEPT** ▶ Why does the concept of cost measurement underlie the five steps in preparing a process cost report?

LO **4, 5**   **DQ4. CONCEPT** ▶ What is the primary cost measurement and cost recognition differences between the FIFO and average costing methods of preparing a process cost report?

LO **6**   **DQ5. CONCEPT** ▶ **BUSINESS APPLICATION** ▶ Why does process costing in the management process reinforce the concepts of cost recognition and cost measurement to produce business results?

SHORT EXERCISES

LO **1**   **Accounting Concepts**

SE1. CONCEPT ▶Match the following statements about process costing with its associated accounting concept:

a. Cost measurement
b. Cost recognition
c. Matching concept

1. Because the processing of a continuous flow of similar products makes it difficult to track costs to individual units, the process costing system provides the cost information for product revenues to be measured against the expenses required to generate them. It provides managers with unit cost information, cost data for management decisions, and ending values for the Materials Inventory, Work in Process, and Finished Goods Inventory accounts.
2. Costs are tracked and accumulated by process, department, or work cell.
3. The report prepared at the end of each period assigns costs to products completed and transferred out and to the products remaining in the process, department, or work cell.

LO 1   **Process Costing Versus Job Order Costing**

SE2. Indicate whether each of the following is a characteristic of job order costing or process costing:

1. Several Work in Process Inventory accounts are used, one for each department or work cell in the process.
2. Costs are measured for each completed job.
3. Costs are grouped by process or department.
4. Costs are measured in terms of units completed in specific time periods.
5. Only one Work in Process Inventory account is used.
6. Costs are assigned to specific jobs or batches of product.

LO 2   **Process Costing and a Work in Process Inventory Account**

SE3. Pro Chemicals uses an automated mixing machine in its Mixing Department to combine three raw materials into a product called Trio. On average, each unit of Trio contains $3 of Material X, $6 of Material Y, $9 of Material Z, $2 of direct labor, and $10 of overhead. Total costs charged to the Mixing Department's Work in Process Inventory account during the month were $210,000. There were no units in beginning or ending work in process inventory. How many units were completed and transferred to finished goods inventory during the month?

LO 3   **Equivalent Production: FIFO Costing Method**

SE4. Pearl Glaze adds direct materials at the beginning of its production process and adds conversion costs uniformly throughout the process. Given the following information from Pearl's records for July and using Steps 1 and 2 of the FIFO costing method, compute the equivalent units of production:

Units in beginning inventory	3,000
Units started during the period	17,000
Units partially completed in prior period	2,500
Percentage of completion of ending work in process inventory	100% for direct materials; 70% for conversion costs
Percentage of completion of beginning inventory in prior period	100% for direct materials; 40% for conversion costs

LO 4   **Determining Unit Cost: FIFO Costing Method**

SE5. Using the information from **SE4** and the data that follow, compute the total cost per equivalent unit.

	Beginning Work in Process	Costs for the Period
Direct materials	$7,600	$20,400
Conversion costs	2,545	32,490

LO 4   **Assigning Costs: FIFO Costing Method**

SE6. Using the data in **SE4** and **SE5,** assign costs to the units transferred out and to the units in ending inventory for July.

LO 5   **Equivalent Production: Average Costing Method**

SE7. Using the same data as in **SE4** but Steps 1 and 2 of the average costing method, compute the equivalent units of production for the month.

LO 5   **Determining Unit Cost: Average Costing Method**

SE8. Using the average costing method and the information from **SE4, SE5,** and **SE7,** compute the total cost per equivalent unit.

LO 5   **Assigning Costs: Average Costing Method**

SE9. Using the data in **SE4, SE5, SE7,** and **SE8** and assuming that Pearl Glaze uses the average costing method, assign costs to the units completed and transferred out and to the units in ending inventory for July.

LO 5   **Equivalent Production: Average Costing Method**

SE10. Real Company adds direct materials at the beginning of its production process and adds conversion costs uniformly throughout the process. Given the following information from Real's records for July, compute the current period's equivalent units of production for direct materials and conversion costs using the average costing method.

Units in beginning inventory	2,000
Units started during the period	13,000
Units partially completed in prior period	500
Percentage of completion of beginning inventory	100% for direct materials; 40% for conversion costs
Percentage of completion of ending work in process inventory	100% for direct materials; 70% for conversion costs

EXERCISES: SET A

LO 1   **Process Costing Versus Job Order Costing**

E1A. Indicate whether the manufacturer of each of the following products should use a job order costing system or a process costing system to accumulate product costs:

1. paint
2. tailor-made tuxedo
3. soft drinks
4. soy milk

5. cups printed with your school insignia
6. water slide for a theme park
7. plastic
8. posters for a concert

LO 2   **Use of Process Costing Information**

E2A. ACCOUNTING CONNECTION ▶ Mom's Bakery makes a variety of baked goods for distribution to grocery stores in the area. The company uses a standard manufacturing process for all items except special-order birthday cakes. It currently uses a process costing system. The owner of the company has the following questions:

1. Did the cost of making special-order birthday cakes exceed the cost budgeted for this month?
2. How much does it cost to make one cheesecake?
3. What is the value of the cupcake inventory at the end of May?
4. What were the costs of the cookies sold during May?
5. At what price should Mom's Bakery sell its famous sweet rolls to the grocery store chains?
6. Were the planned production costs of $3,000 for making pies in May exceeded?

Which of these questions can be answered using information from a process costing system? Which can be best answered using information from a job order costing system? Explain your answers.

LO 2   **Work in Process Inventory Accounts in Process Costing Systems**

E3A. Chemical, Inc., which uses a process costing system, makes a chemical used as a preservative. The manufacturing process involves Departments A and B. The company had the following total costs and unit costs for completed production last month, when it manufactured 10,000 pounds of the chemical. Neither Department A nor Department B had any beginning or ending work in process inventories:

(Continued)

	Total Cost	Unit Cost
Department A:		
Direct materials	$ 9,000	$0.90
Direct labor	2,600	0.26
Overhead	1.300	0.13
Total costs	$12,900	$1.29
Department B:		
Direct materials	$ 3,000	$0.30
Direct labor	700	0.07
Overhead	1,000	0.10
Total costs	$ 4,700	$0.47
Totals	$17,600	$1.76

1. How many Work in Process Inventory accounts would Chemical, Inc., use?
2. What dollar amount of the chemical's production cost was transferred from Department A to Department B last month?
3. What dollar amount was transferred from Department B to the Finished Goods Inventory account?
4. What dollar amount is useful in determining a selling price for 1 pound of the chemical?

LO 3   **Equivalent Production: FIFO Costing Method**

E4A. Brick Company produces bricks. During its first 12 months, it put 600,000 bricks into production and completed and transferred 580,000 bricks to finished goods inventory. The remaining bricks were still in process at the end of the year and were 60 percent complete.

The company's process costing system adds all direct materials costs at the beginning of the production process; conversion costs are incurred uniformly throughout the process. Using the FIFO costing method, compute the equivalent units of production for direct materials and conversion costs for the company's first year, which ended December 31.

LO 3   **Equivalent Production: FIFO Costing Method**

E5A. Suds Enterprises makes Perfecto Shampoo for professional hair stylists. On July 31, it had 5,000 liters of shampoo in process that were 80 percent complete in regard to conversion costs and 100 percent complete in regard to direct materials costs. During August, it put 210,000 liters of direct materials into production. Data for Work in Process Inventory on August 31 were as follows: shampoo, 10,000 liters; stage of completion, 60 percent for conversion costs and 100 percent for direct materials. Using the FIFO costing method, compute the equivalent units of production for direct materials and conversion costs for the month.

LO 3   **Equivalent Production: FIFO Costing Method**

E6A. Eco Savers Corporation produces wood pulp that is used in making paper. The data that follow pertain to the company's production of pulp during September.

| | | Percentage Complete ||
	Tons	Direct Materials	Conversion Costs
Work in process, Aug. 31	50,000	100%	60%
Placed into production	250,000	—	—
Work in process, Sept. 30	80,000	100%	40%

Compute the equivalent units of production for direct materials and conversion costs for September using the FIFO costing method.

LO 4 **Work in Process Inventory Accounts: Total Unit Cost**

E7A. Scientists at Amazing Laboratories, Inc., have just perfected Sparkle, a liquid substance that dissolves silver tarnish. The substance, which is generated by a complex process involving five departments, is very expensive. Cost and equivalent unit data for the latest week follow (units are in ounces).

	Direct Materials		Conversion Costs	
Dept.	Cost	Equivalent Units	Cost	Equivalent Units
A	$12,000	2,000	$33,825	4,100
B	21,835	1,985	14,070	1,005
C	24,102	1,030	20,972	2,140
D	—	—	22,000	2,000
E	—	—	15,560	1,945

Compute the unit cost for each department and the total unit cost of producing 1 ounce of Sparkle.

LO 4 **Determining Unit Cost: FIFO Costing Method**

E8A. Cookware, Inc., manufactures sets of heavy-duty pans. It has just completed production for August. At the beginning of August, its Work in Process Inventory account showed direct materials costs of $31,000 and conversion costs of $29,000. The cost of direct materials used in August was $280,000; conversion costs were $120,000. During the month, the company started and completed 10,000 sets. For August, a total of 14,000 equivalent sets for direct materials and 12,000 equivalent sets for conversion costs have been computed. Using the FIFO costing method, determine the cost per equivalent set for August.

LO 4 **Assigning Costs: FIFO Costing Method**

E9A. The Bakery produces cupcakes. It uses a process costing system. In March, its beginning inventory was 450 units, which were 100 percent complete for direct materials costs and 10 percent complete for conversion costs. The cost of beginning inventory was $655. Units started and completed during the month totaled 14,200. Ending inventory was 410 units, which were 100 percent complete for direct materials costs and 70 percent complete for conversion costs. Costs per equivalent unit for March were $1.40 for direct materials costs and $1.00 for conversion costs. Using the FIFO costing method, compute the cost of goods transferred to the Finished Goods Inventory account, the cost remaining in the Work in Process Inventory account, and the total costs to be accounted for.

LO 4 **Process Cost Report: FIFO Costing Method**

E10A. Toy Truck Corporation produces children's toy trucks using a continuous production process. All direct materials are added at the beginning of the process. In November, the beginning work in process inventory was 420 units, which were 50 percent complete; the ending balance was 400 units, which were 70 percent complete.

During November, 15,000 units were started into production. The Work in Process Inventory account had a beginning balance of $937 for direct materials costs and $370 for conversion costs. In the course of the month, $35,300 of direct materials were added to the process, and $31,689 of conversion costs were assigned. Using the FIFO costing method, prepare a process cost report that computes the equivalent units for November, the product unit cost for the toys, and the ending balance in the Work in Process Inventory account. (Round cost per equivalent unit to the nearest cent.)

LO 5   **Equivalent Production: Average Costing Method**

E11A. Using the data given for Brick Company in **E4A** and assuming that the company uses the average costing method, compute the equivalent units of production for direct materials and conversion costs for the company's first year ended December 31.

LO 5   **Equivalent Production: Average Costing Method**

E12A. Using the data given for Suds Enterprises in **E5A** and assuming that the company uses the average costing method, compute the equivalent units of production for direct materials and conversion costs for August.

LO 5   **Equivalent Production: Average Costing Method**

E13A. Using the data given for Eco Savers Corporation in **E6A** and assuming that the company uses the average costing method, compute the equivalent units of production for direct materials and conversion costs for September.

LO 5   **Determining Unit Cost: Average Costing Method**

E14A. Using the data given for Cookware, Inc., in **E8A** and assuming that the company uses the average costing method, determine the cost per equivalent set for August. Assume equivalent sets are 15,550 for direct materials costs and 14,900 for conversion costs.

LO 5   **Process Cost Report: Average Costing Method**

E15A. Using the data given for Toy Truck Corporation in **E10A** and assuming that the company uses the average costing method, prepare a process cost report that computes the equivalent units for November, the product unit cost for the toys, and the ending balance in the Work in Process Inventory account. (Round cost per equivalent unit to the nearest cent.)

EXERCISES: SET B

Visit the textbook companion website at www.cengagebrain.com to access Exercise Set B for this chapter.

PROBLEMS

LO 4   **Process Costing: FIFO Costing Method**

✔ 1: Total cost of goods manufactured and transferred: $125,013

P1. Juice Extracts Company produces a line of fruit extracts for home use in making wine, jams and jellies, pies, and meat sauces. Fruits enter the production process in pounds, and the product emerges in quarts (1 pound of input equals 1 quart of output). On May 31, 4,250 units were in process. All direct materials had been added, and the units were 70 percent complete for conversion costs. Direct materials costs of $4,607 and conversion costs of $3,535 were attached to the units in beginning work in process inventory. During June, 61,300 pounds of fruit were added at a cost of $71,108. Direct labor for the month totaled $19,760, and overhead costs applied were $31,375. On June 30, 3,400 units remained in process. All direct materials for these units had been added, and 50 percent of conversion costs had been incurred.

REQUIRED

1. Using the FIFO costing method, prepare a process cost report for June.
2. From the information in the process cost report, identify the amount that should be transferred out of the Work in Process Inventory account, and state where those dollars should be transferred.

LO **4**

✔ 3: August total cost of goods
manufactured and transferred: $120,737

Process Costing: One Process and Two Time Periods—FIFO Costing Method

P2. Clean Laboratories produces biodegradable liquid detergents that leave no soap film. The production process has been automated, so the product can now be produced in one operation instead of in a series of heating, mixing, and cooling operations. All direct materials are added at the beginning of the process, and conversion costs are incurred uniformly throughout the process. Operating data for July and August follow.

	July	August
Beginning work in process inventory:		
Units (pounds)	2,300	3,050
Direct materials	$4,699	?*
Conversion costs	$1,219	?*
Production during the period:		
Units started (pounds)	31,500	32,800
Direct materials	$65,520	$66,912
Conversion costs	$54,213	$54,774
Ending work in process inventory:		
Units (pounds)	3,050	3,600

*From calculations at end of July.

The beginning work in process inventory was 30 percent complete for conversion costs. The ending work in process inventory for July was 60 percent complete; for August, it was 50 percent complete. Assume that the loss from spoilage and evaporation was negligible.

REQUIRED

1. Using the FIFO costing method, prepare a process cost report for July.
2. From the information in the process cost report, identify the amount that should be transferred out of the Work in Process Inventory account, and state where those dollars should be transferred.
3. Repeat requirements **1** and **2** for August.

LO **5**

✔ 1: May total cost of goods manufactured
and transferred: $120,100
✔ 1: June total cost of goods
manufactured and transferred: $185,280

Process Costing: Average Costing Method and Two Time Periods

P3. Top Corporation produces a line of beverage lids. The production process has been automated, so the product can now be produced in one operation rather than in the three operations that were needed before the company purchased the automated machinery. All direct materials are added at the beginning of the process, and conversion costs are incurred uniformly throughout the process. Operating data for May and June follow.

	May	June
Beginning work in process inventory:		
Units (May: 40% complete)	220,000	?
Direct materials	$3,440	$400
Conversion costs	$6,480	$420
Production during the month:		
Units started	24,000,000	31,000,000
Direct materials	$45,000	$93,200
Conversion costs	$66,000	$92,796
Ending work in process inventory:		
Units (May: 70% complete; June: 60% complete)	200,000	320,000

1. Using the average costing method, prepare process cost reports for May and June. (Round unit costs to three decimal places.)

(Continued)

2. From the information in the process cost report for May, identify the amount that should be transferred out of the Work in Process Inventory account, and state where those dollars should be transferred.

3. **ACCOUNTING CONNECTION ▶** Compare the product costing results for June with the results for May. What is the most significant change? What are some of the possible causes of this change?

LO 5

✔ 1: Total cost of goods manufactured and transferred: $552,720

Process Costing: Average Costing Method

P4. Energy Products, Inc., makes high-vitamin, calorie-packed wafers that are popular among professional athletes because they supply quick energy. The company produces the wafers in a continuous flow, and it uses a process costing system based on the average costing method. It recently purchased several automated machines so that the wafers can be produced in a single department. All direct materials are added at the beginning of the process. The costs for the machine operators' labor and production-related overhead are incurred uniformly throughout the process.

In February, the company put a total of 231,200 liters of direct materials into production at a cost of $294,780. Two liters of direct materials were used to produce one unit of output (one unit = 144 wafers). Direct labor costs for February were $60,530, and overhead was $181,590. The beginning work in process inventory for February was 14,000 units, which were 100 percent complete for direct materials and 20 percent complete for conversion costs. The total cost of those units was $55,000, $48,660 of which was assigned to the cost of direct materials. The ending work in process inventory of 12,000 units was fully complete for direct materials but only 30 percent complete for conversion costs.

REQUIRED

1. Using the average costing method and assuming no loss due to spoilage, prepare a process cost report for February.

2. From the information in the process cost report, identify the amount that should be transferred out of the Work in Process Inventory account, and state where those dollars should be transferred.

LO 4, 5

✔ 1: Total cost of goods manufactured and transferred: $82,280

Process Costing: FIFO Costing and Average Costing Methods

P5. Goofy Industries specializes in making Go, a high-moisture, low-alkaline wax used to protect and preserve snowboards. The company began producing a new, improved brand of Go on January 1. Materials are introduced at the beginning of the production process. During January, 15,300 pounds were used at a cost of $46,665. Direct labor of $17,136 and overhead costs of $25,704 were incurred uniformly throughout the month. By January 31, 13,600 pounds of Go had been completed and transferred to the finished goods inventory (1 pound of input equals 1 pound of output). Since no spoilage occurred, the leftover materials remained in production and were 40 percent complete on average.

REQUIRED

1. Using the FIFO costing method, prepare a process cost report for January.

2. From the information in the process cost report, identify the amount that should be transferred out of the Work in Process Inventory account, and state where those dollars should be transferred.

3. Repeat requirements 1 and 2 using the average costing method.

ALTERNATE PROBLEMS

LO 4

✔ 1: Total cost of goods manufactured: $627,790

Process Costing: FIFO Costing Method

P6. Canned fruits and vegetables are the main products made by Yummy Foods, Inc. All direct materials are added at the beginning of the Mixing Department's process. When the ingredients have been mixed, they go to the Cooking Department. There the mixture is heated to 100° Celsius and simmered for 20 minutes. When cooled, the mixture goes to the Canning Department for final processing. Throughout the operations, direct labor and overhead costs are incurred uniformly. No direct materials are added in the Cooking Department. Cost data and other information for the Mixing Department for January are as follows.

Production Cost Data	Direct Materials	Conversion Costs
Mixing Department:		
Beginning inventory	$ 28,560	$ 5,230
Current period costs	450,000	181,200
Work in process inventory:		
Beginning inventory (40% complete in prior period)	5,000 liters	
Ending inventory (60% complete)	6,000 liters	
Unit production data:		
Units started during January	90,000 liters	
Units transferred out during January	89,000 liters	

Assume that no spoilage or evaporation loss took place during January.

REQUIRED

1. Using the FIFO costing method, prepare a process cost report for the Mixing Department for January.
2. **ACCOUNTING CONNECTION ▶** Explain how the analysis for the Cooking Department will differ from the analysis for the Mixing Department.

LO **4**

✔ 1: April total cost of goods
manufactured and transferred: $353,368
✔ 3: May total cost of goods manufactured
and transferred: $390,668

Process Costing: One Process and Two Time Periods—FIFO Costing Method

P7. Doover Company produces organic honey, which it sells to health food stores and restaurants. The company owns thousands of beehives. No direct materials other than honey are used. The production operation is a simple one. Impure honey is added at the beginning of the process and flows through a series of filters, leading to a pure finished product. Costs of labor and overhead are incurred uniformly throughout the filtering process. Production data for April and May follow.

	April	May
Beginning work in process inventory:		
Units (liters)	7,100	12,400
Direct materials	$2,480	?*
Conversion costs	$5,110	?*
Production during the period:		
Units started (liters)	288,000	310,000
Direct materials	$100,800	$117,800
Conversion costs	$251,550	$277,281
Ending work in process inventory:		
Units (liters)	12,400	16,900

*From calculations at end of April.

The beginning work in process inventory for April was 80 percent complete for conversion costs, and ending work in process inventory was 20 percent complete. The ending work in process inventory for May was 30 percent complete for conversion costs. Assume no loss from spoilage or evaporation.

REQUIRED

1. Using the FIFO method, prepare a process cost report for April.
2. From the information in the process cost report, identify the amount that should be transferred out of the Work in Process Inventory account, and state where those dollars should be transferred.
3. Repeat requirements **1** and **2** for May.

Process Costing: Average Costing Method and Two Time Periods

✔ 1: July total cost of goods manufactured and transferred: $168,000

✔ 1: August total cost of goods manufactured and transferred: $162,750

P8. Box Corporation produces a line of beverage boxes. The production process has been automated, so the product can now be produced in one operation rather than in the three operations that were needed before the company purchased the automated machinery. All direct materials are added at the beginning of the process, and conversion costs are incurred uniformly throughout the process. Operating data for July and August follow.

	July	August
Beginning work in process inventory:		
Units (July: 20% complete)	20,000	?
Direct materials	$20,000	$6,000
Conversion costs	$30,000	$6,000
Production during the month:		
Units started	70,000	90,000
Direct materials	$34,000	$59,000
Conversion costs	$96,000	$130,800
Ending work in process inventory:		
Units (July: 40% complete; August: 60% complete)	10,000	25,000

1. Using the average costing method, prepare process cost reports for July and August.
2. From the information in the process cost report for July, identify the amount that should be transferred out of the Work in Process Inventory account, and state where those dollars should be transferred.
3. **ACCOUNTING CONNECTION ▶** Compare the product costing results for August with the results for July. What is the most significant change? What are some of the possible causes of this change?

LO 5

Process Costing: Average Costing Method

✔ 1: Total cost of goods manufactured and transferred: $5,463,040

P9. Many of the products made by Plastics Company are standard telephone replacement parts that require long production runs and are produced continuously. A unit for Plastics is a box of parts. During April, direct materials for 25,250 units were put into production. The total cost of direct materials used during April was $2,273,000. Direct labor costs totaled $1,135,000, and overhead was $2,043,000. The beginning work in process inventory contained 1,600 units, which were 100 percent complete for direct materials costs and 60 percent complete for conversion costs. Costs attached to the units in beginning inventory totaled $232,515, which included $143,500 of direct materials costs. At the end of the month, 1,250 units were in ending inventory; all direct materials had been added, and the units were 70 percent complete for conversion costs.

REQUIRED

1. Using the average costing method and assuming no loss due to spoilage, prepare a process cost report for April.
2. From the information in the process cost report, identify the amount that should be transferred out of the Work in Process Inventory account, and state where those dollars should be transferred.

LO 4, 5

Process Costing: FIFO Costing and Average Costing Methods

SPREADSHEET

✔ 1: FIFO total cost of goods manufactured and transferred: $140,892

✔ 3: Average costing total cost of goods manufactured and transferred: $140,892

P10. Sunny Company manufactures and sells several different kinds of soft drinks. Direct materials (sugar syrup and artificial flavor) are added at the beginning of production in the Mixing Department. Direct labor and overhead costs are applied to products throughout the process. For August, beginning inventory for the citrus flavor was 2,400 gallons, 80 percent complete. Ending inventory was 3,600 gallons, 50 percent complete. Production data show 240,000 gallons started during August. A total of 238,800 gallons was completed and transferred to the Bottling Department. Beginning inventory costs were $576 for direct materials and $672 for conversion costs. Current period costs were $57,600 for direct materials and $83,538 for conversion costs.

REQUIRED

1. Using the FIFO costing method, prepare a process cost report for the Mixing Department for August.
2. From the information in the process cost report, identify the amount that should be transferred out of the Work in Process Inventory account, and state where those dollars should be transferred.
3. Repeat requirements **1** and **2** using the average costing method.

CASES

LO **1, 6**   **Conceptual Understanding: Process Costing Systems**

C1. For more than 60 years, **Dow Chemical Company** has made and sold a tasteless, odorless, and calorie-free substance called Methocel. When heated, this liquid plastic (methyl cellulose) has the unusual characteristic (for plastics) of becoming a gel that resembles cooked egg whites. It is used in over 400 food products, including gravies, soups, and puddings. It was also used as wampa drool in *The Empire Strikes Back* and dinosaur sneeze in *Jurassic Park*. What kind of costing system is most appropriate for the manufacture of Methocel? Why is this system most appropriate? Describe the system, and include in the description a general explanation of how costs are determined.

LO **1, 2, 6**   **Ethical Dilemma: Continuing Professional Education**

C2. BUSINESS APPLICATION ▶ Paula Woodward is the head of the Information Systems Department at Mo Manufacturing Company. Roland Randolph, the company's controller, is meeting with her to discuss changes in data gathering that relate to the company's new flexible manufacturing system. Woodward opens the conversation by saying, "Roland, the old job order costing methods just will not work with the new flexible manufacturing system. The new system is based on continuous product flow, not batch processing. We need to change to a process costing system for both data gathering and product costing. Otherwise, our product costs will be way off, and it will affect our pricing decisions. I found out about this at a professional seminar I attended last month. You should have been there."

Randolph responds, "Job order costing has provided accurate information for this product line for more than 15 years. Why should we change just because we've purchased a new machine? We've purchased several machines for this line over the years. And as for your seminar, I don't need to learn about costing methods. I was exposed to them all when I studied management accounting in the 1970s."

Is Randolph's behavior ethical? If not, what has he done wrong? What can Woodward do if Randolph continues to refuse to update the product costing system?

LO **3, 4, 6**   **Interpreting Managerial Reports: Analysis of Product Cost**

SPREADSHEET

C3. BUSINESS APPLICATION ▶ Road Tire Corporation makes several lines of automobile and truck tires. The company operates in a competitive marketplace, so it relies heavily on cost data from its FIFO-based process costing system. It uses that information to set prices for its most competitive tires. The company's radial line has lost some of its market share during each of the past four years. Management believes that price breaks allowed by the company's three biggest competitors are the main reason for the decline in sales.

The company controller has been asked to review the product costing information that supports pricing decisions on the radial line. In preparing her report, she collected the following data for last year, the most recent full year of operations:

(Continued)

	Units	Dollars
Equivalent units:		
Direct materials	84,200	
Conversion costs	82,800	
Manufacturing costs:		
Direct materials		$1,978,700
Direct labor		800,400
Overhead		1,600,800
Unit cost data:		
Direct materials		23.50
Conversion costs		29.00
Work in process inventory:		
Beginning (70% complete)	4,200	
Ending (30% complete)	3,800	

Units started and completed last year totaled 80,400. Attached to the beginning Work in Process Inventory account were direct materials costs of $123,660 and conversion costs of $57,010. A review of the conversion costs revealed, however, an error in the production account. The correct conversion cost being charged to the production account should have been $2,129,616 instead of $2,401,200. This resulted in overly high overhead costs being charged to the production account.

The radial has been selling for $92 per tire. This price was based on last year's unit data plus a 75 percent markup to cover operating costs and profit. The company's three main competitors have been charging about $87 for a tire of comparable quality. The company's process costing system adds all direct materials at the beginning of the process, and conversion costs are incurred uniformly throughout the process.

1. Identify what inaccuracies in costs, inventories, and selling prices result from the company's cost-charging error.
2. Prepare a revised process cost report for 2014. (Round total costs to whole dollars.)
3. What should have been the minimum selling price per tire this year?
4. Suggest ways of preventing such errors in the future.

LO **3, 4, 6**   **Interpreting Managerial Reports: Setting a Selling Price**

C4. BUSINESS APPLICATION ▶ For the past four years, three companies have dominated the soft drink industry, holding a combined 85 percent of market share. Won Cola, Inc., ranks second nationally in soft drink sales. Its management is thinking about introducing a new low-calorie drink called Uncalorie Cola.

Won soft drinks are processed in a single department. All ingredients are added at the beginning of the process. At the end of the process, the beverage is poured into bottles that cost $0.24 per case produced. Direct labor and overhead costs are applied uniformly throughout the process.

Corporate controller Adam Daneen believes that costs for the new cola will be very much like those for the company's Cola Plus drink. Last year, he collected the data that follow about Cola Plus.

	Units*	Costs
Work in process inventory:		
January 1**	2,200	
Direct materials costs		$ 2,080
Conversion costs		620
December 31***	2,000	
Direct materials costs		1,880
Conversion costs		600
Units started during year	458,500	
Costs for year:		
Liquid materials added		430,990
Direct labor and overhead		229,400
Bottles		110,088

* Each unit is a 24-bottle case.
** 50% complete.
*** 60% complete.

The company's variable general administrative and selling costs are $1.10 per unit. Fixed administrative and selling costs are assigned to products at the rate of $0.50 per unit. Each of Won Cola's two main competitors is already marketing a diet cola. Company A's product sells for $4.10 per unit; Company B's, for $4.05. All costs are expected to increase by 10 percent in the next three years. Won Cola tries to earn a profit of at least 15 percent on the total unit cost.

1. What factors should Won Cola, Inc., consider in setting a unit selling price for a case of Uncalorie Cola?
2. Using the FIFO costing method, compute (a) equivalent units for direct materials, cases of bottles, and conversion costs; (b) the total production cost per unit; and (c) the total cost per unit of Cola Plus for the year.
3. What is the expected unit cost of Uncalorie Cola for the year? (Round unit costs to the nearest cent.)
4. Recommend a unit selling price range for Uncalorie Cola, and give the reason(s) for your choice. (Round to the nearest cent.)

LO **2, 3, 4, 6** ## Business Communications: Using the Process Costing System

C5. BUSINESS APPLICATION ▶ You are the production manager for Breakfast Grain Corporation, a manufacturer of four cereal products. The company's best-selling product is Sugaroos, a sugar-coated puffed rice cereal. Yesterday, Clark Winslow, the controller, reported that the production cost for each box of Sugaroos has increased approximately 22 percent in the last four months. Because the company is unable to increase the selling price for a box of Sugaroos, the increased production costs will reduce profits significantly.

Today, you received a memo from Gilbert Rom, the company president, asking you to review your production process to identify inefficiencies or waste that can be eliminated. Once you have completed your analysis, you are to write a memo presenting your findings and suggesting ways to reduce or eliminate the problems. The president will use your information during a meeting with the top management team in ten days.

You are aware of previous problems in the Baking Department and the Packaging Department. Winslow has provided you with process cost reports for the two departments. He has also given you the following detailed summary of the cost per equivalent unit for a box of Sugaroos cereal:

(Continued)

	April	May	June	July
Baking Department:				
Direct materials	$1.25	$1.26	$1.24	$1.25
Direct labor	0.50	0.61	0.85	0.90
Overhead	0.25	0.31	0.34	0.40
Department totals	$2.00	$2.18	$2.43	$2.55
Packaging Department:				
Direct materials	$0.35	$0.34	$0.33	$0.33
Direct labor	0.05	0.05	0.04	0.06
Overhead	0.10	0.16	0.15	0.12
Department totals	$0.50	$0.55	$0.52	$0.51
Total cost per equivalent unit	$2.50	$2.73	$2.95	$3.06

1. In preparation for writing your memo, answer the following questions:
   a. For whom are you preparing the memo? Does this affect the length of the memo? Explain.
   b. Why are you preparing the memo?
   c. What actions should you take to gather information for the memo? What information is needed? Is the information that Winslow provided sufficient for analysis and reporting?
   d. When is the memo due? What can be done to provide accurate, reliable, and timely information?
2. Based on your analysis of the information that Winslow provided, where is the main problem in the production process?
3. Prepare an outline of the sections you would want in your memo.

Continuing Case: Cookie Company

C6. In this segment of our continuing case, you are considering whether process costing is more appropriate for your cookie company than job order costing. List reasons why your company may choose to use process costing instead of job order costing.

CHAPTER 4
Value-Based Systems: Activity-Based Costing and Lean Accounting

BUSINESS INSIGHT
La-Z-Boy, Inc.

La-Z-Boy, Inc., makes thousands of built-to-order sofas and chairs each week at its U.S. plants and generally delivers them in less than three weeks after customers have placed their orders with a retailer. Because of the efficiency with which it assembles and delivers its products, La-Z-Boy has a competitive advantage over its competitors. Critical factors in the company's success are the speed of its supply chain and its use of value-based systems.

1. CONCEPT ▶ *What underlying accounting concepts support the use of value-based systems like activity-based management and lean accounting?*

2. ACCOUNTING APPLICATION ▶ *How can activity-based costing and lean operations help businesses like La-Z-Boy improve business processes and eliminate waste?*

3. BUSINESS APPLICATION ▶ *How can managers of companies like La-Z-Boy plan to remain competitive in a challenging business environment?*

LEARNING OBJECTIVES

LO 1 Describe value-based systems, and discuss their relationship to the supply chain and the value chain.

LO 2 Define *activity-based costing*, and explain how a cost hierarchy and a bill of activities are used.

LO 3 Define the elements of a lean operation, and identify the changes in inventory management that result when a firm adopts its just-in-time operating philosophy.

LO 4 Define and apply *backflush costing*, and compare the cost flows in traditional and backflush costing.

LO 5 Identify the management tools used for continuous improvement, and compare ABM and lean operations.

CONCEPTS
- Relevance
- Reliability

RELEVANT LEARNING OBJECTIVE

LO 1 Describe value-based systems, and discuss their relationship to the supply chain and the value chain.

LO 1 Concepts Underlying Value-Based Systems

Managers operating in volatile business environments that are strongly influenced by customer demands realize that value-based systems, instead of traditional cost-based systems, provide the *relevant* information they need. The information has more relevance because it is predictive and directly relates to the decisions made. **Value-based systems** provide customer-related, activity-based information. They focus on eliminating waste as companies produce and deliver quality products and services. *Reliability* also is important as it assures users that the value-based information is complete, neutral, and free from material error. It is all the information needed for a reliable decision. Managers can use value-based information reliably to compare the value created by products or services with the **full product cost**, which includes not only the costs of direct materials and direct labor, but also the costs of all production and nonproduction activities required to satisfy the customer. For example, the full product cost of a **La-Z-Boy** sofa includes the cost of the shredded foam and upholstery, as well as the costs of taking the sales order, processing the order, packaging and shipping the sofa, and providing subsequent customer service for warranty work.

Value Chain Analysis

Each step in making a product or delivering a service is a link in a chain that adds value to the product or service. This sequence of activities inside the organization that adds value to a company's product or service is known as the **value chain** (illustrated in Exhibit 1). The steps that add value to a product or service—which range from research and development to customer service—are known as **primary processes**. The sequence of primary processes varies, depending on such factors as the size of the company and the types of products or services offered.

The value chain also includes **support services**, such as legal services, human resources, information technology, and management accounting. These services facilitate the primary processes by providing business infrastructure but do not add value to the final product or service. Their roles are critical, however, to making the primary processes as efficient and effective as possible.

Value chain analysis allows a company to focus on its core competencies. A **core competency** is the activity that a company does best. It is what gives a company an advantage over its competitors. For example, **Wal-Mart**'s core competency is achieving the lowest prices, whereas **The Four Seasons Hotel** is known for providing exceptional guest service.

A common result of value chain analysis is outsourcing, which can also be of benefit to a business. **Outsourcing** is the engagement of other companies to perform a process or service in the value chain that is not among an organization's core competencies. For instance, **Wal-Mart** outsources its inventory management to its vendors, who monitor and stock Wal-Mart's stores and warehouses.

Supply Chains

Managers see their organization's internal value chain as part of a larger system. This larger system is the **supply chain** (or the *supply network*)—the path that leads from the suppliers of the materials from which a product is made to the final customer. The supply chain includes both suppliers and suppliers' suppliers, and customers and

Exhibit 1
The Value Chain in a Furniture Company

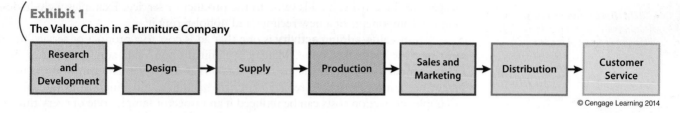

| Research and Development | → | Design | → | Supply | → | Production | → | Sales and Marketing | → | Distribution | → | Customer Service |

© Cengage Learning 2014

customers' customers. It links business to business to business and ultimately to the final consumer.

As Exhibit 2 shows, in the supply chain for a furniture company like **La-Z-Boy**, a farmer supplies cotton to the upholstery manufacturer, which supplies upholstery to the furniture manufacturer. The manufacturer supplies furniture to furniture stores, which in turn supply furniture to the final consumers. Each organization in this supply chain is a customer of an earlier supplier, and each has its own value chain.

Exhibit 2
The Supply Chain in a Furniture Company

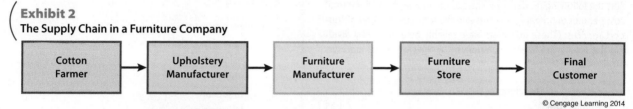

| Cotton Farmer | → | Upholstery Manufacturer | → | Furniture Manufacturer | → | Furniture Store | → | Final Customer |

© Cengage Learning 2014

Using Information from Value Chains and Supply Chains

Understanding value chains and supply chains gives managers a better grasp of their company's internal and external operations. Managers who understand how their company's value-adding activities fit into their suppliers' and customers' value chains can see their company's role in the overall process of creating and delivering products or services. When organizations work cooperatively with others in their supply chain, they can develop new processes that reduce the total costs of their products or services. For example, **La-Z-Boy** places computers for online order entry in its sofa kiosks located in shopping malls. The computers streamline order processing and make the orders more accurate. Even though La-Z-Boy incurs the cost of the computers, the total cost of making and delivering furniture decreases because the cost of order processing decreases.

Process Value Analysis

To improve the *relevance* and *reliability* of information for decision making, managers use **process value analysis (PVA)** to identify and link all the activities involved in the value chain. It analyzes business processes by relating activities to the events that prompt those activities and to the resources that the activities consume. PVA forces managers to look critically at all phases of their operations. PVA improves cost traceability and results in significantly more complete accurate product costs, which in turn improves management decisions and increases profitability. By using PVA to identify non-value-adding activities, companies can improve the relevance and reliability of their data to reduce their costs and redirect their resources to value-adding activities.

Each company in a supply chain is a customer of an earlier supplier. An upholstery company, for example, would be a customer of a cotton farmer and fabric supplier. Its customers might include furniture manufacturers or automobile companies.

Value-Adding and Non-Value-Adding Activities

A **value-adding activity** is one that adds value to a product or service as perceived by the customer. In other words, if customers are willing to pay for the activity, it adds value to the product or service. Examples include designing the components of a new recliner and upholstering it.

A **non-value-adding activity** is one that adds cost to a product or service but does not increase its market value. Managers eliminate non-value-adding activities that are not essential and reduce the costs of those that are, such as legal services, management accounting, machine repair, materials handling, and building maintenance. For example, inspection costs can be reduced if an inspector samples one of every three bolts of upholstery fabric received from a supplier rather than inspecting every one. If the supplier is a reliable source of high-quality upholstery, such a reduction in inspection activity is appropriate.

APPLY IT!

Sort the following product unit costs to determine the relevant total cost per unit of primary processes and the total cost per unit of support services. (These unit costs were reliably determined by dividing the total costs of each component by the number of products produced.)

Research and development	$ 1.25
Human resources	1.35
Design	0.15
Supply	1.10
Legal services	0.40
Production	4.00
Marketing	0.80
Distribution	0.90
Customer service	0.65
Information systems	0.75
Management accounting	0.10
Total cost per unit	$11.45

SOLUTION

Primary processes:	
Research and development	$1.25
Design	0.15
Supply	1.10
Production	4.00
Marketing	0.80
Distribution	0.90
Customer service	0.65
Total cost per unit	$8.85
Support services:	
Human resources	$1.35
Legal services	0.40
Information systems	0.75
Management accounting	0.10
Total cost per unit	$2.60

TRY IT! SE1, SE2, SE3, E1A, E2A, E3A, E4A, E5A, E1B, E2B, E3B, E4B, E5B

ACCOUNTING APPLICATIONS

LO 2 Activity-Based Management

Activity-based management (ABM) identifies all major operating activities, determines the resources consumed by each activity and the cause of the resource usage, and categorizes the activities as adding value to a product or service or not adding value. ABM focuses on reducing or eliminating non-value-adding activities.

Because it provides financial and performance information at the activity level, ABM is useful both for strategic planning and for making tactical and operational decisions about business segments, such as product lines, market segments, and customers. It also helps managers eliminate waste and inefficiencies and redirect resources to activities that add value to the product or service.

Activity-Based Costing

Activity-based costing (ABC) is the tool used in an ABM environment to assign activity costs to cost objects. As access to value chain data has improved, managers have refined the procedures for assigning costs fairly to determine unit costs. Traditional methods of allocating overhead costs to products use such cost drivers as direct labor hours, direct labor costs, or machine hours and one overhead rate. More than 20 years ago, organizations began realizing that these methods did not assign overhead costs accurately and that the resulting inaccuracy in unit costs was causing poor pricing decisions and poor control of overhead costs. In their search for more accurate product costing, many organizations embraced activity-based costing.

Activity-based costing (ABC) calculates a more accurate product cost than traditional methods. It does so by categorizing all indirect costs by activity, tracing the indirect costs to those activities, and assigning those costs to products or services using a cost driver related to the cause of the cost. In other words, ABC reflects the cause-and-effect relationships between costs and individual processes, products, services, or customers.

ABC improves the accuracy in allocating activity-driven costs to cost objects (i.e., products or services). To implement ABC, managers complete the following steps:

- **Step 1**. Identify and classify each activity.
- **Step 2**. Estimate the cost of resources for each activity.
- **Step 3**. Identify a cost driver for each activity, and estimate the quantity of each cost driver.
- **Step 4**. Calculate an activity cost rate for each activity.
- **Step 5**. Assign costs to cost objects based on the level of activity required to make the product or provide the service.

While ABC gives managers greater control over the costs they manage, it has limitations, including the following:

- High measurement costs of collecting accurate data from many activities instead of using just one overhead account may make ABC too costly.
- Some costs are difficult to assign to a specific activity or cost object since they benefit the business in general (e.g., the president's salary) and should not be arbitrarily allocated.
- ABC allocations may add undue complexity to controlling costs.

The Cost Hierarchy and the Bill of Activities

Two tools used in implementing ABC are cost hierarchy and the bill of activities.

Cost Hierarchy A **cost hierarchy** is a framework for classifying activities according to the level at which their costs are incurred. In a manufacturing company, the cost hierarchy typically has four levels, as shown in Exhibit 3.

- **Unit-level activities** are performed each time a unit is produced and are generally considered variable costs. For example, when a furniture manufacturer like **La-Z-Boy** installs a recliner mechanism in a chair, unit-level activities involve the direct material cost of the recliner mechanism, materials handling, and the direct labor cost incurred with connecting the mechanism to the chair frame. Because each chair contains only one mechanism, these activities have a direct correlation to the number of chairs produced.
- **Batch-level activities** are performed each time a batch or production run of goods is produced. Examples of batch-level activities include setup and moving and inspecting mechanisms for the production run of a certain style of furniture. These activities vary with the number of batches prepared or production runs completed.
- **Product-level activities** are performed to support a particular product line. Examples include implementing design, engineering, or marketing changes for a particular brand of product. These activities vary with the number of brands or product designs a company has.
- **Facility-level activities** are performed to support a facility's general manufacturing process and are generally fixed costs. Examples for a furniture manufacturer include maintaining, lighting, securing, and insuring the factory. These activities are generally a fixed amount for a certain time period.

Note that the frequency of activities varies across levels and that the cost hierarchy includes both value-adding and non-value-adding activities.

Exhibit 3
Sample Activities in Cost Hierarchies

	Unit Level Activities performed each time a unit is produced	**Examples** • Install mechanism • Test mechanism
	Batch Level Activities performed each time a batch or production run of goods is produced	**Examples** • Set up installation process • Move mechanisms • Inspect mechanisms
	Product Level Activities performed to support a particular product line	**Example** • Redesign installation process
	Facility Level Activities performed to support a facility's general manufacturing process	**Examples** • Provide facility maintenance • Provide lighting • Provide security

© Cengage Learning 2014

Service organizations can also use a cost hierarchy to group their activities. The four levels typically are the unit level, the batch level, the service level, and the operations level.

Bill of Activities A **bill of activities** is a list of activities and related costs that is used to compute the costs assigned to activities and the product unit cost. More complex bills of activities group activities into activity pools and include activity cost rates and the cost driver levels used to assign costs to cost objects. A bill of activities may be used as the primary document or as a supporting schedule to calculate the product unit cost in both job order and process costing systems and in both manufacturing and service businesses. Exhibit 4 shows a bill of activities for a furniture manufacturer completing an order for 100 chairs.

STUDY NOTE: *A bill of activities summarizes costs relating to a product or service and supports the calculation of the product or service unit cost.*

Exhibit 4
Bill of Activities

Sample Furniture Corporation
Bill of Activities
Chair Order 1.1.12

Activity	Activity Cost Rate	Cost Driver Level	Activity Cost
Unit level:			
Parts production	$40 per machine hour	20 machine hours	$ 800
Assembly	$35 per direct labor hour	10 direct labor hours	350
Packaging and shipping	$10 per unit	100 units	1,000
Batch level:			
Setup	$100 per setup	5 setups	500
Product level:			
Product design	$60 per engineering hour	9 engineering hours	540
Product simulation	$30 per testing hour	3 testing hours	90
Facility level:			
Building occupancy	200% of assembly labor cost	$350 assembly labor cost	700
Total activity costs assigned to order			$3,980
Total units			÷ 100
Activity costs per unit (total activity costs ÷ total units)			$39.80
Cost summary:			
Direct materials			$2,000
Purchased parts			1,000
Activity costs			3,980
Total cost of order			$6,980
Product unit cost (total cost of order ÷ 100 units)			$69.80

APPLY IT!

Bean Bag Convertibles, Inc., has received an order for 100 bean bag sofa convertibles from Furniture Town, LLC. A partially complete bill of activities for that order follows. Fill in the missing data.

Bean Bag Convertibles, Inc.
Bill of Activities
Furniture Town, LLC, Order

Activity	Activity Cost Rate	Cost Driver Level	Activity Cost
Unit level:			
Parts production	$50 per machine hour	5 machine hours	$?
Assembly	$30 per DLH	10 DLH	?
Packing	$3.50 per unit	100 units	?
Batch level:			
Work setup	$25 per setup	4 setups	?
Product level:			
Product design	$160 per design hour	2 design hours	?
Facility level:			
Building occupancy	200% of assembly labor cost	?	?
Total activity costs assigned to job			$?
Total job units			100
Activity costs per unit (total activity costs ÷ total units)			$?
Cost summary:			
Direct materials			$1,000
Purchased parts			500
Activity costs			?
Total cost of order			$?
Product unit cost (total cost ÷ 100 units)			$?

SOLUTION

Bean Bag Convertibles, Inc.
Bill of Activities
Furniture Town, LLC Order

Activity	Activity Cost Rate	Cost Driver Level	Activity Cost
Unit level:			
Parts production	$50 per machine hour	5 machine hours	$ 250
Assembly	$30 per DLH	10 DLH	300
Packing	$3.50 per unit	100 units	350
Batch level:			
Work setup	$25 per setup	4 setups	100
Product level:			
Product design	$160 per design hour	2 design hours	320
Facility level:			
Building occupancy	200% of assembly labor cost	$300	600
Total activity costs assigned to job			$1,920
Total job units			÷ 100
Activity costs per unit (total activity costs ÷ total units)			$19.20
Cost summary:			
Direct materials			$1,000
Purchased parts			500
Activity costs			1,920
Total cost of order			$3,420
Product unit cost (total cost ÷ 100 units)			$34.20

TRY IT! SE4, SE5, E6A, E7A, E8A, E6B, E7B, E8B

LO3 The New Operating Environment and Lean Operations

A **lean operation** focuses on eliminating waste in an organization and on what a customer is willing to pay for. Lean operations emphasize waste that can be eliminated by management analysis of the actions of workers and machines in the process of making products and services.

STUDY NOTE: ABM and lean operations focus on value-adding activities—not costs—to increase income.

To achieve lean operations, a company must redesign its operating systems, plant layout, and basic management methods to conform to several basic concepts:

- Simple is better.
- The quality of the product or service is critical from product design to customer satisfaction.
- The work environment must emphasize continuous improvement.
- Maintaining large inventories wastes resources and may hide poor work.
- Activities or functions that do not add value to a product or service should be eliminated or reduced.
- Goods should be produced only when needed.
- Workers must be multiskilled and must participate in eliminating waste.
- Building and maintaining long-term relationships with suppliers is important.

STUDY NOTE: Traditional environments emphasize functional departments that tend to group similar activities together (e.g., repairs and maintenance).

Application of these lean elements creates a lean operation throughout the company's value chain and guides all employees' work. Piecemeal attempts at lean operations have proved disastrous when the implementation focused on a few lean tools and methodologies instead of understanding how to think lean throughout the organization.

Just-in-Time (JIT)

Managers determined that changes in how inventory was processed traditionally were necessary because:

- Large amounts of an organization's space and money were tied up in inventory.
- The source of poor-quality materials, products, or services was hard to pinpoint.
- The number of non-value-adding activities was growing.
- Accounting for the manufacturing process was becoming ever more complex.

Just-in-time (JIT) is one of the key strategies of a lean operation to reorganize production activities and manage inventory. In a lean operation, the **just-in-time (JIT) operating philosophy** requires that all resources—materials, personnel, and facilities—be acquired and used only as needed to create value for customers. A JIT environment reveals waste and eliminates it by using the principles discussed in the sections that follow.

Business Perspective
The Evolution to Lean Operations

- Eli Whitney perfected the concept of interchangeable parts in 1799, when he produced 10,000 muskets for the U.S. Army for the low price of $13.40 per musket.
- In the late 1890s, Frederick W. Taylor used his ideas of scientific management to standardize work through time studies.
- In the early twentieth century, Frank and Lillian Gilbreth (parents of the authors of *Cheaper by the Dozen*) focused on eliminating waste by studying worker motivation and using motion studies and process charting.
- Starting in 1910, Henry Ford and Charles E. Sorensen arranged all the elements of manufacturing into a continuous system called the *production line*.
- After World War II, Taiichi Ohno and Shigeo Shingo recognized the importance of inventory management, and they perfected the Toyota production system, from which lean operations developed.[1]

Minimum Inventory Levels In the traditional manufacturing environment, parts, materials, and supplies are purchased far in advance and stored until the production department needs them. In contrast, in a JIT environment, materials and parts are purchased and received only when they are needed. The JIT approach lowers costs by reducing the space needed for inventory storage, the amount of materials handling, and the amount of inventory obsolescence. It also reduces the need for inventory control facilities, personnel, and recordkeeping. In addition, it significantly decreases the amount of work in process inventory and the amount of working capital tied up in all inventories.

Pull-Through Production In **pull-through production**, a customer's order triggers the purchase of materials and the scheduling of production for the products that have been ordered. In contrast, with the **push-through production** method used in traditional manufacturing operations, products are manufactured in long production runs and stored in anticipation of customers' orders. With pull-through production, the size of a customer's order determines the size of a production run, and the company purchases materials and parts as needed. Inventory levels are kept low and machines must be set up more frequently as different jobs enter production.

Quick Setup and Flexible Work Cells By placing machines in more efficient locations and standardizing setups, setup time can be minimized in a JIT environment.

In a traditional factory layout, similar machines are grouped together, forming functional departments. Products are routed through these departments in sequence, so that all necessary operations are completed in order. This process can take several days or weeks, depending on the size and complexity of the job. By changing the factory layout so that all the machines needed for sequential processing are placed together, JIT may cut the manufacturing time of a product from days to hours, or from weeks to days. The new cluster of machinery forms a flexible **work cell**, an autonomous production line that can perform all required operations efficiently and continuously. The flexible work cell handles a "family of products"—that is, products of similar shape or size. Product families require minimal setup changes as workers move from one job to the next. The more flexible the work cell is, the greater its potential to minimize total production time.

A Multiskilled Workforce In flexible work cells, one worker may be required to operate several types of machines simultaneously. The worker may have to set up and retool the machines and even perform routine maintenance on them. Under a JIT operating philosophy, multiskilled workers have been very effective in contributing to high levels of productivity.

High Levels of Product Quality A JIT environment results in high-quality products, since high-quality direct materials are used and inspections are made throughout the production process. In a JIT environment, inspection as a separate step does not add value to a product, so inspection is incorporated into ongoing operations. A JIT machine operator inspects the products as they pass through the manufacturing process. If the operator detects a flaw, he or she shuts down the work cell to prevent the production of similarly flawed products while the cause of the problem is being determined. The operator either fixes the problem or helps others find a way to correct it. This integrated inspection procedure, combined with high-quality materials, produces high-quality finished goods.

Effective Preventive Maintenance When a company rearranges its machinery into flexible work cells, each machine becomes an integral part of its cell. If one machine breaks down, the entire work cell stops functioning, and the product cannot easily be routed to another machine while the malfunctioning machine is being repaired. Continuous JIT operations therefore require an effective system of preventive maintenance. Preventing machine breakdowns is considered more important and more cost effective than keeping machines running continuously. Machine operators are trained to perform minor repairs when they detect problems. Machines are serviced regularly—much as

---

STUDY NOTE: Pull-through production represents a change in concept. Instead of producing goods in anticipation of customers' needs, customers' orders trigger the production process.

STUDY NOTE: In the JIT environment, normal operating activities—setup, production, and maintenance—still take place. But the timing of those activities is altered to promote smoother operations and to minimize downtime.

STUDY NOTE: Although separate inspection costs are reduced in a JIT operating environment, some additional time is added to production because the machine operator is now performing the inspection function.

Business Perspective
Lean Operations Improve Hospital Safety and Efficiency

Many hospitals around the country use lean tools to enhance laboratory performance when drawing and processing blood samples, administering patient medications, or supplying sterile IV equipment to operating rooms. Staff participate in value stream mapping to optimize work flows, kaizen (meaning suggest improvements for) different processes to achieve rapid operations, and use JIT principles when managing inventory.

automobiles are—to help guarantee continued operation. The machine operator conducts routine maintenance during downtime periods between orders.

Continuous Improvement of the Work Environment

A JIT operating philosophy fosters loyalty among workers, who are likely to see themselves as part of a team that is deeply involved in the production process. Machine operators must have the skills to run several types of machines, detect defective products, suggest measures to correct problems, and maintain the machinery within their work cells. In addition, each worker is encouraged to suggest improvements to the production process. In Japanese, this is called **kaizen**, meaning "good change." Companies with a JIT operating philosophy receive thousands of employee suggestions and implement a high percentage of them, and they reward workers for suggestions that improve the process. Such an environment fosters workers' initiative and benefits the company.

Accounting for Product Costs in a JIT Operating Environment

When a firm like **La-Z-Boy** shifts to lean operations and adopts a JIT operating philosophy, the changes in the operations will affect how costs are determined and what measures are used to monitor performance. The work cells and the goal of reducing or eliminating non-value-adding activities change the way costs are classified and assigned.

Classifying Costs The traditional production process can be divided into five time frames:

- **Processing time:** The actual amount of time spent working on a product
- **Inspection time:** The time spent looking for product flaws or reworking defective units
- **Moving time:** The time spent moving a product from one operation or department to another
- **Queue time:** The time a product spends waiting to be worked on once it arrives at the next operation or department
- **Storage time:** The time a product spends in materials inventory, work in process inventory, or finished goods inventory

In product costing under JIT, costs associated with processing time are relevant, but costs associated with inspection, moving, queue, and storage time should be reduced or eliminated because they do not add value to the product.

Assigning Costs In a JIT operating environment, managers focus on **throughput time**, the time it takes to move a product through the entire production process. Sophisticated computer monitoring of the work cells allows many costs to be traced directly to the cells in which products are manufactured. As Exhibit 5 shows, several costs that in a traditional environment are treated as indirect costs and applied to products using an overhead rate are treated as the direct costs of a JIT work cell.

- The costs of repairs and maintenance, materials handling, operating supplies, utilities, employee benefits, and indirect labor and supervision can be traced directly to work cells as they are incurred.
- Depreciation charges on machinery are based on units of output, not on time, so depreciation can be charged directly to work cells based on the number of units produced.
- Building occupancy costs, insurance premiums, and property taxes remain indirect costs and must be assigned to the work cells.

Exhibit 5
Direct and Indirect Costs in Traditional and JIT Environments

	Costs in a Traditional Environment	Costs in a JIT Environment
Direct materials	Direct	Direct to work cell
Direct labor	Direct	Direct to work cell
Repairs and maintenance	Indirect	Direct to work cell
Materials handling	Indirect	Direct to work cell
Operating supplies	Indirect	Direct to work cell
Utilities costs	Indirect	Direct to work cell
Supervision	Indirect	Direct to work cell
Depreciation—machinery	Indirect	Direct to work cell
Depreciation—plant	Indirect	Indirect
Supporting service functions	Indirect	Mostly direct to work cell
Building occupancy	Indirect	Indirect
Insurance and taxes	Indirect	Indirect
President's salary	Indirect	Indirect

© Cengage Learning 2014

APPLY IT!

The cost categories in the following list are typical of a furniture manufacturer like Bean Bag Convertibles, Inc. Identify each cost as direct or indirect, assuming that it was incurred in (1) a traditional manufacturing setting and (2) a JIT environment.

a. Direct materials
b. Direct labor
c. Supervisory salaries
d. Electrical power
e. Operating supplies
f. Purchased parts
g. Employee benefits
h. Indirect labor
i. Insurance and taxes, plant

SOLUTION

	1. Traditional Setting	2. JIT Setting
a. Direct materials	Direct	Direct
b. Direct labor	Direct	Direct
c. Supervisory salaries	Indirect	Direct
d. Electrical power	Indirect	Direct
e. Operating supplies	Indirect	Direct
f. Purchased parts	Direct	Direct
g. Employee benefits	Indirect	Direct
h. Indirect labor	Indirect	Direct
i. Insurance and taxes—plant	Indirect	Indirect

TRY IT! SE6, SE9, E10A, E11A, E10B, E11B

LO4 Backflush Costing

We have focused on how managers can trim waste from operations. However, they can also reduce waste in other areas, including the accounting process. Because a lean operation reduces labor costs, the accounting system can combine the costs of direct labor and overhead into the single category of conversion costs. Also, because materials arrive just in time to be used in the production process, there is little reason to maintain a separate Materials Inventory account. Thus, by simplifying cost flows through the accounting records, it is possible to reduce the time it takes to record and account for the costs of the manufacturing process.

Cost Flows in Traditional and Backflush Costing

A lean organization can also streamline its accounting process by using backflush costing. In **backflush costing**, all product costs are first accumulated in the Cost of Goods Sold account. At the end of the period, they are "flushed back," or worked backward, into the appropriate inventory accounts. By having all product costs flow straight to a final destination and working back to determine the proper balances for the inventory accounts, this method saves recording time. As shown in Exhibit 6, it eliminates the need to record several transactions that must be recorded in traditional operating environments.

Exhibit 6
Comparison of Cost Flows in Traditional and Backflush Costing

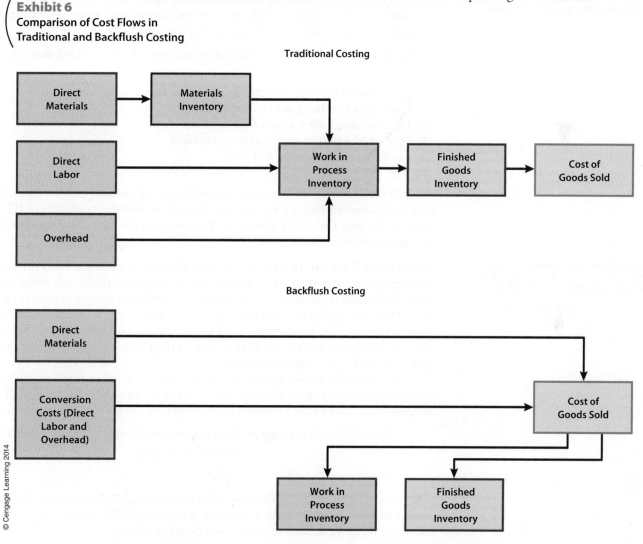

© Cengage Learning 2014

Cost flows differ depending on whether a company is using a traditional costing method or backflush costing.

Traditional Costing Method When a traditional costing method is used:

■ Direct materials costs are entered into the Materials Inventory account upon arrival at the factory.

■ Direct materials costs flow into the Work in Process Inventory account as materials are requisitioned into production. When direct labor is used, its costs are added to the Work in Process Inventory account. Overhead is applied to production using a base like direct labor hours, machine hours, or number of units produced and is added to the other costs in the Work in Process Inventory account.

■ The costs of the finished units are transferred to the Finished Goods Inventory account at the end of the manufacturing process. When the units are sold, their costs are transferred to the Cost of Goods Sold account.

Backflush Costing Method When the backflush costing method is used:

■ Direct materials arrive just in time to be placed into production. The direct materials costs and the **conversion costs** (direct labor and overhead) are immediately charged to the Cost of Goods Sold account.

■ The costs of goods in work in process inventory and in finished goods inventory are determined at the end of the period, and those costs are flushed back to the Work in Process Inventory account and the Finished Goods Inventory account. Once those costs have been flushed back, the Cost of Goods Sold account contains only the costs of units completed and sold during the period.

STUDY NOTE: In backflush costing, entries to the Work in Process Inventory and Finished Goods Inventory accounts are made at the end of the period.

Assume that the following transactions occurred at one of **La-Z-Boy**'s production facilities last month:

1. Purchased $20,000 of direct materials on account.
2. Used all of the direct materials in production.
3. Incurred direct labor costs of $8,000.
4. Applied $24,000 of overhead to production.
5. Completed units costing $51,600.
6. Sold units costing $51,500.

Exhibit 7 shows how these transactions would be entered in T accounts when traditional product costing is used and then shows how backflush costing in a JIT environment would treat the same transactions. You can trace the flow of each cost by following its transaction number.

JIT Costing Method In backflush costing, the cost of direct materials (Transaction 1) is charged directly to the Cost of Goods Sold account. Transaction 2, which is included in the traditional method, is not included when backflush costing is used because there is no Materials Inventory account. The costs of direct labor (Transaction 3) and overhead (Transaction 4) are combined and transferred to the Cost of Goods Sold account. The total in the Cost of Goods Sold account is then $52,000 ($20,000 for direct materials + $32,000 for conversion costs).

Once all product costs for the period have been entered in the Cost of Goods Sold account, the amounts to be transferred back to the inventory accounts are calculated. The amount transferred to the Finished Goods Inventory account is computed as follows.

$$\text{Finished Goods Inventory} = \text{Cost of Completed Units} - \text{Cost of Units Sold}$$
$$= \$51{,}600 - \$51{,}500$$
$$= \$100$$

The remaining difference in the Cost of Goods Sold account represents the cost of the work that is still in production at the end of the period. The amount transferred to the Work in Process Inventory account is computed as follows.

$$\text{Work in Process Inventory} = \text{Costs Charged to Cost of Goods Sold} - \text{Cost of Completed Units}$$
$$= (\$20{,}000 + \$8{,}000 + \$24{,}000) - \$51{,}600$$
$$= \$400$$

The ending balance in the Cost of Goods Sold account, $51,500, is the same as the ending balance when traditional costing is used. The difference is that backflush costing uses fewer accounts and avoids recording several transactions.

Exhibit 7
Comparison of Cost Flows Through T Accounts with Traditional and Backflush Costing

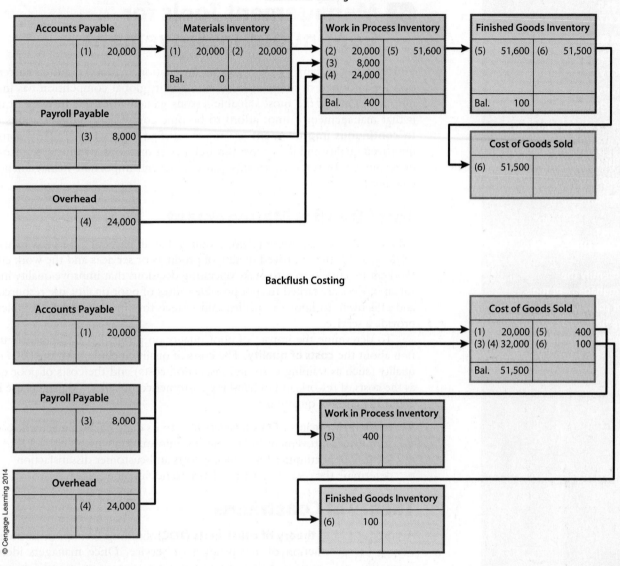

Traditional Costing

Accounts Payable		
	(1)	20,000

Materials Inventory			
(1)	20,000	(2)	20,000
Bal.	0		

Work in Process Inventory			
(2)	20,000	(5)	51,600
(3)	8,000		
(4)	24,000		
Bal.	400		

Finished Goods Inventory			
(5)	51,600	(6)	51,500
Bal.	100		

Payroll Payable		
	(3)	8,000

Overhead		
	(4)	24,000

Cost of Goods Sold		
(6)	51,500	

Backflush Costing

Accounts Payable		
	(1)	20,000

Payroll Payable		
	(3)	8,000

Overhead		
	(4)	24,000

Cost of Goods Sold			
(1)	20,000	(5)	400
(3) (4)	32,000	(6)	100
Bal.	51,500		

Work in Process Inventory		
(5)	400	

Finished Goods Inventory		
(6)	100	

© Cengage Learning 2014

APPLY IT!

For work done during August, Bean Bag Convertibles incurred direct materials costs of $123,450 and conversion costs of $265,200. The company employs a just-in-time operating environment and backflush costing.

At the end of August, the Work in Process Inventory account had been assigned $980 of costs, and the ending balance of the Finished Goods Inventory account was $1,290. There were no beginning inventory balances.

1. How much was charged to the Cost of Goods Sold account during August?
2. What was the ending balance of the Cost of Goods Sold account?

SOLUTION

1. $123,450 + $265,200 = $388,650

2. $388,650 − $980 − $1,290 = $386,380

TRY IT! SE7, E12A, E13A, E12B, E13B

BUSINESS APPLICATIONS

LO5 Management Tools for Continuous Improvement

Today managers have ready access to international markets and to current information for informed decision making. As a result, global competition has increased significantly. One of the most valuable lessons gained from this increase in competition is that management cannot afford to become complacent. Organizations that adhere to **continuous improvement** are never satisfied with what is. They constantly seek improved quality and lower cost through better methods, products, services, processes, or resources. In response to this concept, several important management tools have emerged.

Total Quality Management

Total quality management (TQM) requires that all parts of a business focus on quality. TQM's goal is the improved quality of products or services and the work environment. Workers are empowered to make operating decisions that improve quality in both areas. All employees are tasked to spot possible causes of poor quality, use resources efficiently and effectively to improve quality, and reduce the time needed to complete a task or provide a service.

To determine the impact of poor quality on profits, TQM managers use information about the **costs of quality**. The costs of quality include both the costs of achieving quality (such as training costs and inspection costs) and the costs of poor quality (such as the costs of rework and of handling customer complaints). Managers use information about the costs of quality to:

- relate their organization's business plan to its daily operating activities.
- stimulate improvement by sharing this information with all employees.
- identify opportunities for reducing costs and customer dissatisfaction.
- determine the costs of quality relative to net income.

Theory of Constraints

According to the **theory of constraints (TOC)**, limiting factors, or bottlenecks, occur during the production of any product or service. Once managers identify such a constraint, they can focus their attention and resources on it and achieve significant improvements. TOC thus helps managers set priorities for how they spend their time and resources.

Comparison of ABM and Lean Operations

ABM and lean have several things in common as value-based systems:

- Both analyze processes and identify value-adding and non-value-adding activities.
- Both seek to eliminate waste and reduce non-value-adding activities to improve product or service quality, reduce costs, and improve an organization's efficiency and productivity.
- Both improve the quality of the information that managers use to make decisions about bidding, pricing, product lines, and outsourcing.

The two systems differ in their methods of costing and cost assignment. ABM's tool, ABC, calculates product or service cost by using cost drivers to assign the indirect costs of production to cost objects. ABC is often a fairly complex accounting method used with job order and process costing systems. Note that the ABC method can also be used to examine nonproduction-related activities, such as marketing and shipping.

A lean operation uses JIT and reorganizes many activities so that they are performed within work cells. The costs of those activities become direct costs of the work cell and of the products made in that cell. The total production costs within the cell can then be assigned by using simple cost drivers, such as process hours or direct materials cost. Companies that have implemented lean operations may use backflush costing rather than job order costing or process costing. This approach focuses on the output at the end of the production process and simplifies the accounting system.

Exhibit 8 summarizes the characteristics of ABM and lean operations. A company can use both ABM and lean. ABM and ABC will improve the accuracy of the company's product or service costing and help it to reduce or eliminate business activities that do not add value for its customers. At the same time, the company can apply lean thinking to simplify processes, use resources effectively, and eliminate waste.

STUDY NOTE: *ABM's primary goal is to calculate product or service cost accurately. The primary goal of lean operations is to eliminate waste in business processes.*

Exhibit 8
Comparison of ABM and Lean Operations

	ABM	Lean Operations
Primary purpose	To eliminate or reduce non-value-adding activities	To eliminate or reduce waste in all aspects of a business, including its processes and products or services
Cost assignment	Uses ABC to assign overhead costs to the product by using appropriate cost drivers	Uses JIT and reorganizes production activities into work cells; overhead costs incurred in the work cell become direct costs of the cell's products
Costing method	Integrates ABC with job order or process costing to calculate product costs	May use backflush costing to calculate product costs
Limitation	ABC can involve costly data collection and complex allocations	Requires management to think differently and use different performance measures

© Cengage Learning 2014

To remain competitive in today's business environment, companies have had to rethink their organizational processes and basic operating methods. Managers now focus on creating value for their customers as well as controlling costs throughout their management process. They design their internal value chain and external supply chain to provide customer-related, activity-based information; to track costs; and to eliminate waste and inefficiencies. In this chapter, two value-based systems that help managers improve operating processes and make better decisions as they plan, perform, evaluate, and report were discussed: activity-based management and lean operations. Exhibit 9 summarizes the steps managers take during the management process to manage for value and control costs.

Exhibit 9
Managing for Value and Controlling Costs

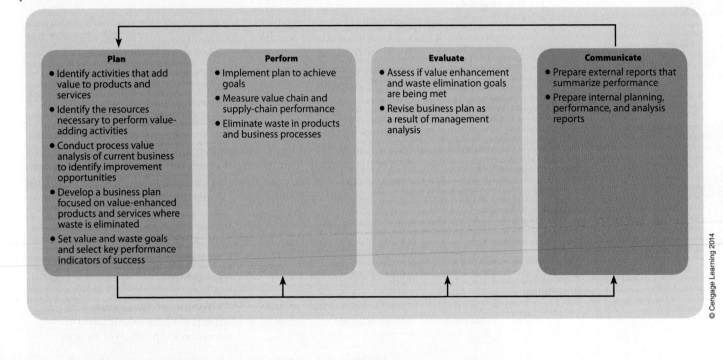

APPLY IT!

Recently, you had dinner with four chief financial officers (CFOs) who were attending a seminar on management tools and approaches to improving operations. The CFOs shared information about their organizations' current operating environments. Excerpts from the conversation appear below. Indicate whether each CFO describes activity-based management (ABM), lean operations, total quality management (TQM), or the theory of constraints (TOC).

- **CFO 1:** We think quality can be achieved through carefully designed production processes. We focus on minimizing the time needed to move, store, queue, and inspect our materials and products. We've reduced inventories by purchasing and using materials only when they're needed.
- **CFO 2:** Your approach is good. But we're more concerned with our total operating environment, so we have a strategy that asks all employees to contribute to the quality of both our products and our work environment. We focus on eliminating poor product quality by reducing waste and inefficiencies in our current operating methods.
- **CFO 3:** Our organization has adopted a strategy for producing high-quality products that incorporates many of your approaches. We also want to manage our resources effectively, and we do it by monitoring operating activities. We analyze all activities to eliminate or reduce the ones that don't add value to products.
- **CFO 4:** But how do you set priorities for your management efforts? We find that we achieve the greatest improvements by focusing our time and resources on the bottlenecks in our production processes.

SOLUTION
CFO 1: Lean operations; CFO 2: TQM; CFO 3: ABM; CFO 4: TOC

TRY IT! SE8, SE9, SE10, E14A, E15A, E14B, E15B

TriLevel Problem

La-Z-Boy, Inc.

The beginning of this chapter focused on **La-Z-Boy, Inc.**, a company that makes built-to-order sofas and chairs. Complete the following requirements in order to answer the questions posed at the beginning of the chapter.

Section 1: Concepts
What underlying accounting concepts support the use of value-based systems like activity-based management and lean accounting?

Section 2: Accounting Applications
How can activity-based costing and lean operations help businesses like La-Z-Boy improve business processes and eliminate waste?

1. Assume that one of La-Z-Boy's production facilities produces more than a dozen styles of convertible sofas. The six-piece modular seating/sleeping style is the most difficult to produce and the most expensive. Campus Stores recently ordered 350 six-piece modular sets. Assume the production facility that received this order has been using a traditional costing system, but its controller is considering a shift to activity-based costing. He therefore wants to use the order from Campus Stores to compare ABC with traditional costing. Costs directly traceable to the order are as follows:

Direct materials	$57,290
Purchased parts	$76,410
Direct labor hours	1,320
Average direct labor pay rate per hour	$14.00

    With the traditional costing approach, the controller applies overhead costs at a rate of 320 percent of direct labor costs.

    For activity-based costing of the Campus Stores order, the controller uses the following data:

Activity	Cost Driver	Activity Cost Rate	Activity Usage
Product design	Engineering hours	$62 per engineering hour	76 engineering hours
Work cell setup	Number of setups	$90 per setup	16 setups
Parts production	Machine hours	$38 per machine hour	380 machine hours
Assembly	Assembly labor hours	$40 per assembly labor hour	500 assembly labor hours
Product simulation	Testing hours	$90 per testing hour	28 testing hours
Packaging and shipping	Product units	$13 per unit	350 units
Building occupancy	Direct labor cost	125% of direct labor cost	$18,480 direct labor cost

    (a) Use the traditional costing approach to compute the total cost and product unit cost of the Campus Stores order.
    (b) Using the cost hierarchy for manufacturing companies, classify each activity of the Campus Stores order according to the level at which it occurs.
    (c) Prepare a bill of activities for the operating costs.
    (d) Use ABC to compute the total cost and product unit cost. Round your answer to the nearest cent.
    (e) What is the difference between the product unit cost you computed using the traditional approach and the one you computed using ABC? Does the use of ABC guarantee cost reduction for every order?

2. Assume that one of La-Z-Boy's production facilities is a lean operation and uses backflush costing in its management of reclining sofa inventory. At the beginning of the month, Work in Process Inventory and Finished Goods Inventory had zero balances. During the month, the following transactions took place:

- Ordered, received, and used materials costing $11,000.
- Direct labor costs incurred, $6,000.
- Overhead costs incurred, $3,000.
- Completed reclining sofas costing $19,000.
- Sold reclining sofas costing $18,500.

Using backflush costing, calculate the ending balance in the Work in Process Inventory and Finished Goods Inventory accounts.

Section 3: Business Applications

How can managers of companies like La-Z-Boy plan to remain competitive in a challenging business environment? To answer this question, match this chapter's manager responsibilities with when they occur within the management process.

a. Plan

b. Perform

c. Evaluate

d. Communicate

1. Identify value-adding activities
2. Prepare external reports
3. Conduct process value analysis to identify improvement opportunities
4. Assess if value and waste goals are met.
5. Prepare internal reports
6. Identify the resources necessary to perform value-adding activities
7. Develop a business plan
8. Implement plan to achieve goals
9. Set value and waste goals and select key performance indicators of success
10. Revise business plan as a result of management analysis
11. Manage and measure value chain and supply chain performance
12. Eliminate waste in products and business processes

SOLUTION

Section 1: Concepts

The concepts of *relevance* and *reliability* underlie value-based systems like activity-based management and lean operations. Value-based systems add relevance since they categorize activities as either adding value to a product or service or not adding value. It enables managers to see their organization as a collection of value-creating activities (a value chain) that operates as part of a larger system that includes suppliers' and customers' value chains (a supply chain). This perspective has a direct bearing on a manager's ability to work with reliable information that is free from material error, complete, and neutral to reduce costs by eliminating waste and inefficiencies and by redirecting resources toward value-adding activities.

Section 2: Accounting Applications

1. (a)

Direct materials	$ 57,290
Purchased parts	76,410
Direct labor	18,480
Overhead (320% of direct labor cost)	59,136
Total cost of order	$211,316
Product unit cost (total costs ÷ 350 units)	$ 603.76

(b) Unit level: Parts production
                   Assembly
                   Packaging and shipping
     Batch level: Work cell setup
     Product level: Product design
                   Product simulation
     Facility level: Building occupancy

(c) and (d)

La-Z-Boy, Inc.
Bill of Activities
Campus Stores Order

Activity	Activity Cost Rate	Cost Driver Level	Activity Cost
Unit level:			
Parts production	$38 per machine hour	380 machine hours	$ 14,440
Assembly	$40 per assembly labor hour	500 assembly labor hours	20,000
Packaging and shipping	$13 per unit	350 units	4,550
Batch level:			
Work cell setup	$90 per setup	16 setups	1,440
Product level:			
Product design	$62 per engineering hour	76 engineering hours	4,712
Product simulation	$90 per testing hour	28 testing hours	2,520
Facility level:			
Building occupancy	125% of direct labor cost	$18,480 direct labor cost	23,100
Total activity costs assigned to job			$ 70,762
Total job units			÷ 350
Activity costs per unit (total activity costs ÷ total units)			$ 202.18*
Cost summary:			
Direct materials			$ 57,290
Purchased parts			76,410
Activity costs (includes labor and overhead)			70,762
Total cost of order			$204,462
Product unit cost (total cost of order ÷ 350 units)			$ 584.18*

*Rounded

(e) Product unit cost using traditional costing approach $603.76
     Product unit cost using activity-based costing approach   584.18
     Difference $ 19.58

Although the product unit cost computed using ABC is lower than the one computed using the traditional costing approach, ABC does not guarantee cost reduction for every product. It does improve cost traceability, which often identifies products that are "undercosted" or "overcosted" by a traditional product costing system.

2. Costs added to Cost of Goods Sold account:

Direct materials	$ 11,000
Conversion costs (direct labor and overhead)	9,000
Total manufacturing costs	$ 20,000
Less: Cost of goods completed	(19,000)
Ending balance of Work in Process Inventory	$ 1,000

Cost of goods completed	$ 19,000
Less: Cost of goods sold	(18,500)
Ending balance of Finished Goods Inventory	$ 500

SOLUTION.

1. a
2. d
3. a
4. c
5. d
6. a
7. a
8. b
9. a
10. c
11. b
12. b

Chapter Review

LO 1 Describe value-based systems, and discuss their relationship to the supply chain and the value chain.

Value-based systems add relevance and reliability since they categorize activities as either adding value to a product or service or not adding value. They enable managers to see their organization as a collection of value-creating activities (a value chain) that operates as part of a larger system that includes suppliers' and customers' value chains (a supply chain). This perspective helps managers work cooperatively both inside and outside their organizations to reduce costs by eliminating waste and inefficiencies and by redirecting resources toward value-adding activities. Process value analysis (PVA) is a technique for analyzing business processes by relating activities to the events that prompt the activities and to the resources that the activities consume. A value-adding activity adds value to a product or service as perceived by the customer. A non-value-adding activity adds cost to a product or service but does not increase its market value.

LO 2 Define *activity-based costing*, and explain how a cost hierarchy and a bill of activities are used.

To implement activity-based costing (ABC), managers (1) identify and classify each activity, (2) estimate the cost of resources for each activity, (3) identify a cost driver for each activity and estimate the quantity of each cost driver, (4) calculate an activity cost rate for each activity, and (5) assign costs to cost objects based on the level of activity required to make the product or provide the service. ABC's primary disadvantage is that it is costly to implement.

A cost hierarchy and a bill of activities help in the implementation of ABC. To create a cost hierarchy, managers classify activities into four levels. Unit-level activities are performed each time a unit is produced. Batch-level activities are performed each time a batch of goods is produced. Product-level activities are performed to support a particular product line or brand. Facility-level activities are performed to support a facility's general manufacturing process. A bill of activities is then used to compute the costs assigned to activities and the product or service unit cost.

LO 3 Define the elements of a lean operation, and identify the changes in inventory management that result when a firm adopts its just-in-time operating philosophy.

One of the primary elements of a lean operation is to produce on a just-in-time (JIT) basis. The elements of a JIT environment are minimum inventory levels, pull-through production, quick setup and flexible work cells, a multiskilled work force, high levels of product quality, effective preventive maintenance, and continuous improvement of the work environment.

In product costing under JIT, processing costs are classified as either direct materials costs or conversion costs. The costs associated with inspection time, moving time, queue time, and storage time are reduced or eliminated. With computerized monitoring of the work cells, many costs that are treated as indirect or overhead costs in traditional manufacturing settings become direct costs since they can be traced directly to work cells. The only costs that remain indirect costs and must be assigned to the work cells are those that cannot be linked to a specific work cell, such as building occupancy, insurance, and property taxes.

LO 4 Define and apply *backflush costing*, and compare the cost flows in traditional and backflush costing.

In backflush costing, all product costs are first accumulated in the Cost of Goods Sold account. At the end of the period, they are "flushed back" into the appropriate inventory accounts. Backflush costing is commonly used to account for product costs in a JIT operating environment. It differs from the traditional costing approach, which records the costs of materials purchased in the Materials Inventory account and uses the Work in Process Inventory account to record the costs of direct materials, direct labor, and overhead during the production process. The objective of backflush costing is to save recording time, which cuts costs.

Identify the management tools used for continuous improvement, and compare ABM and lean operations. | LO 5

Management tools for continuous improvement include total quality management (TQM), the theory of constraints (TOC), activity-based management (ABM), and lean operations. These tools are designed to help businesses meet the demands of a challenging business environment by reducing resource waste and costs and by improving product or service quality, thereby increasing customer satisfaction. As value-based systems, both ABM and lean operations enhance the relevance and reliability of cost information as they seek to eliminate waste and reduce non-value-adding activities. However, ABM uses ABC to assign indirect costs to products using cost drivers, while lean uses JIT to reorganize activities so that they are performed within work cells. The overhead costs incurred in a work cell become direct costs of the products made in that cell. ABM uses job order or process costing to calculate product costs, whereas lean operations may use backflush costing.

Key Terms

activity-based costing (ABC) 127 (LO2)
activity-based management (ABM) 127 (LO2)
backflush costing 135 (LO4)
batch-level activities 128 (LO2)
bill of activities 129 (LO2)
continuous improvement 138 (LO5)
conversion costs 136 (LO4)
core competency 124 (LO1)
cost hierarchy 128 (LO2)
costs of quality 138 (LO5)
facility-level activities 128 (LO2)
full product cost 124 (LO1)
inspection time 133 (LO3)

just-in-time (JIT) operating philosophy 131 (LO3)
kaizen 133 (LO3)
lean operation 131 (LO3)
moving time 133 (LO3)
non-value-adding activity 126 (LO1)
outsourcing 124 (LO1)
primary processes 124 (LO1)
process value analysis (PVA) 125 (LO1)
processing time 133 (LO3)
product-level activities 128 (LO2)
pull-through production 132 (LO3)
push-through production 132 (LO3)
queue time 133 (LO3)

storage time 133 (LO3)
supply chain 124 (LO1)
support services 124 (LO1)
theory of constraints (TOC) 138 (LO5)
throughput time 133 (LO3)
total quality management (TQM) 138 (LO5)
unit-level activities 128 (LO2)
value-adding activity 125 (LO1)
value-based systems 124 (LO1)
value chain 124 (LO1)
work cell 132 (LO3)

Chapter Assignments

DISCUSSION QUESTIONS

LO 1   **DQ1. CONCEPT ▶** Discuss how differentiating between activities that add value and those that do not add value enhance the relevance and reliability of manager information.

LO 2   **DQ2. CONCEPT ▶** Why do the concepts of relevance and reliability underlie the five steps in implementing activity-based costing (ABC)?

LO 2   **DQ3. CONCEPT ▶** Describe how a cost hierarchy and a bill of activities can improve the relevance and reliability of an ABC implementation.

LO 3, 4   **DQ4. CONCEPT ▶** Why does the classification of costs in lean operations improve the relevance and reliability of product costs?

LO 1, 5   **DQ5.   CONCEPT ▶ BUSINESS APPLICATION ▶** Why do value-based systems in the management process reinforce the concepts of relevance and reliability to lead to better business operations?

SHORT EXERCISES

LO 1   ## Concepts

SE1. CONCEPT ▶ Indicate whether each of the following pertains to the accounting concept of reliability or relevance.

a. Predictive value
b. Faithful representation

c. Free from material error
d. Has a direct bearing on a decision

LO 1   ## The Value Chain

SE2. The unit costs that follow were determined by dividing the total costs of each component by the number of products produced. From these unit costs, determine the total cost per unit of primary processes and the total cost per unit of support services.

Research and development	$ 1.00
Human resources	1.45
Design	0.55
Supply	1.10
Legal services	0.60
Production	4.00
Marketing	0.80
Distribution	0.90
Customer service	0.65
Information systems	0.75
Management accounting	0.20
Total cost per unit	$12.00

LO 1   ## Value-Adding and Non-Value-Adding Activities

SE3. Indicate whether the following activities of a gourmet sandwich shop are value-adding (VA) or non-value-adding (NVA).

a. Purchasing sandwich ingredients
b. Storing condiments
c. Making sandwiches

d. Cleaning up the shop
e. Making home deliveries
f. Accounting for sales and costs

LO 2   ## The Cost Hierarchy

SE4. Engineering design is an activity that is vital to the success of any motor vehicle manufacturer. Identify the level at which engineering design would be classified in the cost hierarchy used with ABC for each of the following:

a. A maker of unique editions of luxury automobiles
b. A maker of built-to-order city and county emergency vehicles (orders are usually placed for 10 to 12 identical vehicles)
c. A maker of a line of automobiles sold throughout the world

LO 2   ## The Cost Hierarchy

SE5. Match the four levels of the cost hierarchy to the following activities of a jeans manufacturer that uses activity-based management:

a. Routine maintenance of sewing machines
b. Designing a pattern for a new style
c. Sewing seams on a garment
d. Producing 100 jeans of a certain style in a certain size

LO 3   **Product Costing Changes in a JIT Environment**

SE6. Beauty Products Company is in the process of adopting the JIT operating environment for its lotion-making operations. Indicate which of the following overhead costs are non-value-adding costs (NVA) and which can be traced directly to the new lotion-making work cell (D):

a. Storage containers for work in process inventory
b. Insurance on the storage warehouse
c. Machine electricity
d. Machine repairs
e. Depreciation of the storage container moving equipment
f. Machine setup labor

LO 4   **Backflush Costing**

SE7. For work done during August, Ohir Company incurred direct materials costs of $120,000 and conversion costs of $260,000. The company employs a JIT operating philosophy and backflush costing. At the end of August, the Work in Process Inventory account had been assigned $900 of costs, and the ending balance of the Finished Goods Inventory account was $1,300. There were no beginning inventory balances. How much was charged to the Cost of Goods Sold account during August? What was the ending balance of that account?

LO 5   **Comparison of ABM and Lean**

SE8. ACCOUNTING CONNECTION ▶ Hong Corp. recently installed three just-in-time work cells in its screen-making division. The work cells will make large quantities of similar products for major window and door manufacturers. Should Hong use lean operations with JIT and backflush costing or ABM and ABC to account for product costs? Defend your choice of activity-based system.

LO 5   **TQM and Value**

SE9. Petal Dry Cleaners recently adopted total quality management. The owner has hired you as a consultant. Classify each of the following activities as either value-adding (VA) or non-value-adding (NVA):

a. Providing same-day service
b. Closing the store on weekends
c. Providing free delivery service
d. Having a seamstress on site
e. Making customers pay for parking

LO 5   **Activity-Based Systems**

SE10. ACCOUNTING CONNECTION ▶ Bob Lillie started a retail clothing business two years ago. Lillie's first year was very successful, but sales dropped 50 percent in the second year. A friend who is a business consultant analyzed Lillie's business and came up with two basic reasons for the decline in sales: (1) Lillie has been placing orders late in each season, and (2) shipments of clothing have been arriving late and in poor condition. What measures can Lillie take to improve his business and persuade customers to return?

EXERCISES: SET A

LO 1   **The Supply Chain and Value Chain**

E1A. Indicate which of the following items associated with a hotel are part of the supply chain (S) and which are part of the value chain (V):

a. Travel agency
b. Housekeeping supplies
c. Special events and promotions
d. Customer service
e. Travel bureau website
f. Tour agencies

LO 1   **The Value Chain**

E2A. As shown in the data that follow, a producer of ceiling fans has determined the unit cost of its most popular model. From these unit costs, determine the total cost per unit of primary processes and the total cost per unit of support services.

Research and development	$ 5.00
Human resources	4.50
Design	1.50
Supply	1.00
Legal services	0.50
Production	4.50
Marketing	2.00
Distribution	2.50
Customer service	6.50
Information systems	1.80
Management accounting	0.20
Total cost per unit	$30.00

LO 1   **Management Reports**

E3A. ACCOUNTING CONNECTION ▶ The reports that follow are from a grocery store. Which report would be used for financial purposes, and which would be used for activity-based decision making? Why?

Salaries	$ 1,000	Scan grocery purchases	$ 3,000
Equipment	2,200	Stock fruit	1,000
Freight	5,000	Bake rye bread	500
Supplies	800	Operate salad bar	2,500
Use and occupancy	1,000	Stock can goods	2,000
Total	$10,000	Collapse cardboard boxes	1,000
		Total	$10,000

LO 1   **The Value Chain**

E4A. Edwin Cortez recently opened his own company. In order to improve the business, he will be undertaking the following actions:

a. Engaging an accountant to help analyze progress in meeting the objectives of the company
b. Hiring a company to handle payroll records and employee benefits
c. Developing a logo for labeling and packaging the ceramics
d. Making gift packages by placing gourmet food products in ceramic pots and wrapping them in plastic
e. Engaging an attorney to write contracts
f. Traveling to Mexico himself to arrange for the purchase of products and their shipment back to the company
g. Arranging new ways of taking orders over the Internet and shipping the products
h. Keeping track of the characteristics of customers and the number and types of products they buy

i. Following up with customers to see if they received the products and if they are happy with them

j. Arranging for an outside firm to keep the accounting records

k. Distributing brochures that display the ceramics and refer to the website

1. Classify each of Cortez's actions as one of the value chain's primary processes—research and development, design, supply, production, marketing, distribution, or customer service—or as a support service—human resources, legal services, information systems, or management accounting.

2. **ACCOUNTING CONNECTION ▶** Of these actions, which are the most likely candidates for outsourcing? Why?

LO 1   **Value-Adding and Non-Value-Adding Activities**

E5A. When Cornelia Tyson prepared a process value analysis for her company, she identified the following primary activities. Identify the value-adding activities (VA) and the non-value-adding activities (NVA).

a. Engineering design   c. Product sales
b. Product marketing   d. Materials storage

LO 2   **The Cost Hierarchy**

E6A. Topa Electronics makes speaker systems. Its customers range from new hotels and restaurants that need specifically designed sound systems to nationwide retail outlets that order large quantities of similar products. The following activities are part of the company's operating process:

a. Retail sales commissions   d. Assembly line setup
b. Product design   e. Building security
c. Assembly labor   f. Facility supervision

Classify each activity as unit level (UL), batch level (BL), product level (PL), or facility level (FL).

LO 2   **Bill of Activities**

E7A. Ohfir Corporation has received an order for handheld computers from Townsend, LLC. A partially complete bill of activities for that order follows. Fill in the missing data.

Ohfir Corporation
Bill of Activities for Townsend, LLC
Handheld Computers Order

Activity	Activity Cost Rate	Cost Driver Level	Activity Cost
Unit level:			
Parts production	$50 per machine hour	200 machine hours	$?
Assembly	$20 per DLH	100 DLH	?
Packaging and shipping	$12.50 per unit	400 units	?
Batch level:			
Work cell setup	$100 per setup	16 setups	?
Product level:			
Product design	$60 per engineering hour	80 engineering hours	?
Product simulation	$80 per testing hour	30 testing hours	?
Facility level:			
Building occupancy	200% of direct labor cost	?	?
Total activity costs assigned to job			$?
Total job units			400
Activity costs per unit (total activity costs ÷ total units)			$?
Cost summary:			
Direct materials			$60,000
Purchased parts			80,000
Activity costs			?
Total cost of order			$?
Product unit cost (total cost of order ÷ 400 units)			$?

LO **2**   **Activity Cost Rates**

E8A. Compute the activity cost rates for materials handling, assembly, and design based on the data that follow.

Materials:	
Cloth	$26,000
Fasteners	4,000
Purchased parts	40,000
Materials handling:	
Labor	8,000
Equipment depreciation	5,000
Electrical power	2,000
Maintenance	6,000
Assembly:	
Machine operators	5,000
Design:	
Labor	5,000
Electrical power	1,000
Overhead	8,000

Output totaled 40,000 units. Each unit requires three machine hours of effort. Materials handling costs are allocated to the products based on direct materials cost. Design costs are allocated based on units produced. Assembly costs are allocated based on 500 machine operator hours. (*Hint:* Activity cost rate = Total activity costs ÷ Total allocation base. Examples of an allocation base include total dollars of materials, total machine operator hours, or total units of output.)

LO **3**   **Elements of a Lean Operating Environment**

E9A. The numbered items that follow are concepts that underlie value-based systems, such as ABM and lean operations. Match each concept to the related lettered element(s) of a lean operating environment.

1. Business processes are simplified.
2. The quality of the product or service is critical.
3. Employees are cross-trained.
4. Large inventories waste resources and may hide bad work.
5. Goods should be produced only when needed.
6. Equipment downtime is minimized.

a. Minimum inventory levels
b. Pull-through production
c. Quick machine setups and flexible work cells
d. A multiskilled work force
e. High levels of product quality
f. Effective preventive maintenance

LO **3**   **Comparison of Traditional and JIT Manufacturing Environments**

E10A. Identify which of the following exist in a traditional manufacturing environment and which exist in a JIT operating environment:

a. Large amounts of inventory
b. Complex manufacturing processes
c. A multiskilled labor force
d. Flexible work cells
e. Push-through production methods
f. Materials purchased infrequently but in large lot sizes
g. Infrequent setups

LO 3 **Direct and Indirect Costs in JIT and Traditional Manufacturing Environments**

E11A. The cost categories in the following list are typical of many manufacturing operations:

a. Direct materials:
   (1) Sheet steel
   (2) Iron castings
b. Assembly parts:
   (1) Part 24
   (2) Part 15
c. Direct labor
d. Engineering labor
e. Indirect labor

f. Operating supplies
g. Small tools
h. Depreciation—plant
i. Depreciation—machinery
j. Supervisory salaries
k. Electrical power
l. Insurance and taxes—plant
m. President's salary
n. Employee benefits

Identify each cost as direct or indirect, assuming that it was incurred in (1) a traditional manufacturing setting and (2) a JIT environment.

LO 4 **Backflush Costing**

E12A. Telluride Products Company implemented a JIT work environment in its shovel division eight months ago, and the division has been operating at near capacity since then. At the beginning of May, Work in Process Inventory and Finished Goods Inventory had zero balances. The following transactions took place during the month:

- Ordered, received, and used handles and sheet metal costing $11,340.
- Direct labor costs incurred, $5,400.
- Overhead costs incurred, $8,100.
- Completed shovels costing $24,800.
- Sold shovels costing $24,000.

Using backflush costing, calculate the ending balance in the Work in Process Inventory and Finished Goods Inventory accounts.

LO 4 **Backflush Costing**

E13A. Morning Enterprises produces clocks. It has a JIT assembly process and uses backflush costing to record production costs. Overhead is assigned at a rate of $17 per assembly labor hour. There were no beginning inventories in March. During March, the following operating data were generated:

Cost of direct materials purchased and used	$53,200
Direct labor costs incurred	$27,300
Overhead costs assigned	?
Assembly hours worked	3,840 hours
Ending work in process inventory	$1,050
Ending finished goods inventory	$960

Using T accounts, show the flow of costs through the backflush costing system. What is the total cost of goods sold in March?

LO 5 **Comparison of ABM and Lean Operations**

E14A. Identify each of the following as a characteristic of ABM or lean operations:

a. Backflush costing
b. ABC used to assign overhead costs to the product cost
c. ABC integrated with job order or process costing systems
d. Complexity reduced by using work cells, minimizing inventories, and reducing or eliminating non-value-adding activities
e. Activities reorganized so that they are performed within work cells

LO 5 **Comparison of ABM and Lean Operations**

E15A. BUSINESS APPLICATION ▶ Excerpts from a conversation between two managers about their companies' management systems follow. Identify the manager who works for a company that emphasizes ABM and the one who works for a company that emphasizes a lean operating system.

■ **Manager 1:** We try to manage our resources effectively by monitoring operating activities. We analyze all major operating activities, and we focus on reducing or eliminating the ones that don't add value to our products.

■ **Manager 2:** We're very concerned with eliminating waste. We've designed our operations to reduce the time it takes to move, store, queue, and inspect materials. We've also reduced our inventories by buying and using materials only when we need them.

EXERCISES: SET B

Visit the textbook companion website at www.cengagebrain.com to access Exercise Set B for this chapter.

PROBLEMS

LO 1 **The Value Chain**

✔ 1: Total current cost per unit: $27.60
✔ 1: Total projected cost per unit: $22.25

P1. Reigle Electronics is a manufacturer of cell phones, a highly competitive business. Reigle's phones carry a price of $99, but competition forces the company to offer significant discounts and rebates. As a result, the average price of Reigle's cell phones has dropped to around $50, and the company is losing money. Management is applying value chain analysis to the company's operations in an effort to reduce costs and improve product quality. A study by the company's management accountant has determined the following per unit costs for primary processes:

Primary Process	Cost per Unit
Research and development	$ 2.50
Design	3.50
Supply	4.50
Production	6.70
Marketing	8.00
Distribution	1.90
Customer service	0.50
Total cost	$27.60

To generate a gross margin large enough for the company to cover its overhead costs and earn a profit, Reigle must lower its total cost per unit for primary processes to no more than $20. After analyzing operations, management reached the following conclusions about primary processes:

■ Research and development and design are critical functions because the market and competition require constant development of new features with "cool" designs at lower cost. Nevertheless, management feels that the cost per unit of these processes must be reduced by 10 percent.

■ Six different suppliers currently provide the components for the cell phones. Ordering these components from just two suppliers and negotiating lower prices could result in a savings of 15 percent.

■ The cell phones are currently manufactured in Mexico. By shifting production to China, the unit cost of production can be lowered by 20 percent.

■ Most cell phones are sold through wireless communication companies that are trying to attract new customers with low-priced cell phones. Management believes that these companies should bear more of the marketing costs and that it is feasible to renegotiate its marketing arrangements with them so that they will bear 35 percent of the current marketing costs.

- Distribution costs are already very low, but management will set a target of reducing the cost per unit by 10 percent.
- Customer service is a weakness of the company and has resulted in lost sales. Management therefore proposes increasing the cost per unit of customer service by 50 percent.

REQUIRED

1. Prepare a table showing the current cost per unit of primary processes and the projected cost per unit based on management's proposals for cost reduction. (Round to the nearest cent.)
2. **ACCOUNTING CONNECTION** ▶ Will management's proposals for cost reduction achieve the targeted total cost per unit? What further steps should management take to reduce costs? Which steps that management is proposing do you believe will be the most difficult to accomplish?
3. **ACCOUNTING CONNECTION** ▶ What are the company's support services? What role should these services play in the value chain analysis?

LO **2**

SPREADSHEET

✔ 1: Product unit cost: $90.00
✔ 4: Activity cost per unit: $21.47
✔ 4: Product unit cost: $93.49

Activity-Based Costing

P2. Printware Products, Inc., produces printers for wholesale distributors. It has just completed packaging an order from Hawes Company for 450 printers. Before the order is shipped, the controller wants to compare the unit costs computed under the company's new activity-based costing system with the unit costs computed under its traditional costing system. Printware's traditional costing system assigned overhead costs at a rate of 240 percent of direct labor cost.

Data for the Hawes order are as follows: direct materials, $17,552; purchased parts, $14,856; direct labor hours, 140; and average direct labor pay rate per hour, $17. Data for activity-based costing related to processing direct materials and purchased parts for the Hawes order follow.

Activity	Cost Driver	Activity Cost Rate	Activity Usage
Engineering systems design	Engineering hours	$28 per engineering hour	18 engineering hours
Setup	Number of setups	$36 per setup	12 setups
Parts production	Machine hours	$37 per machine hour	82 machine hours
Product assembly	Assembly hours	$42 per assembly hour	96 assembly hours
Packaging	Number of packages	$5.60 per package	150 packages
Building occupancy	Machine hours	$10 per machine hour	82 machine hours

REQUIRED

1. Use the traditional costing approach to compute the total cost and the product unit cost of the Hawes order.
2. Using the cost hierarchy, identify each activity as unit level, batch level, product level, or facility level.
3. Prepare a bill of activities for the activity costs.
4. Use ABC to compute the total cost and product unit cost of the Hawes order. (Round your answer to the nearest cent.)
5. **ACCOUNTING CONNECTION** ▶ What is the difference between the product unit cost you computed using the traditional approach and the one you computed using ABC? Does the use of ABC guarantee cost reduction for every order?

LO **2**

SPREADSHEET

✔ 3: Product unit cost: $8.67

Activity Cost Rates

P3. Tailgator Company produces four versions of its model J7-21 bicycle seat. The four versions have different shapes, but their processing operations and production costs are identical. During July, the following costs were incurred:

(Continued)

Direct materials:	
Leather	$25,430
Metal frame	39,180
Bolts	3,010
Materials handling:	
Labor	8,232
Equipment depreciation	4,410
Electrical power	2,460
Maintenance	5,184
Assembly:	
Direct labor	13,230
Engineering design:	
Labor	4,116
Electrical power	1,176
Engineering overhead	7,644
Overhead:	
Equipment depreciation	7,056
Indirect labor	30,870
Supervision	17,640
Operating supplies	4,410
Electrical power	10,584
Repairs and maintenance	21,168
Building occupancy overhead	52,920

July's output totaled 29,400 units. Each unit requires three machine hours of effort. Materials handling costs are allocated to the products based on direct materials cost, engineering design costs are allocated based on units produced, and overhead is allocated based on machine hours. Assembly costs are allocated based on direct labor hours, which are estimated at 882 for July.

During July, Tailgator completed 520 bicycle seats for Job 14. The activity usage for Job 14 was as follows: direct materials, $1,150; direct labor hours, 15.

REQUIRED

1. Compute the following activity cost rates: (a) materials handling cost rate, (b) assembly cost rate, (c) engineering design cost rate, and (d) overhead rate.
2. Prepare a bill of activities for Job 14.
3. Use activity-based costing to compute the job's total cost and product unit cost. (Round activity costs to the nearest dollar, and round unit costs to the nearest cent.)

LO 3   **Direct and Indirect Costs in Lean and Traditional Manufacturing Environments**

✔ 3: Direct cost per unit: $12

P4. Zunz Company, a producer of wooden toys, is about to adopt a lean operating environment. In anticipation of the change, Zunz's controller prepared the following list of costs for December:

Wood	$1,200	Insurance—plant	$ 324
Bolts	32	President's salary	4,000
Small tools	54	Engineering labor	2,700
Depreciation—plant	450	Utilities	1,250
Depreciation—machinery	275	Building occupancy	1,740
Direct labor	2,675	Supervision	2,686
Indirect labor	890	Operating supplies	254
Purchased parts	58	Repairs and maintenance	198
Materials handling	74	Employee benefits	2,654

REQUIRED

1. Identify each cost as direct or indirect, assuming that it was incurred in a traditional manufacturing setting.
2. Identify each cost as direct or indirect, assuming that it was incurred in a lean operating environment.
3. Assume that the costs incurred in the lean operating environment are for a work cell that completed 1,250 toy cars in December. Compute the total direct cost and the direct cost per unit for the cars produced.

LO **4**

Backflush Costing

✔ 3: Total cost of goods sold: $564,400

P5. Auto Parts Company produces 12 parts for car bodies and sells them to four automobile assembly companies in Canada. The company implemented lean operating and costing procedures three years ago. Overhead is applied at a rate of $26 per work cell hour used. All direct materials and purchased parts are used as they are received.

One of the company's work cells produces automotive fenders that are completely detailed and ready to install when received by the customer. The cell is operated by four employees and involves a flexible manufacturing system with 14 workstations. Operating details for February for this cell follow.

Beginning work in process inventory	—
Beginning finished goods inventory	$420
Cost of direct materials purchased on account and used	$213,400
Cost of parts purchased on account and used	$111,250
Direct labor costs incurred	$26,450
Overhead costs assigned	?
Work cell hours used	8,260
Costs of goods completed during February	$564,650
Ending work in process inventory	$1,210
Ending finished goods inventory	$670

REQUIRED

1. Using T accounts, show the cost flows through a backflush costing system.
2. Using T accounts, show the cost flows through a traditional costing system.
3. What is the total cost of goods sold for the month?

ALTERNATE PROBLEMS

LO **1**

The Value Chain

Support Services:
✔ 1: Total current cost per unit: $8.00
✔ 1: Total projected cost per unit: $6.40

P6. Comfy Spot is a manufacturer of futon mattresses. Comfy Spot's mattresses are priced at $60, but competition forces the company to offer significant discounts and rebates. As a result, the average price of the futon mattress has dropped to around $50, and the company is losing money. Management is applying value chain analysis to the company's operations in an effort to reduce costs and improve product quality. A study by the company's management accountant has determined the following per unit costs for primary processes and support services:

(Continued)

	Cost per Unit
Primary processes:	
Research and development	$ 5.00
Design	3.00
Supply	4.00
Production	16.00
Marketing	6.00
Distribution	7.00
Customer service	1.00
Total cost per unit	$42.00
Support services:	
Human resources	$ 2.00
Information services	5.00
Management accounting	1.00
Total cost per unit	$ 8.00

To generate a gross margin large enough for the company to cover its overhead costs and earn a profit, Comfy Spot must lower its total cost per unit for primary processes to no more than $32.00 and its support services to no more than $5.00. After analyzing operations, management reached the following conclusions about primary processes and support services:

■ Research and development and design are critical functions because the market and competition require constant development of new features with "cool" designs at lower cost. Nevertheless, management feels that the cost per unit of these processes must be reduced by 20 percent.

■ Ten different suppliers currently provide the components for the futons. Ordering these components from just two suppliers and negotiating lower prices could result in a savings of 15 percent.

■ The futons are currently manufactured in Mali. By shifting production to China, the unit cost of production can be lowered by 40 percent.

■ Management believes that by selling to large retailers like Wal-Mart, it is feasible to lower current marketing costs by 25 percent.

■ Distribution costs are already very low, but management will set a target of reducing the cost per unit by 10 percent.

■ Customer service and support to large customers are key to keeping their business. Management therefore proposes increasing the cost per unit of customer service by 20 percent.

■ By outsourcing its support services, management projects a 20 percent drop in these costs.

REQUIRED

1. Prepare a table showing the current cost per unit of primary processes and support services and the projected cost per unit based on management's proposals.

2. **ACCOUNTING CONNECTION** ▶ Will management's proposals achieve the targeted total cost per unit? What further steps should management take to reduce costs?

3. **ACCOUNTING CONNECTION** ▶ What role should the company's support services play in the value chain analysis?

LO 2   **Activity-Based Costing**

✔ 1: Product unit cost traditional: $7.03
✔ 4: Activity cost per unit: $1.11
✔ 4: Product unit cost: $6.91

P7. Kall Company produces cellular phones. It has just completed an order for 10,000 phones placed by Connect, Ltd. Kall recently shifted to an activity-based costing system, and its controller is interested in the impact that the ABC system had on the Connect order. Data for that order are as follows: direct materials, $36,950; purchased parts, $21,100; direct labor hours, 220; and average direct labor pay rate per hour, $15.

Under Kall's traditional costing system, overhead costs were assigned at a rate of 270 percent of direct labor cost. Data for activity-based costing for the Connect order follow.

Activity	Cost Driver	Activity Cost Rate	Activity Usage
Electrical engineering design	Engineering hours	$19 per engineering hour	32 engineering hours
Setup	Number of setups	$29 per setup	11 setups
Parts production	Machine hours	$26 per machine hour	134 machine hours
Product testing	Number of tests	$32 per test	52 tests
Packaging	Number of packages	$0.0374 per package	10,000 packages
Building occupancy	Machine hours	$9.80 per machine hour	134 machine hours
Assembly	Direct labor hours	$15 per direct labor hour	220 direct labor hours

REQUIRED

1. Use the traditional costing approach to compute the total cost and the product unit cost of the Connect order. (Round unit costs to the nearest cent.)
2. Using the cost hierarchy, identify each activity as unit level, batch level, product level, or facility level.
3. Prepare a bill of activities for the activity costs.
4. Use ABC to compute the total cost and product unit cost of the Connect order. (Round activity costs to the nearest dollar, and round unit costs to the nearest cent.)
5. **ACCOUNTING CONNECTION** ▶ What is the difference between the product unit cost you computed using the traditional approach and the one you computed using ABC? Does the use of ABC guarantee cost reduction for every order?

LO **2**

SPREADSHEET

✔ 3: Product unit cost: $10.43

Activity Cost Rates

P8. Nifty Company produces three models of aluminum skateboards. The models have minor differences, but their processing operations and production costs are identical. During June, the following costs were incurred:

Direct materials:	
Aluminum frame	$162,524
Bolts	3,876
Purchased parts:	
Wheels	74,934
Decals	5,066
Materials handling *(assigned based on direct materials cost)*:	
Labor	17,068
Utilities	4,438
Maintenance	914
Depreciation	876
Assembly line *(assigned based on labor hours)*:	
Labor	46,080
Setup *(assigned based on number of setups)*:	
Labor	6,385
Supplies	762
Overhead	3,953
Product testing *(assigned based on number of tests)*:	
Labor	2,765
Supplies	435
Building occupancy *(assigned based on machine hours)*:	
Insurance	5,767
Depreciation	2,452
Repairs and maintenance	3,781

(Continued)

For June, output totaled 32,000 skateboards. Each board required 1.5 machine hours of effort. During June, Nifty's assembly line worked 2,304 hours, performed 370 setups and 64,000 product tests, and completed an order for 1,000 skateboards placed by Wow Toys Company. The job incurred costs of $5,200 for direct materials and $2,500 for purchased parts. It required 3 setups, 2,000 tests, and 72 assembly line hours.

REQUIRED

1. Compute the following activity cost rates: (a) materials handling cost rate, (b) assembly line cost rate, (c) setup cost rate, (d) product testing cost rate, and (e) building occupancy cost rate.
2. Prepare a bill of activities for the Wow Toys job.
3. Use activity-based costing to compute the job's total cost and product unit cost. (Round unit costs to the nearest cent.)

LO 3

✔ 3: Direct cost per unit: $2.19

Direct and Indirect Costs in JIT and Traditional Manufacturing Environments

P9. Peralto Company, which processes coffee beans into ground coffee, is about to adopt a JIT operating environment. In anticipation of the change, Peralto's controller prepared the following list of costs for the month:

Coffee beans	$5,000	Insurance—plant	$ 300
Bags	100	President's salary	4,000
Small tools	80	Engineering labor	1,700
Depreciation—plant	400	Utilities	1,250
Depreciation—grinder	200	Building occupancy	1,940
Direct labor	1,000	Supervision	400
Indirect labor	300	Operating supplies	205
Labels	20	Repairs and maintenance	120
Materials handling	75	Employee benefits	500

REQUIRED

1. Identify each cost as direct or indirect, assuming that it was incurred in a traditional manufacturing setting.
2. Identify each cost as direct or indirect, assuming that it was incurred in a just-in-time (JIT) environment.
3. Assume that the costs incurred in the JIT environment are for a work cell that completed 5,000 1-pound bags of coffee during the month. Compute the total direct cost and the direct cost per unit for the bags produced. (Carry unit cost to two decimal places.)

LO 4

✔ 3: Total cost of goods sold: $391,520

Backflush Costing

P10. Elly Corporation produces metal fasteners using six work cells, one for each of its product lines. It implemented JIT operations and costing methods two years ago. Overhead is assigned using a rate of $14 per machine hour for the Snap Work Cell. There were no beginning inventories on April 1. All direct materials and purchased parts are used as they are received. Operating details for April for the Snap Work Cell follow.

Cost of direct materials purchased on account and used	$104,500
Cost of parts purchased on account and used	$78,900
Direct labor costs incurred	$39,000
Overhead costs assigned	?
Machine hours used	12,220
Costs of goods completed during April	$392,540
Ending work in process inventory	$940
Ending finished goods inventory	$1,020

REQUIRED

1. Using T accounts, show the flow of costs through a backflush costing system.
2. Using T accounts, show the flow of costs through a traditional costing system.
3. What is the total cost of goods sold for April using a traditional costing system?

CASES

LO **2, 5**

Group Activity: ABM and ABC in a Service Business

C1. MUF, a Chartered Accounting firm, has provided audit and tax services to businesses in the London area for over 50 years. Recently, the firm decided to use ABM and activity-based costing to assign its overhead costs to those service functions. Ginny Fior is interested in seeing how the change from the traditional to the activity-based costing approach affects the average cost per audit job. The following information has been provided to assist in the comparison:

Total direct labor costs	£400,000
Other direct costs	120,000
Total direct costs	£520,000

The traditional costing approach assigned overhead costs at a rate of 120 percent of direct labor costs.

Data for activity-based costing of the audit function follow.

Activity	Cost Driver	Activity Cost Rate	Activity Usage
Professional development	Number of employees	£2,000 per employee	50 employees
Administration	Number of jobs	£1,000 per job	50 jobs
Client development	Number of new clients	£5,000 per new client	29 new clients

Your instructor will divide the class into groups to work through the case. One student from each group should present the group's findings to the class.

1. Using traditional costing and direct labor cost as the cost driver, calculate the total costs for the audit function. What is the average cost per job?
2. Using activity-based costing to assign overhead, calculate the total costs for the audit function. What is the average cost per job?
3. Calculate the difference in total costs between the two approaches. Why would activity-based costing be the better approach for assigning overhead to the audit function?

LO **2, 5**

Interpreting Management Reports: ABC and Selling and Administrative Expenses

C2. Star Kleymeyer, owner of Star Bakery, wants to know the profitability of each of her bakery's customer groups. She is especially interested in the State Institutions customer group, which is one of the company's largest. Currently, the bakery is selling doughnuts and snack foods to ten state institutions in three states. The controller has prepared the following income statement for the State Institutions customer group:

Star Bakery

Income Statement for State Institutions Customer Group

For the Year Ended December 31

Sales ($5 per case × 50,000 cases)	$250,000
Cost of goods sold ($3.50 per case × 50,000 cases)	175,000
Gross margin	$ 75,000
Less: Selling and administrative activity costs (see schedule below)	94,750
Operating income (loss) contributed by State Institutions customer group	$ (19,750)

(Continued)

Schedule of Selling and Administrative Activity Costs

Activity	Activity Cost Rate	Actual Cost Driver Level	Activity Cost
Make sales calls	$60 per sales call	60 sales calls	$ 3,600
Prepare sales orders	$10 per sales order	900 sales orders	9,000
Handle inquiries	$5 per minute	1,000 minutes	5,000
Ship products	$1 per case sold	50,000 cases	50,000
Process invoices	$20 per invoice	950 invoices	19,000
Process credits	$20 per notice	40 notices	800
Process billings and collections	$7 per billing	1,050 billings	7,350
Total selling and administrative activity costs			$94,750

The controller has also provided budget information about selling and administrative activities for the State Institutions customer group. For this year, the planned activity cost rates and the annual cost driver levels for each selling and administrative activity are as follows:

Activity	Planned Activity Cost Rate	Planned Annual Cost Driver Level
Make sales calls	$60 per sales call	59 sales calls
Prepare sales orders	$10 per sales order	850 sales orders
Handle inquiries	$5.10 per minute	1,000 minutes
Ship products	$0.60 per case sold	50,000 cases
Process invoices	$1 per invoice	500 invoices
Process credits	$10 per notice	5 notices
Process billings and collections	$4 per billing	600 billings

You have been called in as a consultant on the State Institutions customer group.

1. Calculate the planned activity cost for each activity.
2. Calculate the differences between the planned activity cost and the State Institutions customer group's activity costs for this year.
3. From your evaluation of the differences calculated in **2** and your review of the income statement, identify the non-value-adding activities and state which selling and administrative activities should be examined.
4. What actions might the company take to reduce the costs of non-value-adding selling and administrative activities?

LO **2, 5**

Decision Analysis: ABC in Planning and Control

C3. Refer to the income statement in **C2** for the State Institutions customer group for the year ended December 31, this year. Star Kleymeyer, owner of Star Bakery, is in the process of budgeting income for next year. She has asked the controller to prepare a budgeted income statement for the State Institutions customer group. She estimates that the selling price per case, the number of cases sold, the cost of goods sold per case, and the activity costs for making sales calls, preparing sales orders, and handling inquiries will remain the same for next year. She has contracted with a new freight company to ship the 50,000 cases at $0.60 per case sold. She has also analyzed the procedures for invoicing, processing credits, billing, and collecting and has decided that it would be less expensive for a customer service agency to do the work. The agency will charge the bakery 1.5 percent of the total sales revenue.

1. Prepare a budgeted income statement for the State Institutions customer group for next year; the year ends December 31.

2. Refer to the information in **C2**. Assuming that the planned activity cost rate and planned annual cost driver level for each selling and administrative activity remain the same next year, calculate the planned activity cost for each activity.

3. Calculate the differences between the planned activity costs (determined in **2**) and the State Institutions customer group's budgeted activity costs for next year (determined in **1**).

4. Evaluate the results of changing freight companies and outsourcing the customer service activities.

LO **3, 5**

Conceptual Understanding: Lean Operations in a Service Business

C4. At an initiation banquet for new members of your business club, you are talking with two college students who are majoring in marketing. In discussing the accounting course they are taking, they mention that they are having difficulty understanding lean operations. They have read that the elements of a company's operating system support the concepts of simplicity, continuous improvement, waste reduction, timeliness, and efficiency. They realize that to understand lean thinking in a complex manufacturing environment, they must first understand lean operations in a simpler service context. They ask you to explain the lean operating philosophy and provide an example.

Briefly explain lean operations. Apply the elements of a JIT operating system to the restaurant where the banquet is being held. Do you believe a lean operating philosophy applies in all restaurant operations? Explain your answer.

LO **3, 5**

Conceptual Understanding: Activities, Cost Drivers, and JIT

C5. Fifteen years ago, Bryce Stabele, together with several financial supporters, founded SA Corporation. Located in Atlanta, the company originally manufactured roller skates, but 12 years ago, on the advice of its marketing department, it switched to making skateboards. More than 4 million skateboards later, SA Corporation finds itself an industry leader in both volume and quality. To retain market share, it has decided to automate its manufacturing process. It has ordered flexible manufacturing systems for wheel assembly and board shaping. Manual operations will be retained for board decorating because some hand painting is involved. All operations will be converted to a JIT environment.

Bryce wants to know how the JIT approach will affect the company's product costing practices and has called you in as a consultant.

1. Summarize the elements of a JIT environment.
2. How will the automated systems change product costing?
3. What are some cost drivers that the company should employ? In what situations should it employ them?

Continuing Case: Cookie Company

C6. As we continue with this case, assume that your company has been using a continuous manufacturing process to make chocolate chip cookies. Demand has been so great that the company has built a special plant that makes only custom-ordered cookies. The cookies are shaped by machines but vary according to the customer's specific instructions. Ten basic sizes of cookies are produced and then customized. Slight variations in machine setup produce the different sizes.

In the past six months, several problems have developed. Even though a computer-controlled machine is used in the manufacturing process, the company's backlog is growing rapidly, and customers are complaining that delivery is too slow. Quality is declining because cookies are being pushed through production without proper inspection. Working capital is tied up in excessive amounts of inventory and storage space. Workers are complaining about the pressure to produce the backlogged orders. Machine breakdowns are increasing. Production control reports are not useful because they are not timely and contain irrelevant information. The company's profitability and cash flow are suffering.

(Continued)

Assume that you have been appointed CEO and that the company has asked you to analyze its problems. The board of directors asks that you complete your preliminary analysis quickly so that you can present it to the board at its midyear meeting.

1. In memo form, prepare a preliminary report recommending specific changes in the manufacturing processes.
2. In preparing the report, answer the following questions:
   a. Why are you preparing the report? What is its purpose?
   b. Who is the audience for this report?
   c. What kinds of information do you need to prepare the report, and where will you find it (i.e., what sources will you use)?
   d. When do you need to obtain the information?

CHAPTER 5
Cost-Volume-Profit Analysis

The types of products and services that a company offers often vary from year to year depending on customer preferences. For example, **Flickr**, which is today a popular website for sharing photos and videos online, evolved from an online game for multiple players called *Game Neverending* that was launched in 2002. The game was shelved in 2004, and the tools used in developing it were then focused on photo exchange capabilities. The site currently claims to host over five billion photos, and it not only provides public and private photo and video storage but also mobile apps and an online community platform. The ongoing challenge for Flickr's management is to offer a mix of services that appeal to customers and that allows the company to optimize its resources, cash, and profits. In this chapter, we describe how managers in any company make such an evaluation.

1. **CONCEPT** ▶ *Why is cost-volume-profit analysis useful for the purposes of comparability and understandability?*

2. **ACCOUNTING APPLICATION** ▶ *How will Flickr's managers decide which products and services to offer?*

3. **BUSINESS APPLICATION** ▶ *How can managers use cost behavior analysis to improve business performance?*

LEARNING OBJECTIVES

LO 1 Define *cost behavior*, and identify variable, fixed, and mixed costs.

LO 2 Separate mixed costs into their variable and fixed components, and prepare a contribution margin income statement.

LO 3 Perform cost-volume-profit (CVP) analysis.

LO 4 Define *breakeven point*, and use contribution margin to determine a company's breakeven point for multiple products.

LO 5 Discuss how managers use CVP analysis in the management process and how they can project the profitability of products and services.

CONCEPTS
- Comparability
- Understandability

RELEVANT LEARNING OBJECTIVE

LO 1 Define *cost behavior*, and identify variable, fixed, and mixed costs.

LO 1 Concepts Underlying Cost Behavior

Cost behavior—the way costs respond to changes in volume or activity—is a factor in almost every decision managers make. Two underlying accounting concepts support the usefulness of cost-volume-profit analysis in decision making: *understandability* and *comparability*. Knowing how costs will behave improves manager comprehension of the meaning of the information they receive, enhancing their *understanding* of it. Knowledge of cost behavior patterns enables managers to identify cost similarities and differences so *comparisons* of alternatives are possible. Thus, when evaluating operations, managers compare how changes in cost and sales affect the profitability of product lines, sales territories, customers, departments, and other segments. Service businesses like **Flickr**, **Facebook**, and **Google** find that understanding cost behavior is useful when planning the optimal mix of services to offer. For example, Google's managers analyze cost behavior of new features for products like Gmail in their online Google Labs and gather user data and feedback before officially deciding to add a new feature.

During the year, managers collect cost behavior data and use it in decision making. Managers must understand and anticipate cost behavior to determine the impact of their actions on operating income and resource optimization. For example, Google's managers must compare the changes in income that can result from buying new, more productive servers or launching an online advertising product like AdWords or AdSense.

Although our focus in this chapter is on cost behavior as it relates to products and services, it is also important to understand the cost behaviors of selling, administrative, and general activities, such as how increasing the number of shipments affects shipping costs, how the number of units sold or total sales revenue affects the cost of sales commissions, and how the number of customers billed affects total billing costs. If managers can predict how costs behave, and whether they are product- or service-related or are for selling, administrative, or general activities, then costs become manageable.

Cost Behavior

Some costs vary with volume or operating activity (variable costs). Others remain fixed as volume changes (fixed costs). Between those two extremes are costs that exhibit characteristics of each type (mixed costs). Exhibit 1 shows examples of each type of cost for different industries.

Variable Costs Total costs that change in direct proportion to changes in productive output (or any other measure of volume) are called **variable costs**. They are referred to as unit-level activities, since the cost is incurred each time a unit is produced or a service is delivered. For example, direct materials, direct labor, operating supplies, and gasoline are variable costs.

Total variable costs go up or down as volume increases or decreases, but the cost per unit remains unchanged. For example, as shown in Exhibit 2, for My Media Place, a hypothetical company that designs and sets up websites for small businesses and individuals, there is a linear relationship between direct labor (webpage designers) and units produced (completed webpages). Each webpage, or unit of output, requires $2.50 of labor cost. Total labor costs grow in direct proportion to the increase in units of output. For two units, total labor costs are $5.00; for six units, the organization incurs $15.00 in labor costs.

Exhibit 1

Examples of Variable, Fixed, and Mixed Costs

Costs	Manufacturing Company—Tire Manufacturer	Merchandising Company—Department Store	Service Company—Bank
	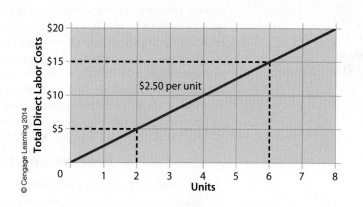		
Variable	• Direct materials • Direct labor (hourly) • Indirect labor (hourly) • Operating supplies • Small tools	• Merchandise to sell • Sales commissions • Shelf stockers (hourly)	• Computer equipment leasing (Based on usage) • Computer operators (hourly) • Operating supplies • Data storage disks

Fixed	• Depreciation, machinery and building (straight-line)
	• Insurance premiums
	• Labor (salaried)
	• Supervisory salaries
	• Property taxes (on machinery and building)
		• Depreciation, equipment and building (straight-line)
		• Insurance premiums
		• Buyers (salaried)
		• Supervisory salaries
		• Property taxes (on equipment and building)
			• Depreciation, furniture and fixtures (straight-line)
			• Insurance premiums
			• Salaries:
			  • Programmers
			  • Systems designers
			  • Bank administrators
			• Rent, buildings

Mixed	• Electrical power • Telephone • Heat	• Electrical power • Telephone • Heat	• Electrical power • Telephone • Heat

© Cengage Learning 2014

Exhibit 2

A Common Variable Cost Behavior Pattern: A Linear Relationship

© Cengage Learning 2014

Variable cost can be computed using the following **variable cost formula**:

Total Variable Cost = Variable Rate × Units Produced

The cost formula for direct labor for My Media Place is computed as follows.

Total Direct Labor Costs = $2.50 × Units Produced

Because variable costs increase or decrease in direct proportion to volume or output, it is important to know an organization's operating capacity. **Operating capacity** is the upper limit of an organization's productive output capability, given its existing resources. It describes what an organization can accomplish in a given period. In our discussions, we assume that operating capacity is constant and that all activity occurs within the limits of current operating capacity.

STUDY NOTE: *Variable costs change in direct proportion to changes in activity; that is, they increase in total with an increase in volume and decrease in total with a decrease in volume, but they remain the same on a per unit basis.*

There are three common measures, or types, of operating capacity:

- **Theoretical capacity** (or *ideal capacity*) is the maximum productive output for a given period in which all machinery and equipment are operating at optimum speed, without interruption. No company ever actually operates at such an ideal level.
- **Practical capacity** (or *engineering capacity*) is theoretical capacity reduced by normal and expected work stoppages, such as machine breakdowns; downtime for retooling, repairs, and maintenance; and employee breaks. Practical capacity is used primarily as a planning goal of what could be produced if all went well; but no company ever actually operates at such a level.
- **Normal capacity** is the average annual level of operating capacity needed to meet expected sales demand. Normal capacity is the realistic measure of what an organization is *likely* to produce, not what it *can* produce. Thus, each variable cost should be related to an appropriate measure of normal capacity. For example, operating costs can be related to machine hours used or total units produced, and sales commissions usually vary in direct proportion to total sales dollars.

The basis for measuring the activity of variable costs should be carefully selected for two reasons:

- An appropriate activity base simplifies cost planning and control.
- Managers must combine (aggregate) many variable costs with the same activity base so that the costs can be analyzed in a reasonable way. Such aggregation also provides information that allows managers to predict future costs.

An **activity base** (or *denominator activity* or *cost driver*) is the activity for which relationships are established. The basic relationships should not change greatly if activity fluctuates around the level of denominator activity. The general guide for selecting an activity base is to relate costs to their most logical or causal factor. For example, direct material and direct labor costs should be considered variable in relation to the number of units produced.

Fixed Costs **Fixed costs**, referred to as facility-level activities, are total costs that remain constant within a relevant range of volume or activity. **Relevant range** is the span of activity in which a company expects to operate. Within the relevant range, it is assumed that both total fixed costs and per unit variable costs are constant.

According to economic theory, all costs tend to be variable in the long run; thus, as the examples in Exhibit 1 suggest, a cost is fixed only within a limited period. A change in plant capacity, labor needs, or other production factors causes fixed costs to increase or decrease. Management usually considers a one-year period when planning and controlling costs; thus fixed costs are expected to be constant within that period.

Fixed cost behavior is expressed mathematically in the **fixed cost formula** as follows.

$$\text{Total Fixed Cost} = \text{Fixed Cost in Relevant Range}$$

Of course, fixed costs change when activity exceeds the relevant range. These costs are called *step costs* or *step-variable*, *step-fixed*, or *semifixed costs*. A **step cost** remains constant in a relevant range of activity and increases or decreases in a step-like manner when activity is outside the relevant range.

For example, assume that one Customer Support Team at My Media Place has the capacity to handle up to 500,000 customer incidents per 8-hour shift. The relevant range, then, is from 0 to 500,000 units. Unfortunately, volume has increased to more than 500,000 incidents per 8-hour shift, taxing current equipment capacity and the quality of customer care. My Media Place must add another Customer Support Team to handle the additional volume. Exhibit 3 shows this behavior pattern. The fixed costs for the first 500,000 units of production are $4,000. Thus, the fixed cost formula for up to 500,000 units is:

$$\text{Total Fixed Cost} = \$4,000$$

But if output goes above 500,000 units, another team must be added, pushing this fixed cost to $8,000.

STUDY NOTE: Because fixed costs are expected to hold relatively constant over the entire relevant range of activity, they can be described as the costs of providing capacity.

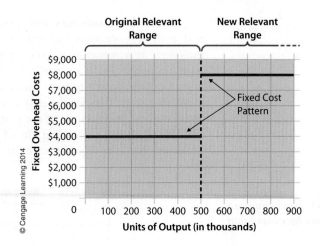

Exhibit 3
A Common Step-Like Fixed
Cost Behavior Pattern

On a per unit basis, fixed costs go down as volume goes up, as long as a firm is operating within the relevant range of activity. Look at how the Customer Support Team cost per unit falls as the volume of activity increases within the relevant range:

Volume of Activity	Support Team Cost per Unit
100,000 units	$4,000 ÷ 100,000 = $0.0400
300,000 units	$4,000 ÷ 300,000 = $0.0133*
500,000 units	$4,000 ÷ 500,000 = $0.0080
600,000 units	$8,000 ÷ 600,000 = $0.0133*

*Rounded

At 600,000 units, the activity level is above the relevant range, which means another team must be added. Thus, the per unit cost changes to $0.0133.

Mixed Costs Mixed costs have both variable and fixed cost components. Part of a mixed cost changes with volume or usage, and part is fixed over a particular period. Electric, telephone, and heating costs are examples of mixed costs. Exhibit 4 depicts My Media Place's total electricity costs. Electric costs include charges per kilowatt-hour used plus a basic monthly service charge. The kilowatt-hour charges are variable because they depend on the amount of use; the monthly service charge is a fixed cost. Notice that the cost line does not start at $0 (compare to Exhibit 2). The cost line starts at the Y axis at the amount of fixed cost, and the variable cost rate determines the slope of the line from that point as kilowatt-hours are consumed.

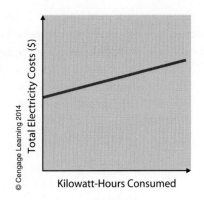

Exhibit 4
Behavior Patterns
of Mixed Costs

Mixed cost behavior is expressed mathematically in the **mixed cost formula** as follows.

Total Mixed Cost = (Variable Rate × Units Produced) + Fixed Cost

Many mixed costs vary with operating activity in a nonlinear fashion. To simplify cost analysis procedures and make mixed costs easier to use, managers and accountants use *linear approximation* to convert nonlinear costs into linear ones. This method relies on the concept of relevant range. For example, My Media Place can examine the linearity of its monthly electricity costs with machine hours worked (in thousands) by plotting its monthly electric bills for the past year as illustrated in Exhibit 5. Since the data appears linear in the relevant range of the past 12 months then a cost formula can be derived for monthly electricity costs using one of the methods explained in Section 2 of this chapter. Those estimated costs can then be treated as part of the other variable and fixed costs.

Exhibit 5
Relevant Range and Linear Approximation

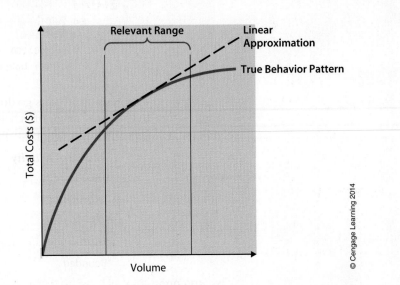

A linear approximation of a nonlinear cost is not a precise measure, but it allows the inclusion of nonlinear costs in cost behavior analysis, and the loss of accuracy is usually not significant. The goal is to help management estimate and control costs and to prepare budgets.

Indicate whether each of the following costs is usually variable (V) or fixed (F):

1. Operating supplies
2. Real estate taxes
3. Gasoline for a delivery truck
4. Property insurance
5. Depreciation expense of computers (calculated with the straight-line method)
6. Depreciation expense of machinery (calculated with the units-of-production method)

SOLUTION

1. V; 2. F; 3. V; 4. F; 5. F; 6. V

TRY IT! SE1, SE2, E1A, E2A, E1B, E2B

ACCOUNTING APPLICATIONS

LO 2 Mixed Costs and the Contribution Margin Income Statement

For cost planning and control purposes, mixed costs must be divided into their variable and fixed components. The separate components can then be grouped with other variable and fixed costs for analysis. Four methods are commonly used to separate mixed cost components. Because the results yielded by each of these methods often differ, managers usually use multiple approaches to find the best possible estimate for a mixed cost.

The Scatter Diagram Method

When there is doubt about the behavior pattern of a particular cost, especially a mixed cost, it helps to plot past costs and related measures of volume in a scatter diagram. A **scatter diagram** is a chart of plotted points that helps determine whether a linear relationship exists between a cost item and its related activity measure. It is a form of linear approximation. If the diagram suggests a linear relationship, a cost line can be imposed on the data by either visual means or statistical analysis. For example, suppose that My Media Place incurred the following machine hours and electricity costs last year:

Month	Machine Hours	Electricity Costs
January	6,250	$ 24,000
February	6,300	24,200
March	6,350	24,350
April	6,400	24,600
May	6,300	24,400
June	6,200	24,300
July	6,100	23,900
August	6,050	23,600
September	6,150	23,950
October	6,250	24,100
November	6,350	24,400
December	6,450	24,700
Totals	75,150	$290,500

Exhibit 6 shows a scatter diagram of these data. The diagram suggests a linear relationship between machine hours and the cost of electricity. If we were to add a line to the diagram to represent the linear relationship, the estimated fixed electricity cost would occur at the point at which the line intersects the vertical axis, or $23,200 of fixed monthly electric costs. The variable cost per machine hour can be estimated by determining the slope of the line, much as is done in Step 1 of the high-low method.

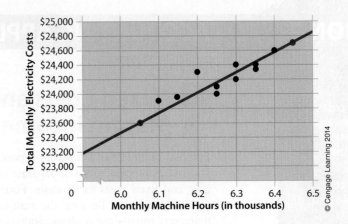

Exhibit 6
Scatter Diagram of Machine Hours and Electricity Costs

STUDY NOTE: *A scatter diagram shows how closely volume and costs are correlated. A tight, closely associated group of data is better suited to linear approximation than a random or circular pattern.*

The High-Low Method

The **high-low method** is another approach to determining the variable and fixed components of a mixed cost, which is based on the premise that only two data points are necessary to define a linear cost-volume relationship. The disadvantage of this method is that if the high or low data points are not representative of the remaining data set, the estimate of variable and fixed costs may not be accurate. Its advantage is that it can be used when only limited data are available. The example that follows illustrates how to use the high-low method for My Media Place.

Step 1. Find the variable rate. To determine the variable rate,

- Select the periods of highest and lowest activity within the accounting period. For My Media Place, the highest-volume machine-hour month was in December (6,450 hours) and the lowest was in August (6,050 hours).
- Find the difference between the highest and lowest amounts for both the machine hours and their related electricity costs.

$$6,450 \text{ hours} - 6,050 \text{ hours} = 400 \text{ hours}$$

$$\$24,700 - \$23,600 = \$1,100$$

- Compute the variable cost per machine hour by dividing the difference in cost by the difference in machine hours.

$$\text{Variable Cost per Machine Hour} = \$1,100 \div 400 \text{ Machine Hours}$$

$$= \$2.75 \text{ per Machine Hour}$$

Step 2. Find the total fixed costs. Compute total fixed costs for a month by putting the known variable rate and the information from the month with the highest volume into the cost formula and solve for the total fixed costs.

$$\text{Total Fixed Costs} = \text{Total Costs} - \text{Total Variable Costs}$$

$$\text{Total Fixed Costs for December} = \$24,700.00 - (6,450 \text{ Hours} \times \$2.75) = \$6,962.50$$

You can check your answer by recalculating total fixed costs using the month with the lowest activity.

$$\text{Total Fixed Costs for August} = \$23,600.00 - (6,050 \text{ Hours} \times \$2.75) = \$6,962.50$$

Step 3. Express the cost formula to estimate the total costs within the relevant range. For My Media Place, this is computed as follows.

$$\text{Total Mixed Cost} = (\text{Variable Rate} \times \text{Volume Level}) + \text{Fixed Costs}$$

$$\text{Total Electricity Costs per Month} = (\$2.75 \times \text{Machine Hours}) + \$6,962.50$$

Remember that the cost formula will work only within the relevant range. In this example, the formula would work for activity between 6,050 machine hours and 6,450 machine hours. To estimate the electricity costs for machine hours outside the relevant range (in this case, below 6,050 machine hours or above 6,450 machine hours), a new cost formula must be calculated.

Statistical Methods

Statistical methods, such as **regression analysis**, mathematically describe the relationship between costs and activities and are used to separate mixed costs into variable and fixed components. Because all data observations are used, the resulting linear equation is more representative of cost behavior than either the high-low or scatter diagram methods. Regression analysis can be performed using one or more activities to predict costs. For example, overhead costs can be predicted using only machine hours (a simple regression analysis), or they can be predicted using both machine hours and labor hours (a multiple regression analysis) because both activities affect overhead. We leave further description of regression analysis to statistics courses, which provide detailed coverage of this method.

The Engineering Method

The **engineering method** separates costs by performing a step-by-step analysis (sometimes called a *time and motion study*) of the tasks, costs, and processes involved. The engineering method is expensive because it is so detailed, and it is generally used to estimate the cost of activities or new products. For example, the U.S. Postal Service conducts periodic audits of how many letters a postal worker should be able to deliver on a particular mail route within a certain period.

Contribution Margin Income Statements

Once an organization's costs are classified as being either variable or fixed, the traditional income statement can be reorganized into a more useful format for internal operations and decision making. Exhibit 7 compares the structure of a traditional and a **contribution margin income statement** (or *variable costing income statement*). A contribution margin income statement emphasizes cost behavior rather than organizational functions. **Contribution margin (CM)** is the amount that remains after all variable costs are subtracted from sales. All variable costs related to production, selling, administration, and general expenses are subtracted from sales to determine the total contribution margin. All fixed costs related to production, selling, administration, and general expenses are subtracted from the total contribution margin to determine operating income.

Like most businesses, the U.S. Postal Service is concerned about delivery time. To determine how many deliveries a postal worker should be able to make within a certain period, it conducts periodic audits using the engineering method.

Richard Susanto/Shutterstock.com

Exhibit 7
Comparison of Income Statements

Traditional Income Statement	Contribution Margin Income Statement
Sales revenue	Sales revenue
– Cost of goods sold, variable	– Cost of goods sold, variable
– Cost of goods sold, fixed	– Operating expenses, variable
= Gross margin	= Contribution margin
– Operating expenses, variable	– Cost of goods sold, fixed
– Operating expenses, fixed	– Operating expenses, fixed
= Operating income	= Operating income

© Cengage Learning 2014

STUDY NOTE: *Although both statements arrive at the same operating income, the traditional approach divides costs into product and period costs, whereas the contribution margin approach divides costs into variable and fixed costs.*

The contribution margin income statement enables managers to view revenue and cost relationships on a per unit basis or as a percentage of sales. If managers understand these relationships, they can determine:

- How many units they must sell to avoid losing money
- What the sales price per unit must be to cover costs
- What their profits will be for a certain dollar amount of sales revenue

Exhibit 8 shows the two ways a contribution margin income statement can be presented.

Exhibit 8
Contribution Margin Income Statement

	Per Unit Relationships	As a Percentage of Sales
Sales revenue	(Sales price per unit × Units sold)	(Sales revenue ÷ Sales revenue)
Less variable costs	(Variable rate per unit × Units sold)	(Variable costs ÷ Sales revenue)
Contribution margin	(Contribution margin per unit × Units sold)	Contribution margin ÷ Sales revenue
Less fixed costs	(Fixed costs)	(Fixed costs ÷ Sales revenue)
Operating income	(Operating income)	(Operating income ÷ Sales revenue)

© Cengage Learning 2014

APPLY IT!

Using the high-low method and the information that follows, compute the monthly variable cost per kilowatt-hour and the monthly fixed electricity cost for a local business. Finally, express the monthly electricity cost formula and its relevant range.

Month	Kilowatt-Hours Used	Electricity Costs
April	90	$450
May	80	430
June	70	420

SOLUTION

Volume	Month	Activity Level	Cost
High	April	90 hours	$450
Low	June	70 hours	420
Difference		20 hours	$ 30

Variable cost per kilowatt-hour = $30 ÷ 20 hours
                                        = $1.50 per hour

Fixed costs for April: $450 − (90 × $1.50) = $315

Fixed costs for June: $420 − (70 × $1.50) = $315

Monthly electricity costs = ($1.50 × Hours) + $315

The cost formula can be used for hourly activity between 70 and 90 hours per month.

TRY IT! SE3, SE4, SE9, E3A, E4A, E5A, E3B, E4B, E5B

LO 3 Cost-Volume-Profit Analysis

Cost-volume-profit (CVP) analysis is an examination of the relationships among cost, volume of output, and profit. CVP analysis usually applies to a single product, product line, or division of a company. For that reason, *profit* is the term used in the CVP equation. In the context of CVP analysis, however, profit and operating income mean the same thing. The CVP equation is expressed as:

$$\text{Sales Revenue} - \text{Variable Costs} - \text{Fixed Costs} = \text{Profit}$$

or as:

$$(\text{Sales Price} \times \text{Units Sold}) - (\text{Variable Rate} \times \text{Units Sold}) - \text{Fixed Costs} = \text{Profit}$$

For example, suppose My Media Place wants to make a profit of $50,000 on one of its services. Each service sells for $95.50 and has variable costs of $80. If 4,000 services are sold during the period, what are the fixed costs?

$$(\$95.50 \times 4{,}000) - (\$80 \times 4{,}000) - \text{Fixed Costs} = \$50{,}000$$

$$\$382{,}000 - \$320{,}000 - \text{Fixed Costs} = \$50{,}000$$

$$\text{Fixed Costs} = \underline{\$12{,}000}$$

APPLY IT!

A local business wants to make a profit of $10,000 each month. It has variable costs of $5 per unit and fixed costs of $20,000 per month. How much must it charge per unit if 6,000 units are sold?

SOLUTION

$$(\text{Sales Price} \times \text{Units Sold}) - (\text{Variable Rate} \times \text{Units Sold}) - \text{Fixed Costs} = \text{Profit}$$

$$(\text{Sales Price} \times 6{,}000) - (\$5 \times 6{,}000) - \$20{,}000 = \$10{,}000$$

$$\text{Sales Price} = \frac{(\$5 \times 6{,}000) + \$20{,}000 + \$10{,}000}{6{,}000 \text{ units}} = \frac{\$60{,}000}{6{,}000} = \$10 \text{ per unit}$$

TRY IT! SE4, SE10, E6A, E12A, E13A, E14A, E6B, E12B, E13B, E14B

LO 4 Breakeven Analysis

The **breakeven point** is the point at which total revenues equal total costs. It is thus the point at which an organization can begin to earn a profit. When a new venture or product line is being planned, the likelihood of the project's success can be quickly measured by finding its breakeven point. If, for instance, the breakeven point is 24,000 units and the total market is only 25,000 units, the margin of safety would be very low, and the idea should be considered carefully. The **margin of safety** is the number of sales units or amount of sales dollars by which actual sales can fall below planned sales without resulting in a loss—in this example, 1,000 units.

The general equation for finding the breakeven point is expressed as:

$$\text{Breakeven Point} = \text{Sales} - \text{Variable Costs} - \text{Fixed Costs}$$

or as:

$$(\text{Sales Price} \times \text{Units Sold}) - (\text{Variable Rate} \times \text{Units Sold}) - \text{Fixed Costs} = \text{Profit}$$

Suppose, for example, that one of the services My Media Place sells is website setups. Variable costs are $50 per unit, and fixed costs average $20,000 per year. A unit is a basic website setup, which sells for $90.

Breakeven in Sales Units The breakeven point for website setup services in sales units is:

$$\text{Sales Price} - \text{Variable Cost} - \text{Fixed Cost} = \$0$$
$$(\$90 \times \text{Sales Units}) - (\$50 \times \text{Sales Units}) - \$20{,}000 = \$0$$
$$(\$40 \times \text{Sales Units}) = \$20{,}000$$
$$\text{Sales Units} = \$20{,}000 \div \$40$$
$$\text{Sales Units} = \underline{500}$$

Breakeven in Sales Dollars The breakeven point in sales dollars is:

$$\$90 \times 500 \text{ units} = \underline{\underline{\$45{,}000}}$$

Breakeven by Scatter Diagram We can make a rough estimate of the breakeven point using a scatter diagram. Exhibit 9 shows My Media Place's breakeven graph, which has five parts:

- A horizontal axis for units of output
- A vertical axis for dollars
- A line running horizontally from the vertical axis at the level of fixed costs
- A total cost line that begins at the point where the fixed cost line crosses the vertical axis and slopes upward to the right (The slope of the line depends on the variable cost per unit.)
- A total revenue line that begins at the origin of the vertical and horizontal axes and slopes upward to the right (The slope depends on the selling price per unit.)

At the point at which the total revenue line crosses the total cost line, revenues equal total costs. The breakeven point, stated in either sales units or dollars of sales, is found by extending broken lines from this point to the axes. As Exhibit 9 shows, My Media Place will break even when it has sold 500 website setups for $45,000.

Exhibit 9
Graphic Breakeven
Analysis

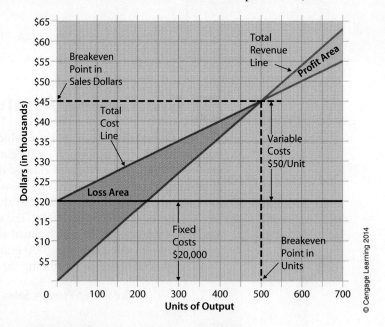

© Cengage Learning 2014

Using an Equation to Determine the Breakeven Point

A simpler method of determining the breakeven point uses contribution margin in an equation. You will recall from the contribution margin income statement that the contribution margin is the amount that remains after all variable costs are subtracted from sales:

$$\text{Sales} - \text{Variable Costs} = \text{Contribution Margin}$$

A product line's contribution margin represents its net contribution to paying off fixed costs and earning a profit. Profit is what remains after fixed costs are paid and subtracted from the contribution margin:

$$\text{Contribution Margin} - \text{Fixed Costs} = \text{Profit}$$

The example that follows uses the contribution margin income statement approach to determine the profitability of one of My Media Place's products.

Symbols		Units Produced and Sold		
		250	**500**	**750**
S	Sales revenue ($90 per unit)	$ 22,500	$45,000	$67,500
VC	Less variable costs ($50 per unit)	12,500	25,000	37,500
CM	Contribution margin ($40 per unit)	$ 10,000	$20,000	$30,000
FC	Less fixed costs	20,000	20,000	20,000
P	Profit (loss)	$(10,000)	$ 0	$10,000

The breakeven point (BE) can be expressed as the point at which contribution margin minus total fixed costs equals zero (or the point at which contribution margin equals total fixed costs).

Breakeven in Sales Units In terms of units of product, the equation for the breakeven point looks like this:

$$(\text{Contribution Margin per Unit} \times \text{Breakeven Point Units}) - \text{Fixed Costs} = \$0$$

It can also be expressed like this:

$$\text{Breakeven (BE) Point Units} = \frac{\text{Fixed Costs (FC)}}{\text{Contribution Margin (CM) per Unit}}$$

For My Media Place, the breakeven point would be computed as follows.

$$\text{Breakeven Point Units} = \frac{\text{Fixed Costs}}{\text{Contribution Margin per Unit}} = \frac{\$20,000}{\$90 - \$50} = \frac{\$20,000}{\$40} = 500 \text{ units}$$

Breakeven in Sales Dollars The breakeven point in total sales dollars may be determined as follows.

$$\text{Breakeven (BE) Point Dollars} = \text{Selling Price (SP)} \times \text{Breakeven (BE) Point Units}$$
$$= \$90 \times 500 \text{ units}$$
$$= \$45,000$$

RATIO

An alternative way of determining the breakeven point in total sales dollars is to divide the fixed costs by the contribution margin ratio. The contribution margin ratio is the contribution margin divided by the selling price:

$$\text{Contribution Margin Ratio} = \frac{\text{Contribution Margin}}{\text{Selling Price}} = \frac{\$40}{\$90} = 0.444^*, \text{ or } 4/9$$

$$\text{Breakeven Point Dollars} = \frac{\text{Fixed Costs}}{\text{Contribution Margin Ratio}} = \frac{\$20,000}{0.444} = \$45,045^*$$

*Rounded

The Breakeven Point for Multiple Products

To satisfy the needs of different customers, most companies sell a variety of products or services that often have different variable and fixed costs and different selling prices.

To calculate the breakeven point for each product, its unit contribution margin must be weighted by the sales mix. The **sales mix** is the proportion of each product's unit sales relative to the company's total unit sales.

Assume that My Media Place sells two types of websites: standard and express. If the company sells 500 units, of which 300 units are standard and 200 are express, the sales mix would be 3:2. The sales mix can also be stated in percentages. Of the 500 units sold, 60 percent (300 ÷ 500) are standard sales, and 40 percent (200 ÷ 500) are express sales (see Exhibit 10).

Exhibit 10
Sales Mix

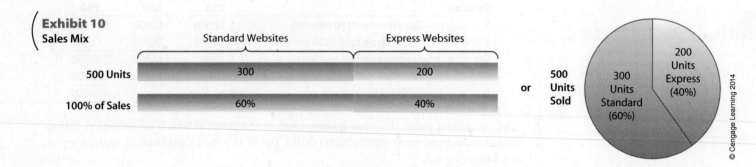

The example that follows illustrates how to compute the breakeven point for multiple products using My Media Place's sales mix of 60 percent standard websites to 40 percent express websites and total fixed costs of $32,000.

Step 1. Compute the weighted-average contribution margin. Multiply the contribution margin for each product by its percentage of the sales mix, as follows.

	Selling Price		Variable Costs		Contribution Margin (CM)		Percentage of Sales Mix		Weighted-Average CM
Standard	$90	−	$50	=	$40	×	60%	=	$24
Express	$40	−	$20	=	$20	×	40%	=	8
Weighted-average contribution margin									$32

Step 2. Calculate the weighted-average breakeven point. Divide total fixed costs by the weighted-average contribution margin:

$$\text{Weighted-Average Breakeven Point Units} = \text{Total Fixed Costs} \div \text{Weighted Average Contribution Margin}$$

$$= \$32{,}000 \div \$32$$

$$= \underline{1{,}000 \text{ units}}$$

Step 3. Calculate the breakeven point for each product. Multiply the weighted-average breakeven point by each product's percentage of the sales mix:

	Weighted-Average Breakeven Point		Sales Mix		Breakeven Point
Standard	1,000 units	×	60%	=	600 units
Express	1,000 units	×	40%	=	400 units

Step 4. Verify results. To verify, determine the contribution margin of each product and subtract the total fixed costs:

Contribution margin:		
Standard	600 × $40	$24,000
Express	400 × $20	8,000
Total contribution margin		$32,000
Less fixed costs		32,000
Profit		$ 0

APPLY IT!

Using the contribution margin approach, find the breakeven point in units for a local business's two products. Product M's selling price per unit is $20, and its variable cost per unit is $11. Product N's selling price per unit is $12, and its variable cost per unit is $6. Fixed costs are $24,000, and the sales mix of Product M to Product N is 2:1.

SOLUTION

Step 1.

	Selling Price		Variable Costs		Contribution Margin (CM)		Percentage of Sales Mix		Weighted-Average CM*
M	$20	−	$11	=	$9	×	66.67%	=	$6
N	$12	−	$ 6	=	$6	×	33.33%	=	2
Weighted-average contribution margin									$8

*Rounded

Step 2.
Weighted-average breakeven point = $24,000 ÷ $8.00 = 3,000 units

Step 3. Breakeven point for each product line:

		Weighted-Average Breakeven Point		Sales Mix		Breakeven Point
M	=	3,000 units	×	0.6667	=	2,000 units
N	=	3,000 units	×	0.3333	=	1,000 units

Step 4. Check:

Contribution margin:						
Product M	=	2,000	×	$9	=	$18,000
Product N	=	1,000	×	$6	=	6,000
Total contribution margin						$24,000
Less fixed costs						24,000
Profit						$ 0

TRY IT! SE5, SE6, SE7, SE8, E5A, E6A, E7A, E8A, E9A, E10A, E11A, E15A, E5B, E6B, E7B, E8B, E9B, E10B, E11B, E15B

BUSINESS APPLICATIONS

**BUSINESS
APPLICATIONS**

■ Planning
■ Performing
■ Evaluating
■ Communicating

**RELEVANT
LEARNING OBJECTIVE**

LO 5 Discuss how managers use CVP analysis in the management process and how they can project the profitability of products and services.

LO 5 Using CVP Analysis to Plan Future Sales, Costs, and Profits

CVP analysis is a general model of financial activity. CVP analysis allows managers to adjust different variables and to evaluate how these changes affect profit. For planning, managers can use CVP analysis to calculate net income when sales volume is known, or they can determine the level of sales needed to reach a targeted amount of net income. CVP analysis is used extensively in budgeting as well, and is also a way of measuring how well an organization's departments are performing. At the end of a period, sales volume and related actual costs are analyzed to find actual net income. A department's performance is measured by comparing actual costs with expected costs, which have been computed by applying CVP analysis to actual sales volume. The result is a performance report on which managers can base the control of operations.

Managers use CVP analysis to measure the effects of alternative courses of action, such as changing variable or fixed costs, expanding or contracting sales volume, and increasing or decreasing selling prices. CVP analysis is useful in making decisions about:

■ product pricing
■ product mix (when an organization makes more than one product or offers more than one service)
■ adding or dropping a product line
■ accepting special orders.

Assumptions Underlying CVP Analysis

CVP analysis is useful only under certain conditions and only when the following assumptions hold true:

■ The behavior of variable and fixed costs can be measured accurately.
■ Costs and revenues have a close linear approximation throughout the relevant range. For example, if costs rise, revenues rise proportionately.
■ Efficiency and productivity hold steady within the relevant range of activity.
■ Cost and price variables also hold steady during the period being planned.
■ The sales mix does not change during the period being planned.
■ Production and sales volume are roughly equal.

If one or more of these conditions and assumptions are absent, the CVP analysis may be misleading.

Applying CVP to Target Profits

The primary goal of a business venture is not to break even, but to generate profits. CVP analysis adjusted for targeted profit can be used to estimate the profitability of a venture. This approach is excellent for "what-if" analysis, in which managers select several scenarios and compute the profit that may be anticipated from each. For instance, what if sales increase by 17,000 units? What effect will the increase have on profit? What if sales increase by only 6,000 units? What if fixed costs are reduced by $14,500? What if the variable unit cost increases by $1.40?

We will continue the My Media Place example to illustrate two ways a business can apply CVP analysis to target profits. Assuming that the company wants to make $4,000 in profit this year, how many website services must it sell to reach the targeted profit?

Contribution Margin Approach Using the contribution margin approach, the number of websites My Media Place must sell to obtain $4,000 in profit would be computed as follows.

$$\text{Sales Revenue} = \text{Variable Costs} + \text{Fixed Costs} + \text{Profit}$$
$$(\$90 \times \text{Targeted Sales Units}) = (\$50 \times \text{Targeted Sales Units}) + \$20{,}000 + \$4{,}000$$
$$(\$40 \times \text{Targeted Sales Units}) = \$24{,}000$$
$$\text{Targeted Sales Units} = \underline{600} \text{ units}$$

Equation Approach Using the equation approach, add the targeted profit to the numerator of the contribution margin breakeven equation and solve for targeted sales in units:

$$\text{Targeted Sales Units} = \frac{\text{Fixed Costs} + \text{Profit}}{\text{Contribution Margin per Unit}}$$

The number of sales units My Media Place needs to generate $4,000 in profit is computed as follows.

$$\text{Targeted Sales Units} = \frac{\$20{,}000 + \$4{,}000}{\$40}$$
$$= \frac{\$24{,}000}{\$40}$$
$$= \underline{600} \text{ units}$$

Contribution Margin Income Statement To summarize My Media Place's plans for the coming year, a contribution income statement can be used, as shown below. The focus of such a statement is on cost behavior, *not* cost function.

My Media Place Contribution Income Statement For the Year Ended December 31		
	Per Unit	**Total for 600 Units**
Sales revenue	$90	$54,000
Less variable costs	50	30,000
Contribution margin	$40	$24,000
Less fixed costs		20,000
Operating income		$ 4,000

Comparing Alternative Options Using CVP My Media Place's planning team wants to consider three alternatives to the original plan shown in the statement.

Alternative 1: Decrease Variable Costs, Increase Sales Volume What if website design labor were outsourced? Based on the planning team's research, the direct labor cost of a website would decrease by $3 to $47 and sales volume would increase by 10 percent to 660 units. How does this alternative affect operating income?

Alternative 1	Per Unit	Total for 660 Units
Sales revenue	$90	$59,400
Less variable costs	47	31,020
Contribution margin	$43	$28,380
Less fixed costs		20,000
Operating income		$ 8,380
Increase in operating income ($8,380 − $4,000)		$ 4,380

Alternative 2: Increase Fixed Costs, Increase Sales Volume What if the Marketing Department suggests that a $500 increase in advertising costs would increase sales volume by 5 percent to 630 units? How does this alternative affect operating income?

Aternative 2	Per Unit	Total for 630 Units
Sales revenue	$90	$56,700
Less variable costs	50	31,500
Contribution margin	$40	$25,200
Less fixed costs		20,500
Operating income		$ 4,700
Increase in operating income ($4,700 − $4,000)		$ 700

Alternative 3: Increase Selling Price, Decrease Sales Volume What is the impact of a $10 increase in selling price on the company's operating income? If the selling price is increased, the planning team estimates that the sales volume will decrease by 15 percent to 510 units. How does this alternative affect operating income?

Alternative 3	Per Unit	Total for 510 Units
Sales revenue	$100	$51,000
Less variable costs	50	25,500
Contribution margin	$ 50	$25,500
Less fixed costs		20,000
Operating income		$ 5,500
Increase in operating income ($5,500 − $4,000)		$ 1,500

Comparative Summary In preparation for a meeting, the planning team at My Media Place compiled the summary presented in Exhibit 11. It compares the three alternatives with the original plan and shows how changes in variable and fixed costs, selling price, and sales volume affect the breakeven point.

Exhibit 11
Comparative Summary of Alternatives

	Original Plan	Alternative 1	Alternative 2	Alternative 3
	Totals for 600 Units	Decrease Direct Materials Costs for 660 Units	Increase Advertising Costs for 630 Units	Increase Selling Price for 510 Units
Sales revenue	$54,000	$59,400	$56,700	$51,000
Less variable costs	30,000	31,020	31,500	25,500
Contribution margin	$24,000	$28,380	$25,200	$25,500
Less fixed costs	20,000	20,000	20,500	20,000
Operating income	$ 4,000	$ 8,380	$ 4,700	$ 5,500
Breakeven point in whole units (FC ÷ CM):				
$20,000 ÷ $40 =	500			
$20,000 ÷ $43 =		466*		
$20,500 ÷ $40 =			513*	
$20,000 ÷ $50 =				400

*Rounded up to next whole unit

© Cengage Learning 2014

The three alternatives differ as follows.

- The decrease in variable costs (direct materials) proposed in Alternative 1 increases the contribution margin per unit (from $40 to $43), which reduces the breakeven point. Because fewer sales dollars are required to cover variable costs, the breakeven point is reached sooner than in the original plan—at a sales volume of 466 units rather than at 500 units.

- In Alternative 2, the increase in fixed costs has no effect on the contribution margin per unit, but it does require the total contribution margin to cover more fixed costs before reaching the breakeven point. Thus, the breakeven point is higher than in the original plan—513 units, as opposed to 500.

- The increase in selling price in Alternative 3 increases the contribution margin per unit, which reduces the breakeven point. Because more sales dollars are available to cover fixed costs, the breakeven point of 400 units is lower than the breakeven point in the original plan.

From a strategic standpoint, which plan should the planning team choose? If they want the highest operating income, they will choose Alternative 1. If, however, they want the company to begin generating operating income more quickly, they will choose the plan with the lowest breakeven point, Alternative 3. Additional quantitative and qualitative information may help the planning team make a better decision. While quantitative information is essential for planning, managers must also be sensitive to qualitative factors, such as product quality, reliability and quality of suppliers, and availability of human and technical resources.

Besides using cost-volume-profit analysis for planning and evaluating purposes, it can be a useful tool in the performing stage of the management process for determining cost behavior and in the communicating stage for providing relevant information for internal decision makers and for summarizing performance in external reports. Exhibit 12 summarizes how CVP analysis relates to the management process.

Exhibit 12
CVP and the Management Process

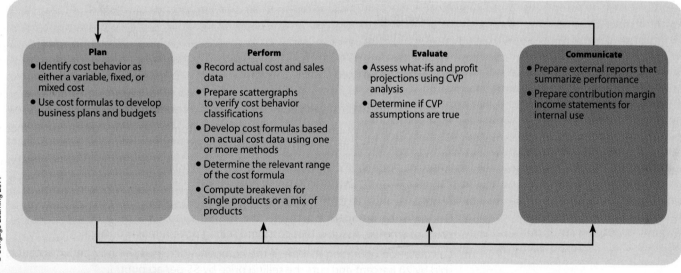

© Cengage Learning 2014

APPLY IT!

A local real estate appraisal business is planning its home appraisal activities for the coming year. The manager estimates that her variable costs per appraisal will be $220, monthly fixed costs are $16,200, and service fee revenue will be $400 per appraisal. How many appraisals will the business have to perform each month to achieve a targeted profit of $18,000 per month?

SOLUTION

Sales Revenue − Variable Costs − Fixed Costs = Profit

($400 × Targeted Sales Units) −
($220 × Targeted Sales Units) − $16,200 = $18,000

$180 × Targeted Sales Units = $34,200

Targeted Sales Units = <u>190</u> appraisals per month

TRY IT! SE9, SE10, E12A, E13A, E14A, E15A, E12B, E13B, E14B, E15B

TriLevel Problem

Flickr

oliveromg/Shutterstock.com

The beginning of this chapter focused on **Flickr**, a company whose business is continually evolving to meet changing customer preferences. Complete the following requirements in order to answer the questions posed at the beginning of the chapter.

Section 1: Concepts
Why is cost-volume-profit analysis useful for the purposes of comparability and understand-ability?

Section 2: Accounting Applications
How will Flickr's managers decide which products and services to offer? Suppose Flickr is considering entering the online digital lockbox business by renting server space to customers to store their movies, music, photos, and other computer files. Its managers believe this service has a large potential market as more individuals and small businesses are starting to move their backup files to secure online servers that can be accessed around the clock. A summary of the data projections for this potential service offering follows.

Selling price per year per customer account	$95
Variable costs per unit:	
Direct supplies	$23
Direct labor	8
Overhead	6
Selling expense	5
Total variable costs per unit	$42
Annual fixed costs:	
Overhead	$195,000
Advertising	55,000
Administrative expense	68,000
Total annual fixed costs	$318,000

1. Compute the annual breakeven point in customer accounts.

2. Assume the company projects sales to 6,500 customer accounts next year. If that projection is accurate, how much profit will it realize?

3. To improve profitability, management is considering the following four alternative courses of action. (In performing the required steps, use the figures from items **1** and **2**, and treat each alternative independently.)

   a. Calculate the number of accounts the business must sell to generate a targeted profit of $95,400. Assume that costs and selling price remain constant.

   b. Calculate the operating income if the company increases the number of accounts sold by 20 percent and cuts the selling price by $5 per account.

   c. Determine the number of accounts that must be sold to break even if advertising costs (fixed costs) increase by $47,700.

   d. Find the number of accounts that must be sold to generate a targeted profit of $120,000 if variable costs decrease by 10 percent.

Section 3: Business Applications

How can managers use cost behavior analysis to improve business performance? To answer this question, match this chapter's manager responsibilities with when they occur within the management process.

a. Plan
b. Perform
c. Evaluate
d. Communicate

1. Use actual data to develop cost formulas
2. Identify variable, fixed, or mixed costs
3. Assess what-ifs and profit projections
4. Use cost formulas to develop business plans and budgets
5. Record actual cost and sales data
6. Determine the relevant range of the cost formula
7. Prepare scatter diagrams to verify cost behavior classifications
8. Prepare external reports
9. Compute breakeven for single products or a mix of products
10. Prepare contribution margin income statements for internal use
11. Determine if CVP assumptions are true

SOLUTION

Concepts

Two underlying accounting concepts support the usefulness of cost-volume-profit analysis: *understandability* and *comparability*. Knowing how costs will behave improves a user's comprehension of the meaning of the information they have received, enhancing their understanding of it. Knowledge of cost behavior patterns enables users to identify cost similarities and differences so comparisons of alternatives are possible. As a result, managers commonly use cost behavior information when they select the course of action that will best generate income for an organization's owners, maintain liquidity for its creditors, and use the organization's resources responsibly. With an understanding of cost behavior patterns, managers can use cost-volume-profit (CVP) analysis to evaluate "what-if" scenarios and to determine selling prices that cover both fixed and variable costs and that take into account the variability of demand for their company's products or services.

Accounting Applications

1. $\text{Breakeven Point Units} = \dfrac{\text{Fixed Costs}}{\text{Contribution Margin per Unit}}$

$$= \frac{\$318,000}{\$95 - \$42} = \frac{\$318,000}{\$53} = \underline{\underline{6,000 \text{ units}}}$$

2. Profit at 6,500 accounts:

Units sold	6,500
Units required to break even	6,000
Units over breakeven	500
Profit = $53 per unit × 500 =	$26,500

Contribution margin equals sales minus all variable costs. Contribution margin per account equals the amount left to cover fixed costs and earn a profit after variable costs have been subtracted from sales dollars. If all fixed costs have been absorbed by the time breakeven is reached, the entire contribution margin of each unit sold in excess of breakeven represents profit.

3. (a) Targeted Sales Units $= \dfrac{\text{Fixed Costs} + \text{Profit}}{\text{Contribution Margin per Unit}}$

$= \dfrac{\$318,000 + \$95,400}{\$53} = \dfrac{\$413,400}{\$53}$

$= 7,800$ units

(b)
Sales revenue [(6,500 × 1.20) accounts at $90 per account]	$702,000
Less variable costs (7,800 units × $42)	327,600
Contribution margin	$374,400
Less fixed costs	318,000
Operating income	$ 56,400

(c) Breakeven Point Units $= \dfrac{\text{Fixed Costs}}{\text{Contribution Margin per Unit}}$

$= \dfrac{\$318,000 + \$47,700}{\$53} = \dfrac{\$365,700}{\$53}$

$= 6,900$ units

(d) Targeted Sales Units $= \dfrac{\text{Fixed Costs} + \text{Profit}}{\text{Contribution Margin per Unit}}$

$= \dfrac{\$318,000 + \$120,000}{\$95 - (\$42 \times 0.9)} = \dfrac{\$438,000}{\$57.20}$

$= 7,658$ units*

*Rounded

Business Applications

1. b
2. a
3. c
4. a
5. b
6. b
7. b
8. d
9. b
10. d
11. c

Chapter Review

Define *cost behavior*, and identify variable, fixed, and mixed costs. **LO 1**

Cost behavior is the way costs respond to changes in volume or activity. Some costs vary in relation to volume or operating activity; other costs remain fixed as volume changes. Total costs that change in direct proportion to changes in productive output (or any other volume measure) are called variable costs. They include hourly wages, the cost of operating supplies, direct materials costs, and the cost of merchandise. Total fixed costs remain constant within a relevant range of volume or activity. They change only when volume or activity exceeds the relevant range—for example, when new equipment or new buildings must be purchased, higher insurance premiums and property taxes must be paid, or additional supervisory personnel must be hired to accommodate increased activity. A mixed cost, such as the cost of electricity, has both variable and fixed cost components.

Separate mixed costs into their variable and fixed components, and prepare a contribution margin income statement. **LO 2**

Mixed costs must be separated into their variable and fixed components, using a variety of methods, including the engineering, scatter diagram, high-low, and statistical methods. When preparing a contribution margin income statement, all variable costs related to production, selling, and administration are subtracted from sales to determine the total contribution margin. Then, all fixed costs are subtracted from the total contribution margin to determine operating income.

Perform cost-volume-profit (CVP) analysis. **LO 3**

Cost-volume-profit analysis is an examination of the cost behavior patterns that underlie the relationships among cost, volume of output, and profit. It is a tool for both planning and control.

Define *breakeven point*, and use contribution margin to determine a company's breakeven point for multiple products. **LO 4**

The breakeven point is the point at which total revenues equal total costs—the point at which net sales equal variable costs plus fixed costs. Once the number of units needed to break even is known, the number can be multiplied by the product's selling price to determine the breakeven point in sales dollars. Contribution margin is the amount that remains after all variable costs have been subtracted from sales. A product's contribution margin represents its net contribution to paying off fixed costs and earning a profit. The breakeven point in units can be computed by using the following formula:

$$\text{Breakeven Point Units} = \frac{\text{Fixed Costs}}{\text{Contribution Margin per Unit}}$$

Sales mix is used to calculate the breakeven point for each product when a company sells more than one product.

Discuss how managers use CVP analysis in the management process and how they can project the profitability of products and services. **LO 5**

CVP relationships provide a general model of financial activity that management can use for short-range planning and for evaluating performance and analyzing alternatives. The addition of targeted profit to the breakeven equation makes it possible to plan levels of operation that yield the desired profit. The formula in terms of contribution margin is:

$$\text{Targeted Sales Units} = \frac{\text{Fixed Costs} - \text{Profit}}{\text{Contribution Margin per Unit}}$$

CVP analysis enables managers to select several "what-if" scenarios and evaluate the outcome of each to determine which will generate the desired results.

Key Terms

activity base 166 (LO1)
breakeven point 173 (LO4)
contribution margin (CM) 171 (LO2)
contribution margin income
    statement 171 (LO2)
cost behavior 164 (LO1)
cost-volume-profit (CVP)
    analysis 173 (LO3)
engineering method 171 (LO2)

fixed cost formula 166 (LO1)
fixed costs 166 (LO1)
high-low method 170 (LO2)
margin of safety 173 (LO4)
mixed cost formula 167 (LO1)
mixed costs 167 (LO1)
normal capacity 166 (LO1)
operating capacity 165 (LO1)
practical capacity 166 (LO1)

regression analysis 171 (LO2)
relevant range 166 (LO1)
sales mix 176 (LO4)
scatter diagram 169 (LO2)
step cost 166 (LO1)
theoretical capacity 166 (LO1)
variable cost formula 165 (LO1)
variable costs 164 (LO1)

Chapter Assignments

DISCUSSION QUESTIONS

LO 1 **DQ1. CONCEPT ▶** Describe how the identification of variable, fixed, and mixed costs increases cost comparability and understanding within the relevant range of volume or activity.

LO 2 **DQ2. CONCEPT ▶** What methods separate mixed costs into their fixed and variable components to better understand cost behavior?

LO 2 **DQ3. CONCEPT ▶** How does the preparation of a contribution margin income statement enhance cost behavior understanding and comparisons?

LO 3, 4 **DQ4. CONCEPT ▶** How does cost-volume-profit (CVP) analysis improve understanding and comparisons when using the contribution margin to determine a company's breakeven point for a single product or multiple products?

LO 5 **DQ5. CONCEPT ▶ BUSINESS APPLICATION ▶** Why does CVP analysis in the management process reinforce the concepts of comparability and understandability to better business profitability?

SHORT EXERCISES

LO 1 **Accounting Concepts**

SE1. CONCEPT ▶ Match the accounting concepts with why they support the decision usefulness of CVP analysis.

a. Understandability
b. Comparability

1. A quality that enables users to identify similarities and differences between alternatives
2. A quality that enables users to comprehend the meaning of the information they receive

LO 1 **Identification of Variable, Fixed, and Mixed Costs**

SE2. Identify the following as (a) fixed costs, (b) variable costs, or (c) mixed costs:

1. Direct materials
2. Electricity
3. Factory building rent
4. Manager's salary
5. Operating supplies

LO 2 **Mixed Costs: High-Low Method**

SE3. Using the high-low method, compute Soho Corporation's monthly variable cost per telephone hour and total fixed costs.

Month	Telephone Hours Used	Telephone Costs
April	95	$4,350
May	90	4,230
June	100	4,680

LO 2, 3 **Contribution Margin Income Statement**

SE4. Prepare a contribution margin income statement if Greenwich, Inc., wants to make a profit of $50,000. It has variable costs of $10 per unit and fixed costs of $20,000. How much must it charge per unit if 5,000 units are sold?

LO 4 **Breakeven Analysis in Units and Dollars**

SE5. How many units must Queens Company sell to break even if the selling price per unit is $9, variable costs are $5 per unit, and fixed costs are $6,000? What is the breakeven point in total dollars of sales?

LO 4 **Contribution Margin in Units**

SE6. Using the contribution margin approach, find the breakeven point in units for Staten Products if the selling price per unit is $11, the variable cost per unit is $4, and the fixed costs are $7,700.

LO 4 **Contribution Margin Ratio**

 SE7. Compute the contribution margin ratio and the breakeven point in total sales dollars for Wall Street Products if the selling price per unit is $16, the variable cost per unit is $8, and the fixed costs are $6,250.

LO 4 **Breakeven Analysis for Multiple Products**

SE8. Using the contribution margin approach, find the breakeven point in units for Suffolk Company's two products. Product A's selling price per unit is $10, and its variable cost per unit is $4. Product B's selling price per unit is $8, and its variable cost per unit is $5. Fixed costs are $14,175, and the sales mix of Product A to Product B is 3:1.

LO 2, 5 **Monthly Costs and the High-Low Method**

SE9. Pup Noir, a private investigation firm, investigated 90 cases in December and had the following costs: direct labor, $190 per case; and service overhead of $20,840. Service overhead for October was $21,150; for November, it was $21,350. The number of cases investigated during October and November was 92 and 95, respectively. Compute the variable and fixed cost components of service overhead using the high-low method. Then determine the variable and fixed costs per case for December. (Round final answers to the nearest dollar where necessary.)

LO 3, 5 **CVP Analysis and Projected Profit**

SE10. If Bronx Watches sells 300 watches at $38 per watch and has variable costs of $18 per watch and fixed costs of $4,000, what is the projected profit?

EXERCISES: SET A

LO 1 **Identification of Variable and Fixed Costs**

E1A. Indicate whether each of the following costs of productive output is usually (a) variable or (b) fixed:

1. License fee for company car
2. Wiring used in radios
3. Machine helper's wages
4. Wood used in bookcases
5. City operating license
6. Machine depreciation based on machine hours used
7. Machine operator's hourly wages
8. Cost of required outside inspection of each unit produced

LO 1 **Variable Cost Analysis**

E2A. Zero Time Oil Change has been in business for six months. The company pays $0.75 per quart for the oil it uses in servicing cars. Each job requires an average of 4 quarts of oil. The company estimates that in the next three months, it will service 250, 280, and 360 cars.

1. Compute the cost of oil for each of the three months and the total cost for all three months.
2. Complete the following sentences by choosing the words that best describe the cost behavior at Zero Time:
   a. Cost per unit (increased, decreased, remained constant).
   b. Total variable cost per month (increased, decreased) as the quantity of oil used (increased, decreased).

LO 2 **Mixed Costs: High-Low Method**

E3A. Madison Company manufactures major appliances. Because of growing interest in its products, it has just had its most successful year. In preparing the budget for next year, its controller compiled the following information:

Month	Volume in Machine Hours	Electricity Cost
July	6,000	$ 60,000
August	5,000	53,000
September	4,500	49,500
October	4,000	46,000
November	3,500	42,500
December	3,000	36,000
Six-month total	26,000	$287,000

Using the high-low method, determine the variable electricity cost per machine hour and the monthly fixed electricity cost. Estimate the total variable electricity costs and fixed electricity costs if 4,800 machine hours are projected to be used next month.

LO 2 **Mixed Costs: High-Low Method**

E4A. When Jerome Company's monthly costs were $80,000, sales were $90,000. When its monthly costs were $60,000, sales were $50,000. Use the high-low method to develop a monthly cost formula for Jerome's coming year.

LO 2, 4 **Contribution Margin Income Statement and Ratio**

E5A. Bowery Company manufactures a single product that sells for $100 per unit. The company projects sales of 400 units per month. Projected costs follow.

Type of Cost	Manufacturing	Nonmanufacturing
Variable	$10,000	$6,000
Nonvariable	13,000	5,000

1. Prepare a contribution margin income statement for the month.
2. What is the contribution margin ratio?
3. What volume, in terms of units, must the company sell to break even?

LO 3, 4 **Contribution Margin Income Statement and Breakeven Analysis**

E6A. Using the data in the contribution margin income statement for Broadway, Inc., that follows, calculate (a) selling price per unit, (b) variable costs per unit, and (c) break-even point in units and in sales dollars.

Broadway, Inc.
Contribution Margin Income Statement
For the Year Ended December 31

Sales (20,000 units)		$16,000,000
Less variable costs:		
Cost of goods sold	$8,000,000	
Selling, administrative, and general	4,000,000	
Total variable costs		12,000,000
Contribution margin		$ 4,000,000
Less fixed costs:		
Overhead	$1,200,000	
Selling, administrative, and general	800,000	
Total fixed costs		2,000,000
Operating income		$ 2,000,000

LO 4   **Breakeven Analysis**

E7A. Meadowlands Design produces head covers for golf clubs. The company expects to generate a profit next year. It anticipates fixed manufacturing costs of $200,500 and fixed general and administrative expenses of $80,000 for the year. Variable manufacturing and selling costs per set of head covers will be $8 and $12, respectively. Each set will sell for $30.

1. Compute the breakeven point in sales units.
2. Compute the breakeven point in sales dollars.
3. If the selling price is increased to $34 per unit and fixed general and administrative expenses are cut to $37,500, what will the new breakeven point be in units?
4. Prepare a graph to illustrate the breakeven point computed in **3**.

LO 4   **Breakeven Point for Multiple Products**

E8A. Eastside Aquarium, Inc., manufactures and sells aquariums, water pumps, and air filters. The sales mix is 1:2:2 (i.e., for every one aquarium sold, two water pumps and two air filters are sold). Using the contribution margin approach, find the breakeven point in units for each product. The company's fixed costs are $52,000. Other information follows.

	Selling Price per Unit	Variable Costs per Unit
Aquariums	$60	$25
Water pumps	20	12
Air filters	10	3

LO 4   **Breakeven Point for Multiple Products**

E9A. Hamburgers and More, Inc., sells hamburgers, drinks, and fries. The sales mix is 1:3:2 (i.e., for every one hamburger sold, three drinks and two fries are sold). Using the contribution margin approach, find the breakeven point in units for each product. The company's fixed costs are $1,020. Other information follows.

	Selling Price per Unit	Variable Costs per Unit
Hamburgers	$0.99	$0.27
Drinks	0.99	0.09
Fries	0.99	0.15

LO 4   **Sales Mix Analysis**

E10A. Marj Plimpton is the owner of a hairdressing salon in New York City. Her salon provides three basic services: shampoo and set, permanent, and cut and blow dry. Its operating results from the past quarter follow.

Type of Service	Number of Customers	Total Sales	Contribution Margin in Dollars
Shampoo and set	1,200	$24,000	$14,700
Permanent	420	21,000	15,120
Cut and blow dry	1,000	15,000	10,000
	2,620	$60,000	$39,820
Total fixed costs			40,000
Profit (loss)			$ (180)

Compute the breakeven point in units based on the weighted-average contribution margin for the sales mix.

LO 2, 5   **Cost Behavior in a Service Business**

E11A. BUSINESS APPLICATION ▶ Jim Lucky, CPA, is the owner of a firm that provides payroll support services. The firm charges $40 per payroll return for the direct professional labor involved in preparing the payroll and submitting the required tax forms. In January, the firm prepared 50 such returns; in February, 100; and in March, 70. Service overhead (telephone and utilities, depreciation on equipment and building, tax forms, office supplies, and wages of clerical personnel) for January was $2,000; for February, $3,500; and for March, $2,700.

1. Using the high-low method, determine the variable and fixed cost components of the firm's Service Overhead account.
2. What would the estimated total cost per tax return be if the firm prepares 80 payroll forms in April?

LO 4, 5   **CVP Analysis and Profit Planning**

E12A. BUSINESS APPLICATION ▶ Cos Cob Systems, Inc., makes heat-seeking missiles. It has recently been offered a government contract from which it may realize a profit. The contract purchase price is $130,000 per missile, but the number of units to be purchased has not yet been decided. The company's fixed costs are budgeted at $4,035,000, and variable costs are $68,500 per unit.

1. Compute the number of units the company should agree to make at the stated contract price to earn a profit of $1,500,000.
2. Using a lighter material, the variable unit cost can be reduced by $1,730, but total fixed overhead will increase by $29,240. How many units must be produced to make $1,500,000 in profit?
3. Given the figures in **2**, how many additional units must be produced to increase profit by $1,264,600?

LO 4, 5   **Planning Future Sales**

E13A. BUSINESS APPLICATION ▶ Short-term automobile rentals are Snap Rentals, Inc.'s specialty. Average variable operating costs have been $20 per day per automobile. The company owns 50 automobiles. Fixed operating costs for the next year are expected to be $150,000. Average daily rental revenue per automobile is expected to be $40. Management would like to earn a profit of $50,000 during the year.

1. Calculate the total number of daily rentals the company must have during the year to earn the targeted profit.
2. On the basis of your answer to **1**, determine the average number of days each automobile must be rented.
3. Determine the total revenue needed to achieve the targeted profit of $50,000.
4. What would the total rental revenue be if fixed operating costs could be lowered by $5,000 and the targeted profit increased to $70,000?

LO 4, 5   **CVP Analysis in a Service Business**

E14A. BUSINESS APPLICATION ▶ Westport Inspection Service specializes in inspecting cars that have been returned to automobile leasing companies at the end of their leases. Westport's charge for each inspection is $60; its average cost per inspection is $15. The owner wants to expand his business by hiring another employee and purchasing an automobile. The fixed costs of the new employee and automobile would be $3,000 per month. How many inspections per month would the new employee have to perform to earn a profit of $1,500?

LO 3, 4, 5   **CVP and Breakeven Analysis and Pricing**

E15A. Americas Company has a plant capacity of 100,000 units per year, but its budget for this year indicates that only 60,000 units will be produced and sold. The entire budget for this year follows.

Sales (60,000 units at $3.75)		$225,000
Less cost of goods produced (based on production of 60,000 units):		
Direct materials (variable)	$60,000	
Direct labor (variable)	30,000	
Variable overhead costs	45,000	
Fixed overhead costs	75,000	
Total cost of goods produced		210,000
Gross margin		$ 15,000
Less selling and administrative expenses:		
Selling (fixed)	$24,000	
Administrative (fixed)	36,000	
Total selling and administrative expenses		60,000
Operating income (loss)		$(45,000)

1. Given the budgeted selling price and cost data, how many units would Americas have to sell to break even? (*Hint:* Be sure to consider selling and administrative expenses.)
2. **BUSINESS APPLICATION ▶** Market research indicates that if Americas were to drop its selling price to $3.70 per unit, it could sell 100,000 units. Would you recommend the drop in price? What would the new operating income or loss be?

EXERCISES: SET B

Visit the textbook companion website at www.cengagebrain.com to access Exercise Set B for this chapter.

PROBLEMS

LO 1, 2, 5

Cost Behavior and Projection for a Service Business

✔ 2: Fixed cost component of mixed cost: $1,145
✔ 3: Average cost per job: $907.76

P1. Wabash Company specializes in refurbishing exterior painted surfaces that have been hard hit by humidity and insect debris. It uses a special technique, called pressure cleaning, before priming and painting the surface. The refurbishing process involves the following steps:

1. Unskilled laborers trim all trees and bushes within two feet of the structure.
2. Skilled laborers clean the building with a high-pressure cleaning machine, using about 6 gallons of chlorine per job.
3. Unskilled laborers apply a coat of primer.
4. Skilled laborers apply oil-based exterior paint to the entire surface.

On average, skilled laborers work 12 hours per job, and unskilled laborers work 8 hours. The refurbishing process generated the following operating results during the year on 500 jobs:

Skilled labor	$20	per hour
Unskilled labor	$8	per hour
Gallons of chlorine used	3,000	gallons at $5.50 per gallon
Paint primer	7,536	gallons at $15.50 per gallon
Paint	6,280	gallons at $16.00 per gallon
Depreciation of paint-spraying equipment	$600	per month depreciation
Lease of two vans	$800	per month total
Rent on storage building	$421	per month

(Continued)

Data on utilities for the year follow:

Month	Number of Jobs	Cost	Hours Worked
January	42	$ 3,950	840
February	37	3,550	740
March	44	4,090	880
April	49	4,410	980
May	54	4,720	1,080
June	62	5,240	1,240
July	71	5,820	1,420
August	73	5,890	1,460
September	63	5,370	1,260
October	48	4,340	960
November	45	4,210	900
December	40	3,830	800
Totals	628	$55,420	12,560

REQUIRED

1. Classify the costs as variable, fixed, or mixed.
2. Using the high-low method, separate mixed costs into their variable and fixed components. Use total hours worked as the basis.
3. Compute the average cost per job for the year. (*Hint:* Divide the total of all costs for the year by the number of jobs completed.) Use estimated hours to determine utilities costs. (Round to two decimal places.)
4. **BUSINESS APPLICATION** ▶ Project the average cost per job for next year if variable costs per job increase 20 percent. (Round to two decimal places.)
5. **ACCOUNTING CONNECTION** ▶ Why can actual utilities costs vary from the amount computed using the utilities cost formula?

LO **4, 5**   **Breakeven Analysis**

✔ 1: Breakeven hours: 7,500 hours

P2. Park & Morgan, a law firm, is considering opening a legal clinic for middle- and low-income clients. The clinic would bill at a rate of $18 per hour. It would employ law students as paraprofessional help and pay them $9 per hour. Other variable costs are anticipated to be $5.40 per hour, and annual fixed costs are expected to total $27,000.

REQUIRED

1. Compute the breakeven point in billable hours.
2. Compute the breakeven point in total billings.
3. **BUSINESS APPLICATION** ▶ Find the new breakeven point in total billings if fixed costs should go up by $2,340.
4. **BUSINESS APPLICATION** ▶ Using the original figures, compute the breakeven point in total billings if the billing rate decreases by $1 per hour, other variable costs decrease by $0.40 per hour, and fixed costs go down by $3,600.

LO **3, 4, 5**   **Planning Future Sales: Contribution Margin Approach**

✔ 1a: Breakeven units: 3,500 units
✔ 3: Selling price: $51

P3. BUSINESS APPLICATION ▶ All Honors Industries is considering a new product for its Trophy Division. The product, which would feature an alligator, is expected to have global market appeal and to become the mascot for many high school and university athletic teams. Expected variable unit costs are as follows: direct materials, $18.50; direct labor, $4.25; production supplies, $1.10; selling costs, $2.80; and other, $1.95. Annual fixed costs are depreciation, building, and equipment, $36,000; advertising, $45,000; and other, $11,400. Plans are to sell the product for $55.

REQUIRED

1. Using the contribution margin approach, compute the number of units the company must sell to (a) break even and (b) earn a profit of $70,224.
2. Using the same data, compute the number of units that must be sold to earn a profit of $139,520 if advertising costs rise by $40,000.
3. Using the original information and sales of 10,000 units, compute the selling price the company must use to make a profit of $131,600. (*Hint:* Calculate contribution margin per unit first.)
4. According to the vice president of marketing, Flora Albert, the most optimistic annual sales estimate for the product would be 15,000 units, and the highest competitive selling price the company can charge is $52 per unit. How much more can be spent on fixed advertising costs if the selling price is $52, the variable costs cannot be reduced, and the targeted profit for 15,000 unit sales is $251,000?

LO **4, 5**

✔ 1a: Breakeven units: 150,000 units
✔ 2: 190,000 units

Breakeven Analysis and Planning Future Sales

P4. Marina Company has a maximum capacity of 200,000 units per year. Variable manufacturing costs are $12 per unit. Fixed overhead is $600,000 per year. Variable selling and administrative costs are $5 per unit, and fixed selling and administrative costs are $300,000 per year. The current sales price is $23 per unit.

REQUIRED

1. What is the breakeven point in (a) sales units and (b) sales dollars?
2. **BUSINESS APPLICATION** ▶ How many units must Marina Company sell to earn a profit of $240,000 per year?
3. **BUSINESS APPLICATION** ▶ A strike at one of the company's major suppliers has caused a shortage of materials, so the current year's production and sales are limited to 160,000 units. To partially offset the effect of the reduced sales on profit, management is planning to reduce fixed costs to $841,000. Variable costs per unit are the same as last year. The company has already sold 30,000 units at the regular selling price of $23 per unit.
   a. What amount of fixed costs was covered by the total contribution margin of the first 30,000 units sold?
   b. What contribution margin per unit will be needed on the remaining 130,000 units to cover the remaining fixed costs and to earn a profit of $210,000 this year?

LO **3, 4, 5**

✔ 1a: 262 loans
✔ 3: Loan application fee: $255

Planning Future Sales for a Service Business

P5. BUSINESS APPLICATION ▶ State Street Lending processes loan applications. The manager of the loan department has established a policy of charging a $250 fee for every loan application processed. Variable costs have been projected as follows: loan consultant's wages, $15.50 per hour (a loan application takes 5 hours to process); supplies, $2.40 per application; and other variable costs, $5.60 per application. Annual fixed costs include depreciation of equipment, $8,500; building rental, $14,000; promotional costs, $12,500; and other fixed costs, $8,099.

REQUIRED

1. Using the contribution margin approach, compute the number of loan applications the company must process to (a) break even and (b) earn a profit of $14,476.
2. Using the same approach and assuming promotional costs increase by $5,662, compute the number of applications the company must process to earn a profit of $20,000.
3. Assuming the original information and the processing of 500 applications, compute the loan application fee the company must charge if the targeted profit is $41,651.
4. The maximum number of loan applications that the department can process is 750. How much more can be spent on promotional costs if the highest fee tolerable to the customer is $280, if variable costs cannot be reduced, and if the targeted profit is $50,000?

ALTERNATE PROBLEMS

LO **1, 2, 5**

Mixed Costs

✔ 1: Total fixed cost: $2,250
✔ 3: Total repairs and maintenance
              cost: $99,824

P6. Officials of the Oakbrook Hills Golf and Tennis Club are in the process of preparing a budget for the year ending December 31. Because the club treasurer has had difficulty with two expense items, the process has been delayed. The two items are mixed costs—expenses for electricity and for repairs and maintenance—and the treasurer has been having trouble breaking them down into their variable and fixed components.

An accountant friend has suggested that he use the high-low method to divide the costs into their variable and fixed parts. The spending patterns and activity measures related to each cost during the past year are as follows:

Month	Electricity Expense		Repairs and Maintenance	
	Amount	Kilowatt-Hours	Amount	Labor Hours
January	$ 7,500	210,000	$ 7,578	220
February	8,255	240,200	7,852	230
March	8,165	236,600	7,304	210
April	8,960	268,400	7,030	200
May	7,520	210,800	7,852	230
June	7,025	191,000	8,126	240
July	6,970	188,800	8,400	250
August	6,990	189,600	8,674	260
September	7,055	192,200	8,948	270
October	7,135	195,400	8,674	260
November	8,560	252,400	8,126	240
December	8,415	246,600	7,852	230
Totals	$92,550	2,622,000	$96,416	2,840

REQUIRED

1. Using the high-low method, compute the variable cost rates used last year for each expense. What was the monthly fixed cost for electricity and for repairs and maintenance? (Round variable cost rate answers to three decimal places.)
2. Compute the total variable cost and total fixed cost for each expense category for last year.
3. **BUSINESS APPLICATION ▶** The treasurer believes that in the coming year, the electricity rate will increase by $0.005 and the repairs rate, by $1.20. Usage of all items and their fixed cost amounts will remain constant. Compute the projected total cost for each category. How will the cost increases affect the club's profits and cash flow?

LO **4, 5**

Breakeven Analysis

✔ 1: Breakeven units: 740 systems
✔ 4: Breakeven units: 790 systems

P7. At the beginning of each year, LED Lighting, Ltd.'s Accounting Department must find the point at which projected sales revenue will equal total budgeted variable and fixed costs. The company produces low-voltage outdoor lighting systems. Each system sells for an average of $435. Variable costs per unit are $210. Total fixed costs for the year are estimated to be $166,500.

REQUIRED

1. Compute the breakeven point in sales units.
2. Compute the breakeven point in sales dollars.
3. **BUSINESS APPLICATION ▶** Find the new breakeven point in sales units if the fixed costs go up by $10,125.
4. **BUSINESS APPLICATION ▶** Using the original figures, compute the breakeven point in sales units if the selling price decreases to $425 per unit, fixed costs go up by $15,200, and variable costs decrease by $15 per unit.

LO **3, 4, 5**

✔ 1a: Breakeven units: 7,900 statues
✔ 2: Target sales units: 16,900 statues

Planning Future Sales: Contribution Margin Approach

P8. BUSINESS APPLICATION ▶ Lipsius Marbles manufactures birdbaths, statues, and other decorative items, which it sells to florists and retail home and garden centers. Its design department has proposed a new product, a frog statue, that it believes will be popular with home gardeners. Expected variable unit costs are direct materials, $9.25; direct labor, $4.00; production supplies, $0.55; selling costs, $2.40; and other, $3.05. The following are fixed costs: depreciation, $33,000; advertising, $40,000; and other, $6,000. Management plans to sell the product for $29.25.

REQUIRED

1. Using the contribution margin approach, compute the number of statues the company must sell to (a) break even and (b) earn a profit of $50,000.
2. Using the same data, compute the number of statues that must be sold to earn a profit of $70,000 if advertising costs rise by $20,000.
3. Using the original data and sales of 15,000 units, compute the selling price the company must charge to make a profit of $101,000.
4. According to the vice president of marketing, if the price of the statues is reduced and advertising is increased, the most optimistic annual sales estimate is 25,000 units. How much more can be spent on fixed advertising costs if the selling price is reduced to $28.00 per statue, the variable costs cannot be reduced, and the targeted profit for sales of 25,000 statues is $120,000?

LO **4, 5**

✔ 1a: Breakeven units: 200,000 units
✔ 2: Sales units: 300,000 units

Breakeven Analysis and Planning Future Sales

P9. Bar Company has a maximum capacity of 500,000 units per year. Variable manufacturing costs are $25 per unit. Fixed overhead is $900,000 per year. Variable selling and administrative costs are $5 per unit, and fixed selling and administrative costs are $300,000 per year. The current sales price is $36 per unit.

REQUIRED

1. What is the breakeven point in (a) sales units and (b) sales dollars?
2. **BUSINESS APPLICATION** ▶ How many units must Bar Company sell to earn a profit of $600,000 per year?
3. **BUSINESS APPLICATION** ▶ A strike at one of the company's major suppliers has caused a shortage of materials, so the current year's production and sales are limited to 400,000 units. To partially offset the effect of the reduced sales on profit, management is planning to reduce fixed costs to $1,000,000. Variable cost per unit is the same as last year. The company has already sold 30,000 units at the regular selling price of $36 per unit.
   a. What amount of fixed costs was covered by the total contribution margin of the first 30,000 units sold?
   b. What contribution margin per unit will be needed on the remaining 370,000 units to cover the remaining fixed costs and to earn a profit of $290,000 this year?

LO **3, 4, 5**

✔ 1a: Breakeven units: 270 loans
✔ 3: Loan application fee: $403

Planning Future Sales for a Service Business

P10. BUSINESS APPLICATION ▶ Last Mortgage, Inc.'s primary business is processing mortgage loan applications. Last year, the manager of the mortgage application department established a policy of charging a $500 fee for every loan application processed. Next year's variable costs have been projected as follows: mortgage processor wages, $30 per hour (a mortgage application takes 3 hours to process); supplies, $10 per application; and other variable costs, $15 per application. Annual fixed costs include depreciation of equipment, $4,950; building rental, $34,000; promotional costs, $45,000; and other fixed costs, $20,000.

(Continued)

REQUIRED

1. Using the contribution margin approach, compute the number of loan applications the company must process to (a) break even and (b) earn a profit of $50,050.
2. Using the same approach and assuming promotional costs increase by $5,450, compute the number of applications the company must process to earn a profit of $60,000.
3. Assuming the original information and the processing of 500 applications, compute the loan application fee the company must charge if the targeted profit is $40,050.
4. The mortgage department can handle a maximum of 750 loan applications. How much more can be spent on promotional costs if the highest fee tolerable to the customer is $400, if variable costs cannot be reduced, and if the targeted profit for the loan applications is $50,000?

CASES

LO 4   ### Ethical Dilemma: Breaking Even and Ethics

C1. Les Pulaski is the supervisor of a new division of Innovation Corporation. Her annual bonus is based on the success of new products and is computed on the number of sales that exceed each new product's projected breakeven point. In reviewing the computations supporting her most recent bonus, Pulaski found that although an order for 7,500 units of a new product called R56 had been refused by a customer and returned to the company, the order had been included in the bonus calculations. She later discovered that the company's accountant had labeled the return an overhead expense and had charged the entire cost of the returned order to the plantwide Overhead account. The result was that product R56 appeared to exceed breakeven by more than 5,000 units and Pulaski's bonus from this product amounted to over $1,000. What actions should Pulaski take? Be prepared to discuss your response in class.

LO 1, 4   ### Group Activity: Cost Behavior and Contribution Margin

C2. Visit a local fast-food restaurant. Observe all aspects of the operation and take notes on the entire process. Describe the procedures used to take, process, and fill an order and deliver the order to the customer. Based on your observations, make a list of the costs incurred by the operation. Identify at least three variable costs and three fixed costs. Can you identify any potential mixed costs? Why is the restaurant willing to sell a large drink for only a few cents more than a medium drink? How is the restaurant able to offer a "value meal" (e.g., sandwich, drink, and fries) for considerably less than those items would cost if they were bought separately? Bring your notes to class and be prepared to discuss your findings.

Your instructor will divide the class into groups to discuss the case. Summarize your group's discussion, and ask one member of the group to present the summary to the rest of the class.

LO 3, 4   ### Conceptual Understanding: CVP Analysis

C3. Based in Italy, Datura, Ltd., is an international importer-exporter of pottery with distribution centers in the United States, Europe, and Australia. The company was very successful in its early years, but its profitability has since declined. As a member of a management team selected to gather information for Datura's next strategic planning meeting, you have been asked to review its most recent contribution margin income statement for the year ended December 31, 2014, which follows.

Datura, Ltd.
Contribution Margin Income Statement
For the Year Ended December 31, 2014

Sales revenue		€13,500,000
Less variable costs:		
Purchases	€6,000,000	
Distribution	2,115,000	
Sales commissions	1,410,000	
Total variable costs		9,525,000
Contribution margin		€ 3,975,000
Less fixed costs:		
Distribution	€ 985,000	
Selling	1,184,000	
General and administrative	871,875	
Total fixed costs		3,040,875
Operating income		€ 934,125

In 2014, Datura sold 15,000 sets of pottery.

1. For each set of pottery sold in 2014, calculate the (a) selling price, (b) variable purchases cost, (c) variable distribution cost, (d) variable sales commission, and (e) contribution margin.
2. Calculate the breakeven point in units and in sales euros.
3. Historically, Datura's variable costs have been about 60 percent of sales. What was the ratio of variable costs to sales in 2014? (Round to two decimal places.) List three actions Datura could take to correct the difference.
4. How would fixed costs have been affected if Datura had sold only 14,000 sets of pottery in 2014?

LO 5 **Business Communications: CVP Analysis Applied**

C4. Refer to the information in C3. In January 2015, the president of Datura, Ltd., conducted a strategic planning meeting. During the meeting, the vice president of distribution noted that because of a new contract with an international shipping line, the company's fixed distribution costs for 2015 would be reduced by 10 percent and its variable distribution costs by 4 percent. The vice president of sales offered the following information:

We plan to sell 15,000 sets of pottery again in 2015, but based on review of the competition, we are going to lower the selling price to €890 per set. To encourage increased sales, we will raise sales commissions to 12 percent of the selling price.

The president is concerned that the changes described by the vice presidents may not improve operating income sufficiently in 2015. If operating income does not increase by at least 10 percent, she will want to find other ways to reduce the company's costs. She asks you to evaluate the situation in a written report. Because it is already January 2015 and changes need to be made quickly, she requests your report within five days.

1. Prepare a budgeted contribution margin income statement for 2015. Your report should show the budgeted (estimated) operating income based on the information provided above and in **C3**. Will the changes improve operating income sufficiently? Explain.
2. In preparation for writing your report, answer the following questions:
   a. Why are you preparing the report?
   b. Who needs the report?
   c. What sources of information will you use?
   d. When is the report due?

LO **5**

SPREADSHEET

Decision Analysis: Planning Future Sales

C5. As noted in **C3** and **C4**, Datura, Ltd., sold 15,000 sets of pottery in 2014. For the next year, 2015, Datura's strategic planning team targeted sales of 15,000 sets of pottery, reduced the selling price to €890 per set, increased sales commissions to 12 percent of the selling price, and decreased fixed distribution costs by 10 percent and variable distribution costs by 4 percent. It was assumed that all other costs would stay the same.

Based on an analysis of these changes, Datura's president is concerned that the proposed strategic plan will not meet her goal of increasing Datura's operating income by 10 percent over last year's income and that the operating income will be less than last year's income. She has come to you for spreadsheet analysis of the proposed strategic plan and for analysis of a special order she just received from an Australian distributor for 4,500 sets of pottery. The order's selling price, variable purchases cost per unit, sales commission, and total fixed costs will be the same as for the rest of the business, but the variable distribution costs will be €160 per unit.

Using a spreadsheet, complete the following tasks:

1. Calculate the targeted operating income for 2015 using just the proposed strategic plan. (Round to the nearest whole number.)
2. Prepare a budgeted contribution margin income statement for 2015 based on just the strategic plan. Do you agree with Datura's president that the company's projected operating income for 2015 will be less than the operating income for 2014? Explain your answer.
3. Calculate the total contribution margin from the Australian sales.
4. Prepare a revised budgeted contribution margin income statement for 2015 that includes the Australian order. (*Hint:* Combine the information from **2** and **3** above.)
5. Does Datura need the Australian sales to achieve its targeted operating income for 2015?

RATIO

Continuing Case: Cookie Company

C6. In this segment of our continuing cookie company case, you will classify the costs of the business as variable, fixed, or mixed; use the high-low method to evaluate utility costs; and prepare a contribution margin income statement.

1. Review your cookie recipe and the overhead costs you identified in previous chapters, and classify the costs as variable, fixed, or mixed costs.
2. Obtain your electric bills for three months, and use the high-low method's cost formula to determine the monthly cost of electricity—that is, monthly electric cost = variable rate per kilowatt-hour + monthly fixed cost. If you do not receive an electric bill, use the following information:

Month	Kilowatt-Hours Used	Electric Costs
August	1,439	$202
September	1,866	230
October	1,146	158

3. a. Prepare a daily contribution margin income statement based on the following assumptions:

My Cookie Company makes only one kind of cookie and sells it for $1.00 per unit. The company projects sales of 500 units per day. Projected daily costs are as follows:

Type of Cost	Manufacturing	Nonmanufacturing
Variable	$100	$50
Nonvariable	120	60

b. What is the contribution margin ratio?
c. What volume, in terms of units, must the company sell to break even each day? (Round to the nearest dollar.)

CHAPTER 6
The Budgeting Process

Framerica Corporation is one of the leading manufacturers of picture frames in North America. Because the company believes its work force is its most valuable asset, one of its priorities is to help employees attain their personal goals. One highly effective way of achieving congruence between a company's goals and its employees' personal aspirations is through a participatory budgeting process—an ongoing dialogue that involves personnel at all levels of the company in making budgeting decisions. This ongoing dialogue provides both managers and lower-level employees with insight into the company's current activities and future direction and motivates them to improve their performance, which, in turn, improves the company's performance.

1. CONCEPT ▶ *What concepts underlie the usefulness of the budgeting process?*

2. ACCOUNTING APPLICATION ▶ *How does the budgeting process translate long-term goals into operating objectives?*

3. BUSINESS APPLICATION ▶ *Why are budgets an essential part of planning, controlling, evaluating, and reporting on business?*

LEARNING OBJECTIVES

 LO 1 Define *budgeting* and describe how it relates to the concepts of comparability and understandability.

 LO 2 Identify the elements of a master budget in different types of organizations and the guidelines for preparing budgets.

LO 3 Prepare the operating budgets that support the financial budgets.

 LO 4 Prepare a budgeted income statement, a cash budget, and a budgeted balance sheet.

LO 5 Explain why budgeting is essential to the management process.

SECTION 1

CONCEPTS

CONCEPTS
■ Comparability
■ Understandability

RELEVANT LEARNING OBJECTIVE

LO 1 Define *budgeting* and describe how it relates to the concepts of comparability and understandability.

LO 1 Concepts Underlying the Budgeting Process

Budgeting is the process of identifying, gathering, summarizing, and communicating financial and nonfinancial information about an organization's future activities. The budgeting process provides managers of all types of organizations the opportunity to match their organizational goals with the resources necessary to accomplish those goals. Budgeting empowers all in the organization to understand organizational goals in terms of their responsibilities and be held accountable for budget plans and results since they can be compared. Budgeting is synonymous with managing an organization. **Budgets** are plans of action based on forecasted transactions, activities, and events.

The concepts of *understandability* and *comparability* underlie the power of budgeting. Budgeting enhances *understandability*, since managers and employees will understand their organizational roles and responsibilities based on how the budget links the organization's strategic plans to its annual plans. Because the budget expresses these plans and objectives in concrete monetary terms, managers and employees are able to understand and act in ways that will achieve them. Budgeting enhances *comparability*, since budget-to-actual comparisons give managers and employees a means of monitoring the results of their actions. As you will see in this chapter, budgeting is not only an essential part of planning; it also helps managers command, control, evaluate, and report on operations.

The Master Budget

A **master budget** consists of a set of operating budgets and a set of financial budgets that detail an organization's financial plans for a specific period, generally a year. When a master budget covers an entire year, some of the operating and financial budgets may show planned results by month or by quarter. As the term implies, **operating budgets** are plans used in daily operations.

Operating budgets include:

■ sales budget
■ production budget
■ direct materials purchases budget
■ direct labor budget
■ overhead budget
■ selling and administrative expenses budget
■ cost of goods manufactured budget

The sales budget is prepared first because it is used to estimate sales volume and revenues. Once managers know the quantity of products or services to be sold and how many sales dollars to expect, they can develop other budgets that will enable them to manage their resources so that they generate profits on those sales.

Operating budgets are also the basis for preparing the **financial budgets**, which are projections of financial results for the period.

Financial budgets include:

■ a budgeted income statement
■ a capital expenditures budget
■ a cash budget
■ a budgeted balance sheet

The budgeted income statement and budgeted balance sheet are also called **pro forma financial statements**, meaning that they show projections rather than actual results. Pro forma financial statements are often used to communicate business plans to external parties. For example, if you apply for a bank loan to start a new business, you would have to present a pro forma income statement and balance sheet showing that you could repay the loan with cash generated by profitable operations.

APPLY IT!

A master budget is a compilation of forecasts for the coming year or operating cycle made by various departments or functions within an organization. What is the most important forecast made in a master budget? List the reasons for your answer.

a. Direct materials purchases in units

b. Sales in units

c. Cash outflows

d. Selling expenses

SOLUTION

b. The amount of estimated sales in units is the most important forecast. It is the key to an accurate master budget. The entire master budget is based on the unit sales forecast.

TRY IT! SE1

SECTION 2 | ACCOUNTING APPLICATIONS

ACCOUNTING APPLICATIONS
- Prepare operating budgets
  - Sales budget
  - Production budget
  - Direct materials purchases budget
  - Direct labor budget
  - Overhead budget
  - Selling and administrative expenses budget
  - Cost of goods manufactured budget
- Prepare financial budgets
  - Budgeted income statement
  - Cash budget
  - Budgeted balance sheet

RELEVANT LEARNING OBJECTIVES

LO 2 Identify the elements of a master budget in different types of organizations and the guidelines for preparing budgets.

LO 3 Prepare the operating budgets that support the financial budgets.

LO 4 Prepare a budgeted income statement, a cash budget, and a budgeted balance sheet.

LO 2 Preparation of a Master Budget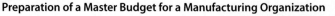

Exhibits 1, 2, and 3 display the elements of a master budget for a manufacturing organization, a retail organization, and a service organization, respectively. As these illustrations indicate, the process of preparing a master budget is similar in all three types of organizations in that each prepares a set of operating budgets that serve as the basis for preparing the financial budgets. The sales budget (or, in service organizations, the service revenue budget) is prepared first because it is used to estimate sales volume and revenues. Once managers know the quantity of products or services to be sold and how many sales dollars to expect, they can develop other budgets that will enable them to manage their resources so that they generate profits on those sales.

Exhibit 1
Preparation of a Master Budget for a Manufacturing Organization

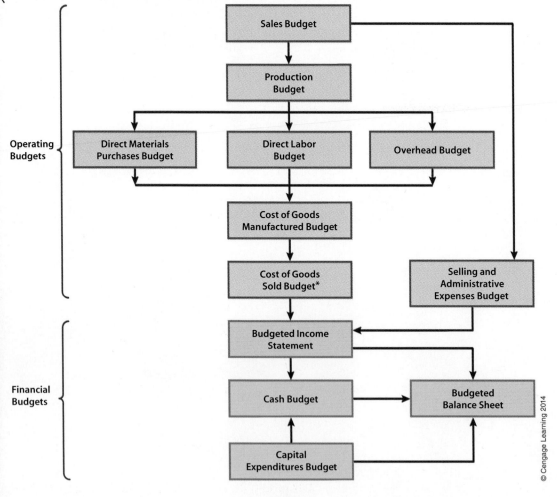

© Cengage Learning 2014

*Some organizations choose to include the cost of goods sold budget in the budgeted income statement.

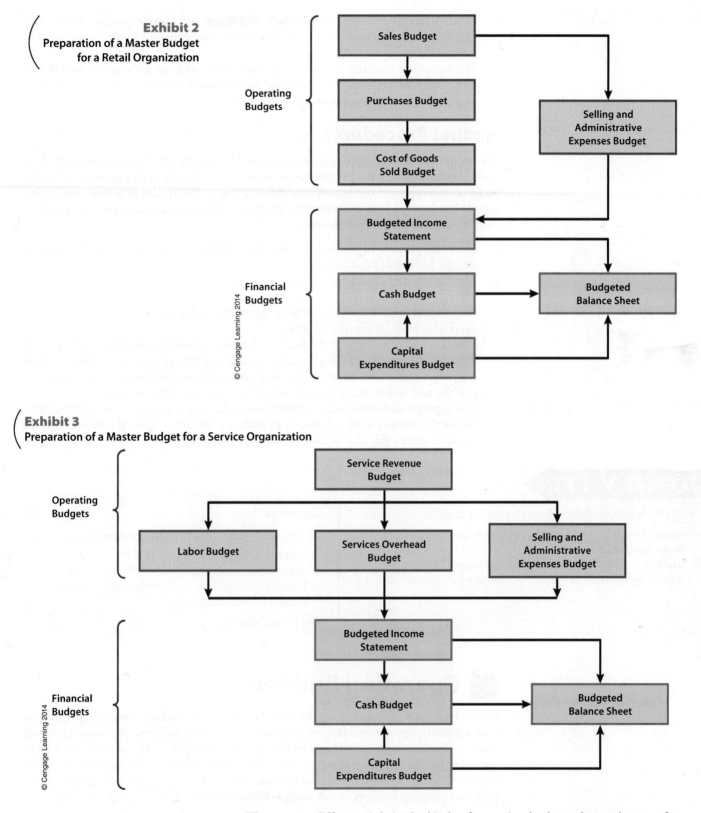

Exhibit 2
Preparation of a Master Budget for a Retail Organization

Exhibit 3
Preparation of a Master Budget for a Service Organization

© Cengage Learning 2014

The process differs mainly in the kinds of operating budgets that each type of organization prepares.

■ The operating budgets of manufacturing organizations, such as **Framerica**, **GM**, and **Harley-Davidson**, include budgets for sales, production, direct materials, direct labor, overhead, selling and administrative expenses, and cost of goods manufactured.

- Retail organizations, such as **Michaels**, **Old Navy**, and **Lowe's**, prepare a sales budget, a purchases budget, a selling and administrative expenses budget, and a cost of goods sold budget.
- The operating budgets of service organizations, such as **Enterprise Rent-A-Car**, **UPS**, and **Amtrak**, include budgets for service revenue (sales), labor, services overhead, and selling and administrative expenses.

Budget Procedures

Because procedures for preparing budgets vary from organization to organization, there is no standard format for budget preparation. The only universal requirement is that budgets communicate the appropriate information to the reader in a clear and understandable manner. Using the following guidelines, managers can improve the quality of budgets in any type of organization:

- Know the purpose of the budget, and clearly identify who is responsible for carrying out the activities in the budget.
- Identify the user group and its information needs.
- Identify sources of accurate, meaningful budget information. Such information may be gathered from documents or from interviews with employees, suppliers, or managers who work in the related areas.
- Establish a clear format for the budget. A budget should begin with a clearly stated heading that includes the organization's name, the type of budget, and the accounting period under consideration. The budget's components should be clearly labeled, and the unit and financial data should be listed in an orderly manner.
- Use appropriate formulas and calculations in deriving the quantitative information.
- Revise the budget until it includes all planning decisions. Several revisions may be required before the final version is ready for distribution.

APPLY IT!

Identify the order in which the following budgets are prepared:

- overhead budget
- production budget
- direct labor budget
- direct materials purchases budget
- sales budget
- budgeted balance sheet
- cash budget
- budgeted income statement

SOLUTION

1. sales budget
2. production budget
3. direct materials purchases budget, direct labor budget, and overhead budget
4. budgeted income statement
5. cash budget
6. budgeted balance sheet

TRY IT! SE1, E1A, E1B

LO3 Operating Budgets

We use Framecraft Company, a hypothetical picture frame making company, to illustrate how a manufacturing organization prepares its operating budgets. Because Framecraft makes only one product—a plastic picture frame—it prepares only one of each type of operating budget as it plans for daily operations in the coming year. Organizations that manufacture a variety of products or provide many types of services may prepare either separate operating budgets or one comprehensive budget for each product or service.

The Sales Budget

The first step in preparing a master budget is to prepare a sales budget. A **sales budget** shows expected sales during a period, expressed in both units and dollars. Sales managers use this information to plan sales- and marketing-related activities and to determine their human, physical, and technical resource needs. Accountants use the information to determine estimated cash receipts for the cash budget.

The following equation is used to determine the total budgeted sales:

Total Budgeted Sales = Estimated Selling Price per Unit × Estimated Sales in Units

Although the calculation is easy, selecting the best estimates for the selling price per unit and the sales demand in units can be difficult. An estimated selling price below the current selling price may be needed if competitors are currently selling the same product or service at lower prices or if the organization wants to increase its share of the market. On the other hand, if the organization has improved the quality of its product or service by using more expensive materials or processes, the estimated selling price may have to be higher than the current price.

The estimated sales volume is very important because it will affect the level of operating activities and the amount of resources needed for operations. To help estimate sales volume, managers often use a **sales forecast**, which is a projection of the estimated sales in units, based on an analysis of external and internal factors.

External factors include:

- the state of the local and national economies
- the state of the industry's economy
- the nature of the competition and its sales volume and selling price

Internal factors include:

- the number of units sold in prior periods
- the organization's credit policies
- the organization's collection policies
- the organization's pricing policies
- any new products that the organization plans to introduce to the market
- the capacity of the organization's manufacturing facilities

Exhibit 4 shows Framecraft's sales budget for the year. The budget shows the estimated number of unit sales and dollar revenue amounts for each quarter and for the entire year. Because the sales forecast indicated a highly competitive marketplace, Framecraft's managers have estimated a selling price of $5 per unit. The sales forecast also indicated highly seasonal sales activity. The estimated sales volume therefore varies from 10,000 to 40,000 per quarter.

Exhibit 4
Sales Budget

Framecraft Company
Sales Budget
For the Year Ended December 31

	Quarter				
	1	2	3	4	Year
Sales in units	10,000	30,000	10,000	40,000	90,000
Selling price per unit	× $5	× $5	× $5	× $5	× $5
Total sales	$50,000	$150,000	$50,000	$200,000	$450,000

© Cengage Learning 2014

The Production Budget

A **production budget** shows the number of units that a company must produce to meet budgeted sales and inventory needs. Production managers use this information to plan for the materials and human resources that production-related activities will require. To prepare a production budget, managers must know the budgeted number of unit sales (which is specified in the sales budget) and the desired level of ending finished goods inventory for each period in the budget year. That level is often stated as a percentage of the next period's budgeted unit sales.

For example, Framecraft's desired level of ending finished goods inventory is 10 percent of the next quarter's budgeted unit sales. (Its desired level of beginning finished goods inventory is 10 percent of the current quarter's budgeted unit sales.)

The following formula identifies the production needs for each period:

$$
\begin{array}{c}
\text{Total Production} \\
\text{Units}
\end{array}
=
\begin{array}{c}
\text{Budgeted Sales in} \\
\text{Units}
\end{array}
+
\begin{array}{c}
\text{Desired Units of} \\
\text{Ending Finished} \\
\text{Goods Inventory}
\end{array}
-
\begin{array}{c}
\text{Desired Units of} \\
\text{Beginning Finished} \\
\text{Goods Inventory}
\end{array}
$$

Exhibit 5 shows Framecraft's production budget for the year. Notice that each quarter's desired total units of ending finished goods inventory become the next quarter's desired total units of beginning finished goods inventory.

Exhibit 5
Production Budget

Framecraft Company Production Budget (Units) For the Year Ended December 31					
	Quarter				
	1	**2**	**3**	**4**	**Year**
Sales in units	10,000	30,000	10,000	40,000	90,000
Plus desired units of ending finished goods inventory	3,000	1,000	4,000	1,500	1,500
Desired total units	13,000	31,000	14,000	41,500	91,500
Less desired units of beginning finished goods inventory	1,000	3,000	1,000	4,000	1,000
Total production units	12,000	28,000	13,000	37,500	90,500

© Cengage Learning 2014

Because unit sales of 15,000 are budgeted for the first quarter of next year, the ending finished goods inventory for the fourth quarter of the year is 1,500 units (0.10 × 15,000 units), which is the same as the desired number of units of ending finished goods inventory for the entire year.

The Direct Materials Purchases Budget

A **direct materials purchases budget** identifies the quantity of purchases required to meet budgeted production and inventory needs and the costs associated with those purchases. A purchasing department uses this information to plan purchases of direct materials. Accountants use the same information to estimate cash payments to suppliers.

To prepare a direct materials purchases budget, managers must know what production needs will be in each period. This information is provided by the production budget. They must also know the desired level of the direct materials inventory for each period and the per-unit cost of direct materials. The desired level of ending direct materials inventory is usually stated as a percentage of the next period's production needs.

For example, Framecraft's desired level of ending direct materials inventory is 20 percent of the next quarter's budgeted production needs. (Its desired level of beginning direct materials inventory is 20 percent of the current quarter's budgeted production needs.)

The following steps are involved in preparing a direct materials purchases budget:

- **Step 1.** Calculate each period's total production needs in units of direct materials using the following formula:

$$\begin{matrix} \text{Total Production Needs} \\ \text{in Units of Direct} \\ \text{Materials} \end{matrix} = \begin{matrix} \text{Total Production} \\ \text{Units} \end{matrix} \times \begin{matrix} \text{Required Amount of} \\ \text{Direct Materials per} \\ \text{Unit} \end{matrix}$$

  Plastic is the only direct material used in Framecraft's picture frames. Framecraft's managers calculate units of production needs in ounces by multiplying the number of frames budgeted for production by the 10 ounces of plastic that each frame requires.

- **Step 2.** Determine the quantity of direct materials to be purchased during each accounting period in the budget using the following formula:

$$\begin{matrix} \text{Total Units} \\ \text{of Direct} \\ \text{Materials to} \\ \text{Be Purchased} \end{matrix} = \begin{matrix} \text{Total Production} \\ \text{Needs in} \\ \text{Units of Direct} \\ \text{Materials} \end{matrix} + \begin{matrix} \text{Desired Units} \\ \text{of Ending} \\ \text{Direct Materials} \\ \text{Inventory} \end{matrix} - \begin{matrix} \text{Desired Units} \\ \text{of Beginning} \\ \text{Direct Materials} \\ \text{Inventory} \end{matrix}$$

  As shown in Exhibit 6, Framecraft's total ounces of direct materials to be purchased in the first quarter are 152,000 ounces and for the year are 911,000 ounces.

- **Step 3.** Calculate the cost of the direct materials purchases using the following formula:

$$\begin{matrix} \text{Cost of Direct} \\ \text{Materials Purchased} \end{matrix} = \begin{matrix} \text{Total Units to} \\ \text{Be Purchased} \end{matrix} \times \begin{matrix} \text{Direct Materials Cost} \\ \text{per Unit} \end{matrix}$$

  Framecraft's Purchasing Department has estimated the cost of the plastic used in the picture frames at $0.05 per ounce.

Exhibit 6 shows Framecraft's direct materials purchases budget for the year. Notice that each quarter's desired units of ending direct materials inventory become the next quarter's desired units of beginning direct materials inventory.

Exhibit 6
Direct Materials Purchases Budget

Framecraft Company
Direct Materials Purchases Budget
For the Year Ended December 31

	Quarter				
	1	2	3	4	Year
Total production units	12,000	28,000	13,000	37,500	90,500
Ounces per unit	× 10	× 10	× 10	× 10	× 10
Total production needs in ounces	120,000	280,000	130,000	375,000	905,000
Plus desired ounces of ending direct materials inventory	56,000	26,000	75,000	30,000	30,000
	176,000	306,000	205,000	405,000	935,000
Less desired ounces of beginning direct materials inventory	24,000	56,000	26,000	75,000	24,000
Total ounces of direct materials to be purchased	152,000	250,000	179,000	330,000	911,000
Cost per ounce	× $0.05	× $0.05	× $0.05	× $0.05	× $0.05
Total cost of direct materials purchases	$ 7,600	$12,500	$ 8,950	$16,500	$ 45,550

© Cengage Learning 2014

Framecraft's budgeted number of units for the first quarter of the following year is 150,000 ounces; its ending direct materials inventory for the fourth quarter of this year is therefore 30,000 ounces (0.20 × 150,000 ounces), which is the same as the number of desired units of ending direct materials inventory for the entire year.

The Direct Labor Budget

A **direct labor budget** shows the direct labor hours needed during a period and the associated costs. Production managers use estimated direct labor hours to plan how many employees will be required during the period and the hours that each will work. Accountants use estimated direct labor costs to plan for cash payments to the workers. Managers of human resources use the direct labor budget in deciding whether to hire new employees or reduce the existing work force. The direct labor budget also serves as a guide in assessing employee training needs and preparing schedules of employee benefits.

The following two steps are used to prepare a direct labor budget:

■ **Step 1.** Estimate the total direct labor hours using the following formula:

$$\text{Total Direct Labor Hours} = \text{Estimated Direct Labor Hours per Unit} \times \text{Total Production Units}$$

Framecraft's Production Department needs an estimated one-tenth (0.10) of a direct labor hour to complete one unit.

■ **Step 2.** Calculate the total budgeted direct labor cost using the following formula:

$$\text{Total Budgeted Direct Labor Costs} = \text{Total Direct Labor Hours} \times \text{Estimated Direct Labor Cost per Hour}$$

A company's human resources department provides an estimate of the hourly labor wage. Framecraft's Human Resources Department estimates a direct labor cost of $6 per hour.

Exhibit 7 shows how Framecraft uses these data and formulas to estimate the total direct labor cost.

Exhibit 7
Direct Labor Budget

Framecraft Company					
Direct Labor Budget					
For the Year Ended December 31					
	Quarter				
	1	**2**	**3**	**4**	**Year**
Total production units	12,000	28,000	13,000	37,500	90,500
Direct labor hours per unit	× 0.10	× 0.10	× 0.10	× 0.10	× 0.10
Total direct labor hours	1,200	2,800	1,300	3,750	9,050
Direct labor cost per hour	× $6	× $6	× $6	× $6	× $6
Total direct labor cost	$7,200	$16,800	$7,800	$22,500	$54,300

© Cengage Learning 2014

The Overhead Budget

An **overhead budget** shows the anticipated manufacturing costs, other than direct materials and direct labor costs, that must be incurred to meet budgeted production needs. It has two purposes:

■ To integrate the overhead cost budgets developed by the managers of production and production-related departments.
■ To group information for the calculation of overhead rates for the next accounting period.

The format for presenting information in an overhead budget is flexible. Grouping information by activities is useful for organizations that use activity-based costing. This approach makes it easier for accountants to determine the application rates for each cost pool.

Exhibit 8
Overhead Budget

Framecraft Company Overhead Budget For the Year Ended December 31					
	Quarter				
	1	**2**	**3**	**4**	**Year**
Total production units	**12,000**	**28,000**	**13,000**	**37,500**	**90,500**
Variable overhead costs:*					
Factory supplies ($0.18)	$ 2,160	$ 5,040	$ 2,340	$ 6,750	$ 16,290
Employee benefits ($0.24)	2,880	6,720	3,120	9,000	21,720
Inspection ($0.09)	1,080	2,520	1,170	3,375	8,145
Maintenance and repairs ($0.16)	1,920	4,480	2,080	6,000	14,480
Utilities ($0.30)	3,600	8,400	3,900	11,250	27,150
Total variable overhead costs	$11,640	$27,160	$12,610	$36,375	$ 87,785
Fixed overhead costs:					
Depreciation—machinery	$ 2,810	$ 2,810	$ 2,810	$ 2,810	$ 11,240
Depreciation—building	3,225	3,225	3,225	3,225	12,900
Supervision	9,000	9,000	9,000	9,000	36,000
Maintenance and repairs	2,150	2,150	2,150	2,150	8,600
Other overhead expenses	3,630	3,630	3,630	3,630	14,520
Total fixed overhead costs	$20,815	$20,815	$20,815	$20,815	$ 83,260
Total overhead costs	$32,455	$47,975	$33,425	$57,190	$171,045

*Amounts in parentheses are unit variable costs.

© Cengage Learning 2014

As Exhibit 8 shows, Framecraft prefers to group overhead information into variable and fixed costs to facilitate CVP analysis. The single overhead rate is computed using the following formula:

Single Overhead Rate = Estimated Total Overhead Costs ÷ Estimated Total Direct Labor Hours

Framecraft's predetermined overhead rate is:

$171,045 ÷ 9,050 direct labor hours = $18.90 per direct labor hour

or

$18.90 per direct labor hour × 0.10 direct labor hour per unit = $1.89 per unit produced

The Selling and Administrative Expenses Budget

A **selling and administrative expenses budget** shows the operating expenses, other than those related to production, that are needed to support sales and overall operations during a period. Accountants use this budget to estimate cash payments for products or services not used in production-related activities.

Framecraft's selling and administrative expenses budget appears in Exhibit 9. The company groups its selling and administrative expenses into variable and fixed

STUDY NOTE: *Selling and administrative expenses are period costs, not product costs.*

© Cengage Learning 2014

Exhibit 9
Selling and Administratives
Expenses Budget

Framecraft Company
Selling and Administrative Expenses Budget
For the Year Ended December 31

	Quarter				
	1	2	3	4	Year
Total sales units	**10,000**	**30,000**	**10,000**	**40,000**	**90,000**
Variable selling and administrative expenses:*					
Delivery expenses ($0.08)	$ 800	$ 2,400	$ 800	$ 3,200	$ 7,200
Sales commissions ($0.10)	1,000	3,000	1,000	4,000	9,000
Accounting ($0.07)	700	2,100	700	2,800	6,300
Other administrative					
Expenses ($0.04)	400	1,200	400	1,600	3,600
Total variable selling and administrative expenses	$ 2,900	$ 8,700	$ 2,900	$11,600	$ 26,100
Fixed selling and administrative expenses:					
Sales salaries	$ 4,500	$ 4,500	$ 4,500	$ 4,500	$ 18,000
Executive salaries	12,750	12,750	12,750	12,750	51,000
Depreciation—office equipment	925	925	925	925	3,700
Taxes and insurance	1,700	1,700	1,700	1,700	6,800
Total fixed selling and administrative expenses	$19,875	$19,875	$19,875	$19,875	$ 79,500
Total selling and administrative expenses	$22,775	$28,575	$22,775	$31,475	$105,600

*Amounts in parentheses are unit variable costs.

components for purposes of cost behavior analysis, CVP analysis, and profit planning. The number of units sold, not produced, are used to compute this budget since selling and administrative costs are triggered by sales, not production.

The Cost of Goods Manufactured Budget

A **cost of goods manufactured budget** summarizes the estimated costs of production during a period. The sources of information for total manufacturing costs are the direct materials, direct labor, and overhead budgets. Most manufacturing organizations anticipate some work in process at the beginning or end of a period. However, Framecraft has a policy of no work in process on December 31 of any year.

Exhibit 10 summarizes the company's estimated costs of production for the year. (The right-hand column of the exhibit shows the sources of key data.) The budgeted, or standard, product unit cost for one picture frame is computed as follows.

Budgeted Product Unit Cost = Cost of Goods Manufactured ÷ Units Produced

$$= \$270,595 \div 90,500 \text{ units}$$

$$= \underline{\$2.99}$$

Exhibit 10
Cost of Goods Manufactured Budget

Framecraft Company Cost of Goods Manufactured Budget For the Year Ended December 31			Source of Data
Direct materials used:			
Direct materials inventory, beginning	$ 1,200*		Direct materials purchases budget
Purchases	45,550		Direct materials purchases budget
Cost of direct materials available for use	$46,750		
Less direct materials inventory, ending	1,500*		Direct materials purchases budget
Cost of direct materials used		$ 45,250	
Direct labor costs		54,300	Direct labor budget
Overhead costs		171,045	Overhead budget
Total manufacturing costs		$270,595	
Work in process inventory, beginning		—**	
Less work in process inventory, ending		—**	
Cost of goods manufactured		$270,595	

*The desired direct materials inventory balance at the beginning of the year is $1,200 (24,000 ounces × $0.05 per ounce); at year end, it is $1,500 (30,000 ounces × $0.05 per ounce).
**It is the company's policy to have no units in process at the beginning or end of the year.

© Cengage Learning 2014

APPLY IT!

Sample Company is preparing a production budget for the year. The company's policy is to maintain a finished goods inventory equal to one-half of the next month's sales. Sales of 4,000 units are budgeted for April. Complete the following monthly production budget for the first quarter to determine how many units should be produced in January, February, and March:

	January	February	March
Sales in units	3,000	2,400	6,000
Add desired units in ending finished goods inventory	?	?	?
Desired total units	?	?	?
Less desired units of beginning finished goods inventory	?	?	?
Total production units	?	?	?

SOLUTION

	January	February	March
Sales in units	3,000	2,400	6,000
Add desired units of ending finished goods inventory	1,200	3,000	2,000
Desired total units	4,200	5,400	8,000
Less desired units of beginning finished goods inventory	1,500	1,200	3,000
Total production units	2,700	4,200	5,000

TRY IT! SE2, SE3, SE4, E2A, E3A, E4A, E5A, E6A, E7A, E2B, E3B, E4B, E5B, E6B, E7B

[LO 4] Financial Budgets

With revenues and expenses itemized in the operating budgets, an organization is able to prepare the financial budgets, which are projections of financial results for the period. Financial budgets include a budgeted income statement, a capital expenditures budget, a cash budget, and a budgeted balance sheet.

The Budgeted Income Statement

A **budgeted income statement** projects an organization's net income for a period based on the revenues and expenses estimated for that period. Exhibit 11 shows Framecraft's budgeted income statement for the year. The company's expenses include 8 percent interest paid on a $70,000 note payable and income taxes paid at a rate of 30 percent. Information about projected sales and costs comes from several operating budgets. (The right-hand column of the exhibit shows the sources of key data.)

At this point, you can review the overall preparation of the operating budgets and the budgeted income statement by comparing the preparation flow in Exhibit 1 with the budgets in Exhibits 4 through 11. Framecraft has no separate budget for cost of goods sold since it is embedded in its budgeted income statement.

Exhibit 11
Budgeted Income Statement

Framecraft Company Budgeted Income Statement For the Year Ended December 31			Source of Data
Sales		$450,000	Sales budget
Cost of goods sold:			
Finished goods inventory, beginning	$ 2,990*		Production budget
Cost of goods manufactured	270,595		Cost of goods manu-factured budget
Cost of goods available for sale	$273,585		
Less finished goods inventory, ending	4,485**		Production budget
Cost of goods sold		269,100	
Gross margin		$180,900	
Selling and administrative expenses		105,600	Selling and admin. expenses budget
Income from operations		$ 75,300	
Interest expense (8% × $70,000)		5,600	
Income before income taxes		$ 69,700	
Income taxes expense (30%)		20,910	
Net income		$ 48,790	

Note: Finished goods inventory balances assume that product unit costs were the same in both years:

*Beginning	**Ending
1,000 units[a]	1,500 units[a]
× $2.99[b]	× $2.99[b]
$2,990	$ 4,485

[a]Production budget (Exhibit 5)
[b]$270,595 ÷ 90,500 units (Exhibits 10 and 5) = $2.99

© Cengage Learning 2014

The Capital Expenditures Budget

A **capital expenditures budget** outlines the anticipated amount and timing of capital outlays for long-term assets during a period. Managers rely on the information in a capital expenditures budget when making decisions about such matters as buying equipment, building a new plant, purchasing and installing a materials handling system, or acquiring another business. Framecraft's capital expenditures budget for the year includes $30,000 for the purchase of a new framemaking machine. The company plans to pay $15,000 in the first quarter of the year, when the order is placed, and $15,000 in the second quarter of the year, when it receives the machine. This information is necessary for preparing the company's cash budget.*

The Cash Budget

A **cash budget** is a projection of the cash that an organization will receive and pay out during a period. It summarizes the cash flow prospects of all transactions considered in the master budget. Exhibit 12 shows how the elements of a cash budget relate to operating, investing, and financing activities.

A cash budget excludes planned noncash transactions, such as depreciation expense, amortization expense, issuance and receipt of stock dividends, uncollectible accounts expense, and gains and losses on sales of assets. Some organizations also exclude deferred taxes and accrued interest from the cash budget.

The following formula is useful in preparing a cash budget:

$$\text{Estimated Ending Cash Balance} = \text{Total Estimated Cash Receipts} - \text{Total Estimated Cash Payments} + \text{Estimated Beginning Cash Balance}$$

Exhibit 12
Elements of a Cash Budget

Activities	Cash Receipts From	Cash Payments For
Operating	• Cash sales • Cash collections on credit sales • Interest income from investments • Cash dividends from investments	• Purchases of materials • Direct labor • Overhead expenses • Selling and administrative expenses • Interest expense • Income taxes
Investing	• Sale of investments • Sale of long-term assets	• Purchases of investments • Purchases of long-term assets
Financing	• Proceeds from loans • Proceeds from issue of stock • Proceeds from issue of bonds	• Loan repayments • Cash dividends to stockholders • Retirement of bonds • Purchases of treasury stock

Note: Classifications of cash receipts and cash payments correspond to those in a statement of cash flows.

© Cengage Learning 2014

In estimating cash receipts and cash payments for the cash budget, many organizations prepare supporting schedules. For example, Framecraft's controller converts credit sales to cash inflows and purchases made on credit to cash outflows and then discloses those conversions to support the cash budget.

---

*We discuss capital expenditures in more detail in a later chapter.

Cash Collections The schedule in Exhibit 13 shows the cash that Framecraft expects to collect from customers during the year. Cash sales represent 20 percent of the company's expected sales; the other 80 percent are credit sales. Experience has shown that Framecraft collects payments for 60 percent of all credit sales in the quarter of sale, 30 percent in the quarter following sale, and 10 percent in the second quarter following sale.

Exhibit 13
Schedule of Expected Cash Collections from Customers

Framecraft Company
Schedule of Expected Cash Collections from Customers
For the Year Ended December 31

	Quarter				
	1	2	3	4	Year
Accounts receivable, beginning	$38,000	$ 10,000	$ —	$ —	$ 48,000
Cash sales	10,000	30,000	10,000	40,000	90,000
Collections of credit sales:					
First quarter ($40,000)	24,000	12,000	4,000	—	40,000
Second quarter ($120,000)	—	72,000	36,000	12,000	120,000
Third quarter ($40,000)	—	—	24,000	12,000	36,000
Fourth quarter ($160,000)	—	—	—	96,000	96,000
Total cash to be collected from customers	$72,000	$124,000	$74,000	$160,000	$430,000

© Cengage Learning 2014

As you can see in Exhibit 13, Framecraft's balance of accounts receivable was $48,000 at the beginning of the budget year. The company expects to collect $38,000 of that amount in the first quarter and the remaining $10,000 in the second quarter. At the end of the budget year, the estimated ending balance of accounts receivable is $68,000 comprised of $ 4,000 from the third quarter's credit sales [($50,000 × 0.80) × 0.10] and $64,000 from the fourth quarter's sales [($200,000 × 0.80) × 0.40]

The expected cash collections for each quarter and for the year appear in the total cash receipts section of the cash budget.

Cash Payments Exhibit 14 shows Framecraft's schedule of expected cash payments for direct materials during the year. This information is summarized in the first line of the cash payments section of the company's cash budget. Framecraft pays 50 percent of the invoices it receives in the quarter of purchase and the other 50 percent in the following quarter.

Exhibit 14
Schedule of Expected Cash Payments for Direct Materials

Framecraft Company
Schedule of Expected Cash Payments for Direct Materials
For the Year Ended December 31

	Quarter				
	1	2	3	4	Year
Accounts payable, beginning	$4,200	$ —	$ —	$ —	$ 4,200
First quarter ($7,600)	3,800	3,800	—	—	7,600
Second quarter ($12,500)	—	6,250	6,250	—	12,500
Third quarter ($8,950)	—	—	4,475	4,475	8,950
Fourth quarter ($16,500)	—	—	—	8,250	8,250
Total cash payments for direct materials	$8,000	$10,050	$10,725	$12,725	$41,500

© Cengage Learning 2014

The beginning balance of accounts payable for the first quarter is given at $4,200. At the end of the budget year, the estimated ending balance of accounts payable is $8,250 (50 percent of the $16,500 of direct materials purchases in the fourth quarter).

Cash Budget Framecraft's cash budget for the year appears in Exhibit 15. (The right-hand column of the exhibit shows the sources of key data.) It shows the estimated cash

Cash Budget

Framecraft Company
Cash Budget
For the Year Ended December 31

| | Quarter | | | | | |
	1	2	3	4	Year	Source of Data
Cash receipts:						
Cash collections from customers	$ 72,000	$124,000	$74,000	$160,000	$430,000	Schedule of expected cash collections from customers
Total cash receipts	$ 72,000	$124,000	$74,000	$160,000	$430,000	
Cash payments:						
Direct materials	$ 8,000	$ 10,050	$10,725	$ 12,725	$ 41,500	Schedule of expected cash payments for direct materials
Direct labor	7,200	16,800	7,800	22,500	54,300	Direct labor budget
Factory supplies	2,160	5,040	2,340	6,750	16,290	Overhead budget
Employee benefits	2,880	6,720	3,120	9,000	21,720	Overhead budget
Inspection	1,080	2,520	1,170	3,375	8,145	Overhead budget
Variable maintenance and repairs	1,920	4,480	2,080	6,000	14,480	Overhead budget
Utilities	3,600	8,400	3,900	11,250	27,150	Overhead budget
Supervision	9,000	9,000	9,000	9,000	36,000	Overhead budget
Fixed maintenance and repairs	2,150	2,150	2,150	2,150	8,600	Overhead budget
Other overhead expenses	3,630	3,630	3,630	3,630	14,520	Overhead budget
Delivery expenses	800	2,400	800	3,200	7,200	Selling and admin. expenses budget
Sales commissions	1,000	3,000	1,000	4,000	9,000	Selling and admin. expenses budget
Accounting	700	2,100	700	2,800	6,300	Selling and admin. expenses budget
Other administrative expenses	400	1,200	400	1,600	3,600	Selling and admin. expenses budget
Sales salaries	4,500	4,500	4,500	4,500	18,000	Selling and admin. expenses budget
Executive salaries	12,750	12,750	12,750	12,750	51,000	Selling and admin. expenses budget
Taxes and insurance	1,700	1,700	1,700	1,700	6,800	Selling and admin. expenses budget
Capital expenditures*	15,000	15,000			30,000	Budgeted income statement
Interest expense	1,400	1,400	1,400	1,400	5,600	Budgeted income statement
Income taxes	5,228	5,227	5,228	5,227	20,910	Budgeted income statement
Total cash payments	$ 85,098	$118,067	$74,393	$123,557	$401,115	
Cash increase (decrease)	$(13,098)	$ 5,933	$ (393)	$ 36,443	$ 28,885	
Beginning cash balance	20,000	6,902	12,835	12,442	20,000	
Ending cash balance	$ 6,902	$ 12,835	$12,442	$ 48,885	$ 48,885	

*The company plans to purchase a machine costing $30,000 and to pay for it in two installments of $15,000 each in the first and second quarters of the year.

receipts and cash payments for the period, as well as the cash increase or decrease. The cash increase or decrease plus the period's beginning cash balance equals the ending cash balance anticipated for the period. As you can see in Exhibit 15, the beginning cash balance for the first quarter is $20,000. Note that each quarter's budgeted ending cash balance becomes the next quarter's beginning cash balance. Also note that equal income tax payments are made quarterly.

Minimum Cash Balance Many organizations maintain a minimum cash balance to provide a margin of safety against uncertainty. If the ending cash balance on the cash budget falls below the minimum level required, short-term borrowing may be necessary to cover planned cash payments during the year. If the ending cash balance is significantly larger than the organization needs, it may invest the excess cash in short-term securities to generate additional income.

For example, if Framecraft wants a minimum of $10,000 cash available at the end of each quarter, its balance of $6,902 at the end of the first quarter indicates that there is a problem. Framecraft can borrow cash to cover the first quarter's cash needs, delay purchasing the new machine until the second quarter, or reduce some of the operating expenses. On the other hand, the balance at the end of the fourth quarter may be higher than the company wants, in which case management might invest a portion of the idle cash in short-term securities.

The Budgeted Balance Sheet

A **budgeted balance sheet** projects an organization's financial position at the end of a period. It uses all estimated data compiled in preparing a master budget and is the final step in the budgeting process. Exhibit 16 presents Framecraft Company's budgeted balance sheet at the end of the year. (The right-hand column of the exhibit shows the sources of key data.) The beginning balances for Land, Notes Payable, Common Stock, and Retained Earnings were $50,000, $70,000, $150,000, and $52,107, respectively.

APPLY IT!

Sample Corporation's budgeted balance sheet for the beginning of the coming year shows total assets of $5,000,000 and total liabilities of $2,000,000. Common stock and retained earnings make up the entire stockholders' equity section of the balance sheet. Common stock remains at its beginning balance of $1,500,000. The projected net income for the year is $350,000. The company plans to pay no cash dividends. What is the balance of retained earnings at the beginning and end of the year?

SOLUTION

Using the accounting equation A = L + SE, knowing that common stock + retained earnings make up the entire SE, and the information given:

Beginning retained earnings:

$5,000,000 = $2,000,000 + $1,500,000 + Beginning RE

Thus, the beginning balance of retained earnings is $1,500,000.

Ending retained earnings:

Beginning retained earnings	$1,500,000
+ Net income	350,000
− Dividends	0
Ending retained earnings	$1,850,000

TRY IT! SE4, SE5, SE6, SE7, SE8, E8A, E9A, E10A, E11A, E12A, E8B, E9B, E10B, E11B, E12B

Exhibit 16
Budgeted
Balance Sheet

Framecraft Company
Budgeted Balance Sheet
December 31

			Source of Data
Assets			
Current assets:			
Cash		$ 48,885	Cash budget
Accounts receivable		68,000[a]	Schedule of expected cash collections from customers
Direct materials inventory		1,500	Cost of goods manufactured budget
Work in process inventory		—	Cost of goods manufactured budget (note)
Finished goods inventory		4,485	Budgeted income statement (note)
Total current assets		$122,870	
Property, plant, and equipment:			
Land		$ 50,000	
Plant and equipment[b]	$200,000		
Less accumulated depreciation[c]	45,000	155,000	
Total property, plant, and equipment		205,000	
Total assets		$327,870	
Liabilities			
Current liabilities:			
Accounts payable		$ 8,250[d]	Schedule of expected cash payments for direct materials
Long-term liabilities:			
Notes payable		70,000	
Total liabilities		$ 78,250	
Stockholders' Equity			
Common stock	$150,000		
Retained earnings[e]	99,620		
Total stockholders' equity		249,620	
Total liabilities and stockholders' equity		$327,870	

[a]The accounts receivable balance at year end is $68,000: $4,000 from the third quarter's sales [($50,000 × 0.80) × 0.10] plus $64,000 from the fourth quarter's sales [($200,000 × 0.80) × 0.40].
[b]The plant and equipment balance includes the $30,000 purchase of a machine.
[c]The accumulated depreciation balance includes depreciation expense of $27,840 for machinery, building, and office equipment ($11,240, $12,900, and $3,700, respectively).
[d]At year end, the estimated ending balance of accounts payable is $8,250 (50 percent of the $16,500 of direct materials purchases in the fourth quarter).
[e]The retained earnings balance at December 31 equals the beginning retained earnings balance plus the net income projected for the year ($50,830 and $48,790, respectively).

SECTION 3

BUSINESS APPLICATIONS

BUSINESS APPLICATIONS
- Planning
- Performing
- Evaluating
- Communicating

RELEVANT LEARNING OBJECTIVE

LO 5 Explain why budgeting is essential to the management process.

LO 5 Budgeting and the Management Process

Budgets are essential to accomplishing an organization's strategic plan. They are used to communicate understandable information, coordinate activities and resource usage, motivate employees, and provide comparative information to evaluate performance. For example, a board of directors may use budgets to determine managers' areas of responsibility and to measure managers' performance in those areas. Budgets are also used to manage and account for cash.

Advantages of Budgeting

Budgeting is advantageous for organizations, because budgets:

- foster organizational communication
- ensure a focus both on future events and on resolving day-to-day issues
- assign resources and the responsibility to use them wisely to managers who are held accountable for their results
- can identify potential constraints before they become problems
- facilitate congruence between organizational and personal goals
- define organizational goals and objectives numerically, against which actual performance results can be evaluated

Budgeting and Goals

Budgeting helps managers achieve both long-term and short-term goals.

Long-Term Goals **Strategic planning** is the process by which management establishes an organization's long-term goals. These goals define the direction that an organization will take and are the basis for making annual operating plans and preparing budgets. Long-term goals cannot be vague. They must set specific tactical targets and timetables and assign responsibility to specific personnel. For example, a long-term goal for a company that currently holds only 4 percent of its product's market share might specify that the vice president of marketing is to develop strategies to ensure that the company controls 10 percent of the market in five years and 15 percent by the end of ten years.

Business Perspective
What Can Cause the Planning Process to Fail?

When chief financial officers were asked what caused their planning process to fail, the six factors they most commonly cited were:[1]

- An inadequately defined strategy
- No clear link between strategy and the operational budget
- Lack of individual accountability for results
- Lack of meaningful performance measures
- Inadequate pay for performance
- Lack of appropriate data

Short-Term Goals Annual operating plans involve every part of an enterprise and are much more detailed than long-term strategic plans. To formulate an annual operating plan, an organization must restate its long-term goals in terms of what it needs to accomplish during the next year. The process entails making decisions about sales and profit targets, human resource needs, and the introduction of new products or services. The short-term goals identified in an annual operating plan are the basis of an organization's operating budgets for the year.

Budgeting Basics

Once long- and short-term goals have been decided, the organization's management plays a central role in coordinating the budgeting process. Managers set the basics of the budgeting process, including assigning budget authority, inviting employee participation, selecting the budget period, and implementing the budget.

Assigning Budget Authority Every budget and budget line item is associated with a specific role or job in an organization. For example, a department manager is responsible for the department's budget, and the marketing vice president is responsible for what is spent on advertising.

Since manager responsibilities and budget authority are linked, managers must explain or take corrective action for any deviations between budget and actual results. Responsibility accounting (which will be discussed in greater detail in the next chapter) authorizes managers to command and be held accountable for the revenues and expenses in their budgets. If managers do not have budget authority over what they need to accomplish their job responsibilities, they lack the control necessary to accomplish their duties and cannot be held accountable for results.

Inviting Employee Participation Because an organization's main activities—such as production, sales, and employee training—take place at its lower levels, the information necessary for establishing a budget flows from the employees and supervisors of those activities through middle managers to senior executives. Each person in this chain of communication thus plays a role in developing a budget, as well as in implementing it. If these individuals have a voice in setting the budget targets, they will be motivated to ensure that their departments attain those targets and stay within the budget. If they do not have a role in the budgeting process, motivation will suffer. The key to a successful budget is therefore **participative budgeting**, a process in which personnel at all levels of an organization actively engage in making decisions about the budget. Participative budgeting depends on joint decision making. Without it, the budgeting process will be authoritative rather than participative, and the budget targets may be unrealistic and impossible to attain.

Selecting the Budget Period Budgets, like the company's fiscal period, generally cover a one-year period of time. An annual operating budget may be divided further into monthly or quarterly periods, depending on the detail of information needed.

The organization's management will decide if they will use a static or continuous budgeting process. **Static budgets** are prepared once a year and do not change during

Business Perspective
Can Budgeting Lead to a Breakdown in Corporate Ethics?

When budgets are used to force performance results, as they were at **WorldCom**, breaches in corporate ethics can occur. One former WorldCom employee described the situation at that company as follows: "You would have a budget, and he [WorldCom CEO Bernard Ebbers] would mandate that you had to be 2% under budget. Nothing else was acceptable."[2] This type of restrictive budget policy appears to have been a factor in many corporate scandals.

the annual budget period. To ensure that its managers have continuously updated operating data against which to measure performance, an organization may select an ongoing budgeting process, called a continuous budget. A **continuous budget** is a 12-month forward-rolling budget that summarizes budgets for the next 12 months. Each month managers prepare a budget for that month, 12 months hence.

Traditional budgeting approaches require managers to justify only budget changes over the past year. An alternative to traditional budgeting is **zero-based budgeting**, which requires that every budget item be justified annually. So each year the budget is built from scratch.

Implementing the Budget The **budget committee,** which includes the controller and many of the organization's top management, has overall responsibility for budget implementation. The budget committee:

■ Oversees each stage in the preparation of the organization's overall budget
■ Mediates any departmental disputes that may arise in the process
■ Gives final approval to the budget

A budget may go through many revisions before it includes all planning decisions and has the approval of the committee. Once approved, periodic reports from department managers allow the committee to monitor the company's progress in attaining budget targets.

Successful budget implementation depends on two factors—clear communication and the support of top management. To ensure their cooperation in implementing the budget, all key persons involved must know what roles they are expected to play and must have specific directions on how to achieve their performance goals. Thus, the budget committee must communicate clearly the performance expectations and budget targets. Equally important, top management must show support for the budget and encourage its implementation. The process will succeed only if middle- and lower-level managers are confident that top management is truly interested in the outcome and is willing to reward personnel for meeting the budget targets. Today, many organizations have employee incentive plans that tie the achievement of budget targets to bonuses or other types of compensation.

As you have seen in this chapter, budgeting is not only an essential part of planning; it also helps managers command, control, evaluate, and report on operations. Exhibit 17 summarizes how budgeting is an integral part of the management process.

Exhibit 17
Budgeting and the Management Process

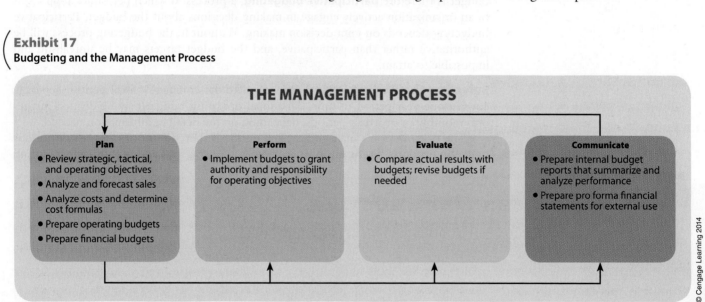

THE MANAGEMENT PROCESS

Plan
● Review strategic, tactical, and operating objectives
● Analyze and forecast sales
● Analyze costs and determine cost formulas
● Prepare operating budgets
● Prepare financial budgets

Perform
● Implement budgets to grant authority and responsibility for operating objectives

Evaluate
● Compare actual results with budgets; revise budgets if needed

Communicate
● Prepare internal budget reports that summarize and analyze performance
● Prepare pro forma financial statements for external use

APPLY IT!

Randi Quelle is the manager of the electronics department in a large discount store. During a recent meeting, Quelle and her supervisor agreed that Quelle's goal for the next year would be to increase the number of flat-screen televisions sold by 20 percent. The department sold 500 TV sets last year. Two salespersons currently work for Quelle. What types of budgets should Quelle use to help her achieve her sales goal? What kinds of information should those budgets provide?

SOLUTION

Budgets and information that might be useful include:

- Breakdown by month of last year's sales to use as a guide to build this year's monthly targets. This would include seasonal sales information.
- Budgets by salesperson, which may indicate a need for a third salesperson.
- Inventory and purchasing information.
- Budgets of sales promotion and advertising.
- Information on customer flow and the best times to sell.

TRY ITI SE9, SE10, E12A, E13A, E14A, E15A, E12B, E13B, E14B, E15B

TriLevel Problem

Framerica Corporation

The beginning of this chapter focused on **Framerica Corporation**. One of Framerica's priorities is to help employees attain personal goals. A participatory budgeting process is a highly effective way to achieve goal congruence between a company's goals and objectives and employee personal aspirations. Complete the following requirements in order to answer the questions posed at the beginning of the chapter.

Section 1: Concepts
What concepts underlie the usefulness of the budgeting process?

Section 2: Accounting Applications
How does the budgeting process translate long-term goals into operating objectives?

Assume Framerica has an Information Processing Division that provides database management services for the professional photographers and artists who buy its frames. Suppose the division uses state-of-the-art equipment and employs five information specialists. Each specialist works an average of 160 hours a month. Assume the division's controller has compiled the following information:

	Actual Data for Past Year		Forecasted Data for This Year		
	November	December	January	February	March
Client billings (sales)	$25,000	$35,000	$25,000	$20,000	$40,000
Selling and administrative expenses	12,000	13,000	12,000	11,000	12,500
Operating supplies	2,500	3,500	2,500	2,500	4,000
Processing overhead	3,200	3,500	3,000	2,500	3,500

Of the client billings, 60 percent are cash sales collected during the month of sale, 30 percent are collected in the first month following sale, and 10 percent are collected in the second month following sale. Operating supplies are paid for in the month of purchase. Selling and administrative expenses and processing overhead are paid in the month following the cost's incurrence.

The division has a bank loan of $12,000 with a 12 percent annual interest rate. Interest is paid monthly, and $2,000 of the loan principal is due on February 28 of next year. Income taxes of $4,550 for this calendar year are due and payable on March 15 of next year. The information specialists earn $8.50 an hour, and all payroll-related employee benefit costs are included in processing overhead. The division anticipates no capital expenditures for the first quarter of the coming year. It expects its cash balance on December 31 of this year to be $13,840.

Prepare a monthly cash budget for the Information Processing Division for the three-month period ending March 31 of this year. Comment on whether the ending cash balances are adequate for the division's cash needs.

Section 3: Business Applications

Why are budgets an essential part of planning, controlling, evaluating, and reporting on business? To answer this question, match this chapter's manager responsibilities with when they occur within the management process.

a. Plan
b. Perform
c. Evaluate
d. Communicate

1. Prepare internal budget reports that summarize and analyze performance
2. Develop operating budgets
3. Grant authority and responsibility of operating objectives by implementing budgets
4. Review strategic, tactical, and operating objectives
5. Compare actual results with budgets
6. Develop financial budgets
7. Prepare pro forma financial statements
8. Analyze and forecast sales
9. Analyze costs and determine cost formulas
10. Revise budgets as needed

SOLUTION

Section 1: Concepts

The budgeting process can be a highly effective way of linking strategic planning to operations. Because the budgets express these goals and objectives in concrete terms, managers and employees are more likely to understand them and are able to act in ways that will achieve them. Budgets give managers and employees a means of monitoring the results of their actions because they can compare operating and financial budgets with actual results. The concepts of *comparability* and *understandability* assure budget accountability, especially when it involves all employees in an ongoing dialogue about a company's activities and direction and engages them in making budgeting decisions.

Section 2: Accounting Applications

Information Processing Division
Monthly Cash Budgets
For the Quarter Ended March 31

	January	February	March	Quarter
Total cash receipts	$28,000	$23,000	$32,500	$83,500
Cash payments:				
Operating supplies	$ 2,500	$ 2,500	$ 4,000	$ 9,000
Direct labor	6,800	6,800	6,800	20,400
Selling & admin. expenses	13,000	12,000	11,000	36,000
Processing overhead	3,500	3,000	2,500	9,000
Interest expense	120	120	100	340
Loan payment	—	2,000	—	2,000
Income tax payment	—	—	4,550	4,550
Total cash payments	$25,920	$26,420	$28,950	$81,290
Cash increase (decrease)	$ 2,080	$ (3,420)	$ 3,550	$ 2,210
Beginning cash balance	13,840	15,920	12,500	13,840
Ending cash balance	$15,920	$12,500	$16,050	$16,050

The details supporting the individual computations in this cash budget are as follows:

	January	February	March
Client billings:			
November	$ 2,500	$ —	$ —
December	10,500	3,500	—
January	15,000	7,500	2,500
February	—	12,000	6,000
March	—	—	24,000
	$28,000	$23,000	$32,500
Operating supplies:			
Paid for in the month purchased	$ 2,500	$ 2,500	$ 4,000
Direct labor:			
5 employees × 160 hours a month × $8.50 an hour	6,800	6,800	6,800
Selling and administrative expenses:			
Paid in the month following incurrence	13,000	12,000	11,000
Processing overhead:			
Paid in the month following incurrence	3,500	3,000	2,500
Interest expense:			
January and February = 1% of $12,000	120	120	—
March = 1% of $10,000	—	—	100
Loan payment	—	2,000	—
Income tax payment	—	—	4,550

The ending cash balances of $15,920, $12,500, and $16,050 for January, February, and March, respectively, appear to be comfortable and not too large for the Information Processing Division.

Section 3: Business Applications

1. d   6. a
2. a   7. d
3. c   8. a
4. a   9. a
5. c   10. c

Chapter Review

Define *budgeting*, and describe how it relates to the concepts of comparability and understandability. **LO 1**

Budgeting is the process of identifying, gathering, summarizing, and communicating financial and nonfinancial information about an organization's future activities. A master budget consists of a set of operating budgets and a set of financial budgets that detail an organization's financial plans for a specific period. The operating budgets serve as the basis for preparing the budgeted income statement, a capital expenditures budget, a cash budget, and a budgeted balance sheet. The concepts of understandability and comparability underlie the power of the budgeting process. Budgeting enhances understandability, since managers and employees understand their organizational roles and responsibilities based on how the master budget links the organization's strategic plans to its annual budget. Budgeting enhances comparability, since budget to actual comparisons gives managers and employees a means of monitoring the results of their actions.

Identify the elements of a master budget in different types of organizations and the guidelines for preparing budgets. **LO 2**

The operating budgets of a manufacturing organization include budgets for sales, production, direct materials purchases, direct labor, overhead, selling and administrative expenses, and cost of goods manufactured. The operating budgets of a retail organization include budgets for sales, purchases, selling and administrative expenses, and cost of goods sold. The operating budgets of a service organization include budgets for service revenue, labor, services overhead, and selling and administrative expenses.

The guidelines for preparing budgets include identifying the purpose of the budget, the user group and its information needs, and the sources of budget information; establishing a clear format for the budget; and using appropriate formulas and calculations to derive the quantitative information.

Prepare the operating budgets that support the financial budgets. **LO 3**

The initial step in preparing a master budget in any type of organization is to prepare a sales budget. Once sales have been estimated, the manager of a manufacturing organization's production department is able to prepare a budget that shows how many units of products must be manufactured to meet the projected sales volume. With that information, other managers are able to prepare budgets for direct materials purchases, direct labor, overhead, selling and administrative expenses, and cost of goods manufactured. A cost of goods sold budget may be prepared separately, or it may be included in the cost of goods manufactured budget for a manufacturing organization. The operating budgets supply the information needed to prepare the financial budgets.

Prepare a budgeted income statement, a cash budget, and a budgeted balance sheet. **LO 4**

With estimated revenues and expenses itemized in the operating budgets, a controller is able to prepare the financial budgets. A budgeted income statement projects an organization's net income for a specific accounting period. A capital expenditures budget estimates the amount and timing of the organization's capital outlays during the period. A cash budget projects its cash receipts and cash payments for the period. Information about cash receipts comes from several sources, including the sales budget, the budgeted income statement, and various financial records. Sources of information about cash payments include the operating budgets, the budgeted income statement, and the capital expenditures budget. The difference between the total estimated cash receipts and total estimated cash payments is the cash increase or decrease anticipated for the period. That total plus the period's beginning cash balance equals the ending cash balance. The final step in developing a master budget is to prepare a budgeted balance sheet, which projects the organization's financial position at the end of the period.

Explain why budgeting is an essential part of the management process. **LO 5**

Budgeting helps managers plan, command, control, evaluate, and report on operations. When managers develop budgets, they match their organizational goals with the resources necessary to accomplish those goals. During the budgeting process, they evaluate operational, tactical, value chain, and capacity issues; assess how resources can be efficiently used; and develop contingency budgets as business conditions change. During the budget period, budgets authorize managers to use resources and provide guidelines to control costs. When managers assess performance, they can compare actual operating results to budget plans and evaluate the variances. In participative budgeting, personnel at all levels actively engage in making decisions about the budget.

Budgets can be static, meaning they do not change during the annual budget period, or continuous, meaning they are forward-moving for the next 12 months. An alternative to traditional budgeting is zero-based budgeting, which requires every budget item to be justified, not just the changes over the past year.

A budget committee made up of the company's controller and top managers has overall responsibility for budget implementation. The committee oversees each stage in the preparation of the master budget, mediates any departmental disputes that may arise during the process, and gives final approval to the budget. After the master budget is approved, periodic reports from department managers enable the committee to monitor the progress in attaining budget targets.

Key Terms

Chapter Assignments

DISCUSSION QUESTIONS

LO 1, 2   **DQ1. CONCEPT ▶** What is a master budget and what are the guidelines that enhance its understandability and comparability?

LO 3, 4   **DQ2.** Why does the preparation of operating budgets before financial budgets increase the usefulness of the budget process?

LO 5   **DQ3. BUSINESS APPLICATION ▶** Why is the difference between a static budget and a continuous budget important in understanding budgets?

LO 5   **DQ4. CONCEPT ▶ BUSINESS APPLICATION ▶** How are understandability and comparability enhanced when knowing who is responsible for the budgeting process?

LO 5   **DQ5. CONCEPT ▶ BUSINESS APPLICATION ▶** Why does the use of budgets in the management process reinforce the concepts of comparability and understandability to better business performance?

SHORT EXERCISES

LO 1, 2   **Budget Usefulness**

SE1. CONCEPT ▶ Budgeting is not only an essential part of planning; but it also helps managers command, control, evaluate, and report on operations. Why are the concepts of understandability and comparability important in budgeting? List the reasons for your answer.

LO 3   **Production Budget**

SE2. Windsor Lock Company's controller is preparing a production budget for the year. The company's policy is to maintain a finished goods inventory equal to one-half of the following month's sales. Sales of 5,000 locks are budgeted for April. Complete the monthly production budget for the first quarter:

	January	February	March
Sales in units	5,000	4,000	6,000
Add desired units of ending finished goods inventory	2,000	?	?
Desired total units	7,000	?	?
Less desired units of beginning finished goods inventory	?	?	?
Total production units	4,500	?	?

LO 3 **Preparing an Operating Budget**

SE3. Hartford Company expects to sell 50,000 units of its product in the coming year. Each unit sells for $50. Sales brochures and supplies for the year are expected to cost $9,000. Two sales representatives cover the southeast region. Each representative's base salary is $20,000, and each earns a sales commission of 5 percent of the selling price of the units he or she sells. The sales representatives supply their own transportation; they are reimbursed for travel at a rate of $0.60 per mile. The company estimates that the sales representatives will drive a total of 70,000 miles next year. Calculate Hartford's budgeted selling expenses for the coming year.

LO 3, 4 **Budgeted Gross Margin**

SE4. Eastport Company's operating budgets reveal the following information: net sales, $400,000; beginning materials inventory, $23,000; materials purchased, $185,000; beginning work in process inventory, $64,700; beginning finished goods inventory, $21,600; direct labor costs, $34,000; overhead applied, $67,000; ending work in process inventory, $61,200; ending materials inventory, $20,000; and ending finished goods inventory, $18,000. Compute Eastport's budgeted gross margin.

LO 4 **Estimating Cash Collections**

CASH FLOW

SE5. Standard Insurance Company specializes in term life insurance contracts. Cash collection experience shows that 40 percent of billed premiums are collected in the month in which they are billed, 50 percent are paid in the first month after they are billed, and 6 percent are paid in the second month after they are billed. Four percent of the billed premiums are paid late (in the third month after they are billed) and include a 10 percent penalty payment. Total billing notices in January were $58,000; in February, $62,000; in March, $66,000; in April, $65,000; in May, $60,000; and in June, $62,000. How much cash does the company expect to collect in May?

LO 4 **Cash Budget**

CASH FLOW

SE6. The projections of direct materials purchases that follow are for Creek Corporation.

	Purchases on Account	Cash Purchases
December 2014	$50,000	$20,000
January 2015	70,000	30,000
February 2015	60,000	25,000
March 2015	70,000	35,000

The company pays for 60 percent of purchases on account in the month of purchase and 40 percent in the month following the purchase. Prepare a monthly schedule of expected cash payments for direct materials for the first quarter of 2015.

LO 4 **Cash Budget**

CASH FLOW

SE7. Eagles Limited needs a cash budget for the month of November. The following information is available:

- The cash balance on November 1 is $5,000.
- Sales for October and November are $80,000 and $60,000, respectively. Cash collections on sales are 30 percent in the month of sale and 68 percent in the month after the sale; 2 percent of sales are uncollectible.
- General expenses budgeted for November are $26,000 (depreciation represents $2,000 of this amount).
- Inventory purchases will total $30,000 in October and $40,000 in November. The company pays for half of its inventory purchases in the month of purchase and for the other half the month after purchase.

- The company will pay $4,000 in cash for office furniture in November. Sales commissions for November are budgeted at $13,000.
- The company maintains a minimum ending cash balance of $4,000 and can borrow from the bank in multiples of $100. All loans are repaid after 60 days.

Prepare a cash budget for Eagles Limited for the month of November.

LO 4   **Budgeted Balance Sheet**

SE8. Bulldog Corporation's budgeted balance sheet for the coming year shows total assets of $4,000,000 and total liabilities of $1,900,000. Common stock and retained earnings make up the entire stockholders' equity section of the balance sheet. Common stock remains at its beginning balance of $1,500,000. The projected net income for the year is $350,000. The company pays no cash dividends. What is the balance of retained earnings at the beginning of the budget period?

LO 5   **Budgeting in a Retail Organization**

SE9. BUSINESS APPLICATION ▶ In a discount department store, the shoe department manager's goal for the next year is to increase the number of pairs of shoes sold by 20 percent. The department sold 8,000 pairs of shoes last year. Two salespeople currently work in the department. What types of budgets should the manager use to help him achieve his sales goal? What kinds of information should those budgets provide?

LO 5   **Budgetary Control**

SE10. BUSINESS APPLICATION ▶ The owner of a tree nursery analyzes her business's results by comparing actual operating results with figures budgeted at the beginning of the year. When the business generates large profits, she often overlooks the differences between actual and budgeted data. But when profits are low, she spends many hours analyzing the differences. If you owned the business, would you use her approach to budgetary control? If not, what changes would you make?

EXERCISES: SET A

LO 2   **Components of a Master Budget**

E1A. Assigning the numbers 1 through 7, identify the order in which the following budgets are prepared.

- direct labor budget
- production budget
- selling, administrative, and general expenses budget
- budgeted income statement
- sales budget
- budgeted balance sheet
- cash budget

LO 3   **Sales Budget**

E2A. Outside Company's quarterly and annual sales for this year follow. Prepare a sales budget for next year based on the estimated percentage increases shown by product class. Show both quarterly and annual totals for each product class.

(Continued)

Outside Company
Actual Sales Revenue
For the Year Ended December 31

Product Class	January–March	April–June	July–September	October–December	Annual Totals	Estimated Percent Increases by Product Class
Backcountry products	$ 44,500	$ 45,500	$ 48,200	$ 47,900	$ 186,100	20%
Marine products	36,900	32,600	34,100	37,200	140,800	5%
Walking products	29,800	29,700	29,100	27,500	116,100	30%
Hiking products	38,800	37,600	36,900	39,700	153,000	10%
Running products	47,700	48,200	49,400	49,900	195,200	25%
Biking products	65,400	65,900	66,600	67,300	265,200	20%
Totals	$263,100	$259,500	$264,300	$269,500	$1,056,400	

LO 3

Production Budget

E3A. Southside Corporation produces and sells a single product. Expected sales for September are 13,000 units; for October, 14,000 units; for November, 9,000 units; for December, 10,000 units; and for January, 15,000 units. The company's desired level of ending finished goods inventory at the end of a month is 10 percent of the following month's expected sales in units. At the end of August, 1,200 units were on hand. How many units need to be produced in the fourth quarter?

LO 3

Direct Materials Purchases Budget

E4A. Eco Door Company manufactures garage door units. The units include hinges, door panels, and other hardware. The controller has provided the information that follows.

Part	Units Needed	Cost
Hinges	4 sets per door	$6.00 per set
Door panels	4 panels per door	$27.00 per panel
Other hardware	1 lock per door	$31.00 per lock
	1 handle per door	$22.50 per handle
	2 roller tracks per door	$16.00 per set of 2 roller tracks
	8 rollers per door	$4.00 per roller

Prepare a direct materials purchases budget for the first quarter of the year based on the budgeted production of 25,000 garage door units. Assume no beginning or ending quantities of direct materials inventory.

LO 2, 3

Purchases Budget

E5A. Spartan Corporation projects the dollar value of the company's cost of goods sold to be $160,000 in June, $169,000 in July, and $154,000 in August. The dollar value of its desired ending inventory is 25 percent of the following month's cost of goods sold.

Compute the total purchases in dollars budgeted for June and the total purchases in dollars budgeted for July.

LO 3

Direct Labor Budget

E6A. Crimson Company has two departments—Dye and Dry—and manufactures three products. Budgeted unit production for the coming year is 21,000 of Product J, 36,000 of Product C, and 30,000 of Product B. The company is currently analyzing direct labor hour requirements for the coming year. Data for each department follow.

	Dye	Dry
Estimated hours per unit:		
Product J	2.0	3.0
Product C	1.0	4.0
Product B	2.5	5.0
Hourly labor rate	$10	$4

Prepare a direct labor budget for the coming year that shows the budgeted direct labor costs for each department and for the company as a whole.

LO 3   Overhead Budget

E7A. As part of the budgeting process, Northview Corporation's CFO is developing the overhead budget for next year for its Evans Division. The division estimates that it will manufacture 150,000 units during the year. The budgeted cost information follows.

	Variable Rate per Unit	Fixed Costs
Indirect materials	$1.00	
Indirect labor	4.00	
Supplies	0.40	
Repairs and maintenance	3.00	$ 50,000
Electricity	0.10	120,000
Factory supervision		160,000
Insurance		25,000
Property taxes		25,000
Depreciation—machinery		82,000
Depreciation—building		72,000

Prepare the division's overhead budget for next year.

LO 4   Cash Collections

E8A. Five Bros., Inc., is an automobile maintenance and repair company with outlets throughout the western United States. The company controller is starting to assemble the cash budget for the fourth quarter. Projected sales for the quarter follow.

	On Account	Cash
October	$400,000	$190,000
November	690,000	220,000
December	750,000	245,000

Cash collection records pertaining to sales on account indicate the following collection pattern:

Month of sale	40%
First month following sale	30%
Second month following sale	28%
Uncollectible	2%

Sales on account during August were $346,000. During September, sales on account were $390,000.

Compute the amount of cash to be collected from customers during each month of the fourth quarter.

LO 4   Cash Collections

E9A. NSW Company collects payment on 50 percent of credit sales in the month of sale, 40 percent in the month following the sale, and 5 percent in the second month following the sale. Its sales budget follows.

(Continued)

Month	Cash Sales	Credit Sales
May	$24,000	$ 40,000
June	30,000	60,000
July	50,000	80,000
August	70,000	100,000

Compute NSW's total cash collections in July and its total cash collections in August.

LO 4   **Cash Budget**

CASH FLOW

E10A. Queensland Enterprises needs a cash budget for the month of June. The following information is available:

- The cash balance on June 1 is $13,000.
- Sales for May and June are $40,000 and $50,000, respectively. Cash collections on sales are 45 percent in the month of sale and 50 percent in the month after the sale; 5 percent of sales are uncollectible.
- General expenses budgeted for June are $20,000 (depreciation represents $1,000 of this amount).
- Inventory purchases will total $40,000 in May and $30,000 in June. The company pays for half of its inventory purchases in the month of purchase and for the other half the month after purchase.
- The company will pay $5,000 in cash for office furniture in June. Sales commissions for June are budgeted at $3,000.
- The company maintains a minimum ending cash balance of $5,000 and can borrow from the bank in multiples of $100. All loans are repaid after 60 days.

Prepare a cash budget for Queensland for the month of June.

LO 4   **Cash Budget**

CASH FLOW

E11A. Citizens Produce Co-op is one of the biggest produce operations in northern Texas. Credit sales to retailers in the area constitute 80 percent of Citizens Produce's business; cash sales to customers at the company's retail outlet make up the other 20 percent. Collection records indicate that Citizens Produce collects payment on 50 percent of all credit sales during the month of sale, 30 percent in the month after the sale, and 20 percent in the second month after the sale.

The company's total sales in May were $60,000; in June, they were $70,000. Anticipated sales in July are $75,000; in August, $80,000; and in September, $90,000. The company's produce purchases are expected to total $45,000 in July, $51,000 in August, and $60,000 in September. The company pays for all purchases in cash.

Projected monthly costs for the quarter include $1,000 for heat, light, and power; $400 for bank fees; $2,000 for rent; $1,120 for supplies; $1,705 for depreciation of equipment; $1,285 for equipment repairs; and $500 for miscellaneous expenses. Other projected costs for the quarter are salaries and wages of $18,700 in July, $19,500 in August, and $20,600 in September.

The company's cash balance at June 30 was $2,000. Effective July 1, the company has a new policy of maintaining a minimum monthly cash balance of $3,000 and can borrow from the bank in multiples of $100.

1. Prepare a monthly cash budget for Citizens Produce Co-op for the quarter ended September 30.
2. **ACCOUNTING CONNECTION ▶** Should Citizens Produce anticipate taking out a loan during the quarter? If so, how much should it borrow, and when?

LO 4, 5   **Budgeted Income Statement**

E12A. Plenair, Inc., is located in France and organizes and coordinates art shows and auctions throughout the world. Its budgeted and actual costs for last year follow.

	Budgeted Cost	Actual Cost
Total operating expenses	€3,140,000	€3,176,868
Net receipts	6,200,000	6,369,200

Because the company sells only services, there is no cost of goods sold (net receipts equal gross margin). Plenair has budgeted the following fixed costs for the coming year: salaries, €1,000,000; advertising expense, €190,000; insurance, €150,000; and space rental costs, €300,000.

Additional information:

a. Net receipts are estimated at €6,400,000.

b. Travel costs are expected to be 11 percent of net receipts.

c. Auctioneer services will be billed at 15 percent of net receipts.

d. Printing costs are expected to be €190,000.

e. Home office costs are budgeted for €30,000.

f. Shipping costs are expected to be 20 percent higher than the €105,000 budgeted in the last year.

g. Miscellaneous expenses for the coming year will be budgeted at €8,000.

1. Prepare the company's budgeted income statement for the coming year using a 40 percent income tax rate,

2. **ACCOUNTING CONNECTION ▶** Should the budget committee be worried about the trend in the company's operations? Explain your answer.

LO 5   **Characteristics of Budgets**

E13A. BUSINESS APPLICATION ▶ You recently attended a workshop on budgeting and overheard the following comments as you walked to the refreshment table:

a. "Budgets are the same regardless of the size of an organization or management's role in the budgeting process."

b. "Budgets can include financial or nonfinancial data. In our organization, we plan the number of hours to be worked and the number of customer contacts we want our salespeople to make."

Do you agree or disagree with each comment? Explain your answers.

LO 5   **Budgeting and Goals**

E14A. BUSINESS APPLICATION ▶ Effective planning of long- and short-term goals has contributed to the success of Multitasker Calendars, Inc. Described below are the actions that the company's management team took during a recent planning meeting. Indicate whether the goals related to those actions are short-term or long-term.

1. Based on the 10-year forecast, the management team made decisions about next year's sales, personnel, material purchases, and profit targets.

2. In forecasting the next 10-year period, the management team considered economic and industry forecasts, product and service projections, and the long-term capital needs of the business.

LO 5   **Budgeting and Goals**

E15A. BUSINESS APPLICATION ▶ Assume that you work in the accounting department of a small shipping services company. Inspired by a recent seminar on budgeting, the company's president wants to develop a budgeting system and has asked you to direct it. Identify the points concerning the initial steps in the budgeting process that you should communicate to the president. Concentrate on principles related to long-term goals and short-term goals.

EXERCISES: SET B

Visit the textbook companion website at www.cengagebrain.com to access Exercise Set B for this chapter.

PROBLEMS

LO 3

Preparing Operating Budgets

P1. Enterprises, Inc.'s principal product is a hammer that carries a lifetime guarantee. Cost and production data for the hammer follow.

Direct materials:
    Anodized steel: 1 kilograms per hammer at $2 per kilogram
    Leather strapping for the handle: 0.5 square meter per hammer at $4 per square meter

Direct labor:
    Forging operation: $24 per labor hour; 6 minutes per hammer
    Leather-wrapping operation: $20 per direct labor hour; 12 minutes per hammer

Overhead:
    Forging operation: rate equals 40 percent of department's direct labor dollars
    Leather-wrapping operation: rate equals 60 percent of department's direct labor dollars

In October, November, and December, Enterprises expects to produce 108,000, 104,000, and 100,000 hammers, respectively. The company has no beginning or ending balances of direct materials inventory or work in process inventory for the year.

REQUIRED

1. For the three-month period ending December 31, prepare monthly production cost information for the hammer. Classify the costs as direct materials, direct labor, or overhead, and show your computations.
2. Prepare a cost of goods manufactured budget for the hammer. Show monthly cost data and combined totals for the quarter for each cost category.

LO 3, 4

Preparing a Comprehensive Budget

P2. Bathworks produces hair and bath products. Bathworks' owner would like to have an estimate of the company's net income in the coming year.

REQUIRED

Project Bathworks's net income next year by completing the operating budgets and budgeted income statement that follows. Assume that the selling price will remain constant.

1. Sales budget:

Bathworks
Sales Budget
For the Year Ended December 31

	Quarter				
	1	2	3	4	Year
Sales in units	4,000	3,000	5,000	5,000	17,000
Selling price per unit	× $6	× ?	× ?	× ?	× ?
Total sales	$24,000	?	?	?	?

2. Production budget:

Bathworks
Production Budget
For the Year Ended December 31

	Quarter				
	1	2	3	4	Year
Sales in units	4,000	?	?	?	?
Plus desired units of ending finished goods inventory[a]	300	?	?	600	600
Desired total units	4,300	?	?	?	?
Less desired units of beginning finished goods inventory[b]	400	?	?	?	400
Total production units	3,900	?	?	?	?

[a]Desired units of ending finished goods inventory = 10% of next quarter's budgeted sales.
[b]Desired units of beginning finished goods inventory = 10% of current quarter's budgeted sales.

3. Direct materials purchases budget:

Bathworks
Direct Materials Purchases Budget
For the Year Ended December 31

	Quarter				
	1	2	3	4	Year
Total production units	3,900	3,200	5,000	5,100	17,200
Ounces per unit	× 4	× 4	× 4	× 4	× 4
Total production needs in ounces	15,600	?	?	?	?
Plus desired ounces of ending direct materials inventory[a]	2,560	?	?	3,600	3,600
	18,160	?	?	?	?
Less desired ounces of beginning direct materials inventory[b]	3,120	?	?	?	3,120
Total ounces of direct materials to be purchased	15,040	?	?	?	?
Cost per ounce	× $0.10	× ?	× ?	× ?	× ?
Total cost of direct materials purchases	$ 1,504	?	?	?	?

[a]Desired ounces of ending direct materials inventory = 20% of next quarter's budgeted production needs in ounces.
[b]Desired ounces of beginning direct materials inventory = 20% of current quarter's budgeted production needs in ounces.

4. Direct labor budget:

Bathworks
Direct Labor Budget
For the Year Ended December 31

	Quarter				
	1	2	3	4	Year
Total production units	3,900	?	?	?	?
Direct labor hours per unit	× 0.10	× ?	× ?	× ?	× ?
Total direct labor hours	390	?	?	?	?
Direct labor cost per hour	× $20	× ?	× ?	× ?	× ?
Total direct labor cost	$7,800	?	?	?	?

(Continued)

5. Overhead budget:

Bathworks
Overhead Budget
For the Year Ended December 31

	Quarter				
	1	2	3	4	Year
Variable overhead costs:					
Factory supplies ($0.05)	$ 195	$?	$?	$?	$?
Employee benefits ($0.25)	975	?	?	?	?
Inspection ($0.10)	390	?	?	?	?
Maintenance and repairs ($0.15)	585	?	?	?	?
Utilities ($0.05)	195	?	?	?	?
Total variable overhead costs	$2,340	$?	$?	$?	$?
Total fixed overhead costs	4,300	?	?	?	?
Total overhead costs	$6,640	$?	$?	$?	$?

Note: The figures in parentheses are variable costs per unit.

6. Selling and administrative expenses budget:

Bathworks
Selling and Administrative Expenses Budget
For the Year Ended December 31

	Quarter				
	1	2	3	4	Year
Variable selling and administrative expenses:					
Delivery expenses ($0.10)	$ 400	$?	$?	$?	$?
Sales commissions ($0.15)	600	?	?	?	?
Accounting ($0.05)	200	?	?	?	?
Other administrative expenses ($0.20)	800	?	?	?	?
Total variable selling and administrative expenses	$2,000	$?	$?	$?	$?
Total fixed selling and administrative expenses	5,000	?	?	?	?
Total selling and administrative expenses	$7,000	$?	$?	$?	$?

Note: The figures in parentheses are variable costs per unit.

7. Cost of goods manufactured budget:

Bathworks
Cost of Goods Manufactured Budget
For the Year Ended December 31

Direct materials used:		
Direct materials inventory, beginning	$?	
Purchases	?	
Cost of direct materials available for use	$?	
Less direct materials inventory, ending	?	
Cost of direct materials used		$?
Direct labor costs		?
Overhead costs		?
Total manufacturing costs		$?
Work in process inventory, beginning		?
Less work in process inventory, ending*		?
Cost of goods manufactured		$?
Units produced		÷ ?
Manufactured cost per unit		$?

* It is the company's policy to have no units in process at the end of the year.

8. Budgeted income statement:

Bathworks
Budgeted Income Statement
For the Year Ended December 31

Sales		$?
Cost of goods sold:		
Finished goods inventory, beginning	$?	
Cost of goods manufactured	?	
Cost of goods available for sale	$?	
Less finished goods inventory, ending	?	
Cost of goods sold		?
Gross margin		$?
Selling and administrative expenses		?
Income from operations		$?
Income taxes expense (30% tax rate)		?
Net income		$?

LO **4**

CASH FLOW

SPREADSHEET

✔ Ending cash balance: $11,260

Cash Budget

P3. All Eyes Security Services Company provides security monitoring services. It employs four security specialists. Each specialist works an average of 180 hours a month. The company's controller has compiled the information that follows.

	Actual Data for Last Year		Forecasted Data for Current Year		
	November	**December**	**January**	**February**	**March**
Security billings (sales)	$30,000	$35,000	$25,000	$20,000	$30,000
Selling and admin. expenses	10,000	11,000	9,000	8,000	10,500
Operating supplies	2,500	3,500	2,500	2,000	3,000
Service overhead	3,000	3,500	3,000	2,500	3,000

Sixty percent of the client billings are cash sales collected during the month of sale; 30 percent are collected in the first month following the sale; and 10 percent are collected in the second month following the sale. Operating supplies are paid for in the month of purchase. Selling and administrative expenses and service overhead are paid in the month following the cost's incurrence.

The company has a bank loan of $12,000 at a 12 percent annual interest rate. Interest is paid monthly, and $2,000 of the loan principal is due on February 28. Income taxes of $2,500 for the last calendar year are due and payable on March 15. The four security specialists each earn $15 an hour, and all payroll-related employee benefit costs are included in service overhead. The company anticipates no capital expenditures for the first quarter of the coming year. It expects its cash balance on December 31 to be $15,000.

REQUIRED

Prepare a monthly cash budget for All Eyes for the three-month period ended March 31.

LO **4**

✔ 2: Net income: $107,982
✔ 3: Total assets: $742,288

Budgeted Income Statement and Budgeted Balance Sheet

P4. Local Bank has asked Wonderware Products, Inc.'s president for a budgeted income statement and budgeted balance sheet for the quarter ended June 30. These pro forma financial statements are needed to support Wonderware's request for a loan.

Wonderware routinely prepares a quarterly master budget. The operating budgets prepared for the quarter ending June 30 have provided the following information:

(Continued)

Projected sales for April are $220,400; for May, $164,220; and for June, $165,980. Direct materials purchases for the period are estimated at $96,840; direct materials usage, at $102,710; direct labor expenses, at $71,460; overhead, at $79,940; selling and administrative expenses, at $143,740; capital expenditures, at $125,000 (to be spent on June 29); cost of goods manufactured, at $252,880; and cost of goods sold, at $251,700.

Balance sheet account balances at March 31 were as follows: Accounts Receivable, $26,500; Materials Inventory, $23,910; Work in Process Inventory, $31,620; Finished Goods Inventory, $36,220; Prepaid Expenses, $7,200; Plant, Furniture, and Fixtures, $498,600; Accumulated Depreciation—Plant, Furniture, and Fixtures, $141,162; Patents, $90,600; Accounts Payable, $39,600; Notes Payable, $105,500; Common Stock, $250,000; and Retained Earnings, $200,988.

Projected monthly cash balances for the second quarter are as follows: April 30, $20,490; May 31, $35,610; and June 30, $39,320. During the quarter, accounts receivable are expected to increase by 30 percent, patents to go up by $6,500, prepaid expenses to remain constant, and accounts payable to go down by 10 percent (Wonderware will make a $5,000 payment on a note payable, $4,100 of which is principal reduction). The federal income tax rate is 30 percent, and the second quarter's tax is paid in July. Depreciation for the quarter will be $6,420, which is included in the overhead budget. The company will pay no dividends.

REQUIRED

1. Determine the June 30 ending balances for Materials Inventory, Work in Process Inventory, and Finished Goods Inventory.
2. Prepare a budgeted income statement for the quarter ended June 30.
3. Prepare a budgeted balance sheet as of June 30.

Basic Cash Budget

LO **4, 5**

✔ March cash receipts from sales on account: $87,360
✔ 1: Ending cash balance: $10,020

P5. Xeriscape Nurseries, Inc., has four divisions. The corporation's controller has been asked to prepare a cash budget for the Northern Division for the first quarter. Projected data supporting this budget follow.

Sales (60% on credit)		Purchases	
November	$160,000	December	$ 90,000
December	200,000	January	98,000
January	120,000	February	100,000
February	160,000	March	104,000
March	140,000		

Collection records of accounts receivable have shown that 40 percent of all credit sales are collected in the month of sale, 50 percent in the month following the sale, and 8 percent in the second month following the sale; 2 percent of the sales are uncollectible. All purchases are paid for in the month of the purchase. Salaries and wages are projected to be $25,000 in January, $33,000 in February, and $21,000 in March. Estimated monthly costs are utilities, $4,220; collection fees, $1,700; rent, $5,300; equipment depreciation, $5,440; supplies, $2,480; small tools, $3,140; and miscellaneous, $1,900. Each of the corporation's divisions maintains a $10,000 minimum cash balance and can borrow from the bank in multiples of $100, as needed. As of December 31, the Southern Division had a cash balance of $10,000.

REQUIRED

1. Prepare a monthly cash budget for Xeriscape Nurseries' Northern Division for the first quarter.
2. **ACCOUNTING CONNECTION** ▶ Should Xeriscape Nurseries anticipate taking out a loan for the Northern Division during the quarter? If so, how much should it borrow, and when?

ALTERNATE PROBLEMS

LO **3**

Preparing Operating Budgets

✔ 1: January total manufacturing costs
budgeted: $780,000
✔ 2: Quarter cost of goods manufactured
budget: $2,242,500

P6. Bobble, Inc.'s principal product is a stainless steel water bottle that carries a lifetime guarantee. Cost and production data for the water bottle follow.

Direct materials:
  Stainless steel: 0.25 kilogram per bottle at $8.00 per kilogram
  Clip for the handle: 1 per bottle at $0.10 each

Direct labor:
  Stamping operation: $30 per labor hour; 2 minutes per bottle

Overhead:
  Stamping operation: rate equals 80 percent of department's direct labor dollars

In January, February, and March, Waterworks expects to produce 200,000, 225,000, and 150,000 bottles, respectively. The company has no beginning or ending balances of direct materials inventory or work in process inventory for the year.

REQUIRED

1. For the three-month period ending March 31, prepare monthly production cost information for the metal water bottle. Classify the costs as direct materials, direct labor, or overhead, and show your computations. (Round to the nearest dollar.)
2. Prepare a cost of goods manufactured budget for the water bottle. Show monthly cost data and combined totals for the quarter for each cost category.

Preparing a Comprehensive Budget

LO **3, 4**

✔ 1: Total annual sales: $175,000
✔ 3: Total annual cost of direct materials
purchases: $36,240
✔ 8: Net income: $60,725

P7. Ginnie Springs Company has been bottling and selling water since 1940. The company's current owner would like to know how a new product would affect the company's net income in the coming year.

REQUIRED

Calculate Ginnie Springs' net income for the new product in the coming year by completing the operating budgets and budgeted income statement that follow. Assume that the selling price will remain constant.

1. Sales budget:

Ginnie Springs Company
Sales Budget
For the Year Ended December 31

	Quarter				
	1	2	3	4	Year
Sales in units	40,000	30,000	50,000	55,000	175,000
Selling price per unit	× $1	× ?	× ?	× ?	× ?
Total sales	$40,000	$?	$?	$?	$?

(Continued)

2. Production budget:

Ginnie Springs Company
Production Budget
For the Year Ended December 31

	Quarter				
	1	2	3	4	Year
Sales in units	40,000	?	?	?	?
Plus desired units of ending					
finished goods inventory[a]	3,000	?	?	6,000	6,000
Desired total units	43,000	?	?	?	?
Less desired units of beginning					
finished goods inventory[b]	4,000	?	?	?	4,000
Total production units	39,000	?	?	?	?

[a]Desired units of ending finished goods inventory = 10% of next quarter's budgeted sales.
[b]Desired units of beginning finished goods inventory = 10% of current quarter's budgeted sales.

3. Direct materials purchases budget:

Ginnie Springs Company
Direct Materials Purchases Budget
For the Year Ended December 31

	Quarter				
	1	2	3	4	Year
Total production units	39,000	32,000	50,500	55,500	?
Ounces per unit	× 20	× 20	× 20	× 20	× 20
Total production needs in ounces	780,000	?	?	?	?
Plus desired ounces of ending					
direct materials inventory[a]	128,000	?	?	240,000	240,000
	908,000	?	?	?	?
Less desired ounces of beginning					
direct materials inventory[b]	156,000	?	?	?	156,000
Total ounces of direct					
materials to be purchased	752,000	?	?	?	?
Cost per ounce	× $0.01	× ?	× ?	× ?	× ?
Total cost of direct					
materials purchases	$ 7,520	?	?	?	?

[a]Desired ounces of ending direct materials inventory = 20% of next quarter's budgeted production needs in ounces.
[b]Desired ounces of beginning direct materials inventory = 20% of current quarter's budgeted production needs in ounces.

4. Direct labor budget:

Ginnie Springs Company
Direct Labor Budget
For the Year Ended December 31

	Quarter				
	1	2	3	4	Year
Total production units	39,000	?	?	?	?
Direct labor hours per unit	×0.001	× ?	× ?	× ?	× ?
Total direct labor hours	39.0	?	?	?	?
Direct labor cost per hour	× $8	× ?	× ?	× ?	× ?
Total direct labor cost	$ 312	$?	$?	$?	$?

5. Overhead budget:

Ginnie Springs Company
Overhead Budget
For the Year Ended December 31

	Quarter				
	1	2	3	4	Year
Variable overhead costs:					
Factory supplies ($0.01)	$ 390	$?	$?	$?	$?
Employee benefits ($0.05)	1,950	?	?	?	?
Inspection ($0.01)	390	?	?	?	?
Maintenance and repairs ($0.02)	780	?	?	?	?
Utilities ($0.01)	390	?	?	?	?
Total variable overhead costs	$3,900	$?	$?	$?	$?
Total fixed overhead costs	1,416	?	?	?	?
Total overhead costs	$5,316	$?	$?	$?	$?

Note: The figures in parentheses are variable costs per unit.

6. Selling and administrative expenses budget:

Ginnie Springs Company
Selling and Administrative Expenses Budget
For the Year Ended December 31

	Quarter				
	1	2	3	4	Year
Variable selling and administrative expenses:					
Delivery expenses ($0.01)	$ 400	$?	$?	$?	$?
Sales commissions ($0.02)	800	?	?	?	?
Accounting ($0.01)	400	?	?	?	?
Other administrative expenses ($0.01)	400	?	?	?	?
Total variable selling and administrative expenses	$2,000	$?	$?	$?	$?
Total fixed selling and administrative expenses	5,000	?	?	?	?
Total selling and administrative expenses	$7,000	$?	$?	$?	$?

Note: The figures in parentheses are variable costs per unit.

7. Cost of goods manufactured budget:

Ginnie Springs Company
Cost of Goods Manufactured Budget
For the Year Ended December 31

Direct materials used:		
Direct materials inventory, beginning	$?	
Purchases	?	
Cost of direct materials available for use	$?	
Less direct materials inventory, ending	?	
Cost of direct materials used		$?
Direct labor costs		?
Overhead costs		?
Total manufacturing costs		$?
Work in process inventory, beginning*		?
Less work in process inventory, ending*		?
Cost of goods manufactured		$?
Units produced		÷ ?
Manufactured cost per unit		$?

* It is the company's policy to have no units in process at the end of the year.

(Continued)

8. Budgeted income statement:

Ginnie Springs Company
Budgeted Income Statement
For the Year Ended December 31

Sales			$?
Cost of goods sold:			
Finished goods inventory, beginning	$?		
Cost of goods manufactured	?		
Cost of goods available for sale	$?		
Less finished goods inventory, ending	?		
Cost of goods sold		?	
Gross margin		$?	
Selling and administrative expenses		?	
Income from operations		$?	
Income taxes expense (30% tax rate)		?	
Net income		$?	

LO 4

CASH FLOW

SPREADSHEET

✔ Ending cash balance: $41,330

Cash Budget

P8. Forensics Company provides fraud monitoring services. It employs five fraud specialists. Each specialist works an average of 200 hours a month. The company's controller has compiled the information that follows.

	Actual Data for Last Year		Forecasted Data for the Current Year		
	November	**December**	**January**	**February**	**March**
Billings (sales)	$100,000	$80,000	$60,000	$50,000	$70,000
Selling and administrative expenses	15,000	12,000	8,000	7,000	10,000
Operating supplies	2,500	3,500	2,500	2,000	3,000
Service overhead	14,000	13,500	13,000	12,500	13,000

Of the client billings, 70 percent are cash sales collected during the month of sale; 20 percent are collected in the first month following the sale; and 10 percent are collected in the second month following the sale. Operating supplies are paid in the month of purchase. Selling and administrative expenses and service overhead are paid in the month the cost is incurred.

The company has a bank loan of $12,000 at a 6 percent annual interest rate. Interest is paid monthly, and $2,000 of the loan principal is due on February 28. Income taxes of $6,500 for last calendar year are due and payable on March 15. The five security specialists each earn $24.00 an hour, and all payroll-related employee benefit costs are included in service overhead. The company anticipates no capital expenditures for the first quarter of the coming year. It expects its cash balance on December 31 to be $5,000.

REQUIRED

Prepare a monthly cash budget for Forensics for the three-month period ended March 31.

LO 4

✔ 2: Net income: $55,580
✔ 3: Total assets: $385,316

Budgeted Income Statement and Budgeted Balance Sheet

P9. Video Company, Inc., produces and markets two popular video games, *High Ranger* and *Star Bounder*. The closing account balances on the company's balance sheet for last year are as follows: Cash, $18,735; Accounts Receivable, $19,900; Materials Inventory, $18,510; Work in Process Inventory, $24,680; Finished Goods Inventory, $21,940; Prepaid Expenses, $3,420; Plant and Equipment, $262,800; Accumulated Depreciation—Plant and Equipment, $55,845; Other Assets, $9,480; Accounts Payable,

$52,640; Mortgage Payable, $70,000; Common Stock, $90,000; and Retained Earnings, $107,804.

Operating budgets for the first quarter of the coming year show the following estimated costs: direct materials purchases, $58,100; direct materials usage, $62,400; direct labor expense, $42,880; overhead, $51,910; selling expenses, $35,820; general and administrative expenses, $60,240; cost of goods manufactured, $163,990; and cost of goods sold, $165,440. Estimated ending cash balances are as follows: January, $34,610; February, $60,190; and March, $51,626. The company will have no capital expenditures during the quarter.

Sales are projected to be $125,200 in January, $105,100 in February, and $112,600 in March. Accounts receivable are expected to double during the quarter, and accounts payable are expected to decrease by 20 percent. Mortgage payments for the quarter will total $6,000, of which $2,000 will be interest expense. Prepaid expenses are expected to go up by $20,000, and other assets are projected to increase by 50 percent over the budget period. Depreciation for plant and equipment (already included in the overhead budget) averages 5 percent of total plant and equipment per year. Federal income taxes (30 percent of profits) are payable in April. The company pays no dividends.

REQUIRED

1. Determine the March 31 ending balances for Materials Inventory, Work in Process Inventory, and Finished Goods Inventory.
2. Prepare a budgeted income statement for the quarter ended March 31.
3. Prepare a budgeted balance sheet as of March 31.

LO **4**   **Comprehensive Cash Budget**

CASH FLOW

✔ Ending cash balance: $36,105

P10. Pur Centers, Inc., operates three fully equipped fitness centers, as well as a medical center that specializes in preventive medicine. The data that follow pertain to the corporation's first quarter.

Cash receipts:
  Memberships: December, 870; January, 880; February, 910; March, 1,030
  Membership dues: $100 per month, payable on the 10th of the month (80 percent collected on time; 20 percent collected one month late)
  Medical examinations: January, $35,610; February, $41,840; March, $45,610
  Special aerobics classes: January, $4,020; February, $5,130; March, $7,130
  High-protein food sales: January, $4,890; February, $5,130; March, $6,280

Cash payments:
  Salaries and wages:
    Corporate officers: 2 at $18,000 per month
    Physicians: 2 at $7,000 per month
    Nurses: 3 at $2,900 per month
    Clerical staff: 2 at $1,500 per month
    Aerobics instructors: 3 at $1,100 per month
    Clinic staff: 6 at $1,700 per month
    Maintenance staff: 3 at $900 per month
    Health-food servers: 3 at $750 per month

  Purchases:
    Muscle-toning machines: January, $14,400; February, $13,800 (no purchases in March)
    Pool supplies: $520 per month
    Health food: January, $3,290; February, $3,460; March, $3,720
    Medical supplies: January, $10,400; February, $11,250; March, $12,640
    Medical uniforms and disposable garments: January, $7,410; February, $3,900; March, $3,450

(Continued)

Medical equipment: January, $11,200; February, $3,400; March $5,900

Advertising: January, $2,250; February, $1,190; March, $2,450

Utilities expense: January, $5,450; February, $5,890; March, $6,090

Insurance:

Fire: January, $3,470

Liability: March, $3,980

Property taxes: $3,760 due in January

Federal income taxes: Last year's taxes of $21,000 due in March

Miscellaneous: January, $2,625; February, $2,800; March, $1,150

Pur Centers' controller anticipates that the beginning cash balance on January 1 will be $14,000.

REQUIRED

Prepare a cash budget for Pur Centers for the first quarter of the year. Use January, February, March, and Quarter as the column headings.

CASES

LO 1, 2, 4, 5   **Conceptual Understanding: Policies for Budget Development**

C1. BUSINESS APPLICATION ▶ Raiders Corporation is a company with annual sales of $50 million. Its budget committee has created the following policy that the company uses each year in developing its master budget for the following calendar year:

May   The company's controller and other members of the budget committee meet to discuss plans and objectives for next year. The controller conveys all relevant information from this meeting to division managers and department heads.

June   Division managers, department heads, and the controller meet to discuss the corporate plans and objectives for next year. They develop a timetable for developing next year's budget data.

July   Division managers and department heads develop budget data. The vice president of sales provides them with final sales estimates, and they complete monthly sales estimates for each product line.

Aug.   Estimates of next year's monthly production activity and inventory levels are completed. Division managers and department heads communicate these estimates to the controller, who distributes them to other operating areas.

Sept.   All operating areas submit their revised budget data. The controller integrates their labor requirements, direct materials requirements, unit cost estimates, cash requirements, and profit estimates into a preliminary master budget.

Oct.   The budget committee meets to discuss the preliminary master budget and to make any necessary corrections, additions, or deletions. The controller incorporates all authorized changes into a final draft of the master budget.

Nov.   The controller submits the final draft to the budget committee for approval. If the committee approves it, it is distributed to all corporate officers, division managers, and department heads.

1. Comment on this policy.
2. What changes would you recommend?

LO 3, 5   **Ethical Dilemma: Ethical Considerations in Budgeting**

C2. BUSINESS APPLICATION ▶ Joakim Keynes is the manager of the Repairs and Maintenance Department of JB Industries. He is responsible for preparing his department's annual budget. Most managers in the company inflate their budget numbers by at least 10 percent because their bonuses depend upon how much below budget their departments operate. Keynes turned in the following information for his department's budget for next year to the company's budget committee:

	Budget This Year	Actual This Year	Budget Next Year
Supplies	$ 20,000	$ 16,000	$ 24,000
Labor	80,000	82,000	96,000
Utilities	8,500	8,000	10,200
Tools	12,500	9,000	15,000
Hand-carried equipment	25,000	16,400	30,000
Cleaning materials	4,600	4,200	5,520
Miscellaneous	2,000	2,100	2,400
Totals	$152,600	$137,700	$183,120

Because the figures for next year are 20 percent above those in this year's budget, the budget committee questioned them. Keynes defended them by saying that he expects a significant increase in activity in his department next year.

What do you think are the real reasons for the increase in the budgeted amounts? What ethical considerations enter into this situation?

LO 4

Conceptual Understanding: Budgeting for Cash Flows

C3. The nature of a company's business affects its need to budget for cash flows.

- **H&R Block** is a service company whose main business is preparing tax returns. Most tax returns are prepared after January 31 and before April 15. For a fee and interest, the company will advance cash to clients who are due refunds. The clients are expected to repay the cash advances when they receive their refunds. Although H&R Block has some revenues throughout the year, it devotes most of the nontax season to training potential employees in tax preparation procedures and to laying the groundwork for the next tax season.

- **Toys"R"Us** is a toy retailer whose sales are concentrated in October, November, and December of one year and January of the next year. Sales continue at a steady but low level during the rest of the year. The company purchases most of its inventory between July and September.

- **Johnson & Johnson** sells the many health care products that it manufactures to retailers, and the retailers sell them to the final customer. Johnson & Johnson offers retailers credit terms.

Discuss the nature of cash receipts and cash disbursements over a calendar year in the three companies we have just described. What are some key estimates that the management of these companies must make when preparing a cash budget?

LO 4, 5

Interpreting Management Reports: Budgeting Procedures

C4. BUSINESS APPLICATION ▶ Since Smart Enterprises inaugurated participative budgeting 10 years ago, everyone in the organization—from maintenance personnel to the president's staff—has had a voice in the budgeting process. Until recently, participative budgeting has worked in the best interests of the company as a whole. Now, however, it is becoming evident that some managers are using the practice solely to benefit their own divisions. The budget committee has therefore asked you, the company's controller, to analyze this year's divisional budgets carefully before incorporating them into the company's master budget.

The Gadget Division was the first of the company's six divisions to submit its budget request for next year. The division's budgeted income statement follows.

(Continued)

Smart Enterprises
Gadget Division
Budgeted Income Statement
For the Years Ended December 31

	Budget for This Year	Budget for Next Year	Increase (Decrease)
Net sales:			
Radios	$ 850,000	$ 910,000	$ 60,000
Appliances	680,000	740,000	60,000
Telephones	270,000	305,000	35,000
Miscellaneous	84,400	90,000	5,600
Net sales	$1,884,400	$2,045,000	$160,600
Less cost of goods sold	750,960	717,500[a]	(33,460)
Gross margin	$1,133,440	$1,327,500	$194,060
Operating expenses:			
Wages			
Warehouse	$ 94,500	$ 102,250	$ 7,750
Purchasing	77,800	84,000	6,200
Delivery/shipping	69,400	74,400	5,000
Maintenance	42,650	45,670	3,020
Salaries:			
Supervisory	60,000	92,250	32,250
Executive	130,000	164,000	34,000
Purchases, supplies	17,400	20,500	3,100
Maintenance	72,400	82,000	9,600
Depreciation	62,000	74,000[b]	12,000
Building rent	96,000	102,500	6,500
Sales commissions	188,440	204,500	16,060
Insurance:			
Fire	12,670	20,500	7,830
Liability	18,200	20,500	2,300
Utilities	14,100	15,375	1,275
Taxes			
Property	16,600	18,450	1,850
Payroll	26,520	41,000	14,480
Miscellaneous	4,610	10,250	5,640
Total operating expenses	$1,003,290	$1,172,145	$168,855
Income from operations	$ 130,150	$ 155,355	$ 25,205

[a] Less expensive merchandise will be purchased in the next year to boost profits.
[b] Depreciation is increased because additional equipment must be bought to handle increased sales.

1. Recast the Gadget Division's budgeted income statement in the following format (round percentages to two decimal places):

	Budget for This Year		Budget for Next Year	
Account	Amount	Percentage of Net Sales	Amount	Percentage of Net Sales

2. Actual results for this year revealed the following information about revenues and cost of goods sold:

	Amount	Percentage of Net Sales
Net sales:		
Radios	$ 780,000	43.94%
Appliances	640,000	36.06
Telephones	280,000	15.77
Miscellaneous	75,000	4.23
Net sales	$1,775,000	100.00%
Less cost of goods sold	763,425	43.01
Gross margin	$1,011,575	56.99%

On the basis of this information and your analysis in **1**, what do you think the budget committee should say to the Gadget Division's managers? Identify any specific areas of the budget that may need to be revised, and explain why the revision is needed.

LO 3, 4

The Budgeting Process

SPREADSHEET

C5. Refer to our development of Framecraft Company's master budget in this chapter. Suppose that because of a new customer in Canada, the company management has decided to increase budgeted sales in the first quarter by 5,000 units. The expenses for this sale will include direct materials, direct labor, variable overhead, and variable selling and administrative expenses. The delivery expense for the Canadian customer will be $0.18 per unit rather than the regular $0.08 per unit. The desired units of beginning finished goods inventory will remain at 1,000 units.

1. Using a spreadsheet, revise Framecraft's budgeted income statement and the operating budgets that support it to reflect the changes described above. (Round manufactured cost per unit to three decimal places, and round income tax expense to the nearest dollar.)
2. What is the change in income from operations? Would you recommend accepting the order from the Canadian customer? If so, why?

Continuing Case: Cookie Company

C6. In this segment of our continuing case, you have decided to open a store where you will sell your company's cookies, as well as coffee, tea, and other beverages. You believe that the store will be able to provide excellent service and undersell the local competition. To fund operations, you are applying for a loan from the Small Business Administration. The loan application requires you to submit two financial budgets—a pro forma income statement and a pro forma balance sheet—within six weeks.

How do the four *w*'s of preparing an accounting report apply in this situation—that is, *why* are you preparing these financial budgets, *who* needs them, *what* information do you need to prepare them, and *when* are they due?

CHAPTER 7
Flexible Budgets and Performance Analysis

BUSINESS INSIGHT
Vail Resorts

Vail Resorts Includes vacation spots like Vail, Breckenridge, Keystone, Heavenly, and Beaver Creek. To help guests enjoy all the activities that these places offer, Vail Resorts instituted an "all-in-one" charge card, which guests can use to pay for anything they might buy at the resort, including meals or snacks, skiing or snowboarding lessons, lift tickets, treatments at the spa, or merchandise from one of the resort's retail shops.

Guests like the all-in-one card because of its convenience, and they can earn points toward free lodging, meals, or lift tickets. The resort's managers like the card system because it is a simple way of collecting vast amounts of both financial and nonfinancial information. Each time a guest makes a purchase, the all-in-one card is electronically scanned. The new data then become part of an integrated management information system, which managers use in a variety of ways to measure and evaluate the resort's performance.

1. CONCEPT ▶ *What concepts guide managers when they evaluate performance?*

2. ACCOUNTING APPLICATION ▶ *How will managers use flexible budgets and other performance measures to analyze the financial and nonfinancial performance of responsibility centers?*

3. BUSINESS APPLICATION ▶ *How can managers achieve a balanced view of a business's well-being and how to improve it?*

LEARNING OBJECTIVES

LO 1 Define a *performance management and evaluation system* and *responsibility accounting*, and describe the roles they play in performance analysis.

LO 2 Use flexible budgets and variable costing to analyze cost center and profit center performance.

LO 3 Analyze investment centers using return on investment, residual income, and economic value added.

LO 4 Describe how the balanced scorecard aligns performance with organizational goals.

LO 5 Explain how properly linked performance incentives and measures add value for all stakeholders in performance management and evaluation.

Blend Images/Fotolia LLC

CONCEPTS
- Comparability
- Understandability

**RELEVANT
LEARNING OBJECTIVE**

LO 1 Define a *performance management and evaluation system* and *responsibility accounting,* and describe the roles they play in performance analysis.

LO 1 Concepts Underlying Performance Analysis

Managers use the concepts of *understandability* and *comparability* as they manage a wide range of financial and nonfinancial data to guide and evaluate performance. If they want satisfactory results, managers must understand the cause-and-effect relationships between their actions and their performance. By measuring and tracking the causal relationships for which they are accountable, managers can improve performance as they command, control, and evaluate the organization.

A **performance management and evaluation system** is a set of procedures that account for and report on both financial and nonfinancial performance so that a company can *understand* how well it is doing, where it is going, and what improvements will make it more profitable. **Performance measures** are quantitative tools that gauge and *compare* an organization's performance in relation to a specific goal or an expected outcome.

- Financial performance measures use monetary information to measure and *compare* the performance of a profit-generating organization or its divisions, departments, product lines, sales territories, or operating activities. Examples include return on investment, net income as a percentage of sales, and the costs of poor quality as a percentage of sales.
- Nonfinancial performance measures use statistics to *understand* how to reduce or eliminate waste and inefficiencies in operating activities. Examples include the number of times an activity occurs or the time taken to perform a task, such as the number of customer complaints; number of orders shipped the same day; or the time taken to fill an order.

What to Measure, How to Measure

Performance measurement is the use of quantitative tools to *understand* an organization's performance in relation to a specific goal or an expected outcome. For performance measurement to succeed, managers must be able to distinguish between what is being measured and the actual measures used to monitor performance and *compare* results. For instance, product or service quality is not a performance measure. It is part of management's strategy to produce the highest-quality product or service possible, given the resources available. Product or service quality thus is what management wants to measure and compare.

As part of their performance management systems, organizations assign resources to specific areas of responsibility and track how the managers of those areas use those resources. For example, **Vail Resorts** assigns resources to its Lodging, Dining, Retail and Rental, Ski School, and Real Estate divisions and holds the managers of those divisions responsible for generating revenue and managing costs. Within each division, other managers are assigned responsibility for such areas as Children and Adult Ski School, Snowboard School, or Private Lessons.

All managers at all levels are then evaluated in terms of their ability to manage their areas of responsibility. To assist in performance management and evaluation, many organizations use responsibility accounting. **Responsibility accounting** is an information system that classifies data according to areas of responsibility and reports each area's activities by including only the revenue, cost, and resource categories that the assigned manager can control. A **responsibility center** is an organizational unit whose manager has been assigned the responsibility of managing a portion of the organization's resources. The activities of a responsibility center dictate the extent of a manager's responsibility. Thus, responsibility accounting establishes accountability—the foundation of performance analysis—by grounding user *comparisons* and *understanding* of an organization.

A report for a responsibility center should contain only the costs, revenues, and resources that the manager of that center can control. Such costs and revenues are called **controllable costs and revenues**, because they are the result of a manager's actions, influence, or decisions. A responsibility accounting system ensures that managers will not be held responsible for items that they cannot change.

Types of Responsibility Centers

There are five types of responsibility centers:

- cost center
- discretionary cost center
- revenue center
- profit center
- investment center

The key characteristics of each type of responsibility center are summarized in Exhibit 1.

Exhibit 1
Types of Responsibility Centers

Responsibility Center	Manager Responsibility	Performance Measures	Examples
Cost center	Only controllable costs, where there are well-defined links between the costs of resources and the resulting products or services	• Comparison of actual costs with flexible and master budget costs • Analysis of resulting variances	**Product:** Manufacturing assembly plants **Service:** Food service for hospital patients
Discretionary cost center	Only controllable costs; the links between the costs of resources and the resulting products or services are *not* well defined	• Comparison of actual noncost-based measures with targets • Determination of compliance with preapproved budgeted spending limits	**Product or service:** Administrative activities such as accounting, human resources, and research and development
Revenue center	Revenue generation	• Comparison of actual revenue with budgeted revenue • Analysis of resulting variances	**Product:** Phone or e-commerce sales for pizza delivery **Service:** Reservation center on Internet
Profit center	Operating income resulting from controllable revenues and costs	• Comparison of actual variable costing income statement with the budgeted income statement	**Product or service:** Local store of a national chain
Investment center	Controllable revenues, costs, and the investment of resources to achieve organizational goals	• Return on investment • Residual income • Economic value added	**Product:** A division of a multinational corporation **Service:** A national office of a multinational consulting firm

© Cengage Learning 2014

Cost Center A responsibility center whose manager is accountable only for controllable costs that have well-defined relationships between the center's resources and certain products or services is called a **cost center**. Manufacturing companies like **Apple** use cost centers to manage assembly plants, where the causal relationship between the costs of resources (direct material, direct labor) and the resulting products is well defined. Service organizations use cost centers to manage activities in which resources are clearly linked with a service that is provided at no additional charge. For example, in nursing homes and hospitals, there is a clear relationship between the costs of food and direct labor and the number of inpatient meals served.

The performance of a cost center is usually evaluated by *comparing* an activity's actual cost with its budgeted cost and analyzing the resulting variances. You will learn more about this performance evaluation process in the chapter on standard costing.

Discretionary Cost Center A responsibility center whose manager is accountable for costs only and in which the relationship between resources and the products or services produced is not well defined is called a **discretionary cost center**. Departments that perform administrative activities, such as accounting, human resources, and legal services, are typical examples of discretionary cost centers. These centers, like cost centers, have approved budgets that set spending limits.

Because the spending and use of resources in discretionary cost centers are not clearly linked to the production of a product or service, cost-based measures usually cannot be used to evaluate performance (although such centers are penalized if they exceed their approved budgets). For example, among the performance measures used to evaluate the research and development activities are the number of patents obtained and the number of cost-saving innovations that are developed. At service organizations, such as **United Way**, a common measure of administrative activities is how low their costs are as a percentage of total contributions.

Research and development units are a type of discretionary cost center in which a manager is accountable for costs only and the relationship between resources and products or services produced is not well defined. A common performance measure used to evaluate research and development activities is the number of patents obtained.

Revenue Center A responsibility center whose manager is accountable primarily for revenue and whose success is based on its ability to generate revenue is called a **revenue center**. Examples of revenue centers are **Hertz**'s national car reservation center and **Amazon**'s ecommerce order department.

A revenue center's performance is usually evaluated by *comparing* its actual revenue with its budgeted revenue and analyzing the resulting variances. Performance measures may include sales dollars, number of customer sales, or sales revenue per minute.

Profit Center A responsibility center whose manager is accountable for both revenue and costs and for the resulting operating income is called a **profit center**. A good example is a local store of a national chain, such as **Wal-Mart** or **Jiffy Lube**.

The performance of a profit center is usually evaluated by *comparing* the figures on its actual income statement with the figures on its master or flexible budget income statement.

Investment Center A responsibility center whose manager is accountable for profit generation and who can also make significant decisions about the resources that the center uses is called an **investment center**. For example, the president of **Harley-Davidson**'s Buell subsidiary and the president of **Brinker International**'s Chili's Grill and Bar can control revenues, costs, and the investment of assets to achieve organizational goals.

The performance of these centers is evaluated using such measures as return on investment, residual income, and economic value added, (which will be discussed later in the chapter). These measures are used in all types of organizations, both manufacturing and service.

Organizational Structure and Performance Reports

Much can be learned about an organization by examining how its managers organize activities and resources. A company's organizational structure formalizes its lines of managerial authority and control. An **organization chart** is a visual representation of an organization's hierarchy of responsibility for the purposes of management control. Within an organization chart, the five types of responsibility centers are arranged by level of management authority and control.

Exhibit 2 shows a typical corporate organization chart for part of the management structure for the Restaurant Division of a hospitality corporation like **Vail Resorts**. Notice that all five types of responsibility centers are represented.

Exhibit 2
**Partial Organization Chart
of the Restaurant Division**

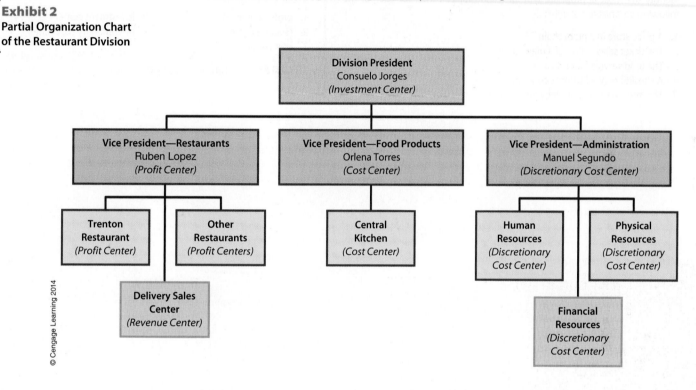

© Cengage Learning 2014

In a responsibility accounting system, the performance reports for each level of management are tailored to each manager's individual needs for information. As information moves up the organizational chart, it is usually condensed. Performance reporting by responsibility level enables an organization to trace the source of a cost, revenue, or resource to the manager who controls it and to evaluate that manager's performance accordingly.

STUDY NOTE: *Only controllable items should be included on a manager's performance report.*

Because performance reports contain information about costs, revenues, and resources, they allow *comparisons* between actual performance and budget expectations. Such comparisons allow management to *understand* and evaluate an individual's performance with respect to responsibility center and company-wide objectives and to recommend changes. Performance reports should contain only costs, revenues, and resources that the manager can control. If a performance report includes items that the manager cannot control, the credibility of the entire responsibility accounting system can be called into question. The content and format of a performance report depend on the nature of the responsibility center. It is up to management to structure and interpret them fairly.

Although performance reports vary in format, they have some common themes:

- All responsibility center reports compare actual results to budgeted figures and focus on the differences.
- Often, comparisons are made to a flexible budget (to be discussed in the next section) as well as to the master budget.
- Only the items that the manager can control are included in the performance report.
- Nonfinancial measures are also examined to achieve a more balanced view of the manager's responsibilities.

APPLY IT!

Identify the most appropriate type of responsibility center for each of the following organizational units:

1. A pizza store in a pizza chain
2. The ticket sales center of a major airline
3. The food service function at a nursing home
4. A subsidiary of a business conglomerate
5. The information technology area of a company

SOLUTION

1. profit center
2. revenue center
3. cost center
4. investment center
5. discretionary cost center

TRY IT! SE1, E1A, E2A, E1B, E2B

SECTION 2

ACCOUNTING APPLICATIONS

LO 2 Performance Evaluation of Cost Centers and Profit Centers

The accuracy of performance analysis depends to a large extent on the type of budget that managers use when *comparing* actual results to a budget. Static, or fixed, budgets forecast revenues and expenses for just one level of sales and just one level of output. The budgets that make up a master budget are usually based on a single level of output; but many things can cause actual output to differ from the estimated output. If a company produces more products than predicted, total production costs will almost always be greater than predicted. Thus, a comparison of actual production costs with master budgeted costs will inevitably show variances.

Flexible Budgets and Performance Analysis

To judge a product or division's performance accurately, the company's managers can use a **flexible budget** (or *variable budget*), which is a summary of expected costs for a range of activity levels. Unlike a static budget, a flexible budget provides forecasted data that can be adjusted for changes in the level of output. In terms of *comparability*, flexible budgets allow managers to compare budgeted and actual costs at any level of output. An important element in preparing a flexible budget is the **flexible budget formula**, an equation that determines the expected, or budgeted, cost for any level of output. The flexible budget formula can be used to create a budget for any level of output in the range of levels given and is computed as follows.

$$\text{Flexible Budgeted Costs} = \left(\text{Variable Cost per Unit} \times \text{Number of Units Produced} \right) + \text{Budgeted Fixed Costs}$$

We will use Winter Wonderland Resort, a hypothetical company, to illustrate how managers use flexible budgets. In the Restaurant Division of Winter Wonderland, the central kitchen evaluates the performance of each food item produced. The flexible budget formula for one of its products, House Dressing, would be computed as follows.

House Dressing Flexible Budget Formula = ($0.33 × Gallons Produced) + $5

A flexible budget for Winter Wonderland's House Dressing appears in Exhibit 3, which shows the estimated costs for 1,000, 1,200, and 1,500 gallons of salad dressing output.

Exhibit 3
Flexible Budget for House Dressing

	Winter Wonderland—Restaurant Division House Dressing Flexible Budget Current Year		
	Units Produced		
Cost Category	**1,000**	**1,200**	**1,500**
Direct materials ($0.25 per gallon)	$250	$300	$375
Direct labor ($0.05 per gallon)	50	60	75
Variable overhead ($0.03 per gallon)	30	36	45
Total variable costs ($0.33 per gallon)	$330	$396	$495
Fixed overhead costs	5	5	5
Total costs	$335	$401	$500

Evaluating Cost Center Performance Using Flexible Budgeting

In the Restaurant Division of a major hospitality company like Winter Wonderland, the central kitchen is where the food products that the restaurants sell are prepared. It is a cost center because its costs have well-defined relationships with the resulting products, which are then transferred to the restaurants for further processing and sale. To ensure each food item is meeting its performance goals, the manager will evaluate each product by *comparing* its actual costs with the corresponding amounts from the budget.

The performance report on House Dressing presented in Exhibit 4 compares data from Winter Wonderland's master budget (prepared at the beginning of the period) and flexible budget (prepared at the end of the period) with the actual results for the period. As you can see, actual costs exceeded budgeted costs. Most managers would consider such a cost overrun significant. But was there really a cost overrun if the amounts budgeted in the master budget are based on an output of 1,000 units of dressing and the actual output was 1,200 units of dressing?

To judge the central kitchen's performance accurately, the company needs to change the budgeted data in the master budget to reflect an output of 1,200 units, as illustrated in Exhibit 4. The flexible budget is used primarily as an evaluation tool at the end of a period. Favorable (positive, or F) and unfavorable (negative, or U) variances between actual costs and the flexible budget can be further examined by using standard costing to compute specific variances for direct materials, direct labor, and variable and fixed overhead.[*]

Exhibit 4
Central Kitchen's Performance Report on House Dressing

	Actual Results	Variance	Flexible Budget	Variance	Master Budget
Gallons produced	**1,200**	**0**	**1,200**	**200 (F)**	**1,000**
Center costs:					
Direct materials ($0.25 per gallon)	$312	$(12) (U)	$300	$(50) (U)	$250
Direct labor ($0.05 per gallon)	72	(12) (U)	60	(10) (U)	50
Variable overhead ($0.03 per gallon)	33	3 (F)	36	(6) (U)	30
Fixed overhead	2	3 (F)	5	0	5
Total cost	$419	$(18) (U)	$401	$(66) (U)	$335
Performance measures:					
Defect-free gallons to total produced	0.98	(0.01) (U)	N/A	N/A	0.99
Average throughput minutes per gallon	11	1 (F)	N/A	N/A	12

Note: In this exhibit and others that appear later in this chapter, (F) indicates a favorable variance, and (U) indicates an unfavorable variance.

© Cengage Learning 2014

Evaluating Profit Center Performance Using Variable Costing

Restaurants are profit centers, since each is accountable for its own revenues and costs and for the resulting operating income. A profit center's performance is usually evaluated by *comparing* its actual income statement results to its budgeted income statement.

One method of preparing profit center performance reports is **variable costing**, which classifies a manager's controllable costs as either variable or fixed. Variable costing produces a variable costing income statement instead of a traditional income statement (also called a *full costing* or *absorption costing income statement*), which is used for external reporting purposes. It is an internally prepared income statement that is useful in performance management and evaluation because it focuses on cost variability and the

STUDY NOTE: *A variable costing income statement has a similar format to the contribution margin income statement used in cost-volume-profit analysis.*

---

[*] Refer to the chapter on standard costing for further information on performance evaluation using variances or the flexible budget.

profit center's contribution to operating income. Under variable costing, variable costs include direct materials costs, direct labor costs, variable overhead costs, and variable selling, administrative, and general costs. Fixed costs include fixed manufacturing costs, like fixed overhead, and fixed selling, administrative, and general costs. The format of a variable costing income statement follows.

Sales
– Variable costs
Contribution margin
– Fixed costs
Operating income

The variable costing income statement differs from the traditional income statement prepared for financial reporting, as shown by the two income statements in Exhibit 5 for Trenton Restaurant, which is part of Winter Wonderland's Restaurant Division. In the traditional income statement, all manufacturing costs are assigned to the cost of goods sold. In the variable costing income statement, only the variable manufacturing costs are included in the variable cost of goods sold. Fixed manufacturing costs are considered costs of the current period and are listed with fixed selling expenses after the contribution margin has been computed.

Exhibit 5
Variable Costing Income Statement Versus Traditional Income Statement for Trenton Restaurant (Amounts in Thousands)

Variable Costing Income Statement		Traditional Income Statement	
Sales	$ 2,500	Sales	$ 2,500
Variable cost of goods sold	(1,575)	Cost of goods sold	
Variable selling expenses	(325)	($1,575 + $170)	(1,745)
Contribution margin	$ 600	Gross margin	$ 755
Fixed manufacturing costs	(170)	Variable selling expenses	(325)
Fixed selling expenses	(230)	Fixed selling expenses	(230)
Profit center operating income	$ 200	Profit center operating income	$ 200

© Cengage Learning 2014

In addition to tracking financial performance measures, a manager of a profit center may also want to measure and evaluate nonfinancial information, such as the number of food orders processed and the average amount of a sales order at Trenton Restaurant. The resulting report, based on variable costing and flexible budgeting, is shown in Exhibit 6.

Exhibit 6
Performance Report Based on Variable Costing and Flexible Budgeting for Trenton Restaurant (Amounts in Thousands)

	Actual Results	Variance	Flexible Budget	Variance	Master Budget
Meals served	750	0	750	250 (U)	1,000
Sales (average meal $2.85)	$ 2,500.00	$ 362.50 (F)	$ 2,137.50	$ 712.50 (U)	$ 2,850.00
Controllable variable costs:					
Variable cost of goods sold ($1.50)	(1,575.00)	(450.00) (U)	(1,125.00)	(375.00) (F)	(1,500.00)
Variable selling expenses ($0.40)	(325.00)	(25.00) (U)	(300.00)	(100.00) (F)	(400.00)
Contribution margin	$ 600.00	$ 112.50 (U)	$ 712.50	$ 237.50 (U)	$ 950.00
Controllable fixed costs:					
Fixed manufacturing expenses	(170.00)	(30.00) (F)	(200.00)	0.00	(200.00)
Fixed selling expenses	(230.00)	(20.00) (F)	(250.00)	0.00	(250.00)
Profit center operating income	$ 200.00	$ 62.50 (U)	$ 262.50	$ 237.50 (U)	$ 500.00
Nonfinancial performance measures:					
Number of orders processed	300	50 (F)	N/A	N/A	250
Average sales order	$8.34	$3.06 (U)	N/A	N/A	$11.40

© Cengage Learning 2014

APPLY IT!

Complete the following performance report for a profit center for the month ended December 31:

	Actual Results	Variance	Master Budget
Sales	$?	$ 20 (F)	$ 120
Controllable variable costs:			
Variable cost of goods sold	(25)	(10) (U)	?
Variable selling and administrative expenses	(15)	? (?)	(5)
Contribution margin	$100	$? (?)	$ 100
Controllable fixed costs	?	10 (F)	60
Profit center income	$ 50	$ 10 (F)	$?
Nonfinancial performance measures:			
Number of orders processed	50	20 (F)	?
Average daily sales	$?	$0.66 (F)	$4.00
Number of units sold	100	40 (F)	?

SOLUTION

**Profit Center
Performance Report
For the Month Ended December 31**

	Actual Results	Variance	Master Budget
Sales	$140	$ 20 (F)	$120
Controllable variable costs:			
Variable cost of goods sold	(25)	(10) (U)	(15)
Variable selling and administrative expenses	(15)	(10) (U)	(5)
Contribution margin	$100	$ 0	$100
Controllable fixed costs	50	10 (F)	60
Profit center operating income	$ 50	$ 10 (F)	$ 40
Nonfinancial performance measures:			
Number of orders processed	50	20 (F)	30
Average daily sales	$4.66	$0.66 (F)	$4.00
Number of units sold	100	40 (F)	60

TRY IT! SE2, SE3, SE4, E3A, E4A, E5A, E6A, E3B, E4B, E5B, E6B

Performance Evaluation of Investment Centers

 LO3

The evaluation of an investment center's performance requires more than a comparison of controllable revenues and costs with budgeted amounts. Because the managers of investment centers also control resources and invest in assets, other performance measures must be used to hold them accountable for revenues, costs, and the capital investments that they control. In this section, we focus on the traditional performance evaluation measures of return on investment and residual income and the relatively new performance measure of economic value added.

RATIO Return on Investment

Traditionally, the most common performance measure that takes into account both operating income and the assets invested to earn that income is **return on investment (ROI)**, which is computed as follows.

Computing Return on Investment (ROI)

Formula

$$\text{Return on Investment (ROI)} = \frac{\text{Operating Income}}{\text{Assets Invested}}$$

In this formula, assets invested is the average of the beginning and ending asset balances for the period.

Properly measuring the income and the assets specifically controlled by a manager is critical to the quality of this performance measure. Using ROI, it is possible to evaluate the manager of any investment center, whether it is an entire company or a unit within a company, such as a subsidiary, division, or other business segment.

Example Winter Wonderland's Restaurant Division had actual operating income of $610, and the average assets invested were $800. The master budget called for $890 in operating income and $1,000 in invested assets. As shown in Exhibit 7, the budgeted

Exhibit 7
Performance Report Based on Return on Investment for the Restaurant Division

	Actual Results	Variance	Master Budget
Operating income	$610	$(280) (U)	$890
Assets invested	$800	$200 (F)	$1,000
Performance measure:			
ROI*	76%	(13%) (U)	89%

*ROI = Operating Income ÷ Assets Invested
Actual = $890 ÷ $1,000
   = 0.89 = 89%
Master = $610 ÷ $800
   = 0.7625 = 76% (rounded)

© Cengage Learning 2014

ROI for the division would be 89 percent, and the actual ROI would be 76 percent. The actual ROI was lower than the budgeted ROI because the division's actual operating income was lower than expected relative to the actual assets invested.

The basic ROI equation, Operating Income ÷ Assets Invested, can be rewritten to show the many elements within the aggregate ROI number that a manager can influence. Two important indicators of performance are profit margin and asset turnover.

STUDY NOTE: *Profit margin focuses on the income statement, and asset turnover focuses on the balance sheet aspects of ROI.*

- **Profit margin** is the ratio of operating income to sales. It represents the percentage of each sales dollar that results in profit.
- **Asset turnover** is the ratio of sales to average assets invested. It indicates the productivity of assets, or the number of sales dollars generated by each dollar invested in assets.

A single ROI number is a composite index of many cause-and-effect relationships and interdependent financial elements. The following formula recognizes the many interrelationships that affect ROI:

$$\text{ROI} = \frac{\text{Operating Income}}{\text{Sales}} \times \frac{\text{Sales}}{\text{Assets Invested}} = \frac{\text{Operating Income}}{\text{Assets Invested}}$$

ROI = Profit Margin × Asset Turnover

Profit margin and asset turnover help explain changes in return on investment for a single investment center or differences in return on investment among investment centers. Therefore, the formula ROI = Profit Margin × Asset Turnover is useful for analyzing and interpreting the elements that make up a business's overall return on investment.

ROI is affected by a manager's decisions about pricing, product sales mix, capital budgeting for new facilities, product sales volume, and other financial matters. A manager can improve ROI by increasing sales, decreasing costs, or decreasing assets.

Business Application If ROI is overemphasized, investment center managers may react by making business decisions that favor their personal ROI performance at the expense of company-wide profits or the long-term success of other investment centers. To avoid such problems, other performance measures should always be used in conjunction with ROI—for example, *comparisons* of revenues, costs, and operating income with budget amounts or past trends; sales growth percentages; market share percentages; or other key variables in the organization's activity. ROI should also be compared with budgeted goals and with past ROI trends because changes in this ratio over time can be more revealing than any single number.

Residual Income

Because of the pitfalls of using ROI as a performance measure, **residual income (RI)** is another approach to evaluating investment centers. Residual income is the operating income that an investment center earns above a minimum desired return on invested assets. Residual income is not a ratio but a dollar amount—the amount of profit left after subtracting a predetermined desired income target for an investment center.

Computing Residual Income (RI)

Formula

$$\text{Residual Income} = \text{Operating Income} - (\text{Desired ROI} \times \text{Assets Invested})$$

STUDY NOTE: *ROI is expressed as a percentage, and residual income is expressed in dollars.*

As in the computation of ROI, assets invested is the average of the center's beginning and ending asset balances for the period.

The desired RI will vary from investment center to investment center depending on the type of business and the level of risk assumed.

Example Exhibit 8 shows Winter Wonderland's Restaurant Division's performance report based on residual income. The residual income performance target is to exceed a 20 percent return on assets invested in the division.

Exhibit 8
Performance Report Based on Residual Income for the Restaurant Division

	Actual Results	Variance	Master Budget
Operating income	$610	$(280) (U)	$890
Assets invested	$800	$200 (F)	$1,000
Desired ROI			20%
Performance measures:			
ROI	76%	(13%) (U)	89%
Residual income*	$450	$(240) (U)	$690

*Residual Income = Operating Income − (Desired ROI × Assets Invested)

$$\text{Actual} = \$610 - (20\% \times \$800)$$
$$= \$450$$
$$\text{Master} = \$890 - (20\% \times \$1,000)$$
$$= \$690$$

© Cengage Learning 2014

Note that the division's residual income is $450, which was lower than the $690 that was projected in the master budget.

Comparisons with other residual income figures will strengthen the analysis. To add context to the analysis of the division and its manager, questions such as the following need to be answered:

- How did the division's residual income this year compare with its residual income in previous years?
- Did the actual residual income exceed the budgeted residual income?
- How did this division's residual income compare with the amounts generated by other investment centers of the company?

Concept For their residual income figures to be *comparable*, all investment centers must have equal access to resources and similar asset investment bases. Some managers may be able to produce larger residual incomes simply because their investment centers are larger rather than because their performance is better.

Economic Value Added

More and more businesses are using the shareholder wealth created by an investment center, or the **economic value added (EVA™)**, as an indicator of performance.[1] The calculation of EVA can be quite complex because it makes various cost of capital and accounting principles adjustments. The **cost of capital** is the minimum desired rate of return on an investment, such as the assets invested in an investment center.

Basically, the computation of EVA is similar to that of RI, except that after-tax operating income is used instead of pretax operating income. Also, a cost of capital percentage is multiplied by the center's invested assets less current liabilities instead of a desired ROI percentage being multiplied by invested assets. Like RI, EVA is expressed in dollars. EVA is computed as follows.

STUDY NOTE: *The EVA number is a composite index drawn from many cause-and-effect relationships and interdependent financial elements.*

Computing Economic Value Added (EVA)

Formula

EVA = After-Tax Operating Income − [Cost of Capital × (Total Assets − Current Liabilities)]

Example Exhibit 9 shows a basic computation of EVA for Winter Wonderland's Restaurant Division. The division's after-tax operating income is $400. Its cost of capital is 12 percent, its total assets are $800, and its current liabilities are $250. The report shows that the division has added $334 to its economic value after taxes and cost of capital. In other words, the division produced after-tax profits of $334 in excess of the cost of capital required to generate those profits.

Exhibit 9
Performance Report Based on Economic Value Added for the Restaurant Division

Performance measures:	Actual Results	Variance	Master Budget
ROI	76%	(13%) (U)	89%
Residual income	$450	$(240) (U)	$690
Economic value added*	$334		

*EVA = After-Tax Operating Income − [Cost of Capital × (Total Assets − Current Liabilities)]
= $400 − [12% × ($800 − $250)]
= $334

© Cengage Learning 2014

The factors that affect the computation of EVA are the managers' decisions on pricing, product sales volume, taxes, cost of capital, capital investments, and other financial matters. A manager can improve the economic value of an investment center by increasing sales, decreasing costs, decreasing assets, or lowering the cost of capital.

Concept The economic value of an investment center and its cost of capital will be more meaningful if the current economic value added is *compared* to EVAs from previous periods, target EVAs, and EVAs from other investment centers.

APPLY IT!

Brew Mountain Company sells coffee and hot beverages. Its Coffee Cart Division sells to skiers as they come off the mountain. The Coffee Cart Division's balance sheet showed that the company had invested assets of $30,000 at the beginning of the year and $50,000 at the end of the year. During the year, the division's operating income was $80,000 on sales of $120,000.

1. Compute the division's residual income if the desired ROI is 20 percent.
2. Compute the return on investment for the division.
3. Compute the economic value added for the company if total corporate assets are $600,000, current liabilities are $80,000, after-tax operating income is $70,000, and the cost of capital is 12 percent.

SOLUTION

1. $80,000 − {20% × [($30,000 + $50,000) ÷ 2]} = $72,000
2. $80,000 ÷ [($30,000 + $50,000) ÷ 2] = 200%
3. $70,000 − [12% × ($600,000 − $80,000)] = $7,600

TRY IT! SE5, SE6, SE7, E7A, E8A, E9A, E7B, E8B, E9B

BUSINESS APPLICATIONS

**RELEVANT
LEARNING OBJECTIVES**

LO 4 Describe how the balanced scorecard aligns performance with organizational goals.

LO 5 Explain how properly linked performance incentives and measures add value for all stakeholders in performance management and evaluation.

LO 4 Performance Measurement

To be effective, a performance management system must consider both operating results and multiple performance measures, such as return on investment, residual income, and economic value added. Comparing actual results to budgeted figures adds meaning to the evaluation. Performance measures such as ROI, RI, and EVA indicate whether an investment center is effective in coordinating its own goals with company-wide goals because these measures take into account both operating income and the assets used to produce that income. However, all three measures are limited by their focus on short-term financial performance. To obtain a fuller picture, management needs to *understand* and *compare* all stakeholders' performance perspectives to ensure a more balanced view of a business's well-being and how to improve it. To do this, managers must collaborate with other managers to develop a group of measures, such as the balanced scorecard.

Organizational Goals and the Balanced Scorecard

The **balanced scorecard** is a framework that links the perspectives of an organization's four basic stakeholder groups—financial (investor), learning and growth (employee), internal business processes, and customer—with the organization's mission and vision, performance measures, strategic and tactical plans, and resources. To succeed, an organization must add value for all groups in both the short and the long term. Thus, an organization will determine each group's objectives and translate them into performance measures that have specific, quantifiable performance targets. Ideally, managers should be able to see how their actions contribute to the achievement of organizational goals and understand how their compensation is related to their actions. The balanced scorecard assumes that an organization will get only what it measures. The balanced scorecard adds dimension to the management process. Managers plan, perform, evaluate, and communicate the organization's performance from multiple perspectives. By balancing the needs of all stakeholders, managers are more likely to achieve their objectives in both the short and the long term. We will use Winter Wonderland to illustrate how managers use the balanced scorecard.

Planning During the planning stage, the balanced scorecard provides a framework that enables managers to translate their organization's vision and strategy into operational terms. Managers evaluate the company's vision from the perspective of each stakeholder group and seek to answer one key question for each group:

- **Financial (investor):** To achieve our organization's vision, how should we appear to our shareholders?
- **Learning and growth (employee):** To achieve our organization's vision, how should we sustain our ability to improve and change?
- **Internal business processes:** To succeed, in which business processes must our organization excel?
- **Customer:** To achieve our organization's vision, how should we appeal to our customers?

These key questions align the organization's strategy from all perspectives.

The answers to the questions result in performance objectives that are mutually beneficial to all stakeholders. Once the organization's objectives are set, managers can select performance measures and set performance targets to translate the objectives into

Business Perspective
"Tableau de Bord and the Balanced Scorecard"

The *tableau de bord*, or "dashboard," was developed by French engineers around 1900 as a concise performance measurement system that helped managers understand the cause-and-effect relationships between their decisions and the resulting performance. The indicators, both financial and nonfinancial, allowed managers at all levels to monitor their progress in terms of the mission and objectives of their unit and of their company overall. The dashboard focuses on and supports an organization's strategic plan.

Source: A. Bourguignon, "The American Balanced Scorecard versus the French Tableau de Bord: The Ideological Dimension," *Management Accounting Research,* Jan. 2004, Vol. 15, Issue 2 (Elsevier), pp. 107–134.

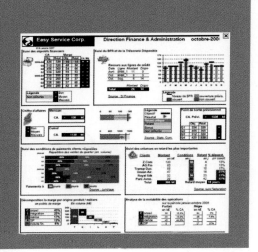

an action plan. For example, if Winter Wonderland's collective vision and strategy is to please guests, its managers might establish the following overall objectives:

Perspective	Objective
Financial (investor)	Increase guests' spending at the resort.
Learning and growth (employee)	Continually cross-train employees in each other's duties to sustain premium-quality service for guests.
Internal business processes	Leverage market position by introducing and improving innovative marketing and technology-driven advances that clearly benefit guests.
Customer	Create new premium-price experiences and facilities for vacations in all seasons.

These overall objectives are then translated into specific performance objectives and measures for specific managers. Exhibit 10 summarizes how Winter Wonderland's managers might link their organization's vision and strategy to objectives, then link the objectives to logical performance measures, and, finally, set performance targets for a ski lift manager. As a result, a ski lift manager will have a variety of performance measures that balance the perspectives and needs of all stakeholders.

Performing Managers use the mutually agreed-upon strategic and tactical objectives for the entire organization as the basis for decision making within their individual areas of responsibility. This practice ensures that they consider the needs of all stakeholder groups and shows how measuring and managing performance for some stakeholder groups can lead to improved performance for another stakeholder group. Specifically, improving the performance of leading indicators like internal business processes and learning and growth will create improvements for customers, which in turn will result in improved financial performance (a lagging indicator). For example, when making decisions about available ski lift capacity, the ski lift manager will balance such factors as lift ticket sales, snow conditions, equipment reliability, trained staff availability, and length of wait for ski lifts.

The balanced scorecard provides a way of linking the lead performance indicators of employees, internal business processes, and customer needs to the lag performance indicator of external financial results. In other words, if managers can foster excellent

STUDY NOTE: *Although their perspectives differ, stakeholder groups may be interested in the same measurable performance goals. For example, both the customer and internal business processes perspectives desire high-quality products.*

Exhibit 10
Sample Balanced Scorecard of Linked Objectives, Performance Measures, and Targets

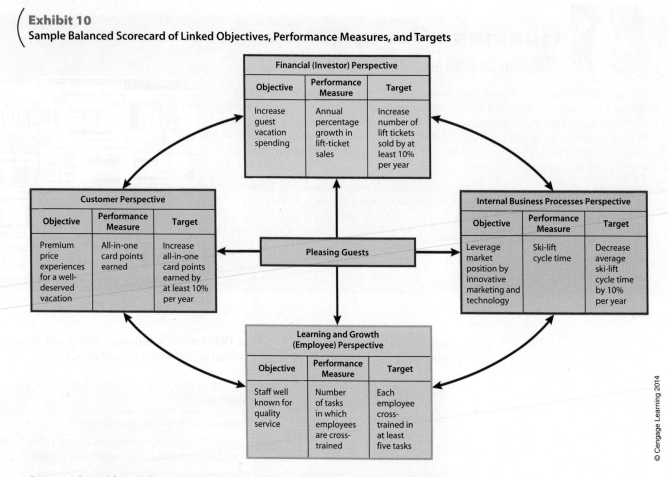

Source: Adapted from Robert S. Kaplan and David P. Norton, "Using the Balanced Scorecard as a Strategic Management System," *Harvard Business Review*, January–February 1996.

performance for three of the stakeholder groups, good financial results will occur for the investor stakeholder group. When managers understand the causal and linked relationship between their actions and their company's overall performance, they can see new ways to be more effective. For example, a ski lift manager may hypothesize that shorter waiting lines for the ski lifts would improve customer satisfaction and lead to more visits to the ski lift. The manager could test this possible cause-and-effect relationship by measuring and tracking the length of ski lift waiting lines and the number of visits to the ski lift. If a causal relationship exists, the manager can improve the performance of the ski lift operation by doing everything possible to ensure that waiting lines are short because a quicker ride to the top will result in improved results for the operation and for other perspectives as well.

Evaluating The balanced scorecard enables a company to determine whether it is making continuous improvement in its operations. Managers *compare* performance objectives and targets with actual results to determine if the targets were met, what measures need to be changed, and what strategies or objectives need revision. For example, the ski lift manager would analyze the reasons for performance gaps and make recommendations to improve the performance of the ski lift area.

A company will also *compare* its performance with that of similar companies in the same industry. **Benchmarking** determines a company's competitive advantage by comparing its performance with that of its closest competitors. **Benchmarks** are measures of the best practices in an industry.

Communicating A variety of reports enable managers to monitor and evaluate performance measures that add value for stakeholder groups. For example, a database makes it possible to prepare financial performance reports, customer statements, internal business process reports for targeted performance measures and results, and performance appraisals of individual employees.

Performance Evaluation and the Management Process

Exhibit 11 summarizes the ways in which performance measures and evaluation support and inform the management process.

Exhibit 11

Performance Evaluation and the Management Process

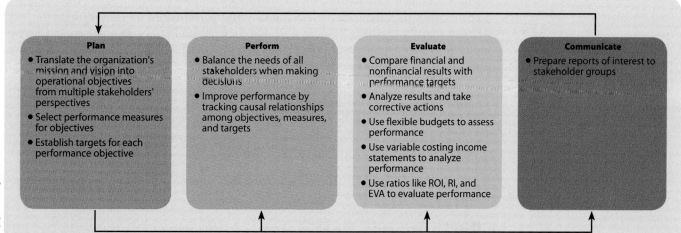

© Cengage Learning 2014

Plan	Perform	Evaluate	Communicate
• Translate the organization's mission and vision into operational objectives from multiple stakeholders' perspectives	• Balance the needs of all stakeholders when making decisions	• Compare financial and nonfinancial results with performance targets	• Prepare reports of interest to stakeholder groups
• Select performance measures for objectives	• Improve performance by tracking causal relationships among objectives, measures, and targets	• Analyze results and take corrective actions	
• Establish targets for each performance objective		• Use flexible budgets to assess performance	
		• Use variable costing income statements to analyze performance	
		• Use ratios like ROI, RI, and EVA to evaluate performance	

APPLY IT!

Connie's Takeout caters to resort employees who want a good meal at home but do not have time to prepare it. Connie's has developed the following business objectives:

1. To provide fast, courteous service
2. To manage the inventory of food carefully
3. To have repeat customers
4. To be profitable and grow

Connie's has also developed the following performance measures:

5. Growth in revenues per quarter and net income
6. Average unsold food at the end of the business day as a percentage of the total food purchased that day
7. Average customer time at the counter before being waited on
8. Percentage of customers providing repeat business

Match each of these objectives and performance measures with the four perspectives of the balanced scorecard: financial perspective, learning and growth perspective, internal business processes perspective, and customer perspective.

SOLUTION

Financial perspective: 4, 5; learning and growth perspective: 1, 7; internal business processes perspective: 2, 6; customer perspective: 3, 8

TRY IT! SE8, SE9, E10A, E11A, E12A, E13A, E10B, E11B, E12B, E13B

LO5 Performance Incentives and Goals

The effectiveness of a performance management and evaluation system depends on how well it coordinates the goals of responsibility centers, managers, and the entire company. Two factors are key to the successful coordination of goals:

■ The logical linking of goals to measurable objectives and targets
■ The tying of appropriate compensation incentives to the achievement of the targets—that is, performance-based pay

Linking Goals, Performance Objectives, Measures, and Performance Targets

The causal links among an organization's goals, performance objectives, measures, and targets must be apparent. For example, if a company seeks to be an environmental steward, as Winter Wonderland does, it may choose the following linked goal, objective, measure, and performance target:

Goal	Objective	Measure	Performance Target
To be an environmental steward	To reduce, reuse, and recycle	Number of tons recycled per year	To recycle at least one pound per guest

You may recall that the balanced scorecard also links objectives, measures, and targets, as shown in Exhibit 10.

Performance-Based Pay

The tying of appropriate compensation incentives to performance targets increases the likelihood that the goals of responsibility centers, managers, and the entire organization will be well coordinated. Unfortunately, this linkage does not always happen. Responsibility center managers are more likely to achieve their performance targets if their compensation depends on it. **Performance-based pay** is the linking of employee compensation to the achievement of measurable business targets.

Cash bonuses, awards, profit-sharing plans, and stock options are common types of incentive compensation. Cash bonuses are usually given to reward an individual's short-term performance. A bonus may be stated as a fixed dollar amount or as a percentage of a target figure, such as 5 percent of operating income or 10 percent of the dollar increase in operating income. An award may be a trip or some other form of recognition for desirable individual or group performance. For example, many companies sponsor a trip for all managers who have met their performance targets during a specified period. Other companies award incentive points that employees may redeem for goods or services. (Awards can be used to encourage both short-term and long-term performance.) Profit-sharing plans reward employees with a share of the company's profits. Employees often receive company stock as recognition of their contribution to a profitable period. Using stock as a reward encourages employees to think and act as both investors and employees and encourages a stable work force. In terms of the balanced scorecard, employees assume two stakeholder perspectives and take both a short- and a long-term viewpoint. Companies use stock to motivate employees to achieve financial targets that increase the company's stock price.

The Coordination of Goals

What performance incentives and measures should a company use to manage and evaluate performance? What actions and behaviors should an organization reward? Which incentive compensation plans work best? The answers to such questions depend on the facts and circumstances of each organization. To determine the right performance incentives for their organization, employees and managers must answer several questions:

- When should the reward be given—now or sometime in the future?
- Whose performance should be rewarded—that of responsibility centers, individual managers, or the entire company?
- How should the reward be computed?
- On what should the reward be based?
- What performance criteria should be used?
- Does the performance incentive plan address the interests of all stakeholders?

The effectiveness of a performance management and evaluation system relies on the coordination of responsibility center, managerial, and company goals. Performance can be optimized by linking goals to measurable objectives and targets and by tying appropriate compensation incentives to the achievement of the targets. Each organization's unique circumstances will determine the correct mix of measures and compensation incentives for that organization. If management values the perspectives of all of its stakeholder groups, its performance management and evaluation system will balance and benefit all interests.

APPLY IT!

Necessary Toys, Inc., has adopted the balanced scorecard to motivate its managers to work toward the companywide goal of leading its industry in innovation. Identify the four stakeholder perspectives that would link to the following objectives, measures, and targets:

Perspective	Objective	Measure	Target
	Successful product introductions	New-product market share	Capture 80 percent of new-product market within one year
	Agile product design and production processes	Time to market (the time between a product idea and its first sales)	Time to market less than one year for 80 percent of product introductions
	Workforce with cutting-edge skills	Percentage of employees cross-trained on work- group tasks	100 percent of work group cross-trained on new tasks within 30 days
	Profitable new products	New-product ROI	New-product ROI of at least 75 percent

SOLUTION

Goal: To lead the industry in innovation

Perspective	Objective	Measure	Target
Customer	Successful product introductions	New-product market share	Capture 80 percent of new-product market within one year
Internal business processes	Agile product design and production processes	Time to market (the time between a product idea and its first sales)	Time to market less than one year for 80 percent of product introductions
Learning and growth (employee)	Workforce with cutting-edge skills	Percentage of employees cross-trained on work- group tasks	100 percent of work group cross-trained on new tasks within 30 days
Financial (investor)	Profitable new products	New-product ROI	New-product ROI of at least 75 percent

TRY IT! SE10, E14A, E15A, E14B, E15B

TriLevel Problem

Vail Resorts

The beginning of this chapter focused on **Vail Resorts**, a well-known vacation destination for skiers. Complete the following requirements in order to answer the questions posed at the beginning of the chapter.

Section 1: Concepts
What concepts guide managers when they evaluate performance?

Section 2: Accounting Applications
How will managers use flexible budgets and other performance measures to analyze the financial and nonfinancial performance of responsibility centers?

Winter Wonderland Resorts is a major hospitality company like Vail Resorts. Winter Wonderland's general manager is responsible for guest activities, administration, and food and lodging and is also solely responsible for Winter Wonderland's capital investments. The following organization chart shows the resort's various activities and the levels of authority that the general manager has established:

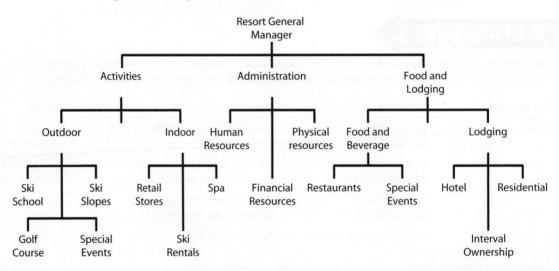

Three divisional managers receive compensation based on their division's performance and have the authority to make employee compensation decisions for their division. Alexandra Patel manages the Food and Lodging Division. The Food and Lodging Division's master budget and actual results for the year ended June 30 follow.

	A	B	C
1	**Winter Wonderland Resort**		
2	**Food and Lodging Division**		
3	**For the Year Ended June 30**		
4	(Dollar amounts in thousands)		
5		**Master**	**Actual**
6		**Budget**	**Results**
7	Guest days	4,000	4,100
8	Sales	$38,000	$40,000
9	Variable cost of sales	24,000	25,000
10	Variable selling and administrative expenses	4,000	4,250
11	Fixed cost of sales	2,000	1,800
12	Fixed selling and administrative expenses	2,500	2,500
13			

1. What types of responsibility centers are (a) Administration, (b) Food and Lodging, and (c) Resort General Manager?
2. Assume that Food and Lodging is a profit center. Prepare a performance report using variable costing and flexible budgeting. Determine the variances between actual results and the corresponding figures in the flexible budget and the master budget.
3. Assume that the divisional managers have been assigned responsibility for capital expenditures and that their divisions are thus investment centers. Food and Lodging is expected to generate a desired ROI of at least 30 percent on average assets invested of $10,000,000.

    (a) Compute the division's return on investment and residual income using the average assets invested in both the actual and budget calculations.

    (b) Using the ROI and residual income, evaluate Alexandra Patel's performance as divisional manager.

4. Compute the division's actual economic value added if the division's assets are $12,000,000, current liabilities are $3,000,000, after-tax operating income is $4,500,000, and the cost of capital is 20 percent.

Section 3: Business Applications

How can managers achieve a balanced view of a business's well-being and how to improve it? To answer this question, match this chapter's manager responsibilities with when they occur within the management process.

a. Plan
b. Perform
c. Evaluate
d. Communicate

1. Establish performance targets of each objective
2. Track causal relationships to improve performance
3. Use flexible budgets to assess performance
4. Translate the organization's mission and vision into objectives from multiple stakeholder perspectives
5. Use variable costing income statements to analyze performance
6. Prepare reports
7. When making decisions, balance all stakeholder needs
8. Use ratios like ROI, RI, and EVA to evaluate performance
9. Compare results with performance targets
10. Analyze results and take corrective actions
11. Select performance measures for objectives

SOLUTION

Section 1: Concepts

Managers use the concepts of *understandability* and *comparability* as they manage a wide range of financial and nonfinancial data to guide and evaluate performance. If they want satisfactory results for their responsibility centers, managers must understand the cause-and-effect relationships between their actions and their responsibility center's performance. To do this, managers use performance analysis tools like flexible budgets; variable costing income statements; and ROI, RI, and EVA ratio analyses to compare plans, actions, and results. By measuring and tracking the causal relationships that they are accountable for, managers can improve performance and thereby add value for all of their organization's stakeholders. A balanced scorecard approach enables managers to understand and compare the perspectives of all the organization's stakeholders: financial (investors), learning and growth (employees), internal business processes, and customers as they command, control, and evaluate the organization.

Section 2: Accounting Applications

1. (a) discretionary cost center
   (b) profit center
   (c) investment center

2.

	A	B	C
1	**Winter Wonderland Resort**		
2	**Food and Lodging Division**		
3	**For the Year Ended June 30**		
4	(Dollar amounts in thousands)		
5		**Actual**			**Flexible**			**Master**
6		**Results**	**Variance**		**Budget**	**Variance**		**Budget**
7	Guest days	4,100	—		4,100	100	(F)	4,000
8	Sales	$40,000	$1,050	(F)	$38,950	$950	(F)	$38,000
9	Controllable variable costs							
10	Variable cost of sales	25,000	400	(U)	24,600	600	(U)	24,000
11	Variable selling and							
12	administrative							
13	expenses	4,250	150	(U)	4,100	100	(U)	4,000
14	Contribution margin	$10,750	$ 500	(F)	$10,250	$250	(F)	$10,000
15	Controllable fixed costs							
16	Fixed cost of sales	1,800	200	(F)	2,000	—		2,000
17	Fixed selling and							
18	administrative							
19	expenses	2,500	—		2,500	—		2,500
20	Division operating income	$ 6,450	$ 700	(F)	$ 5,750	$250	(F)	$ 5,500
21								

3. (a) Return on investment:

Actual results: $6,450,000 ÷ $10,000,000 = <u>64.50%</u>

Flexible budget: $5,750,000 ÷ $10,000,000 = <u>57.50%</u>

Master budget: $5,500,000 ÷ $10,000,000 = <u>55.00%</u>

Residual income:

Actual results: $6,450,000 − (30% × $10,000,000) = <u>$3,450,000</u>

Flexible budget: $5,750,000 − (30% × $10,000,000) = <u>$2,750,000</u>

Master budget: $5,500,000 − (30% × $10,000,000) = <u>$2,500,000</u>

(b) Alexandra Patel's performance as the divisional manager of Food and Lodging exceeds company performance expectations. Actual ROI was 64.5 percent, whereas the company expected an ROI of 30 percent, and the flexible budget and the master budget showed projections of 57.5 percent and 55.0 percent, respectively. Residual income also exceeded expectations. The Food and Lodging Division generated $3,450,000 in residual income when the flexible budget and master budget had projected RIs of $2,750,000 and $2,500,000, respectively. The performance report for the division shows 100 more guest days than had been anticipated and a favorable controllable fixed cost variance. As a manager, Patel will investigate the unfavorable variances associated with her controllable variable costs.

4. Economic value added:

$$\$4,500,000 - [20\% \times (\$12,000,000 - \$3,000,000)] = \underline{\underline{\$2,700,000}}$$

Section 3: Business Applications

1. a	7. b
2. b	8. c
3. c	9. c
4. a	10. c
5. c	11. a
6. d	

Chapter Review

Define a *performance management and evaluation system* and *responsibility accounting*, and describe the roles they play in performance analysis. LO 1

An effective performance management and evaluation system accounts for and reports on both financial and nonfinancial performance so that an organization can understand how well it is doing, where it is going, and what improvements will make it more profitable. Each organization must develop a unique set of performance measures to compare and evaluate based on areas of responsibility that are appropriate to its specific situation. Responsibility accounting classifies data according to areas of responsibility and reports each area's activities by including only the revenue, cost, and resource categories that the assigned manager can control. There are five types of responsibility centers: cost, discretionary cost, revenue, profit, and investment. Performance reporting by responsibility center allows the source of a cost, revenue, or resource to be traced to the manager who controls it and thus makes it easier to understand, compare, and evaluate a manager's performance. The content and format of a performance report depend on the nature of the responsibility center.

Use flexible budgets and variable costing to analyze cost center and profit center performance. LO 2

The performance of a cost center can be evaluated by comparing its actual costs with the corresponding amounts in the flexible and master budgets. A flexible budget is a summary of anticipated costs for a range of activity levels. It provides forecasted cost data that can be adjusted for changes in the level of output. A flexible budget is derived by multiplying actual unit output by predetermined standard unit costs for each cost item in the report. The resulting variances between actual costs and the flexible budget can be examined further by using standard costing to compute specific variances for direct materials, direct labor, and overhead.

The performance of a profit center is usually evaluated by comparing the profit center's actual income statement results with its budgeted income statement. When variable costing is used, the controllable costs of the profit center's manager are classified as variable or fixed. The resulting performance report takes the form of a contribution margin income statement instead of a traditional income statement. The variable costing income statement is useful because it focuses on cost variability and the profit center's contribution to operating income.

Analyze investment centers using return on investment, residual income, and economic value added. **LO 3**

Traditionally, the most common performance measure has been return on investment (ROI). The basic formula is ROI = Operating Income ÷ Assets Invested. Return on investment can also be examined in terms of profit margin and asset turnover. In this case, ROI = Profit Margin × Asset Turnover, where Profit Margin = Operating Income ÷ Sales, and Asset Turnover = Sales ÷ Assets Invested. Residual income (RI) is the operating income that an investment center earns above a minimum desired return on invested assets. It is expressed as a dollar amount: Residual Income = Operating Income − (Desired ROI × Assets Invested). It is the amount of profit left after subtracting a predetermined desired income target for an investment. Today, businesses are increasingly using the shareholder wealth created by an investment center, or economic value added (EVA), as a performance measure. The calculation of economic value added can be quite complex because of the various adjustments it involves. Basically, it is similar to the calculation of residual income: EVA = After-Tax Operating Income − [Cost of Capital × (Total Assets − Current Liabilities)]. A manager can improve the economic value of an investment center by increasing sales, decreasing costs, decreasing assets, or lowering the cost of capital.

Describe how the balanced scorecard aligns performance with organizational goals. **LO 4**

Besides answering basic questions about what to measure and how to measure, management must collaborate to develop a group of measures, such as the balanced scorecard, that will help them determine how to improve performance. The balanced scorecard is a framework that links the perspectives of an organization's four basic stakeholder groups—financial (investor), learning and growth (employee), internal business processes, and customer—with its mission and vision, performance measures, strategic and tactical plans, and resources. The balanced scorecard assumes that an organization will get what it measures. Ideally, managers should see how their actions help to achieve organizational goals and understand how their compensation is linked to their actions. Managers may use benchmarking to determine a company's competitive advantage by comparing its performance with that of its industry peers.

Explain how properly linked performance incentives and measures add value for all stakeholders in performance management and evaluation. **LO 5**

The effectiveness of a performance management and evaluation system depends on how well it coordinates the goals of responsibility centers, managers, and the entire company. Performance can be optimized by linking goals to measurable objectives and targets and tying appropriate compensation incentives to the achievement of those targets. Common types of incentive compensation are cash bonuses, awards, profit-sharing plans, and stock options. If management values the perspectives of all of its stakeholder groups, its performance management and evaluation system will balance and benefit all interests.

Key Terms and Ratios

Chapter Assignments

DISCUSSION QUESTIONS

LO 1   **DQ1. CONCEPT** ▶ Jackie Jefferson, a new employee at Foster, Inc., is learning about the various types of performance reports. Describe the typical contents of a performance report for each type of responsibility center. Why do these reports enhance the understandability and comparability of the data presented?

LO 2, 3, 4   **DQ2. CONCEPT** ▶ What tools can managers use to enhance the understandability and comparability of performance analysis?

LO 2   **DQ3. CONCEPT** ▶ How does the flexible budget formula enhance understandability and comparability when preparing a flexible budget?

LO 2   **DQ4. CONCEPT** ▶ Why is a variable costing income statement more useful than a traditional income statement for understanding and evaluating a profit center's performance?

LO 4, 5   **DQ5. CONCEPT** ▶ **BUSINESS APPLICATION** ▶ How does the balanced scorecard empower managers to understand and compare the interests of all the organization's stakeholders?

SHORT EXERCISES

LO 1   **Responsibility Centers**

SE1. Identify each of the following as a cost center, a discretionary cost center, a revenue center, a profit center, or an investment center:

a. Center A's manager is responsible for generating cash inflows and incurring costs with the goal of making money for the company. The manager has no responsibility for assets.

b. Center B produces a product that is not sold to an external party but transferred to another center for further processing.

c. Center C's manager is responsible for the telephone order operations of a large retailer.

d. Center D designs, produces, and sells products to external parties. The manager makes both long-term and short-term decisions.

e. Center E provides human resource support for the other centers in the company.

LO 2   **Preparing a Flexible Budget**

SE2. Prepare a flexible budget for 20,000, 22,000, and 24,000 units of output, using the information that follows.

Variable costs:	
Direct materials	$1.00 per unit
Direct labor	$4.00 per unit
Variable overhead	$8.00 per unit
Total budgeted fixed overhead	$180,800

LO 2   **Cost Center Performance Report**

SE3. Complete the following performance report for cost center S for the month ended September 30:

(Continued)

	Actual Results	Variance	Flexible Budget	Variance	Master Budget
Units produced	80	0	?	(20) (U)	100
Center costs:					
Direct materials	$ 84	$?	$ 80	$?	$100
Direct labor	150	?	?	40 (F)	200
Variable overhead	?	(20) (U)	240	?	300
Fixed overhead	270	?	250	?	250
Total cost	$?	$(34) (U)	$?	$120 (F)	$850
Performance measures:					
Defect-free units to total produced	80%	?	N/A	N/A	90%
Average throughput minutes per unit	11	?	N/A	N/A	10

LO 2

Profit Center Performance Report

SE4. Complete the following performance report for profit center P for the month ended December 31:

	Actual Results	Variance	Master Budget
Sales	$?	$ 20 (F)	$120
Controllable variable costs:			
Variable cost of goods sold	(25)	(10) (U)	?
Variable selling and administrative expenses	(15)	? (?)	(5)
Contribution margin	$100	$? (?)	$100
Controllable fixed costs	?	20 (F)	60
Profit center operating income	$ 60	$ 20 (F)	$?
Performance measures:			
Number of orders processed	50	20 (F)	?
Average daily sales	$?	$0.68 (F)	$4.00
Number of units sold	100	40 (F)	?

LO 3

Return on Investment

SE5. Complete the profit margin, asset turnover, and return on investment calculations for investment centers D and V. (Round to two decimal places.)

	Center D	Center V
Sales	$1,600	$2,000
Operating income	$400	$200
Average assets invested	$3,200	$1,250
Profit margin	?	?
Asset turnover	?	?
ROI	?	?

LO 3

Residual Income

SE6. Complete the operating income, ending assets invested, average assets invested, and residual income calculations for investment centers H and F.

	Center H	Center F
Sales	$20,000	$25,000
Operating income	$1,500	$?
Beginning assets invested	$4,000	$ 500
Ending assets invested	$6,000	$?
Average assets invested	$?	$1,000
Desired ROI	20%	20%
Residual income	$?	$600

LO 3 **Economic Value Added**

SE7. Complete the current liabilities, total assets − current liabilities, and economic value added calculations for investment centers M and N.

	Center M	Center N
Sales	$15,000	$18,000
After-tax operating income	$1,000	$1,100
Total assets	$4,000	$5,000
Current liabilities	$1,000	$?
Total assets − current liabilities	$?	$3,500
Cost of capital	15%	15%
Economic value added	$?	$?

LO 4 **The Balanced Scorecard: Stakeholder Values**

SE8. BUSINESS APPLICATION ▶ In the balanced scorecard approach, stakeholder groups with different perspectives value different performance goals. Sometimes, however, they may be interested in the same goal. Indicate which stakeholder groups—financial (F), learning and growth (L), internal business processes (P), and customer (C)—value the performance goals that follow.

a. high wages
b. safe products
c. low-priced products
d. improved return on investment
e. job security
f. cost-effective production processes

LO 4 **Balanced Scorecard**

SE9. BUSINESS APPLICATION ▶ One of your college's overall goals is customer satisfaction. In light of that goal, match each of the stakeholders' perspectives that follow with the appropriate objective.

Perspective	Objective
a. Financial (investor)	1. Customer satisfaction means that the faculty (employees) engages in cutting-edge research.
b. Learning and growth (employee)	2. Customer satisfaction means that students receive their degrees in four years.
c. Internal business processes	3. Customer satisfaction means that the college has a winning athletics program.
d. Customer	4. Customer satisfaction means that fund-raising campaigns are successful.

LO 5 **Coordination of Goals**

SE10. BUSINESS APPLICATION ▶ One of your college's goals is customer satisfaction. In view of that goal, identify each of the following as a linked objective, a measure, or a performance target.

1. To have successful fund-raising campaigns
2. Number of publications per year per tenure-track faculty
3. To increase the average donation by 10 percent
4. Average number of dollars raised per donor
5. To have faculty engage in cutting-edge research
6. To increase the number of publications per faculty member by at least one per year

EXERCISES: SET A

LO 1   ## Responsibility Centers

E1A. Identify the most appropriate type of responsibility center for each of the organizational units that follow.

a. The sheets and towels laundry facility of a large hotel chain
b. The online order department of a retailer
c. A manufacturing department of a large corporation
d. An urgent care clinic in a community hospital
e. A famous brand of a large corporation

LO 1   ## Organization Chart

E2A. Higgly Industries wants to formalize its management structure by designing an organization chart. The company has a president, a board of directors, and two vice presidents. Four discretionary cost centers—Business Office, Personnel, Technology Services, and Physical Plant—report to one of the vice presidents. The other vice president has one production facility with three cost centers reporting to her. Draw the company's organization chart.

LO 2   ## Preparing a Flexible Budget

E3A. Bexar Company's fixed overhead costs for the year are expected to be as follows: depreciation, $80,000; supervisory salaries, $90,000; property taxes and insurance, $25,000; and other fixed overhead, $15,000. Total fixed overhead is thus expected to be $210,000. Variable costs per unit are expected to be as follows: direct materials, $15.00; direct labor, $10.00; operating supplies, $2.00; indirect labor, $3.50; and other variable overhead costs, $2.50. Prepare a flexible budget for the following levels of production: 25,000 units, 30,000 units, and 35,000 units. What is the flexible budget formula for the year ended December 31?

LO 2   ## Performance Report for a Cost Center

E4A. Keystone, LLC, owns a peach processing plant. Last month, the plant generated the following information: peaches processed, 60,000 pounds; direct materials, $6,200; direct labor, $12,500; variable overhead, $17,600; and fixed overhead, $15,000. There were no beginning or ending inventories. Average daily pounds processed (25 business days) were 2,400. Average rate of processing was 300 pounds per hour.

At the beginning of the month, Keystone had budgeted costs of peaches, $5,000; direct labor, $10,000; variable overhead, $15,000; and fixed overhead, $14,000. The monthly master budget was based on producing 50,000 pounds of peaches each month. This means that the plant had been projected to process 2,000 pounds daily at the rate of 250 pounds per hour.

Prepare a performance report for the month for the peach processing plant. Include a flexible budget and the computation of variances in your report. Indicate whether the variances are favorable (F) or unfavorable (U) to the performance of the plant.

LO 2   ## Variable Costing Income Statement

E5A. Vegan, LLC, owns a chain of gourmet vegetarian take-out markets. Vegan's income statement in the traditional reporting format for the month follows.

Vegan, LLC
Income Statement
For the Month

Sales	$890,000
Cost of goods sold	607,000
Gross margin	$283,000
Selling and administrative expenses:	
Variable	(44,500)
Fixed	(72,300)
Operating income	$166,200

Total fixed production costs for the month were $140,000.

Prepare an income statement for Vegan, LLC, for the month, using the variable costing format.

LO 2   **Traditional and Variable Costing Income Statements**

E6A. Roofing tile is Tops Corporation's major product. It sold 88,400 cases of tile during the year. Variable cost of goods sold was $848,640; variable selling expenses were $132,600; fixed overhead was $166,680; fixed selling expenses were $152,048; and fixed administrative expenses were $96,450. The selling price was $18 per case. There were no partially completed jobs in process at the beginning or the end of the year. Finished goods inventory had been used up at the end of the previous year. Prepare the calendar year-end income statement for Tops using:

1. the traditional reporting format
2. the variable costing format

LO 3   **Investment Center Performance**

E7A. ACCOUNTING CONNECTION ▶ Flowers Associates is evaluating the performance of three divisions: Daisies, Pansies, and Tulips. Using the data that follow, compute the return on investment and residual income for each division, compare the divisions' performance, and comment on the factors that influenced performance.

	Daisies	**Pansies**	**Tulips**
Sales	$50,000	$50,000	$50,000
Operating income	$10,000	$10,000	$20,000
Assets invested	$25,000	$12,500	$25,000
Desired ROI	30%	30%	30%

LO 3   **Economic Value Added**

E8A. ACCOUNTING CONNECTION ▶ Game, LLP, is evaluating the performance of three divisions: Rock, Scissors, and Paper. Using the data that follow, compute the economic value added by each division, and comment on each division's performance.

	Rock	**Scissors**	**Paper**
Sales	$50,000	$50,000	$50,000
After-tax operating income	$5,000	$5,000	$20,000
Total assets	$25,000	$12,500	$25,000
Current liabilities	$5,000	$5,000	$5,000
Cost of capital	15%	15%	15%

LO 3   **Return on Investment and Economic Value Added**

E9A. The balance sheet for NuBone Corporation's New Products Division showed invested assets of $200,000 at the beginning of the year and $300,000 at the end of the year. During the year, the division's operating income was $12,500 on sales of $500,000.

(Continued)

1. Compute the division's residual income if the desired ROI is 6 percent.
2. Compute the following performance measures for the division: (a) profit margin, (b) asset turnover, and (c) return on investment. (Round profit margin percentage to one decimal place.)
3. Recompute the division's ROI under each of the following independent assumptions.
   a. Sales increase from $500,000 to $600,000, causing operating income to rise from $12,500 to $30,000.
   b. Invested assets at the beginning of the year are reduced from $200,000 to $100,000. (Round percentage to two decimal places.)
   c. Operating expenses are reduced, causing operating income to rise from $12,500 to $20,000.
4. Compute the company's EVA if total corporate assets are $500,000, current liabilities are $80,000, after-tax operating income is $50,000, and the cost of capital is 8 percent.

LO 4   Balanced Scorecard

E10A. BUSINESS APPLICATION ▶ Online Products is considering adopting the balanced scorecard and has compiled the following list of possible performance measures. Select the balanced scorecard perspective that best matches each performance measure.

Balanced Scorecard Perspective	Performance Measure
a. Financial (investor)	1. Economic value added
b. Learning and growth (employee)	2. Employee turnover
c. Internal business processes	3. Average daily sales
d. Customer	4. Defect-free units
	5. Number of repeat customer visits
	6. Employee training hours

LO 4   Performance Measures

E11A. BUSINESS APPLICATION ▶ Wendy Jefferson wants to measure her division's product quality. Link an appropriate performance measure with each balanced scorecard perspective.

Product Quality	Possible Performance Measures
a. Financial (investor)	1. Number of defective products returned
b. Learning and growth (employee)	2. Number of products failing inspection
c. Internal business processes	3. Increased market share
d. Customer	4. Savings from employee suggestions

LO 4   The Balanced Scorecard

E12A. BUSINESS APPLICATION ▶ Unique Exclusive sells antiques to discerning clients. The business has developed the following business objectives:

1. To buy only the antiques that sell
2. To have repeat customers
3. To be profitable and grow
4. To keep employee turnover low

The business also developed the following performance measures:

5. Growth in revenues and net income per quarter
6. Average unsold antiques at the end of the month as a percentage of the total antiques purchased that month
7. Number of unemployment claims
8. Percentage of repeat customers

Match each of these objectives and performance measures with the four perspectives of the balanced scorecard: financial perspective, learning and growth perspective, internal business processes perspective, and customer perspective.

LO **4**   ### The Balanced Scorecard

E13A. BUSINESS APPLICATION ▶ Your college's overall goal is to add value to the communities it serves. In light of that goal, match each of the stakeholders' perspectives that follow with the appropriate objective.

Perspective	Objective
a. Financial (investor)	1. Adding value means that the annual operating budget balances.
b. Learning and growth (employee)	2. Adding value means that students can enroll in courses of their choice.
c. Internal business processes	3. Adding value means that the college has winning interscholastic teams.
d. Customer	4. Adding value means that the faculty engages in meaningful teaching and research.

LO **5**   ### Performance Incentives

E14A. BUSINESS APPLICATION ▶ MOG Consulting is advising Triangle Industries on the short-term and long-term effectiveness of cash bonuses, awards, profit sharing, and stock as performance incentives. Prepare a chart identifying the effectiveness of each incentive as either long-term or short-term or both.

LO **5**   ### Goal Congruence

E15A. BUSINESS APPLICATION ▶ Tech Toys, Inc., has adopted the balanced scorecard to motivate its managers to work toward the companywide goal of leading its industry in innovation. Identify the four stakeholder perspectives that would link to the following objectives, measures, and targets:

Perspective	Objective	Measure	Target
	Agile production processes	Time to market (the time between a product idea and its first sales)	Time to market less than 8 months for 70 percent of product introductions
	Profitable new products	New-product RI	New-product RI of at least $50,000
	Successful product introductions	New-product market share	Capture 65 percent of new-product market within 8 months
	Workforce with cutting-edge skills	Percentage of employees cross-trained on work-group tasks	80 percent of work group cross-trained on new tasks within 20 days

EXERCISES: SET B

Visit the textbook companion website at www.cengagebrain.com to access Exercise Set B for this chapter.

PROBLEMS

LO **2**   ### Preparing a Flexible Budget and Evaluating Performance

P1. Beverage Products Company specializes in 12-ounce drinking glasses. The president asks the controller to prepare a performance report for April. The following report was handed to her a few days later:

✔ 1: Total variable overhead cost per unit: $0.35
✔ 1: Total costs using 55,000 units: $29,750
✔ 3: Total variable overhead costs over budget: $794.00

(Continued)

Cost Category (Variable Unit Cost)	Budgeted Costs*	Actual Costs	Difference Under (Over) Budget
Direct materials ($0.10)	$ 5,000	$ 4,975	$ 25
Direct labor ($0.12)	6,000	5,850	150
Variable overhead:			
Indirect labor ($0.03)	1,500	1,290	210
Supplies ($0.02)	1,000	960	40
Heat and power ($0.03)	1,500	1,325	175
Other ($0.05)	2,500	2,340	160
Fixed overhead:			
Heat and power	3,500	3,500	—
Depreciation	4,200	4,200	—
Insurance and taxes	1,200	1,200	—
Other	1,600	1,600	—
Totals	$28,000	$27,240	$760

*Based on normal capacity of 50,000 units.

In discussing the report with the controller, the president stated, "Profits have been decreasing in recent months, but this report indicates that our production process is operating efficiently."

REQUIRED

1. Prepare a flexible budget for the company using production levels of 45,000 units, 50,000 units, and 55,000 units.
2. What is the flexible budget formula?
3. Assume that the company produced 45,560 units in April and that all fixed costs remained constant. Prepare a revised performance report similar to the one above, using actual production in units as a basis for the budget column. (Do not round your answers.)
4. **ACCOUNTING CONNECTION ▶** Which report is more meaningful for performance evaluation, the original one or the revised one? Why?

LO **1, 2**   **Evaluating Cost Center Performance**

SPREADSHEET

East Coast plant:
✔ 1: Total variance between actual results and flexible budget: $0
✔ 1: Total variance between flexible budget and master budget: $752,000F
✔ 1: Performance measure: Cans processed per hour: 4,566U

P2. Metal Products, LLC, manufactures metal beverage containers. The division that manufactures soft-drink beverage cans for the North American market has two plants that operate 24 hours a day, 365 days a year. The plants are evaluated as cost centers. Small tools and supplies are considered variable overhead. Depreciation and rent are considered fixed overhead. For the month, the master budget for a plant and the actual operating results of the two North American plants, East Coast and West Coast, follow.

	Master Budget	East Coast Actual	West Coast Actual
Center costs:			
Rolled aluminum ($0.01)	$4,000,000	$3,492,000	$5,040,000
Lids ($0.005)	2,000,000	1,980,000	2,016,000
Direct labor ($0.0025)	1,000,000	864,000	1,260,000
Small tools and supplies ($0.0013)	520,000	432,000	588,000
Depreciation and rent	480,000	480,000	480,000
Total cost	$8,000,000	$7,248,000	$9,384,000
Performance measures:			
Cans processed per hour	45,662	41,096	47,945
Average daily pounds of scrap metal	5	6	7
Cans processed (in millions)	400	360	420

REQUIRED

1. Prepare a performance report for the East Coast plant. Include a flexible budget and variance analysis.
2. Prepare a performance report for the West Coast plant. Include a flexible budget and variance analysis.
3. **ACCOUNTING CONNECTION** ▶ Compare the two plants, and comment on their performance.
4. **ACCOUNTING CONNECTION** ▶ Explain why a flexible budget should be prepared.

LO **1, 2, 3**

✔ 1: Total variance between actual and flexible budget operating income: $1,900U
✔ 1: Total variance between flexible and master budget operating income: $1,800U

Evaluating Profit and Investment Center Performance

P3. The managing partner of the law firm Sewell, Bagan, and Clark, LLP, makes asset acquisition and disposal decisions for the firm. As managing partner, she supervises the partners in charge of the firm's three branch offices. Those partners have the authority to make employee compensation decisions. The partners' compensation depends on the profitability of their branch office. Vanessa Smith manages the City Branch, which has the following master budget and actual results for the year ended December 31.

	Master Budget	Actual Results
Billed hours	5,000	4,900
Revenue	$ 250,000	$ 254,800
Controllable variable costs:		
Direct labor	(120,000)	(137,200)
Variable overhead	(90,000)	(34,300)
Contribution margin	$ 90,000	$ 83,300
Controllable fixed costs:		
Rent	(30,000)	(30,000)
Other administrative expenses	(45,000)	(42,000)
Branch operating income	$ 15,000	$ 11,300

REQUIRED

1. Assume that the City Branch is a profit center. Prepare a performance report that includes a flexible budget. Determine the variances between actual results, the flexible budget, and the master budget.
2. **ACCOUNTING CONNECTION** ▶ Evaluate Vanessa Smith's performance as manager of the City Branch.
3. Assume that the branch managers are assigned responsibility for capital expenditures and that the branches are thus investment centers. City Branch is expected to generate a desired ROI of at least 30 percent on average invested assets of $40,000.
   a. Compute the branch's return on investment and residual income. (Round percentages to two decimal places.)
   b. **ACCOUNTING CONNECTION** ▶ Using the ROI and residual income, evaluate Vanessa Smith's performance as branch manager.

LO **3**

✔ 1: This year return on investment: 31.08%
✔ 2: This year residual income: $32,232

Return on Investment and Residual Income

P4. The financial results for the past two years for Ornamental Iron, a division of Iron Horse Company, follow.

(Continued)

Iron Horse Company
Ornamental Iron Division
Balance Sheet
December 31

	This Year	Last Year
Assets		
Cash	$ 5,000	$ 3,000
Accounts receivable	10,000	8,000
Inventory	30,000	32,000
Other current assets	600	600
Plant assets	128,300	120,300
Total assets	$173,900	$163,900
Liabilities and Stockholders' Equity		
Current liabilities	$ 13,900	$ 10,000
Long-term liabilities	90,000	93,900
Stockholders' equity	70,000	60,000
Total liabilities and stockholders' equity	$173,900	$163,900

Iron Horse Company
Ornamental Iron Division
Income Statement
For the Years Ended December 31

	This Year	Last Year
Sales	$ 180,000	$160,000
Cost of goods sold	(100,000)	(90,000)
Selling and administrative expenses	(27,500)	(26,500)
Operating income	$ 52,500	$ 43,500
Income taxes	17,850	14,790
After-tax operating income	$ 34,650	$ 28,710

REQUIRED

1. Compute the division's profit margin, asset turnover, and return on investment for this year and last year. Beginning total assets for last year were $157,900. Round to two decimal places.
2. The desired return on investment for the division has been set at 12 percent. Compute the division's residual income for this year and last year.
3. The cost of capital for the division is 8 percent. Compute the division's economic value added for this year and last year.
4. **ACCOUNTING CONNECTION** ▶ Before drawing conclusions about this division's performance, what additional information would you want?

LO **4**   ## The Balanced Scorecard and Benchmarking

P5. BUSINESS APPLICATION ▶ Howski Associates is an independent insurance agency that sells business, automobile, home, and life insurance. Maya Doyle, senior partner of the agency, recently attended a workshop at the local university in which the balanced scorecard was presented as a way of focusing all of a company's functions on its mission. After the workshop, she met with her managers in a weekend brainstorming session. The group determined that Howski's mission was to provide high-quality, innovative, risk-protection services to individuals and businesses. To ensure that the agency would fulfill this mission, the group established the following objectives:

- To provide a sufficient return on investment by increasing sales and maintaining the liquidity needed to support operations
- To add value to the agency's services by training employees to be knowledgeable and competent
- To retain customers and attract new customers
- To operate an efficient and cost-effective office support system for customer agents

To determine the agency's progress in meeting these objectives, the group established the following performance measures:

- Number of new ideas for customer insurance
- Percentage of customers who rate services as excellent
- Average time for processing insurance applications
- Number of dollars spent on training
- Growth in revenues for each type of insurance
- Average time for processing claims
- Percentage of employees who complete 40 hours of training during the year
- Percentage of new customer leads that result in sales
- Cash flow
- Number of customer complaints
- Return on assets
- Percentage of customers who renew policies
- Percentage of revenue devoted to office support system (information systems, accounting, orders, and claims processing)

REQUIRED

1. Prepare a balanced scorecard for Howski by stating the agency's mission and matching its four objectives to the four stakeholder perspectives: the financial, learning and growth, internal business processes, and customer. Indicate which of the agency's performance measures would be appropriate for each objective.

2. Howski is a member of an association of independent insurance agents that provides industry statistics about many aspects of operating an insurance agency. What is benchmarking, and in what ways would the industry statistics assist Howski in further developing its balanced scorecard?

ALTERNATE PROBLEMS

LO 2

Flexible Budgets and Performance Evaluation

✔ 2: Budgeted variable cost per home: $10,922.50
✔ 3: Operating income under budget: $10,003

P6. Realtors, Inc., specializes in the sale of residential properties. It earns its revenue by charging a percentage of the sales price. Commissions for sales persons, listing agents, and listing companies are its main costs. Business has improved steadily over the last 10 years. The managing partner of Realtors, Inc., receives a report summarizing the company's performance each year. The report for the most recent year follows.

Realtors, Inc.
Performance Report
For the Year Ended December 31

	Budget*	Actual**	Difference Under (Over) Budgeted
Total selling fees	$2,052,000	$2,242,200	$(190,200)
Variable costs:			
Sales commissions	$1,102,950	$1,205,183	$(102,233)
Automobile	36,000	39,560	(3,560)
Advertising	93,600	103,450	(9,850)
Home repairs	77,400	89,240	(11,840)
General overhead	656,100	716,970	(60,870)
Total variable costs	$1,966,050	$2,154,403	$(188,353)
Fixed costs:			
General overhead	60,000	62,300	(2,300)
Total costs	$2,026,050	$2,216,703	$(190,653)
Operating income	$ 25,950	$ 25,497	$ 453

*Budgeted data are based on 180 units sold.
**Actual data for 200 units sold.

(Continued)

REQUIRED

1. **ACCOUNTING CONNECTION ▶** Analyze the performance report. What does it say about the company's performance? Is the performance report reliable? Explain your answer.
2. Calculate the budgeted selling fee and budgeted variable costs per home sale.
3. Prepare a performance report using a flexible budget based on the actual number of home sales.
4. **ACCOUNTING CONNECTION ▶** Analyze the report you prepared in requirement 3. What does it say about the company's performance? Is the report reliable? Explain your answer.
5. **ACCOUNTING CONNECTION ▶** What recommendations would you make to improve the company's performance next year?

LO **1, 2**

Evaluating Cost Center Performance

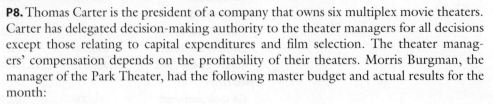

North plant:
✔ 1: Total variance between actual results and flexible budget: $52,000F
✔ 1: Total variance between flexible budget and master budget: $775,000F
✔ 1: Performance measure: Bottles processed per hour: 7,450U

P7. Reuse Products, LLC, manufactures plastic beverage bottles. The division that manufactures water bottles for the North American market has two plants that operate 24 hours a day, 365 days a year. The plants are evaluated as cost centers. Small tools and supplies are considered variable overhead. Depreciation and rent are considered fixed overhead. For the month, the master budget for a plant and the actual operating results of the two North American plants, North and South, follow.

Cost Category (Variable Unit Cost)	Master Budget	North Actual	South Actual
Center costs:			
Plastic pellets ($0.009)	$4,500,000	$3,880,000	$5,500,000
Caps ($0.004)	2,000,000	1,990,000	2,000,000
Direct labor ($0.002)	1,000,000	865,000	1,240,000
Small tools and supplies ($0.0005)	250,000	198,000	280,000
Depreciation and rent	450,000	440,000	480,000
Total cost	$8,200,000	$7,373,000	$9,500,000
Performance measures:			
Bottles processed per hour	69,450	62,000	70,250
Average daily pounds of scrap	5	6	7
Bottles processed (in millions)	500	450	520

REQUIRED

1. Prepare a performance report for the North plant. Include a flexible budget and variance analysis.
2. Prepare a performance report for the South plant. Include a flexible budget and variance analysis.
3. **ACCOUNTING CONNECTION ▶** Compare the two plants, and comment on their performance.
4. **ACCOUNTING CONNECTION ▶** Explain why a flexible budget should be prepared.

LO **1, 2, 3**

Evaluating Profit and Investment Center Performance

✔ 1: Total variance between actual and flexible budget operating income: $6,000F
✔ 1: Total variance between flexible and master budget operating income: $20,000U

P8. Thomas Carter is the president of a company that owns six multiplex movie theaters. Carter has delegated decision-making authority to the theater managers for all decisions except those relating to capital expenditures and film selection. The theater managers' compensation depends on the profitability of their theaters. Morris Burgman, the manager of the Park Theater, had the following master budget and actual results for the month:

	Master Budget	Actual Results
Tickets sold	120,000	110,000
Revenue—tickets	$ 840,000	$ 880,000
Revenue—concessions	480,000	330,000
Total revenue	$1,320,000	$1,210,000
Controllable variable costs:		
Concessions	(120,000)	(99,000)
Direct labor	(420,000)	(330,000)
Variable overhead	(540,000)	(550,000)
Contribution margin	$ 240,000	$ 231,000
Controllable fixed costs:		
Rent	(55,000)	(55,000)
Other administrative expenses	(45,000)	(50,000)
Theater operating income	$ 140,000	$ 126,000

REQUIRED

1. Assuming that the theaters are profit centers, prepare a performance report for the Park Theater. Include a flexible budget. Determine the variances between actual results, the flexible budget, and the master budget.
2. **ACCOUNTING CONNECTION** ▶ Evaluate Burgman's performance as manager of the Park Theater.
3. Assume that the managers are assigned responsibility for capital expenditures and that the theaters are thus investment centers. Park Theater is expected to generate a desired ROI of at least 6 percent on average invested assets of $2,000,000.
   a. Compute the theater's return on investment and residual income. (Round percentages to one decimal place.)
   b. **ACCOUNTING CONNECTION** ▶ Using the ROI and residual income, evaluate Burgman's performance as manager.

LO **3**   **Return on Investment and Residual Income**

P9. LET Company's financial results for the past two years follow.

✔ 1: This year return on investment: 36.40%
✔ 2: This year residual income: $50,160

LET Company
Balance Sheet
December 31

	This Year	Last Year
Assets		
Cash	$ 9,000	$ 4,000
Accounts receivable	40,000	50,000
Inventory	30,000	25,000
Other current assets	1,000	1,000
Plant assets	120,000	100,000
Total assets	$200,000	$180,000
Liabilities and Stockholders' Equity		
Current liabilities	$ 10,000	$ 10,000
Long-term liabilities	20,000	10,000
Stockholders' equity	170,000	160,000
Total liabilities and stockholders' equity	$200,000	$180,000

(Continued)

LET Company
Income Statement
For the Years Ended December 31

	This Year	Last Year
Sales	$ 247,000	$ 204,000
Cost of goods sold	(150,000)	(115,000)
Selling and administrative expenses	(27,840)	(17,600)
Operating income	$ 69,160	$ 71,400
Income taxes	20,160	29,400
After-tax operating income	$ 49,000	$ 42,000

REQUIRED

1. Compute the company's profit margin, asset turnover, and return on investment for this year and last year. Beginning total assets for last year were $160,000. (Round percentages to two decimal places.)
2. The desired return on investment for the company has been set at 10 percent. Compute LET's residual income for this year and last year.
3. The cost of capital for the company is 5 percent. Compute the company's economic value added for this year and last year.
4. **ACCOUNTING CONNECTION** ▶ Before drawing conclusions about this company's performance, what additional information would you want?

LO 4   ## The Balanced Scorecard and Benchmarking

P10. BUSINESS APPLICATION ▶ Resource College is a liberal arts school that provides local residents the opportunity to take college courses and earn bachelor's degrees. Yolanda Howard, the school's provost, recently attended a workshop in which the balanced scorecard was presented as a way of focusing all of an organization's functions on its mission. After the workshop, she met with her administrative staff and college deans in a weekend brainstorming session. The group determined that the college's mission was to provide high-quality courses and degrees to individuals to add value to their lives. To ensure that the college would fulfill this mission, the group established the following objectives:

- To provide a sufficient return on investment by increasing tuition revenues and maintaining the liquidity needed to support operations
- To add value to the college's courses by encouraging faculty to be lifelong learners
- To retain students and attract new students
- To operate efficient and cost-effective student support systems

To determine the college's progress in meeting these objectives, the group established the following performance measures:

- Number of faculty publications
- Percentage of students who rate college as excellent
- Average time for processing student applications
- Number of dollars spent on professional development
- Growth in revenues for each department
- Average time for processing transcript requests
- Percentage of faculty who annually do 40 hours of professional development
- Percentage of new student leads that result in enrollment
- Cash flow
- Number of student complaints
- Return on assets
- Percentage of returning students
- Percentage of revenue devoted to student services systems (registrar, computer services, financial aid, and student health)

REQUIRED

1. Prepare a balanced scorecard for Resource by stating the college's mission and matching its four objectives to the four stakeholder perspectives: the financial, learning and growth, internal business processes, and customer perspectives. Indicate which of the college's performance measures would be appropriate for each objective.

2. Resource College is a member of an association of independent liberal arts schools that provides industry statistics about many aspects of operating a college. What is benchmarking, and in what ways would the association's statistics assist Resource College in further developing its balanced scorecard?

CASES

Interpreting Management Reports: Responsibility Centers

LO 1

C1. Wood4Fun makes wooden playground equipment for the institutional and consumer markets. The company strives for low-cost, high-quality production because it operates in a highly competitive market in which product price is set by the marketplace and is not based on production costs. The company is organized into responsibility centers. The vice president of manufacturing is responsible for three manufacturing plants. The vice president of sales is responsible for four sales regions. Recently, these two vice presidents began to disagree about whether the manufacturing plants are cost centers or profit centers. The vice president of manufacturing views the plants as cost centers because the managers of the plants control only product-related costs. The vice president of sales believes the plants are profit centers because product quality and product cost strongly affect company profits.

1. Identify the controllable performance that Wood4Fun values and wants to measure. Give at least three examples of performance measures that Wood4Fun could use to monitor such performance.
2. For the manufacturing plants, what type of responsibility center is most consistent with the controllable performance Wood4Fun wants to measure?
3. For the sales regions, what type of responsibility center is most appropriate?

Conceptual Understanding: Types of Responsibility Centers

LO 1, 2

C2. Yuma Foods acquired Aldo's Tortillas several years ago. Aldo's has continued to operate as an independent company, except that Yuma Foods has exclusive authority over capital investments, production quantity, and pricing decisions because Yuma has been Aldo's only customer since the acquisition. Yuma uses return on investment to evaluate the performance of Aldo's manager. The most recent performance report follows.

Yuma Foods
Performance Report for Aldo's Tortillas
For the Year Ended June 30

Sales	$6,000
Variable cost of goods sold	(3,000)
Variable administrative expenses	(1,000)
Variable corporate expenses (% of sales)	(600)
Contribution margin	$1,400
Fixed overhead (includes depreciation of $100)	(400)
Fixed administrative expenses	(500)
Operating income	$ 500
Average assets invested	$5,500
Return on investment	9.09%*

*Rounded

(Continued)

1. Analyze the items listed in the performance report, and identify the items that Aldo controls and those that Yuma controls. In your opinion, what type of responsibility center is Aldo's Tortillas? Explain your response. (Round to two decimal places.)

2. Prepare a revised performance report for Aldo's Tortillas and an accompanying memo to the president of Yuma Foods that explains why it is important to change the content of the report. Cite some basic principles of responsibility accounting to support your recommendation.

LO 3

Decision Analysis: Return on Investment and Residual Income

C3. Suppose Alexandra Patel, the manager of the Food and Lodging Division at Winter Wonderland Resort, has hired you as a consultant to help her examine her division's performance under several different circumstances.

1. Type the data that follow into a spreadsheet to compute the division's actual return on investment and residual income. (Data are from parts **3** and **4** of this chapter's TriLevel Problem.) Match your data entries to the rows and columns shown below. (*Hint:* Remember to format each cell for the type of numbers it holds, such as percentage, currency, or general. Round profit margin to two decimal places.)

	A	B	C	D
1				**Investment Center**
2				**Food and Lodging Division**
3				**Actual Results**
4	Sales			$40,000,000
5	Operating income			$ 6,450,000
6	Average assets invested			$10,000,000
7	Desired ROI			30%
8	Return on investment			=(D5/D6)
9	Profit margin			=(D5/D4)
10	Asset turnover			=(D4/D6)
11	Residual income			=(D5−(D7*D6))
12				

2. Patel would like to know how the figures would change if Food and Lodging had a desired ROI of 40 percent and average assets invested of $10,000,000. Revise your spreadsheet from **1** to compute the division's return on investment and residual income under those conditions.

3. Patel also wants to know how the figures would change if Food and Lodging had a desired ROI of 30 percent and average assets invested of $12,000,000. Revise your spreadsheet from **1** to compute the division's return on investment and residual income under those conditions.

4. Does the use of formatted spreadsheets simplify the computation of ROI and residual income? Do such spreadsheets make it easier to perform "what-if" analyses?

LO 3, 5

Conceptual Understanding: Economic Value Added and Performance

C4. Sevilla Consulting offers environmental consulting services worldwide. The managers of branch offices are rewarded for superior performance with bonuses based on the economic value that the office adds to the company. Last year's operating results for the entire company and for its three offices, expressed in millions of U.S. dollars, follow.

	Worldwide	Europe	Americas	Asia
Cost of capital	9%	10%	8%	12%
Total assets	$210	$70	$70	$70
Current liabilities	80	10	40	30
After-tax operating income	15	5	5	5

1. Compute the economic value added for each office worldwide. What factors affect each office's economic value added? How can an office improve its economic value added? (Round to two decimal places.)
2. **BUSINESS APPLICATION** ▶ If managers' bonuses are based on economic value added to office performance, what specific actions will managers be motivated to take?
3. Is economic value added the only performance measure needed to evaluate investment centers adequately? Explain your response.

LO **4, 5**   ## Group Activity: Performance Measures and the Balanced Scorecard

C5. BUSINESS APPLICATION ▶ Working in a group of four to six students, select a local business. The group should become familiar with the background of the business by interviewing its manager or accountant. Each group member should identify several performance objectives for the business and link each objective with a specific stakeholder's perspective from the balanced scorecard. (Select at least one performance objective for each perspective.) For each objective, ask yourself, "If I were the manager of the business, how would I set performance measures for each objective?" Then prepare an email stating the business's name, location, and activities and your linked performance objectives and perspectives. Also list possible measures for each performance objective.

In class, members of the group should compare their individual emails and compile them into a group report by having each group member assume a different stakeholder perspective (add government and community if you want more than four perspectives). Each group should be ready to present all perspectives and the group's report on performance objectives and measures in class.

Continuing Case: Cookie Company

C6. As we continue with this case, assume that your cookie store is now part of a national chain. The store has been consistently profitable, and sales remain satisfactory despite a temporary economic downturn in your area.

At the first of the year, corporate headquarters set a targeted return on investment of 20 percent for your store. The store currently averages $140,000 in invested assets (beginning invested assets, $130,000; ending invested assets, $150,000) and is projected to have an operating income of $30,800. You are considering whether to take one or both of the following actions before the end of the year:

- Hold off recording and paying $5,000 in bills owed until the start of the next fiscal year.
- Write down to zero value $3,000 in store inventory (nonperishable containers) that you have been unable to sell.

Currently, your bonus is based on store profits. Next year, corporate headquarters is changing its performance incentive program so that bonuses will be based on a store's actual return on investment.

1. What effect would each of the actions that you are considering have on the store's operating income this year? In your opinion, is either action unethical?
2. Independent of question **1**, how would the inventory write-down affect next year's income and return on investment if the inventory is sold for $4,000 next year, when corporate headquarters changes its performance incentive plan for store managers? In your opinion, do you have an ethical dilemma? (Round ROI to the nearest whole percentage.)

CHAPTER 8
Standard Costing and Variance Analysis

Known for its floor-cleaning home robots, Roomba and Scooba, **iRobot** is a leader in the emerging robotics industry. Its PackBot, a combat-proven mobile robot, has saved many lives by performing hazardous reconnaissance, search, and bomb disposal duties in battle zones worldwide.

As iRobot develops the next generation of robots for military, industrial, and home use, its managers will continue to keep the business highly profitable by using design specifications to set standard costs for the company product lines. Managers in all types of companies use these figures as performance targets and as benchmarks against which to measure actual spending trends and monitor changes in business conditions.

1. CONCEPT ▶ *Why is standard costing and variance analysis useful?*

2. ACCOUNTING APPLICATION ▶ *How can iRobot's managers evaluate the performance of its cost centers?*

3. BUSINESS APPLICATION ▶ *Why does the setting of performance standards help managers control costs and improve performance?*

LEARNING OBJECTIVES

 Define *standard costs*, and explain why standard costing is useful.

 Compute standard unit costs, and describe the role of flexible budgets in variance analysis to control costs.

 Compute and analyze direct materials variances.

 Compute and analyze direct labor variances.

 Compute and analyze overhead variances.

LO 6 Explain how variances are used to evaluate a business's performance.

CONCEPTS

CONCEPTS
- Comparability
- Understandability

RELEVANT LEARNING OBJECTIVE

LO 1 Define *standard costs*, and explain why standard costing is useful.

LO 1 Concepts Underlying Standard Costing

Managers find standard costing useful due to the concepts of understandability and comparability. *Understandability* applies because the **standard costs** are realistic estimates of costs based on analyses of both past and projected operating costs and conditions. They are usually stated in terms of cost per unit. They provide a standard, or predetermined performance level for use in standard costing. *Comparability* applies because **standard costing** is a method of cost control that is used to compare the difference, or **variance**, between standard and actual performance. This method differs from actual and normal costing methods in that it uses estimated costs exclusively to compute all three elements of product cost—direct materials, direct labor, and overhead.

Standard costing is especially effective for understanding and managing cost centers. Recall that a *cost center* is a responsibility center in which there are well-defined links between the cost of the resources (direct materials, direct labor, and overhead) and the resulting products or services.

Managers find standard costing and variance analysis useful to develop budgets, to control costs, and to prepare reports. Managers set standard costs based on realistic estimates of operating costs and then use the standards to prepare flexible budgets. Flexible budgets improve the understanding and accuracy of their variance analysis since these budgets compare actual costs and a budget based on the same amount of output. By analyzing variances between standard and actual costs, managers gain insight into the causes of those differences. Once they have identified an operating problem that is causing a cost variance, they can devise a solution that results in better control of costs.

Standard costing can be used in any type of business. Both manufacturers and service businesses can use standard costing in conjunction with a job order costing, process costing, or activity-based costing system to compare actual performance results for materials, labor, and overhead with their predetermined performance standards. However, a disadvantage to using standard costing is that it can be expensive and time-consuming to gather all the needed information. The estimated costs are based not just on past costs, but also on engineering estimates, forecasted demand, worker input, time and motion studies, and type and quality of direct materials.

In the next section, we describe how standard unit costs are computed and used to prepare flexible budgets and how managers use the variance between standard and actual costs to evaluate performance and control costs.

APPLY IT!

Kellman Corporation is considering adopting the standard costing method. Dan Osterheld, the Midwest Division's manager, attended a corporate meeting at which the controller discussed the proposal. Osterheld asked, "How will this new method help me understand my division's performance? Does performance comparability improve if my division uses this new method?" Help prepare the controller's response to Osterheld by deciding whether the following statements are true or false. If false, make the statement true.

1. Standard costing helps managers compare actual cost results to a standard or predetermined performance level.
2. At the end of the period, variance analysis will only identify areas of cost efficiency.
3. Standard costing helps managers understand where to focus efforts for improvement.

SOLUTION

1. True
2. False

   At the end of the period, variance analysis will identify areas of cost efficiency and inefficiency.
3. True

TRY IT! SE1, SE2, E1A, E1B

ACCOUNTING APPLICATIONS

LO 2 Variance Analysis

Variance analysis is the process of computing the differences between standard costs and actual costs and identifying the causes of those differences. By examining the differences, or variances, between standard and actual costs, managers can gather valuable information about improving the accuracy of variance analysis and controlling costs.

Computing Standard Costs

A fully integrated standard costing system uses standard costs for all the elements of product cost: direct materials, direct labor, and overhead. Standard costs are recorded in inventory accounts for materials, work in process, and finished goods, as well as the Cost of Goods Sold account. Actual costs are recorded separately so that managers can compare what should have been spent (the standard costs) with the actual costs incurred in the cost center.

A standard unit cost for a manufactured product has the following six elements:

■ Direct materials price standard   ■ Direct materials quantity standard
■ Direct labor rate standard   ■ Direct labor time standard
■ Variable overhead rate standard   ■ Fixed overhead rate standard

To compute a standard unit cost, it is necessary to identify and analyze each of these elements. (Note that a standard unit cost for a service includes only the elements that relate to direct labor and overhead.)

Standard Direct Materials Cost

The **standard direct materials cost** is the price that should be paid for the materials and is computed as follows.

$$\text{Standard Direct Materials Cost} = \text{Direct Materials Price Standard} \times \text{Direct Materials Quantity Standard}$$

In this equation, the **direct materials price standard** is a careful estimate of the cost of a specific direct material in the next period. An organization's purchasing department is responsible for developing price standards for all direct materials and for making the actual purchases. When estimating a direct materials price standard, the purchasing department must take into account all possible price increases, changes in available quantities, and new sources of supply.

The **direct materials quantity standard** is an estimate of the amount of direct materials, including scrap and waste, that will be used in a period. It is influenced by product engineering specifications, the quality of direct materials, the age and productivity of machinery, and the quality and experience of the work force. Production managers or managerial accountants usually establish and monitor standards for direct materials quantity, but engineers, purchasing agents, and machine operators may also contribute to the development of these standards.

We will use ICU, which makes surveillance robots, to illustrate how standard costs are used to compute total unit cost. ICU has recently updated the standards for its Watch Dog product. Direct materials price standards are now $9.20 per square foot for casing materials and $20.17 for each mechanism. Direct materials quantity standards are 0.025 square foot of casing materials per robot and one mechanism per robot. Thus, the direct materials costs of making one robot are:

Direct materials costs:	
Casing ($9.20 per sq. ft. × 0.025 sq. ft.)	$ 0.23
One mechanism	20.17

Standard Direct Labor Cost

The **standard direct labor cost** for a product, task, or job order is the cost necessary to produce that product, task, or job order and is computed as follows.

$$\text{Standard Direct Labor Cost} = \text{Direct Labor Rate Standard} \times \text{Direct Labor Time Standard}$$

In this equation, the **direct labor rate standard** is the hourly direct labor rate that is expected to prevail during the next period for each function or job classification. Although rate ranges are established for each type of worker and rates vary within those ranges according to each worker's experience and length of service, an average standard rate is developed for each task. Even if the person making the product is paid more or less than the standard rate, the standard rate is used to calculate the standard direct labor cost.

The **direct labor time standard** is the expected labor time required for each department, machine, or process to complete the production of one unit or one batch of output. In many cases, standard time per unit is a small fraction of an hour. Current time and motion studies of workers and machines, as well as records of their past performance, provide the data for developing this standard. The direct labor time standard should be revised whenever a machine is replaced or the quality of the labor force changes.

For ICU, for example, direct labor time standards are 0.01 hour per robot for the Case Stamping Department and 0.05 hour per robot for the Assembly Department. Direct labor rate standards are $8.00 per hour for the Case Stamping Department and $10.20 per hour for the Assembly Department. Thus, the direct labor costs of making one robot in each department are:

Direct labor costs:

Case Stamping Department ($8.00 per hour × 0.01 hour per robot)	$0.08
Assembly Department ($10.20 per hour × 0.05 hour per robot)	0.51

Standard Overhead Cost

The **standard overhead cost** is the sum of the estimates of variable and fixed overhead costs in the next period. It is based on standard overhead rates that are computed in much the same way as the predetermined overhead rate discussed in an earlier chapter. Unlike that rate, however, the standard overhead rate has two parts:

■ variable costs
■ fixed costs

The reason for computing the standard variable and fixed overhead rates separately is that their cost behavior differs.

The **standard variable overhead rate** is computed by dividing the total budgeted variable overhead costs by an expression of capacity, such as the budgeted number of standard machine hours or standard direct labor hours.* Using standard direct labor hours as the base, the formula is as follows.

$$\text{Standard Variable Overhead Rate} = \frac{\text{Total Budgeted Variable Overhead Costs}}{\text{Total Budgeted Number of Standard Direct Labor Hours}}$$

For ICU, for example, the standard variable overhead rate is $12.00 per direct labor hour. Thus, the variable overhead cost of making one robot is:

Variable overhead cost ($12.00 per hour × 0.06 hour per robot)	$0.72

The **standard fixed overhead rate** is computed by dividing the total budgeted fixed overhead costs by an expression of capacity, usually normal capacity in terms of standard

---

*Other bases may be used if machine hours or direct labor hours are not good predictors, or drivers, of variable overhead costs.

hours or units. The denominator is expressed in the same terms as the variable overhead rate. Using normal capacity in terms of standard direct labor hours as the denominator, the formula is as follows.

$$\frac{\text{Standard Fixed}}{\text{Overhead Rate}} = \frac{\text{Total Budgeted Fixed Overhead Costs}}{\text{Normal Capacity in Terms of Standard Direct Labor Hours}}$$

For ICU, for example, the standard fixed overhead rate is $9.00 per direct labor hour. Thus, the fixed overhead cost of making one robot is:

Fixed overhead cost ($9.00 per hour × 0.06 hour per robot) $0.54

Recall that *normal capacity* is the level of operating capacity needed to meet expected sales demand. Using it as the application base ensures that all fixed overhead costs have been applied to units produced by the time normal capacity is reached.

Total Standard Unit Cost

Using standard costs eliminates the need to calculate unit costs from actual cost data every week or month or for each batch of goods produced. Once standard costs for direct materials, direct labor, and variable and fixed overhead have been developed, a total standard unit cost can be computed at any time. We used ICU to illustrate how standard costs are used to compute total unit cost. The standard cost of making one robot would be computed as follows.

STUDY NOTE: *The total standard unit cost of $22.25 represents the desired cost of producing one robot.*

Direct materials costs:	
Casing ($9.20 per sq. ft. × 0.025 sq. ft.)	$ 0.23
One mechanism	20.17
Direct labor costs:	
Case Stamping Department ($8.00 per hour × 0.01 hour per robot)	0.08
Assembly Department ($10.20 per hour × 0.05 hour per robot)	0.51
Variable overhead ($12.00 per hour × 0.06 hour per robot)	0.72
Total standard variable cost of one robot	$21.71
Fixed overhead ($9.00 per hour × 0.06 hour per robot)	0.54
Total standard unit cost	$22.25

The Role of Flexible Budgets in Variance Analysis

The accuracy of variance analysis depends to a large extent on the type of budget that managers use when comparing variances. Static, or fixed, budgets forecast revenues and expenses for just one level of sales and just one level of output. The budgets that make up a master budget are usually based on a single level of output; but many things can cause actual output to differ from the estimated output. If a company produces more products than predicted, total production costs will almost always be greater than predicted. Thus, a comparison of actual production costs with fixed budgeted costs will inevitably show variances.

The performance report in Exhibit 1 compares data from ICU's static master budget with the actual costs of the company's Watch Division, the division responsible for manufacturing the Watch Dog. As you can see, actual costs exceeded budgeted costs by $5,539. Most managers would consider such a cost overrun significant. But was there really a cost overrun? The budgeted amounts are based on an output of 17,500 units when the actual output was 19,100 units.

The total standard unit cost of producing a video game controller or a robot like the Watch Dog represents the desired production cost. It is based on the standards established for direct materials costs, direct labor costs, and variable and fixed overhead.

Exhibit 1
Performance Report Using
Data from a Static Budget

ICU, Inc.
Performance Report—Watch Division
For the Year Ended December 31

Cost Category	Master Budgeted Costs*	Actual Costs**	Difference Under (Over) Budget
Direct materials	$357,000	$361,000	$(4,000)
Direct labor	10,325	11,779	(1,454)
Variable overhead:			
Indirect materials	3,500	3,600	(100)
Indirect labor	5,250	5,375	(125)
Utilities	1,750	1,810	(60)
Other	2,100	2,200	(100)
Fixed overhead:			
Supervisory salaries	4,000	3,500	500
Depreciation	2,000	2,000	—
Utilities	450	450	—
Other	3,000	3,200	(200)
Totals	$389,375	$394,914	$(5,539)

*Budgeted costs are based on an output of 17,500 units.

**Actual output was 19,100 units.

© Cengage Learning 2014

To judge the division's performance accurately, ICU's managers can use a flexible budget. Recall that a *flexible* (or *variable*) *budget* is a summary of expected costs for a range of activity levels. Unlike a static budget, a flexible budget provides forecasted data that can be adjusted for changes in the level of output. The flexible budget in Exhibit 2 is based on standard unit cost data from the static master budget in Exhibit 1. Variable unit costs have been multiplied by the 19,100 units actually produced to arrive at the

Exhibit 2
Performance Report Using
Data from a Flexible Budget

ICU, Inc.
Performance Report—Watch Division
For the Year Ended December 31

Cost Category	Flexible Budgeted Costs*	Actual Costs	Difference Under (Over) Budget
Direct materials ($20.40)**	$389,640	$361,000	$28,640
Direct labor ($0.59)	11,269	11,779	(510)
Variable overhead:			
Indirect materials ($0.20)	3,820	3,600	220
Indirect labor ($0.30)	5,730	5,375	355
Utilities ($0.10)	1,910	1,810	100
Other ($0.12)	2,292	2,200	92
Fixed overhead:			
Supervisory salaries	4,000	3,500	500
Depreciation	2,000	2,000	—
Utilities	450	450	—
Other	3,000	3,200	(200)
Totals	$424,111	$394,914	$29,197

*Budgeted costs are based on actual output of 19,100 units.

**Amounts in parentheses in the Cost Category column are variable unit costs.

© Cengage Learning 2014

total flexible budgeted costs, and fixed overhead information has been carried over from Exhibit 1. In this report, actual costs are $29,197 less than the amount budgeted. In other words, the flexible budget shows that the Watch Division's performance in this period actually exceeded budget targets by $29,197.

The rest of this chapter will discuss how to explain the variances between actual costs and the flexible budget by using standard costing to analyze specific variances for direct materials, direct labor, variable overhead, and fixed overhead.

Using Variance Analysis to Control Costs

As Exhibit 3 shows, using variance analysis to control costs is a four-step process:

- **Step 1.** Managers compute the amount of the variance. If the amount is insignificant—actual operating results are close to those anticipated—no corrective action is needed.
- **Step 2.** If the variance is significant, managers analyze the variance to identify its cause.
- **Step 3.** In identifying the cause, they then select performance measures that will enable them to track the activities that need to be monitored, analyze the results, and determine the action needed to correct the problem.
- **Step 4.** The final step is to take the appropriate corrective action.

Exhibit 3
Variance Analysis: A Four-Step Approach to Controlling Costs

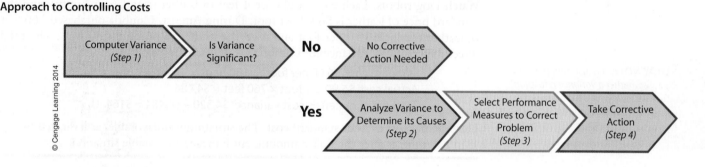

© Cengage Learning 2014

Although computing the amount of a variance is important, it does nothing to prevent the variance from recurring. To control costs, managers must determine the cause of the variance and select performance measures that will help them track the problem and find the best solution for it.

APPLY IT!

Using the information that follows, compute the total standard unit cost of a 5-pound bag of sugar.

Direct materials quantity standard	5 pounds per unit
Direct materials price standard	$0.05 per pound
Direct labor time standard	0.01 hour per unit
Direct labor rate standard	$10.00 per hour
Variable overhead rate standard	$0.15 per machine hour
Fixed overhead rate standard	$0.10 per machine hour
Machine hour standard	0.5 hour per unit

SOLUTION

Direct materials cost ($0.05 × 5 pounds)	$0.25
Direct labor cost ($10.00 × 0.01 hour)	0.10
Variable overhead ($0.15 × 0.5 machine hour)	0.08*
Fixed overhead ($0.10 × 0.5 machine hour)	0.05
Total standard unit cost	$0.48

*Rounded

TRY IT! SE3, SE4, E2A, E3A, E2B, E3B

LO3 Computing and Analyzing Direct Materials Variances

To control cost center operations, managers compute and analyze variances for whole cost categories, such as total direct materials costs, as well as variances for elements of those categories, such as the price and quantity of each direct material. The more detailed their analysis of direct materials variances, the more effective they will be in controlling costs.

Computing Total Direct Materials Cost Variance

Total Direct Materials Cost Variance

Performance Measure The **total direct materials cost variance** measures the difference between what the actual total materials cost and what they should have cost according to the flexible budget for the good units produced. *Good units* are the total units produced less units that are scrapped or need to be reworked—in other words, the salable units.

Formula

$$\text{Total Direct Materials Cost Variance} = \text{Standard Cost*} - \text{Actual Cost**}$$

*Standard Cost = Standard Price × Standard Quantity
**Actual Cost = Actual Price × Actual Quantity

Example Cambria Company is a manufacturer that makes leather bags to carry the Watch Dog robots. Each bag should use 4 feet of leather (standard quantity), and the standard price of leather is $6.00 per foot. During August, Cambria purchased 760 feet of leather costing $5.90 per foot and used the leather to produce 180 bags. The total direct materials cost variance for Cambria is calculated as follows.

> Standard cost: $6.00 per foot × (180 bags × 4 feet per bag) = $4,320
> Actual cost: $5.90 per foot × 760 feet = $4,484
> Total direct materials cost variance: $4,320 – $4,484 = $164 (U)

STUDY NOTE: *It is just as important to identify whether a variance is favorable or unfavorable as it is to compute the variance. This information is necessary for analyzing the variance and taking corrective action.*

Here, actual cost exceeds standard cost. The situation is unfavorable, as indicated by the U in parentheses after the dollar amount. An F means a favorable situation.

Computing Total Direct Materials Price Variance

To find the area or people responsible for the variance, the total direct materials cost variance must be broken down into two parts: the direct materials price variance and the direct materials quantity variance.

Direct Materials Price Variance

Performance Measure The **direct materials price variance** (or *direct materials spending* or *rate variance*) measures the difference between what the purchased materials actually cost and what they should have cost according to the flexible budget standard.

Formula

$$\text{Direct Materials Price Variance} = (\text{Standard Price} - \text{Actual Price}) \times \text{Actual Quantity}$$

Example For Cambria, the direct materials price variance is computed as follows.

> Direct Materials Price Variance = ($6.00 – $5.90) × 760 feet = $76 (F)

Because the price that the company paid for the direct materials was less than the standard price, the variance is favorable.

Computing Total Direct Materials Quantity Variance

Direct Materials Quantity Variance

Performance Measure The **direct materials quantity variance** (or *direct materials efficiency* or *usage variance*) measures the difference between the quantity of materials actually used to make the product and what the design standard called for.

Formula

Direct Materials Quantity Variance = Standard Price × (Standard Quantity – Actual Quantity)

Example For Cambria, it is computed as follows.

Direct Materials Quantity Variance = $6 × [(180 bags × 4 feet) – 760 feet] = $240 (U)

Because more leather than the standard quantity was used in the production process, the direct materials quantity variance is unfavorable.

Summary of Direct Materials Variances

The net of the direct materials price variance and the direct materials quantity variance should equal the total direct materials cost variance. The following check shows that the variances for Cambria were computed correctly:

Direct materials price variance	$ 76 (F)
Direct materials quantity variance	240 (U)
Total direct materials cost variance	$164 (U)

Variance analyses are sometimes easier to interpret in diagram form, as shown for Cambria in Exhibit 4. Notice that although direct materials are purchased at actual cost, they are entered in the Materials Inventory account at standard price. Thus, the direct materials price variance of $76 (F) is obvious when the costs are recorded. As Exhibit 4 shows, the standard price multiplied by the standard quantity is the amount entered in the Work in Process Inventory account.

Exhibit 4
Diagram of Direct Materials Variance Analysis

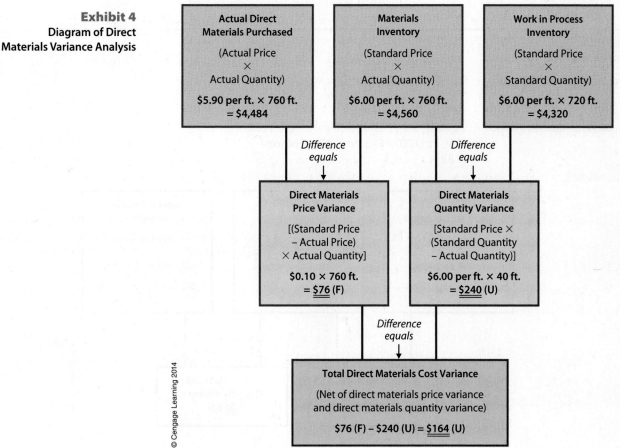

Business Application

Cambria's managers were concerned because the company had been experiencing direct materials price and quantity variances for some time. Moreover, as our analysis shows, the price variances were always favorable and the quantity variances were always unfavorable. By tracking the purchasing activity for three months, the managers discovered that the company's purchasing agent, without any authorization, had been purchasing a lower grade of leather at a reduced price. After careful analysis, the engineering manager determined that the substitute leather was not appropriate and that the company should resume purchasing the grade of leather originally specified. In addition, an analysis of scrap and rework revealed that the inferior quality of the substitute leather was causing the unfavorable quantity variance. By tracking the purchasing activity, Cambria's managers were able to solve the problems.

APPLY IT!

Using the information that follows, compare the actual and standard cost and usage data for the production of 5-pound bags of sugar, and compute the direct materials price and direct materials quantity variances using formulas or diagram form.

Direct materials quantity standard	5 pounds per unit
Direct materials price standard	$0.05 per pound
Direct materials purchased and used	55,100 pounds
Price paid for direct materials	$0.04 per pound
Number of good units produced	11,000 units

SOLUTION

Using formulas:

Direct Materials Price Variance   = (Standard Price – Actual Price) × Actual Quantity

    = ($0.05 – $0.04) × 55,100 pounds

    = $551 (F)

Direct Materials Quantity Variance = Standard Price × (Standard Quantity – Actual Quantity)

    = $0.05 × [(11,000 × 5 pounds) – 55,100 pounds]

    = $5 (U)

In diagram form:

Actual Direct Materials Purchased	Materials Inventory	Work in Process Inventory
(Actual Price × Actual Quantity)	(Standard Price × Actual Quantity)	(Standard Price × Standard Quantity)
$0.04 × 55,100 lbs. = $2,204	$0.05 × 55,100 = $2,755	$0.05 × (11,000 × 5) = $2,750

Direct Materials Price Variance $551 (F)	Direct Materials Quantity Variance $5 (U)

© Cengage Learning 2014

TRY IT! SE5, SE6, E4A, E5A, E6A, E4B, E5B, E6B

LO4 Computing and Analyzing Direct Labor Variances

The procedure for computing and analyzing direct labor cost variances parallels the procedure for finding direct materials variances. Again, the more detailed the analysis, the more effective managers will be in controlling costs.

Computing Total Direct Labor Cost Variance

Total Direct Labor Cost Variance

Performance Measure The **total direct labor cost variance** measures the difference between what the actual total labor cost and what it should have cost according to the flexible budget for the good units produced.

Formula

$$\text{Total Direct Labor Cost Variance} = \text{Standard Cost}^* - \text{Actual Cost}^{**}$$

*Standard Cost = Standard Price × Standard Quantity
**Actual Cost = Actual Price × Actual Quantity

Example At Cambria, each leather bag requires 2.4 standard direct labor hours, and the standard direct labor rate is $8.50 per hour. During August, 450 direct labor hours were used to make 180 bags at an average pay rate of $9.20 per hour. Cambria's total direct labor cost variance is computed as follows.

Standard cost: $8.50 per hour × (180 bags × 2.4 hours per bag) = $3,672
Actual cost: $9.20 per hour × 450 hours = $4,140
Total direct labor cost variance: $3,672 – $4,140 = $468 (U)

Both the actual direct labor hours per bag and the actual direct labor rate varied from the standard.

For effective performance evaluation, management must know how much of the total cost arose from different direct labor rates and how much from different numbers of direct labor hours. This information is found by computing the direct labor rate variance and the direct labor efficiency variance.

Computing Direct Labor Rate Variance

Direct Labor Rate Variance

Performance Measure The **direct labor rate variance** (or *direct labor spending variance*) measures the difference between what the direct labor actually cost and what it should have cost according to the flexible budget standard.

Formula

$$\text{Direct Labor Rate Variance} = (\text{Standard Rate} - \text{Actual Rate}) \times \text{Actual Hours}$$

Example For Cambria, it is computed as follows.

Direct Labor Rate Variance = ($8.50 – $9.20) × 450 hours = $315 (U)

Computing Direct Labor Efficiency Variance

Direct Labor Efficiency Variance

Performance Measure The **direct labor efficiency variance** (or *direct labor quantity* or *usage variance*) measures the difference between the labor quantity actually used to make the product and what the design standard called for. It is computed as follows.

Formula

$$\text{Direct Labor Efficiency Variance} = \text{Standard Rate} \times (\text{Standard Hours Allowed} - \text{Actual Hours})$$

Example For Cambria, it is computed this way:

$$\text{Direct Labor Efficiency Variance} = \$8.50 \times [(180 \text{ bags} \times 2.4 \text{ hours}) - 450 \text{ hours}] = \underline{\$153} \text{ (U)}$$

Summary of Direct Labor Variances The net of the direct labor rate variance and the direct labor efficiency variance should equal the total direct labor cost variance. The following check shows that the variances were computed correctly:

Direct labor rate variance	$315 (U)
Direct labor efficiency variance	153 (U)
Total direct labor cost variance	$468 (U)

Exhibit 5 summarizes Cambria's direct labor variances. Unlike direct materials variances, the direct labor rate and efficiency variances are usually computed and recorded at the same time.

Exhibit 5
Diagram of Direct Labor Variance Analysis

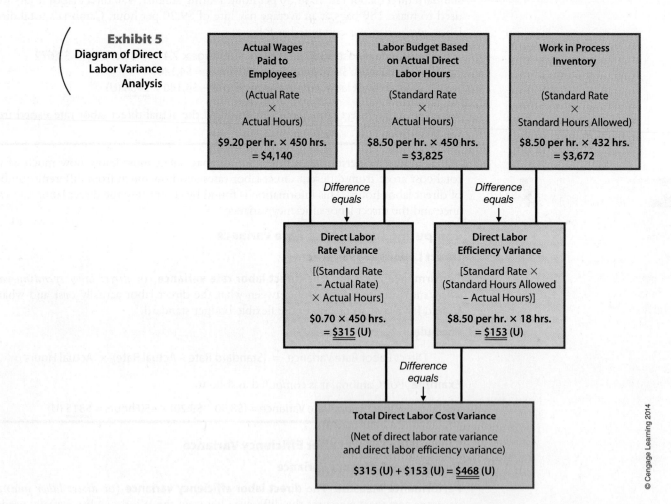

Business Perspective
What Do You Get When You Cross a Vacuum Cleaner with a Gaming Console?

The transfer of technology ideas developed for government purposes to everyday consumer use is common—for example, the Internet and computers. But what about transferring technology from home use to the battlefield? **iRobot Corporation**[1] applied the technology it uses in its Roomba vacuum cleaner to create Small Unmanned Ground Vehicles (SUGVs). These robots, such as the PackBot, have cameras that see both during the day and at night, flexible treads that allow them to climb stairs, and radio links that connect them to an operator at a gaming-like console and to the military command center.

Business Application

Because Cambria's direct labor rate variance and direct labor efficiency variance were unfavorable, its managers investigated the causes of these variances. An analysis of employee time cards revealed that the Bag Assembly Department had replaced an assembly worker who was ill with a machine operator from another department. The machine operator made $9.20 per hour, whereas the assembly worker earned the standard $8.50 per hour rate. When questioned about the unfavorable efficiency variance, the assembly supervisor identified two causes. First, the machine operator had to learn assembly skills on the job, so his assembly time was longer than the standard time per bag. Second, the materials handling people were partially responsible because they delivered parts late on five different occasions. Because the machine operator was a temporary replacement, Cambria's managers took no corrective action; but they decided to keep a close eye on the materials handling function by tracking delivery times and the number of delays for the next three months. Once they have collected and analyzed the new data, they will take whatever action is needed to correct the scheduling problem.

APPLY IT!

Using the information that follows, compare the standard cost and usage data for the production of 5-pound bags of sugar, and compute the direct labor rate and direct labor efficiency variances using formulas or diagram form.

Direct labor time standard	0.01 hour per unit
Direct labor rate standard	$10.00 per hour
Direct labor hours used (actual)	100 hours
Total cost of direct labor	$1,010
Number of good units produced	11,000 units

SOLUTION

Using formulas:

Direct Labor Rate Variance = (Standard Rate – Actual Rate) × Actual Hours

= [$10.00 – ($1,010 ÷ 100 hours)] × 100 hours

= $10 (U)

Direct Labor Efficiency Variance = Standard Rate × (Standard Hours Allowed – Actual Hours)

= $10 × [(11,000 × 0.01 hour) – 100 hours]

= $100 (F)

(Continued)

In diagram form:

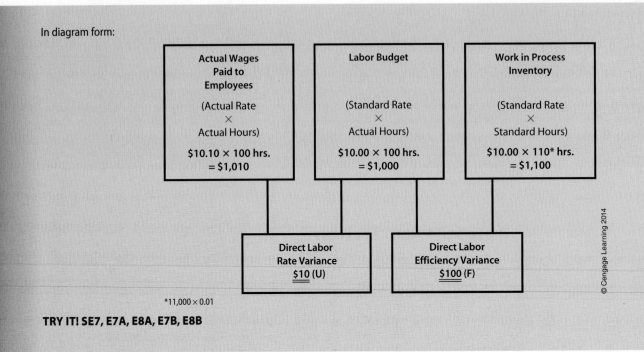

*11,000 × 0.01

TRY IT! SE7, E7A, E8A, E7B, E8B

LO 5 Computing and Analyzing Overhead Variances

Controlling variable and fixed overhead costs is more difficult than controlling direct materials and direct labor costs because the responsibility for overhead costs is hard to assign. Fixed overhead costs may be unavoidable past costs, such as depreciation and lease expenses, which are not under the control of any department manager. If variable overhead costs can be related to departments or activities, however, some control is possible.

Computing Total Overhead Cost Variance

Total Overhead Cost Variance

Performance Measure Analyses of overhead variances differ in degree of detail. The basic approach is to compute the **total overhead cost variance**, which is the difference between what actual overhead cost and what it should have cost according to the flexible budget for the good units produced.

Formula

Total Overhead Cost Variance = Standard Cost* – Actual Cost**

*Standard Cost = Standard Rate × Standard Hours for the Good Units Produced
**Actual cost is given.

Example Recall how overhead is applied to production using a standard or predetermined overhead rate. A standard overhead rate has two parts: a variable rate and a fixed rate. For Cambria, these standard overhead rates are as follows.

Variable overhead rate (from the flexible budget)	$5.75 per direct labor hour
Standard fixed overhead rate [$1,300 total budgeted fixed overhead ÷ 400 direct labor hours (normal capacity)]	3.25 per direct labor hour
Total standard overhead rate	$9.00 per direct labor hour

Cambria's total overhead cost variance would therefore be computed as follows.

Standard cost: $9.00 per hour × (180 bags × 2.4 hours per bag) = $3,888
Actual cost (given): Variable $2,500 + Fixed $1,600 = $4,100
Total direct materials cost variance: $3,888 − $4,100 = $212 (U)

This amount can be divided into a variable overhead variance and a fixed overhead variance.

Variable Overhead Variances

Total Variable Overhead Cost Variance

Performance Measure The **total variable overhead cost variance** measures the difference between what the actual variable overhead cost and what it should have cost according to the flexible budget for the good units produced.

Formula

Total Variable Overhead Cost Variance = Overhead Applied* − Actual Overhead
*Overhead Applied = Standard Rate × Standard Hours for the Good Units Produced

Example At Cambria, each leather bag requires 2.4 standard direct labor hours, and the standard variable overhead rate is $5.75 per direct labor hour. For the month, the company incurred $2,500 of actual variable overhead costs. The total variable overhead cost variance is computed as follows.

Overhead applied: $5.75 per hour × (180 bags × 2.4 hours per bag) = $2,484
Total variable overhead cost variance: $2,484 − $2,500 = $16 (U)

Exhibit 6 shows an analysis of Cambria's variable overhead variances.

Exhibit 6
**Diagram of Variable
Overhead Variance Analysis**

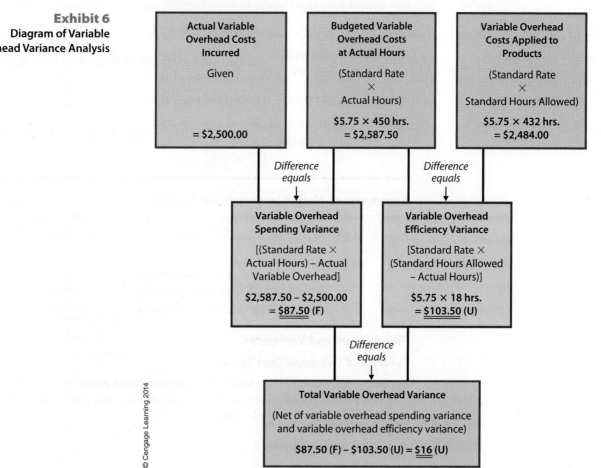

© Cengage Learning 2014

For effective performance evaluation, managers must know how much of the total cost arose from variable overhead spending deviations and how much from variable overhead application deviations (i.e., applied and actual direct labor hours). This information is found by computing the variable overhead spending variance and the variable overhead efficiency variance.

Computing Variable Overhead Spending Variance

Variable Overhead Spending Variance

Performance Measure The **variable overhead spending variance** (or *variable overhead rate variance*) measures the difference between what variable overhead actually cost and what it should have cost according to the flexible budget standard.

Formula

$$\text{Variable Overhead Spending Variance} = (\text{Standard Rate} \times \text{Actual Hours}) - \text{Actual Variable Overhead Cost}$$

Example For Cambria, it is computed as follows:

$$\text{Variable Overhead Spending Variance} = (\$5.75 \times 450 \text{ hours}) - \$2,500$$

$$= \underline{\$87.50} \text{ (F)}$$

Computing Variable Overhead Efficiency Variance

Variable Overhead Efficiency Variance

Performance Measure The **variable overhead efficiency variance** measures the difference between the labor hours actually worked to make the product and the labor hours that should have been worked to produce the number of products made.

Formula

$$\text{Variable Overhead Efficiency Variance} = \text{Standard Rate} \times (\text{Standard Hours Allowed} - \text{Actual Hours})$$

Example For Cambria, it is computed as follows.

$$\text{Variable Overhead Efficiency Variance} = \$5.75 \times [(180 \text{ bags} \times 2.4 \text{ hours}) - 450 \text{ hours}]$$

$$= \underline{\$103.50} \text{ (U)}$$

Summary of Variable Overhead Variances The net of the variable overhead spending variance and the variable overhead efficiency variance should equal the total variable overhead variance. The following check shows that these variances have been computed correctly:

Variable overhead spending variance	$ 87.50 (F)
Variable overhead efficiency variance	103.50 (U)
Total variable overhead cost variance	$ 16.00 (U)

Fixed Overhead Variances

Total Fixed Overhead Cost Variance

Performance Measure The **total fixed overhead cost variance** measures the difference between what the actual fixed overhead cost and what was applied according to the flexible budget for the good units produced.

Formula

$$\text{Total Fixed Overhead Cost Variance} = \text{Fixed Overhead Applied*} - \text{Actual Fixed Overhead}$$

*Fixed Overhead Applied = Standard Rate × Standard Hours for the Good Units Produced

STUDY NOTE: *The procedure for finding the total fixed overhead cost variance differs from the procedure used for finding direct materials, direct labor, and variable overhead variances.*

Example At Cambria, each bag requires 2.4 standard direct labor hours, and the standard fixed overhead rate is $3.25 per direct labor hour. As we noted earlier, the standard fixed overhead rate is found by dividing budgeted fixed overhead ($1,300) by normal capacity, which was set by the master budget at the beginning of the period. In this case, because normal capacity is 400 direct labor hours, the fixed overhead rate is $3.25 per direct labor hour ($1,300 ÷ 400 hours). For the month, Cambria incurred $1,600 of actual fixed overhead costs. The total fixed overhead variance is computed as follows.

Fixed overhead applied: $3.25 per hour × (180 bags × 2.4 hours per bag) = $1,404
Total fixed overhead variance: $1,404 – $1,600 = $196 (U)

Exhibit 7 shows an analysis of Cambria's fixed overhead variances.

Exhibit 7
Diagram of Fixed Overhead Variance Analysis

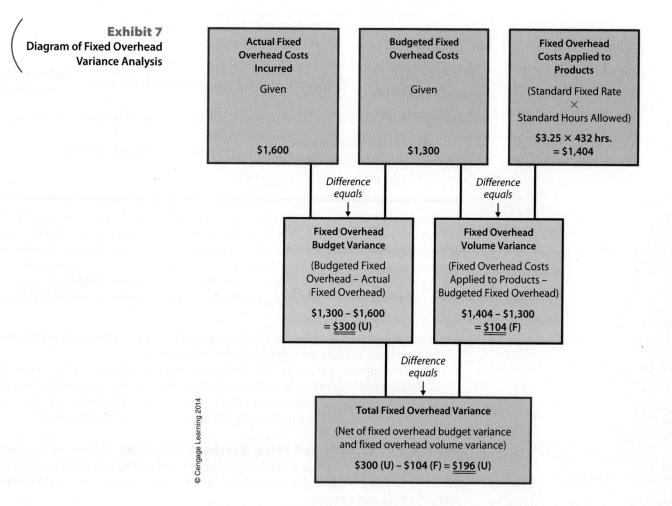

© Cengage Learning 2014

For effective performance evaluation, managers break down the total fixed overhead cost variance into two additional variances: the fixed overhead budget variance and the fixed overhead volume variance.

Computing Fixed Overhead Budget Variance

Fixed Overhead Budget Variance

Performance Measure The **fixed overhead budget variance** (or *budgeted fixed overhead variance*) measures the difference between what fixed overhead actually cost and what was budgeted.

Formula

$$\frac{\text{Fixed Overhead Budget}}{\text{Variance}} = \text{Budgeted Fixed Overhead} - \text{Actual Fixed Overhead}$$

Example For Cambria, it is computed as follows.

$$\text{Fixed Overhead Budget Variance} = \$1,300 - \$1,600 = \underline{\$300} \text{ (U)}$$

Computing Fixed Overhead Volume Variance

Fixed Overhead Volume Variance

Performance Measure The **fixed overhead volume variance** measures the difference between budgeted fixed overhead costs and the fixed overhead costs applied to products based on the standard fixed rate and standard hours allowed.

Formula

$$\frac{\text{Fixed Overhead}}{\text{Volume Variance}} = (\text{Standard Fixed Rate} \times \text{Standard Hours Allowed}) - \frac{\text{Budgeted Fixed}}{\text{Overhead}}$$

Example For Cambria, the fixed overhead volume variance is computed as follows.

$$\frac{\text{Fixed Overhead}}{\text{Volume Variance}} = [\$3.25 \times (180 \text{ bags} \times 2.4 \text{ hours})] - \$1,300$$

$$= \underline{\$104} \text{ (F)}$$

Because the fixed overhead volume variance measures the use of existing facilities and capacity, a volume variance will occur if more or less than normal capacity is used. At Cambria, 400 direct labor hours are considered normal use of facilities. Because fixed overhead costs are applied on the basis of standard hours allowed, Cambria's overhead was applied on the basis of 432 hours, even though the fixed overhead rate was computed using 400 hours. Thus, more fixed costs would be applied to products than were budgeted.

- When capacity exceeds the expected amount, the result is a favorable overhead volume variance because fixed overhead was overapplied.
- When a company operates at a level below the normal capacity in units, the result is an unfavorable volume variance. Not all of the fixed overhead costs will be applied to units produced. In other words, fixed overhead is underapplied, and the cost of goods produced does not include the full budgeted cost of fixed overhead.

Summary of Variable and Fixed Overhead Variances The net of the variable and fixed overhead variances should equal the total overhead cost variance. Checking the computations, we find that the variable and fixed overhead variances do equal the total overhead cost variance:

Variable overhead spending variance	$ 87.50 (F)
Variable overhead efficiency variance	103.50 (U)
Fixed overhead budget variance	300.00 (U)
Fixed overhead volume variance	104.00 (F)
Total overhead cost variance	$212.00 (U)

Exhibits 6 and 7 summarize the analysis of overhead variances. The total overhead cost variance is also the amount of overapplied or underapplied overhead. Recall that actual variable and fixed overhead costs are recorded as they occur, that variable and fixed overhead are applied to products as they are produced, and that the overapplied or underapplied overhead is computed and reconciled at the end of each period. By breaking down the total overhead cost variance into its variable and fixed components, managers can more accurately control costs and reconcile their causes. An analysis of these two overhead variances will help explain why the amount of overhead applied to units produced is different from the actual overhead costs incurred.

Business Application

In analyzing the unfavorable total overhead cost variance of $212, the manager of Cambria's Bag Assembly Department found the following causes for the variances that contributed to it.

■ Although the variable overhead spending variance was favorable ($87.50 less than expected because of savings on purchases), the inefficiency of the machine operator who substituted for an assembly worker created unfavorable variances for both direct labor efficiency and variable overhead efficiency. As a result, the manager is going to consider the feasibility of implementing a program for cross-training employees.

■ After reviewing the fixed overhead costs, the Bag Assembly Department's manager concluded that higher-than-anticipated factory insurance premiums were the reason for the unfavorable fixed overhead budget variance and were the result of an increase in the number of insurance claims filed by employees. To obtain more specific information, the manager will study the insurance claims filed over a three-month period.

■ Finally, since the 432 standard hours were well above the normal capacity of 400 direct labor hours, fixed overhead was overapplied, and it resulted in a $104 (F) volume variance. The overutilization of capacity was traced to high demand that pressed the company to use almost all its capacity. Management decided not to do anything about the fixed overhead volume variance because it fell within an anticipated seasonal range.

APPLY IT!

Sutherland Products uses standard costing. The following information about overhead was generated during August:

Standard variable overhead rate	$2 per machine hour
Standard fixed overhead rate	$3 per machine hour
Actual variable overhead costs	$443,200
Actual fixed overhead costs	$698,800
Budgeted fixed overhead costs	$700,000
Standard machine hours per unit produced	12
Good units produced	18,940
Actual machine hours	228,400

Compute the variable overhead spending and efficiency variances and the fixed overhead budget and volume variances using formulas or diagram form.

(Continued)

SOLUTION

Using formulas:

Variable Overhead Spending Variance = (Standard Rate × Actual Hours) − Actual Variable Overhead Cost
= ($2 × 228,400 hours) − $443,200
= $13,600 (F)

Variable Overhead Efficiency Variance = Standard Rate × (Standard Hours Allowed − Actual Hours)
= $2 × [(18,940 × 12) − 228,400 hours]
= $2,240 (U)

Fixed Overhead Budget Variance = Budgeted Fixed Overhead − Actual Fixed Overhead
= $700,000 − $698,800
= $1,200 (F)

Fixed Overhead Volume Variance = (Standard Rate × Standard Hours Allowed) − Budgeted Fixed Overhead
= [$3 × (18,940 × 12)] − $700,000
= $18,160 (U)

In diagram form:

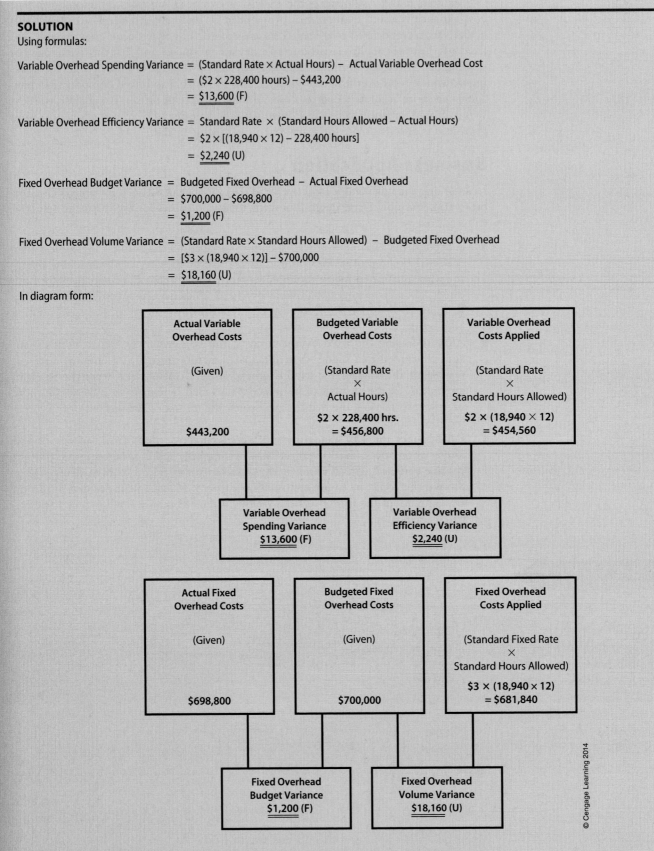

© Cengage Learning 2014

TRY IT! SE8, SE9, E9A, E10A, E11A, E12A, E13A, E14A, E9B, E10B, E11B, E12B, E13B, E14B

LO 6 Using Cost Variances to Evaluate Managers' Performance

To ensure that the evaluation of a business's performance is effective and fair, a company's policies should be based on input from managers and employees and should specify the procedures that managers are to use when doing the following:

- Preparing operational plans
- Assigning responsibility for carrying out the operational plans
- Communicating the operational plans to key personnel
- Evaluating performance in each area of responsibility
- Identifying the causes of significant variances from the operational plan
- Taking corrective action to eliminate problems

Exhibit 8 frames these manager responsibilities for standard costing and variance analysis within the management process of planning, performing, evaluating and reporting on cost center operations.

Exhibit 8
Variance Analysis and The Management Process

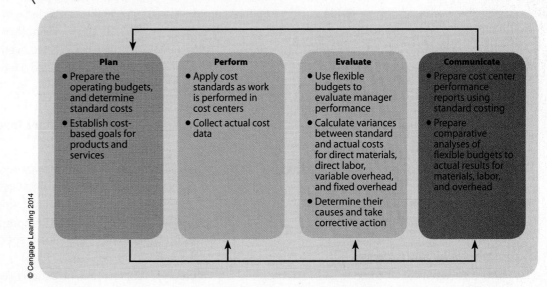

© Cengage Learning 2014

Variance analysis is usually more effective at pinpointing efficient and inefficient operating areas than are basic comparisons of budgeted and actual data. A managerial performance report based on standard costs and related variances should identify the causes of each significant variance, the personnel involved, and the corrective actions taken. It should be tailored to the cost center manager's specific areas of responsibility and explain clearly how the manager's department met or did not meet operating expectations. Managers should be held accountable only for the cost areas under their control.

Exhibit 9 shows a performance report for the manager of Cambria's Bag Assembly Department. The report summarizes all cost data and variances for direct materials, direct labor, and overhead. In addition, it identifies the causes of the variances and the corrective actions taken.

Exhibit 9
Managerial Performance
Report Using Variance Analysis

Cambria Company
Managerial Performance Report—Bag Assembly Department
For the Month Ended August 31

Productivity Summary:

Normal capacity in units	167 bags
Normal capacity in direct labor hours (DLH)	400* DLH
Good units produced (actual)	180 bags
Performance level (standard hours allowed for good units produced)	432 DLH

*Rounded

Cost and Variance Analysis:

	Standard Costs	Actual Costs	Total Variance	Variance Breakdown	
				Amount	Type
Direct materials	$ 4,320	$ 4,484	$164 (U)	$ 76.00 (F)	Direct materials price variance
				240.00 (U)	Direct materials quantity variance
Direct labor	3,672	4,140	468 (U)	315.00 (U)	Direct labor rate variance
				153.00 (U)	Direct labor efficiency variance
Variable overhead	2,484	2,500	16 (U)	87.50 (F)	Variable overhead spending variance
				103.50 (U)	Variable overhead efficiency variance
Fixed overhead	1,404	1,600	196 (U)	300.00 (U)	Fixed overhead budget variance
				104.00 (F)	Fixed overhead volume variance
Totals	$11,880	$12,724	$844 (U)	$844.00 (U)	

Causes of Variances	**Actions Taken**
Direct materials price variance:	
New direct materials purchased at reduced price	New direct materials deemed inappropriate; resumed purchasing materials originally specified
Direct materials quantity variance:	
Poor quality of new direct materials	New direct materials deemed inappropriate; resumed using direct materials originally specified
Direct labor rate variance:	
Machine operator who had to learn assembly	Temporary replacement; no action taken on the job skills
Direct labor efficiency variance:	
Machine operator who had to learn assembly	Temporary replacement; no action taken on the job skills
Late delivery of parts to assembly floor	Material delivery times and number of delays being tracked
Variable overhead spending variance:	
Cost savings on purchases	No action necessary
Variable overhead efficiency variance:	
Machine operator who had to learn assembly	A cross-training program for employees is under consideration
Fixed overhead budget variance:	
Large number of factory insurance claims	Study of insurance claims being conducted
Fixed overhead volume variance:	
High number of orders caused by demand	No action necessary

Remember that the mere occurrence of a variance does not indicate that a manager of a cost center has performed poorly. However, if a variance occurs consistently, and no cause is identified and no corrective action is taken, it may well indicate poor managerial performance. Exhibit 9 shows that the causes of the variances have been identified and corrective actions are being taken, indicating that the manager of Cambria's Bag Assembly Department has the operation under control.

APPLY IT!

Jayson Dunn, the production manager at Sample Industries, recently received his performance report from the company's controller. The report contained the following information:

	Actual Cost	Standard Cost	Variance
Direct materials	$38,200	$36,600	$1,600 (U)
Direct labor	19,450	19,000	450 (U)
Variable overhead	62,890	60,000	2,890 (U)

The controller asked Dunn to respond to his performance report. Help Dunn prepare his response by deciding whether the following statements are true or false. If false, make the statement true.

1. Dunn is responsible for all the variances listed on his performance report.
2. Before Dunn can answer the controller's query, the total variances given to him need to be broken down into their component parts. Then, and only then, will Dunn find out how well or poorly he performed.

SOLUTION

1. False
   Dunn is responsible only for the direct materials quantity variance, the direct labor efficiency variance, and the variable overhead efficiency variance listed on his performance report.
2. True

TRY IT! SE10, E15A, E15B

TriLevel Problem

iRobot Corporation

The beginning of this chapter focused on **iRobot Corporation**, a manufacturer of robots for military, industrial, and home use. Complete the following requirements in order to answer the questions posed at the beginning of the chapter.

Section 1: Concepts
Why is standard costing and variance analysis useful?

Section 2: Accounting Applications
How can iRobot's managers evaluate the performance of its cost centers? Assume iRobot has begun producing carrier bags for its robots. Suppose these high-quality, heavy-duty bags are made in a single cost center using a standard costing system. Assume the standard variable costs for one bag (a unit) are as follows.

Direct materials (3 sq. meters @ $12.50 per sq. meter)	$37.50
Direct labor (1.2 hours @ $9.00 per hour)	10.80
Variable overhead (1.2 hours @ $5.00 per direct labor hour)	6.00
Total standard variable cost per unit	$54.30

The center's master budget was based on its normal capacity of 15,000 direct labor hours. Its budgeted fixed overhead costs for the year were $54,000. During the year, the company produced and sold 12,200 bags, and it purchased and used 37,500 square meters of direct materials; the purchase cost was $12.40 per square meter. The average labor rate was $9.20 per hour, and 15,250 direct labor hours were worked. The center's actual variable overhead costs for the year were $73,200, and its fixed overhead costs were $55,000.

Using the data given, compute the following using formulas or diagram form:

1. Standard hours allowed for good output
2. Standard fixed overhead rate
3. Direct materials cost variances:
   (a) Direct materials price variance
   (b) Direct materials quantity variance
   (c) Total direct materials cost variance
4. Direct labor cost variances:
   (a) Direct labor rate variance
   (b) Direct labor efficiency variance
   (c) Total direct labor cost variance
5. Variable overhead cost variances:
   (a) Variable overhead spending variance
   (b) Variable overhead efficiency variance
   (c) Total variable overhead cost variance
6. Fixed overhead cost variances:
   (a) Fixed overhead budget variance
   (b) Fixed overhead volume variance
   (c) Total fixed overhead cost variance

Section 3: Business Applications

Why does the setting of performance standards help managers control costs and improve performance? To answer this question, match this chapter's manager responsibilities with when they occur within the management process.

a. Plan
b. Perform
c. Evaluate
d. Communicate

1. Prepare operating budgets
2. Apply cost standards as work is performed in cost centers
3. Establish product and service cost goals
4. Collect actual cost data
5. Determine standard costs
6. Calculate variances
7. Use flexible budgets to evaluate performance
8. Prepare comparative reports using flexible budgets
9. Determine cause of variances and take corrective action
10. Prepare cost center performance reports using standard costing

SOLUTION

Section 1: Concepts

Managers find standard costing and variance analysis useful because they enhance *comparability* and *understandability*. When evaluating cost centers, managers use standard costs to prepare a flexible budget, which will improve the accuracy of their cost comparisons and variance analysis. This comparison of actual costs and a budget based on the same amount of output can provide managers with understandable objective data that they can use to assess the center's performance in terms of its key success factor—cost. By analyzing variances between standard and actual costs, they gain insight into the causes of those differences. Once they understand the operating problem that is causing a cost variance, they can devise a solution that results in better control of costs.

Section 2: Accounting Applications

1. Standard Hours Allowed = Good Units Produced × Standard Direct Labor Hours per Unit

$$= 12{,}200 \text{ units} \times 1.2 \text{ hours}$$

$$= \underline{14{,}640} \text{ hours}$$

2. Standard Fixed Overhead Rate $= \dfrac{\text{Budgeted Fixed Overhead Cost}}{\text{Normal Capacity}}$

$$= \dfrac{\$54{,}000}{15{,}000 \text{ Direct Labor Hours}}$$

$$= \underline{\$3.60} \text{ per Direct Labor Hour}$$

3. Direct Materials Cost Variances:

   Using formulas:

   (a) Direct Materials Price Variance = (Standard Price − Actual Price) × Actual Quantity

   $$= (\$12.50 - 12.40) \times 37{,}500 \text{ sq. meters}$$

   $$= \underline{\$3{,}750} \text{ (F)}$$

   (b) Direct Materials Quantity Variance = Standard Price × (Standard Quantity Allowed − Actual Quantity)

   $$= \$12.50 \times [(12{,}200 \times 3) - 37{,}500]$$

   $$= \underline{\$11{,}250} \text{ (U)}$$

   (c) Total Direct Materials Cost Variance = Direct Materials Price Variance + Direct Materials Quantity Variance

   $$= \$3{,}750 \text{ (F)} + \$11{,}250 \text{ (U)}$$

   $$= \underline{\underline{\$7{,}500}} \text{ (U)}$$

In diagram form:

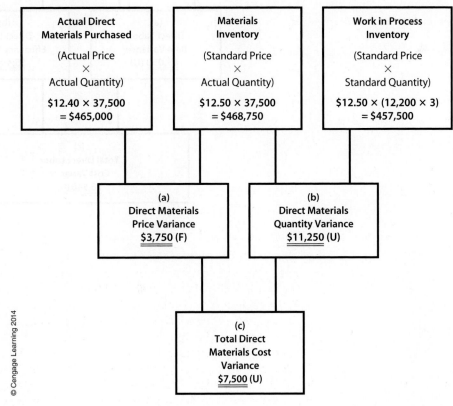

4. Direct Labor Cost Variances:

Using formulas:

(a) Direct Labor Rate Variance $=$ (Standard Rate − Actual Rate) × Actual Hours

$=$ ($9.00 − $9.20) × 15,250 hours

$=$ $3,050 (U)

(b) Direct Labor Efficiency Variance $=$ Standard Rate × (Standard Hours Allowed − Actual Hours)

$=$ $9.00 × [(12,200 units produced × 1.2 hours) − 15,250]

$=$ $5,490 (U)

(c) Total Direct Labor Cost Variance $=$ $\dfrac{\text{Direct Labor Rate}}{\text{Variance}}$ $+$ $\dfrac{\text{Direct Labor Efficiency}}{\text{Variance}}$

$=$ $3,050 (U) + $5,490 (U)

$=$ $8,540 (U)

In diagram form:

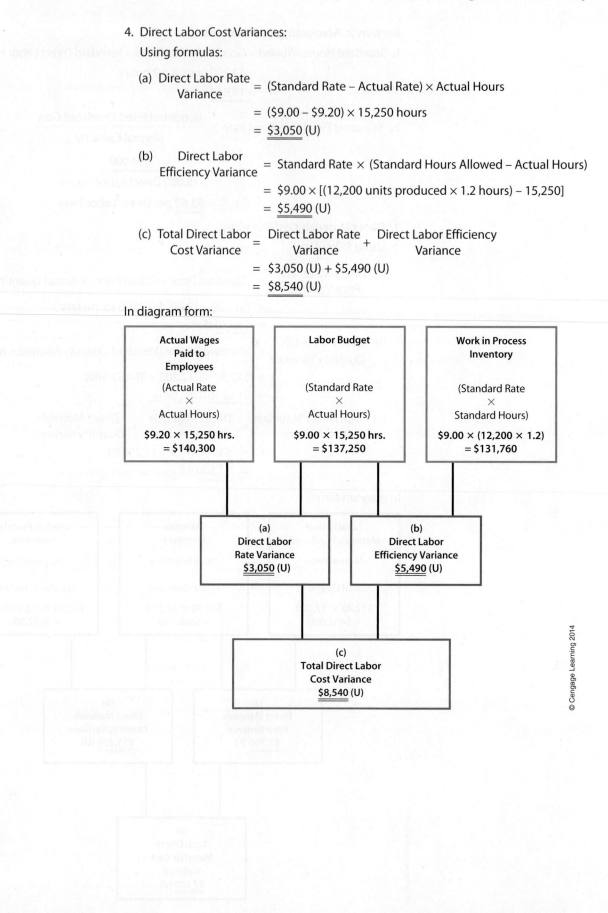

© Cengage Learning 2014

5. Variable Overhead Cost Variances:

Using formulas:

(a) Variable Overhead Spending Variance = (Standard Rate × Actual Hours) − Actual Variable Overhead Cost

= ($5 × 15,250) − $73,200

= $3,050 (F)

(b) Variable Overhead Efficiency Variance = Standard Rate × (Standard Hours Allowed − Actual Hours)

= $5 × [(12,200 units produced × 1.2 hours) − 15,250 hours]

= $3,050 (U)

(c) Total Variable Overhead Cost Variance = Variable Overhead Spending Variance + Variable Overhead Efficiency Variance

= $3,050 (F) + $3,050 (U)

= $0

In diagram form:

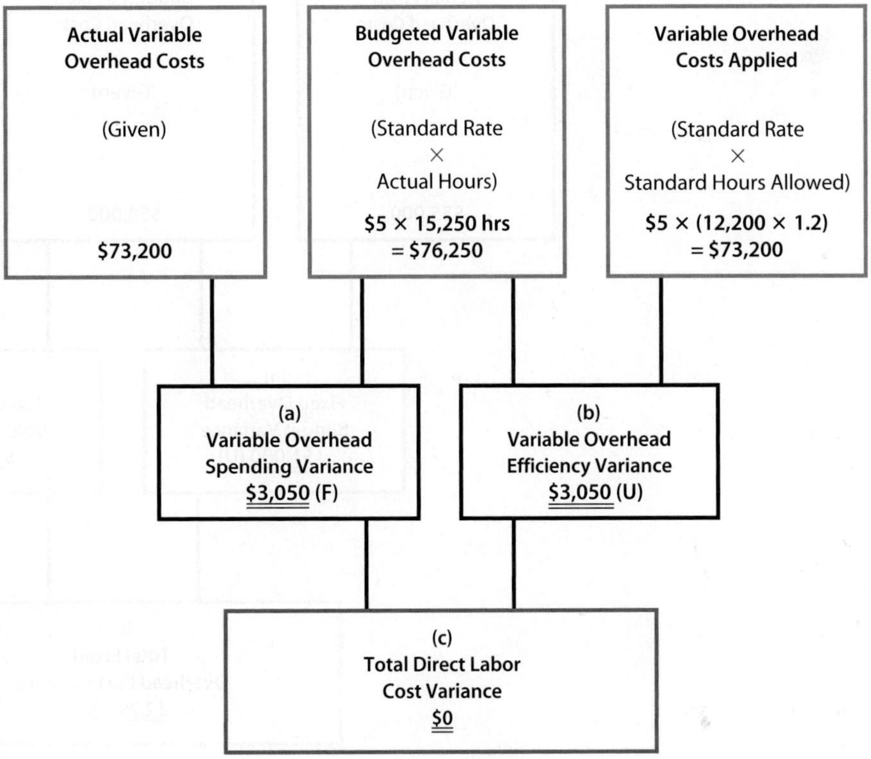

Actual Variable Overhead Costs	Budgeted Variable Overhead Costs	Variable Overhead Costs Applied
(Given)	(Standard Rate × Actual Hours)	(Standard Rate × Standard Hours Allowed)
$73,200	$5 × 15,250 hrs = $76,250	$5 × (12,200 × 1.2) = $73,200

(a) Variable Overhead Spending Variance $3,050 (F)

(b) Variable Overhead Efficiency Variance $3,050 (U)

(c) Total Direct Labor Cost Variance $0

© Cengage Learning 2014

6. Fixed Overhead Cost Variances:
   Using formulas:

   (a) Fixed Overhead
        Budget Variance = Budgeted Fixed Overhead − Actual Fixed Overhead

   $$= \$54,000 - \$55,000$$

   $$= \underline{\$1,000 \text{ (U)}}$$

   (b) Fixed Overhead
        Volume Variance = (Standard Rate × Standard Hours Allowed) − Budgeted Fixed
                                                                      Overhead

   $$= [\$3.60 \times (12,200 \text{ units produced} \times 1.2)] - \$54,000$$

   $$= \underline{\$1,296 \text{ (U)}}$$

   (c) Total Fixed Overhead   _   Fixed Overhead Budget   _   Fixed Overhead
        Cost Variance   =   Variance   +   Volume Variance

   $$= \$1,000 \text{ (U)} + \$1,296 \text{ (U)}$$

   $$= \underline{\underline{\$2,296 \text{ (U)}}}$$

In diagram form:

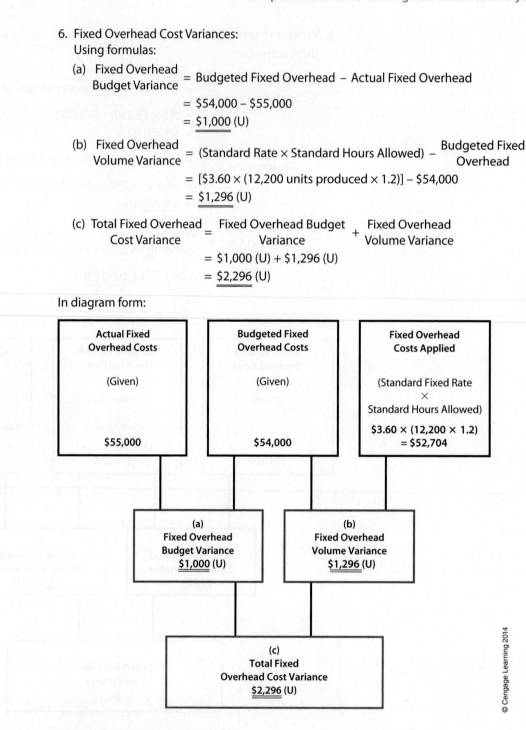

© Cengage Learning 2014

Section 3: Business Applications

1. a   6. c
2. b   7. c
3. a   8. d
4. b   9. c
5. a   10. d

Chapter Review

Define *standard costs*, and explain why standard costing is useful. **LO 1**

Standard costs are realistic estimates of costs based on analyses of both past and projected operating costs and conditions. They provide an understandable standard, or predetermined, performance level for use in standard costing, which includes a comparison measure of the variance between standard and actual performance.

Compute standard unit costs, and describe the role of flexible budgets in variance analysis to control costs. **LO 2**

A standard unit cost has six elements. A total standard unit cost is computed by adding the following costs: direct materials costs (direct materials price standard times direct materials quantity standard), direct labor costs (direct labor rate standard times direct labor time standard), and overhead costs (standard variable and standard fixed overhead rates times standard direct labor hours allowed per unit). Standard unit costs are used to develop a flexible budget. A flexible budget is a summary of anticipated costs for a range of activity levels. It provides forecasted cost data that can be adjusted for changes in level of output. The variable cost per unit and total fixed costs presented in a flexible budget are components of the flexible budget formula, which determines the budgeted cost for any level of output. A flexible budget improves the accuracy of variance analysis, which is a four-step approach to controlling costs. First, managers compute the amount of the variance. If the amount is significant, managers then analyze the variance to identify its cause. They then select performance measures that will enable them to track those activities, analyze the results, and determine the action needed to correct the problem. Their final step is to take the appropriate corrective action.

Compute and analyze direct materials variances. **LO 3**

The direct materials price variance is computed by finding the difference between the standard price and the actual price per unit and multiplying it by the actual quantity purchased. The direct materials quantity variance is the difference between the standard quantity that should have been used and the actual quantity used, multiplied by the standard price. An analysis of these variances enables managers to identify what is causing them and to formulate plans for correcting related operating problems.

Compute and analyze direct labor variances. **LO 4**

The direct labor rate variance is computed by determining the difference between the standard direct labor rate and the actual rate and multiplying it by the actual direct labor hours worked. The direct labor efficiency variance is the difference between the standard hours allowed for the number of good units produced and the actual hours worked multiplied by the standard direct labor rate. Managers analyze these variances to find the causes of differences between standard direct labor costs and actual direct labor costs.

Compute and analyze overhead variances. **LO 5**

The total overhead variance is equal to the amount of under- or overapplied overhead costs for an accounting period. An analysis of the variable and fixed overhead variances will help explain why the amount of overhead applied to units produced differs from the actual overhead costs incurred. The total overhead cost variance can be broken down into a variable overhead spending variance, a variable overhead efficiency variance, a fixed overhead budget variance, and a fixed overhead volume variance.

Explain how variances are used to evaluate a business's performance. **LO 6**

To ensure that performance evaluation is effective and fair, a company's evaluation policies should be based on input from managers and employees and should be specific about the procedures that managers are to follow. The evaluation process becomes more accurate when performance reports for cost centers include variances from standard costs. A performance report based on standard costs and related variances should identify the causes of each significant variance, along with the personnel involved and the corrective actions taken. It should be tailored to the cost center manager's specific areas of responsibility.

Key Terms

Chapter Assignments

DISCUSSION QUESTIONS

LO **1, 2**   **DQ1. CONCEPT** ▶ Describe how the six elements of a standard unit cost increase cost comparability and understandability.

LO **2**   **DQ2.** What role do flexible budgets play in improving the understanding of variance analysis?

LO **2, 3, 4, 5**   **DQ3.** Why does the four-step process of variance analysis enhance a cost center's ability to control costs?

LO **6**   **DQ4. CONCEPT** ▶ **BUSINESS APPLICATION** ▶ What should be included in a management report to further understandability and comparability when evaluating a cost center?

LO **6**   **DQ5. CONCEPT** ▶ **BUSINESS APPLICATION** ▶ Why does the use of standard costing and variance analysis in the management process reinforce the concepts of comparability and understandability to better business performance?

SHORT EXERCISES

LO **1**   ### Standard Costing Concepts

SE1. CONCEPT ▶ Columbus Corporation is considering adopting the standard costing method to enhance the understandability and comparability of accounting information. Prepare several reasons in support of why understandability and comparability will be enhanced.

LO **1**   ### Purposes of Standard Costs

SE2. ACCOUNTING CONNECTION ▶ Suppose you are a management consultant and a client asks you the advantages and disadvantages of using standard costs in cost accounting systems. Prepare your response, listing the advantages and disadvantages of using standard costs.

LO 2   **Computing a Standard Unit Cost**

SE3. Using the information that follows, compute the total standard unit cost of Product WW+.

Direct materials quantity standard	1 pound per unit
Direct materials price standard	$10.00 per pound
Direct labor time standard	0.5 hour per unit
Direct labor rate standard	$12.00 per hour
Variable overhead rate standard	$6.00 per machine hour
Fixed overhead rate standard	$11.00 per machine hour
Machine hour standard	4 hours per unit

LO 2   **Analyzing Cost Variances**

SE4. ACCOUNTING CONNECTION ▶ Dancing Waters produces fountains. The company analyzes only variances that differ by more than 5 percent from the standard cost. The controller computed the following direct labor efficiency variances for May:

	Direct Labor Efficiency Variance	Standard Direct Labor Cost
Product 4	$1,200 (U)	$24,000
Product 6	3,200 (F)	42,800
Product 7	2,000 (U)	42,000
Product 9	1,600 (F)	34,000
Product 12	2,800 (U)	50,000

For each product, determine the variance as a percentage of the standard cost (round to one decimal place). Then identify the products for which variances should be analyzed and suggest possible causes for the variances.

LO 3   **Direct Materials Variances**

SE5. Clean Plate Company produces placemats. Each placemat calls for 0.2 meters of vinyl material; the material should cost $1 per meter. In June, the company manufactured and sold 100,000 placemats. During the month, it used 20,200 meters of vinyl material. The total cost of the material was $19,796. Compute the direct materials price and direct materials quantity variances for June.

LO 3   **Direct Materials Variances**

SE6. Using the standard unit costs that you computed in **SE3** and the actual cost and usage data that follow, compute the direct materials price and direct materials quantity variances.

Direct materials purchased and used (pounds)	21,800
Price paid for direct materials	$10.10 per pound
Number of good units produced	21,000 units

LO 4   **Direct Labor Variances**

SE7. Using the standard unit costs that you computed in **SE3** and the actual cost and usage data that follow, compute the direct labor rate and direct labor efficiency variances.

Direct labor hours used	11,000 hours
Total cost of direct labor	$134,200
Number of good units produced	21,000 units

LO 5 **Overhead Variances**

SE8. Meanwhile Products uses standard costing. The following information about overhead was generated during August:

Standard variable overhead rate	$2.50 per machine hour
Standard fixed overhead rate	$3.00 per machine hour
Actual variable overhead costs	$60,100
Actual fixed overhead costs	$68,800
Budgeted fixed overhead costs	$70,000
Standard machine hours per unit produced	2.8
Good units produced	8,000
Actual machine hours	24,200

Compute the variable overhead spending and efficiency variances and the fixed overhead budget and volume variances.

LO 5 **Fixed Overhead Rate and Variances**

SE9. Point Manufacturing Company uses the standard costing method. The company's main product is a fine-quality pen that normally takes 5.1 hours to produce. Normal annual capacity is 20,000 direct labor hours, and budgeted fixed overhead costs for the year were $10,000. During the year, the company produced and sold 4,000 units. Actual fixed overhead costs were $10,200. Compute the fixed overhead rate per direct labor hour, and determine the fixed overhead budget and volume variances.

LO 6 **Evaluating Managerial Performance**

SE10. BUSINESS APPLICATION ▶ ZMT Products' controller gave the production manager a report containing the following information:

	Actual Cost	Standard Cost	Variance
Direct materials	$50,000	$48,200	$1,800 (U)
Direct labor	7,550	7,000	550 (U)
Variable overhead	52,000	50,000	2,000 (U)

The controller asked for a response. How would you respond? What additional information might you need to prepare your response?

EXERCISES: SET A

LO 1 **Uses of Standard Costs**

E1A. ACCOUNTING CONNECTION ▶ Asa Wentz, the new controller at Market Research Company, is concerned that the company's methods of cost control do not accurately track the operations of the business. She plans to suggest to Tyson Getz, the company's president, that the company start using standard costing for budgeting and cost control. The new method could be incorporated into the existing accounting system. The anticipated cost of adopting it and training managers is around $80,000. Prepare a memo from Wentz to Getz that defines standard costing and outlines its uses and benefits.

LO 2 **Computing Standard Costs**

E2A. Flossmoor Corporation uses standard costing and is in the process of updating its direct materials and direct labor standards for Product 2B. The following data have been accumulated:

Direct materials: In the previous period, 20,000 units were produced, and 32,000 square yards of direct materials at a cost of $128,000 were used to produce them.

Direct labor: In the previous period, 20,000 units were produced and 58,000 direct labor hours were worked—34,000 hours on machine H and 24,000 hours on machine K. Machine H operators earned $10 per hour, and machine K operators earned $9 per hour last period. A new labor union contract calls for a 10 percent increase in labor rates for the coming period.

Using this information as the basis for the new standards, compute the direct materials quantity and price standards and the direct labor time and rate standards for each machine for the coming accounting period.

LO 2   **Computing a Total Standard Unit Cost**

E3A. Weather Balloons, Inc., makes reusable weather-detecting balloons. Because of a recent recession, management has ordered that standard costs be recomputed. New direct materials price standards are $600 per set for electronic components and $13 per square meter for heavy-duty canvas. Direct materials quantity standards include one set of electronic components and 100 square meters of heavy-duty canvas per balloon. Direct labor time standards are 26 hours per balloon for the Electronics Department and 21 hours per balloon for the Assembly Department. Direct labor rate standards are $20 per hour for the Electronics Department and $15 per hour for the Assembly Department. Standard overhead rates are $18 per direct labor hour for the standard variable overhead rate and $10 per direct labor hour for the standard fixed overhead rate. Compute the total standard unit cost of one weather balloon.

LO 3   **Direct Materials Price and Quantity Variances**

E4A. Natural Company produces organic twig brooms. Each broom calls for 1 pound of wood; the wood should cost $0.25 per pound. In July, the division manufactured and sold 500,000 brooms. During the month, it used 495,000 pounds of wood, and the total cost of the material was $128,700. Normal monthly capacity was set at 580,000 brooms. Calculate Natural's material price and quantity variances for wood for the month.

LO 3   **Direct Materials Price and Quantity Variances**

E5A. LIFT Elevator Company manufactures small hydroelectric elevators. One of the direct materials used is heavy-duty carpeting for the floor of the elevator. The direct materials quantity standard for May was 6 square yards per elevator. During May, the purchasing agent purchased this carpeting at $20 per square yard; the standard price for the period was $22. Fifty elevators were completed and sold during the month; the Production Department used an average of 6.5 square yards of carpet per elevator. Calculate the company's direct materials price and quantity variances for carpeting for May.

LO 3   **Direct Materials Variances**

E6A. Creative Productions manufactured and sold 800 products at $10,000 each during the past year. At the beginning of the year, production had been set at 1,000 products, and direct materials standards had been set at 10 pounds of direct materials at $12 per pound for each product produced. During the year, the company purchased and used 7,900 pounds of direct materials with a cost of $12.02 per pound. Calculate the company's direct materials price and quantity variances for the year.

LO 4   **Direct Labor Variances**

E7A. At the beginning of last year, Creative Productions set direct labor standards of 2 hours at $25 per hour for each product produced. During the year, 1,700 direct labor hours were actually worked at an average cost of $26 per hour. Using this information and the applicable information in **E6A**, calculate the company's direct labor rate and efficiency variances for the year.

LO **4**

Direct Labor Rate and Efficiency Variances

E8A. For the past two years, NE Company's best-selling product has been a titanium engine block. Standard direct labor hours per block are 2.0 hours. All direct labor employees are paid $24 per hour. During July, NE produced 16,000 blocks. Actual direct labor hours and costs for the month were 31,000 hours and $775,000, respectively.

1. Compute the direct labor rate variance for blocks during July.
2. Using the same data, compute the direct labor efficiency variance for engine blocks during July. Check your answer, assuming that the total direct labor cost variance is $7,000 (U).

LO **5**

Variable Overhead Variances

E9A. At the beginning of last year, Creative Productions set variable overhead standards of 5 machine hours at a rate of $15 per hour for each product produced. During the year, 4,800 machine hours were used at a cost of $15.10 per hour. Using this information and the applicable information in E6A, calculate the company's variable overhead spending and efficiency variances for the year.

LO **5**

Fixed Overhead Variances

E10A. At the beginning of last year, Creative Productions set budgeted fixed overhead costs at $46,000 and budgeted production at 1,000 products. During the year, actual fixed overhead costs were $50,000. Using this information and the applicable information in E6A, calculate the company's fixed overhead budget and volume variances for the year. Assume that fixed overhead is applied based on units of product.

LO **5**

Variable Overhead Variances for a Service Business

E11A. MUF Architects, LLP, billed clients for 6,000 hours of design work for the month. Actual variable overhead costs for the month were $910,000, and 6,050 hours were worked. At the beginning of the year, a variable overhead standard of $150 per design hour had been developed based on a budget of 5,000 design hours each month. Calculate the company's variable overhead spending and efficiency variances for the month.

LO **5**

Fixed Overhead Variances for a Service Business

E12A. Engineering Associates billed clients for 10,000 hours of engineering work for the month. Actual fixed overhead costs for the month were $1,450,000. At the beginning of the year, a fixed overhead standard of $140 per engineering hour had been developed based on a budget of 10,500 engineering hours each month. Calculate the company's fixed overhead budget and volume variances for the month.

LO **5**

Overhead Variances

E13A. Quay Company produces handmade scallop buckets and sells them to distributors along Florida's Gulf Coast. The company incurred $10,500 of actual overhead costs ($9,500 variable; $1,000 fixed) in March. Budgeted standard overhead costs for March were $1 of variable overhead costs per direct labor hour and $1,200 of fixed overhead costs. Normal capacity was set at 10,000 direct labor hours per month. In March, the company produced 8,100 clamming buckets by working 9,000 direct labor hours. The time standard is 0.9 direct labor hour per bucket. Compute (a) the variable overhead spending and efficiency variances and (b) the fixed overhead budget and volume variances for March. (Round to the nearest dollar.)

LO **5**

Overhead Variances

E14A. Goldencoast Industries uses standard costing and a flexible budget for cost planning and control. Its monthly budget for overhead costs is $100,000 of fixed costs plus $5 per machine hour. Monthly normal capacity of 100,000 machine hours is used to compute the standard fixed overhead rate. During the month, 104,000 machine hours were used. Only 102,500 standard machine hours were allowed for good units produced during the month. Actual overhead costs incurred during the month totaled $511,000 of variable costs and $94,500 of fixed costs. Compute (a) the under- or overapplied overhead for the month and (b) the variable overhead spending and efficiency variances and the fixed overhead budget and volume variances.

LO 6

Evaluating Managerial Performance

E15A. BUSINESS APPLICATION ▶ Layton Davis oversees projects for Pace Construction Company. Recently, the company's controller sent him a performance report regarding the construction of the Highlands Bank, a project that Davis supervised. Included in the report was an unfavorable direct labor efficiency variance of $900 for roof structures. What types of information does Davis need to analyze before he can respond to this report?

EXERCISES: SET B

Visit the textbook companion website at www.cengagebrain.com to access Exercise Set B for this chapter.

PROBLEMS

LO 2

✔ 2: Total standard unit cost per entrance last year: $9,542

Computing and Using Standard Costs

P1. Modular houses are Homes, Inc.'s specialty. The company's best-selling model is a three-bedroom, 1,400-square-foot house with an impressive front entrance. Last year, the standard costs for the six basic direct materials used in manufacturing the entrance were as follows: wood framing materials, $2,140; deluxe front door, $480; door hardware, $260; exterior siding, $710; electrical materials, $580; and interior finishing materials, $1,520. Three types of direct labor are used to build the entrance: carpenter, 30 hours at $36 per hour; door specialist, 4 hours at $24 per hour; and electrician, 8 hours at $50 per hour. Last year, the company used an overhead rate of 40 percent of total direct materials cost.

This year, the cost of wood framing materials is expected to increase by 20 percent, and a deluxe front door will cost $496. The cost of the door hardware will increase by 10 percent, and the cost of electrical materials will increase by 20 percent. Exterior siding cost should decrease by $15 per unit. The cost of interior finishing materials is expected to remain the same. The carpenter's wages will increase by $1 per hour, and the door specialist's wages should remain the same. The electrician's wages will increase by $0.50 per hour. Finally, the overhead rate will decrease to 30 percent of total direct materials cost.

REQUIRED

1. Compute the total standard cost of direct materials per entrance for last year.
2. Using your answer to requirement **1**, compute the total standard unit cost per entrance for last year.
3. Compute the total standard unit cost per entrance for this year. (Round to the nearest dollar.)

LO 3, 4

✔ 1: Direct materials price variance, $1,204 (F)
✔ 1: Direct materials quantity variance, $6 (U)
✔ 2: Direct labor rate variance, $1,000 (U)
✔ 2: Direct labor efficiency variance, $108 (F)

Direct Materials and Direct Labor Variances

P2. Party Balloons Company produces mylar balloons. The company's direct materials standards for its deluxe balloon include 3 ounces of mylar. Standard prices for the year were $0.030 per ounce. Direct labor standards for the deluxe balloon specify 0.01 hour of direct labor at a standard direct labor rate of $18 per hour.

During January, the company made 200,600 deluxe balloons. Actual production data follow.

Direct materials	602,000 ounces @ $0.028 per ounce
Direct labor	2,000 hours @ $18.50 per hour

REQUIRED

1. Compute the direct materials price and quantity variances.
2. Compute the direct labor rate and efficiency variances.

Direct Materials and Direct Labor Variances

P3. Winners Trophy Company produces trophies. The company's direct materials standards for its deluxe trophy include 1 pound of metal and 10 ounces of wood for the base. Standard prices for the year were $3 per pound of metal and $0.45 per ounce of wood. Direct labor standards for the deluxe trophy specify 0.2 hour of direct labor in the Molding Department and 0.4 hour in the Trimming/Finishing Department. Standard direct labor rates are $20 per hour in the Molding Department and $18.00 per hour in the Trimming/Finishing Department.

During January, the company made 16,400 deluxe trophies. Actual production data follow.

Direct materials:	
Metal	16,640 pounds @ $2.95 per pound
Wood	164,400 ounces @ $0.48 per ounce
Direct labor:	
Molding	3,400 hours @ $19.80 per hour
Trimming/Finishing	6,540 hours @ $18.10 per hour

REQUIRED

1. Compute the direct materials price and quantity variances for metal and wood.
2. Compute the direct labor rate and efficiency variances for the Molding and Trimming/Finishing Departments.

Overhead Variances

P4. Copa Corporation's accountant left for vacation before completing the monthly cost variance report. The corporation's president has asked you to complete the report. The following data are available (capacities are expressed in machine hours):

Actual machine hours	17,100
Standard machine hours allowed	17,500
Actual variable overhead	(a)
Standard variable overhead rate	$2.50
Variable overhead spending variance	$750 (F)
Variable overhead efficiency variance	(b)
Actual fixed overhead	(c)
Budgeted fixed overhead	$153,000
Fixed overhead budget variance	$1,300 (U)
Fixed overhead volume variance	$4,500 (F)
Normal capacity in machine hours	(d)
Standard fixed overhead rate	(e)
Fixed overhead applied	(f)

REQUIRED

Analyze the data and fill in the missing amounts. [*Hint:* Use the structure of Exhibits 6 and 7 to guide your analysis. Solve for (f) before solving for (e) and (d).]

Computing Variances and Evaluating Performance

P5. Clean Sweep Company produces all-vinyl mats. Each doormat calls for 0.5 meter of vinyl material; the material should cost $3 per meter. Standard direct labor hours and labor cost per doormat are 0.3 hour and $6 (0.3 hour × $20 per hour), respectively. Currently, the division's standard variable overhead rate is $1.50 per direct labor hour, and its standard fixed overhead rate is $0.80 per direct labor hour.

In August, the division manufactured and sold 50,000 doormats. During the month, it used 25,200 meters of vinyl material; the total cost of the material was $73,080. The total actual overhead costs for August were $28,200, of which $18,200 was variable. The total number of direct labor hours worked was 10,800, and the factory payroll for direct labor for the month was $214,920. Budgeted fixed overhead for August was $9,280. Normal monthly capacity for the year was set at 58,000 doormats.

REQUIRED

1. Compute for August the (a) direct materials price variance, (b) direct materials quantity variance, (c) direct labor rate variance, (d) direct labor efficiency variance, (e) variable overhead spending variance, (f) variable overhead efficiency variance, (g) fixed overhead budget variance, and (h) fixed overhead volume variance.
2. **BUSINESS APPLICATION** ▶ Prepare a performance report based on your variance analysis, and suggest possible causes for each variance.

ALTERNATE PROBLEMS

Computing Standard Costs for Direct Materials

P6. BUSINESS APPLICATION ▶ Old Hands, Ltd., assembles clock movements for grandfather clocks. Each movement has four components: the clock facing, the clock hands, the time movement, and the spring assembly. For the current year, the company used the following standard costs: clock facing, $15.90; clock hands, $12.70; time movement, $66.10; and spring assembly, $52.50.

Prices of materials are expected to change next year. Old Hands will purchase 60 percent of the facings from Company A at $18.50 each and the other 40 percent from Company B at $18.80 each. The clock hands are purchased from Hardware, Inc., and will cost $15.50 per set next year. Old Hands will purchase 30 percent of the time movements from Company Q at $68.50 each, 20 percent from Company R at $69.50 each, and 50 percent from Company S at $71.90 each. The manufacturer that supplies Old Hands with spring assemblies has announced that it will increase its prices by 20 percent.

REQUIRED

1. Determine the total standard direct materials cost per unit for next year.
2. Suppose that because Old Hands has guaranteed Hardware that it will purchase 2,500 sets of clock hands next year, the cost of a set of clock hands has been reduced by 20 percent. Find the total standard direct materials cost per clock.
3. Suppose that to avoid the increase in the cost of spring assemblies, Old Hands purchased substandard ones from a different manufacturer at $50 each; 20 percent of them turned out to be unusable and could not be returned. Assuming that all other data remain the same, compute the total standard direct materials unit cost. Spread the cost of the defective materials over the good units produced.

Direct Materials and Direct Labor Variances

P7. Flat Cups Company produces collapsible beverage containers. The company's direct materials standards for its 16-ounce beverage bottle include 5 ounces of biodegradable plastic. Standard prices for the year were $0.011 per ounce. Direct labor standards for the beverage bottle specify 0.04 hours of direct labor at a standard direct labor rate of $20 per hour.

During January, the company made 100,000 16-ounce beverage bottles. Actual production data follow.

Direct materials	500,100 ounces @ $0.012 per ounce
Direct labor	3,990 hours @ $20.50 per hour

(Continued)

REQUIRED

1. Compute the direct materials price and quantity variances.
2. Compute the direct labor rate and efficiency variances.

Direct Materials and Direct Labor Variances

P8. Green Packaging Company makes plant-based baskets for food wholesalers. Each basket requires 0.8 gram of material G and 0.6 gram of an additive that includes color and hardening agents. The standard prices are $0.15 per gram of material G and $0.09 per gram of additive. Two kinds of direct labor—molding and trimming/packing—are required to make the baskets. The direct labor time and rate standards for a batch of 100 baskets are as follows: molding, 1.0 hour per batch at an hourly rate of $12; and trimming/packing, 1.2 hours per batch at $10 per hour.

During the year, the company produced 48,000 baskets. It used 38,600 grams of material G at a total cost of $5,404 and 28,950 grams of additive at $2,895. Actual direct labor included 480 hours for molding at a total cost of $5,664 and 560 hours for trimming/packing at $5,656.

REQUIRED

1. Compute the direct materials price and quantity variances for both material G and the additive.
2. Compute the direct labor rate and efficiency variances for the molding and trimming/packing processes.

Overhead Variances

P9. Exact Corporation's accountant left for vacation before completing the monthly cost variance report. The corporation's president has asked you to complete the report. The following data are available (capacities are expressed in machine hours):

Actual machine hours	20,100
Standard machine hours allowed	20,500
Actual variable overhead	(a)
Standard variable overhead rate	$2.00
Variable overhead spending variance	$250 (F)
Variable overhead efficiency variance	(b)
Actual fixed overhead	(c)
Budgeted fixed overhead	$153,000
Fixed overhead budget variance	$500 (U)
Fixed overhead volume variance	$750 (F)
Normal capacity in machine hours	(d)
Standard fixed overhead rate	(e)
Fixed overhead applied	(f)

REQUIRED

Analyze the data and fill in the missing amounts. [*Hint:* Use the structure of Exhibits 6 and 7 to guide your analysis. Solve for (f) before solving for (e) and (d).]

Computing Variances and Evaluating Performance

P10. Last year, Panacea Laboratories, Inc., researched and perfected a cure for the common cold. Called Cold-Gone, the product sells for $28.00 per package, each of which contains five tablets. Standard unit costs for this product were developed late last year for use this year. Per package, the standard unit costs were as follows: chemical ingredients, 6 ounces at $1.00 per ounce; packaging, $1.20; direct labor, 0.8 hour at $14.00 per hour; standard variable overhead, $4.00 per direct labor hour; and standard fixed overhead, $6.40 per direct labor hour. Normal capacity is 46,875 units per week.

In the first quarter of this year, demand for the new product rose well beyond the expectations of management. During those three months, the peak season for colds, the company produced and sold over 500,000 packages of Cold-Gone. During the first week in April, it produced 50,000 packages but used materials for 50,200 packages costing $60,240. It also used 305,000 ounces of chemical ingredients costing $292,800. The total cost of direct labor for the week was $579,600; direct labor hours totaled 40,250. Total variable overhead was $161,100, and total fixed overhead was $242,000. Budgeted fixed overhead for the week was $240,000.

REQUIRED

1. Compute for the first week of April (a) all direct materials price variances, (b) all direct materials quantity variances, (c) the direct labor rate variance, (d) the direct labor efficiency variance, (e) the variable overhead spending variance, (f) the variable overhead efficiency variance, (g) the fixed overhead budget variance, and (h) the fixed overhead volume variance.

2. **BUSINESS APPLICATION ▶** Prepare a performance report based on your variance analysis, and suggest possible causes for each significant variance.

CASES

LO 2

Ethical Dilemma: An Ethical Question Involving Standard Costs

C1. Lopez Industries, Inc., develops standard costs for all its direct materials, direct labor, and overhead costs. It uses these costs to price products, cost inventories, and evaluate the performance of purchasing and production managers. It updates the standard costs whenever costs, prices, or rates change by 3 percent or more. It also reviews and updates all standard costs each December; this practice provides current standards that are appropriate for use in valuing year-end inventories on the company's financial statements.

Jaye Elgar is in charge of standard costing at Lopez. On November 30, she received a memo from the chief financial officer informing her that Lopez was considering purchasing another company and that she and her staff were to postpone adjusting standard costs until late February; they were instead to concentrate on analyzing the proposed purchase.

In the third week of November, prices on more than 20 of Lopez's direct materials had been reduced by 10 percent or more, and a new labor union contract had reduced several categories of labor rates. A revision of standard costs in December would have resulted in lower valuations of inventories, higher cost of goods sold because of inventory write-downs, and lower net income for the year. Elgar believed that the company was facing an operating loss and that the assignment to evaluate the proposed purchase was designed primarily to keep her staff from revising and lowering standard costs. She questioned the chief financial officer about the assignment and reiterated the need for updating the standard costs, but she was again told to ignore the update and concentrate on the proposed purchase. Elgar and her staff were relieved of the evaluation assignment in early February. The purchase never materialized.

Assess Elgar's actions in this situation. Did she follow all ethical paths to solving the problem? What are the consequences of failing to adjust the standard costs?

LO 1, 2

Group Activity: Standard Costs and Variance Analysis

C2. Domino's Pizza is a major purveyor of home-delivered pizzas. Although customers can pick up their orders at the shops where Domino's makes its pizzas, employees deliver most orders to customers' homes, and they use their own cars to do it.

Specify what standard costing for a Domino's pizza shop would entail. Where would you obtain the information for determining the cost standards? In what ways would the standards help in managing a pizza shop? If necessary to gain a better understanding of the operation, visit a pizzeria (it does not have to be a Domino's).

(Continued)

Your instructor will divide the class into groups to discuss the case. Summarize your group's discussion, and select one person from your group to report the group's findings to the class.

Business Communication: Preparing Performance Reports

C3. BUSINESS APPLICATION ▶ Terry Correy, Pine Valley Spa's president, is concerned about the spa's operating performance during March. He budgeted his costs carefully so that he could reduce the annual membership fees. He now needs to evaluate those costs to make sure that the spa's profits are at the level he expected.

He has asked you, the spa's controller, to prepare a performance report on labor and overhead costs for March. He also wants you to analyze the report and suggest possible causes for any problems that you find. He wants to attend to any problems quickly, so he has asked you to submit your report as soon as possible. The following information for the month is available:

	Budgeted Costs	Actual Costs
Variable costs:		
Operating labor	$10,880	$12,150
Utilities	2,880	3,360
Repairs and maintenance	5,760	7,140
Fixed overhead costs:		
Depreciation, equipment	2,600	2,680
Rent	3,280	3,280
Other	1,704	1,860
Totals	$27,104	$30,470

Correy's budget allows for eight employees to work 160 hours each per month. During March, nine employees worked an average of 150 hours each.

1. Answer the following questions:
   a. Why are you preparing this performance report?
   b. Who will use the report?
   c. What information do you need to develop the report? How will you obtain that information?
   d. When are the performance report and the analysis needed?

2. With the limited information available to you, compute the labor rate variance, the labor efficiency variance, and the variable and fixed overhead variances.

3. Prepare a performance report for the spa for March. Analyze the report, and suggest causes for any problems that you find.

Decision Analysis: Developing a Flexible Budget and Analyzing Overhead Variances

C4. BUSINESS APPLICATION ▶ The controller at FT Industries has asked you, her new assistant, to analyze the following data related to projected and actual overhead costs for October:

Variable Overhead Costs	Standard Variable Costs per Machine Hour (MH)	Actual Variable Costs in October
Indirect materials and supplies	$1.10	$ 2,380
Indirect machine setup labor	2.50	5,090
Materials handling	1.40	3,950
Maintenance and repairs	1.50	2,980
Utilities	0.80	1,490
Miscellaneous	0.10	200
Totals	$7.40	$16,090

Fixed Overhead Costs	Budgeted Fixed Overhead	Actual Fixed Overhead in October
Supervisory salaries	$ 3,630	$ 3,630
Machine depreciation	8,360	8,580
Other	1,210	1,220
Totals	$13,200	$13,430

For October, the number of good units produced was used to compute the 2,100 standard machine hours allowed.

1. Prepare a monthly flexible budget for operating activity at 2,000 machine hours, 2,200 machine hours, and 2,500 machine hours.
2. Develop a flexible budget formula.
3. The company's normal operating capacity is 2,200 machine hours per month. Compute the fixed overhead rate at this level of activity. Then break the rate down into rates for each element of fixed overhead.
4. Prepare a detailed comparative cost analysis for October. Include all variable and fixed overhead costs. Format your analysis by using columns for the following five elements: cost category, cost per machine hour, costs applied, actual costs incurred, and variance.
5. Develop an overhead variance analysis for October that identifies the variable overhead spending and efficiency variances and the fixed overhead budget and volume variances.
6. Prepare an analysis of the variances. Could a manager control some of the fixed costs? Defend your answer.

LO **4, 5**

Conceptual Understanding: Standard Costing in a Service Company

C5. AAA Life Insurance Company's (ALIC) most popular life insurance policy is P20A—a permanent, 20-year life annuity policy. This policy sells in $10,000 increments depending on the policyholder's needs and age. ALIC devotes an entire department to supporting and marketing the P20A policy. Because both the support staff and the salespersons contribute to each P20A policy, ALIC categorizes them as direct labor for purposes of variance analysis, cost control, and performance evaluation. For unit costing, each $10,000 increment is considered one unit; thus, a $90,000 policy is counted as nine units. Standard unit cost information for January is as follows.

Direct labor:	
Policy support staff (3 hours at $12.00 per hour)	$ 36.00
Policy salespersons (8.5 hours at $14.20 per hour)	120.70
Operating overhead:	
Variable operating overhead (11.5 hours at $26.00 per hour)	299.00
Fixed operating overhead (11.5 hours at $18.00 per hour)	207.00
Standard unit cost	$662.70

Actual costs incurred for the 265 units sold during January were as follows.

Direct labor:	
Policy support staff (848 hours at $12.50 per hour)	$10,600
Policy salespersons (2,252.5 hours at $14.00 per hour)	31,535
Operating overhead:	
Variable operating overhead	78,440
Fixed operating overhead	53,400

Normal monthly capacity is 260 units, and the budgeted fixed operating overhead for January was $53,820.

1. Compute the standard hours allowed in January for policy support staff and policy salespersons.
2. What should the total standard costs for January have been? What were the total actual costs that the company incurred in January? Compute the total cost variance for the month.

(Continued)

3. Compute the direct labor rate and efficiency variances for policy support staff and policy salespersons.
4. Compute the variable and fixed operating overhead variances for January.
5. Identify possible causes for each variance and suggest possible solutions.

Continuing Case: Cookie Company

C6. In this segment of our continuing case, assume that you have been using standard costing to plan and control costs at your cookie store. In a meeting with your budget team, which includes managers and employees from the Purchasing, Product Design, and Production departments, you ask all team members to describe any operating problems they encountered in the last quarter. You explain that you will use this information to analyze the causes of significant cost variances that occurred during the quarter.

For each of the following situations, identify the direct materials and/or direct labor variance(s) that could be affected, and indicate whether the variances are favorable or unfavorable.

1. The production department uses highly skilled, highly paid workers.
2. Machines were improperly adjusted.
3. Direct labor personnel worked more carefully than they had in the past to manufacture the product.
4. The Product Design Department replaced a direct material with one that was less expensive and of lower quality.
5. The Purchasing Department bought higher-quality materials at a higher price.
6. A major supplier used a less-expensive mode of transportation to deliver the raw materials.
7. Work was halted for 2 hours because of a power failure.

CHAPTER 9
Short-Run Decision Analysis

Bank of America is one of the world's largest financial institutions. It has received many awards for its online services and initiatives in preventing online fraud and identity theft. Bank of America's managers believe the trend to online commerce is good for business, and as customers gain confidence in dealing with their finances online, they plan to offer more online products and services. In looking for safe and innovative ways to meet customers' needs, the managers will make short-run decisions that will affect the bank's profits, resources, and opportunities.

1. **CONCEPT ▶** Why is the concept of cost-benefit important when making short-run decisions?

2. **ACCOUNTING APPLICATION ▶** How does incremental analysis ensure a wise allocation of resources involved in short-run decisions?

3. **BUSINESS APPLICATION ▶** How can incremental analysis help managers improve performance and take advantage of business opportunities?

LEARNING OBJECTIVES

LO 1 Describe how the concept of cost-benefit is useful when making short-run decisions.

LO 2 Perform incremental analysis for outsourcing decisions.

LO 3 Perform incremental analysis for special order decisions.

LO 4 Perform incremental analysis for segment profitability decisions.

LO 5 Perform incremental analysis for sales mix decisions involving constrained resources.

LO 6 Perform incremental analysis for sell-or-process-further decisions.

LO 7 Describe why short-run decision analysis is critical for business success.

CONCEPT
■ Cost-benefit

**RELEVANT
LEARNING OBJECTIVE**

LO 1 Describe how the
concept of cost-
benefit is useful when
making short-run decisions.

LO1 Concepts Underlying Decision Analysis

The concept of *cost-benefit* holds that the benefits to be gained from a course of action or alternative should be greater than the costs of implementing it. Cost-benefit is an accounting convention or rule of thumb that supports both short-run and long-run decision making. It considers both quantitative and qualitative cost and benefit measures to facilitate cost-benefit comparisons between alternatives for sound business decisions. Managers frequently take the following actions when applying the cost-benefit concept to short-run decisions:

■ **Step 1.** Discover a problem or need.
■ **Step 2.** Identify all reasonable courses of action that can solve the problem or meet the need.
■ **Step 3.** Prepare a thorough analysis of each possible solution, identifying its total costs, savings, benefits, other financial effects, and any qualitative factors.
■ **Step 4.** Select the best course of action.

Later, each decision is reviewed to determine whether it produced the forecasted results by examining how each decision was carried out and how its actual costs and benefits affected the organization. If results fell short, managers identify and prescribe corrective action. This post-decision audit supplies feedback about the results of the decision. If the solution is not completely satisfactory or if the problem remains, the process of evaluating costs and benefits of alternatives begins again.

Short-run decision analysis is the systematic examination of any decision whose effects will be felt over the course of the next year or less. In making such decisions, managers analyze not only quantitative cost and benefit factors relating to profitability and liquidity, they also analyze qualitative factors. In the course of a year, managers may make many short-run decisions that involve the evaluation of the costs and benefits of short-term actions, such as whether to make a product or service or buy it from an outside supplier, whether to accept a special order, whether to keep or drop an unprofitable segment, and whether to sell a product as is or process it further. If resources are limited, they may also have to decide on the most appropriate product mix.

Concepts Underlying Incremental Analysis

Once managers have determined that a problem or need is worthy of consideration and have identified alternative courses of action, they must evaluate the costs and benefits of each alternative. The method of comparing alternatives by focusing on the differences in their projected revenues and costs is called **incremental analysis**. If incremental analysis excludes revenues or costs that stay the same or that do not change between the alternatives, it is called *differential analysis*.

Irrelevant Costs and Revenues A cost that changes between alternatives is known as a **differential cost** (or *incremental cost*). For example, suppose that Home State Bank's managers are deciding which of two ATM machines—C or W—to buy. The ATMs have the same purchase price but different revenue and cost characteristics. The company currently owns ATM B, which it bought three years ago for $15,000 and which has accumulated depreciation of $9,000, and carries a book value of $6,000. ATM B is now obsolete as a result of advances in technology and cannot be sold or traded in.

A manager has prepared the following comparison of the annual revenue and operating cost estimates for the two new machines:

	ATM C	ATM W
Increase in revenue	$16,200	$19,800
Increase in annual operating costs:		
Direct materials	4,800	4,800
Direct labor	2,200	4,100
Variable overhead	2,100	3,050
Fixed overhead (depreciation included)	5,000	5,000

STUDY NOTE: *Sunk costs cannot be recovered and are irrelevant in short-run decision making.*

Incremental Analysis The first step in the incremental analysis is to eliminate any irrelevant revenues and costs. *Irrelevant revenues* are those that will not differ between the alternatives. *Irrelevant costs* include costs that will not differ between the alternatives and sunk costs. A **sunk cost** is a cost that was incurred because of a previous decision and cannot be recovered through the current decision. For Home State Bank, the costs of direct materials and fixed overhead (depreciation included) are irrelevant costs because they are the same under both alternatives. In addition, ATM B's book value is a sunk cost because it represents money that was spent in the past and so does not affect the decision about whether to replace ATM B with a new one. ATM B would be of interest only if it could be sold or traded in, and if the amount received for it would be different, depending on which new ATM was chosen. In that case, the amount of the sale or trade-in value would be relevant to the decision because it would affect the future cash flows of the alternatives.

Once the irrelevant revenues and costs have been identified, the incremental analysis can be prepared using only the differential revenues and costs that will change between the alternative ATMs, as shown in Exhibit 1. The analysis shows that ATM W would produce $750 more in operating income than ATM C. Because the costs of buying the two ATMs are the same, this report would favor the purchase of ATM W.

Exhibit 1
Incremental Analysis

Home State Bank
Incremental Analysis

	ATM C	ATM W	Difference in Favor of ATM W
Increase in revenue	$16,200	$19,800	$ 3,600
Increase in annual operating costs that differ between alternatives:			
Direct labor	$ 2,200	$ 4,100	$(1,900)
Variable overhead	2,100	3,050	(950)
Total increase in operating costs	$ 4,300	$ 7,150	$(2,850)
Resulting change in operating income	$11,900	$12,650	$ 750

© Cengage Learning 2014

Opportunity Costs Because incremental analysis focuses on only the quantitative differences among the alternatives, it simplifies management's evaluation of a decision and reduces the time needed to choose the best course of action. However, incremental analysis is only one input to the final decision. Management needs to consider qualitative issues. For instance, the manufacturer of ATM C might have a reputation for better quality or service than the manufacturer of ATM W.

Operating Central Park in New York city involves maintenance, employee, and equipment costs. But the largest cost is actually the opportunity cost of the tens of billions of dollars the city could get by leasing the land to real estate developers.

Opportunity costs are the benefits that are forfeited or lost when one alternative is chosen over another. In other words, opportunity costs arise when the choice of one course of action eliminates the possibility of another course of action. Opportunity costs often come into play when a company is operating at or near capacity and must choose which products or services to offer. For example, suppose that Home State Bank, which currently services 20,000 debit cards, has the option of offering 15,000 premium debit cards, which is a higher-priced product, but it cannot do both. The amount of income from the 20,000 debit cards is an opportunity cost of the premium debit cards.

APPLY IT!

Credit Bank has assembled the following monthly information related to the purchase of a new automated teller machine:

	Machine A	Machine B
Increase in revenue	$4,200	$5,100
Increase in annual operating costs:		
Direct materials	1,200	1,200
Direct labor	1,200	1,600
Variable overhead	2,500	2,900
Fixed overhead (including depreciation)	1,400	1,400

Use incremental analysis to determine the cost-benefit difference in favor of Machine B.

SOLUTION

Credit Bank
Incremental Analysis

	Machine A	Machine B	Difference in Favor of Machine B
Increase in revenue	$4,200	$5,100	$ 900
Increase in operating costs that differ between alternatives:			
Direct labor	$1,200	$1,600	$(400)
Variable overhead	2,500	2,900	(400)
Total increase in operating costs	$3,700	$4,500	$(800)
Resulting change in operating income	$ 500	$ 600	$ 100

TRY IT! SE1, SE2, E1A, E1B

ACCOUNTING APPLICATIONS

LO 2 Incremental Analysis for Outsourcing Decisions

Outsourcing is the use of suppliers outside the organization to perform services or produce goods that could be performed or produced internally. **Make-or-buy decisions**, which are decisions about whether to make a part internally or buy it from an external supplier, may lead to outsourcing. A company may decide to outsource entire operating activities, such as warehousing or human resources, that have traditionally been performed in-house. Outsourcing can reduce a company's investment in physical assets and human resources, which can improve cash flow. It can also help a company reduce its operating costs and improve operating income. For example, because **Amazon.com** outsources the distribution of most of its products, it has been able to reduce its storage and distribution costs enough to offer product discounts of up to 40 percent off the list price.

Outsourcing Analysis

In manufacturing companies, a common decision facing managers is whether to make or buy some or all of the parts used in product assembly. The goal is to select the more profitable choice by identifying the costs of each alternative and their effects on revenues and existing costs. Managers need the following information for this analysis:

Information About Making	Information About Buying
• Variable costs of making the item	• Purchase price of item
• Need for additional machinery	• Rent or cash flow to be generated from vacated space in the factory
• Incremental fixed costs	• Salvage value of unused machinery

For example, for the past five years, Box Company has purchased packing cartons from Pappe, Inc., an outside supplier, at a cost of $1.25 per carton. Effective immediately, Pappe is raising the price 20 percent, to $1.50 per carton. Box has space and idle machinery that could be adjusted to produce the cartons. Annual production and usage would be 20,000 cartons. Box estimates the cost of direct materials at $0.84 per carton. Workers, who will be paid $8.00 per hour, can process 20 cartons per hour ($0.40 per carton). The cost of variable overhead will be $4 per direct labor hour, and 1,000 direct labor hours will be required. Fixed overhead includes $4,000 of depreciation per year and $6,000 of other fixed costs. The idle machines will continue to be idle if the cartons are purchased. Should Box continue to outsource the cartons?

Exhibit 2 presents an incremental analysis of the two alternatives. All relevant costs are listed. Because the machinery has already been purchased, and neither the

Exhibit 2
Incremental Analysis: Outsourcing Decision

	Box Company Outsourcing Decision Incremental Analysis		
	Make	**Outsource**	**Difference in Favor of Make**
Direct materials (20,000 × $0.84)	$16,800	$ —	$(16,800)
Direct labor (20,000 × $0.40)	8,000	—	(8,000)
Variable overhead (1,000 hours × $4)	4,000	—	(4,000)
Purchase price (20,000 × $1.50)	—	30,000	30,000
Totals	$28,800	$30,000	$ 1,200

© Cengage Learning 2014

STUDY NOTE: *Remember to exclude irrelevant information (such as depreciation and other fixed costs). Only costs that change between the alternatives should be used in incremental analysis.*

machinery nor the required factory space has any other use, the depreciation costs and other fixed overhead costs are the same for both alternatives. Therefore, they are not relevant to the decision. The cost of making the needed cartons is $28,800. The cost of buying 20,000 cartons at the increased purchase price will be $30,000. Since the company would save $1,200 by making the cartons, management should decide to make the cartons.

APPLY IT!

Office Associates, Inc., is currently operating at less than capacity. The company thinks it could cut costs by outsourcing office cleaning to an independent cleaning service for $75 a week. Currently, a general office worker is employed for $10 an hour to do light cleaning and other general office duties. Cleaning the office usually takes one hour a day to perform and consumes $10 of supplies, $2 of variable overhead, and $18 of fixed overhead each week. Should Office Associates continue to perform office cleanings, or should it outsource them?

SOLUTION

Costs per Cleaning	Continue to Perform Cleanings	Outsource Cleanings	Difference in Favor of Continuing to Perform Cleanings
Employee labor	$50	$—	$(50)
Supplies	10	—	(10)
Variable overhead	2	—	(2)
Outside cleaning service	—	75	75
Totals	$62	$75	$ 13

Office Associates should continue to perform office cleanings itself.

TRY IT! SE3, SE4, E2A, E3A, E2B, E3B

LO3 Incremental Analysis for Special Order Decisions

Managers are often faced with **special order decisions**, which are decisions about whether to accept or reject special orders at prices below the normal market prices. Special order decisions must be consistent with the company's strategic plan and tactical objectives and must take into account not only costs and revenues but also relevant qualitative factors, such as the impact of the special order on regular customers, the potential of the special order to lead into new sales areas, and the customer's ability to maintain an ongoing relationship that includes good ordering and paying practices.

Before a company accepts a special product order, it must be sure that excess capacity exists to complete the order and that the order will not reduce unit sales from its full-priced regular product line. In addition, a special order should be accepted only if it maximizes operating income. In many situations, sales commission expenses are excluded from a special order decision analysis because the customer approached the company directly. In addition, the fixed costs of existing facilities usually do not change if a company accepts a special order, and therefore these costs are usually irrelevant to the decision. If additional fixed costs must be incurred to fill the special order, they would be relevant to the decision. Examples of relevant fixed costs are the purchase of additional machinery, an increase in supervisory help, and an increase in insurance premiums required by a specific order.

Special Order Analysis: Price and Relevant Cost Comparison

One approach to a special order decision is to compare the price of the special order with the relevant costs of producing, packaging, and shipping the order. The relevant costs include the variable costs, variable selling costs (if any), and other costs directly associated with the special order (e.g., freight, insurance, and packaging and labeling the product). For example, suppose Home State Bank has been approved to provide and service four ATMs at a special event. The event sponsors want the fee reduced to $0.50 per ATM transaction. At past special events, ATM use has averaged 2,000 transactions per machine. Home State Bank has four idle ATMs and determined the following additional information:

ATM Cost Data for Annual Use of One Machine (400,000 Transactions)	
Direct materials	$0.10
Direct labor	0.05
Variable overhead	0.20
Fixed overhead ($100,000 ÷ 400,000)	0.25
Advertising ($60,000 ÷ 400,000)	0.15
Other fixed selling and administrative expenses ($120,000 ÷ 400,000)	0.30
Cost per transaction	$1.05
Regular fee per transaction	$1.50

Should Home State Bank accept the special event offer?

An incremental analysis of the decision appears in Exhibit 3. The report shows the contribution margin for Home State Bank's operations both with and without the special order for the four machines. Fixed costs are not included because the only costs affected by the order are direct materials, direct labor, and variable overhead. The net result of accepting the special order is a $1,200 increase in contribution margin (and, correspondingly, in operating income). The analysis reveals that Home State Bank should accept the special order. The $1,200 increase is verified by the following contribution margin calculation:

Special order sales [(2,000 transactions × 4 machines) × $0.50]		$4,000
Less variable costs:		
Direct materials (8,000 transactions × $0.10)	$ 800	
Direct labor (8,000 transactions × $0.05)	400	
Variable overhead (8,000 transactions × $0.20)	1,600	
Total variable costs		2,800
Special order contribution margin		$1,200

Exhibit 3
Incremental Analysis: Special Order Decision

Home State Bank
Special Order Decision
Incremental Analysis

	Without Order	With Order	Difference in Favor of Accepting Order
Sales	$2,400,000	$2,404,000	$ 4,000
Less variable costs:			
Direct materials	$ 160,000	$ 160,800	$ (800)
Direct labor	80,000	80,400	(400)
Variable overhead	320,000	321,600	(1,600)
Total variable costs	$ 560,000	$ 562,800	$(2,800)
Contribution margin	$1,840,000	$1,841,200	$ 1,200

Special Order Analysis: Minimum Bid Price for Special Order

Another approach to this kind of decision is to prepare a special order bid price by calculating a minimum selling price for the special order. The bid price must cover the relevant costs and an estimated profit. For example, assume that the event sponsor asks Home State Bank what its minimum special order price is. If the incremental costs for the special order are $2,800, the relevant cost per transaction is $0.35 ($2,800 ÷ 8,000). The special order price should cover this cost and generate a profit. If Home State Bank would like to earn $800 from the special order, the special order price should be $0.45 [$0.35 cost per transaction plus $0.10 profit per transaction ($800 ÷ 8,000 transactions)].

APPLY IT!

Sample Company has received an order for Product EZ at a special selling price of $26 per unit (suggested retail price is $30). This order is over and above normal production, and budgeted production and sales targets for the year have already been exceeded. Capacity exists to satisfy the special order. No selling costs will be incurred in connection with this order. Unit costs to manufacture and sell Product EZ are as follows: direct materials, $7.00; direct labor, $10.00; variable overhead, $8.00; fixed manufacturing costs, $5.00; variable selling costs, $3.00; and fixed general and administrative costs, $9.00. Should Sample accept the order?

SOLUTION

Variable costs to produce Product EZ:

Direct materials	$ 7.00
Direct labor	10.00
Variable overhead	8.00
Total variable costs to produce	$25.00

Sample should accept the special order, because the offered price of $26 exceeds the variable manufacturing costs of $25.

TRY IT! SE5, SE6, E4A, E5A, E4B, E5B

LO 4 Incremental Analysis for Segment Profitability Decisions

Another type of operating decision that management must make is whether to keep or drop unprofitable segments, such as product lines, services, sales territories, divisions, departments, stores, or outlets. Management must select the alternative that maximizes operating income. The objective of the decision analysis is to identify the segments that have a negative segment margin so that managers can drop them or take corrective action.

A **segment margin** is a segment's sales revenue minus its direct costs (direct variable costs and direct fixed costs traceable to the segment). Such costs are assumed to be **avoidable costs**. An avoidable cost could be eliminated if management were to drop the segment.

▲ If a segment has a positive segment margin—that is, the segment's revenue is greater than its direct costs—it is able to cover its own direct costs and contribute a portion of its revenue to cover common costs and add to operating income. In that case, management should keep the segment.

▼ If a segment has a negative segment margin—that is, the segment's revenue is less than its direct costs—management should eliminate the segment.

However, certain common costs will be incurred regardless of the decision. Those are unavoidable costs, and the remaining segments must have sufficient contribution margin to cover their own direct costs and the common costs.

Segment Profitability Analysis

An analysis of segment profitability includes the preparation of a segmented income statement using variable costing to identify variable and fixed costs. The fixed costs that are traceable to the segments are called *direct fixed costs*. The remaining fixed costs are *common costs* and are not assigned to segments.

Business Perspective
Why Banks Prefer e-Banking

After performing segment analysis of online banking and face-to-face banking, bank managers worldwide are encouraging customers to do their banking over the Internet. Banks have found that linking global Internet access with customer relationship management (CRM), customer-friendly financial software, and online bill payment in a secure banking environment can reduce costs, increase service and product availability, and boost earnings.[1]

Suppose Home State Bank wants to determine if it should eliminate its Safe Deposit Division. Managers prepare a segmented income statement, separating variable and fixed costs to calculate the contribution margin. They separate the total fixed costs of $84,000 further by directly tracing $55,500 to Bank Operations and $16,500 to the Safe Deposit Division. The remaining $12,000 are common fixed costs. Exhibit 4 shows the segment margins for Bank Operations and the Safe Deposit Division and the operating income for the total company.

Exhibit 4
Segmented Income Statement

Home State Bank
Segmented Income Statement
For the Year Ended December 31, 2014

	Bank Operations	Safe Deposit Division	Total Company
Sales	$135,000	$15,000	$150,000
Less variable costs	52,500	7,500	60,000
Contribution margin	$ 82,500	$ 7,500	$ 90,000
Less direct fixed costs	55,500	16,500	72,000
Segment margin	$ 27,000	$ (9,000)	$ 18,000
Less common fixed costs			12,000
Operating income			$ 6,000

© Cengage Learning 2014

Situation 1 Exhibit 5 demonstrates that dropping the Safe Deposit Division will increase operating income by $9,000. Unless the bank can increase the division's segment margin by increasing sales revenue or by reducing direct costs, management should drop the segment. The incremental approach to analyzing this decision isolates the segment and focuses on its segment margin, as shown in the last column of Exhibit 5. The decision to drop a segment also requires a careful review of the other segments to see whether they will be affected.

Situation 2 Exhibit 6 assumes that the Bank Operations' sales volume and variable costs will decrease 20 percent if management eliminates the Safe Deposit Division. The reduction in sales volume stems from the loss of customers who purchase products from both divisions. The analysis shows that dropping the division would reduce both the segment margin and the bank's operating income by $7,500. In this situation, Home State Bank would want to keep the Safe Deposit Division.

Exhibit 5
Incremental Analysis:
Segment Profitability
Decision (Situation 1)

Home State Bank
Segment Profitability Decision
Incremental Analysis—Situation 1

	Keep Safe Deposit Division	Drop Safe Deposit Division	Difference in Favor of Dropping Safe Deposit Division
Sales	$150,000	$135,000	$(15,000)
Less variable costs	60,000	52,500	7,500
Contribution margin	$ 90,000	$ 82,500	$ (7,500)
Less direct fixed costs	72,000	55,500	16,500
Segment margin	$ 18,000	$ 27,000	$ 9,000
Less common fixed costs	12,000	12,000	0
Operating income	$ 6,000	$ 15,000	$ 9,000

© Cengage Learning 2014

Exhibit 6
Incremental Analysis:
Segment Profitability
Decision (Situation 2)

Home State Bank
Segment Profitability Decision
Incremental Analysis—Situation 2

	Keep Safe Deposit Division	Drop Safe Deposit Division	Difference in Favor of Keeping Safe Deposit Division
Sales	$150,000	$108,000	$(42,000)
Less variable costs	60,000	42,000	18,000
Contribution margin	$ 90,000	$ 66,000	$(24,000)
Less direct fixed costs	72,000	55,500	16,500
Segment margin	$ 18,000	$ 10,500	$ (7,500)
Less common fixed costs	12,000	12,000	0
Operating income	$ 6,000	$ (1,500)	$ (7,500)

© Cengage Learning 2014

APPLY IT!

Sample Company is evaluating its two divisions, East Division and West Division. Data for East Division include sales of $500,000, variable costs of $250,000, and fixed costs of $400,000, 50 percent of which are traceable to the division. West Division's data for the same period include sales of $600,000, variable costs of $350,000, and fixed costs of $450,000, 60 percent of which are traceable to the division. Should either division be considered for elimination?

SOLUTION

	East Division	West Division	Total Company
Sales	$500,000	$600,000	$1,100,000
Less variable costs	250,000	350,000	600,000
Contribution margin	$250,000	$250,000	$ 500,000
Less direct fixed costs	200,000	270,000	470,000
Divisional income	$ 50,000	$ (20,000)	$ 30,000
Less common fixed costs			380,000
Operating income (loss)			$ (350,000)

The company should keep East Division because it is profitable. West Division does not seem to be profitable and should be considered for elimination. The home office and its very heavy overhead costs are causing the company's loss.

TRY IT! SE7, E6A, E6B

LO5 Incremental Analysis for Sales Mix Decisions

Limits on resources like machine time or available labor may restrict the types or quantities of products or services that a company can provide. The question is, which products or services contribute the most to profitability in relation to the amount of capital assets or other constrained resources needed to offer those items? To satisfy customers' demands and maximize operating income, management will make a **sales mix decision** to offer the most profitable combination of products and services. To decide on the optimal sales mix of products or services, managers calculate the contribution margin per constrained resource (such as labor hours or machine hours) for each product or service.

Sales Mix Analysis

The objective of a sales mix decision is to select the alternative that maximizes the contribution margin per constrained resource. The decision analysis, which uses incremental analysis to identify the relevant costs and revenues, consists of two steps.

- **Step 1.** Calculate the contribution margin per unit for each product or service affected by the constrained resource as follows.

    Contribution Margin per Unit = Selling Price per Unit – Variable Costs per Unit

- **Step 2.** Calculate the contribution margin per unit of the constrained resource as follows.

$$\frac{\text{Contribution Margin per Unit}}{\text{of Constrained Resources}} = \frac{\text{Contribution Margin per Unit}}{\text{Quantity of the Constrained Resource Required per Unit}}$$

Suppose Home State Bank offers three types of loans: commercial loans, auto loans, and home loans. The product line data follows.

	Commercial Loans	Auto Loans	Home Loans
Current loan application demand	20,000	30,000	18,000
Processing hours per loan application	2.0	1.0	2.5
Loan origination fee	$24.00	$18.00	$32.00
Variable processing costs	$12.50	$10.00	$18.75
Variable selling costs	$6.50	$5.00	$6.25

The current loan application capacity is 100,000 processing hours.

Ranking the Order Which loan type should be advertised and promoted first because it is the most profitable for the bank? Which should be second? Which last? Exhibit 7 shows the sales mix analysis. It indicates that the auto loans should be promoted first because they provide the highest contribution margin per processing hour. Home loans should be second, and commercial loans should be last.

Number of Units How many of each type of loan should the bank sell to maximize its contribution margin based on the current loan application capacity of 100,000 processing hours? What is the total contribution margin for that combination? To begin the analysis, compare the current loan application capacity with the total capacity required to meet the current loan demand. The company needs 115,000 processing hours to meet the current loan demand, calculated as follows.

Processing hours for commercial loans (20,000 loans × 2 processing hours per loan)	40,000
Processing hours for auto loans (30,000 loans × 1 processing hour per loan)	30,000
Processing hours for home loans (18,000 × 2.5 processing hours per loan)	45,000
Total processing hours	115,000

Because the 115,000 processing hours needed exceeds the current capacity of 100,000 processing hours, management must determine the sales mix that maximizes the company's contribution margin, which will also maximize its operating income.

The calculations in Exhibit 8 show that Home State Bank should sell 30,000 auto loans, 18,000 home loans, and 12,500 commercial loans. The total contribution margin is as follows.

Auto loans (30,000 loans × $3.00 per loan)	$ 90,000
Home loans (18,000 loans × $7.00 per loan)	126,000
Commercial loans (12,500 loans × $5.00 per loan)	62,500
Total contribution margin	$278,500

Exhibit 7
Incremental Analysis:
Sales Mix Decision
Involving Constrained
Resources
(Ranking the Order)

Home State Bank
Sales Mix Decision: Ranking the Order of Loans
Incremental Analysis

	Commercial Loans	Auto Loans	Home Loans
Loan origination fee per loan	$24.00	$18.00	$32.00
Less variable costs:			
Processing	$12.50	$10.00	$18.75
Selling	6.50	5.00	6.25
Total variable costs	$19.00	$15.00	$25.00
Contribution margin per loan	$ 5.00	$ 3.00	$ 7.00
Processing hours per loan	÷ 2.0	÷ 1.0	÷ 2.5
Contribution margin per processing hour	$ 2.50	$ 3.00	$ 2.80

© Cengage Learning 2014

Exhibit 8
Incremental Analysis:
Sales Mix Decision
Involving Constrained
Resources
(Number of Units)

Home State Bank
Sales Mix Decision: Number of Units to Make
Incremental Analysis

	Processing Hours
Total processing hours available	100,000
Less processing hours to produce auto loans (30,000 loans × 1 processing hour per loan)	30,000
Balance of processing hours available	70,000
Less processing hours to produce home loans (18,000 loans × 2.5 processing hours per loan)	45,000
Balance of processing hours available	25,000
Less processing hours to produce commercial loans (12,500 loans × 2 processing hours per loan)	25,000
Balance of processing hours available	0

© Cengage Learning 2014

APPLY IT!

Surf, Inc., makes three kinds of surfboards, but it has a limited number of machine hours available to make them. Product line data are as follows. In what order should the surfboard product lines be produced?

	Fiberglass	Plastic	Graphite
Machine hours per unit	4	1	2
Selling price per unit	$1,500	$800	$1,300
Variable manufacturing cost per unit	500	200	800
Variable selling costs per unit	200	350	200

SOLUTION

	Fiberglass	Plastic	Graphite
Selling price per unit	$1,500	$800	$1,300
Less variable costs:			
Manufacturing	$ 500	$200	$ 800
Selling	200	350	200
Total unit variable costs	$ 700	$550	$1,000
Contribution margin per unit	$ 800	$250	$ 300
Machine hours per unit	÷ 4	÷ 1	÷ 2
Contribution margin per machine hour	$ 200	$250	$ 150

Surf should produce plastic first, then fiberglass, and finally graphite surfboards.

TRY IT! SE8, E7A, E8A, E9A, E7B, E8B, E9B

LO 6 Incremental Analysis for Sell-or-Process-Further Decisions

STUDY NOTE: *Products are made by combining materials or by dividing materials, as in oil refining or ore extraction.*

Some companies offer products or services that can either be sold in a basic form or be processed further and sold as a more refined product or service to a different market. A **sell-or-process-further decision** is a decision about whether to sell a joint product at the split-off point or sell it after further processing. **Joint products** are two or more products made from a common material or process that cannot be identified as separate products or services during some or all of the processing. Only at a specific point, called the **split-off point**, do joint products or services become separate and identifiable. At that point, a company may choose to sell the product or service as is or to process it into another form for sale to a different market.

Sell-or-Process-Further Analysis

The objective of a sell-or-process-further decision is to select the alternative that maximizes operating income. The decision analysis entails calculating the **incremental revenue** as follows.

$$\begin{array}{c} \text{Incremental} \\ \text{Revenue} \end{array} = \begin{array}{c} \text{Total Revenue if} \\ \text{Product/Service Is Sold} \\ \text{at Split-Off Point} \end{array} - \begin{array}{c} \text{Total Revenue if} \\ \text{Product/Service Is Sold} \\ \text{after Further Processing} \end{array}$$

▲ If the incremental *revenue* is greater than the incremental costs of processing further, a decision to process the product or service further would be justified.

▲ If the incremental *costs* are greater than the incremental revenue, a decision to sell the product or service at the split-off point would be in order.

STUDY NOTE: *Joint costs are irrelevant in a sell-or-process-further decision.*

The common costs shared by two or more products before they are split off are called **joint costs** (or *common costs*). Although accountants assign joint costs to products or services when valuing inventories and calculating cost of goods sold, joint costs are not relevant to a sell-or-process-further decision because they are incurred *before* the split-off point and do not change if further processing occurs.

For example, as part of the company's strategic plan, Home State Bank's management is looking for new markets for banking services, and management is considering whether it would be profitable to bundle banking services. The bank is considering adding two levels of service beyond its current Basic Checking account services: Premier Checking and Personal Banker. The three levels have the following bundled features:

- **Basic Checking:** Online checking account, debit card, and online bill payment with a required minimum average balance of $500
- **Premier Checking:** Paper and online checking, a debit card, a credit card, and a small life insurance policy equal to the maximum credit limit on the credit card for customers who maintain a minimum average balance of $1,000
- **Personal Banker:** All of the features of Premier Checking plus a safe deposit box, a $5,000 personal line of credit at the prime interest rate, financial investment advice, and a toaster upon opening the account for customers who maintain a minimum average balance of $5,000

Assume that the bank can earn sales revenue of 5 percent on its checking account balances and that the total cost of offering basic checking services is currently $50,000. The bank's accountant provided these data for each level of service:

Product	Sales Revenue	Additional Costs
Basic Checking	$ 25	$ 0
Premier Checking	50	30
Personal Banker	250	200

Should the bank offer any additional services? The decision analysis in Exhibit 9 indicates that the bank should offer Personal Banker services in addition to Basic Checking accounts. Notice that the $50,000 joint costs of Basic Checking were ignored because they are sunk costs that will not influence the decision.

Exhibit 9
Incremental Analysis: Sell-or-Process-Further Decision

Home State Bank
Sell-or-Process-Further Decision
Incremental Analysis

	Premier Checking	Personal Banker
Incremental revenue per account if processed further:		
Process further	$50	$250
Split-off—Basic Checking	25	25
Incremental revenue	$25	$225
Less incremental costs	30	200
Operating income (loss) from processing further	$ (5)	$ 25

© Cengage Learning 2014

APPLY IT!

In an attempt to provide superb customer service, Anytime Movie Access is considering expanding its product offerings from single movie or game pay-per-view to complete movie or game evenings. Each evening would include unlimited online access to movies or games and a coupon for candy, popcorn, and drinks. The company's accountant has compiled the information that follows. Determine which products Anytime Movie Access should offer.

Product	Sales Revenue if No Additional Services	Sales Revenue if Processed Further into Unlimited Evening	Additional Processing Costs
Movie	$2	$10	$5
Game	1	6	5

SOLUTION

	Movie Evening	Game Evening
Incremental revenue if processed further:		
Process further	$10	$6
Split-off	2	1
Incremental revenue	$ 8	$5
Less incremental costs	5	5
Operating income from further processing	$ 3	$0

Anytime Movie Access should promote movie evenings first, then movies, and finally games or game evenings. There is no difference in profitability between the sale of games and the sale of game evenings.

TRY IT! SE9, E10A, E11A, E10B, E11B

SECTION 3

BUSINESS APPLICATIONS

BUSINESS
APPLICATIONS
■ Planning
■ Performing
■ Evaluating
■ Communicating

RELEVANT
LEARNING OBJECTIVE

LO 7 Describe why short-run decision analysis is critical for business success.

LO 7 The Management Process

Managers use both financial and nonfinancial quantitative and qualitative information to analyze the effects of past and potential business actions on their organization's resources and profits. Although many business problems are unique and cannot be solved by following strict rules, managers often use a suite of short-run decision-making methods and tools. Those decision methods and tools were the focus of this chapter. Exhibit 10 summarizes the tools and methods managers use to ensure a wise allocation of resources and at the same time minimize the business risks involved.

Exhibit 10
Short-Run Decisions and the Management Process

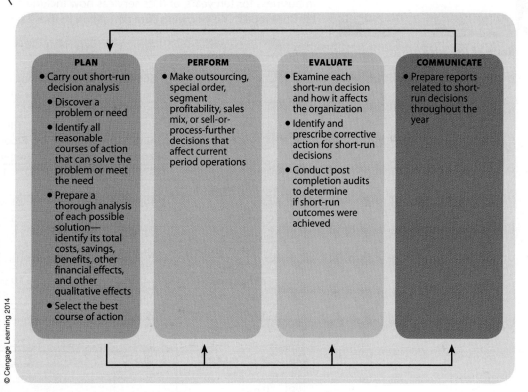

PLAN	PERFORM	EVALUATE	COMMUNICATE
• Carry out short-run decision analysis • Discover a problem or need • Identify all reasonable courses of action that can solve the problem or meet the need • Prepare a thorough analysis of each possible solution—identify its total costs, savings, benefits, other financial effects, and other qualitative effects • Select the best course of action	• Make outsourcing, special order, segment profitability, sales mix, or sell-or-process-further decisions that affect current period operations	• Examine each short-run decision and how it affects the organization • Identify and prescribe corrective action for short-run decisions • Conduct post completion audits to determine if short-run outcomes were achieved	• Prepare reports related to short-run decisions throughout the year

© Cengage Learning 2014

APPLY IT!

When managers make short-run decisions that are critical to their business, they ask questions. From the list that follows, select the questions a manager might ask.

1. When should products and services be outsourced?
2. Which capital budget proposal should be accepted?
3. When is a business segment profitable?
4. When resource constraints exist, what is the best sales mix?
5. When should products or services be sold as is or processed further into different products or services?
6. When should a special order for service or products be accepted?

SOLUTION

All are examples of questions managers might ask when making short-term decisions that are critical to their business's success.

TriLevel Problem

Bank of America

The beginning of this chapter focused on **Bank of America**. Complete the following requirements in order to answer the questions posed at the beginning of the chapter.

Section 1: Concepts
Why is the concept of cost-benefit important when making short-run decisions?

Section 2: Accounting Applications
How does incremental analysis ensure a wise allocation of resources involved in short-run decisions?

Suppose a loan officer at a bank like Bank of America has been analyzing Home Services, Inc., to determine whether the bank should grant it a loan. Home Services has been in business for ten years, and its services now include tree trimming and auto, boat, and tile floor repair. The following data pertaining to those services were available for analysis:

	A	B	C	D	E	F	G
1			Home Services, Inc.				
2			Segmented Income Statement				
3			For the Year Ended December 31, 2014				
4							
5					Tile		
6			Auto	Boat	Floor	Tree	Total
7			Repair	Repair	Repair	Trimming	Impact
8	Sales		$297,500	$114,300	$126,400	$97,600	$635,800
9	Less variable costs						
10	Direct labor		$119,000	$ 40,005	$ 44,240	$34,160	$237,405
11	Operating supplies		14,875	5,715	6,320	4,880	31,790
12	Small tools		11,900	4,572	5,056	7,808	29,336
13	Replacement parts		59,500	22,860	25,280	—	107,640
14	Truck costs		—	11,430	12,640	14,640	38,710
15	Selling costs		44,625	17,145	18,960	9,760	90,490
16	Other variable costs		5,950	2,286	2,528	1,952	12,716
17	Total variable costs		$255,850	$104,013	$115,024	$73,200	$548,087
18	Contribution margin		$ 41,650	$ 10,287	$ 11,376	$24,400	$ 87,713
19	Less direct fixed costs		35,800	16,300	24,100	5,200	81,400
20	Segment margin		$ 5,850	$ (6,013)	$ (12,724)	$19,200	$ 6,313
21	Less common fixed						
22	costs						32,100
23	Operating income						
24	(loss)						$ (25,787)
25							

Home Services' profitability has decreased over the past two years, and to increase the likelihood that the company will qualify for a loan, the loan officer has advised its owner, Dale Bandy, to determine which service lines are not meeting the company's profit targets. Once Bandy has identified the unprofitable service lines, he can either eliminate them or set higher prices. If he sets higher prices, those prices will have to cover all variable and fixed operating, selling, and general administration costs.

1. Analyze the performance of the four service lines. Should Dale Bandy eliminate any of them? Explain your answer.

2. Why might Bandy want to continue providing unprofitable service lines?

3. Identify possible causes of a service's poor performance. What actions do you think Bandy should take to make his company a better loan candidate?

Section 3: Business Applications

How can incremental analysis help managers improve performance and take advantage of business opportunities?

To answer this question, match this chapter's managerial responsibilities with when they occur within the management process.

a. Plan
b. Perform
c. Evaluate
d. Communicate

1. Carry out short-run decision analysis: discover a problem or need
2. Prepare reports related to short-run decisions throughout the year.
3. Examine each short-run decision and how it affects the organization.
4. Identify and prescribe corrective action for short-run decisions.
5. Make outsourcing, special order, segment profitability, sales mix, or sell-or-process-further decisions that affect current period operations.
6. Conduct post completion audits to determine if short-run outcomes were achieved.

SOLUTION

Section 1: Concepts

The concept of *cost-benefit* is used to evaluate short-run decisions so that the benefits to be gained from a course of action or alternative can be compared to the costs of implementing it. For an alternative to be feasible, its benefits must outweigh its costs. Cost-benefit is an accounting convention or rule of thumb that considers both quantitative and qualitative cost and benefit measures to facilitate comparisons between alternatives for sound business decisions. Managers frequently take the following actions when applying the cost-benefit concept:

- **Step 1.** Discover a problem or need.
- **Step 2.** Identify all reasonable courses of action that can solve the problem or meet the need.
- **Step 3.** Prepare a thorough analysis of each possible solution, identifying its total costs, savings, benefits, other financial effects, and any qualitative factors.
- **Step 4.** Select the best course of action.

Section 2: Accounting Applications

1. In deciding whether to eliminate any of the four service lines, Dale Bandy should concentrate on those that have a negative segment margin. If the revenues from a service line are less than the sum of its variable and direct fixed costs, then other service lines must cover some of the losing line's costs and carry the burden of the common fixed costs.

   By looking at the segmented income statement, Dale Bandy can see that the company will improve its operating income by $18,737 ($6,013 + $12,724) if he eliminates the boat and tile floor repair services, both of which have a negative segment margin. Bandy's decision can also be supported by the following analysis:

	A	B	C	D	E
1			Home Services, Inc.		
2			Segment Profitability Decision		
3					
4					Difference in
5					Favor of
6			Keep	Drop	Dropping
7			Boat Repair	Boat Repair	Boat Repair
8			and	and	and
9			Tile Floor Repair	Tile Floor Repair	Tile Floor Repair
10	Sales		$635,800	$395,100	$(240,700)
11	Less variable costs		548,087	329,050	219,037
12	Contribution margin		$ 87,713	$ 66,050	$ (21,663)
13	Less direct fixed costs		81,400	41,000	40,400
14	Segment margin		$ 6,313	$ 25,050	$ 18,737
15	Less common fixed costs		32,100	32,100	—
16	Operating income (loss)		$ (25,787)	$ (7,050)	$ 18,737

2. Bandy may want to continue offering the unprofitable service lines if their elimination would have a negative effect on the sale of the auto repair or tree trimming services.

3. The following are among the possible causes of a service's poor performance:

   a. Service fees set too low

   b. Inadequate advertising

   c. Excessively high direct labor costs

   d. Other variable costs

   e. Poor management of fixed costs

   f. Excessive supervision costs

    To improve profitability and make the company a better candidate for a bank loan, Bandy should eliminate non-value-adding costs, increase service fees, or increase the volume of services provided to customers.

Section 3: Business Applications

1. a   4. c

2. d   5. b

3. c   6. c

Chapter Review

Describe how the concept of cost-benefit is useful when making short-run decisions.   **LO 1**

The concept of cost-benefit considers both quantitative and qualitative cost and benefit measures to facilitate comparisons between alternatives for sound business decisions. Managers apply the cost-benefit concept when following the four decision-making steps: (1) discover a problem or need; (2) identify all reasonable courses of action that can solve the problem or meet the need; (3) prepare a thorough analysis of each possible solution, identifying its total costs, savings, benefits, other financial effects, and any qualitative factors; and (4) select the best course of action.

Incremental analysis helps managers compare alternative courses of action by focusing on the cost and benefit differences in projected revenues and costs. Any data that relate to future costs, revenues, or uses of resources and that will differ among alternative courses of action are considered relevant decision information. Examples of relevant information are projected sales or estimated costs, such as the costs of direct materials or direct labor, which differ for each alternative. The manager analyzes relevant information to determine which alternative contributes the most to profits or incurs the lowest costs. Only data that differ for each alternative are considered. Differential or incremental costs are costs that vary among alternatives and thus are relevant to the decision. Sunk costs are past costs that cannot be recovered. They are irrelevant to the decision process. Opportunity costs are revenue or income forgone as a result of choosing an alternative.

Perform incremental analysis for outsourcing decisions. LO 2

Outsourcing (including make-or-buy) decision analysis helps managers decide whether to use suppliers from outside the organization to perform services or provide goods that could be performed or produced internally. An incremental analysis of the expected costs and revenues for each alternative is used to identify the best alternative.

Perform incremental analysis for special order decisions. LO 3

A special order decision is a decision about whether to accept or reject a special order at a price below the normal market price. One approach is to compare the special order price with the relevant costs to see if a profit can be generated. Another approach is to prepare a special order bid price by calculating a minimum selling price for the special order. Generally, fixed costs are irrelevant to a special order decision because such costs are covered by regular sales activity and do not differ among alternatives.

Perform incremental analysis for segment profitability decisions. LO 4

Segment profitability decisions involve the review of product lines, services, sales territories, divisions, or departments. Managers often must decide whether to add or drop a segment. A segment with a negative segment margin may be dropped. A segment margin is a segment's sales revenue minus its direct costs, which include variable costs and avoidable fixed costs. Avoidable costs are traceable to a specific segment. If the segment is eliminated, the avoidable costs will also be eliminated.

Perform incremental analysis for sales mix decisions involving constrained resources. LO 5

Sales mix decisions require the selection of the most profitable combination of sales items when a company makes more than one product or service using a common constrained resource. The product or service generating the highest contribution margin per constrained resource is offered and sold first.

Perform incremental analysis for sell-or-process-further decisions. LO 6

Sell-or-process-further decisions require managers to choose between selling a joint product at its split-off point or processing it into a more refined product. Managers compare the incremental revenues and costs of the two alternatives. Joint processing costs are irrelevant to the decision because they are identical for both alternatives. A product should be processed further only if the incremental revenues generated exceed the incremental costs incurred.

Describe why short-run decision analysis is critical for business success. LO 7

Managers use both financial and nonfinancial quantitative and qualitative information to analyze the effects of past and potential business actions on their organization's resources and profits on a daily basis. Although many business problems are unique and cannot be solved by following strict rules, managers often use a suite of short-run decision-making methods and tools. Those decision methods and tools were the focus of this chapter. During the management process, as managers plan, perform, evaluate, and report on business operations, they utilize these tools and methods to ensure a wise allocation of resources and, at the same time, minimize the daily business risks involved.

Key Terms

avoidable costs 338 (LO4)
differential cost 332 (LO1)
incremental analysis 332 (LO1)
incremental revenue 343 (LO6)
joint costs 343 (LO6)
joint products 343 (LO6)
make-or-buy decisions 335 (LO2)

opportunity costs 334 (LO1)
outsourcing 335 (LO2)
sales mix decision 340 (LO5)
segment margin 338 (LO4)
sell-or-process-further
 decision 343 (LO6)

short-run decision
 analysis 332 (LO1)
special order decisions 336 (LO3)
split-off point 343 (LO6)
sunk cost 333 (LO1)

Chapter Assignments

DISCUSSION QUESTIONS

LO 1, 7 **DQ1. CONCEPT ▶ BUSINESS APPLICATION ▶** How do managers use the concept of cost-benefit for short-run decisions during the planning phase of the management process?

LO 1, 7 **DQ2. CONCEPT ▶ BUSINESS APPLICATION ▶** How do managers use the concept of cost-benefit for short-run decisions during the performing phase of the management process?

LO 1, 7 **DQ3. CONCEPT ▶ BUSINESS APPLICATION ▶** How do managers use the concept of cost-benefit for short-run decisions during the evaluating phase of the management process?

LO 1, 7 **DQ4. CONCEPT ▶ BUSINESS APPLICATION ▶** How do managers use the concept of cost-benefit for short-run decisions during the communicating phase of the management process?

SHORT EXERCISES

LO 1 **Qualitative and Quantitative Information in Short-Run Decision Analysis**

SE1. The owner of a Mexican restaurant is deciding whether to take fish tacos off the menu. State whether each item of decision information that follows is qualitative or quantitative. If the information is quantitative, specify whether it is financial or nonfinancial.

1. The time needed to prepare the fish
2. The daily number of customers who order the tacos
3. Whether competing Mexican restaurants have this entrée on the menu
4. The labor cost of the chef who prepares the fish tacos
5. The fact that the president of a nearby company who brings ten guests with him each week always orders fish tacos

LO **1**   **Using Incremental Analysis**

SE2. Fortress Hill Corporation has assembled the following information related to the purchase of a new cable car:

	Peaks Machine	Valley Machine
Increase in revenue	$44,200	$49,300
Increase in annual operating costs:		
Direct materials	12,200	12,200
Direct labor	10,200	10,600
Variable overhead	24,500	26,900
Fixed overhead (including depreciation)	12,400	12,400

Using incremental analysis and only relevant information, compute the difference in favor of the Valley machine.

LO **2**   **Outsourcing Decision**

SE3. Will Company assembles products from a group of interconnecting parts. The company produces some of the parts and buys some from outside vendors. The vendor for Part X has just increased its price by 35 percent, to $10 per unit for the first 5,000 units and $9 per additional unit ordered each year. The company uses 7,500 units of Part X each year. Unit costs if the company makes the part are as follows.

Direct materials	$3.50
Direct labor	2.00
Variable overhead	4.00
Variable selling costs for the assembled product	3.75

Should Will Company continue to purchase Part X or begin making it?

LO **2**   **Outsourcing Decision**

SE4. Dental Associates, Inc., is currently operating at less than capacity. The company thinks it could cut costs by outsourcing dental cleaning to an independent dental hygienist for $50 per cleaning. Currently, a dental hygienist is employed for $30 an hour. A dental cleaning usually takes one hour to perform and consumes $10 of dental supplies, $8 of variable overhead, and $16 of fixed overhead. Should Dental Associates continue to perform dental cleanings, or should it begin to outsource them?

LO **3**   **Special Order Decision**

SE5. Hadley Company has received a special order request for Product R3P at a selling price of $20 per unit. This order is over and above normal production, and budgeted production and sales targets for the year have already been exceeded. Capacity exists to satisfy the special order. No selling costs will be incurred in connection with this order. Unit costs to manufacture and sell Product R3P are as follows: direct materials, $7.60; direct labor, $3.75; variable overhead, $9.25; fixed overhead, $4.85; variable selling costs, $2.75; and fixed general and administrative costs, $6.75. Should Hadley accept the order?

LO **3**   **Special Order Decision**

SE6. Wong Accounting Services is considering a special order that it received from one of its corporate clients. The special order calls for Wong to prepare the individual tax returns of the corporation's four largest shareholders. The company has idle capacity

(Continued)

that could be used to complete the special order. The following data have been gathered about the preparation of individual tax returns:

Materials cost per page	$1
Average hourly labor rate	$60
Standard hours per return	4
Standard pages per return	10
Variable overhead cost per page	$0.50
Fixed overhead cost per page	$0.50

Wong would be satisfied with a $40 gross profit per return. Compute the minimum bid price for the entire order.

LO 4 **Segment Profitability Decision**

SE7. ACCOUNTING CONNECTION ▶ Peruna Company is evaluating its two divisions, North Division and South Division. Data for North Division include sales of $530,000, variable costs of $290,000, and fixed costs of $260,000, 50 percent of which are traceable to the division. South Division's efforts for the same period include sales of $610,000, variable costs of $340,000, and fixed costs of $290,000, 60 percent of which are traceable to the division. Should Peruna consider eliminating either division? Is there any other problem that needs attention? Explain your answer.

LO 5 **Sales Mix Decision**

SE8. Blizzard, Inc., makes three kinds of snowboards, but it has a limited number of machine hours available to make them. Product line data are as follows:

	Wood	Plastic	Graphite
Machine hours per unit	1.25	1.0	1.5
Selling price per unit	$100	$120	$200
Variable manufacturing cost per unit	$45	$50	$100
Variable selling costs per unit	$15	$26	$37

In what order should the snowboard product lines be produced?

LO 6 **Sell-or-Process-Further Decision**

SE9. Gomez Industries produces three products from a single operation. Product A sells for $4 per unit, Product B for $6 per unit, and Product C for $10 per unit. When B is processed further, there are additional unit costs of $3, and its new selling price is $10 per unit. Each product is allocated $2 of joint costs from the initial production operation. Should Product B be processed further, or should it be sold at the end of the initial operation?

LO 6 **Sell-or-Process-Further Decision**

SE10. In an attempt to provide superb customer service, Richard V. Meats is considering the expansion of its product offerings from whole hams and turkeys to complete ham and turkey dinners. Each dinner would include a carved ham or turkey, two side dishes, and six rolls or cornbread. The company's accountant has compiled the following relevant information:

Product	Sales Revenue if No Additional Service	Sales Revenue if Processed Further	Additional Processing Costs
Ham	$30	$50	$15
Turkey	20	35	15

A cooked, uncarved ham costs the company $20 to prepare. A cooked, uncarved turkey costs $15 to prepare. Use incremental analysis to determine which products the company should offer.

EXERCISES: SET A

LO 1

Incremental Analysis

E1A. Coffee Culture Company's managers must decide which of two coffee grinders—Y or Z—to buy. The grinders have the same purchase price but different revenue and cost characteristics. The company currently owns Grinder X, which it bought three years ago for $10,000 and which has accumulated depreciation of $9,000 and a book value of $1,000. Grinder X is now obsolete as a result of advances in technology and cannot be sold or traded in.

The accountant has collected the following annual revenue and operating cost estimates for the two new machines:

	Grinder Y	Grinder Z
Increase in revenue	$15,000	$18,000
Increase in annual operating costs:		
Direct materials	4,500	4,500
Direct labor	3,000	4,000
Variable overhead	2,000	3,000
Fixed overhead (depreciation included)	4,000	4,000

1. Identify the relevant data in this problem.
2. Prepare an incremental analysis to aid the managers in their decision.
3. **ACCOUNTING CONNECTION ▶** Should the company purchase Grinder Y or Grinder Z? Explain your answer.

LO 2

Outsourcing Decision

E2A. ACCOUNTING CONNECTION ▶ Cyber Queen Services' manager must decide whether to hire a new employee or to outsource some of the web design work to Kai Yu, a freelance graphic designer. If she hires a new employee, she will pay $30 per design hour for the employee to work 500 hours and incur service overhead costs of $2 per design hour. She will also redirect the use of a computer and server to generate $4,000 in additional revenue from web page maintenance work. If she outsources the work to Kai Yu, she will pay $34 per design hour for 500 hours of work. Should Cyber Queen Services hire a new designer or outsource the work to Kai Yu? Explain your answer.

LO 2

Outsourcing Decision

E3A. One component of a radio produced by Audio Systems, Inc., is currently being purchased for $225 per 100 parts. Management is studying the possibility of manufacturing that component. Annual production (usage) at Audio is 70,000 units; fixed costs (all of which remain unchanged whether the part is made or purchased) are $38,500; and variable costs are $0.95 per unit for direct materials, $0.55 per unit for direct labor, and $0.60 per unit for variable overhead. Using incremental analysis, decide whether Audio Systems should manufacture the part or continue to purchase it from an outside vendor.

LO 3

Special Order Decision

E4A. Antiquities, Inc., produces antique-looking books. Management has just received a request for a special order of 2,000 books and must decide whether to accept it. Venus Company, the purchaser, is offering to pay $22.00 per book, plus $3.00 per book for shipping costs.

The variable production costs per book include $9.20 for direct materials, $4.00 for direct labor, and $3.80 for variable overhead. The current year's production is 22,000 books, and maximum capacity is 25,000 books. Fixed costs, including overhead, advertising, and selling and administrative costs, total $80,000. The usual selling price is $25.00 per book. Shipping costs, which are additional, average $3.00 per book.

Determine whether Antiquities should accept the special order.

LO 3 **Special Order Decision**

E5A. Fun Sporting Goods, Inc., manufactures a complete line of sporting equipment. Lei Enterprises operates a large chain of discount stores. Lei has approached Fun with a special order for 20,000 deluxe baseballs. Instead of being packaged separately, the balls are to be packed in boxes containing 500 baseballs each. Lei is willing to pay $2.50 per baseball. Fun's standard annual expected production is 400,000 baseballs, but Fun is on track to produce 410,000 baseballs as the current year's production. Fun's maximum production capacity is 450,000 baseballs. The following additional information is available:

Standard unit cost data for 400,000 baseballs:	
Direct materials	$ 1.00
Direct labor	0.50
Overhead:	
Variable	0.60
Fixed ($100,000 ÷ 400,000)	0.25
Packaging per unit	0.20
Advertising ($60,000 ÷ 400,000)	0.15
Other fixed selling and administrative expenses ($120,000 ÷ 400,000)	0.30
Product unit cost	$ 3.00
Unit selling price	$ 4.00
Total estimated bulk packaging costs for special order (20,000 baseballs: 500 per box)	$2,000

1. Should Fun Sporting Goods accept Lei's offer?
2. What would be the minimum order price per baseball if Fun would like to earn a profit of $3,000 from the special order?

LO 4 **Elimination of Unprofitable Segment Decision**

E6A. Gold's Glass, Inc., has three divisions: Commercial, Nonprofit, and Residential. The segmented income statement for last year revealed the following:

Gold's Glass, Inc.
Divisional Profit Summary and Decision Analysis

	Commercial Division	Nonprofit Division	Residential Division	Total Company
Sales	$300,000	$523,000	$837,000	$1,660,000
Less variable costs	157,000	425,000	472,000	1,054,000
Contribution margin	$143,000	$ 98,000	$365,000	$ 606,000
Less direct fixed costs	114,000	116,000	139,000	369,000
Segment margin	$ 29,000	$ (18,000)	$226,000	$ 237,000
Less common fixed costs				168,000
Operating income				$ 69,000

1. How will Gold's Glass be affected if the Nonprofit Division is dropped?
2. Assume the elimination of the Nonprofit Division causes the sales of the Residential Division to decrease by 10 percent. How will Gold's Glass be affected if the Nonprofit Division is dropped?

LO 5 **Constrained Resource Usage**

E7A. ZE, Inc., manufactures two products that require both machine processing and labor operations. Although there is unlimited demand for both products, ZE could devote all its capacities to a single product. Unit prices, cost data, and processing requirements follow.

	Product E	Product Z
Unit selling price	$75	$200
Unit variable costs	$25	$80
Machine hours per unit	0.4	1.2
Labor hours per unit	2.0	6.0

Next year, the company will be limited to 160,000 machine hours and 120,000 labor hours. Fixed costs for the year are $1,000,000.

1. **ACCOUNTING CONNECTION** ▶ Compute the most profitable combination of products to be produced next year. Explain your answer.
2. Prepare an income statement using the contribution margin format for the product volume computed in **1**.

LO **5**   **Sales Mix Decision**

E8A. GAME Enterprises manufactures three computer games called Rocket Star, Game Master, and Rock Warrior. The product line data follow.

	Rocket Star	Game Master	Rock Warrior
Current unit sales demand	20,000	30,000	18,000
Machine hours per unit	2.0	1.0	2.5
Selling price per unit	$20.00	$16.00	$30.00
Unit variable manufacturing costs	$12.50	$10.00	$18.75
Unit variable selling costs	$6.50	$5.00	$6.25

The current production capacity is 100,000 machine hours.

1. Which computer game should be manufactured first? Which should be manufactured second? Which last?
2. How many of each type of computer game should be manufactured and sold to maximize the company's contribution margin based on the current production activity of 100,000 machine hours? What is the total contribution margin for that combination?

LO **5**   **Sales Mix Decision**

E9A. ACCOUNTING CONNECTION ▶ Web Services, a small company owned by Simon Orozco, provides web page services to small businesses. His services include the preparation of basic pages and custom pages. The following summary of information will be used to make several short-run decisions for Web Services:

	Basic Pages	Custom Pages
Service revenue per page	$200	$750
Variable costs per page	77	600
Contribution margin per page	$123	$150

Total annual fixed costs are $78,000.

One of Web Services' two graphic designers, Taylor Campbell, is planning to take maternity leave in July and August. As a result, there will only be one designer available to perform the work, and design labor hours will be a resource constraint. Orozco plans to help the other designer complete the projected 160 orders for basic pages and 30 orders for custom pages for those two months. However, he wants to know which type of page Web Services should advertise and market. Although custom pages have a higher contribution margin per service, each custom page requires 12.5 design hours, whereas basic pages require only 1 design hour per page. On which page type should his company focus? Explain your answer.

LO **6**

Sell-or-Process-Further Decision

E10A. ACCOUNTING CONNECTION ▶ Beef Products, Inc., processes cattle. It can sell the meat as sides of beef or process it further into final cuts (steaks, roasts, and hamburger). As part of the company's strategic plan, management is looking for new markets for meat or meat by-products. The production process currently separates hides and bones for sale to other manufacturers. However, management is considering whether it would be profitable to process the hides into leather and the bones into fertilizer. The costs of the cattle and of transporting, hanging, storing, and cutting sides of beef are $100,000. The company's accountant provided these data:

Product	Sales Revenue if Sold at Split-Off	Sales Revenue if Sold After Further Processing	Additional Processing Costs
Meat	$100,000	$200,000	$80,000
Bones	20,000	40,000	25,000
Hides	50,000	60,000	5,000

Should the products be processed further? Explain your answer.

LO **6**

Sell-or-Process-Further Decision

E11A. ACCOUNTING CONNECTION ▶ Four Star Pizza manufactures make-at-home frozen pizza and calzone kits and sells them for $5 each. It is currently considering a proposal to manufacture and sell fully prepared products. The following relevant information has been gathered by management:

Product	Sales Revenue if No Additional Processing	Sales Revenue if Processed Further	Additional Processing Costs
Pizza	$5	$15	$6
Calzone	5	10	6

Use incremental analysis to determine which products Four Star should offer. Explain your answer.

EXERCISES: SET B

Visit the textbook companion website at www.cengagebrain.com to access Exercise Set B for this chapter.

PROBLEMS

LO **2**

Outsourcing Decision

✔ 1: Incremental cost to make: $93,750
✔ 2: Variable unit cost to make: $16

P1. Freeze Refrigerator Company purchases ice makers and installs them in its products. The ice makers cost $138 per case, and each case contains 12 ice makers. The supplier recently gave advance notice that the price will rise by 50 percent immediately. Freeze Refrigerator Company has idle equipment that with only a few minor changes could be used to produce similar ice makers.

Cost estimates have been prepared under the assumption that the company could make the product itself. Direct materials would cost $100.80 per 12 ice makers. Direct labor required would be 10 minutes per ice maker at a labor rate of $18.00 per hour. Variable overhead would be $4.60 per ice maker. Fixed overhead, which would be incurred under either decision alternative, would be $32,420 a year for depreciation and $234,000 a year for other costs. Production and usage are estimated at 75,000 ice makers a year. (Assume that any idle equipment cannot be used for any other purpose.)

REQUIRED

1. Prepare an incremental analysis to determine whether the ice makers should be made within the company or purchased from the outside supplier at the higher price.
2. Compute the variable unit cost to (a) make one ice maker and (b) buy one ice maker.

LO **3**

✔ 1: Contribution margin
from order: $6,420
✔ 2: Total variable costs per unit: $621.50

Special Order Decision

P2. On March 26, Buoy Industries received a special order request for 120 ten-foot aluminum fishing boats. Operating on a fiscal year ending May 31, the company already has orders that will allow it to produce at budget levels for the period. However, extra capacity exists to produce the 120 additional boats.

The terms of the special order call for a selling price of $675 per boat, and the customer will pay all shipping costs. No sales personnel were involved in soliciting the order.

The ten-foot fishing boat has the following cost estimates:

- Direct materials, aluminum, two 49 × 89 sheets at $155 per sheet
- Direct labor, 14 hours at $15.00 per hour
- Variable overhead, $7.25 per direct labor hour
- Fixed overhead, $4.50 per direct labor hour
- Variable selling expenses, $46.50 per boat
- Variable shipping expenses, $57.50 per boat

REQUIRED

1. Prepare an analysis for Buoy's management to use in deciding whether to accept or reject the special order. What decision should be made?
2. To make an $8,000 profit on this order, what would be the lowest possible price that Buoy could charge per boat?

LO **4**

SPREADSHEET

✔ 1: Revised operating income: $77,000
✔ 2: URL Services segment margin: $131,000

Elimination of Unprofitable Segment Decision

P3. URL Services has two divisions: Basic Webpages and Custom Webpages. Ricky Vega, Custom's manager, wants to find out why Custom is not profitable. He has prepared the reports that follow.

URL Services
Segmented Income Statement
For the Year Ended December 31

	Basic Webpages (1,000 units)	Custom Webpages (200 units)	Total Company
Service revenue	$200,000	$150,000	$350,000
Less variable costs:			
Direct professional labor: design	$ 32,000	$ 80,000	$112,000
Direct professional labor: install	30,000	4,000	34,000
Direct professional labor: maintain	15,000	36,000	51,000
Total variable costs	$ 77,000	$120,000	$197,000
Contribution margin	$123,000	$ 30,000	$153,000
Less direct fixed costs:			
Depreciation on computer equipment	$ 6,000	$ 12,000	$ 18,000
Depreciation on servers	10,000	20,000	30,000
Total direct fixed costs	$ 16,000	$ 32,000	$ 48,000
Segment margin	$107,000	$ (2,000)	$105,000
Less common fixed costs:			
Building rent			$ 24,000
Supplies			1,000
Insurance			3,000
Telephone			1,500
Website rental			500
Total common fixed costs			$ 30,000
Operating income			$ 75,000

(Continued)

URL Services
Custom Webpages Division
Segment Profitability Decision
Incremental Analysis

	Design	Install	Maintain	Total
Service revenue	$ 60,000	$25,000	$65,000	$150,000
Less variable costs	80,000	4,000	36,000	120,000
Contribution margin	$(20,000)	$21,000	$29,000	$ 30,000
Less direct fixed costs	6,000	13,000	13,000	32,000
Segment margin	$(26,000)	$ 8,000	$16,000	$ (2,000)

1. How will URL Services be affected if the Custom Webpages Division is eliminated?
2. How will URL Services be affected if the Design segment of Custom Webpages is eliminated?
3. **ACCOUNTING CONNECTION ▶** What should Ricky Vega do? What additional information would be helpful to him in making the decision?

LO **5, 7**

Sales Mix Decision

SPREADSHEET

✔ 2: Product C5 contribution margin per machine hour: $2.50

P4. Common Chemical Company's management is evaluating its product mix in an attempt to maximize profits. For the past two years, Common has produced four products, and all have large markets in which to expand market share. Common's controller has gathered data from current operations and wants you to analyze them for him. Sales and operating data are as follows.

	Product A1	Product B7	Product C5	Product D9
Variable production costs	$71,000	$91,000	$91,920	$97,440
Variable selling costs	$10,200	$5,400	$12,480	$30,160
Fixed production costs	$20,400	$21,600	$29,120	$18,480
Fixed administrative costs	$3,400	$5,400	$6,240	$10,080
Total sales	$122,000	$136,000	$156,400	$161,200
Units produced and sold	85,000	45,000	26,000	14,000
Machine hours used*	17,000	18,000	20,800	16,800

*Common's scarce resource, machine hours, is being used to full capacity.

REQUIRED

1. Compute the machine hours needed to produce one unit of each product.
2. Determine the contribution margin per machine hour for each product.
3. Which product line(s) should be targeted for market share expansion?

LO **6, 7**

Sell-or-Process-Further Decision

✔ 1: Incremental contribution margin for bagels with cream cheese: $1.50
✔ 1: Incremental contribution margin for bagel sandwiches: $2.00
✔ 3: Operating income from further processing bagel sandwiches with cheese: $0.50

P5. Bakers Bagels, Inc., produces and sells 20 types of bagels by the dozen. Bagels are priced at $6.00 per dozen (or $0.50 each) and cost $0.20 per unit to produce. The company is considering processing the bagels further into two products: bagels with cream cheese and bagel sandwiches. It would cost an additional $0.50 per unit to produce bagels with cream cheese, and the new selling price would be $2.50 each. It would cost an additional $1.00 per sandwich to produce bagel sandwiches, and the new selling price would be $3.50 each.

REQUIRED

1. Identify the relevant per-unit costs and revenues for the alternatives. Are there any sunk costs?
2. Based on the information in requirement 1, should Bakers Bagels expand its product offerings?
3. **ACCOUNTING CONNECTION ▶** Suppose that Bakers Bagels did expand its product line to include bagels with cream cheese and bagel sandwiches. Based on customer feedback, the company determined that it could further process those two products

into bagels with cream cheese and fruit and bagel sandwiches with cheese. The company's accountant compiled the following information:

Product (per unit)	Sales Revenue if Sold without Further Processing	Sales Revenue if Processed Further	Additional Processing Costs
Bagels with cream cheese	$2.50	$3.50	Fruit: $1.00
Bagel sandwiches	3.50	4.50	Cheese: 0.50

Perform an incremental analysis to determine if Bakers Bagels should process its products further. Explain your findings.

ALTERNATE PROBLEMS

LO **2**

Outsourcing Decision

✔ 2: Variable unit cost to make: $28.00

P6. Sisters Restaurant purchases cheesecakes and offers them as dessert items on its menu. The cheesecakes cost $24 each, and a cake contains 8 pieces. The supplier recently gave notice that the price will rise by 20 percent immediately. Sisters has idle equipment that, with only a few minor changes, could be used to produce similar cheesecakes.

Cost estimates have been prepared under the assumption that the company could make the product itself. Direct materials would cost $7.00 per cheesecake. Direct labor required would be 0.5 hour per cheesecake at a labor rate of $24.00 per hour. Variable overhead would be $9.00 per cheesecake. Fixed overhead, which would be incurred under either decision alternative, would be $35,200 a year for depreciation and $230,000 a year for other costs. Production and usage are estimated at 3,600 cheesecakes a year. (Assume that any idle equipment cannot be used for any other purpose.)

REQUIRED

1. Prepare an incremental analysis to determine whether the cheesecakes should be made within the company or purchased from the outside supplier at the higher price.
2. Compute the variable unit cost to (a) make one cheesecake and (b) buy one cheesecake.

LO **3**

Special Order Decision

✔ 1: Total variable costs per thousand: $48.50

P7. Leisure Resorts, Ltd., has approached EZ Printers, Inc., with a special order to produce 300,000 two-page brochures. Most of EZ's work consists of recurring short-run orders. Leisure Resorts is offering a one-time order, and EZ has the capacity to handle the order over a two-month period.

Leisure Resorts' management has stated that the company would be unwilling to pay more than $48 per 1,000 brochures. EZ's controller assembled the following cost data for this decision analysis:

Direct materials (paper)	$26.80 per 1,000 brochures
Direct labor costs	$6.80 per 1,000 brochures
Direct materials (ink)	$4.40 per 1,000 brochures
Variable production overhead	$6.20 per 1,000 brochures
Machine maintenance (fixed cost)	$1.00 per direct labor dollar
Other fixed production overhead	$2.40 per direct labor dollar
Variable packing costs	$4.30 per 1,000 brochures
General and administrative expenses (fixed costs) to be allocated	$5.25 per direct labor dollar

REQUIRED

1. Prepare an analysis for EZ's management to use in deciding whether to accept or reject Leisure Resorts' offer. What decision should be made?
2. What is the lowest possible price EZ can charge per thousand and still make a $6,000 profit on the order?

LO 4

SPREADSHEET

✔ 1: Revised operating income: $94,000
✔ 2: Security Services segment
margin: $148,000

Elimination of Unprofitable Segment Decision

P8. Security Services has two divisions: Basic Monitoring and Custom Monitoring. Rachel Sims, Custom's manager, wants to find out why the Custom Monitoring Division is not profitable. She has prepared the reports that follow.

Security Services
Segmented Income Statement
For the Year Ended December 31

	Basic Monitoring (1,000 locations)	Custom Monitoring (200 locations)	Total Company
Service revenue	$250,000	$100,000	$350,000
Less variable costs:			
Direct professional labor: design	$ 25,000	$ 40,000	$ 65,000
Direct professional labor: install	20,000	14,000	34,000
Direct professional labor: maintain	5,000	16,000	21,000
Total variable costs	$ 50,000	$ 70,000	$120,000
Contribution margin	$200,000	$ 30,000	$230,000
Less direct fixed costs:			
Depreciation on computer equipment	$ 6,000	$ 14,000	$ 20,000
Depreciation on servers	50,000	20,000	70,000
Total direct fixed costs	$ 56,000	$ 34,000	$ 90,000
Segment margin	$144,000	$ (4,000)	$140,000
Less common fixed costs:			
Building rent			$ 34,000
Supplies			2,000
Insurance			6,000
Telephone			2,500
Equipment rental			5,500
Total common fixed costs			$ 50,000
Operating income			$ 90,000

Security Services
Custom Monitoring Division
Segment Profitability Decision
Incremental Analysis

	Design	Install	Maintain	Total
Service revenue	$50,000	$25,000	$25,000	$100,000
Less variable costs	50,000	10,000	10,000	70,000
Contribution margin	$ 0.00	$15,000	$15,000	$ 30,000
Less direct fixed costs	8,000	13,000	13,000	34,000
Segment margin	$(8,000)	$ 2,000	$ 2,000	$ (4,000)

1. How will Security Services be affected if the Custom Monitoring Division is eliminated?
2. How will Security Services be affected if the Design segment of Custom Monitoring is eliminated?
3. **ACCOUNTING CONNECTION** ▶ What should Rachel Sims do? What additional information would be helpful to her in making the decision?

LO 5, 7

Sales Mix Decision

SPREADSHEET

P9. Dr. Stott, who specializes in internal medicine, wants to analyze his sales mix to find out how the time of his physician assistant, Connie Mortiz, can be used to generate the highest operating income.

✔ 1: Office visits contribution
margin per hour: $100
✔ 2: Three hours for office visits
✔ 2: Total daily contribution margin: $820

Mortiz sees patients in Dr. Stott's office, consults with patients over the telephone, and conducts one daily weight-loss support group attended by up to 50 patients. Statistics for the three services are as follows.

	Office Visits	Phone Calls	Weight-Loss Support Group
Maximum number of patient billings per day	20	40	50
Hours per billing	0.25	0.10	1.0
Billing rate	$50	$25	$10
Variable costs	$25	$12	$5

Mortiz works seven hours a day.

REQUIRED

1. Determine the best sales mix. Rank the services offered in order of their profitability.
2. Based on the ranking in requirement **1**, how much time should Mortiz spend on each service in a day? (*Hint:* Remember to consider the maximum number of patient billings per day.) What would be the daily total contribution margin generated by Mortiz?
3. Dr. Stott believes the ranking is incorrect. He knows that the daily 60-minute meeting of the weight-loss support group has 50 patients and should continue to be offered. If the new ranking for the services is (1) weight-loss support group, (2) phone calls, and (3) office visits, how much time should Mortiz spend on each service in a day? What would be the total contribution margin generated by Mortiz, assuming the weight-loss support group has the maximum number of patient billings?
4. **ACCOUNTING CONNECTION ▶** Which ranking would you recommend? What additional amount of total contribution margin would be generated if your recommendation were to be accepted?

LO **6, 7**

Sell-or-Process-Further Decision

✔ 1: Total costs for brochures: $26,200
✔ 2: Incremental loss to income: $2,400

P10. CU, Inc., developed a promotional program for a local shopping center a few years ago. Having invested $360,000 in developing the original promotion campaign, the firm is ready to present its client with an add-on contract offer that includes the original promotion areas of (1) a TV advertising campaign, (2) a series of brochures for mass mailing, and (3) a special rotating BIG SALE schedule for 10 of the 28 tenants in the shopping center. The revenue terms from the original contract with the shopping center and the offer for the add-on contract, which extends the original contract terms, follow.

	Original Contract Terms	Extended Contract Including Add-On Terms
TV advertising campaign	$520,000	$ 580,000
Brochure series	210,000	230,000
Rotating BIG SALE schedule	170,000	190,000
Totals	$900,000	$1,000,000

CU estimates that the following additional costs will be incurred by extending the contract:

	TV Campaign	Brochures	BIG SALE Schedule
Direct labor	$30,000	$ 9,000	$7,000
Variable overhead costs	22,000	14,000	6,000
Fixed overhead costs*	12,000	4,000	2,000

*80 percent are direct fixed costs applied to this contract.

(Continued)

REQUIRED

1. Compute the costs that will be incurred for each part of the add-on portion of the contract.

2. **ACCOUNTING CONNECTION** ▶ Should CU offer the add-on contract, or should it ask for a final settlement check based on the original contract only? Defend your answer.

3. **ACCOUNTING CONNECTION** ▶ If management of the shopping center indicates that the terms of the add-on contract are negotiable, how should CU respond?

CASES

LO 1, 7

Conceptual Understanding: Defining and Identifying Relevant Information

C1. BUSINESS APPLICATION ▶ Big Burgers is in the fast-food restaurant business. One component of its marketing strategy is to increase sales by expanding in foreign markets. It uses both financial and nonfinancial quantitative and qualitative information when deciding whether to open restaurants abroad. Big decided to open a restaurant in Prague (Czech Republic) five years ago. The following information helped the managers in making that decision:

Financial Quantitative Information

- Operating information
- Estimated food, labor, and other operating costs (e.g., taxes, insurance, utilities, and supplies)
- Estimated selling price for each food item
- Capital investment information
- Cost of land, building, equipment, and furniture
- Financing options and amounts

Nonfinancial Quantitative Information

- Estimated daily number of customers, hamburgers to be sold, employees to work
- High-traffic time periods
- Income of people living in the area
- Ratio of population to number of restaurants in the market area
- Traffic counts in front of similar restaurants in the area

Qualitative Information

- Government regulations, taxes, duties, tariffs, political involvement in business operations
- Property ownership restrictions
- Site visibility
- Accessibility of store location
- Training process for local managers
- Hiring process for employees
- Local customs and practices

Big Burgers has hired you as a consultant and given you an income statement comparing the operating incomes of its five restaurants in Eastern Europe. You have noticed that the Prague location is operating at a loss (including unallocated fixed costs) and must decide whether to recommend closing that restaurant.

Review the information used in making the decision to open the restaurant. Identify the types of information that would also be relevant in deciding whether to close the restaurant. What additional information would be relevant in making your decision?

LO 1, 7

Group Activity: Identifying Relevant Decision Information

C2. BUSINESS APPLICATION ▶ Select two destinations for a one-week vacation, and gather information about them from brochures, magazines, travel agents, the Internet, and friends. Then list the relevant quantitative and qualitative information in order of its importance to your decision. Analyze the information, and select a destination.

Which factors were most important to your decision? Why? Which were least important? Why? How would the process of identifying relevant information differ if the president of your company asked you to prepare a budget for the next training meeting, to be held at a location of your choice?

Your instructor will divide the class into groups and ask each group to discuss this case. One student from each group will summarize his or her group's findings and debrief the entire class.

LO **6, 7**

Conceptual Understanding: Decision to Add a New Department

C3. *(CMA adapted)* Cakes Company's management is considering a proposal to install a third production department in its factory building. With the company's existing production setup, direct materials are processed through the Mixing Department to produce Materials A and B in equal proportions. The Shaping Department then processes Material A to yield Product C. Material B is sold as is at $20.25 per pound. Product C has a selling price of $100.00 per pound. There is a proposal to add a Baking Department to process Material B into Product D. It is expected that any quantity of Product D can be sold for $30.00 per pound.

Costs per pound under this proposal appear here.

	Mixing Department (Materials A and B)	Shaping Department (Product C)	Baking Department (Product D)
Costs from Mixing Department	—	$52.80	$13.20
Direct materials	$20.00	—	—
Direct labor	6.00	9.00	3.50
Variable overhead	4.00	8.00	4.00
Fixed overhead:			
Traceable (direct, avoidable)	2.25	2.25	1.80
Allocated (common, unavoidable)	0.75	0.75	0.75
Totals	$33.00	$72.80	$23.25

1. If sales and production levels are expected to remain constant in the foreseeable future, and there are no foreseeable alternative uses for the factory space, should Cakes Company add a Baking Department and produce Product D, if 100,000 pounds of D can be sold? Show calculations of incremental revenues and costs to support your answer.

2. **BUSINESS APPLICATION** ▶ List at least two qualitative reasons why Cakes Company may not want to install a Baking Department and produce Product D, even if this decision appears profitable.

3. **BUSINESS APPLICATION** ▶ List at least two qualitative reasons why Cakes Company may want to install a Baking Department and produce Product D, even if it appears that this decision is unprofitable.

Continuing Case: Cookie Company

C4. As the CEO of your cookie company, you are interested in how public companies with a segment that includes cookies report their operating results. Because public companies are required to report on their segments, it is possible to evaluate the performance of comparable segments of different companies.

Access the website of **Kraft Foods, Inc.,** which markets Nabisco cookies (www .kraftfoodscompany.com/About), and the website of **Kellogg Company**, which markets Keebler cookies (www.kelloggcompany.com). Find information about these companies' major segments. Which segments are comparable, and which are not comparable? Which segments of these companies do you think include their brand of cookies?

CHAPTER 10
Capital Investment Analysis

BUSINESS INSIGHT
Air Products and Chemicals, Inc.

Air Products and Chemicals, Inc., is an industrial producer of gases that are piped directly to steel mills and other factories from small unmanned gas plants located near customers. What makes Air Products and Chemicals competitive is its use of "lights-out" systems, which link the unmanned plants to the Internet so that managers can monitor operations at any time and from anywhere. Automated systems of this kind are expensive, and managers must carefully weigh the risks and rewards of investing in them.

1. **CONCEPT ▶** Why is the concept of cost-benefit important when making capital budgeting decisions?

2. **ACCOUNTING APPLICATION ▶** How does capital budgeting ensure a wise allocation of resources and minimize the risks involved in long-run decisions?

3. **BUSINESS APPLICATION ▶** Why is capital investment analysis critical for the business performance of a company like Air Products and Chemicals?

LEARNING OBJECTIVES

 Define *capital investment analysis*, and state why the concept of cost-benefit is important when making long-term investment decisions.

 Identify the types of projected costs and revenues used to evaluate alternatives for capital investment.

LO 3 Analyze capital investment proposals using the net present value method.

LO 4 Analyze capital investment proposals using the payback period method and the accounting rate-of-return method.

LO 5 Describe why capital investment analysis is critical for business success.

SECTION 1

CONCEPTS

CONCEPT

■ Cost-benefit

**RELEVANT
LEARNING OBJECTIVE**

LO 1 Define *capital
investment analysis*,
and state why the concept of
cost-benefit is important
when making long-term
investment decisions.

LO 1 Concepts Underlying Long-Term Decision Analysis

The concept of *cost-benefit* holds that the benefits to be gained from a course of action or alternative should be greater than the costs of providing it. Cost-benefit is an accounting convention or rule of thumb that supports long-run decision making. It considers both quantitative and qualitative cost and benefit measures to facilitate cost-benefit comparisons between alternatives for sound business decisions.

Capital investment decisions are decisions about when and how much to spend on capital facilities and other long-term projects. For example, **Air Products and Chemicals, Inc.**, will make decisions about installing new equipment, replacing old equipment, expanding service by renovating or adding to existing equipment, buying a building, or acquiring another company.

Capital Investment Analysis

Each decision made about a capital investment is vitally important because it involves a large amount of money and commits a company to a course of action for years to come. **Capital investment analysis** (or *capital budgeting*) involves the evaluation of alternative proposals for large capital investments, including considerations for financing the projects. Managers frequently follow six key steps when applying the cost-benefit concept to the capital budgeting process.

Step 1. Identify Capital Investment Needs Managers identify capital investment opportunities from past sales experience, changes in sources and quality of materials, employees' suggestions, bottlenecks caused by obsolete equipment, new production or distribution methods, or customer complaints. In addition, capital investment needs are identified through proposals to add new products to the product line, expand capacity in existing product lines, reduce production costs of existing products without altering operating levels, or automate existing production processes.

Step 2. Prepare Formal Requests for Capital Investments Each request includes a complete description of the investment under review; the reasons a new investment is needed; the alternative means of satisfying the need; the timing, estimated costs, and related cost savings of each alternative; and the investment's engineering specifications, if necessary.

Step 3. Conduct a Preliminary Screening Organizations that have a highly developed system for capital investment analysis require that all proposals go through preliminary screening. The purpose of preliminary screening is to ensure that the only proposals to receive serious review are those that both meet company strategic goals and produce the minimum rate of return set by management.

Step 4. Establish the Acceptance-Rejection Standard An acceptance-rejection standard may be expressed as a minimum rate of return or a minimum cash flow payback period. If the number of acceptable requests exceeds the funds available for capital investments, the proposals must be ranked according to their rates of return. Acceptance-rejection standards are used to identify projects that are expected to yield inadequate or marginal returns. They also identify proposed projects for which high product demand and high financial returns are expected.

Management can evaluate proposed capital investments using the net present value method, payback period method, and/or accounting rate-of-return method to determine whether the projects meet the minimum acceptance-rejection standard.

Step 5. Evaluate Proposals Proposals are evaluated by verifying decision variables and applying established proposal evaluation methods. The key decision variables are expected life, estimated cash flow, and investment cost. Three commonly used methods of evaluating proposed capital investments are: net present value method, payback period method, and accounting rate-of-return method. Using one or more evaluation methods and the minimum acceptance-rejection standard, management evaluates all proposals. Management will also consider qualitative factors, such as availability and training of employees, competition, anticipated future technological improvements, and the proposal's impact on other company operations.

Step 6. Make Capital Investment Decisions The proposals that meet the standards of the evaluation process are given to the appropriate manager for final review. When deciding which requests to implement, the manager must consider the funds available. The acceptable proposals are ranked, and the highest-ranking proposals are funded first. Often there will not be enough money to fund all proposals. The final capital investment budget is then prepared by allocating funds to the selected proposals.

The Minimum Rate of Return on Investment

Most companies set a **minimum rate of return** to guard their profitability, and any capital expenditure proposal that fails to produce that rate of return is automatically refused. The minimum rate of return is often referred to as a *hurdle rate*, because it is the rate that must be exceeded, or hurdled. If the return from a capital investment falls below the minimum rate of return, the funds can be used more profitably in another part of the organization. Projects that produce poor returns will ultimately have a negative effect on an organization's profitability.

Ranking Capital Investment Proposals Even after management evaluates and selects proposals under the minimum acceptance-rejection standard, there are often too many proposals to fund adequately. At that point, managers must rank the proposals according to their rates of return, or profitability, and begin a second selection process.

Suppose that **Air Products and Chemicals, Inc.**, has $4,500,000 to spend this year for capital improvements and that five acceptable proposals are competing for those funds. The company's current minimum rate of return is 18 percent, and it is considering the following proposals:

Project	Rate of Return	Capital Investment	Cumulative Investment
A	32%	$1,460,000	$1,460,000
B	30%	1,890,000	3,350,000
C	28%	460,000	3,810,000
D	24%	840,000	4,650,000
E	22%	580,000	5,230,000
Total		$5,230,000	

The proposals are listed in the order of their rates of return. As you can see, Projects A, B, and C have the highest rates of return and together will cost a total of $3,810,000. That leaves $690,000 in capital funds for other projects. Project D should be examined first to see if it could be implemented for $150,000 less. If not, then Project E should be selected. The selection of Projects A, B, C, and E means that $110,000 in capital funds will be uncommitted for the year.

APPLY IT!

The supervisor of one of the "lights out" facilities has $1,000,000 to spend on new lights out equipment to improve operations. How should the manager proceed if the company's current minimum rate of return is 16 percent and it is considering the following proposals?

Proposal	Rate of Return	Capital Investment
L	12%	$ 600,000
M	20%	900,000
N	18%	100,000
O	14%	800,000
P	15%	800,000
Total		$3,200,000

SOLUTION

The manager should proceed with proposals M and N since they have the highest rates of return over the 16% minimum and together will cost a total of $1,000,000.

TRY IT! SE1, SE2, E1A, E14A, E1B, E14B

SECTION 2   **ACCOUNTING APPLICATIONS**

CASH FLOW **LO 2** # Capital Investment Analysis Measures and Methods

When evaluating a proposed capital investment, managers must predict how the new asset will perform and how it will benefit the company.

Expected Benefits from a Capital Investment

Managers must measure and evaluate all the investment alternatives consistently. The measure of expected benefit depends on the method of analyzing capital investment alternatives. The benefits from a capital investment can be measured by net income and net cash flows and cost savings.

Net Income Net income is calculated in the usual way:

$$\text{Revenue} - \text{Expenses} = \text{Net Income}$$

Managers must determine the increases in net income that will result from each capital investment alternative.

Net Cash Flows and Cost Savings A more widely used measure of expected benefit is projected cash flows. **Net cash inflows** are the balance of increases in projected cash receipts over increases in projected cash payments resulting from a capital investment, computed as follows.

$$\frac{\text{Projected Capital Investment}}{\text{Cash Receipts}} - \frac{\text{Projected Capital Investment}}{\text{Cash Payments}} = \text{Net Cash Inflows}$$

In some cases, equipment replacement decisions involve situations in which revenues are the same among alternatives. In such cases, the benefits are measured by the **cost savings**, or the decrease in operating costs that will result from the proposed capital investments. Either net cash inflows or cost savings can be used as the basis for an evaluation, but the two measures should not be confused.

■   If the analysis involves cash receipts, net cash inflows are used.
■   If the analysis involves only cash outlays, cost savings are used.

Equal Versus Unequal Cash Flows

Projected cash flows may be the same for each year of an asset's life, or they may vary from year to year. Unequal annual cash flows are common and must be analyzed for each year of an asset's life. Proposed projects with equal annual cash flows require less detailed analysis.

Carrying Value of Assets

Carrying value (or *book value*) is the undepreciated portion of the original cost of a fixed asset—that is, the asset's cost less its accumulated depreciation. When a decision to replace an asset is being evaluated, the carrying value of the old asset is irrelevant because it is a past, or historical, cost and will not be altered by the decision. Net proceeds from the asset's sale or disposal are relevant, however, because the proceeds affect cash flows and may differ for each alternative.

Depreciation Expense and Income Taxes

Income taxes alter the amount and timing of cash flows of projects under consideration by for-profit companies. To assess the benefits of a capital project, a company must include the effects of taxes in its capital investment analyses. Corporate income tax rates vary and can change yearly.

Depreciation expense is deductible when determining income taxes.* Thus, depreciation expense influences the amount of income taxes that a company pays and can lead to significant tax savings.

To examine how taxes affect capital investment analysis, assume that **Air Products and Chemicals, Inc.**, has a tax rate of 30 percent. It is considering a capital project that will make the following annual contribution to operating income:

Cash revenues	$ 400,000
Cash expenses	(200,000)
Depreciation	(100,000)
Operating income before income taxes	$ 100,000
Income taxes at 30%	(30,000)
Operating income	$ 70,000

The net cash inflows for this project can be determined in either of two ways:

1. Net cash inflows—receipts and disbursements:

Revenues (cash inflows)	$400,000
Cash expenses (outflows)	(200,000)
Income taxes (outflows)	(30,000)
Net cash inflows	$170,000

2. Net cash inflows—income adjustment procedure:

Income after income taxes	$ 70,000
Add back noncash expenses (depreciation)	100,000
Less noncash revenues	—
Net cash inflows	$170,000

In both computations, the net cash inflows are $170,000, and the total effect of income taxes is to lower the net cash inflows by $30,000.

Disposal or Residual Values

Proceeds from the sale of an old asset are current cash inflows and are relevant to evaluating a proposed capital investment. Projected disposal or residual values of replacement equipment are also relevant because they represent future cash inflows and usually differ among alternatives. Remember that the *residual value* (or *disposal* or *salvage value*) of an asset will be received at the end of the asset's estimated life.

APPLY IT!

Palmer Company has a tax rate of 25 percent. It is considering a capital project that will make the following annual contribution to operating income:

Cash revenues	$ 500,000
Cash expenses	(300,000)
Depreciation	(150,000)
Operating income before income taxes	$ 50,000
Income taxes at 25%	(12,500)
Operating income	$ 37,500

1. Determine the net cash inflows for this project in two different ways. Are net cash flows the same under either approach?
2. What is the impact of income taxes on net cash flows?

SOLUTION

1. The net cash inflows for this project can be determined in two ways:

   (a)   Net cash inflows—receipts and disbursements:

Revenues (cash inflows)	$500,000
Cash expenses (outflows)	(300,000)
Income taxes (outflows)	(12,500)
Net cash inflows	$187,500

   (b)   Net cash inflows—income adjustment procedure

Income after income taxes	$ 37,500
Add back noncash expenses (depreciation)	150,000
Less noncash revenues	—
Net cash inflows	$187,500

In both computations, the net cash inflows are $187,500.

2. The total effect of income taxes is to lower the net cash inflows by $12,500.

TRY IT! SE3, E2A, E2B

---

* You may recall that the annual depreciation expense computation using the straight-line method is the asset's cost less its residual value, divided by the asset's useful life.

LO3 The Net Present Value Method

A variety of methods can help managers make cost-benefit decisions about when and how much to spend on capital facilities and other long-term projects. One of the most popular methods is the *net present value method*. The net present value method incorporates the time value of money, which is discussed in Appendix A. You may wish to review this material prior to reading further.

The **net present value method** evaluates a capital investment by discounting its future cash flows to their present values and subtracting the amount of the initial investment from their sum, as follows.

Net Present Value = Present Value of Future Net Cash Inflows − Cost of Investment

All proposed capital investments are evaluated in the same way, and the projects with the highest net present value—the amount that exceeds the initial investment—are selected for implementation.

Advantages of the Net Present Value Method

A significant advantage of the net present value method is that it incorporates the time value of money into the analysis of proposed capital investments. Future cash inflows and outflows are discounted by the company's minimum rate of return to determine their present values. The minimum rate of return should at least equal the company's average cost of capital.

When dealing with the time value of money, use discounting to find the present value of an amount to be received in the future. To determine the present values of future amounts of money, use Tables 1 and 2 in Appendix A. Remember that Table 1 deals with a single payment or amount and Table 2 is used for a series of equal periodic amounts. Tables 1 and 2 are used to discount each future cash inflow and cash outflow over the life of the asset to the present.

- If the net present value is positive (the total of the discounted net cash inflows exceeds the cash investment at the beginning), the rate of return on the investment will exceed the company's minimum rate of return, or hurdle rate, and the project can be accepted.
- If the net present value is negative (the cash investment at the beginning exceeds the discounted net cash inflows), the return on the investment is less than the minimum rate of return and the project should be rejected.
- If the net present value is zero (if discounted cash inflows equal discounted cash outflows), the project meets the minimum rate of return and can be accepted.

The Net Present Value Method Illustrated

Suppose that **Air Products and Chemicals, Inc.**, is considering the purchase of a new "lights out" unit. The company's minimum rate of return is 16 percent. Management must decide between two models.

- Model M costs $17,500 and will have an estimated residual value of $2,000 after five years. It is projected to produce cash inflows of $6,000, $5,500, $5,000, $4,500, and $4,000 during its five-year life.
- Model N costs $21,000 and will have an estimated residual value of $2,000. It is projected to produce cash inflows of $6,000 per year for five years.

Model M Analysis Because Model M is expected to produce unequal cash inflows, Table 1 in Appendix A is used to determine the present value of each cash inflow from each year of the machine's life. The net present value of Model M is determined as follows.

Model M

Year	Net Cash Inflows	16% Factor	Present Value
1	$6,000	0.862	$ 5,172.00
2	5,500	0.743	4,086.50
3	5,000	0.641	3,205.00
4	4,500	0.552	2,484.00
5	4,000	0.476	1,904.00
Residual value	2,000	0.476	952.00
Total present value of cash inflows			$17,803.50
Less purchase price of Model M			17,500.00
Net present value			$ 303.50

All the factors for this analysis can be found in the column for 16 percent in Table 1. The factors are used to discount the individual cash flows, including the expected residual value, to the present. The amount of the investment in Model M is deducted from the total present value of the cash inflows to arrive at the net present value of $303.50. Since the entire investment of $17,500 in Model M is a cash outflow at the beginning— that is, at time zero—no discounting of the $17,500 purchase price is necessary. Because the net present value is positive, the proposed investment in Model M will achieve at least the minimum rate of return.

Model N Analysis Because Model N is expected to produce equal cash receipts in each year of its useful life, Table 2 in Appendix A is used to determine the combined present value of those future cash inflows. However, Table 1 is used to determine the present value of the machine's residual value because it represents a single payment, not an annuity. The net present value of Model N is calculated as follows.

Model N

Year	Net Cash Inflows	16% Factor	Present Value
1–5	$6,000	3.274	$19,644.00
Residual value	2,000	0.476	952.00
Total present value of cash inflows			$20,596.00
Less purchase price of Model N			21,000.00
Net present value			$ (404.00)

Table 2 is used to determine the factor of 3.274 (found in the column for 16 percent and the row for five periods). Because the residual value is a single inflow in the fifth year, the factor of 0.476 must be taken from Table 1 (the column for 16 percent and the row for five periods). The result is a net present value of ($404). Because the net present value is negative, the proposed investment in Model N will not achieve the minimum rate of return and should be rejected.

Analysis Recap The two analyses show that Model M should be chosen because it has a positive net present value and would exceed the company's minimum rate of return. Model M is the better choice because it is expected to produce cash inflows sooner and will thus produce a proportionately greater present value.

Business Perspective
What Is Total Cost of Ownership, and Why Is It Important?

The concept of total cost of ownership (TCO) was developed to determine the total lifetime costs of owning an information technology (IT) asset, such as a computer system. TCO includes both the direct and indirect costs associated with the acquisition, deployment, operation, support, and retirement of the asset. Today, TCO is the industry standard for evaluating and comparing the costs associated with long-lived asset acquisitions. For example, if you buy a printer, TCO includes the direct costs of buying the printer, the annual supplies costs of ink and paper, and the indirect costs of maintaining it. Thus, the decision about which printer to buy is not based solely on the cost of the printer, but on all costs related to it over its useful lifetime.

APPLY IT!

Woods Communications, Inc., is considering purchasing a new piece of data transmission equipment. Estimated annual net cash inflows for the new equipment are $575,000. The equipment costs $2 million, has a five-year life, and will have no residual value at the end of the five years. The company's minimum rate of return is 12 percent. Compute the net present value of the equipment. Should the company purchase it?

SOLUTION

Net Present Value = Present Value of Future Net Cash Inflows − Cost of Equipment

$$= (\$575{,}000 \times 3.605^*) - \$2{,}000{,}000$$

$$= \$2{,}072{,}875 - \$2{,}000{,}000$$

$$= \underline{\$72{,}875}$$

*From Table 1 in Appendix A.

The solution is positive, so the company should purchase the equipment. A positive answer means that the investment will yield more than the minimum 12 percent return required by the company.

TRY IT! SE4, SE5, SE6, SE7, E3A, E4A, E5A, E6A, E7A, E8A, E3B, E4B, E5B, E6B, E7B, E8B

LO4 Other Methods of Capital Investment Analysis

STUDY NOTE: *Payback period is expressed in time, net present value is expressed in money, and accounting rate of return is expressed as a percentage.*

CASH FLOW

STUDY NOTE: *The payback period method measures the estimated length of time necessary to recover in cash the cost of an investment.*

The net present value method is the best method for capital investment analysis. However, two other commonly used methods are the payback period method and the accounting rate-of-return method.

The Payback Period Method

Because cash is an essential measure of a business's health, many managers estimate the cash flow that an investment will generate. Their goal is to determine the minimum time it will take to recover the initial investment. If two investment alternatives are being studied, management should choose the investment that pays back its initial cost in the shorter time. That period of time is known as the *payback period*, and the method of evaluation is called the **payback period method**. The payback period method is simple to use, but it does not consider the time value of money.

Payback Calculation The payback period is computed as follows.

$$\text{Payback Period} = \frac{\text{Cost of Investment}}{\text{Annual Net Cash Inflows}}$$

Suppose that **Air Products and Chemicals, Inc.**, is interested in purchasing a new server that costs $51,000 and has a residual value of $3,000. Assume that estimates for the proposal include revenue increases of $17,900 a year and operating cost increases of $11,696 a year (including depreciation and taxes). To evaluate this proposed capital investment, use the following steps.

Step 1 Determine the cost of the investment. For Air Products and Chemicals, it is $51,000.

Step 2 Determine the annual net cash inflows, which are the annual cash revenues minus the cash expenses. Eliminate the effects of all noncash revenue and expense items included in the analysis of net income to determine cash revenues and cash expenses. In this case, the only noncash expense or revenue is machine depreciation. To eliminate it from operating expenses, you must first calculate depreciation expense. To calculate this amount, you must know the asset's life and the depreciation method. Suppose Air Products and Chemicals uses the straight-line method of depreciation, and the new server will have a ten-year service life. The annual depreciation is computed as follows.

$$\text{Annual Depreciation} = \frac{\text{Cost} - \text{Residual Value}}{\text{Years}}$$

$$= \frac{\$51{,}000 - \$3{,}000}{10 \text{ Years}}$$

$$= \underline{\$4{,}800} \text{ per year}$$

Thus, cash expenses are equal to the operating cost of $11,696 reduced by the depreciation expense of $4,800, or $6,896. The annual net cash inflows are $11,004, or cash revenue increases of $17,900 less cash expenses of $6,896.

Step 3 Compute the payback period.

$$\text{Payback Period} = \frac{\text{Cost of Machine}}{\text{Cash Revenue} - \text{Cash Expenses}}$$

$$= \frac{\$51{,}000}{\$17{,}900 - (\$11{,}696 - \$4{,}800)}$$

$$= \frac{\$51{,}000}{\$11{,}004}$$

$$= \underline{4.6} \text{ years*}$$

*Rounded

If the company's desired payback period is five years or less, this proposal would be approved.

Unequal Annual Net Cash Inflows If a proposed capital investment has unequal annual net cash inflows, the payback period is determined as follows.

$$\text{Payback Period} = \text{Cost of Investment} - \text{Unequal Annual Net Cash Inflows*}$$

*In chronological order until a zero balance is reached.

When a zero balance is reached, the payback period has been determined. This will often occur in the middle of a year. The portion of the final year is computed by dividing the amount needed to reach zero (the unrecovered portion of the investment) by the entire year's estimated cash inflow.

Advantages and Disadvantages The payback period method is especially useful in areas in which technology changes rapidly, such as in Internet companies, and when risk is high, such as when investing in emerging countries. However, this approach has several disadvantages:

- The payback period method does not measure profitability.
- It ignores differences in the present values of cash flows from different periods; thus, it does not adjust cash flows for the time value of money.
- The payback period method emphasizes the time it takes to recover the investment rather than the long-term return on the investment.
- It ignores all future cash flows after the payback period is reached.

The Accounting Rate-of-Return Method

The **accounting rate-of-return method** is an imprecise but easy way to measure the estimated performance of a capital investment, since it uses financial statement information.

This method does not use an investment's cash flows but considers the financial reporting effects of the investment instead. The accounting rate-of-return method measures expected performance using two variables: the estimated annual net income from the project and average investment cost.

Accounting Rate-of-Return Calculation The basic equation follows.

$$\text{Accounting Rate of Return} = \frac{\text{Average Annual Net Income}}{\text{Average Investment Cost}}$$

Step 1 Compute the average annual net income. Use the cost and revenue data prepared for evaluating the project—that is, revenues minus operating expenses (including depreciation and taxes).

Step 2 Compute the average investment cost in a proposed capital facility as follows.

$$\text{Average Investment Cost} = \left(\frac{\text{Total Investment} - \text{Residual Value}}{2} \right) + \text{Residual Value}$$

Step 3 Compute the accounting rate of return. For example, assume the same facts as before for Air Products and Chemicals' interest in purchasing a server. Also assume that the company's management will consider only projects that promise to yield more than a 16 percent return. To determine if the company should invest in the machine, compute the accounting rate of return as follows.

$$\text{Accounting Rate of Return} = \frac{\$17,900 - \$11,696}{\left(\dfrac{\$51,000 - \$3,000}{2} \right) + \$3,000}$$

$$= \underline{23\%^*}$$

*Rounded

The projected rate of return is higher than the 16 percent minimum, so management should think seriously about making the investment.

Advantages and Disadvantages The accounting rate-of-return method is easy to understand and apply. However, it has several disadvantages.

- Because net income is averaged over the life of the investment, it is not a reliable figure, as actual net income may vary considerably from the estimates.
- It ignores cash flows.
- It does not consider the time value of money; thus, future and present dollars are treated as equal.

APPLY IT!

Part One: Payback Period Method
Segovia, Inc., is considering purchasing new data transmission equipment. Estimated annual net cash inflows from the new equipment are $575,000. The equipment costs $2 million and will have no residual value at the end of its five-year life. Compute the payback period for the equipment. Does this method yield a positive or negative response to the proposal to buy the equipment, assuming that the company has set a maximum payback period of four years?

Part Two: Accounting Rate-of-Return Method
Conaton, Inc., is considering whether to purchase a delivery truck that will cost $26,000, last six years, and have an estimated residual value of $6,000. Average annual net income from the delivery truck is estimated at $4,000. The company's owners want to earn an accounting rate of return of 20 percent. Compute the average investment cost and the accounting rate of return. Should the company make the investment?

SOLUTION

Part One: Payback Period Method

Payback Period = Cost of Investment ÷ Annual Net Cash Inflows

= $2,000,000 ÷ $575,000

= 3.5 years*

*Rounded

The piece of equipment should be purchased because its payback period is less than the company's maximum payback period of 4 years.

TRY IT! SE8, SE9, E9A, E9B

Part Two: Accounting Rate-of-Return Method

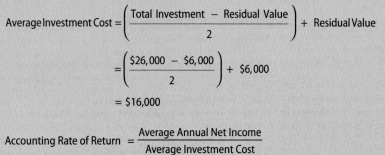

$$\text{Average Investment Cost} = \left(\frac{\text{Total Investment} - \text{Residual Value}}{2} \right) + \text{Residual Value}$$

$$= \left(\frac{\$26,000 - \$6,000}{2} \right) + \$6,000$$

$$= \$16,000$$

$$\text{Accounting Rate of Return} = \frac{\text{Average Annual Net Income}}{\text{Average Investment Cost}}$$

$$= \frac{\$4,000}{\$16,000}$$

$$= 25\%$$

The project will exceed the desired return of 20% and should be undertaken.

TRY IT! SE10, E10A, E11A, E12A, E13A, E10B, E11B, E12B, E13B

BUSINESS APPLICATIONS

LO5 The Management Process

Once a capital investment decision has been made, the implementation of the project is critical to its success. A project must be scheduled, and its development, construction, or purchase must be overseen. Controls must be established to make sure the project is completed on time, within budget, and at the desired level of quality. Upon completion, the project should be audited to determine if it is meeting the company's goals and targets set forth in the planning phase. Finally, to communicate results, project reports should be prepared and distributed within the organization. These reports should include comparisons of budgeted expenditures and actual expenditures.

Managers use quantitative and qualitative information to analyze the effects of capital investment decisions on their organization's resources and profits. Although many capital budgeting problems are unique and cannot be solved by following strict rules, managers often use the present value, payback, and accounting rate-of-return methods. Exhibit 1 summarizes the tools and methods managers use to ensure a wise allocation of resources, to make sound, ethical decisions that will enhance customers' and other stakeholders' value, to earn a profit, and to minimize business risks.

Exhibit 1
Capital Investment Analysis and the Management Process

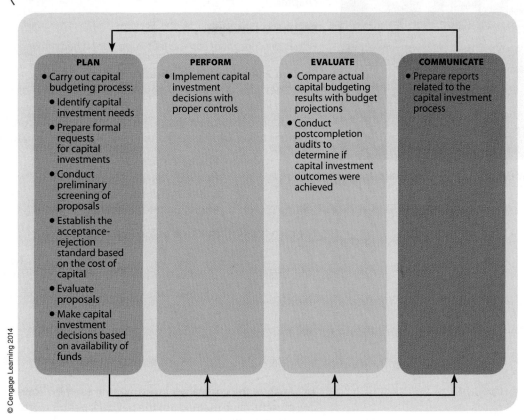

© Cengage Learning 2014

APPLY IT!

Arrange the steps of the capital budgeting process in their proper order:

a. Identify capital investment needs
b. Conduct preliminary screening of proposals
c. Evaluate proposals
d. Prepare formal requests for capital investments
e. Make decisions based on availability of funds
f. Establish the acceptance-rejection standard based on the cost of capital

SOLUTION

1. a; 2. d; 3. b; 4. f; 5. c; and 6. e

TRY IT! E14A, E14B

TriLevel Problem

Air Products and Chemicals, Inc.

Keith Wood/Corbis

The beginning of this chapter focused on **Air Products and Chemicals, Inc.,** Complete the following requirements in order to answer the questions posed at the beginning of the chapter.

Section 1: Concepts
Why is the concept of cost-benefit important when making capital budgeting decisions?

Section 2: Accounting Applications
How does capital budgeting ensure a wise allocation of resources and minimize the risks involved in long-run decisions?

Suppose that Air Products and Chemicals, Inc., is considering building a new communications tower and has gathered the following information:

Purchase price	$600,000
Residual value	$100,000
Desired payback period	3 years
Minimum rate of return	15%

The cash flow estimates are as follows.

Year	Cash Inflows	Cash Outflows	Net Cash Inflows	Projected Net Income
1	$ 500,000	$260,000	$240,000	$115,000
2	450,000	240,000	210,000	85,000
3	400,000	220,000	180,000	55,000
4	350,000	200,000	150,000	25,000
Totals	$1,700,000	$920,000	$780,000	$280,000

1. Analyze the company's investment in the new tower. In your analysis, use (a) the net present value method, (b) the payback period method, and (c) the accounting rate-of-return method.

2. Summarize your findings from requirement 1, and recommend a course of action.

Section 3: Business Applications

Why is capital investment analysis critical for the business performance of a company like Air Products and Chemicals?

To answer this question, match this chapter's managerial responsibilities with when they occur within the management process.

a. Plan
b. Perform
c. Evaluate
d. Communicate

1. Implement capital investment decision with proper controls
2. Carry out capital budgeting process
3. Compare actual capital budgeting results with budget projections
4. Prepare reports related to the capital investment process
5. Conduct postcompletion audits to determine if capital investment outcomes were achieved

SOLUTION

Section 1: Concepts

The concept of *cost-benefit* is used to evaluate long-run decisions so that the benefits to be gained from a course of action or alternative can be compared to the costs of providing it. For an alternative to be feasible, its benefits must outweigh its costs. Cost-benefit is an accounting convention or rule of thumb that considers both quantitative and qualitative cost and benefit measures to facilitate comparisons between alternatives for sound business decisions.

Section 2: Accounting Applications

1. (a) Net present value method (factors are from Table 1 in Appendix A):

Year	Net Cash Inflows	Present Value Factor	Present Value
1	$240,000	0.870	$208,800
2	210,000	0.756	158,760
3	180,000	0.658	118,440
4	150,000	0.572	85,800
4	100,000 (residual value)	0.572	57,200
Total present value			$629,000
Less cost of original investment			600,000
Net present value			$ 29,000

(b) Payback period method:

Total cash investment		$ 600,000
Less cash flow recovery:		
Year 1	$240,000	
Year 2	210,000	
Year 3 (10/12 of $180,000)	150,000	(600,000)
Unrecovered investment		$ 0

Payback period: 2 years, 10 months, or 2.833 years

(c) Accounting rate-of-return method:

$$\text{Accounting Rate of Return} = \frac{\text{Average Annual Net Income}}{\text{Average Investment Cost}}$$

$$= \frac{\$280,000 \div 4}{\left(\dfrac{\$600,000 - \$100,000}{2}\right) + \$100,000}$$

$$= \frac{\$70,000}{\$350,000}$$

$$= 0.20 = 20\%$$

2.   Summary of decision analysis:

	Decision Measures	
	Desired	Calculated
Net present value	—	$29,000
Accounting rate of return	15%	20%
Payback period	3 years	2.833 years

Based on the calculations in requirement **1**, the company should invest in the communication tower.

Section 3: Business Applications

1. b   4. d

2. a   5. c

3. c

Chapter Review

Define *capital investment analysis*, and state why the concept of cost-benefit is important when making long-term investment decisions. LO 1	The concept of cost-benefit considers both quantitative and qualitative cost and benefit measures to facilitate comparisons between alternatives for sound business decisions. Capital investment analysis, or capital budgeting, consists of identifying the need for a capital investment, analyzing courses of action to meet that need, preparing reports for management, choosing the best alternative, and dividing funds among competing resource needs. The minimum rate of return, or hurdle rate, is used as a screening mechanism to eliminate from further consideration capital investment requests with anticipated inadequate returns.
Identify the types of projected costs and revenues used to evaluate alternatives for capital investment. LO 2	The accounting rate-of-return method requires measures of net income. Other methods evaluate net cash inflows or cost savings. The analysis process must take into consideration whether each period's cash flows will be equal or unequal. Unless the after-income-tax effects on cash flows are being considered, carrying values and depreciation expense of assets awaiting replacement are irrelevant. Net proceeds from the sale of an old asset and estimated residual value of a new facility represent future cash flows and must be a part of the estimated benefit of a project. Depreciation expense on replacement equipment is relevant to evaluations based on after-income-tax cash flows.
Analyze capital investment proposals using the net present value method. LO 3	The net present value method incorporates the time value of money into the analysis of a proposed capital investment. A minimum required rate of return is used to discount an investment's expected future cash flows to their present values. The present values are added together, and the amount of the initial investment is subtracted from their total. If the resulting amount, called the net present value, is positive, the rate of return on the investment will exceed the required rate of return, and the investment should be accepted. If the net present value is negative, the return on the investment will be less than the minimum rate of return, and the investment should be rejected.
Analyze capital investment proposals using the payback period method and the accounting rate-of-return method. LO 4	The payback period method of evaluating a capital investment focuses on the minimum length of time needed to get the amount of the initial investment back in cash. The accounting rate-of-return method requires measures of net income. With the accounting rate-of-return method, managers evaluate two or more capital investment proposals and then select the alternative that yields the highest ratio of average annual net income to average cost of investment. Both of these methods are very rough measures that do not consider the time value of money. As a result, the net present value method is preferred.

<table>
<tr><td>Describe why capital investment analysis is critical for business success.</td><td>LO 5</td><td>Managers often use the present value, payback, and accounting rate-of-return methods during the management process as they plan, perform, evaluate, and report on business operations. They utilize these capital budgeting tools to ensure a wise allocation of resources, to make sound, ethical decisions that will enhance customers' and other stakeholders' value, to earn a profit, and to minimize business risks.</td></tr>
</table>

Key Terms

accounting rate-of-return
  method 374 (LO4)
capital investment
  analysis 366 (LO1)

capital investment
  decisions 366 (LO1)
carrying value 369 (LO2)
cost savings 369 (LO2)

minimum rate of return 367 (LO1)
net cash inflows 369 (LO2)
net present value method 371 (LO3)
payback period method 373 (LO4)

Chapter Assignments

DISCUSSION QUESTIONS

LO 1, 5   **DQ1. CONCEPT ▶ BUSINESS APPLICATION ▶** How do managers use the concept of cost-benefit for capital budgeting decisions during the planning phase of the management process?

LO 1, 5   **DQ2. CONCEPT ▶ BUSINESS APPLICATION ▶** How do managers use the concept of cost-benefit for capital budgeting decisions during the performing phase of the management process?

LO 1, 5   **DQ3. CONCEPT ▶ BUSINESS APPLICATION ▶** How do managers use the concept of cost-benefit for capital budgeting decisions during the evaluating phase of the management process?

LO 1, 5   **DQ4. CONCEPT ▶ BUSINESS APPLICATION ▶** How do managers use the concept of cost-benefit for capital budgeting decisions during the communicating phase of the management process?

SHORT EXERCISES

LO 1   **Manager's Role in Capital Investment Decisions**

SE1. The Logistics Department's supervisor has suggested to the plant manager that a new machine costing $285,000 be purchased to improve material handling operations for the plant's newest product line. How should the plant manager proceed with this request?

LO 1   **Ranking Capital Investment Proposals**

SE2. ACCOUNTING CONNECTION ▶ Zelolo Corp. has the following capital investment requests pending from its three divisions:

Project Request	Capital Investment	Projected Rate of Return
Request 1	$ 60,000	11%
Request 2	110,000	14%
Request 3	130,000	16%
Request 4	160,000	13%
Request 5	175,000	12%
Request 6	230,000	15%

(Continued)

Zelolo's minimum rate of return is 13 percent, and $500,000 is available for capital investment this year. Which requests will be honored, and in what order? Explain your answer.

LO 2   **Capital Investment Analysis and Revenue Measures**

SE3. ACCOUNTING CONNECTION ▶ Admiralty Corporation is analyzing a proposal to switch its factory over to a lights-out operation. To do so, it must acquire a fully auto-mated machine. The machine will be able to produce an entire product line in a single operation. Projected annual net cash inflows from the machine are $180,000, and pro-jected net income is $120,000. Why is the projected net income lower than the pro-jected net cash inflows? Identify possible causes for the $60,000 difference.

LO 3   **Net Present Value Method**

SE4. ACCOUNTING CONNECTION ▶ Sandcastles, Inc.'s management has recently been looking at a proposal to purchase a new brick molding machine. With the new machine, the company would not have to buy bricks. The estimated useful life of the machine is 15 years, and the purchase price, including all setup charges, is $400,000. The residual value is estimated to be $40,000. The net addition to the company's cash inflow as a result of the savings from making the bricks is estimated to be $70,000 a year. Sandcas-tle's management has decided on a minimum rate of return of 14 percent. Using the net present value method to evaluate this capital investment, determine whether the com-pany should purchase the machine. Support your answer. (*Hint:* Use Tables 1 and 2 in Appendix A.)

LO 3   **Net Present Value Method**

SE5. ACCOUNTING CONNECTION ▶ Noway Jose Communications, Inc., is considering pur-chasing a new piece of computerized data transmission equipment. Estimated annual net cash inflows for the new equipment are $590,000. The equipment costs $2 million, it has a five-year life, and it will have no residual value at the end of the five years. The company has a minimum rate of return of 12 percent. Compute the net present value of the piece of equipment. Should the company purchase it? Why?. (*Hint:* Use Table 2 in Appendix A.)

LO 4   **Payback Period Method**

SE6. Refer to the information in **SE5** for Noway Jose Communications, Inc. Compute the payback period for the piece of equipment. (Round to one decimal place.) Does this method yield a positive or a negative response to the proposal to buy the equipment, assuming that the company sets a maximum payback period of four years?

LO 4   **Payback Period Method**

SE7. ACCOUNTING CONNECTION ▶ Territories Cable, Inc., is considering purchasing new data transmission equipment. Estimated annual cash revenues for the new equip-ment are $1 million, and operating costs (including depreciation of $400,000) are $825,000. The equipment costs $2 million, it has a five-year life, and it will have no residual value at the end of the five years. Compute the payback period for the piece of equipment. (Round to one decimal place.) Does this method yield a positive or a nega-tive response to the proposal to buy the equipment if the company has set a maximum payback period of four years? Explain your answer.

LO 4   **Accounting Rate-of-Return Method**

SE8. Doorstep Cleaners is considering whether to purchase a delivery truck that will cost $50,000, last six years, and have an estimated residual value of $5,000. Average annual net income from the delivery service is estimated to be $4,000. Doorstep Cleaners' owners seek to earn an accounting rate of return of 10 percent. Compute the average investment cost and the accounting rate of return. (Round percentages to one decimal place.) Should the investment be made?

LO 3 **Residual Value and Present Value**

SE9. Annelle Coiner is developing a capital investment analysis for her supervisor. The proposed capital investment has an estimated residual value of $5,500 at the end of its five-year life. The company uses an 8 percent minimum rate of return. What is the present value of the residual value? (Round to the nearest dollar.) (*Hint:* Use Table 1 in Appendix A.)

LO 3 **Time Value of Money**

SE10. ACCOUNTING CONNECTION ▶ Sherry Rudd recently inherited a trust fund from a distant relative. On January 2, the bank managing the trust fund notified Rudd that she has the option of receiving a lump-sum check for $200,000 or leaving the money in the trust fund and receiving an annual year-end check for $20,000 for each of the next 20 years. Rudd likes to earn at least a 5 percent return on her investments. What should she do?

EXERCISES: SET A

LO 1 **Ranking Capital Investment Proposals**

E1A. Emerald Bay Furniture Company's managers have gathered all of the capital investment proposals for the year, and they are ready to make their final selections. The following proposals and related rate-of-return amounts were received during the period:

Project	Capital Investment	Rate of Return
AB	$ 450,000	19%
CD	500,000	28%
EF	654,000	12%
GH	800,000	32%
IJ	320,000	23%
KL	240,000	18%
MN	180,000	16%
OP	400,000	26%
QR	560,000	14%
ST	1,200,000	22%
UV	1,600,000	20%

Assume that the company's minimum rate of return is 15 percent and that $5,000,000 is available for capital investments during the year.

1. List the acceptable capital investment proposals in order of profitability.
2. **ACCOUNTING CONNECTION** ▶ Which proposals should be selected for this year? Why?

LO 2 **Income Taxes and Net Cash Flow**

CASH FLOW

E2A. Santa Rita Company has a tax rate of 20 percent on taxable income. It is considering a capital project that will make the following annual contribution to operating income:

Cash revenues	$ 360,000
Cash expenses	(160,000)
Depreciation	(140,000)
Operating income before income taxes	$ 60,000
Income taxes at 20%	(12,000)
Operating income	$ 48,000

1. Determine the net cash inflows for this project in two different ways. Are net cash inflows the same under either approach?
2. What is the impact of income taxes on net cash inflows?

LO 3   **Using the Present Value Tables**

E3A. For each of the following situations, identify the correct factor to use from Tables 1 or 2 in Appendix A. Also, compute the appropriate present value.

1. Annual net cash inflows of $10,000 for five years, discounted at 6 percent
2. An amount of $20,000 to be received at the end of ten years, discounted at 4 percent
3. The amount of $10,000 to be received at the end of two years, and $7,000 to be received at the end of years 4, 5, and 6, discounted at 10 percent

LO 3   **Using the Present Value Tables**

E4A. For each of the following situations, identify the correct factor to use from Tables 1 or 2 in Appendix A. Also, compute the appropriate present value.

1. Annual net cash inflows of $22,500 for a period of twelve years, discounted at 14 percent
2. The following five years of cash inflows, discounted at 10 percent:

Year 1	$35,000	Year 4	$40,000
Year 2	20,000	Year 5	50,000
Year 3	30,000		

3. The amount of $70,000 to be received at the beginning of year 7, discounted at 14 percent

LO 3   **Net Present Value Method**

E5A. Tuen and Associates wants to buy an automated coffee roaster/grinder/brewer. This piece of equipment would have a useful life of six years, would cost $190,000, and would increase annual net cash inflows by $50,000. Assume that there is no residual value at the end of six years. The company's minimum rate of return is 14 percent. Using the net present value method, prepare an analysis to determine whether the company should purchase the machine. (*Hint:* Use Tables 1 and 2 in Appendix A.)

LO 3   **Net Present Value Method**

E6A. ACCOUNTING CONNECTION ▶ Full Service Station is planning to invest in automatic car wash equipment valued at $210,000. The owner estimates that the equipment will increase annual net cash inflows by $40,000. The equipment is expected to have a ten-year useful life with an estimated residual value of $20,000. The company requires a 14 percent minimum rate of return. Using the net present value method, prepare an analysis to determine whether the company should purchase the equipment. How important is the estimate of residual value to this decision? (*Hint:* Use Tables 1 and 2 in Appendix A.)

LO 3   **Net Present Value Method**

E7A. Assume the same facts for Full Service Station as in **E6A,** except that the company requires a 20 percent minimum rate of return. Using the net present value method, prepare an analysis to determine whether the company should purchase the equipment. (*Hint:* Use Tables 1 and 2 in the Appendix A.)

LO 3   **Present Value Computations**

E8A. Two machines—Machine M and Machine P—are being considered in a replacement decision. Both machines have about the same purchase price and an estimated ten-year life. The company uses a 12 percent minimum rate of return as its acceptance-rejection standard. The estimated net cash inflows for each machine follow.

Year	Machine M	Machine P
1	$12,000	$17,500
2	12,000	17,500
3	14,000	17,500
4	19,000	17,500
5	20,000	17,500
6	22,000	17,500
7	23,000	17,500
8	24,000	17,500
9	25,000	17,500
10	20,000	17,500
Residual value	14,000	12,000

1. Compute the present value of future cash flows for each machine, using Tables 1 and 2 in Appendix A.
2. Which machine should the company purchase, assuming that both involve the same capital investment?

LO 4   **Payback Period Method**

E9A. Eco Wet, Inc., a manufacturer of gears for lawn sprinklers, is thinking about adding a new fully automated machine. This machine can produce gears that the company now produces on its third shift. The machine has an estimated useful life of ten years and will cost $500,000. The residual value of the new machine is $50,000. Gross cash revenue from the machine will be about $420,000 per year, and related operating expenses, including depreciation, should total $400,000. Depreciation is estimated to be $80,000 annually. The payback period should be five years or less. Use the payback period method to determine whether the company should invest in the new machine. Show the computations that support your answer.

LO 4   **Accounting Rate-of-Return Method**

E10A. Assume the same facts as in **E9A** for Eco Wet, Inc. Management has decided that only capital investments that yield at least an 8 percent return will be accepted. Using the accounting rate-of-return method, decide whether the company should invest in the machine. (Round percentages to one decimal place.) Show the computations that support your decision.

LO 4   **Accounting Rate-of-Return Method**

E11A. Sound Perfection, Inc., a manufacturer of stereo speakers, is thinking about adding a new machine. This machine can produce speaker parts that the company now buys from outsiders. The machine has an estimated useful life of 14 years and will cost $450,000. The residual value of the new machine is $50,000. Gross cash revenue from the machine will be about $300,000 per year, and related cash expenses should total $210,000. Depreciation is estimated to be $30,000 annually. Sound Perfection's management has decided that only capital investments that yield at least a 20 percent return will be accepted. Using the accounting rate-of-return method, decide whether the company should invest in the machine. Show the computations that support your decision.

LO 4   **Accounting Rate-of-Return Method**

E12A. Assume the same facts as in **E11A** for Sound Perfection, Inc. Management has decided that only capital investments that yield at least a 25 percent return will be

(Continued)

accepted. Using the accounting rate-of-return method, decide whether the company should invest in the machine. Show the computations that support your decision.

LO **4**   ## Accounting Rate-of-Return Method

E13A. Boink Corporation manufactures metal hard hats for on-site construction workers. Recently, management has tried to raise productivity to meet the growing demand from the real estate industry. The company is now thinking about buying a new stamping machine. Management has decided that only capital investments that yield at least a 14 percent return will be accepted. The new machine would cost $325,000, revenue would increase by $98,400 per year, the residual value of the new machine would be $32,500, and operating cost increases (including depreciation) would be $75,000. Using the accounting rate-of-return method, decide whether the company should invest in the machine. (Round percentages to one decimal place.) Show the computations that support your decision.

LO **1, 5**   ## Capital Investment Analysis

E14A. BUSINESS APPLICATION ▶ Genette Henderson was just promoted to supervisor of building maintenance for Ford Valley Theater complex. Allpoints Entertainment, Inc., Henderson's employer, uses a company-wide system for evaluating capital investment requests from its 22 supervisors. Henderson has approached you, the corporate controller, for advice on preparing her first proposal. She would also like to become familiar with the entire decision-making process.

1. What advice would you give Henderson before she prepares her first capital investment proposal?
2. Explain the role of capital investment analysis in the management process, including the key steps taken during planning.

EXERCISES: SET B

Visit the textbook companion website at www.cengagebrain.com to access Exercise Set B for this chapter.

PROBLEMS

LO **3, 5**   ## Net Present Value Method

✔ 1: Present value of future
cash flows: $99,672
✔ 2: Net present value: $112,465

P1. Sonja and Sons, Inc., owns and operates a group of apartment buildings. Management wants to sell one of its older four-family buildings and buy a new building. The old building, which was purchased 25 years ago for $100,000, has a 40-year estimated life. The current market value is $80,000, and if it is sold, the cash inflow will be $67,675. Annual net cash inflows from the old building are expected to average $16,000 for the remainder of its estimated useful life.

The new building will cost $300,000. It has an estimated useful life of 25 years. Net cash inflows are expected to be $50,000 annually.

Assume that (1) all cash flows occur at year end, (2) the company uses straight-line depreciation, (3) the buildings will have a residual value equal to 10 percent of their purchase price, and (4) the minimum rate of return is 14 percent. (*Hint:* Use Tables 1 and 2 in Appendix A.)

REQUIRED

1. Compute the present value of future cash flows from the old building.
2. What will the net present value of cash flows be if the company purchases the new building?
3. **ACCOUNTING CONNECTION ▶** Should the company keep the old building or purchase the new one? Why?

LO **3, 5**

✔ 1: Net present value: $35,540
✔ 2: Net present value: ($5,430)

Net Present Value Method

P2. Better Plastics' management has recently been looking at a proposal to purchase a new plastic-injection-style molding machine. With the new machine, the company would not have to buy small plastic parts to use in production. The estimated useful life of the machine is 15 years, and the purchase price, including all setup charges, is $400,000. The residual value is estimated to be $40,000. The net addition to the company's cash inflow as a result of the savings from making the parts is estimated to be $70,000 a year. Better Plastics' management has decided on a minimum rate of return of 14 percent. (*Hint:* Use Tables 1 and 2 in Appendix A.)

REQUIRED

1. Using the net present value method to evaluate this capital investment, determine whether the company should purchase the machine. Support your answer.
2. If management had decided on a minimum rate of return of 16 percent, should the machine be purchased? Show computations to support your answer.

LO **4, 5**

✔ 1: Accounting rate of return for HZT machine: 13.4%
✔ 2: Payback period for HZT machine: 6.1 years

Accounting Rate-of-Return and Payback Period Methods

P3. Raab Company is expanding its production facilities to include a new product line, a sporty automotive tire rim. Tire rims can now be produced with little labor cost using new computerized machinery. The controller has advised management about two such machines. Details about each machine follow.

	XJS Machine	HZT Machine
Cost of machine	$500,000	$550,000
Residual value	50,000	55,000
Net income	34,965	40,670
Annual net cash inflows	91,215	90,170

The company's minimum rate of return is 12 percent. The maximum payback period is six years.

REQUIRED

1. For each machine, compute the projected accounting rate of return. (Round percentages to one decimal place.)
2. Compute the payback period for each machine. (Round to one decimal place.)
3. **ACCOUNTING CONNECTION** ▶ Based on the information from requirements 1 and 2, which machine should be purchased? Why?

LO **2, 3, 4, 5**

✔ 1a: Net present value: ($26,895)
✔ 1b: Accounting rate of return: 8.2%
✔ 1c: Payback period: 3.7 years

Capital Investment Decision: Comprehensive

P4. Edge Company's production vice president believes keeping up-to-date with technological changes is what makes the company successful and feels that a machine introduced recently would fill an important need. The machine has an estimated useful life of four years, a purchase price of $250,000, and a residual value of $25,000. The company controller has estimated average annual net income of $11,250 and the following cash flows for the new machine:

	Cash Flow Estimates		
Year	Cash Inflows	Cash Outflows	Net Cash Inflows
1	$325,000	$250,000	$75,000
2	320,000	250,000	70,000
3	315,000	250,000	65,000
4	310,000	250,000	60,000

The company uses a 12 percent minimum rate of return and a three-year payback period for capital investment evaluation purposes.

(Continued)

REQUIRED

1. Analyze the data about the machine. Use the following evaluation approaches in your analysis:

   a. the net present value method (Round to the nearest dollar.)

   b. the accounting rate-of-return method. (Round percentage to one decimal place.)

   c. the payback period method (Round to one decimal place.)
      (*Hint:* Use Tables 1 and 2 in Appendix A.)

2. **ACCOUNTING CONNECTION ▶** Summarize the information generated in requirement **1,** and make a recommendation.

ALTERNATE PROBLEMS

LO **3, 5**

✔ 1: Present value of future cash flows: $92,536.50
✔ 2: Net present value: $222,646

Comparison of Alternatives: Net Present Value Method

P5. City Sights, Ltd., operates a tour and sightseeing business. Its trademark is the use of trolley buses. Each vehicle has its own identity and is specially made for the company. Gridlock, the oldest bus, was purchased 15 years ago and has 5 years of its estimated useful life remaining. The company paid $25,000 for Gridlock, and the bus could be sold today for $20,000. Gridlock is expected to generate average annual net cash inflows of $24,000 for the remainder of its estimated useful life.

Management wants to replace Gridlock with a modern-looking vehicle called Phantom. Phantom has a purchase price of $140,000 and an estimated useful life of 20 years. Net cash inflows for Phantom are projected to be $40,000 per year.

Assume that (1) all cash flows occur at year end, (2) each vehicle's residual value equals 10 percent of its purchase price, and (3) the minimum rate of return is 10 percent. (*Hint:* Use Tables 1 and 2 in Appendix A.)

REQUIRED

1. Compute the present value of the future cash flows from Gridlock.

2. Compute the net present value of cash flows if Phantom were purchased.

3. **ACCOUNTING CONNECTION ▶** Should City Sights keep Gridlock or purchase Phantom?

LO **3, 5**

✔ 1: Net present value: $16,573
✔ 2: Net present value: ($7,080)

Net Present Value Method

P6. Mansion is a famous restaurant in the French Quarter of New Orleans. Bouillabaisse Sophie is Mansion's house specialty. Management is considering purchasing a machine that would prepare all the ingredients, mix them automatically, and cook the dish to the restaurant's specifications. The machine will function for an estimated 12 years, and the purchase price, including installation, is $250,000. Estimated residual value is $25,000. This labor-saving device is expected to increase net cash inflows by an average of $42,000 per year during its estimated useful life. For capital investment decisions, the restaurant uses a 12 percent minimum rate of return. (*Hint:* Use Tables 1 and 2 in Appendix A.)

REQUIRED

1. Using the net present value method, determine if the company should purchase the machine. Support your answer.

2. If management had decided on a minimum rate of return of 14 percent, should the machine be purchased? Show computations to support your answer.

LO **4, 5**

✔ 1: Accounting rate of return for Autom machine: 16.8%
✔ 2: Payback period for Autom machine: 6.5 years

Accounting Rate-of-Return and Payback Period Methods

P7. Cute Car Company is expanding its production facilities to include a new product line, an energy-efficient sporty convertible. The car can be produced with little labor cost using computerized machinery. There are two such machines to choose from. Details about each machine follow.

	GoGo Machine	Autom Machine
Cost of machine	$300,000	$325,000
Residual value	30,000	32,500
Net income	25,000	30,000
Annual net cash inflows	60,000	50,000

The company's minimum rate of return is 15 percent. The maximum payback period is six years. (Round to one decimal place.)

REQUIRED

1. For each machine, compute the projected accounting rate of return.
2, Compute the payback period for each machine.
3. Based on the information from requirements **1** and **2**, which machine should be purchased?

LO **2, 3, 4, 5**

Capital Investment Decision: Comprehensive

P8. Express Corporation wants to buy a new stamping machine. The machine will provide the company with a new product line: pressed food trays for kitchens. Two machines are being considered; the data for each machine follows.

✔ 1: Net present value for LKR machine: $4,658
✔ 2: Accounting rate of return for LKR machine: 23.7%
✔ 3: Payback period for LKR machine: 4.9 years

	ETZ Machine	LKR Machine
Cost of machine	$350,000	$370,000
Net income	$39,204	$48,642
Annual net cash inflows	$64,404	$75,642
Residual value	$28,000	$40,000
Estimated useful life in years	10	10

The company's minimum rate of return is 16 percent, and the maximum allowable payback period is 5.0 years.

REQUIRED

1. Compute the net present value for each machine. (Round to the nearest dollar.)
2. Compute the accounting rate of return for each machine. (Round percentages to one decimal place.)
3. Compute the payback period for each machine. (Round to one decimal place.)
4. **ACCOUNTING CONNECTION** ▶ From the information generated in requirements **1**, **2**, and **3**, decide which machine should be purchased. Why?

CASES

LO **1, 5**

Evaluation of Proposed Capital Investments

C1. Tanashi Corporation's board of directors met to review a number of proposed capital investments that would improve the quality of company products. One production-line manager requested purchasing new computer-integrated machines to replace the older machines in one of the ten production departments at the Tokyo plant. Although the manager had presented quantitative information to support the purchase of the new machines, the board members asked the following important questions:

1. Why do we want to replace the old machines? Have they deteriorated? Are they obsolete?
2. Will the new machines require less cycle time?
3. Can we reduce inventory levels or save floor space by replacing the old machines?
4. How expensive is the software used with the new machines?

(Continued)

5. Will we be able to find highly skilled employees to maintain the new machines? Or can we find workers who are trainable? What would it cost to train workers? Would the training disrupt the staff by causing relocations?

6. Would the implementation of the machines be delayed because of the time required to recruit and train new workers?

7. How would the new machines affect the other parts of the manufacturing systems? Would the company lose some of the flexibility in its manufacturing systems if it introduced the new machines?

The board members believe that the qualitative information needed to answer their questions could lead to the rejection of the project, even though it would have been accepted based on the quantitative information.

1. Identify the questions that can be answered with quantitative information. Give an example of the quantitative information that could be used.

2. Identify the questions that can be answered with qualitative information. Explain why this information could negatively influence the capital investment decision even though the quantitative information suggests a positive outcome.

LO 3 Using Net Present Value

C2. McCall Syndicate owns four resort hotels in Europe. Because the Paris operation (Hotel 1) has been booming over the past five years, management has decided to build an addition to the hotel. This addition will increase the hotel's capacity by 20 percent. A construction company has bid to build the addition at a cost of $30,000,000. The building will have an increased residual value of $3,000,000.

Daj Van Dyke, the controller, has started an analysis of the net present value for the project. She has calculated the annual net cash inflows by subtracting the increase in cash operating expenses from the increase in cash inflows from room rentals. Her partially completed schedule follows:

Year	Net Cash Inflows
1–20 (each year)	$3,900,000

Capital investment projects must generate a 12 percent minimum rate of return to qualify for consideration.

Using net present value analysis, evaluate the proposal and make a recommendation to management. Explain how your recommendation would change if management were willing to accept a 10 percent minimum rate of return. (*Hint:* Use Tables 1 and 2 in Appendix A.)

LO 3, 5 Net Present Value of Cash Flows

C3. CPC Corporation is an international plumbing equipment and supply company located in southern California. The Pipe Division's manager is considering purchasing a computerized copper pipe machine that costs $120,000.

The machine has a six-year life, and its expected residual value after six years of use will be 10 percent of its original cost. Cash revenue generated by the new machine is projected to be $50,000 in year 1 and will increase by $10,000 each year for the next five years. Variable cash operating costs will be materials and parts, 25 percent of revenue; machine labor, 5 percent of revenue; and overhead, 15 percent of revenue. First-year sales and marketing cash outflows are expected to be $10,500 and will decrease by 10 percent each year over the life of the new machine. Anticipated cash administrative expenses will be $2,500 per year. The company uses a 15 percent minimum rate of return for all capital investment analyses.

1. Prepare a spreadsheet to compute the net present value of the anticipated cash flows for the life of the proposed new machine. (Round to the nearest dollar.) Use the following format:

	A	B	C	D	E	F	G	H	I	J
1					Projected Cash Outflows					
2	Future Time Period	Projected Cash Revenue	Materials and Parts	Machine Labor	Overhead	Sales and Marketing	Adminis-trative Expenses	Projected Net Cash Inflows	15% Factor	Present Value
3										

Should the company invest in the new machine?

2. After careful analysis, the controller has determined that the variable rate for materials and parts can be reduced to 22 percent of revenue. Will this reduction in cash out-flow change the decision about investing in the new machine? Explain your answer. (Round to the nearest dollar.)

3. The marketing manager has determined that the initial estimate of sales and marketing cash expenses was too high and has reduced that estimate by $1,000. The 10 percent annual reductions are still expected to occur. Together with the change in **2**, will this reduction affect the initial investment decision? Explain your answer. (Round to the nearest dollar.)

LO **2, 3, 5**   **Interpreting Management Reports: Capital Investment Analysis**

C4. Angelo Bank is planning to replace some old ATM machines and has decided to use the York Machine. Anita Chavez, the controller, has prepared the analysis shown here. She has recommended purchasing the machine based on the positive net present value shown in the analysis.

The York Machine has an estimated useful life of five years and an expected residual value of $35,000. Its purchase price is $385,000. Two existing ATMs, each having a carrying value of $25,000, can be sold to a neighboring bank for a total of $50,000. Annual operating cash inflows are expected to increase in the following manner:

Year 1	$79,900
Year 2	76,600
Year 3	79,900
Year 4	83,200
Year 5	86,500

Angelo Bank uses straight-line depreciation. The minimum rate of return is 12 percent.

Angelo Bank
Capital Investment Analysis
Net Present Value Method

Year	Net Cash Inflows	Present Value Factor	Present Value
1	$85,000	0.909	$ 77,265
2	80,000	0.826	66,080
3	85,000	0.751	63,835
4	90,000	0.683	61,470
5	95,000	0.621	58,995
5 (residual value)	35,000	0.621	21,735
Total present value			$ 349,380
Initial investment		$385,000	
Less proceeds from the sale of existing ATM machines		50,000	
Net capital investment			335,000
Net present value			$ 14,380

1. Analyze Chavez's work. (Round to the nearest dollar.) What changes need to be made in her capital investment analysis?

2. What would be your recommendation to bank management about the purchase of the York Machine?

LO 5   **Ethical Understanding: Capital Investment Decisions and the Globally Competitive Business Environment**

C5. Bramer Corporation's controller, Mara Jossen, was asked to prepare a capital investment analysis for a robot-guided aluminum window machine. This machine would automate the entire window-casing manufacturing line. She has just returned from an international seminar on the subject of qualitative inputs into the capital investment decision process and is eager to incorporate those new ideas into the analysis. In addition to the normal net present value analysis (which produced a significant negative result), Jossen factored in figures for customer satisfaction, scrap reduction, reduced inventory needs, and reputation for quality. With the additional information included, the analysis produced a positive response to the decision question.

1. When the chief financial officer finished reviewing Jossen's work, he threw the papers on the floor and said, "What kind of garbage is this! You know it's impossible to quantify such things as customer satisfaction and reputation for quality. How do you expect me to go to the board of directors and explain your work? I want you to redo the entire analysis and follow only the traditional approach to net present value. Get it back to me in two hours!"

2. What is Jossen's dilemma? What ethical courses of action are available to her?

LO 2, 3, 4, 5   **Continuing Case: Cookie Company**

C6. Suppose your cookie company is now a corporation that has granted franchises to more than 50 stores. Currently, only 10 of the 50 stores have computerized machines for mixing cookie dough. Because of a tremendous increase in demand for cookie dough, you, as the corporation's president, are considering purchasing 10 more computerized mixing machines by the end of this month. You are writing a memo evaluating this purchase that you will present at the board of directors' meeting next week.

According to your research, the 10 new machines will cost a total of $320,000. They will function for an estimated five years and should have a total residual value of $32,000. All of your corporation's capital investments are expected to produce a 20 percent minimum rate of return, and they should be recovered in three years or less. All fixed assets are depreciated using the straight-line method. The forecasted increase in operating results for the aggregate of the 10 new machines follows.

	Cash Flow Estimates	
Year	**Cash Inflows**	**Cash Outflows**
1	$310,000	$210,000
2	325,000	220,000
3	340,000	230,000
4	300,000	210,000
5	260,000	180,000

1. In preparation for writing your memo, answer the following questions:

   a. What kinds of information do you need to prepare this memo?
   b. Why is the information relevant?
   c. Where would you find the information?
   d. When would you want to obtain the information?

2. Using the following methods, analyze the purchase of the machines and decide if your corporation should purchase them.

   a. the net present value method
   b. the accounting rate-of-return method (Round percentages to one decimal place.)
   c. the payback period method (Round to one decimal place.)

CHAPTER 11
Pricing Decisions, Including Target Costing and Transfer Pricing

Lab 126, a subsidiary of **Amazon.com**, dominates the e-book market with its Kindle readers and applications for other handheld devices. Competition between Lab 126 and its competitors is very keen, and there is constant pressure to offer more technology-rich features. Lab 126 managers are expected to make money, use resources wisely, and operate profitably. To fulfill these expectations, managers must know a lot about how to price products or services.

1. CONCEPT *How are pricing and the concept of revenue recognition related?*

2. ACCOUNTING APPLICATION *How do companies determine the price of products?*

3. BUSINESS APPLICATION *How does managerial accounting help managers during the management process with pricing decisions?*

LEARNING OBJECTIVES

LO 1 Explain how the pricing of goods and services relates to the concept of revenue recognition.

LO 2 Describe economic pricing concepts, including the auction-based pricing method used on the Internet.

LO 3 Use cost-based pricing methods to develop prices.

LO 4 Describe target costing, and use it to analyze pricing decisions and evaluate a new product opportunity.

LO 5 Describe how transfer pricing is used for transferring goods and services and evaluating performance within a division or segment.

LO 6 Relate pricing issues to the management process.

CONCEPTS
- ■ Recognition
- ■ Matching rule (accrual accounting)

RELEVANT LEARNING OBJECTIVES

LO 1 Explain how the pricing of goods and services relates to the concept of revenue recognition.

LO 2 Describe economic pricing concepts, including the auction-based pricing method used on the Internet.

LO 1 Concepts Underlying Pricing Decisions

Establishing a product or service price depends on a manager's ability to analyze the marketplace for customers' price reactions and to know when to apply various cost-based or market-based approaches to pricing. Setting appropriate prices is one of the most difficult decisions that managers must make, and managers rely on managerial accounting information to make these decisions.

Revenue Recognition and Pricing Policies

The prices managers set have a significant impact on business operations, both externally and internally, since revenue is computed by multiplying the product or service price by the quantity sold. On the income statement, these revenues are generally *recognized* when goods are transferred or services are rendered, and they are *matched* with the costs incurred to generate them. The resulting difference is a net profit or loss, the fundamental measure of an organization's profitability. Thus, a manager's ability to set prices is essential to the long-term survival of any profit-oriented enterprise.

Organizational goals, objectives, and strategic plans that guide and control an organization's activities should include a pricing policy. A pricing policy is one way in which companies differentiate themselves from their competitors. Compare, for example, the pricing policies of luxury brands like **Lexus** and **Nordstrom** with those of cost-driven companies like **Toyota** or **Wal-Mart**. Consider also how prices are set on **eBay** and **Priceline.com**. Although all these companies are successful, their pricing policies differ significantly because each company has different pricing objectives.

Companies may also use pricing policies to differentiate among their own brands. For example, **Gap, Inc.**, uses price to differentiate the Gap brand from the brand of its subsidiary, **Old Navy**. **Mercedes-Benz** uses price to differentiate the Smart Car from the Mercedes. Thus, for each product brand, the company has identified the market segment that it intends to serve and has developed pricing objectives to meet the needs of that market.

Pricing Policy Objectives

Possible objectives of a pricing policy include the following:

- **Identifying and adhering to both short-run and long-run pricing strategies.** The pricing strategies of companies that produce standard items or commodities for a competitive marketplace will differ from the pricing strategies of companies that make custom-designed items. In a competitive market, companies can reduce prices to draw sales away from competing companies. They can also continuously add value-enhancing features and upgrades to their products and services to create the impression that customers are receiving more for their money. In contrast, a company that makes custom-designed items can be more conservative in its pricing strategy.
- **Maximizing profits.** Maximizing profits has traditionally been the underlying objective of any pricing policy.
- **Maintaining or gaining market share.** One key indicator of profit potential is an increasing share of the market. Maintaining or gaining market share is closely related to pricing strategies. However, market share is important only if sales are profitable. To increase market share by reducing prices below cost can be economically disastrous unless such a move is accompanied by strategies that compensate for the lost revenues.
- **Setting socially responsible prices.** To enhance their standing with the public and thus ensure their long-term survival, companies also consider whether their prices are socially responsible. The pricing policies of many companies now take into consideration a variety of social concerns, including environmental factors, the influence of an aging population, legal constraints, and ethical issues.

- **Maintaining a minimum rate of return on investment.** Organizations view each product or service as an investment. They will not invest in making a product or providing a service unless it will provide a minimum return. When setting prices, an organization adds a markup percentage to each product's costs of production in order to maintain a minimum return on investment. This markup percentage is closely related to the objective of profit maximization.
- **Being customer focused.** Taking customers' needs into consideration when setting prices or increasing a product's value to customers is important for at least three reasons:
  - Sensitivity to customers is necessary to sustain sales growth.
  - Customers' acceptance is crucial to success in a competitive market.
  - Prices should reflect the enhanced value that the company adds to the product or service, which is another way of saying that prices are customer-driven.

External and Internal Pricing Factors

When making and evaluating pricing decisions, managers must consider many factors. As shown in Exhibit 1, some of those factors relate to the external market, and others relate to internal constraints.

- The external factors include demand for the product, customer needs, competition, and quantity and quality of competing products or services.
- The internal factors include constraints caused by costs, desired return on investment, quality and quantity of materials and labor, and allocation of scarce resources.

Exhibit 1
External and Internal Factors Affecting Pricing Decisions

When Making and Evaluating Pricing Decisions

External Factors

Demand for the product

Customer needs

Competition

Quantity and quality of competing products

© Cengage Learning 2014

Internal Factors

Constraints caused by reduced costs

Desired return on investment

Materials and labor

Allocation of scarce resources

APPLY IT! ➤

Towne's Tire Outlet features more than a dozen brands of tires. Information about two of the brands—Gripper and Roadster—follows.

	Gripper	Roadster
Selling price:		
Single tire, installed	$125	$110
Set of four tires, installed	460	400
Cost per tire	90	60

Selling prices include installation costs, which are $20 per tire.

1. Compute each brand's net unit selling price after installation for both a single tire and a set of four.
2. Was cost the main consideration in setting those prices?
3. What other factors could have influenced those prices?

SOLUTION

1.

	Gripper		Roadster	
	One Tire	Four Tires	One Tire	Four Tires
Selling price	$125	$460	$110	$400
Less installation cost	20	80	20	80
Net selling price	$105	$380	$ 90	$320
Unit selling price	$105	$ 95	$ 90	$ 80

2. The Gripper tire costs the company $30 more than the Roadster tire, but there is only a $15 difference between the two selling prices. The low cost of the Roadster allows the company to sell it at a significantly lower price than the higher-cost Gripper. Therefore, customers perceive the Roadster to be a better purchase value than the Gripper. The company is not using cost as a major consideration in its pricing decisions.
3. Other pricing considerations include local competition, quality versus price, and demand for the tires.

TRY IT! SE1, E1A, E1B

LO2 Economic Pricing Concepts

The economic approach to pricing is based on microeconomic theory. Although each product has its own set of revenues and costs, microeconomic theory states that profit will be greatest when the difference between total revenue and total cost is the greatest.

Total Revenue and Total Cost Curves

It may seem that if a company could produce an infinite number of products, it would realize the maximum profit. But this is not the case, and microeconomic theory explains why. Exhibit 2 shows the economist's view of a break-even chart. It contains two break-even points, between which is a large space labeled "profit area."

Total Revenues Notice that the total revenue line is curved rather than straight. The theory behind this is that as a product is marketed, because of competition and other factors, price reductions will be necessary if the firm is to sell additional units. Total revenue will continue to increase, but the rate of increase will diminish as more units are sold. Therefore, the slope of the total revenue line declines, and the line curves toward the right.

Total Costs Costs react in an opposite way. Over the assumed relevant range, variable and fixed costs are fairly predictable, with fixed costs remaining constant and variable costs being the same per unit. The result is a straight line for total costs. However, following microeconomic theory, costs per unit will increase as more units are sold because fixed costs, such as supervision and depreciation, will increase. Competition causes marketing costs to rise. As the company pushes for more and more products from limited facilities, repair and maintenance costs also increase. As the push from management increases, total costs per unit rise at an accelerating rate. The result is that the slope of the total cost line in Exhibit 2A increases, and the line begins curving upward. The total revenue line and the total cost line then cross again. Beyond that point, the company suffers a loss on additional sales.

Profit Maximization Profits are maximized at the point where the difference between total revenue and total cost is the greatest. In Exhibit 2A, this point is 6,000 units of sales.

Exhibit 2
Microeconomic
Pricing Theory

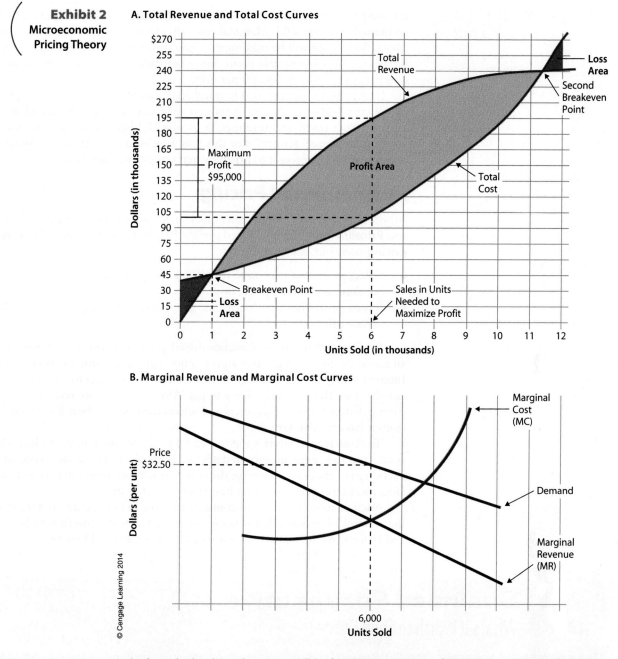

A. Total Revenue and Total Cost Curves

B. Marginal Revenue and Marginal Cost Curves

At that sales level, total revenue will be $195,000; total cost, $100,000; and profit, $95,000. In theory, if one additional unit is sold, profit per unit will drop because total cost is rising at a faster rate than total revenues. As you can see, if the company sells 11,000 units, total profits will be almost entirely depleted by the rising costs. Therefore, 6,000 sales units is the optimal operating level, and the price charged at that level is the optimal price.

Marginal Revenue and Marginal Cost Curves

Economists use marginal revenue and marginal cost to help determine the optimal price for a product or service. **Marginal revenue** is the change in total revenue caused by a one-unit change in output. **Marginal cost** is the change in total cost caused by a one-unit change in output. Graphic curves for marginal revenue and marginal cost are created by measuring and plotting the rate of change in total revenue and total cost at various activity levels.

If marginal revenue and marginal cost for each unit sold were plotted on a graph, the lines would resemble those in Exhibit 2B. Notice that the marginal cost line crosses the marginal revenue line at 6,000 units. After that point, profit per unit will decrease as additional units are sold. Marginal cost will exceed marginal revenue for each unit sold over 6,000. Profit will be maximized when the marginal revenue and marginal cost lines intersect. By projecting this point onto the product's demand curve, you can locate the optimal price, which is $32.50 per unit.

If all the information used in microeconomic theory were certain, picking the optimal price would be fairly easy. Although an analysis relies on projected amounts for unit sales, product costs, and revenues, it usually highlights cost patterns and the unanticipated influences of demand. For this reason, it is important that managers consider the microeconomic approach to pricing when setting product prices.

Auction-Based Pricing

In recent years, as a result of auctions hosted by Internet companies like **eBay**, **Yahoo**, and **Priceline.com**, auction-based pricing has skyrocketed in popularity. **Auction-based pricing** occurs in one of two ways:

- Sellers post what they have to sell, ask for price bids, and accept a buyer's offer to purchase at a certain price, or
- Buyers post what they want, ask for prices, and accept a seller's offer to sell at a certain price.

To illustrate the seller's auction-based price, suppose a corporation like **Intel** has an excess of silicon chips after a production run. The company posts a message on the Internet asking for the quantity of silicon chips that prospective buyers are willing to buy and the price that they are willing to pay. After the offers are received, the company prepares a demand curve of all offers and selects the one that best fits the quantity of silicon chips it has available for sale.

To illustrate the buyer's auction-based price, consider an individual who wants to fly round-trip to Europe on certain dates and posts his or her needs on one of the Internet's auction markets. After receiving the offers to sell round-trip tickets to Europe, the individual will accept the offer that best suits his or her needs.

Auction-based pricing will continue to grow in importance as a result of the escalating amount of business that is being conducted over the Internet by both organizations and individuals. Just about anything can be bought or sold via the Internet.

Business Perspective
What's It Worth to Shop Online?

The Internet makes it possible to price efficiently at the level of marginal costs. For instance, at websites like **Priceline.com**, travelers pick a destination and a price they are willing to pay for air or hotel reservations. The price must be guaranteed by credit card. An airline or hotel has a limited amount of time to accept or reject the bid. If the bid is accepted, the buyer is obligated to pay for the air or hotel reservation. The hotels and airlines are often willing to accept the low bid prices because the marginal cost of filling an additional seat on an airplane or an extra room in a hotel is very low.

© Cengage Learning 2014

APPLY IT!

Assume that a product has the total cost and total revenue curves pictured in Exhibit 2A. The difference between total revenue and total cost is the same at the 4,000- and 9,000-unit levels. Which of these two levels of activity would you chose as goals for total sales over the life of the product?

SOLUTION

4,000. If the same total profit will be made at both the 4,000- and the 9,000-unit levels, it does not make economic sense to produce the additional 5,000 units.

TRY IT! SE2, E2A, E2B

SECTION 2 ACCOUNTING APPLICATIONS

LO 3 Cost-Based Pricing Methods

In some areas of the economy, such as government contracts, cost-based pricing is widely used because a good starting point for developing a price is to base it on the cost of producing a good or service. Two pricing methods based on cost are gross margin pricing and return on assets pricing. Remember that in a competitive environment, market prices and conditions also influence price. However, if prices do not cover a company's costs, the company will eventually fail.

To illustrate the two methods of cost-based pricing, we will use Bookit Company. Bookit buys parts from outside vendors and assembles them into basic e-book readers. In the previous accounting period, the company produced 14,750 readers. The total costs and unit costs incurred follow.

	Total Costs	Unit Costs
Variable production costs:		
Direct materials and parts	$ 88,500	$ 6.00
Direct labor	66,375	4.50
Variable overhead	44,250	3.00
Total variable production costs	$199,125	$13.50
Fixed overhead	154,875	10.50
Total production costs	$354,000	$24.00
Selling, general, and administrative expenses:		
Selling expenses	$ 73,750	$ 5.00
General expenses	36,875	2.50
Administrative expenses	22,125	1.50
Total selling, general, and administrative expenses	$132,750	$ 9.00
Total costs and expenses	$486,750	$33.00

No changes in unit costs are expected this period. The desired profit for the period is $110,625. The company uses assets totaling $921,875 in producing the e-book readers and expects a 14 percent return on those assets.

Gross Margin Pricing

The **gross margin pricing method** (or the *income statement method*) emphasizes the use of income statement information to determine a selling price. (Gross margin is the difference between sales and the total production costs of those sales.) In gross margin pricing, the price is computed using a markup percentage based on a product's total production costs. The markup percentage is designed to include all costs other than those used in the computation of gross margin. Therefore, the gross margin markup percentage covers selling, general, and administrative expenses and the desired profit. Because an accounting system often provides management with unit production cost data, both variable and fixed, this method of determining selling price can be easily applied.

Gross Margin Calculations With gross margin pricing, there are three ways of determining a price.

1. The first approach uses the two formulas that follow.

$$\text{Markup Percentage} = \frac{\text{Desired Profit} + \text{Total Selling, General, and Administrative Expenses}}{\text{Total Production Costs}}$$

$$\begin{array}{c}\text{Gross Margin-Based} \\ \text{Price}\end{array} = \begin{array}{c}\text{Total Production} \\ \text{Costs per Unit}\end{array} + \left(\begin{array}{c}\text{Markup} \\ \text{Percentage}\end{array} \times \begin{array}{c}\text{Total Production} \\ \text{Costs per Unit}\end{array} \right)$$

For Bookit, the markup percentage and selling price are computed as follows.

$$\text{Markup Percentage} = \frac{\$110{,}625 + \$132{,}750}{\$354{,}000}$$

$$= 68.75\%$$

$$\text{Gross Margin-Based Price} = \$24.00 + (68.75\% \times \$24.00)$$

$$= \underline{\$40.50}$$

The numerator in the markup percentage formula is the sum of the desired profit ($110,625) and the total selling, general, and administrative expenses ($132,750). The denominator contains all production costs: variable costs of $199,125 and fixed production costs of $154,875. The gross margin markup is 68.75 percent of total production costs, or $16.50. Adding $16.50 to the total production costs per unit yields a selling price of $40.50.

STUDY NOTE: *Gross margin-based price per unit equals total production, selling, general, and administrative costs per unit plus a desired profit per unit.*

2. The second way to express the gross margin-based price is to state the formula in terms of a company's desire to recover all of its costs and make a profit. This approach ignores the computation of the markup percentage, achieves the same gross margin-based price, and is stated as follows.

$$\text{Gross Margin-Based Price} = \frac{\substack{\text{Total Production Costs} + \text{Total Selling, General,} \\ \text{and Administrative Expenses} + \text{Desired Profit}}}{\text{Total Units Produced}}$$

Using this formula, the gross margin-based price for Bookit is computed as follows.

$$\text{Gross Margin-Based Price} = \frac{\$354{,}000 + \$132{,}750 + \$110{,}625}{14{,}750 \text{ Units}}$$

$$= \$597{,}375 \div 14{,}750$$

$$= \underline{\$40.50}$$

3. The third way the gross margin-based price can be determined is on a per-unit basis.

$$\begin{aligned}\text{Gross Margin-Based Price} = \ &\text{Direct Materials} + \text{Direct Labor} \\ &+ \text{Variable Overhead} + \text{Fixed Overhead} \\ &+ \text{Selling, General, and Administrative Expenses} \\ &+ \text{Desired Profit per Unit}\end{aligned}$$

Applying this formula to Bookit's data, the computations are as follows.

$$\begin{aligned}\text{Gross Margin-Based Price} = \ &\$6.00 + \$4.50 + \$3.00 + \$10.50 + \$5.00 \\ &+ \$2.50 + \$1.50 + (\$110{,}625 \div 14{,}750) \\ &= \underline{\$40.50}\end{aligned}$$

Return on Assets Pricing

The **return on assets pricing method** (or *balance sheet method*) focuses on earning a specified rate of return on the assets employed in the operation. This changes the objective of the price determination process from earning a return on the income statement to earning a return on the business's resources on the balance sheet. Because this approach focuses on a desired minimum rate of return on assets, it is also known as the *balance sheet approach to pricing*.

Return on Assets Calculations There are two formulas for finding the return on assets price.

1. Return on Assets-Based Price = Total Costs and Expenses per Unit
   + (Desired Rate of Return
   × Cost of Assets Employed per Unit)

2. Return on Assets-Based Price =

$$\left(\frac{\text{Total Production Costs} + \text{Total Selling, General, and Administrative Expenses}}{\text{Units to Be Produced}} \right) + \left(\frac{\text{Desired Rate of Return} \times \text{Total Cost of Assets Employed}}{\text{Units to Be Produced}} \right)$$

Recall that Bookit has an asset base of $921,875. It plans to produce 14,750 units and would like to earn a 14 percent return on assets. If the company uses return on assets pricing, the selling price per unit would be calculated as follows.

$$\text{Return on Assets-Based Price} = \$24.00 + \$9.00$$
$$+ [14\% \times (\$921,875 \div 14,750)]$$
$$= \underline{\underline{\$41.75}}$$

or as

$$\text{Return on Assets-Based Price} = [(\$354,000 + \$132,750) \div 14,750]$$
$$+ [14\% \times (\$921,875 \div 14,750)]$$
$$= \$33.00 + \$8.75$$
$$= \underline{\underline{\$41.75}}$$

Summary of Cost-Based Pricing Methods

Exhibit 3 summarizes the two cost-based pricing methods. If Bookit Company uses return on assets pricing and has a desired rate of return of 14 percent, it will need to set a higher selling price ($41.75) than it would under the gross margin method ($40.50).

Companies select their pricing methods based on their degree of trust in a cost base. The cost bases from which they can choose are (1) total product costs per unit and (2) total costs and expenses per unit.

■ Often, total product costs per unit are readily available, which makes gross margin pricing a good way to compute selling prices. However, gross margin pricing depends on an accurate forecast of units because the fixed cost per-unit portion of total production costs will vary if the actual number of units produced differs from the estimated number of units.

■ Return on assets pricing is also a good pricing method if the assets used to manufacture a product can be identified and their cost determined. If this is not the case, the method yields inaccurate results.

Business Perspective
Pricing a Six-Pack

The average cost of a six-pack of beer continues to rise. That's because **Anheuser-Busch**, maker of Bud Light and Budweiser—the world's largest-selling brands of beer—generally raises prices to keep pace with the consumer price index, and competitors have historically followed the company's price lead.[1]

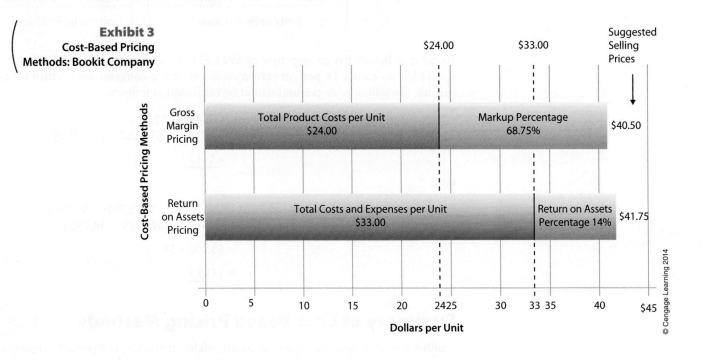

Exhibit 3
Cost-Based Pricing Methods: Bookit Company

Pricing Services

A service business's approach to pricing differs from that of a manufacturer. Although a service has no physical substance, it must still be priced and billed to the customer. Most service organizations use a form of **time and materials pricing** (or *parts and labor pricing*) to arrive at the price of a service. With this method, service companies, such as appliance repair shops, home-remodeling specialists, and automobile repair shops, arrive at prices by using two computations: one for direct labor and one for materials and parts. Markup percentages are added to the costs of materials and labor to cover the cost of overhead and provide a profit factor. If the service does not require materials and parts, then only direct labor costs are used in developing the price. Professionals, such as attorneys, accountants, and consultants, apply a factor representing all overhead costs to the base labor costs to establish a price for their services.

Time and Materials Price Calculation The formula used in time and materials pricing follows.

$$\text{Time and Materials Price} = \frac{\text{Material Cost}}{\text{per Unit}} + \left(\frac{\text{Markup \% × Material}}{\text{Cost per Unit}}\right) + \frac{\text{Labor Cost}}{\text{per Unit}} + \left(\frac{\text{Markup \% × Labor}}{\text{Cost per Unit}}\right)$$

To illustrate, suppose that the owner of an auto repair shop has just completed work on a customer's car. The parts used to repair the vehicle cost $840. The company's 40 percent markup rate on parts covers parts-related overhead costs and profit. The repairs required 4 hours of labor by a certified repair specialist, whose wages are $35 per hour. The company's overhead markup rate on labor is 80 percent. The repair shop will compute the bill as follows.

Repair parts used	$840	
Overhead charges: $840 × 40%	336	
Total parts charges		$1,176
Labor charges: 4 hours @ $35 per hour	$140	
Overhead charges: $140 × 80%	112	
Total labor charges		252
Total billing		$1,428

Factors Affecting Cost-Based Pricing Methods

Once a cost-based price has been determined, the decision maker must also consider such factors as competitors' prices, customers' expectations, and the cost of substitute products and services. Pricing is a risky part of operating a business, and care must be taken when establishing the selling price.

APPLY IT!

Gillson Industries has just patented a new product called Shine, an automobile wax for lasting protection against the elements. The company's controller has developed the following annual information:

Variable production costs	$1,110,000
Fixed overhead	540,000
Selling expenses	225,000
General and administrative expenses	350,000
Desired profit	250,000
Cost of assets employed	1,000,000

Annual demand for the product is expected to be 250,000 cans. On average, the company now earns a 10 percent return on assets.

1. Compute the projected unit cost for one can of Shine.
2. Using gross margin pricing, compute the markup percentage and selling price for one can.
3. Using return on assets pricing, compute the unit price for one can.

SOLUTION

1.

Costs Categories	Total Projected Cost
Variable production costs	$1,110,000
Fixed overhead	540,000
Total production costs	$1,650,000
Selling expenses	$ 225,000
General and administrative expenses	350,000
Total selling, general, and administrative expenses	$ 575,000
Total costs and expenses	$2,225,000
Total cost per unit ($2,225,000 ÷ 250,000 units)	$ 8.90

(Continued)

2.

$$\text{Markup Percentage} = \frac{\text{Desired Profit} + \text{Total Selling, General, and Administrative Expenses}}{\text{Total Production Costs}}$$

$$= \frac{\$250,000 + \$575,000}{\$1,650,000} = 50.0\%$$

Gross Margin-Based Price = Total Production Costs per Unit + (Markup Percentage × Total Production Costs per Unit)

= ($1,650,000 ÷ 250,000) + [50.0% × ($1,650,000 ÷ 250,000)]

= $9.90

3.

Return on Assets-Based Price = Total Costs and Expenses per Unit + (Desired Rate of Return × Cost of Assets Employed per Unit)

= $8.90 + [10% × ($1,000,000 ÷ 250,000)]

= $8.90 + $0.40

= $9.30

TRY IT! SE3, SE4, E3A, E4A, E5A, E6A, E7A, E3B, E4B, E5B, E6B, E7B

LO4 Pricing Based on Target Costing

Target costing (or *target pricing*) is a pricing method designed to enhance a company's ability to compete, especially in markets for new or emerging products, such as the e-book readers described in this chapter's Business Insight. Target costing reverses the procedure used by the cost-based methods. Target costing:

- identifies the price at which a product will be competitive in the marketplace
- defines the desired profit to be made on the product
- computes the target cost for the product by subtracting the desired profit from the competitive market price

Target Costing Calculation The formula used in target costing follows.

$$\text{Target Price} - \text{Desired Profit} = \text{Target Cost}$$

Once the target cost has been established, the company's engineers and product designers use it as the maximum cost to be incurred for the materials and other resources needed to design and manufacture the product. It is their responsibility to create the product at or below its target cost.

Pricing based on target costing may not seem revolutionary, but a detailed look at its underlying principles reveals its strategic superiority:

- Target costing gives managers the ability to control or dictate the costs of a new product at the planning stage of the product's life cycle.
- In a competitive environment, the use of target costing enables managers to analyze a product's potential before they commit resources to its production.

Exhibit 4 compares the timing of a pricing decision that uses a traditional approach with one that uses target costing. The stages of the product life cycle, from the generation

Exhibit 4
Comparison of Price Decision Timing

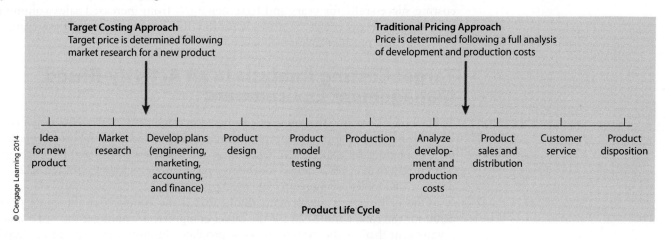

Target Costing Approach
Target price is determined following market research for a new product

Traditional Pricing Approach
Price is determined following a full analysis of development and production costs

| Idea for new product | Market research | Develop plans (engineering, marketing, accounting, and finance) | Product design | Product model testing | Production | Analyze develop-ment and production costs | Product sales and distribution | Customer service | Product disposition |

Product Life Cycle

© Cengage Learning 2014

of the product idea to the final disposition of the product, are identified at the base of the figure.

- When traditional cost-based pricing practices are used, prices cannot be set until production has taken place and costs have been incurred and analyzed. At that point, a profit factor is added to the product's cost, and the product is ready to be offered to customers.

- In contrast, under target costing, the pricing decision takes place immediately after the market research for a new product has been completed. The market research not only reveals the potential demand for the product but also identifies the maximum price that a customer would be willing to pay for it. Once the price is determined, target costing enables the company's engineers to design the product with a fixed maximum target cost on which to base the product's features.

STUDY NOTE: *Remember that when desired profit is defined as a percentage of target cost, target price is equal to 100 percent of target cost plus the percentage of target cost desired as profit.*

Target costing enables IKEA to offer its products at competitive prices and ensures that a product will earn a profit as soon as it is introduced. This method identifies the price at which a product will be competitive in the marketplace, defines the desired profit to be made on the product, and computes the target cost by subtracting the desired profit from the competitive market price.

Differences Between Cost-Based Pricing and Target Costing

The increased emphasis on product design allows a company to engineer the target cost into the product before manufacturing begins. A new product is designed only if its projected costs are equal to or lower than its target cost. The company can thus focus on holding costs down while it plans and designs the product, before the costs are actually committed and incurred.

- **Committed costs** are the costs of design, development, engineering, testing, and production that are engineered into a product or service at the design stage of development.
- **Incurred costs** are the actual costs incurred in making the product.

When cost-based pricing is used, it is very difficult to control costs from the planning phase through the production phase. Under that approach, concern about reducing costs begins only after the product has been produced. This often leads to random efforts to cut costs, which can reduce product quality and further erode the customer base. Under target costing, the product is expected to produce a profit as soon as it is marketed. Cost-cutting improvements in a product's design and production methods can still be made, but profitability is built into the selling price from the beginning. Companies like **Sony** and **IKEA** have used target costing successfully for years and have benefited from increased sales volume each time they have cut prices because of production improvements. These companies never sacrifice product quality.

Target Costing Analysis in an Activity-Based Management Environment

To see how a company that uses activity-based management implements target costing, consider Elsinore Company's approach to new product decisions. A customer is seeking price quotations for a special-purpose router and a wireless palm-sized tablet computer. The current market-price ranges for the two products are as follows: router, $320–$380 per unit; and tablet computer, $750–$850 per unit.

One of Elsinore's salespersons thinks that if the company could quote prices of $300 for the router and $725 for the tablet computer, it would get the order and gain a significant share of the market for those products. Elsinore's usual profit markup is 25 percent of total unit cost.

The company's design engineers and accountants put together the following specifications and costs for the new products:

Activity-based cost rates:

Materials handling	$ 1.30 per dollar of direct materials and purchased parts cost
Production	$ 3.50 per machine hour
Product delivery	$24.00 per router
	$30.00 per computer

	Router	Computer
Projected unit demand	26,000	18,000
Per-unit data:		
Direct materials cost	$25.00	$65.00
Purchased parts cost	$15.00	$45.00
Manufacturing labor:		
Hours	2.6	4.8
Hourly labor rate	$12.00	$15.00
Assembly labor:		
Hours	3.4	8.2
Hourly labor rate	$14.00	$16.00
Machine hours	12.8	28.4

The three steps used in arriving at the target cost follow.

- **Step 1. Find the target cost per unit.** The target cost for each product is computed as follows.

$$\text{Router} = \$300.00 \div 1.25 = \$240.00^*$$
$$\text{Computer} = \$725.00 \div 1.25 = \$580.00$$

$$^*\text{Target Price} - \text{Desired Profit} = \text{Target Cost}$$
$$\$300.00 - 0.25X = X$$
$$\$300.00 = 1.25X$$
$$X = \frac{\$300.00}{1.25} = \$240.00$$

- **Step 2. Find the projected unit cost.** The projected total unit cost of production and delivery is as follows.

	Router	Computer
Direct materials cost	$ 25.00	$ 65.00
Purchased parts cost	15.00	45.00
Total cost of direct materials and parts	$ 40.00	$110.00
Manufacturing labor:		
Router (2.6 hours × $12.00)	31.20	
Computer (4.8 hours × $15.00)		72.00
Assembly labor:		
Router (3.4 hours × $14.00)	47.60	
Computer (8.2 hours × $16.00)		131.20
Activity-based costs:		
Materials handling:		
Router ($40.00 × $1.30)	52.00	
Computer ($110.00 × $1.30)		143.00
Production:		
Router (12.8 machine hours × $3.50)	44.80	
Computer (28.4 machine hours × $3.50)		99.40
Product delivery:		
Router	24.00	
Computer		30.00
Projected total unit cost	$239.60	$585.60

- **Step 3. Make a decision.** Using the target costing approach and the following data, we can determine whether Elsinore should produce the new products:

	Router	Computer
Target unit cost	$240.00	$580.00
Less projected unit cost	239.60	585.60
Difference	$ 0.40	$ (5.60)

The router can be produced below its target cost, so it should be produced. As currently designed, the tablet computer cannot be produced at or below its target cost, so Elsinore should either redesign it or drop plans to produce it.

APPLY IT! ▶

Success Ltd. is considering a new product and must make a go or no-go decision when its planning team meets tomorrow. Market research shows that the unit selling price that would be agreeable to potential customers is $1,000, and the company's desired profit is 25 percent of target cost. The design engineer's preliminary estimate of the product's design, production, and distribution costs is $775 per unit. Using target costing, should the company market the new product?

SOLUTION
Yes. The company should market the new product. The target cost for the product is $800 ($1,000 ÷ 1.25). The engineer's projected cost is $775, or $25 below the amount needed to earn the desired profit.

TRY IT! SE5, SE6, E8A, E9A, E10A, E11A, E8B, E9B, E10B, E11B

LO5 Pricing for Internal Providers of Goods and Services

So far, we have focused on how a company sets prices for consumers outside the organization. We now look at how an organization prices its products and services for internal transfers between divisions or segments.

As a business grows, its day to day operations may be more manageable if it is organized into divisions or operating segments. A separate manager is assigned to control the operations of each segment. Such a business is called a **decentralized organization**. Each division or segment often sells its goods and services both inside and outside the organization.

For example, the beverage division of **Pepsico** sells its drink products to internal customers like **KFC** and **Taco Bell** restaurants. It also sells to external customers like **Safeway** and **Wal-Mart**. **Anheuser-Busch**'s beer segment produces and sells its products internally to **Sea World** amusement parks, as well as externally to unrelated entities like airlines and grocery stores.

Transfer Pricing

When divisions or segments within a company exchange goods or services and assume the role of customer or supplier for each other, they use transfer prices. A **transfer price** is the price at which goods and services are charged and exchanged between a company's divisions or segments.

- Transfer prices affect the revenues and costs of the divisions involved.
- They do not affect the revenues and costs of the company as a whole.

The transfer price shifts part of the profits from the divisions or centers that externally charge for their goods or services to the divisions or centers that do not externally bill for their services and products. Transfer pricing enables a business to assess both the internal and the external profitability of its products or services. The three basic kinds of transfer prices are:

- Cost-plus transfer prices
- Market transfer prices
- Negotiated transfer prices

Cost-Plus Transfer Price A **cost-plus transfer price** is based on either the full cost or the variable costs incurred by the producing division plus an agreed-on profit percentage. The weakness of the cost-plus pricing method is that cost recovery is guaranteed to the selling division. Guaranteed cost recovery prevents the company from detecting inefficient operating conditions and the incurrence of excessive costs, and it may even inappropriately reward inefficient divisions that incur excessive costs. This reduces overall company profitability and shareholder value.

Market Transfer Price A **market transfer price** (or *external market price*) is based on the price that could be charged if a segment could buy from or sell to an external party. Some experts believe that the use of a market transfer price is preferable to the other methods. It forces the division that is "selling" or transferring the product or service to another division to be competitive with market conditions, and it does not penalize the "buying" or receiving division by charging it a higher price than it would have to pay if it bought from outside the firm.

However, using market prices may lead the selling division to ignore negotiation attempts from the buying division manager and to sell directly to outside customers. If this causes an internal shortage of materials and forces the buying division to purchase materials from the outside, overall company profits may decline even if the selling division makes a profit. Such use of market prices works against a company's overall operating objectives. Therefore, when market prices are used to develop transfer prices, they are usually used only as a basis for negotiation.

Negotiated Transfer Price A **negotiated transfer price** is arrived at through bargaining between the managers of the buying and selling divisions or segments. Such a

STUDY NOTE: *Transfer pricing is not used for external pricing; it is used to set prices for transfers among a company's departments, divisions, or segments.*

STUDY NOTE: *Cost-plus transfer pricing is similar to the gross margin pricing method.*

transfer price may be based on an agreement to use a cost plus a profit percentage. The negotiated price will be between the negotiation floor (the selling division's variable cost) and the negotiation ceiling (the market price). This approach allows for cost recovery while still allowing the selling division to return a profit.

Developing a Transfer Price

To illustrate the development of the three kinds of transfer prices, we will use Simple Box Company, which makes cardboard boxes. As shown in Exhibit 5, this company has two divisions: the Pulp Division and the Cardboard Division. The Pulp Division produces pulp for the Cardboard Division. The Cardboard Division may also purchase pulp from outside suppliers.

Exhibit 5
Transfer Price Alternatives at Simple Box Company

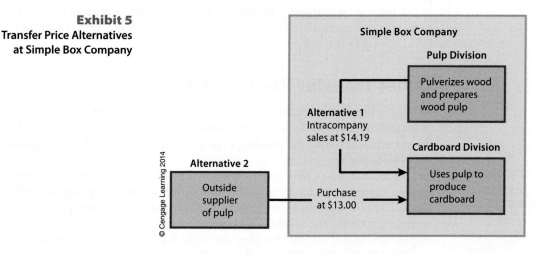

Exhibit 6 shows the development of a cost-plus transfer price for the Pulp Division. The Pulp Division's manager has created a one-year budget based on the expectation that the Cardboard Division will require 480,000 pounds of pulp. Unit costs appear in the last column.

Exhibit 6
Transfer Price Computation

Simple Box Company
Pulp Division—Transfer Price Computation

Cost Categories	Budgeted Costs	Cost per Unit
Direct materials:		
Wood	$1,584,000	$ 3.30
Scrap wood	336,000	0.70
Direct labor:		
Shaving/cleaning	768,000	1.60
Pulverizing	1,152,000	2.40
Blending	912,000	1.90
Overhead:		
Variable	936,000	1.95
Fixed	504,000	1.05
Subtotals	$6,192,000	$12.90
Costs allocated from corporate office	144,000	
Target profit, 10% of division's costs	619,200	1.29
Total costs and profit	$6,955,200	
Cost-plus transfer price		$14.19

© Cengage Learning 2014

Cost-Plus Transfer Price Notice that allocated corporate overhead is not included in the computation of the transfer price. Only the variable costs of $11.85 ($3.30 + $0.70 + $1.60 + $2.40 + $1.90 + $1.95) and the fixed cost of $1.05 related to the Pulp Division are included. The profit markup of 10 percent adds $1.29, producing the final cost-plus transfer price of $14.19.

Market Price Management could now dictate that the $14.19 price be used. However, the Cardboard Division's manager could point out that it is possible to purchase pulp from an outside supplier for $13.00 per pound. Use of the $13.00 price would represent a market-based approach.

Negotiated Transfer Price The best solution might be to agree on a negotiated transfer price between the variable costs of $11.85, the floor, and the outside market price of $13.00, the ceiling. The negotiation process will facilitate each manager's role in maximizing companywide profits and earning the 10 percent minimum return. Many times, the managers will split the difference and negotiate a price of $12.43 (rounded) [($11.85 + $13.00) ÷ 2].

Other Transfer Price Issues

At Simple Box Company, both managers brought their concerns to the attention of top management, and a settlement was reached. The negotiated transfer price allows the two divisions to share the final product's companywide profits when the boxes are sold on the outside market.

Additional issues may arise if the Cardboard Division chooses to purchase from outside suppliers. Because the Pulp Division has adequate capacity to fulfill the Cardboard Division's demands, it should sell to that division at any price that recovers its incremental costs. The incremental costs of intracompany sales include all variable costs of production and distribution plus any avoidable fixed costs that are directly traceable to intracompany sales. If the Cardboard Division can acquire products from outside suppliers at an annual cost that is less than the Pulp Division's incremental costs, then purchases should be made from the outside supplier because it will enhance the company's overall profits. Before making such a decision, a thorough analysis of the Pulp Division's operations should be conducted.

Using Transfer Prices to Measure Performance

Because a transfer price contains an estimated amount of profit, a manager's ability to meet a targeted profit can be measured. Although transfer prices are often called *artificial* or *created* prices, they and their related policies are closely connected with performance evaluation.

When transfer prices are used, a division can be evaluated as a profit center, even if it does not sell to outsiders, because using transfer prices to value the division's output creates simulated revenues for the division. Although the operating income is not based on real sales to outsiders, it is a valuable performance measure if the transfer prices are realistic.

Exhibit 7 shows a performance report for Simple Box Company's Pulp Division. The Pulp Division produced and transferred 42,000 pounds as budgeted at a negotiated transfer price of $13.00 per pound. (The budgeted costs are based on the costs per unit in Exhibit 6.) The performance report shows that the Pulp Division's actual gross margin was ($1,725), whereas the budgeted gross margin was $4,200. The difference of $5,925 stems from cost overages in various materials, labor, and variable overhead accounts. Those differences will need to be investigated, as they would be for any division.

Exhibit 7
Performance Report
Using Transfer Prices

Simple Box Company
Pulp Division—Performance Report
For March

	Budget	Actual	Difference Under/(Over) Budget
Sales to Carboard Division (42,000 lbs.)	$546,000	$546,000	$ 0
Costs Controllable by Manager			
Cost of goods sold:			
Direct materials:			
Wood	$138,600	$140,250	$(1,650)
Scrap wood	29,400	29,750	(350)
Direct labor:			
Shaving/cleaning	67,200	68,000	(800)
Pulverizing	100,800	102,000	(1,200)
Blending	79,800	80,750	(950)
Overhead:			
Variable	81,900	82,875	(975)
Fixed	44,100	44,100	—
Total cost of goods sold	$541,800	$547,725	$(5,925)
Gross margin from sales	$ 4,200	$ (1,725)	$ 5,925
Costs Uncontrollable by Manager			
Cost allocated from corporate office	12,600	12,600	—
Operating (loss)	$ (8,400)	$ (14,325)	$ 5,925

© Cengage Learning 2014

The use of transfer prices to simulate revenues allows further evaluation. For instance, the measures of operating income (loss) can be compared with the amount of capital the company has invested in the Pulp Division to determine whether the division is making an adequate return on the company's investment. The impact on the division of uncontrollable costs from the corporate office can also be assessed.

APPLY IT!

The Molding Process Division at Trophy Products has been treated as a cost center since the company was founded in 1968. Recently, management decided to change the performance evaluation approach and treat the company's processing divisions as profit centers. Each division is expected to earn a 20 percent profit on its total production costs. One of Trophy's products is a plastic base for a display chest. The Molding Process Division supplies this base to the Cabinet Process Division, and it also sells the base to another company. Molding's total production cost for the base is $27.40. It sells the base to the other company for $38.00. What should the transfer price for the plastic base be?

SOLUTION

In addition to the traditional approaches of transferring the product from one process to the next at variable or full cost, management should consider the following three options when setting the transfer price for the plastic base:

Cost plus profit: $27.40 + ($27.40 × 20%) = $32.88
Market price: $38.00
Negotiated price: Any price between $27.40 and $38.00

Managers of the Molding Process Division have the option of selling the division's output to the outside company and earning more than the 20 percent minimum return. They should also be able to earn more than 20 percent internally. A price at the midpoint of the negotiated price range, $32.70, seems fair.

TRY IT! SE7, SE8, SE9, E12A, E13A, E12B, E13B

SECTION 3

BUSINESS APPLICATIONS

BUSINESS APPLICATIONS
- Planning
- Performing
- Evaluating
- Communicating

RELEVANT LEARNING OBJECTIVE

LO 6 Relate pricing issues to the management process.

LO 6 Pricing and the Management Process

For an organization to stay in business, its selling price must:

- be competitive with the competition's price
- be acceptable to customers
- recover all costs incurred in bringing the product or service to market
- return a profit

If a manager deviates from any of these four pricing rules, there must be a specific short-run objective that accounts for the change. Breaking those pricing rules for a long period will force a company into bankruptcy. Exhibit 8 illustrates the elements of pricing that managers need to consider at each step in the management process.

Exhibit 8
Pricing and the Management Process

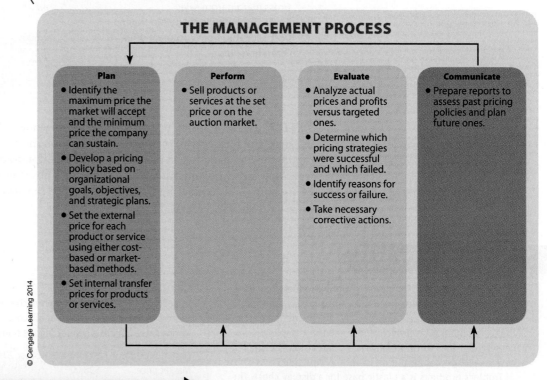

THE MANAGEMENT PROCESS

Plan
- Identify the maximum price the market will accept and the minimum price the company can sustain.
- Develop a pricing policy based on organizational goals, objectives, and strategic plans.
- Set the external price for each product or service using either cost-based or market-based methods.
- Set internal transfer prices for products or services.

Perform
- Sell products or services at the set price or on the auction market.

Evaluate
- Analyze actual prices and profits versus targeted ones.
- Determine which pricing strategies were successful and which failed.
- Identify reasons for success or failure.
- Take necessary corrective actions.

Communicate
- Prepare reports to assess past pricing policies and plan future ones.

© Cengage Learning 2014

APPLY IT!

For an organization to stay in business, which of the following is *not true* when setting its selling price? The selling price must

a. return a profit

b. be acceptable to customers

c. be acceptable to competitors

d. be competitive with the competition's price

e. recover all costs incurred in bringing the product or service to market

SOLUTION

c.

TRY IT! SE10, E14A, E14B

TriLevel Problem

Lab 126

The beginning of this chapter focused on **Lab 126**, an Amazon subsidiary that makes Kindle e-readers and e-reader applications for other handheld devices. Complete the following requirements in order to answer the questions posed at the beginning of the chapter.

Section 1: Concepts
How are pricing and the concept of revenue recognition related?

Section 2: Accounting Applications
How do companies determine the price of products?

Suppose that Undercovers Company makes a complete line of covers (a plain cover, a deluxe cover, and a trendy cover) for e-book readers like the Kindle. The covers are produced on an assembly line, beginning with the Stamping Department and continuing through the Sewing, Detailing, and Packaging departments. The projected costs of each cover and the percentages for assigning unavoidable fixed and common costs follow.

Cost Categories	Total Projected Costs	Plain Cover	Deluxe Cover	Trendy Cover
Direct materials:				
Leather	$137,000	$62,500	$29,000	$45,500
Magnet	5,250	2,500	1,000	1,750
Clip	9,250	3,750	2,000	3,500
Package	70,500	30,000	16,000	24,500
Direct labor:				
Stamping	53,750	22,500	12,000	19,250
Sewing	94,000	42,500	20,000	31,500
Detailing	107,500	45,000	24,000	38,500
Packaging	44,250	17,500	11,000	15,750
Indirect labor	173,000	77,500	36,000	59,500
Operating supplies	30,000	12,500	7,000	10,500
Variable overhead	90,500	40,000	19,000	31,500
Fixed overhead	120,000	45%	25%	30%
Distribution expenses	105,000	40%	20%	40%
Variable marketing expenses	123,000	$55,000	$26,000	$42,000
Fixed marketing expenses	85,400	40%	25%	35%
General and administrative expenses	47,600	40%	25%	35%

Undercovers' policy is to earn a minimum of 30 percent over total cost on each type of cover produced. Expected sales for the year are: plain, 50,000 units; deluxe, 20,000 units; and trendy, 35,000 units. Assume no change in inventory levels, and round all answers to two decimal places.

1. Using the gross margin pricing method, compute the selling price for each kind of cover.

2. The competition is selling a similar plain cover for around $14. Should this influence Undercovers' pricing decision? Give reasons for your answer.

Section 3: Business Applications

How does managerial accounting help managers during the management process with pricing decisions? To answer this question, match this chapter's manager responsibilities with when they occur within the management process.

a. Plan
b. Perform
c. Evaluate
d. Communicate

1. Prepare reports to assess past pricing policies and plan future ones.
2. Identify the maximum price the market will accept and the minimum price the company can sustain.
3. Develop a pricing policy based on organizational goals, objectives, and strategic plans.
4. Analyze actual prices and profits versus targeted ones.
5. Set the external price for each product or service using either cost-based or market-based methods.
6. Take necessary corrective actions.
7. Sell products or services at the set price or on the auction market.
8. Determine which pricing strategies were successful and which failed.
9. Identify reasons for success or failure.
10. Set internal transfer prices for products or services.

SOLUTION

Section 1: Concepts

The prices managers set have a significant impact on business operations, since revenue is computed by multiplying the product or service price by the quantity sold. Revenues are generally *recognized* when goods are transferred or services are rendered. On the income statement, the recognition of revenues is *matched* with the costs incurred to generate those revenues, resulting in the recognition of a net profit or loss, the fundamental measure of an organization's profitability. Thus, a manager's ability to set prices is essential to the long-term survival of any profit-oriented enterprise. There are various approaches that managers use to establish the prices of goods and services. Each approach may very well produce a different price for the same product or service. The process of establishing a correct price is, in fact, more of an art than a science. No one pricing method is superior because each business and market segment differs. Successful managers, like those at Lab 126, generally use several pricing approaches.

Early in the e-book reader market, there was little competition, and new models may have been priced to recover the product's cost and earn a certain amount of profit. Now that new products with desirable features, such as text-to-speech, are being introduced and the market has become very competitive, Lab 126's managers might use target costing to set a price for a new reader. To do so, they would subtract their desired profit from the proposed market price to arrive at the maximum target cost. A team of engineering, accounting, and sales managers would then analyze each proposed product feature to verify that the product could be designed and manufactured at or below the target cost.

Section 2: Accounting Applications

Before the selling prices are computed, the cost analysis must be completed and restructured to supply the information that is required for the pricing computations.

Cost Categories	Total Projected Costs	Plain Cover	Deluxe Cover	Trendy Cover
Total direct materials	$ 222,000	$ 98,750	$ 48,000	$ 75,250
Total direct labor	299,500	127,500	67,000	105,000
Indirect labor	173,000	77,500	36,000	59,500
Operating supplies	30,000	12,500	7,000	10,500
Variable overhead	90,500	40,000	19,000	31,500
Fixed overhead	120,000	54,000	30,000	36,000
Total production costs	$ 935,000	$410,250	$207,000	$317,750
Distribution expenses	$ 105,000	$ 42,000	$ 21,000	$ 42,000
Variable marketing expenses	123,000	55,000	26,000	42,000
Fixed marketing expenses	85,400	34,160	21,350	29,890
General and administrative expenses	47,600	19,040	11,900	16,660
Total selling, general, and administrative expenses	$ 361,000	$150,200	$ 80,250	$130,550
Total costs	$1,296,000	$560,450	$287,250	$448,300
Desired profit (30%)	$ 388,800	$168,135	$ 86,175	$134,490

1.

Markup percentage formula:

$$\text{Markup Percentage} = \frac{\text{Desired Profit} + \text{Total Selling, General, and Administrative Expenses}}{\text{Total Production Costs}}$$

Gross margin pricing formula:

Gross Margin-Based Price = Total Production Costs per Unit + (Markup Percentage × Total Production Costs per Unit)

Plain: $\text{Markup Percentage} = \dfrac{\$168,135 + \$150,200}{\$410,250} = 77.60\%*$

   Gross Margin-Based Price = ($410,250 ÷ 50,000) + [77.60% × ($410,250 ÷ 50,000)] = $14.57*

Deluxe: $\text{Markup Percentage} = \dfrac{\$86,175 + \$80,250}{\$207,000} = 80.40\%*$

   Gross Margin-Based Price = ($207,000 ÷ 20,000) + [80.40% × ($207,000 ÷ 20,000)] = $18.67*

Trendy: $\text{Markup Percentage} = \dfrac{\$134,490 + \$130,550}{\$317,750} = 83.41\%*$

   Gross Margin-Based Price = ($317,750 ÷ 35,000) + [83.41% × ($317,750 ÷ 35,000)] = $16.65*

*Rounded

2. If the quality and design of the competition's plain cover are similar to those of Undercovers' plain cover, Undercovers' management should consider reducing the price of its cover to the $14.00 range. At $14.57, Undercovers has a 30 percent profit built into its price. The plain cover's break-even is at $11.21 (rounded, $14.57 ÷ 1.3). Therefore, the company could reduce its price below the competitor's price and still make a significant profit.

Section 3: Business Applications

1. d		6. c	
2. a		7. b	
3. a		8. c	
4. c		9. c	
5. a		10. a	

Chapter Review

Explain how the pricing of goods and services relates to the concept of revenue recognition. **LO 1**

The prices managers set have a strong relationship with revenue recognition since revenue is computed by multiplying the product or service price by the quantity sold. When goods are transferred or services are rendered is generally when revenue is recognized. Costs are then matched with the revenues they generated and the difference is shown on the income statement as a net profit or loss, the fundamental measure of an organization's profitability. Thus, it is important that an organization's activities be guided by a pricing policy. A pricing policy is one way companies differentiate themselves from their competitors. Possible pricing policy objectives include (1) identifying and adhering to both short-run and long-run pricing strategies, (2) maximizing profits, (3) maintaining or gaining market share, (4) setting socially responsible prices, (5) maintaining a minimum rate of return on investment, and (6) being customer focused.

Describe economic pricing concepts, including the auction-based pricing method used on the Internet. **LO 2**

Microeconomic theory states that profits will be maximized when the difference between total revenue and total cost is greatest. Total revenue then increases more slowly, because as a product is marketed, price reductions are necessary to sell more units. Total cost increases when larger quantities are produced because fixed costs change. Profit is maximized at the point where the marginal revenue and marginal cost curves intersect. Auction-based pricing is growing in importance as a pricing mechanism as more companies and individuals are conducting business over the Internet. Basically, the Internet allows sellers and buyers to solicit bids and transact exchanges in an open market environment.

Use cost-based pricing methods to develop prices. **LO 3**

Cost-based pricing methods include gross margin pricing and return on assets pricing. Under these two methods, a markup representing a percentage of production costs or a desired rate of return is added to the total costs. A pricing method often used by service businesses is time and materials pricing.

Describe target costing, and use it to analyze pricing decisions and evaluate a new product opportunity. **LO 4**

Target costing (1) identifies the price at which a product will be competitive in the marketplace, (2) defines the desired profit to be made on the product, and (3) computes the target cost for the product by subtracting the desired profit from the competitive market price. Target costing gives managers the ability to control or dictate the costs of a new product at the planning stage. Under a traditional pricing system, managers cannot control costs until after the product has been manufactured. To identify a new product's target cost, the following formula is applied:

$$\text{Target Price} - \text{Desired Profit} = \text{Target Cost}$$

The target cost is then given to the engineers and product designers, who use it as a maximum cost to be incurred for materials and other resources needed to design and manufacture the product. It is their responsibility to create the product at or below its target cost. Sometimes, the cost requirements cannot be met. In such a case, the organization should try to adjust the product's design and the approach to production. If those attempts fail, the organization should either invest in new equipment and procedures or abandon its plans to market the product.

Describe how transfer pricing is used for transferring goods and services and evaluating performance within a division or segment. **LO 5**

A transfer price is the price at which goods and services are charged and exchanged between a company's divisions or segments. There are three primary approaches to developing transfer prices: (1) the price may be based on the cost of the item up to the point at which it is transferred to the next department or process; (2) the price may be based on market value if the item has an existing external market; or (3) the price may be negotiated by the managers of the buying and selling divisions. A cost-plus transfer price is the sum of costs incurred by the producing division plus an agreed-on profit percentage. A market-based transfer price is based on external market prices. In most cases, a negotiated transfer price is used; that is, a price is reached through bargaining between the managers of the selling and buying divisions. A division's performance may be evaluated by using transfer prices as the basis for determining revenues.

Relate pricing issues to the management process. **LO 6**

Managers use various pricing approaches throughout the management process to plan, use, evaluate, and report on the prices of goods and services. Each approach may very well produce a different price for the same product or service. The process of establishing a correct price is, in fact, more of an art than a science and is guided by four selling price principles. The price must be: competitive with the competition's price, be acceptable to customers, recover all costs incurred in bringing the product or service to market, and return a profit.

Key Terms

auction-based pricing 398 (LO2)
committed costs 405 (LO4)
cost-plus transfer price 408 (LO5)
decentralized organization 408 (LO5)
**gross margin pricing
   method** 399 (LO3)

incurred costs 405 (LO4)
marginal cost 397 (LO2)
marginal revenue 397 (LO2)
market transfer price 408 (LO5)
**negotiated transfer
   price** 408 (LO5)

**return on assets pricing
   method** 400 (LO3)
target costing 404 (LO4)
**time and materials
   pricing** 402 (LO3)
transfer price 408 (LO5)

Chapter Assignments

DISCUSSION QUESTIONS

LO 1 **DQ1. CONCEPT** ▶ How do product or service prices set by managers impact the revenue recognized by an organization?

LO 1 **DQ2.** Why is setting an appropriate price one of the most difficult decisions a manager makes?

LO 1, 6 **DQ3. BUSINESS APPLICATION** ▶ How does a pricing policy help companies differentiate their brands from their competitors?

LO 1, 6 **DQ4. BUSINESS APPLICATION** ▶ List some of the objectives of a pricing policy.

LO 1, 6 **DQ5. BUSINESS APPLICATION** ▶ What are some of the internal and external factors that affect pricing decisions?

SHORT EXERCISES

LO 1   ## External Factors That Influence Prices

SE1. ACCOUNTING CONNECTION ▶ Your client is about to introduce a very high-quality product that will remove an invasive form of pepper plant in the southern United States. The Marketing Department has established a price of $37 per gallon, and the company controller has projected total production, selling, and distribution costs of $26 per gallon. What other factors should your client consider before introducing the product into the marketplace?

LO 2   ## Traditional Economic Pricing Concept

SE2. ACCOUNTING CONNECTION ▶ You are to decide the total demand for a particular product. The product you are evaluating has the total cost and total revenue curves pictured in Exhibit 2A. The difference between total revenue and total cost is the same at the 5,000- and 8,000-unit levels. If you had to choose between those two levels of activity as goals for total sales over the life of the product, which would you prefer? Why?

LO 3   ## Cost-Based Price Setting

SE3. Kinder Company has collected the following data for one of its product lines: total production costs, $300,000; total selling, general, and administrative expenses, $112,600; desired profit, $67,400; and production costs per unit, $40. Using the gross margin pricing method, compute a suggested selling price for this product that would yield the desired profit.

LO 3   ## Pricing a Service

SE4. Eileen van Gelder runs a home repair business. Recently she gathered the following cost information about the repair of a client's deck: replacement wood, $650; deck screws and supplies, $112; and labor, 12 hours at $14 per hour. Van Gelder applies a 40 percent overhead rate to all direct costs of a job. Compute the total billing price for the repair of the deck.

LO 4   ## Committed Costs and Target Costing

SE5. ACCOUNTING CONNECTION ▶ Nat Osborn is a designer for Base Enterprises. In a discussion about a proposed new product, Osborn stated that the product's projected target cost was $6.50 below the committed costs identified by design estimates. Should the company proceed with the new product? Explain your answer, and include a definition of committed cost in your analysis.

LO 4   ## Pricing Using Target Costing

SE6. ACCOUNTING CONNECTION ▶ MTZ Furniture is considering a new product and must make a go or no-go decision before tomorrow's planning team meeting. Market research shows that the unit selling price agreeable to potential customers is $1,600, and the company's desired profit is 22 percent of target cost. The designer's preliminary estimate of the product's design, production, and distribution costs is $1,380 per unit. Using target costing, determine whether the company should market the new product. (Round to the nearest dollar.)

LO 5   ## Decision to Use Transfer Prices

SE7. ACCOUNTING CONNECTION ▶ The production process at Premium Castings includes eight processes, each of which is currently treated as a cost center with a specific set of operations to perform on each casting produced. Following the fourth process's operations, the rough castings have an external market. The fourth process must also supply the fifth process with its direct materials. Premium's management wants to develop a new approach to measuring process performance. Is Premium a candidate for using transfer prices? Explain your answer.

LO **5**   **Cost-Based Versus Market-Based Transfer Prices**

SE8. ACCOUNTING CONNECTION ▶ Refer to the information in **SE7**. Should Premium Castings use cost-based, market-based, or negotiated transfer prices? Why?

LO **5**   **Developing a Negotiated Transfer Price**

SE9. The Cookie Division at Sweet Products has been treated as a cost center since the company was founded. Recently, management decided to change the performance evaluation approach and treat its processing divisions as profit centers. Each division is expected to earn a 20 percent profit on its total production costs. One of Sweet's products is chocolate chip cookie dough. The Cookie Division supplies this dough to the Packaged Cookies Division, and it also sells it to another company. Cookie Division's total production cost for the dough is $2.40 per pound. It sells the dough to the other company for $5.00 a pound. What should the transfer price for a pound of cookie dough be?

LO **6**   **Rules for Establishing Prices**

SE10. BUSINESS APPLICATION ▶ Jay Patel is planning to open a pizza restaurant next month in Flora, Alabama. He plans to sell his large pizzas for a base price of $18 plus $2 for each topping selected. When asked how he arrived at the base price, he said that his cousin developed that price for his pizza restaurant in New York City. What pricing rules has Patel not followed?

EXERCISES: SET A

LO **1**   **External and Internal Pricing Factors**

E1A. Ready Tires features more than a dozen brands of tires in many sizes. Two of the brands are RoadPlus and RoadPower. Information about the two brands follows.

	RoadPlus	RoadPower
Selling price:		
Tire, installed	$180	$170
Cost per tire	120	80

As shown, selling prices include installation costs. Each tire costs $20 to install.

1. Compute each brand's net unit selling price after installation.
2. **ACCOUNTING CONNECTION** ▶ Was cost the main consideration in setting those prices?
3. **ACCOUNTING CONNECTION** ▶ What other factors could have influenced those prices?

LO **2**   **Traditional Economic Pricing Theory**

E2A. InStyle, a product design firm, has just completed a contract to develop a wireless entry system. The wireless key fob needs to be recharged only once a week and can be used worldwide. Initial fixed costs for this product are $4,000. The designers estimate that the product will break even at the $5,000/100-unit mark. Total revenues will again equal total costs at the $25,000/900-unit point. Marginal cost is expected to equal marginal revenue when 550 units are sold.

1. Sketch total revenue and total cost curves for this product. Mark the vertical axis at each $5,000 increment and the horizontal axis at each 100-unit increment.
2. Based on your total revenue and total cost curves in **1**, at what unit selling price will profits be maximized? (Round to the nearest cent.)

LO 3   **Price Determination**

E3A. Soft Industries has just patented a new lotion with lasting sun protection. The company's controller has developed the following annual information for use in price determination meetings:

Variable production costs	$ 450,000
Fixed overhead	250,000
Selling expenses	100,000
General and administrative expenses	75,000
Desired profit	315,000
Cost of assets employed	1,000,000

Annual demand for the product is expected to be 500,000 tubes. On average, the company now earns an 8 percent return on assets.

1. Compute the projected unit cost for one tube of lotion.
2. Using gross margin pricing, compute the markup percentage and selling price for one tube.
3. Using return on assets pricing, compute the unit price for one tube of lotion.

LO 3   **Pricing a Service**

E4A. Iowa has just passed a law making it mandatory to have every chicken inspected at least once a year for a variety of communicable diseases. Cluck Enterprises is considering entering this inspection business. After extensive studies, Cluck's owner has developed the following annual projections:

Direct service labor	$275,000
Variable service overhead costs	25,000
Fixed service overhead costs	200,000
Selling expenses	100,500
General and administrative expenses	59,500
Minimum desired profit	100,000
Cost of assets employed	800,000

The owner believes his company could inspect 2,000,000 chickens per year. On average, the company now earns a 6 percent return on assets.

1. Compute the projected cost of inspecting each chicken.
2. Using gross margin pricing, determine the price to charge for inspecting each chicken.
3. Using return on assets pricing, compute the unit price to charge for this inspection service. (Round to two decimal places.)

LO 3   **Cost-Based Pricing**

E5A. Metro Transit is determining the price for its newest prepaid fare card. The fare card can be used at any transportation station or retail outlet—no PIN number or signature is required. The following annual information has been developed for use in upcoming price determination meetings:

Variable processing costs	$40 million
Fixed processing costs	4 million
Selling expenses (fixed)	4 million
General and administrative expenses (fixed)	2 million
Desired profit	90 million
Cost of assets employed	5 billion

Annual usage is expected to be 5 billion transactions. On average, the company now earns a 5 percent return on assets.

1. Compute the projected cost of one transaction.
2. Using gross margin pricing, compute the price to charge per transaction. (Round to three decimal places.)
3. Using return on assets pricing, compute the price to charge per transaction.

LO 3 **Pricing Services**

E6A. Watt Car Repair specializes in repairing electric cars. The company uses a 60 percent markup rate on parts to cover parts-related overhead costs and profit margin. It uses a 200 percent markup rate on labor to cover labor-related overhead costs and profit margin. Compute the bill for a recent job that used the following parts and labor:

Material and repair parts used	$300
Labor used	5 hours at $40 per hour

LO 3 **Time and Materials Pricing**

E7A. Orange Remodeling Service specializes in renovating older homes. Last week the company was asked to bid on the following remodeling job. The list of materials and labor needed to complete the job follows.

Materials		**Labor**	
Lumber	$ 5,000	Carpenter	$ 4,000
Nails/bolts	200	Floor specialist	2,000
Paint	1,800	Painter	2,000
Glass	3,000	Supervisor	1,000
Doors	500	Helpers	3,000
Hardware	500	Total	$12,000
Supplies	1,000		
Total	$12,000		

Orange uses an overhead markup percentage for materials (50 percent) and for labor (60 percent). Those markups cover all operating costs. In addition, Orange expects to make at least a 30 percent profit on all jobs. Compute the price that Orange should quote for the job.

LO 4 **Target Costing and Pricing**

E8A. Lovebug Company has determined that its new automotive hood screen would gain widespread customer acceptance if the company could price it at or under $30. Anticipated labor hours and costs for each unit of the new product follow.

Direct materials cost	$5
Direct labor cost	
Manufacturing labor:	
Hours	0.2
Hourly labor rate	$10
Assembly labor:	
Hours	0.5
Hourly labor rate	$15
Machine hours	1

The company currently uses the following three activity-based cost rates:

Materials handling	$0.30 per dollar of direct materials
Production	$5.00 per machine hour
Product delivery	$0.50 per unit

ACCOUNTING CONNECTION ▶ The company's minimum desired profit is 40 percent over total production and delivery cost. Compute the target cost for the new hood screen, and determine if the company should market it. (Round to two decimal places.)

LO 4 **Target Costing**

E9A. ACCOUNTING CONNECTION ▶ Assume the same facts as in **E8A** except that the company's minimum desired profit has been revised to 20 percent over production and delivery costs as a result of a recent economic downturn. Compute the revised target cost for the new hood screen, and determine if the company should market it.

LO 4

Target Costing

E10A. Suppose that Sleek Manufacturing is developing a new table targeted to sell for less than $10 and that it is considering the two production alternatives that follow. Rank the alternatives, assuming that the company's minimum desired profit is 40 percent over total production costs. (Round to two decimal places.)

	Alternative A	Alternative B
Direct material costs	$2	$2
Direct labor cost	0.25 hour at $10 per hour	0.20 hour at $12 per hour
Overhead costs	50 percent of direct labor costs	$0.40 per dollar of direct materials

LO 4

Target Costing

E11A. Management at Pew Co. is considering the development of an automated machine called the AutoMate. After conferring with the design engineers, the controller's staff assembled the following data about this product:

Target selling price	$500 per unit
Desired profit percentage	50% of total unit cost
Projected unit demand	5,000 units
Activity-based cost rates:	
Materials handling	1% of direct materials and purchased parts cost
Engineering	$20 per unit
Production and assembly	$10 per machine hour
Delivery	$7 per unit
Marketing	$4 per unit
Per-unit data:	
Direct materials cost	$160
Purchased parts cost	$40
Manufacturing labor:	
Hours	2
Hourly labor rate	$15
Assembly labor:	
Hours	3
Hourly labor rate	$10
Machine hours	4

1. Compute the product's target cost. (Round to the nearest dollar.)
2. Compute the product's projected unit cost based on the design engineers' estimates.
3. **ACCOUNTING CONNECTION ▶** Should management produce and market the Auto-Mate? Defend your answer.

LO 5

Transfer Price Comparison

E12A. Michelle Nicholas is developing a transfer price for the housing section of an automatic garage door opener. The housing for the opener is made in Department H. It is then passed on to Department G, where final assembly occurs. Unit costs for the housing follow.

Cost Categories	Unit Costs
Direct materials	$3.00
Direct labor	2.00
Variable overhead	1.00
Fixed overhead	2.50
Profit markup, 25% of cost	?

An outside vendor can supply the housing for $10.00 per unit.

1. Develop a cost-plus transfer price for the housing. (Round to two decimal places.)
2. **ACCOUNTING CONNECTION** ▶ What should the transfer price be? Support your answer.

LO 5   **Transfer Pricing**

E13A. Quality Company's Seconds Store offers refurbished or factory seconds products to the public at substantially reduced prices. The controller is developing transfer price alternatives to present to management to determine the best price to use when transferring products from the factory to the store, using the following data:

Unit price if sold to outside retailers	$20
Variable product cost per unit	$8
Fixed product cost per unit	$6
Seconds Store profit markup	50%

1. What is the market-based transfer price alternative?
2. What is the minimum transfer price alternative?
3. Compute the cost-plus transfer price alternative assuming cost includes variable costs only.

LO 6   **Pricing Policy Objectives**

E14A. BUSINESS APPLICATION ▶ Bulls Eye, Ltd., is an international merchandising company that retails medium-priced goods. Its retail outlets are located throughout the United States, France, Germany, and Great Britain. Management wants to maintain the company's image of providing the highest possible quality at the lowest possible prices. Selling prices are developed to draw customers away from competitors' stores. First-of-the-month sales are regularly held at all stores, and customers are accustomed to this practice. Company buyers are carefully trained to seek out quality goods at inexpensive prices. Sales are targeted to increase a minimum of 5 percent per year. All sales should yield a 15 percent return on assets. Sales personnel are expected to wear a uniform while working. All stores are required to be clean and well organized. Competitors' prices are checked daily. Identify Bulls Eye's pricing policy objectives.

EXERCISES: SET B

Visit the textbook companion website at www.cengagebrain.com to access Exercise Set B for this chapter.

PROBLEMS

LO 3   **Pricing Decision**

✔ 1: Total costs and expenses: $12,492,000
✔ 2: Gross margin-based price: $24.03

P1. Chill Industries specializes in the assembly of home appliances. One division focuses most of its efforts on assembling a convection toaster. Projected costs of this product follow.

Cost Description	Budgeted Costs
Toaster casings	$ 960,000
Electrical components	2,220,000
Direct labor	3,600,000
Variable indirect assembly costs	780,000
Fixed indirect assembly costs	1,740,000
Selling expenses	1,536,000
General operating expenses	840,000
Administrative expenses	816,000

(Continued)

The projected costs are based on an estimated demand of 600,000 convection toasters per year. The company wants to make a $1,923,000 profit.

Competitors have just published their wholesale prices for the coming year. They range from $21.60 to $22.64 per toaster. The Chill convection toaster is known for its high quality and modern look. It competes with products at the top end of the price range. Even with its reputation, however, every $0.20 increase above the top competitor's price causes a drop in demand of 60,000 units below the original estimate. Assume that all price changes are in $0.20 increments.

REQUIRED

1. Prepare a schedule of total projected costs and unit costs.
2. Use gross margin pricing to compute the anticipated selling price. (Round to two decimal places.)
3. **ACCOUNTING CONNECTION ▶** Based on competitors' prices, what should the Chill toaster sell for (assume a constant unit cost)? Defend your answer. (*Hint:* Determine the total profit at various sales levels.)
4. **ACCOUNTING CONNECTION ▶** Would your pricing structure in requirement **3** change if the company had only limited competition at its quality level? If so, in what direction? Explain why.

LO **3**   **Pricing Decisions**

✔ 1a: Lawn mower return on assets-based price: $114.60
✔ 1b: Lawn edger gross margin-based price: $54

P2. (*CMA adapted*) Cutting Edge Company manufactures lawn equipment for retail stores. Ron Ellington, the vice president of marketing, has proposed that the company introduce two new products: a GPS lawn mower and a laser-guided lawn edger. Ellington has requested that the Profit Planning Department develop preliminary selling prices for the two new products for his review.

Profit Planning has followed the company's standard policy for developing potential selling prices. It has used all data available for each product. The data accumulated by Profit Planning follows.

	Lawn Mower	Lawn Edger
Estimated annual demand in units	20,000	18,000
Estimated unit manufacturing costs	$100.00	$30.00
Estimated unit selling and administrative expenses	$5.00	Not available
Assets employed in manufacturing	$480,000	Not available

Cutting Edge plans to use an average of $1,200,000 in assets to support operations in the current year. The condensed budgeted income statement that follows reflects the planned return on assets of 40 percent ($480,000 ÷ $1,200,000) for the entire company for all products.

Cutting Edge Company
Budgeted Income Statement
For the Year Ended May 31
(in thousands)

Revenue	$2,880
Cost of goods sold	1,600
Gross margin	$1,280
Selling and administrative expenses	800
Operating income	$ 480

REQUIRED

1. Use the budgeted income statement to calculate a potential selling price for (a) the lawn mower, using return on assets pricing, and (b) the lawn edger, using gross margin pricing.
2. **ACCOUNTING CONNECTION ▶** Could a selling price for the lawn mower be calculated using return on assets pricing? Explain your answer.

3. **ACCOUNTING CONNECTION** ▶ Which of the two pricing methods—return on assets pricing or gross margin pricing—is more appropriate for decision analysis? Explain your answer.

4. **ACCOUNTING CONNECTION** ▶ Discuss the additional steps Ron Ellington is likely to take in setting an actual selling price for each of the two products after he receives their potential selling prices (as calculated in requirement **1**.)

LO **3**

Time and Materials Pricing in a Service Business

✔ 3: Total materials and parts: $4,966.50
Materials overhead: $6,456.45
✔ Direct labor: $1,412.40
✔ Direct labor overhead: $1,977.36

P3. Acme Maintenance, Inc., repairs heavy construction equipment and vehicles. Recently, Turnkey Construction Company had one of its giant earthmovers overhauled and its tires replaced. Repair work for a vehicle of that size usually takes from one week to ten days. The vehicle must be lifted up so that maintenance workers can gain access to the engine. Parts are normally so large that a crane must be used to put them into place.

The company uses the time and materials pricing system and data from the previous year to compute markup percentages for overhead related to parts and materials and overhead related to direct labor. It adds markups of 130 percent to the cost of materials and parts and 140 percent to the cost of direct labor to cover overhead and profit. The following materials, parts, and direct labor are needed to repair the giant earthmover:

Quantity	Unit Price	Hours	Hourly Rate
Materials and parts:		Direct labor:	
24 Spark plugs	$ 3.40	42 Mechanic hours	$18.20
20 Oil, quarts	2.90	54 Assistant mechanic hours	12.00
12 Hoses	11.60		
1 Water pump	764.00		
30 Coolant, quarts	6.50		
18 Clamps	5.90		
1 Distributor cap	128.40		
1 Carburetor	214.10		
4 Tires	820.00		

REQUIRED

Prepare a complete billing for this job. Include itemized amounts for each type of materials, parts, and direct labor. Follow the time and materials pricing approach, and show the total price for the job.

LO **4**

Pricing Using Target Costing

✔ 1: Target cost for Speed-Calc 5: $88 .00
2: Projected total unit cost for Speed-Calc 4: $74.22
✔ 2: Projected total unit cost for Speed-Calc 5: $84.84

P4. Yuan Hwang Corp. is considering marketing two new graphing calculators, named Speed-Calc 4 and Speed-Calc 5. According to recent market research, the two products will surpass the current competition in both speed and quality and would be welcomed in the market. Customers would be willing to pay $98 for Speed-Calc 4 and $110 for Speed-Calc 5, based on their projected design capabilities. Both products have many uses, but the primary market interest comes from college students. Current production capacity exists for the manufacture and assembly of the two products. The company has a minimum desired profit of 25 percent above all costs for all of its products. Current activity-based cost rates follow.

Materials/parts handling	$1.20 per dollar of direct materials and purchased parts cost
Production	$8.00 per machine hour
Marketing/delivery	$4.40 per unit of Speed-Calc 4
	$6.20 per unit of Speed-Calc 5

(Continued)

Design engineering and accounting estimates to produce the two new products follow.

	Speed-Calc 4	Speed-Calc 5
Projected unit demand	100,000	80,000
Per-unit data:		
Direct materials cost	$5.50	$7.50
Computer chip cost	$10.60	$11.70
Production labor:		
Hours	1.2	1.3
Hourly labor rate	$16.00	$16.00
Assembly labor:		
Hours	0.6	0.5
Hourly labor rate	$12.00	$12.00
Machine hours	1	1.2

REQUIRED

1. Compute the target costs for each product.
2. Compute the projected total unit cost of production and delivery.
3. **ACCOUNTING CONNECTION** ▶ Using the target costing approach, decide whether the products should be produced.

LO **5**   ## Developing Transfer Prices

✔ 1: Cost-plus transfer price: $19.20

SPREADSHEET

P5. BUSINESS APPLICATION ▶ Sand Company has two divisions, Glass Division and Instrument Division. For several years, Glass Division has manufactured a special glass container, which it sells to Instrument Division at the prevailing market price of $20. Glass Division produces the glass containers only for Instrument Division and does not sell the product to outside customers. Annual production and sales volume is 20,000 containers. A unit cost analysis for Glass Division follows.

Cost Categories	Costs per Container
Direct materials	$ 3.50
Direct labor, 1/4 hour	2.30
Variable overhead	7.50
Avoidable fixed costs: $30,000 ÷ 20,000 units	1.50
Corporate overhead: $3.60 per direct labor hour	4.50
Variable shipping costs	1.20
Unit cost	$20.50

Corporate overhead represents the allocated joint fixed costs of production—building depreciation, property taxes, insurance, and executives' salaries. A profit markup of 20 percent is used to determine transfer prices.

REQUIRED

1. What would be the appropriate transfer price for Glass Division to use in billing its transactions with Instrument Division?
2. If Glass Division decided to sell some containers to outside customers, would your answer to requirement 1 change? Defend your response.
3. What factors concerning transfer price should management consider when transferring products between divisions?

ALTERNATE PROBLEMS

LO **3**   ## Pricing Decision

✔ 1: Total costs and expenses: $5,658,800
✔ 2: Gross margin-based price: $27.68

P6. Connect, Ltd., designs and assembles low-priced portable Internet devices. It estimates that there will be 235,000 requests for its most popular model. Budgeted costs for this product for the year follow.

Description	Budgeted Costs
Casing	$ 432,400
Battery chamber	545,200
Electronics	1,151,500
Direct labor	1,598,000
Variable indirect assembly costs	789,600
Fixed indirect assembly costs	338,400
Selling expenses	493,500
General operating expenses	183,300
Administrative expenses	126,900

The budget is based on the demand previously stated. The company wants to earn an annual operating income of $846,000.

Last week, four competitors released the following wholesale prices for the year: Competitor A, $25.68; Competitor B, $24.58; Competitor C, $23.96; Competitor D, $25.30.

Connect's portable devices are known for their high quality. However, every $1 price increase above the top competitor's price causes a 55,000-unit drop in demand from the original estimate. (Assume all price changes occur in $1 increments.)

REQUIRED

1. Prepare a schedule of total projected costs and unit costs.
2. Use gross margin pricing to compute the anticipated selling price. (Round to two decimal places.)
3. **ACCOUNTING CONNECTION** ▶ Based on competitors' prices, what should Connect's portable device sell for (assume a constant unit cost)? Defend your answer. (*Hint:* Determine the total operating income at various sales levels.)
4. **ACCOUNTING CONNECTION** ▶ Would your pricing structure in requirement **3** change if the company had only limited competition at this quality level? If so, in what direction? Explain why.

LO **3**   **Pricing Decisions**

✔ 1a: Electric stapler return on assets-based price: $20
✔ 1b: Electric pencil sharpener gross margin-based price: $25.00

P7. (*CMA adapted*) Offix Company manufactures office equipment for retail stores. Carole Windsor, the vice president of marketing, has proposed that Offix introduce two new products: an electric stapler and an electric pencil sharpener. Windsor has requested that the Profit Planning Department develop preliminary selling prices for the two new products for her review.

Profit Planning has followed the company's standard policy for developing potential selling prices. It has used all data available for each product. The data accumulated by Profit Planning follows.

	Electric Stapler	Electric Pencil Sharpener
Estimated annual demand in units	16,000	12,000
Estimated unit manufacturing costs	$14.00	$15.00
Estimated unit selling and administrative expenses	$3.00	Not available
Assets employed in manufacturing	$240,000	Not available

Offix plans to use an average of $1,200,000 in assets to support operations in the current year. The condensed budgeted income statement that follows reflects the planned return on assets of 20 percent ($240,000 ÷ $1,200,000) for the entire company for all products.

Offix Company
Budgeted Income Statement
For the Year Ended May 31
(in thousands)

Revenue	$2,400
Cost of goods sold	1,440
Gross margin	$ 960
Selling and administrative expenses	720
Operating income	$ 240

(Continued)

REQUIRED

1. Use the budgeted income statement to calculate a potential selling price for (a) the stapler, using return on assets pricing, and (b) the pencil sharpener, using gross margin pricing. (Round to two decimal places.)

2. **ACCOUNTING CONNECTION ▶** Could a selling price for the electric pencil sharpener be calculated using return on assets pricing? Explain your answer.

3. **ACCOUNTING CONNECTION ▶** Which of the two pricing methods—return on assets pricing or gross margin pricing—is more appropriate for decision analysis? Explain your answer.

4. **ACCOUNTING CONNECTION ▶** Discuss the additional steps Carole Windsor is likely to take in setting an actual selling price for each of the two products after she receives their potential selling prices (as calculated in requirement **1**.)

LO **3**

Time and Materials Pricing in a Service Business

P8. Route 66 Car Repair performs routine maintenance on rental vehicles. Recently, the local auto rental business had its fleet serviced. The company uses the time and materials pricing system and data from the previous year to compute markup percentages for overhead related to parts and materials and overhead related to direct labor. It adds markups of 100 percent to the cost of materials and parts and 120 percent to the cost of direct labor to cover overhead and profit. The following materials, parts, and direct labor are needed to repair the rental fleet:

Quantity	Unit Price	Hours	Hourly Rate
Materials and parts:		Direct labor:	
24 Spark plugs	$ 0.50	38 Mechanic hours	$28.20
50 Oil, quarts	2.50	61 Assistant mechanic hours	14.00
12 Hoses	11.20		
1 Sun visor	13.50		
36 Coolant, quarts	6.50		
4 Clamps	5.50		
5 Emergency kits	12.40		
40 Washer fluid	1.25		
4 Tires	300.00		

REQUIRED

Prepare a complete billing for this job. Include itemized amounts for each type of materials, parts, and direct labor. Follow the time and materials pricing approach, and show the total price for the job.

LO **4**

Pricing Using Target Costing

P9. Queen Tool Company designs and produces a line of high-quality machine tools and markets them throughout the world. Its main competition comes from French, British, and Korean companies. Five competitors have recently introduced two highly specialized machine tools, Y14 and Z33. The prices charged for Y14 range from $625 to $675 per tool, and the price range for Z33 is from $800 to $840 per tool. Queen is contemplating entering the market for these two products. Market research has indicated that if Queen can sell Y14 for $650 per tool and Z33 for $750 per tool, it will be successful in marketing the products worldwide. The company's profit markup is 25 percent over all costs to produce and deliver a product. Current activity-based cost rates follow.

Materials handling	$1.30 per dollar of direct materials and purchased parts cost
Production	$4.40 per machine hour
Product delivery	$34.00 per unit of Y14
	$40.00 per unit of Z33

✔ 8: Total materials and parts: $1,852.90
✔ Materials overhead: $1,852.90
✔ Direct labor: $1,925.60
✔ Direct labor overhead: $2,310.72

✔ 1: Target cost for product Y14: $520 .00
✔ 2: Projected total unit cost for product Y14: $502.10
✔ 2: Projected total unit cost for product Z33: $623.40

Design engineering and accounting estimates for the production of the two new products follow.

	Product Y14	Product Z33
Projected unit demand	75,000	95,000
Per-unit data:		
Direct materials cost	$50.00	$60.00
Purchased parts cost	$65.00	$70.00
Manufacturing labor:		
Hours	6.2	7.4
Hourly labor rate	$14.00	$14.00
Assembly labor:		
Hours	4.6	9.2
Hourly labor rate	$12.00	$12.00
Machine hours	14	16

REQUIRED

1. Compute the target cost for each product.
2. Compute the total projected unit cost of producing and delivering each product.
3. **ACCOUNTING CONNECTION** ▶ Using target costing, decide whether the products should be produced.

LO **5**

✔ 1 Cost-plus transfer price: $34.08

Developing Transfer Prices

P10. BUSINESS APPLICATION ▶ Tim Corporation produces sound equipment for home use. The Research and Development (R&D) Division is responsible for continually evaluating and updating critical electronic parts used in the corporation's products. Two years ago, R&D took on the added responsibility of producing all microchip circuit boards for the company's sound equipment. One of Tim's specialties is a sound dissemination board (SDB) that greatly enhances the quality of Tim's speakers.

Demand for the SDB has increased significantly in the past year. As a result, R&D has increased its production and assembly labor force. Three outside customers now want to purchase the SDB. To date, R&D has been producing SDBs for internal use only.

The R&D controller wants to create a transfer price for the SDBs that will apply to all intracompany transfers. Estimated demand over the next six months is 235,000 SDBs for internal use and 165,000 SDBs for external customers, for a total of 400,000 units. The following data show cost projections for the next six months:

Materials and parts	$2,600,000
Direct labor	1,920,000
Supplies	100,000
Indirect labor	580,000
Other variable overhead costs	200,000
Fixed overhead, SDBs	1,840,000
Other fixed overhead, corporate	560,000
Variable selling expenses, SDBs	1,480,000
Fixed selling expenses, corporate	520,000
General corporate operating expenses	880,000
Corporate administrative expenses	680,000

A profit markup of at least 20 percent must be added to total unit cost for internal transfer purposes. Outside customers are willing to pay $35 for each SDB. All categories of fixed costs are assumed to be unavoidable.

REQUIRED

1. Prepare a table that shows the total budgeted costs and the cost per unit for each component of the budget. Also show the profit markup and the cost-plus transfer price.
2. Should R&D use the computed transfer price? Explain the factors that influenced your decision.

CASES

LO **1, 6**

Conceptual Understanding: Ethics in Pricing

C1. BUSINESS APPLICATION ▶ Karnes Company has been doing business in Shanghai for the past three years. The company produces leather handbags that are in great demand there. When Karnes's sales person Harriet Pakay was recently in Shanghai, Kai Choy, the purchasing agent for Chen Enterprises, approached her to arrange for a purchase of 2,500 handbags. Karnes's usual price is $75 per bag. Kai Choy wanted to purchase the handbags at $65 per bag. After an hour of haggling, they agreed to a final price of $68 per item. When Pakay returned to her hotel room after dinner, she found an envelope containing five new $100 bills and a note that said, "Thank you for agreeing to our order of 2,500 handbags at $68 per bag. My company's president wants you to have the enclosed gift for your fine service." Pakay later learned that Kai Choy was following her company's normal business practice. What should Harriet Pakay do? Is the gift hers to keep? Be prepared to justify your opinion.

LO **3, 4**

Conceptual Understanding: Product Pricing in a Foreign Market

C2. Torner, Inc., is an international corporation that manufactures and sells home care products. Today a meeting is being held at corporate headquarters in New York City. The purpose of the meeting is to discuss changing the price of the laundry detergent the company manufactures and sells in Brazil. During the meeting, a conflict develops between Karl Mickleson, the corporate sales manager, and José Tapral, the Brazilian Division's sales manager.

Mickleson insists that the selling price of the laundry detergent should be increased to the equivalent of U.S. $3. This increase is necessary because the Brazilian Division's costs are higher than those of other international divisions. The Brazilian Division is paying high interest rates on notes payable for the acquisition of a new manufacturing plant. In addition, a stronger, more expensive ingredient has been introduced into the laundry detergent, which has caused the product cost to increase by $0.20.

Tapral believes that the laundry detergent's selling price should remain at $2.50 for several reasons. He argues that the market for laundry detergent in Brazil is highly competitive. Labor costs are low, and the costs of distribution are small because the target market is limited to the Rio de Janeiro metropolitan area. Inflation is extremely high in Brazil, and the Brazilian government continues to impose policies to control inflation. Because of these controls, Tapral insists, buyers will resist any price hikes.

1. What selling price do you believe Torner, Inc., should set for the laundry detergent? Explain your answer. Do you believe Torner should let the Brazilian Division set the selling price for laundry detergent in the future? When should corporate headquarters set prices?
2. Based on the information given, should cost-based pricing or target costing be used to set the selling price for laundry detergent in Brazil? Explain your answer.

LO **4**

Internet Case: Target Costing and the Internet

C3. Assume that you work for a company that wants to develop a product to compete with the Kindle. You have been assigned the task of using target costing to help in its development. Do a search for Kindle product reviews and product specifications and get price quotes. Why would your company's management want to use target costing to help in its development of a competitive e-book reader? What retail price would you suggest be used as a basis for target costing? Assuming a desired profit of 25 percent of selling price, what is the resulting target cost? What actions should the company take now?

LO **4** **Decision Analysis: Target Costing**

C4. Treadwell Electronics, Inc., produces circuit boards for electronic devices that are made by more than a dozen customers. Competition among the producers of circuit boards is keen, with over 30 companies bidding on every job request from those customers. The circuit boards can vary widely in their complexity, and their unit prices can range from $250 to more than $500.

Treadwell's controller is concerned that the cost planning projection for a new complex circuit board, the CX35, is almost 6 percent above its target cost. The controller has asked the Engineering Design Department to review its design and projections and come up with alternatives that will reduce the proposed product's costs to equal to or below the target cost. The following information was used to develop the initial cost projections:

Target selling price	$590.00 per unit
Desired profit percentage	25% of total unit cost
Projected unit demand	13,600 units
Per-unit data:	
Direct materials cost	$56.00
Purchased parts cost	$37.00
Manufacturing labor:	
Hours	4.5
Hourly labor rate	$14.00
Assembly labor:	
Hours	5.2
Hourly labor rate	$15.00
Machine hours	26
Activity-based cost rates:	
Materials handling	10% of direct materials and purchased parts cost
Engineering	$13.50 per unit
Production	$8.20 per machine hour
Product delivery	$24.00 per unit
Marketing	$6.00 per unit

1. Compute the product's target cost.
2. Compute the product cost of the original estimate to verify that the controller's calculations were correct.
3. Rework the product cost calculations for each of the following alternatives recommended by the design engineers:
   a. Cut product quality, which will reduce direct materials cost by 20 percent and purchased parts cost by 15 percent.
   b. Increase the quality of direct materials, which will increase direct materials cost by 20 percent but will reduce machine hours by 10 percent, manufacturing labor hours by 16 percent, and assembly labor hours by 20 percent.
4. What decision should Treadwell's management make about the new product? Defend your answer.

LO **5** **Interpreting Managerial Reports: Transfer Pricing**

C5. BUSINESS APPLICATION ▶ Dalton Industries, Inc., has two major operating divisions, the Furniture Division and the Electronics Division. The company's main product is a deluxe entertainment center. The centers' components (shelving, drawers, and glass cabinet doors) are manufactured by the Furniture Division, and the Electronics Division produces all electronic components (HDTV receivers, portable electronics docking stations, speakers, etc.) and assembles the sets. The company has a decentralized organizational structure.

(Continued)

The Furniture Division not only supplies entertainment centers to the Electronics Division but also sells shelving, drawers, and cabinet doors to other manufacturers. The following unit cost breakdown for a deluxe entertainment center was developed based on a typical sales order of 40 entertainment centers:

Direct materials	$ 32.00
Direct labor	15.00
Variable overhead	12.00
Fixed overhead	18.00
Variable selling expenses	9.00
Fixed selling expenses	6.00
Fixed general and administrative expenses	8.00
Total unit cost	$100.00

The Furniture Division's usual profit margin is 20 percent, and the regular selling price of a deluxe entertainment center is $120. The division's managers recently decided that $120 will also be the transfer price for all intracompany transactions.

Managers at the Electronics Division are unhappy with that decision. They claim that the Furniture Division will show superior performance at the expense of the Electronics Division. Competition recently forced the company to lower its prices. Because of the newly established transfer price for the cabinet, the Electronics Division's portion of the profit margin on deluxe entertainment centers was lowered to 18 percent. To counteract the new intracompany transfer price, the managers of the Electronics Division announced that effective immediately, all furniture components of each center (shelving, drawers, and glass cabinet doors) will be purchased from an outside supplier, in lots of 200 entertainment centers at a unit price of $110 per center. The company president, Jack Dalton, has called a meeting of both divisions to negotiate a fair intracompany transfer price. The following prices were listed as possible alternatives:

Current market price	$120 per entertainment center
Current outside purchase price (This price is based on a large-quantity purchase discount. It will cause increased storage costs for the Electronics Division.)	$110 per entertainment center
Total unit manufacturing costs plus a 20 percent profit margin: $77.00 + $15.40	$92.40 per entertainment center
Total unit costs excluding variable selling expenses plus a 20 percent profit margin: $91.00 + $18.20	$109.20 per entertainment center

1. What price should be established for intracompany transactions? Defend your answer by showing the shortcomings of each alternative.
2. If there were an outside market for all units produced by the Furniture Division at the $120 price, would you change your answer to **1**? Why?

Continuing Case: Cookie Company

C6. Your company produces cookies in a two-step process. The Mixing Division prepares the cookie dough and transfers it to the Baking Division, which bakes the cookies and packs all finished cookies for shipment.

At a recent meeting of your company's board of directors, the manager of the Baking Division made this statement: "That Mixing Division is robbing us blind!" Because of the board's concern about this statement, the company controller gathered the following data for the past year:

	Mixing Division	Baking Division
Sales:		
Regular	$700,000	$1,720,000
Deluxe	900,000	3,300,000
Direct materials:		
Cookie dough (from Mixing Division)	—	1,600,000
Cookie ingredients	360,000	—
Box inserts	—	660,000
Boxes	—	1,560,000
Direct labor	480,000	540,000
Variable overhead	90,000	240,000
Fixed divisional overhead—avoidable	150,000	210,000
Selling and general operating expenses	132,000	372,000
Company administrative expenses	84,000	108,000

During the year, the two divisions completed and transferred or shipped 200,000 regular cookie boxes and 150,000 deluxe cookie boxes. Transfer prices used by the Mixing Division follow.

Regular	$3.50
Deluxe	6.00

The regular box wholesales for $8.60 and the deluxe box for $22.00. The company uses a predetermined formula to allocate administrative costs to the divisions. Management has indicated that the transfer price should include a 20 percent profit factor on total division costs.

1. Prepare a performance report on the Mixing Division.
2. Prepare a performance report on the Baking Division.
3. Compute each division's rate of return on controllable cost (cost of goods sold) and on total division costs. (Round percentages to two decimal places.)
4. Do you agree with the statement made by the manager of the Baking Division? Explain your response.
5. What procedures would you recommend to the board of directors?

CHAPTER 12
Quality Management and Measurement

Through its innovative approach to social networking, **Facebook** has changed the rules of human interactions. To maintain a competitive advantage, the company utilizes a system that can capture all kinds of information in huge, secure databases. The quality of a Facebook user's experience has many dimensions. Not only must service be defect-free and dependable, but it must also embody such quality intangibles as prestige and good taste. Facebook managers must meet or exceed a variety of user expectations and create innovative new products and services for their ever-evolving social utility and ecommerce business model. In this chapter, we describe measures of quality and how managers can use these measures to evaluate operating performance.

1. CONCEPT ▶ *What underlying accounting concepts support quality management and measurement?*

2. ACCOUNTING APPLICATION ▶ *What measures of quality can be used to evaluate operating performance?*

3. BUSINESS APPLICATION ▶ *Why does quality help managers improve company performance and maintain a competitive edge?*

LEARNING OBJECTIVES

LO1 Discuss quality and how it relates to the accounting concepts of relevance and understandability.

LO2 Identify the awards and organizations that promote quality.

LO3 Describe total quality management (TQM), and identify financial and nonfinancial measures of quality.

LO4 Use measures of quality to evaluate operating performance.

LO5 Describe a management information system, and explain how it enhances management decision making.

Ken Brown/PictureLake/iStockphoto.com

CONCEPTS
- Relevance
- Understandability

RELEVANT LEARNING OBJECTIVES

LO 1 Discuss quality and how it relates to the accounting concepts of relevance and understandability.

LO 2 Identify the awards and organizations that promote quality.

LO 1   Concepts Underlying Quality

To the average person, *quality* means that one product or service is better than another—perhaps because of its design, its durability, or some other attribute. In a business setting, however, **quality** is the result of an operating environment in which a product or service meets or conforms to a customer's specifications the first time it is produced or delivered.

Managers operating in volatile business environments that are strongly influenced by customer demands realize that value-based systems, instead of traditional cost-based systems, provide the relevant information they need. The information has more *relevance* because it is predictive and directly relates to the decisions made. This relevance enhances a manager's *understandability* of the environment in which their business operates, including the ever-changing e-business environment. Managers must understand both their customers and the responsiveness of their company's value chain as they make decisions to improve quality.

Before the advent of TQM over 20 years ago, managers assumed that there was a trade-off between the costs and the benefits of improving quality. **Total quality management (TQM)** is an organizational environment in which all business functions work together to build quality into the firm's products or services. In economic terms, a **return on quality (ROQ)** results when the marginal revenues possible from a higher-quality good or service exceed the marginal costs of providing that higher quality. In other words, managers must weigh the high costs of consistent quality against the resulting higher revenues, and they must base the quality standards for a good or service on the expected return on quality.

In the 1980s, quality gave organizations a competitive edge in the global market-place. Managers realized they needed more than data from cost-based systems and ROQ to understand the business environment. This need for more relevant information led W. Edwards Deming and other advocates of TQM to stress quality as a means of enhancing an organization's efficiency and profits. As a result, managers focused on increasing customer satisfaction and product or service quality, and organizations recognized the value of producing highly reliable products. Companies emphasized **kaizen**, or the gradual and ongoing improvement of products and processes while reducing costs. Quality control methods such as statistical analysis, computer-aided design, and Six Sigma (discussed next) eliminated defects in the design and manufacture of products. Today more than 90 percent of the *Fortune* 500 companies use a combination of those methods for relevant information for decision making and to understand their businesses.

In 1978, **Motorola** was losing market share as a result of aggressive competition from high-quality Japanese goods. In response, Motorola set the goal of **Six Sigma** quality, which meant that its customers would perceive the company's products and services as perfect. It used the DMAIC (define, measure, analyze, improve, control) and DMADV (define, measure, analyze, design, verify) methods to improve both existing processes and new ones. Motorola applied the Six Sigma quality standard to all aspects of its operations—not just to production. Even Motorola's Corporate Finance Department measures defects per unit, tracking its number of errors per monthly close and the time it takes to close the books each month.

Thousands of companies, including **Amazon.com**, have embraced the data-driven approach of Six Sigma to reduce errors. However, Six Sigma has its drawbacks, including diminishing worker morale and invention, and many companies are rethinking Six Sigma as a business cure-all.

Two respected techniques made popular by Six Sigma, benchmarking and process mapping, are still widely used and allow managers to understand and measure quality improvements.

- **Benchmarking** is the measurement of the gap between the quality of a company's process and the quality of a parallel process at the best-in-class company. For example, **Motorola** improved its order-processing system by studying order processing at **Lands' End**.

■ **Process mapping** is a method of using a visual diagram to indicate process inputs, outputs, constraints, and flows to help managers identify unnecessary efforts and inefficiencies in a business process. Quality problems and their causes are visually tracked using charts and diagrams. As a result, customer satisfaction with a product or service and with the buying experience, both before and after the sale, is enhanced.

Service businesses also recognize the importance of quality and seek to maximize customers' satisfaction with their services. For example, **Disney** theme parks minimize customers' impatience as they wait in long lines by having Disney characters interact and play with the crowd. A potential customer problem becomes another opportunity to deliver Disney magic.

In summary, a manager's concept of quality must continuously evolve to add information *relevance* to both long-term and short-term decision making. Quality performance measures aid managers in understanding the dynamic business environment. Quality has many dimensions. A product or service must not only be defect-free and dependable, but it must also embody such intangibles as brand prestige and life style. The accounting concepts of relevance and *understandability* help managers meet or exceed a variety of expectations about customer service and the creation of innovative new products and services.

APPLY IT!

Match the abbreviations that follow with the words they represent.

1. TQM
2. DMADV
3. ROQ
4. DMAIC

a. Return on quality
b. Total quality management
c. Define, measure, analyze, improve, control
d. Define, measure, analyze, design, verify

SOLUTION
1. b; 2. d; 3. a; 4. c

TRY IT! SE1, SE2

ᴸᴼ2 Recognition of Quality

Many awards and organizations have been established to recognize and promote the importance of quality. Three of the most prestigious awards are the Deming prizes, the EFQM Excellence Award, and the Malcolm Baldrige Quality Award. In addition, the International Organization for Standardization works to promote quality standards worldwide.

Deming Prizes

In the early 1950s, the Japanese Union of Scientists and Engineers established the **Deming Prize** to honor individuals or groups who have contributed to the development and dissemination of total quality control. Consideration for the prize was originally limited to Japanese companies, but interest in it was so great that the rules were revised to allow the participation of companies outside Japan who operate in Japan. Today, the organization awards several Deming Prizes to companies and individuals who achieve distinctive results by carrying out total quality control.

EFQM Excellence Award

Since the 1990s, the nonprofit European Foundation for Quality Management has presented the **EFQM Excellence Award** annually to businesses and organizations operating in Europe that excel in quality management. The EFQM has also developed a quality framework, called the EFQM Excellence Model, about what an organization does, how they do it, and what an organization achieves. Managers can use the model as a diagnostic tool to analyze the cause-and-effect relationships between the model's enabling and the results criteria to self-assess their organizations. The enablers and the results criteria follow:

- Enablers: Leadership; Strategy; People; Partnerships and Resources; and Processes, Products, and Services
- Results: Customer, People, Society, and Key

Malcolm Baldrige National Quality Award

In 1987, the U.S. Congress created the **Malcolm Baldrige National Quality Award** to recognize U.S. organizations for their achievements in quality and business performance and to raise awareness of the importance of quality and performance excellence. Organizations are evaluated on the basis of the Baldrige performance excellence criteria, which are divided into the following seven categories:

- Leadership
- Strategic planning
- Customer focus
- Measurement, analysis, and knowledge management
- Workforce focus
- Operations focus
- Results

Thousands of organizations throughout the world accept the Baldrige criteria as the standards for performance excellence and use them for training and self-assessment. Award winners are showcased annually on the Internet and are encouraged to share their best practices with others.[1]

ISO Standards

The International Organization for Standardization (ISO) is a worldwide federation of national standards bodies.[2] It promotes standardization with a view to facilitating the international exchange of goods and services. For example, by developing a standard format for credit cards, standard film speed codes, and standard graphical symbols for use on equipment and diagrams, the ISO has saved time and money for both individuals and businesses worldwide.

To standardize quality management and quality assurance, the ISO developed the **ISO 9000** series. The ISO 9000 series guidelines cover the design, development, production, final inspection and testing, installation, and servicing of products, processes, and services. Because many organizations do business only with ISO-certified companies, these guidelines have been adopted worldwide. To become ISO certified, an organization must pass a rigorous third-party audit of its manufacturing and service processes. As a result, certified companies have detailed documentation of their operations. The eight quality management principles of ISO 9000 follow.

- Customer focus
- Leadership
- Involvement of people
- Process approach
- System approach to management
- Continual involvement
- Factual approach to decision making
- Mutually beneficial supplier relationships

STUDY NOTE: *Some ISO standards vary between countries. For example, the standard size of computer paper in the United States is different from the standard size in European countries.*

Other popular standards include ISO 14000, ISO 26000, and ISO 31000.

- The **ISO 14000** series provides a management framework to minimize the harmful environmental effects of business activities and continually improve environmental performance.
- **ISO 26000** provides social responsibility guidance.
- **ISO 31000** outlines risk management principles and guidelines.

APPLY IT!

Match the organizations that follow with the quality principles or criteria they use. (*Hint:* Some principles or criteria may be used more than once.)

1. European Foundation for Quality Management
2. Baldrige Performance Excellence Program
3. International Organization for Standardization 9000

   a. Leadership
   b. Strategy or Strategic planning
   c. People or Involvement of people
   d. Customer focus or Customer results
   e. Mutually beneficial supplier relationships or Partnerships and resources
   f. Results or Key results

SOLUTION
1. a. b. c. d. e. f.
2. a. b. d. f.
3. a. c. d. e.

TRY IT! SE3, E1A, E1B

SECTION 2

ACCOUNTING APPLICATIONS

LO 3 Financial and Nonfinancial Measures of Quality

Over the past two decades, organizations have defined quality in terms of what their customers value. Organizations believe that customers want the highest-quality goods and services and that customers' willingness to pay for high quality will result in improved profits. As a result, organizations strive to exceed customers' expectations and improve the quality of their products or services. Quality is not something that a company can simply add at some point in the production process or assume will happen automatically. Inspections can detect bad products, but they do not ensure quality. Managers need to create a total quality management (TQM) environment to help them meet the goal of producing high-quality, reasonably priced products or services.

To create a TQM environment, managers take the following steps:

- **Step 1.** Identify and manage the financial measures of quality, or the costs of quality.
- **Step 2.** Analyze operating performance using nonfinancial measures.
- **Step 3.** Require that all processes and products or services be improved continuously.

Financial Measures of Quality

The **costs of quality** are the costs that are specifically associated with the achievement or nonachievement of product or service quality. They can make up a significant portion of a product's or service's total cost. Therefore, controlling the costs of quality strongly affects profitability. Today's managers should be able to identify the activities associated with improving quality and should be aware of the cost of resources used to achieve high quality.

The costs of quality have the following two components:

- **Costs of conformance:** The costs of good quality that are incurred to ensure the successful development of a product or service. In other words, the costs of building quality into products and services by doing it right the first time.
- **Costs of nonconformance:** The costs of poor quality that are incurred to correct defects in a product or service.

The costs of conformance are made up of prevention costs and appraisal costs.

- **Prevention costs:** The costs associated with the prevention of defects and failures in products and services.
- **Appraisal costs:** The costs of activities that measure, evaluate, or audit products, processes, or services to ensure their conformance to quality standards and performance requirements.

The costs of nonconformance include internal failure costs and external failure costs.

- **Internal failure costs:** Costs incurred to correct mistakes found by the company when defects are discovered before a product or service is delivered to a customer.
- **External failure costs:** Costs incurred to correct mistakes discovered by customers after the delivery of a defective product or service.

Exhibit 1 gives examples of each cost category. Note that there is an inverse relationship between the costs of conformance and the costs of nonconformance. For example, if a company spends money on the costs of conformance, the costs of nonconformance should be reduced. However, if little attention is paid to the costs of conformance, the costs of nonconformance may escalate.

Exhibit 1
Costs of Conformance and Nonconformance

Costs of Conformance to Customer Standards

Prevention Costs:

- Technical support for vendors
- Integrated system development
- Quality improvement projects
- Quality training of employees
- Design review of products and processes

- Quality-certified suppliers
- Quality circles
- Preventive maintenance
- Statistical process control
- Process engineering

Appraisal Costs:

- Inspection of materials, processes, and machines
- End-of-process sampling and testing
- Vendor audits and sample testing

- Maintenance of test equipment
- Quality audits of products and processes
- Field testing

Costs of Nonconformance to Customer Standards

Internal Failure Costs:

- Scrap and rework
- Reinspection and retesting of rework
- Quality-related downtime
- Scrap disposal losses

- Failure analysis
- Inventory control and scheduling
- Downgrading because of defects

External Failure Costs:

- Lost sales
- Restoration of reputation
- Warranty claims and adjustments
- Customer complaint processing

- Returned goods and replacements
- Investigation of defects
- Product recalls
- Product-liability settlements

© Cengage Learning 2014

An organization's overall goal is to avoid costs of nonconformance because both internal and external failures affect customers' satisfaction and the organization's profitability. High initial costs of conformance are justified when they minimize the total costs of quality over the life of a product or service.

RATIO **Quality Ratios**

Common quality ratios and the formulas showing how to compute them follow.

$$\text{Total Costs of Quality as a Percentage of Net Sales} = \frac{(\text{Costs of Conformance} + \text{Costs of Nonconformance})}{\text{Net Sales}}$$

$$\text{Ratio of Costs of Conformance to Total Costs of Quality} = \frac{\text{Costs of Conformance}}{(\text{Costs of Conformance} + \text{Costs of Nonconformance})}$$

$$\text{Ratio of Costs of Nonconformance to Total Costs of Quality} = \frac{\text{Costs of Nonconformance}}{(\text{Costs of Conformance} + \text{Costs of Nonconformance})}$$

$$\text{Costs of Nonconformance as a Percentage of Net Sales} = \frac{\text{Costs of Nonconformance}}{\text{Net Sales}}$$

For example, consider the data for Garin's Cycle Shop that follow.

Total sales	$7,000
Costs of quality:	
Prevention	$ 400
Appraisal	500
Internal failure	200
External failure	300

The quality ratios for Garin's would be computed as follows.

Costs of Conformance	= Prevention Costs + Appraisal Costs
	= $400 + $500 = $900
Costs of Nonconformance	= Internal Failure Costs + External Failure Costs
	= $200 + $300 = $500
Total Costs of Quality as a Percentage of Net Sales	= (Costs of Conformance + Costs of Nonconformance) / Net Sales
	= ($900 + $500) ÷ $7,000
	= 20%
Ratio of Costs of Conformance to Total Costs of Quality	= Costs of Conformance ÷ (Costs of Conformance + Costs of Nonconformance)
	= $900 ÷ ($900 + $500)
	= 0.64 to 1
Ratio of Costs of Nonconformance to Total Costs of Quality	= Costs of Nonconformance ÷ (Costs of Conformance + Costs of Nonconformance)
	= $500 ÷ ($900 + $500)
	= 0.36 to 1
Costs of Nonconformance as a Percentage of Net Sales	= $500 ÷ $7,000 = 7.14%

Nonfinancial Measures of Quality

By measuring the costs of quality, a company learns how much it has spent in its efforts to improve product or service quality. But critics say that tracking historical data to monitor quality performance does little to enhance quality. What managers need is a measurement and evaluation system that signals poor quality early enough to allow problems to be corrected before a defective product or service reaches the customer. Implementing a policy of continuous improvement satisfies this need for and is the second stage of total quality management.

Nonfinancial measures of performance are used to supplement cost-based measures. Although cost control is still an important consideration, a commitment to ongoing improvement encourages activities that enhance quality at every stage, from design to delivery. By controlling the leading nonfinancial performance measures of activities, managers can ultimately maximize the resulting financial return from operations. Five categories of nonfinancial measures of quality are discussed in the sections that follow:

- Product design
- Vendor performance
- Production performance
- Delivery cycle time
- Customer satisfaction

Product Design Problems with quality often are the result of poor design. Most automated production operations use **computer-aided design (CAD)**, a computer-based engineering system with a built-in program to identify poorly designed parts or manufacturing processes, which means that engineers can correct these problems before production begins. Among the measures that managers consider are:

- number and types of design defects detected
- average time between defect detection and correction
- number of unresolved design defects at the time of product introduction

Vendor Performance Instead of dealing with dozens of suppliers in a quest for the lowest cost, companies now analyze their vendors to determine which ones are most reliable, furnish high-quality goods, have a record of timely deliveries, and charge competitive prices. Once a company has identified such vendors, they become an integral part of the production team's effort to ensure a continuing supply of high-quality materials. Vendors may even contribute to product design to ensure that the correct materials are being used.

Managers use measures of quality (such as defect-free materials as a percentage of total materials received) and measures of delivery (such as timely deliveries as a percentage of total deliveries) to identify reliable vendors and monitor their performance.

Production Performance Management must always be concerned about the wasted time and money that can be traced to defective products, scrapped parts, machine maintenance, and downtime. To minimize such concerns, more and more companies have adopted **computer-integrated manufacturing (CIM) systems**, in which production and its support operations are coordinated by computers. Within a CIM system, computer-aided manufacturing (CAM) may be used to coordinate and control production activities, or a flexible manufacturing system (FMS) may be used to link together automated equipment into a flexible production network.

In CIM systems, most direct labor hours are replaced by machine hours, and very little direct labor cost is incurred. In addition, a significant part of variable product cost is replaced by the cost of expensive machinery, a fixed cost. Today, the largest item on a company's balance sheet is often automated machinery and equipment. Each piece of equipment has a specific capacity, above which continuous operation is threatened. When managers evaluate such machines, their measures have two objectives:

- To evaluate the performance of each piece of equipment in relation to its capacity
- To evaluate the performance of maintenance personnel in following a prescribed maintenance program

Measures of production quality, parts scrapped, equipment utilization, machine downtime, and machine maintenance time help managers monitor production performance.

Delivery Cycle Time To evaluate their responsiveness to customers, companies examine their **delivery cycle time**, which is the time between the acceptance of an order and the final delivery of the product or service. When a customer places an order, it is important for a salesperson to be able to promise an accurate delivery date. On-time delivery is important not only to customers but also to companies, because a decrease in delivery cycle time can lead to a significant increase in income from operations.

The formula to compute delivery cycle time follows.

Delivery Cycle Time = Purchase-Order Lead Time + Production Cycle Time + Delivery Time

- **Purchase-order lead time** is the time it takes a company to take and process an order and organize so that production can begin.
- **Production cycle time** is the time it takes to make a product.
- **Delivery time** is the time between the completion of a product and its receipt by the customer.

Managers should establish measures that emphasize the importance of minimizing the delivery cycle time for each order. They should also track the average purchase-order lead time, production cycle time, and delivery time for all orders. Trends should be highlighted, and reports should be readily available. Other measures designed to monitor delivery cycle time include order backlogs, on-time delivery performance, percentage of orders filled, and waste time. The formula to compute waste time follows.

Waste Time = Production Cycle Time − (Average Process Time + Average Setup Time)

Customer Satisfaction The sale and shipment of a product does not mark the end of performance measurement. Measures used to determine the degree of customer satisfaction include the following:

- the number and types of customer complaints
- the number and causes of warranty claims
- the percentage of shipments returned by customers (or the percentage of shipments accepted by customers)

Several companies have developed their own customer satisfaction indexes from these measures so that they can compare different product lines over different time periods.

As a way of enhancing customer satisfaction for those waiting in line at Walt Disney World theme parks, characters interact with and entertain guests.

Shanghai Daily/AP Images

Overview Exhibit 2 lists the nonfinancial measures used to monitor quality. These measures help a company continuously produce higher-quality products, improve production processes, and reduce throughput time and costs.

Exhibit 2
Nonfinancial Measures of Quality

Measure of Product Design Quality	
• Product design flaws	Number and types of design defects detected
	Average time between defect detection and correction
	Number of unresolved design defects at time of product introduction
Measures of Vendor Performance	
• Vendor quality	Defect-free materials as a percentage of total materials received; prepared for each vendor
• Vendor delivery	Timely deliveries of materials as a percentage of total deliveries; prepared for each vendor
Measures of Production Performance	
• Production quality	Number of defective products per thousand produced
• Parts scrapped	Number and type of materials spoiled during production
• Equipment utilization rate	Productive machine time as a percentage of total time available for production
• Machine downtime	Amount of time each machine is idle
• Machine maintenance time	Amount of time each machine is idle for maintenance and upgrades
Measures of Delivery Cycle Time	
• On-time deliveries	Shipments received by promised date as a percentage of total shipments
• Orders filled	Orders filled as a percentage of total orders received
• Average process time	Average time required to make a product available for shipment
• Average setup time	Average amount of time elapsed between the acceptance of an order and the beginning of production
• Purchase-order lead time	Time it takes a company to process an order and organize so that production can begin
• Production cycle time	Time it takes to make a product
• Delivery time	Time between a product's completion and its receipt by customer
• Delivery cycle time	Time between the acceptance of an order and the final delivery of the product or service (purchase-order lead time + production cycle time + delivery time)
• Waste time	Production cycle time − (average process time + average setup time)
• Production backlog	Number and type of units waiting to begin processing
Measures of Customer Satisfaction	
• Customer complaints	Number and types of customer complaints
• Warranty claims	Number and causes of claims
• Returned orders	Shipments returned as a percentage of total shipments

Measuring Service Quality

Many of the costs-of-quality categories and several of the nonfinancial measures of quality can be applied directly to services and can be adopted by any type of service company.

- Flaws in service design lead to poor-quality services.
- Timely service delivery is as important as timely product shipments.
- Customer satisfaction in a service business can be measured by services accepted or rejected, the number of complaints, and the number of returning customers.
- Poor service development leads to internal and external failure costs.

APPLY IT!

Internal reports on quality at Social Utility Company generated the following information for the Apps Division for the first three months of the year:

Total sales	$60,000,000
Costs of quality:	
Prevention	$ 523,000
Appraisal	477,000
Internal failure	1,360,000
External failure	640,000

Compute the following:

1. Total costs of quality as a percentage of sales
2. Ratio of costs of conformance to total costs of quality
3. Ratio of costs of nonconformance to total costs of quality
4. Costs of nonconformance as a percentage of total sales

SOLUTION

Costs of Conformance	= Prevention Costs + Appraisal Costs
	= $523,000 + $477,000 = $1,000,000
Costs of Nonconformance	= Internal Failure Costs + External Failure Costs
	= $1,360,000 + $640,000 = $2,000,000
1. Total Costs of Quality as a Percentage of Sales	= $3,000,000 ÷ $60,000,000 = 5%
2. Ratio of Costs of Conformance to Total Costs of Quality	= Costs of Conformance ÷ (Costs of Conformance + Costs of Nonconformance)
	= $1,000,000 ÷ ($1,000,000 + $2,000,000)
	= 0.33 to 1
3. Ratio of Costs of Nonconformance to Total Costs of Quality	= Costs of Nonconformance ÷ (Costs of Conformance + Costs of Nonconformance)
	= $2,000,000 ÷ ($1,000,000 + $2,000,000)
	= 0.67 to 1
4. Costs of Nonconformance as a Percentage of Total Sales	= $2,000,000 ÷ $60,000,000 = 3.33%

TRY IT! SE4, SE5, SE6, SE7, E2A, E3A, E4A, E5A, E6A, E2B, E3B, E4B, E5B, E6B

LO 4   Measuring Quality: An Illustration

Using many of the examples of the costs of quality identified in Exhibit 1 and the nonfinancial measures of quality listed in Exhibit 2, the sections that follow demonstrate how a company measures and evaluates its progress toward the goal of achieving total quality management.

Evaluating the Costs of Quality

As demonstrated in Exhibit 3, three companies—Able, Baker, and Cane—have taken different approaches to achieving product quality. All three companies are the same size, each having generated $15 million in sales last year. Each company spent between 10.22 and 10.48 percent of its sales dollars on quality costs.

Key Quality Performance Questions   Using the information in Exhibit 3, we can evaluate each company's approach to quality enhancement by analyzing the costs of quality and by answering the questions that follow.

- **Which company is most likely to succeed in the competitive marketplace?**

  Able spent the most money on costs of quality. What is more important, however, is that the company spent 80 percent of that money on costs of conformance, which

Exhibit 3
Analysis of the Costs of Quality

	Able Co.	Baker Co.	Cane Co.
Annual Sales	$15,000,000	$15,000,000	$15,000,000
Costs of conformance to customer standards			
Prevention Costs			
Quality training of employees	$ 210,000	$ 73,500	$ 136,500
Process engineering	262,500	115,500	189,000
Design review of products	105,000	42,000	84,000
Preventive maintenance	157,500	84,000	115,500
Subtotal	$ 735,000	$ 315,000	$ 525,000
Appraisal Costs			
End-of-process sampling and testing	$ 126,000	$ 63,000	$ 73,500
Inspection of materials	199,500	31,500	115,500
Quality audits of products	84,000	21,000	42,000
Vendor audits and sample testing	112,500	52,500	63,000
Subtotal	$ 522,000	$ 168,000	$ 294,000
Total costs of conformance	$ 1,257,000	$ 483,000	$ 819,000
Costs of nonconformance to customer standards			
Internal Failure Costs			
Scrap and rework	$ 21,000	$ 189,000	$ 126,000
Reinspection of rework	15,750	126,000	73,500
Quality-related downtime	42,000	231,000	178,500
Scrap disposal losses	26,250	84,000	52,500
Subtotal	$ 105,000	$ 630,000	$ 430,500
External Failure Costs			
Warranty claims	$ 47,250	$ 94,500	$ 84,000
Returned goods and replacements	15,750	68,250	36,750
Investigation of defects	26,250	78,750	57,750
Customer complaint processing	120,750	178,500	126,000
Subtotal	$ 210,000	$ 420,000	$ 304,500
Total costs of nonconformance	$ 315,000	$ 1,050,000	$ 735,000
Total costs of quality	$ 1,572,000	$ 1,533,000	$ 1,554,000
Total costs of quality as a percentage of sales	10.48%	10.22%	10.36%
Ratio of costs of conformance to total costs of quality	0.80 to 1	0.32 to 1	0.53 to 1
Ratio of costs of nonconformance to total costs of quality	0.20 to 1	0.68 to 1	0.47 to 1
Costs of nonconformance as a percentage of sales	2.10%	7.00%	4.90%

will reap benefits in years to come. The company's focus on the costs of conformance means that only a small amount had to be spent on internal and external failure costs. The resulting high-quality products will lead to high customer satisfaction.

■ **Which company has serious problems with its product quality?**

Baker spent the least on costs of quality. However, over 68 percent of its costs of quality ($1,050,000 of a total of $1,533,000) was spent on internal and external failure costs. Scrap costs, reinspection costs, the cost of downtime, warranty costs, and customer complaint costs were all high. Baker's products are very low in quality, which will lead to hard times in the future.

■ **What do you think will happen to the total costs of quality for each company over the next five years? Why?**

Able: When money is spent on costs of conformance early in a product's life cycle, quality is integrated into the development and production processes. Once a high level of quality has been established, total costs of quality should be lower in future years.

Baker: Baker's costs of conformance will have to increase significantly if the company expects to stay in business. It is spending 7 percent of its sales revenue on internal and external failure costs. Because the marketplace is not accepting its products, its competitors have the upper hand and the company is in a weak position.

Cane: Cane is taking a middle road. This company is spending a little more than half (53 percent) of its cost-of-quality dollars on conformance, so product quality should be increasing. However, the company is still incurring high internal and external failure costs. Cane's managers must learn to prevent such costs if they expect the company to remain competitive.

Evaluating Nonfinancial Measures of Quality

Exhibit 4 presents nonfinancial measures for each company for three years—2013, 2014, and 2015.

Exhibit 4
Analysis of Nonfinancial
Measures of Quality

	Able Co.	Baker Co.	Cane Co.
Vendor Performance			
Percentage of defect-free materials			
2013	98.20%	94.40%	95.20%
2014	98.40%	93.20%	95.30%
2015	98.60%	93.10%	95.20%
Production Performance			
Production quality level (product defects per million)			
2013	1,400	4,120	2,710
2014	1,340	4,236	2,720
2015	1,210	4,340	2,680
Delivery Cycle Time			
Percentage of on-time deliveries			
2013	94.20%	76.20%	84.10%
2014	94.60%	75.40%	84.00%
2015	95.40%	73.10%	83.90%
Customer Satisfaction			
Percentage of returned orders			
2013	1.30%	6.90%	4.20%
2014	1.10%	7.20%	4.10%
2015	0.80%	7.60%	4.00%
Number of customer complaints			
2013	22	189	52
2014	18	194	50
2015	12	206	46

© Cengage Learning 2014

From the information in Exhibit 4, we can evaluate each company's experience in its pursuit of total quality management. The trends shown tend to support the findings in the analysis of the costs of quality in Exhibit 3.

■ **Able:** For Able, 98.2 percent of the materials received from suppliers in 2013 were of high quality, and the quality has been increasing over the three years. The product defect rate, measured in number of defects per million, has been decreasing rapidly, proof that the costs of conformance are having a positive effect. The percentage of on-time deliveries has been increasing, and both the percentage of returned orders and the number of customer complaints have been decreasing, which means that customer acceptance and satisfaction have been increasing.

- **Baker:** Baker's experience is not encouraging. The number of high-quality shipments of materials from vendors has been decreasing, the product defect rate has been increasing (it seems to be out of control), on-time deliveries were bad to begin with and have been getting worse, more goods have been returned each year, and customer complaints have been on the rise. All these signs reflect the company's high costs of nonconformance.

- **Cane:** Cane is making progress toward higher quality, but its progress is very slow. Most of the nonfinancial measures show a very slight positive trend. More money needs to be spent on the costs of conformance.

A graphic analysis can be very useful when a manager is comparing the performance of several operating units. Mere columns of numbers do not always adequately depict differences in operating performance and may be difficult to interpret. In such cases, a chart or graph can help managers see what the data are saying. For example, the bar graph in Exhibit 5 illustrates the amounts that Able, Baker, and Cane are spending on costs of quality. It clearly shows that

- Able is focusing on costs of conformance and has low costs of nonconformance.
- Baker, in contrast, is paying over $1,000,000 in costs of nonconformance because it has not tried to increase spending on prevention and appraisal.
- Cane spends slightly more on costs of conformance than on costs of nonconformance, but, like Baker, it is spending too much on failure costs.

Exhibit 5
Comparison of Costs of Quality: Conformance Versus Nonconformance

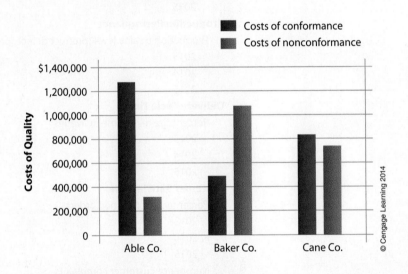

APPLY IT!

Essex Corporation has two departments, C and D, which produce two separate product lines. Essex has been implementing total quality management over the past year. Conformance and nonconformance cost ratios of quality for the year for each department are presented below. Which department is committed to TQM?

	Dept. C	Dept. D	Totals
Total costs of quality as a percentage of sales	5.00%	5.00%	5.00%
Ratio of costs of conformance to total costs of quality	0.70 to 1	0.35 to 1	0.51 to 1
Ratio of costs of nonconformance to total costs of quality	0.30 to 1	0.65 to 1	0.49 to 1
Costs of nonconformance as a percentage of sales	1.50%	3.25%	2.45%

SOLUTION

Department C is taking a more serious approach to implementing TQM. It is spending more than twice as much on costs of conformance as on costs of nonconformance. Department D is doing almost the opposite.

TRY IT! SE8, E7A, E8A, E9A, E10A, E11A, E12A, E13A, E7B, E8B, E9B, E10B, E11B, E12B, E13B

BUSINESS APPLICATIONS

- Management Information System (MIS)
- Planning
- Performing
- Evaluating
- Communicating

RELEVANT LEARNING OBJECTIVE

LO 5 Describe a management information system, and explain how it enhances management decision making.

LO 5 The Role of Management Information Systems in Quality Management

Many traditional management information systems contain only financial data. However, in today's competitive business environment, the information system should identify, monitor, and maintain continuous, detailed analyses of a company's activities, use social media and mobile technologies, and provide managers with timely measures of operating results. This kind of **management information system (MIS)** is designed to support such philosophies as lean operations, activity-based management (ABM), and total quality management (TQM).

By focusing on activities, rather than costs, an MIS provides managers with information that is needed to increase responsiveness to customers and reduce processing time. More accurate product and service costs lead to improved pricing decisions. Nonvalue-adding activities are highlighted, and managers can work to reduce or eliminate them. An MIS can also analyze the profitability of individual customers or users and look at all aspects of serving them. Overall, the MIS identifies resource usage and cost for each activity and fosters managerial decisions that lead to continuous improvement throughout the organization.

Enterprise Resource Planning Systems and Software as a Service

An MIS can be designed as a fully integrated database system known as an **enterprise resource planning (ERP) system**. An ERP system combines the management of all major business activities (e.g., purchasing, manufacturing, marketing, sales, logistics, and order fulfillment) with support activities (e.g., accounting and human resources) to form one easy-to-access, centralized data warehouse. Advantages of an ERP system are its integration and ability to communicate within an organization and with other businesses' databases. But an ERP system is costly to implement and maintain, can be less than user friendly, and leave many frustrated.

The emerging alternative is **software as a service (SaaS)**. SaaS utilizes the Internet, social media, and mobile technologies to manage all business activities on demand. Advantages of SaaS include low acquisition costs, quick implementations, predictable pricing, reduced internal support staff, and a potentially more agile ability to innovate. Currently, its primary disadvantage is data security and internal controls as multiple company data may co-exist on a shared web infrastructure as multi-tenants. One of the fastest growing companies that provides SaaS is **Workday, Inc.**

Managers' Use of MIS

Managers today use their management information systems' detailed, real-time financial and nonfinancial information about customers, inventory, resources, and the supply chain to manage quality. Without the flexibility and power of database and management information systems like ERP or SaaS, managers would be at a disadvantage in today's rapidly changing and highly competitive business environment.

Planning Managers use the MIS database to obtain relevant and reliable information for formulating strategic plans, making forecasts, and preparing budgets. For example, managers at **Amazon.com** use their MIS to develop forecasts and budgets for existing operations and to create plans for new value-adding products and services.

Performing Managers use the financial and nonfinancial information in the MIS database to implement decisions about personnel, resources, and activities that will minimize waste and improve the quality of their organization's products or services. At **Amazon .com**, managers use their supply-chain and value-chain software to manage operations in ways that ensure accurate order fulfillment and timely delivery.

Evaluating Managers identify and track financial and nonfinancial performance measures to evaluate all major business functions. By enabling the timely comparison of actual performance with expected performance, **Amazon.com**'s MIS allows managers to reward good performance promptly, take speedy corrective actions, and analyze and revise performance measurement plans.

Communicating Managers can use an MIS to generate customized reports that evaluate performance and provide useful information for decision making. For example, managers at **Amazon.com** can consolidate customer profiles from their company's sophisticated database into a real-time report available on their desktops to continuously monitor the changing buying habits of their customers.

MIS and the Management Process The steps managers take during the management process for quality management and measurement are summarized in Exhibit 6.

Exhibit 6
Management Information Systems and The Management Process

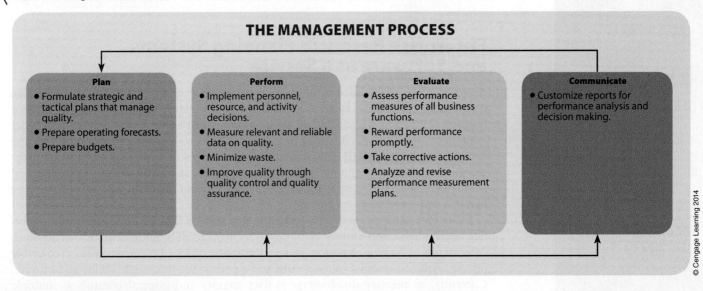

© Cengage Learning 2014

APPLY IT!

Match the four stages of the management process with the examples that follow.

1. Plan
2. Perform
3. Evaluate
4. Communicate

a. Databases can be used to develop forecasts and budgets for existing operations and to create plans for new value-adding products and services.

b. Timely comparison of actual performance with expected performance can be made by managers to reward good performance promptly, take speedy corrective actions, and analyze and revise performance measurement plans.

c. Managers can use supply-chain and value-chain information to manage operations in ways that ensure accurate order fulfillment and timely delivery.

d. Managers can consolidate customer profiles from their company's database into a real-time report available on their desktops to continuously monitor the changing buying habits of their customers.

SOLUTION
1. a;　2. c;　3. b;　4. d

TRY IT! SE9, SE10, E14A, E14B

TriLevel Problem

Facebook

The beginning of this chapter focused on **Facebook**, a social utilities company. Complete the following requirements in order to answer the questions posed at the beginning of the chapter.

Section 1: Concepts
What underlying accounting concepts support quality management and measurement?

Section 2: Accounting Applications
What measures of quality can be used to evaluate operating performance?

Suppose that, three months ago, one of Facebook's application developers installed a new production system in its New Apps Division. A lean approach is now followed for everything from ordering supplies to the delivery of apps. The division's manager is very interested in the initial results of the venture. The following data have been collected for your analysis:

	A	B	C	D	E	F	G	H	I
1					Week				
2		1	2	3	4	5	6	7	8
3	Warranty claims	2	4	1	1	–	5	7	11
4	Average setup time								
5	(hours)	0.30	0.25	0.25	0.30	0.25	0.20	0.20	0.15
6	Purchase-order lead								
7	time (hours)	2.4	2.3	2.2	2.3	2.4	2.4	2.4	2.5
8	Production cycle time								
9	(minutes)	2.7	2.6	2.5	2.6	2.6	2.6	2.6	2.7
10	Average process time								
11	(minutes)	1.90	1.90	1.85	1.80	1.90	1.95	1.95	1.90
12	Customer complaints	12	12	10	8	9	7	6	4
13	Production backlog								
14	(units)	9,210	9,350	9,370	9,420	9,410	8,730	8,310	7,950
15	Machine downtime								
16	(hours)	86.5	83.1	76.5	80.1	90.4	100.6	120.2	124.9
17	Equipment utilization								
18	rate (%)	98.2	98.6	98.9	98.5	98.1	97.3	96.6	95.7
19	On-time deliveries (%)	93.2	94.1	96.5	95.4	92.1	90.5	88.4	89.3
20	Machine maintenance								
21	time (hours)	34.6	32.2	28.5	22.1	18.5	12.6	19.7	26.4
22									

1. Analyze the nonfinancial measures of quality of the division for the eight-week period. Focus on the following areas of performance:

   a. Production performance
   b. Delivery cycle time
   c. Customer satisfaction

2. Summarize your findings in a report to the division's manager.

Section 3: Business Applications
Why does quality help managers improve company performance and maintain a competitive edge?

To answer this question, match this chapter's manager responsibilities with when they occur within the management process.

a. Plan
b. Perform
c. Evaluate
d. Communicate

1. Customize reports for performance analysis and decision making.
2. Assess performance measures of all business functions.
3. Implement personnel, resource, and activity decisions.
4. Formulate strategic and tactical plans that manage quality.
5. Reward performance promptly.
6. Measure relevant and reliable data on quality.
7. Prepare operating forecasts.
8. Take corrective actions.
9. Minimize waste.
10. Prepare budgets.
11. Analyze and revise performance measurement plans.
12. Improve quality through quality control and quality assurance.

SOLUTION

Section 1: Concepts

The concepts of *relevance* and *understandability* underlie quality. Doing business over the Internet has added a rich dimension to quality as managers try to understand the ever-changing e-business environment. Managers need on-demand quality performance measures to support their decision making as they strive to satisfy users today and create innovative products and services for tomorrow. At **Facebook**, the quality of a user's experience is enhanced by the company's management information system. By maintaining user profiles based on previous visits and activities, Facebook can greet users as they return to the site with a web page customized to their preferences. Facebook's managers also use their information system's highly developed infrastructure to meet the changing expectations of a diverse customer base. In understanding its users and the responsiveness of the company's value chain, these managers use relevant nonfinancial and financial quality measures for decision making and performance management.

Section 2: Accounting Application

1. (*Note*: The data given were reorganized as shown below, and one additional piece of information, average waste time, was calculated from the data.)

	A	B	C	D	E	F	G	H	I	J	K
1						Week					Weekly
2			1	2	3	4	5	6	7	8	Average
3	a.	**Production Performance**									
4		Machine downtime (hours)	86.5	83.1	76.5	80.1	90.4	100.6	120.2	124.9	95.3
5		Equipment utilization rate (%)	98.2	98.6	98.9	98.5	98.1	97.3	96.6	95.7	97.7
6		Machine maintenance time (hours)	34.6	32.2	28.5	22.1	18.5	12.6	19.7	26.4	24.3
7	b.	**Delivery Cycle Time**									
8		On-time deliveries (%)	93.2	94.1	96.5	95.4	92.1	90.5	88.4	89.3	92.4
9		Average setup time (hours)	0.30	0.25	0.25	0.30	0.25	0.20	0.20	0.15	0.24
10		Purchase-order lead time (hours)	2.4	2.3	2.2	2.3	2.4	2.4	2.4	2.5	2.4
11		Production cycle time (minutes)	2.7	2.6	2.5	2.5	2.5	2.6	2.6	2.7	2.6
12		Average process time (minutes)	1.90	1.90	1.85	1.80	1.90	1.95	1.95	1.90	1.89
13		Production backlog (units)	9,210	9,350	9,370	9,420	9,410	8,730	8,310	7,950	8,969
14		Average waste time (hours)	0.50	0.45	0.40	0.50	0.45	0.45	0.45	0.65	0.48
15	c.	**Customer Satisfaction**									
16		Customer complaints	12	12	10	8	9	7	6	4	8.5
17		Warranty claims	2	4	1	1	—	5	7	11	3.9
18											

2. The analysis of the operating data for the division for the last eight weeks revealed the following:

- **Production Performance:** Machine downtime is increasing. Also, the equipment utilization rate is down. Machine maintenance time originally decreased, but it has increased in the past two weeks. Department managers should be aware of these potential problem areas.
- **Delivery Cycle Time:** The company is having trouble maintaining the averages for delivery cycle time established eight weeks ago. On-time delivery percentages are slipping. Waste time is increasing, which is contrary to goals. Backlogged orders are decreasing, which is a good sign from a lean viewpoint, but could spell problems in the future. On the positive side, setup time seems to be under control. Emphasis needs to be placed on reducing lead time, cycle time, and process time.
- **Customer Satisfaction:** Customer satisfaction seems to be improving, as the number of complaints is decreasing rapidly. However, warranty claims have risen significantly in the past three weeks, which may be a signal of quality problems.

Overall, the company can see good signs from the new equipment, but needs to pay special attention to all potential problem areas.

Section 3: Business Applications

1.	d	7.	a
2.	c	8.	c
3.	b	9.	b
4.	a	10.	a
5.	c	11.	c
6.	b	12.	b

Chapter Review

Discuss quality and how it relates to the accounting concepts of relevance and understandability. LO 1

Quality is the result of an operating environment in which a product or service meets or conforms to a customer's specifications the first time it is produced or delivered. Quality has many dimensions that extend beyond the mere creation and delivery of a product or service. Quality performance measures help support decision making as managers try to satisfy customers today and create innovative products and services for tomorrow. Total quality management is an organizational environment in which all business functions work together to build quality into a firm's products or services.

Identify the awards and organizations that promote quality. LO 2

The importance of quality has been acknowledged worldwide through the granting of numerous awards, certificates, and prizes for quality. Three of the most prestigious awards are the Deming Prizes, the EFQM Excellence Award, and the Malcolm Baldrige Quality Award. In addition, the International Organization for Standardization promotes quality management through standards like the ISO 9000 and 14000 series of standards.

Describe total quality management (TQM), and identify financial and nonfinancial measures of quality. LO 3

The costs of quality are measures of the costs that are specifically related to the achievement or non-achievement of product or service quality. The costs of quality have two components. One is the cost of conforming to a customer's product or service standards by preventing defects and failures and by appraising quality and performance. The other is the cost of non-conformance—the costs incurred when defects are discovered before a product is shipped and the costs incurred after a defective product or faulty service is delivered to the customer. The objective of TQM is to reduce or eliminate the costs of nonconformance, the internal and external failure costs that are associated with customer dissatisfaction.

Use measures of quality to evaluate operating performance. **LO 4**

Nonfinancial measures of quality are related to product design, vendor performance, production performance, delivery cycle time, and customer satisfaction. Those measures, together with the costs of quality, help a firm meet its goal of continuously improving product or service quality and the production process.

Describe a management information system, and explain how it enhances management decision making. **LO 5**

A management information system (MIS) focuses on the management of activities, not on costs. Thus, an MIS provides managers with improved knowledge of the internal and external processes for which they are responsible or access. The MIS can integrate a company as a company-based ERP system or be Internet-based like SaaS, where data are available on demand and support social media and mobile technologies.

As managers plan, they use the MIS database to obtain relevant and reliable information for formulating strategic plans, making forecasts, and preparing budgets. They use financial and nonfinancial information in the MIS database to implement decisions about personnel, resources, and activities that will minimize waste and improve the quality of their organization's products or services. By enabling the timely comparison of actual to expected performance, the MIS allows managers to reward performance promptly, take speedy corrective actions, and analyze and revise performance measurement plans.

Key Terms

appraisal costs 440 (LO3)	**EFQM Excellence Award** 437 (LO2)	**management information system (MIS)** 449 (LO5)
benchmarking 436 (LO1)	**enterprise resource planning (ERP) system** 449 (LO5)	**prevention costs** 440 (LO3)
computer-aided design (CAD) 442 (LO3)	**external failure costs** 440 (LO3)	**process mapping** 437 (LO1)
computer-integrated manufacturing (CIM) systems 443 (LO3)	**internal failure costs** 440 (LO3)	**production cycle time** 443 (LO3)
costs of conformance 440 (LO3)	**ISO 9000** 438 (LO2)	**purchase-order lead time** 443 (LO3)
costs of nonconformance 440 (LO3)	**ISO 14000** 439 (LO2)	**quality** 436 (LO1)
costs of quality 440 (LO3)	**ISO 26000** 439 (LO2)	**return on quality (ROQ)** 436 (LO1)
delivery cycle time 443 (LO3)	**ISO 31000** 439 (LO2)	**Six Sigma** 436 (LO1)
delivery time 443 (LO3)	**kaizen** 436 (LO1)	**software as a service (SaaS)** 449 (LO5)
Deming Prize 437 (LO2)	**Malcolm Baldrige National Quality Award** 438 (LO2)	**total quality management (TQM)** 436 (LO1)

Chapter Assignments

DISCUSSION QUESTIONS

LO 1, 5   **DQ1. CONCEPT ▶ BUSINESS APPLICATION ▶** How do managers use the concept of relevance during the management process?

LO 1, 5   **DQ2. CONCEPT ▶ BUSINESS APPLICATION ▶** How do managers use the concept of understandability during the management process?

LO 1, 5   **DQ3. BUSINESS APPLICATION ▶** How do companies continue to anticipate customer needs now that e-commerce has changed the way goods and services are obtained?

LO 1, 5   **DQ4. BUSINESS APPLICATION ▶** You have been asked to develop a plan for installing a management information system in your company. What kind of information will you need to gather to make an informed decision about all aspects of the management process?

SHORT EXERCISES

LO 1 **Return on Quality**

SE1. For many years, Greg Pirolo has used return on quality (ROQ) to evaluate quality. What assumptions about quality did he make?

LO 1 **Quality and Cycle Time**

SE2. Motorola's Finance Department has adapted the concept of delivery cycle time to include the measurement of cycle times for processing customer credit memos, invoices, and orders. Why would such performance measures contribute to Motorola's quest for Six Sigma quality?

LO 2 **Quality Award Recipients**

SE3. What types of organizations are represented by recent recipients of the Malcolm Baldrige Award? Consult the website at www.nist.gov/baldrige/.

LO 3 **Costs of Quality in a Service Business**

SE4. ABC Insurance Agency incurred the following activity costs related to service quality. Identify those that are costs of conformance (CC) and those that are costs of nonconformance (NC).

Policy processing improvements	$76,400
Customer complaints response	34,100
Policy writer training	12,300
Policy error losses	82,700
Policy proofing	39,500

LO 3 **Measures of Quality**

SE5. Internal reports on quality at Lakelawn Press Company generated the following information for the School Division for the first three months of the year:

Total sales	$50,000,000
Costs of quality:	
Prevention	$ 523,000
Appraisal	77,000
Internal failure	860,000
External failure	640,000

Compute the following. (Round to two decimal places.)

1. Total costs of quality as a percentage of sales
2. Ratio of costs of conformance to total costs of quality
3. Ratio of costs of nonconformance to total costs of quality
4. Costs of nonconformance as a percentage of total sales

LO 3 **Nonfinancial Measures of Quality**

SE6. ACCOUNTING CONNECTION ▶ For a fast-food restaurant that specializes in deluxe hamburgers, identify two nonfinancial measures of good product quality and two nonfinancial measures of poor product quality.

LO 3 **Vendor Quality**

SE7. ACCOUNTING CONNECTION ▶ Cite some specific measures of vendor quality that Nikki Mile could use when she installs a quality-certification program for the vendors that supply her company, Emboss It, Inc., with direct materials.

LO 4 **Measures of Delivery Cycle Time**

SE8. ACCOUNTING CONNECTION ▶ Quality Products, Inc., has developed a set of non-financial measures to evaluate on-time product delivery for one of its best-selling cosmetics. The following data have been generated for the past four weeks:

Week	Purchase-Order Lead Time	Production Cycle Time	Delivery Time
1	3.0 days	3.5 days	4.0 days
2	2.3 days	3.5 days	3.5 days
3	2.4 days	3.3 days	3.4 days
4	2.5 days	3.2 days	3.3 days

Compute the total delivery cycle time for each week. Evaluate the delivery performance. Is there an area that needs management's attention?

LO 5 **Traits of a Management Information System**

SE9. BUSINESS APPLICATION ▶ What kinds of information does a management information system capture? How do managers use such information?

LO 5 **Continuous Improvement**

SE10. BUSINESS APPLICATION ▶ May Patt is the controller for Patt Industries. She has been asked to develop a plan for installing a management information system in her company. The president has already approved the concept and has given Patt the go-ahead. What kind of information will Patt need to give managers to help them with their decision making?

EXERCISES: SET A

LO 2 **Awards for Quality**

E1A. The International Organization for Standardization facilitates international exchange. List at least two examples of their more popular standards.

LO 3 **Costs of Conformance in a Service Business**

E2A. Hollis Home Health Care, LLP, incurred the service-related activity costs for the month that follow.

Total sales	$50,000
Quality training of employees	400
Vendor audits	200
Quality-certified vendors	200
Preventive maintenance	300
Quality sampling of services	400
Field testing of new services	250
Quality circles	50
Quality improvement projects	150
Technical service support	75
Inspection of services rendered	175

Prepare an analysis of the costs of conformance by identifying the prevention costs and appraisal costs, and compute the percentage of sales represented by prevention costs, appraisal costs, and total costs of conformance.

LO 3 **Costs of Nonconformance in a Service Business**

E3A. Home Health Care, LLP, incurred the service-related activity costs for the month that follow.

Total sales	$24,000
Reinspection of rework	50
Investigation of service defects	300
Lawsuits	100
Quality-related downtime	75
Failure analysis	50
Customer complaint processing	500
Retesting of service scheduling	25
Restoration of reputation	0
Lost sales	100
Replacement services	500

Prepare an analysis of the costs of nonconformance by identifying the internal failure costs and external failure costs, and compute the percentage of sales represented by internal failure costs, external failure costs, and total costs of nonconformance. (Round percentages to two decimal places.)

LO 3 **Measures of Quality in a Service Business**

E4A. Rehab Health Care, LLC, incurred the service-related activity costs for the month that follow.

Total sales	$40,000
Customer complaint processing	1,000
Employee training	400
Reinspection and retesting	500
Design review of service procedures	300
Technical support	200
Investigation of service defects	800
Sample testing of vendors	100
Inspection of supplies	150
Quality audits	250
Quality-related downtime	300

Prepare an analysis of the costs of quality for Rehab Health Care. Categorize the costs as (a) costs of conformance, with subsets of prevention costs and appraisal costs, or (b) costs of nonconformance, with subsets of internal failure costs and external failure costs. Compute the percentage of sales represented by prevention costs, appraisal costs, total costs of conformance, internal failure costs, external failure costs, total costs of nonconformance, and total costs of quality. Also compute the ratio of costs of conformance to total costs of quality and the ratio of costs of nonconformance to total costs of quality.

LO 3 **Costs of Quality**

E5A. La Coupe Corporation produces and supplies automotive manufacturers with the mechanisms used to adjust the positions of front seating units. Several competitors have recently entered the market, and management is concerned that the quality of the company's current products may be surpassed by the quality of the new competitors'

(Continued)

products. The controller was asked to conduct an analysis of the efforts in January to improve product quality. His analysis generated the following costs of quality:

Training of employees	$50,400
Customer service	13,600
Reinspection of rework	28,000
Quality audits	30,300
Design review	49,500
Warranty claims	7,100
Sample testing of materials	26,400
Returned goods	98,700
Preventive maintenance	45,700
Quality engineering	41,800
Setup for testing new products	41,100
Scrap and rework	44,200
Losses caused by vendor scrap	65,800
Product simulation	29,400

1. Prepare a detailed analysis of the costs of quality.
2. **ACCOUNTING CONNECTION** ▶ Comment on the company's current efforts to improve product quality.

LO 3   **Measuring Costs of Quality**

E6A. Lola Corporation has two departments that produce two separate product lines. The company has been implementing total quality management over the past year. Revenue and costs of quality for that year follow.

	Dept. R	Dept. Q	Totals
Annual sales	$10,200,000	$10,000,000	$20,200,000
Costs of quality:			
Prevention costs	$ 106,000	$ 204,500	$ 310,500
Appraisal costs	104,001	99,999	204,000
Internal failure costs	194,000	97,500	291,500
External failure costs	144,000	60,000	204,000
Totals	$ 548,001	$ 461,999	$ 1,010,000

Which department is taking a more serious approach to implementing TQM? Base your answer on the following computations. (Round to two decimal places.)

1. Total costs of quality as a percentage of sales
2. Ratio of costs of conformance to total costs of quality
3. Ratio of costs of nonconformance to total costs of quality
4. Costs of nonconformance as a percentage of sales

LO 4   **Measures of Product Design Quality**

E7A. ACCOUNTING CONNECTION ▶ Vu It, Inc.'s management's goal was to be the first to market with its newest product, TV sunglasses. Comment on how the company's measures of product design quality, which follow, compare with the industry benchmarks.

Measures of Product Design Quality	Vu It, Inc.	Industry Benchmark
Number of design defects detected	20	20
Unresolved design defects at time of product introduction	5	2
Average time between defect detection and correction (hours)	2	4
Time to market (time from design idea to market) (days)	50	80

LO 4   **Measures of Vendor Performance**

E8A. ACCOUNTING CONNECTION ▶ Howe Curtin, the manager of a hotel that caters to traveling businesspeople, is reviewing the nonfinancial measures of quality for the hotel's dry-cleaning service. Six months ago, he contracted with a local dry-cleaning company to provide the service to hotel guests. The cleaner promised a four-hour turnaround on all dry-cleaning orders. Comment on the following measures for the last six months:

	January	February	March	April	May	June
Percentage of complaints	2%	3%	2%	3%	3%	2%
Percentage of on-time deliveries	100%	85%	100%	90%	80%	100%
Number of orders	500	600	600	700	800	800

LO 4   **Measures of Production Performance**

E9A. Analyze the following nonfinancial measures of quality for Sweet Express, Inc., a supplier of novelty candy boxes, for a recent four-week period. Focus specifically on measures of production performance.

Measures of Quality	Week 1	Week 2	Week 3	Week 4
Percentage of defective products per million produced	0.9%	0.7%	0.5%	0.4%
Equipment utilization rate	89%	90%	89%	90%
Machine downtime (hours)	11	9	12	11
Machine maintenance time (hours)	9	8	8	9
Machine setup time (hours)	3	4	5	3

LO 4   **Measures of Delivery Cycle Time**

E10A. Compute the missing numbers for **a**, **b**, **c**, and **d** for the delivery cycle time for Companies M, N, Q, and P.

Company	Purchase-Order Lead Time	Production Cycle Time	Delivery Time	Total Delivery Cycle Time
M	**a**	2	1	5
N	2	5	**b**	10
Q	10	**c**	15	32
P	2	7	3	**d**

LO 4   **Analysis of Waste Time**

E11A. ACCOUNTING CONNECTION ▶ Calculate the missing numbers for **a**, **b**, **c**, and **d** to analyze the waste time for the following orders. Comment on your findings.

Name of Order	Production Cycle Time	Average Process Time	Average Setup Time	Waste Time
Jones	6	**a**	2	1
Huang	**b**	8	4	3
Gonzales	8	4	**c**	2
Poon	7	3	1	**d**

LO 4   **Nonfinancial Measures of Quality and TQM**

E12A. ACCOUNTING CONNECTION ▶ "A satisfied customer is the most important goal of this company!" was the opening remark of the corporate president, Alicia Les, at Wonder Tube Company's monthly executive committee meeting. The company manufactures tube products for customers in 16 western states. It has four divisions, each

(Continued)

producing a different type of tubing material. Les, a proponent of total quality management, was reacting to the latest measures of quality from the four divisions. The data for the four divisions follow.

	Brass Division	Plastics Division	Aluminum Division	Copper Division	Company Averages
Vendor on-time delivery	96.30%	90.50%	97.20%	87.10%	92.61%
Production quality rates (defective parts per million)	1,300	2,600	1,200	4,300	2,400
On-time shipments	87.10%	76.30%	89.70%	73.50%	81.65%
Returned orders	1.00%	4.00%	0.75%	6.00%	3.00%
Number of customer complaints	20	52	6	58	34
Number of warranty claims	6	11	3	13	9

Why was Les upset? Which division or divisions do not appear to have satisfied customers? What criteria did you use to make your decision?

LO 4   ## Nonfinancial Data Analysis

E13A. Strong Company makes racing bicycles. Its Lightspeed model is considered the top of the line in the industry. Three months ago, to improve quality and reduce production time, Strong purchased and installed a computer-integrated manufacturing system for the Lightspeed model. Management is interested in cutting time in all phases of the delivery cycle. The controller's office gathered the following data for the past four-week period:

	Week			
	1	2	3	4
Average process time (hours)	23.6	23.4	22.8	22.2
Average setup time (hours)	1.5	1.4	1.3	1.2
Customer complaints	8	7	9	9
Delivery time (hours)	34.0	35.0	36.0	38.0
On-time deliveries (%)	97.1	96.7	96.2	95.3
Production backlog (units)	8,030	8,040	8,020	8,030
Production cycle time (hours)	28.5	27.9	27.2	26.4
Purchase-order lead time (hours)	38.5	36.2	35.5	34.1
Warranty claims	3	4	3	2

Analyze the performance of the Lightspeed model for the four-week period, focusing specifically on product delivery cycle time and on customer satisfaction. (Round the weekly averages to two decimal places.)

LO 5   ## Adapting to Changing Information Needs

E14A. BUSINESS APPLICATION ▶ "What's all the fuss about managers needing to focus on activities instead of costs?" demanded Lucy LaVern, the controller of Wishes, Inc. "The bottom line is all that matters, and our company's current management information system is just fine for figuring that out. I know that our system is eight years old, but if it isn't broken, why should we fix it?" How would you respond to Lucy?

EXERCISE: SET B

Visit the textbook companion website at www.cengagebrain.com to access Exercise Set B for this chapter.

PROBLEMS

LO **3**

SPREADSHEET

✔1 and 2: Kenicott Company:
Total prevention costs: $678,000
✔1 and 2: Total appraisal costs: $445,000
✔1 and 2: Total internal failure costs:
$319,200
✔1 and 2: Total external failure costs:
$538,650

Costs and Nonfinancial Measures of Quality

P1. Inturn Enterprises, Inc., operates as three autonomous companies, each with a chief executive officer who oversees its operations. At a recent corporate meeting, the company CEOs agreed to adopt total quality management and to track, record, and analyze their costs and nonfinancial measures of quality. All three companies are operating in highly competitive markets. Sales and quality-related data for September follow.

	Avondale Company	Kenicott Company	Silvertone Company
Annual sales	$11,000,000	$13,000,000	$10,553,800
Costs of quality:			
Vendor audits	$ 69,000	$ 184,800	$ 130,800
Quality audits	58,000	115,000	141,500
Failure analysis	188,500	92,400	16,350
Design review of products	80,500	176,700	218,000
Scrap and rework	207,000	160,800	21,200
Quality-certified suppliers	48,000	105,000	231,000
Preventive maintenance	92,000	158,400	163,500
Warranty adjustments	149,000	105,600	49,050
Product recalls	201,250	198,000	80,050
Quality training of employees	149,500	237,900	272,500
End-of-process sampling and testing	34,500	145,200	202,700
Reinspection of rework	126,500	66,000	27,250
Returned goods	163,103	72,600	16,350
Customer complaint processing	109,250	162,450	38,150
Total costs of quality	$ 1,676,103	$ 1,980,850	$ 1,608,400
Nonfinancial measures of quality:			
Number of warranty claims	60	32	10
Customer complaints	107	52	18
Defective parts per million	4,610	2,190	1,012
Returned orders	9.20%	4.10%	0.90%

REQUIRED

1. Prepare an analysis of the costs of quality for the three divisions. Categorize the costs as (a) costs of conformance, with subsets of prevention costs and appraisal costs, or (b) costs of nonconformance, with subsets of internal failure costs and external failure costs. Compute the total costs in each category for each company.
2. For each company compute the percentage of sales represented by prevention costs, appraisal costs, total costs of conformance, internal failure costs, external failure costs, total costs of nonconformance, and total costs of quality. (Round to two decimal places.)
3. **ACCOUNTING CONNECTION** ▶ Interpret the cost-of-quality data for each company. Is its product of high or low quality? Why? Is each company headed in the right direction to be competitive?
4. **ACCOUNTING CONNECTION** ▶ Evaluate the nonfinancial measures of quality in terms of customer satisfaction. Are the results consistent with your analysis in requirement **3**? Explain your answer.

Analysis of Nonfinancial Data

P2. Convenience Enterprises, Inc., manufactures several lines of small machinery. Before the company installed automated equipment, the total delivery cycle time for its Coin machine models averaged about three weeks. Last year, management decided to purchase a new computer-integrated manufacturing system for the Coin line. A summary of operating data for the past eight weeks for the Coin line follows.

	Week							
	1	**2**	**3**	**4**	**5**	**6**	**7**	**8**
Average process time (hours)	7.20	7.20	7.10	7.40	7.60	7.20	6.80	6.60
Average setup time (hours)	2.20	2.20	2.10	1.90	1.90	1.80	2.00	1.90
Customer complaints	5	6	4	7	6	8	9	9
Delivery time (hours)	36.20	37.40	37.20	36.40	35.90	35.80	34.80	34.20
Equipment utilization rate (%)	98.10	98.20	98.40	98.10	97.80	97.60	97.80	97.80
Machine downtime (hours)	82.30	84.20	85.90	84.30	83.40	82.20	82.80	80.40
Machine maintenance time (hours)	50.40	52.80	49.50	46.40	47.20	45.80	44.80	42.90
On-time deliveries (%)	92.40	92.50	93.20	94.20	94.40	94.10	95.80	94.60
Production backlog (units)	15,230	15,440	15,200	16,100	14,890	13,560	13,980	13,440
Production cycle time (hours)	12.20	12.60	11.90	11.80	12.20	11.60	11.20	10.60
Purchase-order lead time (hours)	26.20	26.80	26.50	25.90	25.70	25.30	24.80	24.20
Warranty claims	2	2	3	2	3	4	3	3

REQUIRED

1. Analyze the performance of the Coin machine line for the eight-week period. Focus on performance in the following areas. (Round to two decimal places.)
   a. Production performance
   b. Delivery cycle time, including computations of delivery cycle time and waste time
   c. Customer satisfaction

2. **ACCOUNTING CONNECTION ▶** Summarize your findings in a report to the company's president, Deborah Shimon.

Costs of Quality

P3. Barbara Speiss, regional manager of Candy Heaven, is evaluating the performance of four candy kitchens in her region. In accordance with the company's costs-of-quality standards of performance, the four locations provided the following data for the past six months:

	Alta	Provo	Snowbird	Copper
Sales	$1,800,000	$1,500,000	$1,400,000	$1,200,000
Prevention costs	$ 32,000	$ 48,000	$ 16,000	$ 20,000
Appraisal costs	42,000	32,000	18,000	25,000
Internal failure costs	24,000	21,000	42,000	30,000
External failure costs	33,000	16,000	45,000	25,000
Total costs of quality	$ 131,000	$ 117,000	$ 121,000	$ 100,000

REQUIRED

1. For each location, compute the percentages of sales represented by prevention costs, appraisal costs, total costs of conformance, internal failure costs, external failure costs, total costs of nonconformance, and total costs of quality. (Round to two decimal places.)
2. For each location, calculate the ratio of costs of conformance to costs of quality and the ratio of costs of nonconformance to costs of quality. (Round to two decimal places.)
3. **ACCOUNTING CONNECTION ▶** Interpret the cost-of-quality data for each location. Rank the locations in terms of quality.

LO **3, 4** **Interpreting Measures of Quality**

P4. ACCOUNTING CONNECTION ▶ Circuit Corporation supplies integrated circuitry to major appliance manufacturers in all parts of the world. Producing a high-quality product in each of the company's four divisions is the mission of management. Each division is required to record and report its efforts to achieve quality in all of its primary product lines. The following information for the most recent three-month period was submitted to the chief financial officer:

	Macon Division		Dothan Division		Valdosta Division		Columbia Division	
	Amount	% of Revenue	Amount	% of Revenue	Amount	% of Revenue	Amount	% of Revenue
Costs of Conformance								
Prevention costs:								
Quality training of employees	$ 4,400		$ 15,600		$ 23,600		$ 8,900	
Process engineering	3,100		19,700		45,900		9,400	
Preventive maintenance	5,800		14,400		13,800		11,100	
Total prevention costs	$ 13,300	0.95%	$ 49,700	3.11%	$ 83,300	5.55%	$ 29,400	1.73%
Appraisal costs:								
End-of-process sampling and testing	$ 3,500		$ 19,500		$ 21,400		$ 6,900	
Quality audits of products	6,100		11,900		17,600		8,700	
Vendor audits	4,100		10,100		9,800		7,300	
Total appraisal costs	$ 13,700	0.98%	$ 41,500	2.59%	$ 48,800	3.25%	$ 22,900	1.35%
Total costs of conformance	$ 27,000	1.93%	$ 91,200	5.70%	$132,100	8.80%	$ 52,300	3.08%
Costs of Nonconformance								
Internal failure costs:								
Quality-related downtime	$ 26,800		$ 8,300		$ 6,500		$ 22,600	
Scrap and rework	17,500		9,100		7,800		16,200	
Scrap disposal losses	31,200		7,200		3,600		19,900	
Total internal failure costs	$ 75,500	5.39%	$ 24,600	1.54%	$ 17,900	1.19%	$ 58,700	3.45%
External failure costs:								
Warranty claims	$ 22,600		$ 4,400		$ 2,500		$ 17,100	
Customer complaint processing	31,600		8,100		6,400		22,300	
Returned goods	29,900		5,600		3,100		19,800	
Total external failure costs	$ 84,100	6.01%	$ 18,100	1.13%	$ 12,000	0.80%	$ 59,200	3.48%
Total costs of nonconformance	$159,600	11.40%	$ 42,700	2.67%	$ 29,900	1.99%	$117,900	6.93%
Total costs of quality	$186,600	13.33%	$133,900	8.37%	$162,000	10.79%	$170,200	10.01%
Ratios of Nonfinancial Measures:								
Number of sales to number of warranty claims	168 to 1		372 to 1		996 to 1		225 to 1	
Number of products produced to number of products reworked	1,420 to 1		3,257 to 1		6,430 to 1		2,140 to 1	
Change in throughput time (positive amount means time reduction)	(−4.615%)		2.163%		5.600%		(−1.241%)	
Total number of deliveries to number of late deliveries	86 to 1		168 to 1		290 to 1		128 to 1	

REQUIRED

1. Rank the divisions in order of their apparent product quality.
2. What three measures were most important in your rankings in 1? Why?
3. Which division is most successful in its bid to improve quality? What measures illustrate its high-quality rating?
4. Consider the two divisions producing the lowest-quality products. What actions would you recommend to the management of each division? Where should their quality dollars be spent?

ALTERNATE PROBLEMS

Costs and Nonfinancial Measures of Quality

P5. Stainless Company operates as three autonomous divisions. Each division has a general manager in charge of product development, production, and distribution. Management recently adopted total quality management, and the divisions now track, record, and analyze their costs and nonfinancial measures of quality. All three divisions are operating in highly competitive marketplaces. Sales and quality-related data for April follow.

	North Division	West Division	South Division
Annual sales	$8,500,000	$9,500,000	$13,000,000
Costs of quality:			
Field testing	$ 51,600	$ 112,800	$ 183,950
Quality audits	17,200	79,100	109,650
Failure analysis	103,100	14,700	92,700
Quality training of employees	60,200	188,000	167,700
Scrap and rework	151,000	18,800	154,800
Quality-certified suppliers	34,400	94,000	108,200
Preventive maintenance	65,800	148,000	141,900
Warranty claims	107,500	42,300	106,050
Customer complaint processing	151,500	108,100	154,800
Process engineering	94,600	235,000	232,200
End-of-process sampling and testing	24,700	178,600	141,900
Scrap disposal losses	77,400	23,500	64,500
Returned goods	152,500	16,200	45,150
Product recalls	64,500	32,900	64,500
Total costs of quality	$1,156,000	$1,292,000	$ 1,768,000
Nonfinancial measures of quality:			
Defective parts per million	3,410	1,104	1,940
Returned orders	7.40%	1.10%	3.20%
Customer complaints	62	12	30
Number of warranty claims	74	16	52

REQUIRED

1. Prepare an analysis of the costs of quality for the three divisions. Categorize the costs as (a) costs of conformance, with subsets of prevention costs and appraisal costs, or (b) costs of nonconformance, with subsets of internal failure costs and external failure costs. Compute the total costs for each category for each division.

2. For each division, compute the percentage of sales represented by prevention costs, appraisal costs, total costs of conformance, internal failure costs, external failure costs, total costs of nonconformance, and total costs of quality.

3. **ACCOUNTING CONNECTION** ▶ Interpret the cost-of-quality data for each division. Is each division's product of high or low quality? Explain your answers. Are the divisions headed in the right direction to be competitive?

4. **ACCOUNTING CONNECTION** ▶ Evaluate the nonfinancial measures of quality in terms of customer satisfaction. Are the results consistent with your analysis in requirement **3**? Explain your answers.

Analysis of Nonfinancial Data

P6. Electronics Company is known for its high-quality products and on-time deliveries. Six months ago, it installed a computer-integrated manufacturing system in its Small Components Department. The new equipment produces the entire component, so the finished product is ready to be shipped when needed. During the past eight-week period, the controller's staff gathered the data that follow.

	Week							
	1	**2**	**3**	**4**	**5**	**6**	**7**	**8**
Average process time (hours)	10.90	11.10	10.60	10.80	11.20	11.80	12.20	13.60
Average setup time (hours)	2.50	2.60	2.60	2.80	2.70	2.40	2.20	2.20
Customer complaints	11	10	23	15	9	7	5	6
Delivery time (hours)	26.20	26.40	26.10	25.90	26.20	26.60	27.10	26.40
Equipment utilization rate (%)	96.20	96.10	96.30	97.20	97.40	96.20	96.40	95.30
Machine downtime (hours)	106.40	108.10	120.20	110.40	112.80	102.20	124.60	136.20
Machine maintenance time (hours)	64.80	66.70	72.60	74.20	76.80	66.60	80.40	88.20
On-time deliveries (%)	97.20	97.50	97.60	98.20	98.40	96.40	94.80	92.60
Production backlog (units)	10,246	10,288	10,450	10,680	10,880	11,280	11,350	12,100
Production cycle time (hours)	16.50	16.40	16.30	16.10	16.30	17.60	19.80	21.80
Purchase-order lead time (hours)	15.20	15.10	14.90	14.60	14.60	13.20	12.40	12.60
Warranty claims	4	8	2	1	6	4	2	3

REQUIRED

1. Analyze the performance of the Small Components Department for the eight-week period. Focus on performance in the following areas: (a) production performance, (b) delivery cycle time (include computations of delivery cycle time and waste time), and (c) customer satisfaction. (Round to two decimal places.)

2. **ACCOUNTING CONNECTION** ▶ Summarize your findings in a report to the department's superintendent, Pierre Jour.

LO **3**

Costs of Quality

✔1: Subchapter S Portal percentage of sales represented by prevention costs: 0.20%
✔1: Subchapter S Portal appraisal costs: 0.35%
✔1: Subchapter S Portal total internal failure costs: 0.40%
✔1: Subchapter S Portal total external failure costs: 0.69%
✔2: Ratio of costs of conformance to costs of quality, Subchapter S Portal: 0.34 to 1
✔2: Ratio of costs of nonconformance to costs of quality, Subchapter S Portal: 0.66 to 1

P7. Charles Caroll, the regional manager of Quik File, Inc., is evaluating the performance of four ecommerce tax preparation sites in his region. The following data for the past six months were presented to him by each site in accordance with the company's costs-of-quality standards of performance:

	Partnership Portal	Corporation Portal	Subchapter S Portal	Sole Proprietorship Portal
Sales	$5,000,000	$10,000,000	$8,000,000	$6,000,000
Prevention costs	$ 62,000	$ 58,000	$ 16,000	$ 20,000
Appraisal costs	32,000	42,000	28,000	15,000
Internal failure costs	54,000	31,000	32,000	40,000
External failure costs	23,000	26,000	55,000	35,000
Total costs of quality	$ 171,000	$ 157,000	$ 131,000	$ 110,000

REQUIRED

1. For each site, compute the percentages of sales represented by prevention costs, appraisal costs, total costs of conformance, internal failure costs, external failure costs, total costs of nonconformance, and total costs of quality. (Round to two decimal places.)

2. For each site, calculate the ratio of costs of conformance to costs of quality and the ratio of costs of nonconformance to costs of quality. (Round to two decimal places.)

3. **ACCOUNTING CONNECTION** ▶ Interpret the cost-of-quality data for each site. Rank the sites in terms of quality.

LO **3, 4**

Interpreting Measures of Quality

✔1 and 2: Division A total prevention costs: $20,200
✔1 and 2: Division A total appraisal costs: $26,100
✔1 and 2: Division A total internal failure costs: $61,600
✔1 and 2: Division A total external failure costs: $50,200
✔1 and 2: Division A number of sales to number of warranty claims: 295 to 1

P8. Salmon Corporation has five divisions, each manufacturing a product line that competes in the global marketplace. The company is planning to compete for the Malcolm Baldrige Award, so management requires that each division record and report its efforts to achieve quality in its product line. The information below was submitted to the company's controller for the most recent six-month period.

(Continued)

	A	B	C	D	E	F
1		Division A	Division B	Division C	Division D	Division E
2	**Total Revenue**	$886,000	$1,040,000	$956,000	$1,225,000	$1,540,000
3	**Costs of Quality**					
4	Customer complaint processing	$10,400	$12,600	$12,300	$10,100	$15,600
5	Scrap and rework	26,800	13,500	38,700	11,900	34,800
6	Quality audit of products	13,600	28,400	6,300	25,600	11,700
7	Returned goods	18,700	11,400	38,400	11,300	36,000
8	Warranty claims	21,100	6,400	36,200	6,500	42,600
9	Quality training of employees	8,900	12,600	4,600	11,400	4,200
10	Preventive maintenance	11,300	18,700	8,300	13,600	6,300
11	Failure analysis	34,800	9,800	46,900	10,200	56,900
12	Inspection of materials	12,500	18,700	7,800	17,500	5,600
13	**Nonfinancial Measure of Quality**					
14	Number of warranty claims versus	22	12	46	12	62
15	number of sales	6,500	8,900	7,200	9,800	9,600
16	Number of products reworked versus	150	140	870	70	900
17	number of products manufactured	325,000	456,000	365,000	450,000	315,600

REQUIRED

1. Prepare an analysis of the costs of quality for each division. Categorize the costs as costs of conformance or costs of nonconformance. (Round to two decimal places.)

2. For each division, compute the percentage of total revenue for each of the four cost-of-quality categories and the ratios for the nonfinancial data. (Round percentages to two decimal places.)

3. Rank the divisions in order of their apparent product quality.

4. **ACCOUNTING CONNECTION** ▶ What three measures were most important in your rankings in requirement 3? Why?

5. **ACCOUNTING CONNECTION** ▶ Which division has been most successful in its bid to improve quality? What measures illustrate its high quality rating?

6. **ACCOUNTING CONNECTION** ▶ Consider the two divisions producing the lowest-quality products. What actions would you recommend to the management of each division? Where should their quality dollars be spent?

CASES

LO 1

Conceptual Understanding: Quality Measures and Techniques

C1. Motorola's Total Customer Satisfaction (TCS) Teams are cross-functional teams that use customer-focused methods to solve quality and process problems. According to Motorola's website, one TCS Team success story involved an international supplier with quality and delivery problems. These problems required additional order expediting and rework and were causing customer dissatisfaction. The TCS Team's report to management disclosed the following:

- By evaluating and revising the product's design with input from the international supplier, the team created a more robust finished product.
- The team's adoption of process capability studies, together with continuous monitoring, resulted in improved quality for the international supplier.
- When sourcing was moved to a local supplier, the number of times the inventory turned over annually improved. It went from 26 to 52 times a year.
- Over the three-year life of the product, the team's changes resulted in $831,438 in cost savings.

1. From the TCS Team's report, identify the key issues involved in solving the international supplier's quality and process problems.
2. How could the team have applied the process-based techniques of benchmarking and process mapping to improve quality?

LO **3, 4**   ## Conceptual Understanding: Evaluating Performance Measures

C2. Harn Company and Ocala Company compete in the same industry. Each company is located in a large western city, and each employs between 300 and 350 people. Both companies have adopted a total quality management approach, and both want to improve their ability to compete in the marketplace. They have installed common performance measures to help track their quest for quality and a competitive advantage.

During the most recent three-month period, Harn and Ocala generated the data that follow.

	Harn Company		Ocala Company	
Performance Measures	**Financial**	**Nonfinancial**	**Financial**	**Nonfinancial**
Production performance:				
Equipment utilization rate		89.4%		92.1%
Machine downtime (in machine hours)		720		490
Delivery cycle time:				
On-time deliveries		92.1%		96.5%
Purchase-order lead time (hours)		17		18
Production cycle time (hours)		14		16
Waste time (hours)		3		2
Customer satisfaction:				
Customer complaints		28		24
Scrap and rework costs	$14,390		$13,680	
Field service costs	9,240		7,700	

1. For each measure, indicate which company has the better performance.
2. Which company is more successful in achieving a total quality environment and an improved competitive position? Explain your answer.

LO **3, 4**   ## Interpreting Management Reports: Reports on Quality Data

C3. Jack Knome is chief executive officer of Red Tundra Machinery, Inc. The company adopted a JIT operating environment five years ago. Since then, each segment of the company has been converted, and a complete computer-integrated manufacturing system operates in all parts of the company's five plants. Processing of Red Tundra's products now averages less than four days once the materials have been put into production.

Knome is worried about customer satisfaction and has asked you, as the controller, for some advice and help. He has also asked the Marketing Department to perform a quick survey of customers to determine weak areas in customer relations. A summary of four customers' replies follows.

- **Customer A:** Customer for five years; waits an average of six weeks for delivery; located 1,200 miles from plant; returns an average of 3 percent of products; receives 90 percent on-time deliveries; never hears from salesperson after placing order; likes quality or would go with competitor.
- **Customer B:** Customer for seven years; waits an average of five weeks for delivery; orders usually sit in backlog for at least three weeks; located 50 miles from plant; returns about 5 percent of products; receives 95 percent on-time deliveries; has great rapport with salesperson; salesperson is why this customer is loyal.

(Continued)

- **Customer C:** Customer for twelve years; waits an average of seven weeks for delivery; located 1,500 miles from plant; returns about 4 percent of products; receives 92 percent on-time deliveries; salesperson is available but of little help in getting faster delivery; customer is thinking about dealing with another source for its product needs.

- **Customer D:** Customer for fifteen years; very pleased with company's product; waits almost five weeks for delivery; located 120 miles from plant; returns only 2 percent of goods received; rapport with salesperson is very good; follow-up service of salesperson is excellent; would like delivery cycle time reduced to equal that of competitors; usually deals with three-week backlog.

1. Identify the areas of concern, and give at least three examples of reports that will help managers improve the company's response to customer needs.

2. Assume that you are asked to write a report that will provide information about customer satisfaction. In preparation for writing the report, answer the following questions:
   a. What kinds of information do you need to prepare this report?
   b. Why is this information relevant?
   c. Where would you find this information (i.e., what sources would you use)?
   d. When would you want to obtain this information?

LO 5   **Ethical Dilemma: MIS and Ethics**

C4. BUSINESS APPLICATION ▶ Three months ago, Max Enterprises hired a consultant, Stacy Stone, to assist in the design and installation of a new management information system for the company. Mike Carney, one of Max's systems design engineers, was assigned to work with Stone on the project. During the three-month period, Stone and Carney met six times and developed a tentative design and installation plan for the MIS. Before the plan was to be unveiled to top management, Carney asked his supervisor, Toby Bohoven, to look it over and comment on the design.

Included in the plan was the consolidation of three engineering functions into one. Both of the supervisors of the other two functions had seniority over Bohoven, so he believed that the design would lead to his losing his management position. He communicated this to Carney and ended his comments with the following statement: "If you don't redesign the system to accommodate all three of the existing engineering functions, I will give you an unsatisfactory performance evaluation for this year!"

How should Carney respond to Bohoven's assertion? Should he handle the problem alone, keeping it inside the company, or communicate the comment to Stone? Outline Carney's options, and be prepared to discuss them in class.

Continuing Case: Cookie Company

C5. In this chapter, in preparation for developing a website for your company, you will compare the quality of cookie manufacturers' websites. Visit three sites from the following list:

- www.cheryls.com
- www.davidscookies.com
- www.famous-amos.com
- www.mrsfields.com

What features does each site offer its customers? Do the sites offer both pre- and post-sale assistance? In your opinion, how have these websites affected the way cookies are sold? What features will your company's website have?

CHAPTER 13

LEARNING OBJECTIVES

 LO 1 Describe the principal purposes and concepts underlying the statement of cash flows, and identify its components and format.

 LO 2 Use the indirect method to determine cash flows from operating activities.

 LO 3 Determine cash flows from investing activities.

LO 4 Determine cash flows from financing activities.

LO 5 Analyze the statement of cash flows.

www.amazon.com/ref=gno_logo

amazon.com

Hello. Sign in to get

Your Amazon.com

Shop All Departments

Search   All Depar

Unlimited Instant Videos

MP3s & Cloud Player

Annette Shaff/Shutterstock.com

THE STATEMENT OF CASH FLOWS

Business Insight
Amazon.com, Inc.

Founded in 1995, **Amazon.com, Inc.**, is now the largest online merchandising company in the world and one of the 500 largest companies in the United States. The company's financial focus is on "long-term sustainable growth" in cash flows.

Strong cash flows are critical to achieving and maintaining liquidity. If cash flows exceed the amount a company needs for operations and expansion, it will not have to borrow additional funds. It can use its excess cash to reduce debt, thereby lowering its debt to equity ratio and improving its financial position. That, in turn, can increase the market value of its stock.

Amazon.com's Financial Highlights summarize key components of the company's statement of cash flows.[1]

AMAZON.COM'S FINANCIAL HIGHLIGHTS:
Consolidated Statement of Cash Flows (In millions)

	2011	2010	2009
Net cash provided by operating activities	$ 3,903	$ 3,495	$ 3,293
Net cash provided by (used in) investing activities	(1,930)	(3,360)	(2,337)
Net cash provided by (used in) financing activities	(482)	181	(280)
Foreign currency effects	1	17	(1)
Increase (decrease) in cash and equivalents	$ 1,492	$ 333	$ 675

1. **CONCEPT** ▶ How do relevance and classification apply to the statement of cash flows?

2. **ACCOUNTING APPLICATION** ▶ How is the statement of cash flows prepared using the indirect method?

3. **BUSINESS APPLICATION** ▶ Are Amazon.com's operations generating sufficient operating cash flows?

SECTION 1   CONCEPTS

CONCEPTS
- Relevance
- Classification
- Disclosure

**RELEVANT
LEARNING OBJECTIVE**

LO 1 Describe the principal
purposes and
concepts underlying the
statement of cash flows, and
identify its components and
format.

LO 1 Concepts Underlying the Statement
CASH FLOW of Cash Flows

Cash flows enable a company to pay expenses, debts, employees' wages, and taxes and to invest in the assets it needs for its operations. Without sufficient cash flows, a company cannot grow and prosper. Because of the importance of cash flows, one must be alert to the possibility that items may be incorrectly *classified* in a statement of cash flows and that the statement may not fully *disclose* all pertinent information. This chapter identifies the classifications used in a statement of cash flows and explains how to analyze the statement.

The **statement of cash flows** shows how a company's operating, investing, and financing activities have affected cash during a period. It explains the net increase (or decrease) in cash during the period. For purposes of this statement, **cash** is defined as including both cash and cash equivalents. **Cash equivalents** are investments that can be quickly converted to cash. They have a maturity of 90 days or less when they are purchased, and they include the following:

- Money market accounts
- Commercial paper (short-term corporate notes)
- U.S. Treasury bills

A company invests in cash equivalents to earn interest on cash that would otherwise be temporarily idle. Suppose, for example, that a company has $1,000,000 that it will not need for 30 days. To earn a return on this amount, the company could place the cash in an account that earns interest (such as a money market account), lend the cash to another corporation by purchasing that corporation's short-term notes (commercial paper), or purchase a short-term obligation of the U.S. government (a Treasury bill).

Cash equivalents should not be confused with short-term investments, also called **marketable securities**. Marketable securities have a maturity of more than 90 days but are intended to be held only until cash is needed for current operations. Purchases of marketable securities are treated as cash outflows, and sales of marketable securities are treated as cash inflows. Conversely, transfers between the Cash account and cash equivalents are not treated as cash inflows or cash outflows.

Relevance of the Statement of Cash Flows

The statement of cash flows provides information about a company's cash receipts and cash payments during a period, as well as about a company's operating, investing, and financing activities. Some information about those activities may be inferred from other financial statements, but the statement of cash flows summarizes *all* transactions that affect cash.

International Perspective
IFRS How Universal Is the Statement of Cash Flows?

Despite the importance of the statement of cash flows in assessing the liquidity of companies in the United States, there has been considerable variation in its use and format in other countries. For example, in many countries, the statement shows the change in working capital rather than the change in cash and cash equivalents. Although the European Union's principal directives for financial reporting do not address the statement of cash flows, international accounting standards require it, and international financial markets expect it to be presented. As a result, most multinational companies include the statement in their financial reports. Most European countries adopted the statement of cash flows when the European Union adopted international accounting standards.

The information provided by the statement of cash flows is relevant to management in operating the business, as well as to investors and creditors in making investment and lending decisions. Management uses the statement of cash flows to:

■ assess liquidity (e.g., to determine whether short-term financing is needed to pay current liabilities).
■ determine dividend policy.
■ evaluate the effects of major policy decisions involving investments and financing needs.

Investors and creditors use the statement of cash flows to assess a company's ability to:

■ manage cash flows.
■ generate positive future cash flows.
■ pay its liabilities.
■ pay dividends and interest.
■ anticipate the need for additional financing.

Classification of Cash Flows

Amazon.com is the largest online retailer in the world and one of the 500 largest companies in the United States. Exhibit 1 shows the company's consolidated statements of cash flows for 2011, 2010, and 2009. As you can see, this statement has three major classifications: operating, investing, and financing activities.

The *classifications* of operating, investing, and financing activities are illustrated in Exhibit 2 and summarized next.

Operating Activities The first section of the statement of cash flows is cash flow from operating activities. **Operating activities** involve the cash inflows and outflows from activities that enter into the determination of net income. Cash inflows in this category include cash receipts from the sale of goods and services and from the sale of trading securities. **Trading securities** are a type of marketable security that a company buys and sells for making a profit in the near term as opposed to holding them indefinitely for investment purposes. Cash inflows from operating activities also include interest received on loans and dividends received on investments. Cash outflows from operating activities include cash payments for wages, inventory, expenses, interest, taxes, and the purchase of trading securities.

Investing Activities The second section of the statement of cash flows is cash flows from investing activities. **Investing activities** involve the acquisition and sale of property, plant, and equipment and other long-term assets, including long-term investments. They also involve the acquisition and sale of short-term marketable securities, other than trading securities, and the making and collecting of loans. Cash flows provided by investing activities include the cash received from selling marketable securities and long-term assets and from collecting on loans. Cash flows used by investing activities include the cash expended on purchasing these securities and assets and the cash lent to borrowers. Cash outflows for property, plant, and equipment, or capital expenditures, are usually shown separately from cash inflows from sales of these assets, as they are in **Amazon.com**'s statement in Exhibit 1. However, when the inflows are not material, some companies combine these two lines to show the net amount of outflow.

Financing Activities The third section of the statement of cash flows is cash flows from financing activities. **Financing activities** involve obtaining resources from stockholders and creditors. Cash inflows include the proceeds from stock issues and from short- and long-term borrowing. Cash outflows include the repayments of loans (excluding interest) and payments to stockholders, including cash dividends. Treasury stock transactions are also considered financing activities. Repayments of accounts payable or accrued liabilities are not considered repayments of loans. They are classified as cash outflows under operating activities.

Cash Balances A reconciliation of the beginning and ending balances of cash appears at the bottom of the statement. These cash balances will tie into the cash balances on the balance sheet.

STUDY NOTE: Operating activities involve the day-to-day sale of goods and services, investing activities involve long-term assets and investments, and financing activities deal with stockholders' equity accounts and debt (borrowing).

Exhibit 1
Consolidated Statement of Cash Flows

Amazon.com, Inc.
Consolidated Statements of Cash Flows

(In millions)	For the Years Ended		
	2011	**2010**	**2009**
Operating Activities:			
Net income	$ 631	$ 1,152	$ 902
Adjustments to reconcile net income to net cash from operating activities:			
Depreciation and amortization	1,083	568	378
Stock-based compensation	557	424	341
Other operating expense (income), net	154	106	103
Losses (gains) on sales of marketable securities, net	(4)	(2)	(4)
Other expense (income), net	(56)	(79)	(15)
Deferred income taxes	136	4	81
Excess tax benefits from stock-based compensation	(62)	(259)	(105)
Changes in operating assets and liabilities:			
Inventories	(1,777)	(1,019)	(531)
Accounts receivable, net and other	(866)	(295)	(481)
Accounts payable	2,997	2,373	1,859
Accrued expenses and other	1,067	740	300
Additions to unearned revenue	1,064	687	1,054
Amortization of previously unearned revenue	(1,021)	(905)	(589)
Net cash provided by operating activities	$ 3,903	$ 3,495	$ 3,293
Investing Activities:			
Purchases of fixed assets, including internal-use software and website development	(1,811)	(979)	(373)
Acquisitions, net of cash received and other	(705)	(352)	(40)
Sales and maturities of marketable securities and other investments	6,843	4,250	1,966
Purchases of marketable securities and other investments	(6,257)	(6,279)	(3,890)
Net cash provided by (used in) investing activities	$(1,930)	$(3,360)	$(2,337)
Financing Activities:			
Excess tax benefits from exercises of stock options	62	259	105
Common stock repurchased (treasury stock)	(277)	—	—
Proceeds from long-term debt and other	177	143	87
Repayments of long-term debt and capital lease obligations	(444)	(221)	(472)
Net cash provided by (used in) financing activities	$ (482)	$ 181	$ (280)
Foreign-currency effect on cash and cash equivalents	1	17	(1)
Net (decrease) increase in cash and cash equivalents	$ 1,492	$ 333	$ 675
Cash and cash equivalents, beginning of year	3,777	3,444	2,769
Cash and cash equivalents, end of year	$ 5,269	$ 3,777	$ 3,444

Source: Amazon.com, Inc., *Annual Report*, 2011 (adapted).

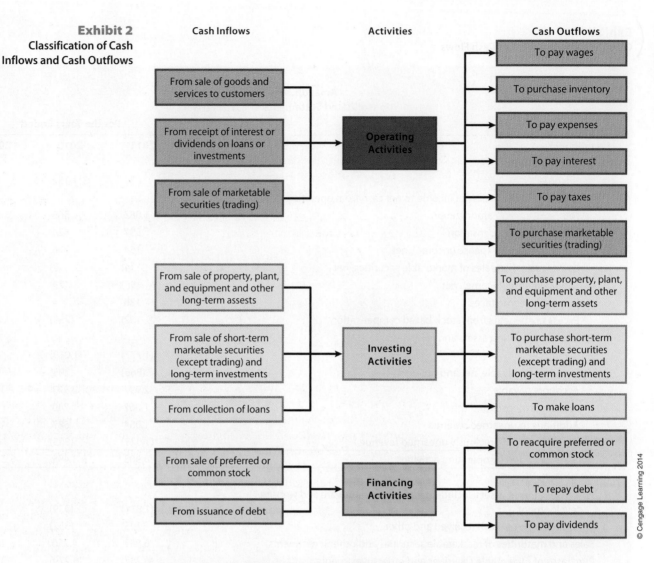

Exhibit 2
Classification of Cash Inflows and Cash Outflows

Required Disclosure of Noncash Investing and Financing Transactions

Companies occasionally engage in significant **noncash investing and financing transactions**. These transactions involve *only* long-term assets, long-term liabilities, or stockholders' equity. For instance, a company might exchange a long-term asset for a long-term liability, settle a debt by issuing capital stock, or take out a long-term mortgage to purchase real estate. Although noncash transactions represent significant investing and financing activities, they are not reflected in the body of the statement of cash flows because they do not affect current cash inflows or outflows. They will, however, affect future cash flows. For this reason, they must be *disclosed* in a separate schedule, usually following the statement of cash flows.

Alternate Presentations of Operating Activities

There are two ways of presenting operating activities on the statement of cash flows.

■ The **direct method** converts each item on the income statement from the accrual basis to the cash basis. The operating activities section of the statement of cash flows under the direct method follows in simplified format.

Cash Flows from Operating Activities		
Cash receipts from:		
Sales	xxx	
Interest	xxx	xxx
Less cash payments for:		
Purchases	xxx	
Operating expenses	xxx	
Interest payments	xxx	
Income taxes	xxx	xxx
Cash flows from operating activities		xxx

■ The **indirect method** does not require the conversion of each item on the income statement. It lists only the items necessary to convert net income to cash flows from operations in the following format:

Cash Flows from Operating Activities	
Net income	xxx
Adjustments to reconcile net income to net cash flows	
from operating activities:	
Plus non-cash expenses	xxx
Plus or minus changes in current assets	
and current liabilities	xxx
Cash flows from operating activities	xxx

STUDY NOTE: *The direct and indirect methods relate only to the operating activities section of the statement of cash flows. They are both acceptable for financial reporting purposes.*

The direct and indirect methods always produce the same amount of cash flows from operating activities. The direct method presentation of operating cash flows is more straightforward than that of the indirect method, but it is more difficult to implement in practice. Few accounting systems provide the data easily to make the calculations necessary for the direct method. Further, when the direct method is presented, preparation and *disclosure* of the indirect method of presenting cash flows from operating activities is also required.

Analysts prefer the indirect method to the direct method because it begins with net income and derives cash flows from operations. Analysts can readily identify the factors that cause cash flows from operations to differ from net income. Companies prefer the indirect method because it is easier and less expensive to prepare. As a result, the indirect method is the overwhelming choice of most companies and accountants. A survey of large companies shows that 98 percent use this method.[2]

International Perspective

IFRS The Direct Method May Become More Important Under IFRS

In the interest of converging U.S. GAAP with international financial reporting standards (IFRS), the IASB is promoting the use of the direct method, even though it is more costly for companies to prepare. IFRS will continue to require a reconciliation of net income and net cash flows from operating activities similar to what is now done in the indirect method. For example, **CVS**'s statement of cash flows is one of the few U.S. companies to use the direct method with a reconciliation. Thus, its approach is very similar to what all companies may do if the U.S. adopts IFRS.

© loops7 / iStockphoto.com

© Cengage Learning 2014

APPLY IT!

Mango Corporation engaged in the transactions that follow. Identify each transaction as (a) an operating activity, (b) an investing activity, (c) a financing activity, (d) a noncash transaction, or (e) not on the statement of cash flows.

1. Purchased office equipment, a long-term investment.
2. Decreased accounts receivable.
3. Sold land at cost.
4. Issued long-term bonds for plant assets.
5. Increased inventory.
6. Issued common stock.
7. Repurchased common stock.
8. Issued notes payable.
9. Increased income taxes payable.
10. Purchased a 60-day Treasury bill.
11. Purchased a long-term investment.
12. Declared and paid a cash dividend.

SOLUTION

1. b; 2. a; 3. b; 4. d; 5. a; 6. c; 7. c; 8. c;
9. a; 10. e (cash equivalent); 11. b; 12. c

TRY IT! SE1, SE6, E1A, E1B

ACCOUNTING APPLICATIONS

LO 2 CASH FLOW Step 1: Determining Cash Flows from Operating Activities

As shown in Exhibit 3, preparing a statement of cash flows involves four steps:

- **Step 1:** Determine cash flows from operating activities.
- **Step 2:** Determine cash flows from investing activities.
- **Step 3:** Determine cash flows from financing activities.
- **Step 4:** Prepare the statement of cash flows.

In this section, we begin with determining cash flows from operating activities.

Exhibit 3
Preparation of the Statement of Cash Flows

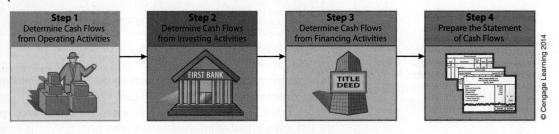

| Step 1 Determine Cash Flows from Operating Activities | Step 2 Determine Cash Flows from Investing Activities | Step 3 Determine Cash Flows from Financing Activities | Step 4 Prepare the Statement of Cash Flows |

© Cengage Learning 2014

To demonstrate the preparation of the statement of cash flows, we will use data for Eureka Corporation. Eureka's income statement for 2014 is presented in Exhibit 4, and its balance sheets for December 31, 2014 and 2013 appear in Exhibit 5. Exhibit 5 also shows the balance sheet accounts that we use for analysis and whether the change in each account is an increase or a decrease.

Exhibit 4
Income Statement

Eureka Corporation Income Statement For the Year Ended December 31, 2014		
Sales		$698,000
Cost of goods sold		520,000
Gross margin		$178,000
Operating expenses (including depreciation expense of $37,000)		147,000
Operating income		$ 31,000
Other income (expenses):		
Interest expense	$(23,000)	
Interest income	6,000	
Gain on sale of investments	12,000	
Loss on sale of plant assets	(3,000)	(8,000)
Income before income taxes		$ 23,000
Income taxes expense		7,000
Net income		$ 16,000

© Cengage Learning 2014

Exhibit 5

Comparative Balance Sheets Showing Changes in Accounts

Eureka Corporation
Comparative Balance Sheets
December 31, 2014 and 2013

	2014	2013	Change	Increase or Decrease
Assets				
Current assets:				
Cash	$ 47,000	$ 15,000	$ 32,000	Increase
Accounts receivable (net)	47,000	55,000	(8,000)	Decrease
Inventory	144,000	110,000	34,000	Increase
Prepaid expenses	1,000	5,000	(4,000)	Decrease
Total current assets	$ 239,000	$185,000	$ 54,000	
Investments	$ 115,000	$127,000	$ (12,000)	Decrease
Plant assets	$ 715,000	$505,000	$210,000	Increase
Less accumulated depreciation	(103,000)	(68,000)	(35,000)	Increase
Total plant assets	$612,000	$437,000	$175,000	
Total assets	$ 966,000	$749,000	$217,000	
Liabilities				
Current liabilities:				
Accounts payable	$ 50,000	$ 43,000	$ 7,000	Increase
Accrued liabilities	12,000	9,000	3,000	Increase
Income taxes payable	3,000	5,000	(2,000)	Decrease
Total current liabilities	$ 65,000	$ 57,000	$ 8,000	
Long-term liabilities:				
Bonds payable	295,000	245,000	50,000	Increase
Total liabilities	$ 360,000	$302,000	$ 58,000	
Stockholders' Equity				
Common stock, $5 par value	$ 276,000	$200,000	$ 76,000	Increase
Additional paid-in capital	214,000	115,000	99,000	Increase
Retained earnings	141,000	132,000	9,000	Increase
Treasury stock	(25,000)	0	(25,000)	Increase
Total stockholders' equity	$ 606,000	$447,000	$159,000	
Total liabilities and stockholders' equity	$ 966,000	$749,000	$217,000	

The income statement indicates how successful a company has been in earning an income from its operating activities. However, because that statement is prepared on an accrual basis, it does not reflect the inflow and outflow of cash related to operating activities. Revenues are recorded even though the company may not yet have received the cash, and expenses are recorded even though the company may not yet have expended the cash. Thus, to ascertain cash flows from operations in step 1 in preparing the statement of cash flows, the figures on the income statement must be converted from an accrual basis to a cash basis.

As Exhibit 6 shows, the indirect method focuses on adjusting items on the income statement to reconcile net income to net cash flows from operating activities. These items include the following:

- Depreciation, amortization, and depletion
- Gains and losses
- Changes in the balances of current asset and current liability accounts.

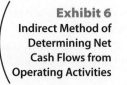

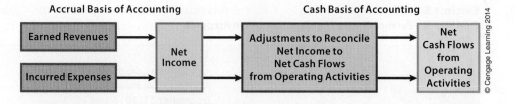

These adjusting items can be seen in the schedule in Exhibit 7, which shows the reconciliation of Eureka's net income to net cash flows from operating activities. Each adjusting item requires a different type of analysis as illustrated in the sections that follow.

Exhibit 7
Schedule of Cash
Flows from
Operating Activities:
Indirect Method

Eureka Corporation		
Schedule of Cash Flows from Operating Activities		
For the Year Ended December 31, 2014		
Cash flows from operating activities:		
Net income		$16,000
Adjustments to reconcile net income to net cash		
flows from operating activities:		
Depreciation	$ 37,000	
Gain on sale of investments	(12,000)	
Loss on sale of plant assets	3,000	
Changes in current assets and current liabilities:		
Decrease in accounts receivable	8,000	
Increase in inventory	(34,000)	
Decrease in prepaid expenses	4,000	
Increase in accounts payable	7,000	
Increase in accrued liabilities	3,000	
Decrease in income taxes payable	(2,000)	14,000
Net cash flows from operating activities		$30,000

© Cengage Learning 2014

Depreciation, Amortization, and Depletion

STUDY NOTE: *Operating expenses on the income statement include depreciation expense, which does not require a cash outlay.*

Although the cash payments made for plant assets, intangible assets, and natural resources appear in the investing activities section of the statement of cash flows, the depreciation expense, amortization expense, and depletion expense associated with these assets appear in the operating activities section. The amount of these expenses can usually be found in the income statement or in a note to the financial statements.

Depreciation

Financial Statement Information Eureka's income statement (Exhibit 4) shows $37,000 of depreciation expense.

Journal Entry

			Dr.	Cr.
A = L + SE		Depreciation Expense	37,000	
−37,000 −37,000		Accumulated Depreciation		37,000
		To record annual depreciation on plant assets		

Cash Flow Analysis
Depreciation $37,000

When depreciation expense is recorded, the Cash account is not affected. Thus, net income needs to be adjusted upward by the amount of depreciation, or $37,000, because depreciation expense involves no current outlay of cash even though it appears on the income statement. Amortization and depletion expenses are handled in exactly the same way as depreciation expense.

Gains and Losses

Like depreciation expense, gains and losses that appear on the income statement do not affect cash flows from operating activities and need to be subtracted from or added to net income. The actual cash flows from these transactions are reflected in the investing and financing activities sections of the statement of cash flows.

Gain—Sale of Investments

Financial Statement Information Eureka's income statement (Exhibit 4) shows a $12,000 gain on the sale of investments.

Cash Flow Analysis

Gain on sale of investments	($12,000)

This amount is subtracted from net income to reconcile net income to net cash flows from operating activities. The reason for doing this is that the $12,000 is included in the investing activities section of the statement of cash flows as part of the cash from the sale of the investment. Because the gain has already been included in the calculation of net income, the $12,000 gain must be subtracted to prevent double counting.

Loss—Sale of Plant Assets

Financial Statement Information Eureka's income statement shows a $3,000 loss on the sale of plant assets.

Cash Flow Analysis

Loss on sale of plant assets	$3,000

As was the case with depreciation expense, a loss on the sale of assets is added to net income to reconcile net income to net cash flows from operating activities. The cash received associated with the transaction that resulted in this loss is reflected in the investing activities section of the statement of cash flows.

Changes in Current Assets

As explained in this section and the next, changes in current assets and current liabilities require a different approach to reconcile net income to cash flows from operating activities.

Decreases in current assets other than cash have positive effects on cash flows, and increases in current assets have negative effects on cash flows:

▼ A *decrease* in a current asset frees up invested cash, thereby increasing cash flow.

▲ An *increase* in a current asset consumes cash, thereby decreasing cash flow.

Decrease in Current Assets—Accounts Receivable

Financial Statement Information Eureka's balance sheet (Exhibit 5) shows an $8,000 decrease in accounts receivable. We can conclude that collections were $8,000 more than sales recorded for the year.

Cash Flow Analysis

Decrease in account receivable	$8,000

Because net sales in 2014 were $698,000, the total cash received from sales can be calculated as follows.

Net Sales + Additional Cash Collections = Total Cash Collections Received
$698,000 + $8,000 = $706,000

The effect on Accounts Receivable can be illustrated as follows.

	Accounts Receivable			
Sales to Customers	Beg. Bal.	55,000	Cash Collections 706,000 →	**Cash Receipts from Customers**
→	Net Sales	698,000		
	End. Bal.	**47,000**		

To reconcile net income to net cash flows from operating activities, the $8,000 decrease in accounts receivable is added to net income.

Increase in Current Assets—Inventory

Financial Statement Information Eureka's balance sheet (Exhibit 5) shows a $34,000 increase in inventory.

Cash Flow Analysis

Increase in inventory   ($34,000)

Because the cost of goods sold in 2014 was $520,000, the total cash paid for inventory can be calculated as follows, as was done with accounts receivable.

Cost of Goods Sold + Additional Purchases = Total Purchases
$520,000 + $34,000 = $554,000

	Inventory			
Purchases from Supplier	Beg. Bal.	110,000	Cost of Goods Sold 520,000 →	**Cost of Goods Sold to Customers**
→	Total Purchases	554,000		
	End. Bal.	**144,000**		

Thus, Eureka expended $34,000 more in cash for purchases than it included in the cost of goods sold on its income statement. Because of this expenditure, net income is higher than net cash flows from operating activities, so $34,000 must be deducted from net income.

Decrease in Current Assets—Prepaid Expenses

Financial Statement Information Continuing with current assets, Eureka's balance sheet (Exhibit 5) shows a $4,000 decrease in prepaid expenses.

Cash Flow Analysis

Decrease in prepaid expenses $4,000

Using the same logic, the decrease shown on the balance sheet is added to net income because Eureka expended less cash on prepaid expenses than was included on the income statement.

Changes in Current Liabilities

The effect that changes in current liabilities have on cash flows is the opposite of the effect of changes in current assets:

▲ An *increase* in a current liability represents a postponement of a cash payment, which frees up cash and increases cash flow in the current period; thus, it is added to net income.

▼ A *decrease* in a current liability consumes cash, which decreases cash flow; thus, it is deducted from net income.

Increase in Current Liabilities—Accounts Payable

Financial Statement Information Eureka's balance sheet (Exhibit 5) shows a $7,000 increase in accounts payable.

Cash Flow Analysis

Increase in accounts payable	$7,000

This means that Eureka paid $7,000 less to creditors than the amount indicated in the cost of goods sold on its income statement, illustrated as follows.

Purchases on Account* – Amount Unpaid = Total Cash Payments
$554,000 – $7,000 = $547,000

The following T account illustrates this relationship:

Cash Payments to Suppliers	Accounts Payable		
→ Payments on Account 547,000	Beg. Bal.	43,000	
	Purchases on Account	554,000* ←	Purchases
	End. Bal.	**50,000**	

*Purchases = Cost of Goods Sold ($520,000) + Increase in Inventory ($34,000)

Thus, $7,000 must be added to net income to reconcile net income to net cash flows from operating activities.

Increase in Current Liabilities—Accrued Liabilities

Financial Statement Information Eureka's balance sheet (Exhibit 5) shows a $3,000 increase in accrued liabilities.

Cash Flow Analysis

Increase in accrued liabilities	$3,000

Using the same logic as with the increase in accounts payable, this amount is added to net income. The increase in accrued liabilities was created by an adjusting entry that also increases expenses but does not use cash in the current period. Since expenses decrease net income, the increase in accrued expenses needs to be added to net income.

Decrease in Current Liabilities—Income Taxes Payable

Financial Statement Information Eureka's balance sheet (Exhibit 5) shows a $2,000 decrease in income taxes payable.

Cash Flow Analysis

Decrease in income taxes payable	($2,000)

This amount is deducted from net income because the decrease in income taxes payable means the company paid this year's taxes plus an amount from the prior year, as follows.

Income Taxes Expense + Additional Payment = Total Income Taxes Payments
$7,000 + $2,000 = $9,000

Cash Paid for Income Taxes	Income Taxes Payable		
→ Income Taxes Payments 9,000	Beg. Bal.	5,000	Income Taxes Expense for the Year
	Income Taxes Expense	7,000 ←	
	End. Bal.	**3,000**	

Schedule of Cash Flows from Operating Activities

In summary, Exhibit 7 shows that by using the indirect method, net income of $16,000 has been adjusted by reconciling items totaling $14,000 to arrive at net cash flows from operating activities of $30,000:

Net Income +/– Reconciling Items = Cash Flows from Operating Activities
$16,000 + $14,000 = $30,000

Although Eureka's net income was $16,000, the company actually had net cash flows of $30,000 from operating activities to use for purchasing assets, reducing debts, and paying dividends. The rules for reconciling items from the income statement that do not affect cash flows can be summarized as follows.

	Add to or Deduct from Net Income
Depreciation expense	✚ Add
Amortization expense	✚ Add
Depletion expense	✚ Add
Losses	✚ Add
Gains	─ Deduct

The following summarizes the adjustments from the balance sheet for increases and decreases in current assets and current liabilities:

	Add to Net Income ✚	Deduct from Net Income ─
Current assets:		
Accounts receivable (net)	▼ Decrease	▲ Increase
Inventory	▼ Decrease	▲ Increase
Prepaid expenses	▼ Decrease	▲ Increase
Current liabilities:		
Accounts payable	▲ Increase	▼ Decrease
Accrued liabilities	▲ Increase	▼ Decrease
Income taxes payable	▲ Increase	▼ Decrease

Business Perspective
What Is EBITDA, and Is It Any Good?

Some companies and analysts like to use EBITDA (an acronym for Earnings Before Interest, Taxes, Depreciation, and Amortization) as a shortcut measure of cash flows from operations. But experiences of the past decade have caused many analysts to reconsider this measure of performance. For instance, when **WorldCom** transferred $3.8 billion from expenses to capital expenditures in one year, it touted its EBITDA. At the time, the firm was, in fact, nearly bankrupt. The demise of **Vivendi**, the big French company that imploded when it did not have enough cash to pay its debts and that also touted its EBITDA, is another reason that analysts have had second thoughts about relying on this measure of performance.

Some analysts are now saying that EBITDA is "to a great extent misleading" and that it "is a confusing metric.... Some take it for a proxy for profits and some take it for a proxy for cash flow, and it's neither."[3] Cash flows from operations and free cash flow, both of which take into account interest, taxes, and depreciation, are better and more comprehensive measures of a company's ability to generate sufficient cash flows.

APPLY IT!

For the year ended June 30, 2015, RAK Corporation's net income was $7,400. Its depreciation expense was $2,000. During the year, its accounts receivable increased by $4,400, inventories increased by $7,000, prepaid rent decreased by $1,400, accounts payable increased by $14,000, salaries payable increased by $1,000, and income taxes payable decreased by $600. The company also had an $1,800 gain on the sale of investments. Use the indirect method to prepare a schedule of cash flows from operating activities.

SOLUTION

RAK Corporation
Schedule of Cash Flows from Operating Activities
For the Year Ended June 30, 2015

Cash flows from operating activities:		
Net income		$ 7,400
Adjustments to reconcile net income to net cash flows from operating activities:		
Depreciation	$ 2,000	
Gain on sale of investments	(1,800)	
Changes in current assets and current liabilities:		
Increase in accounts receivable	(4,400)	
Increase in inventories	(7,000)	
Decrease in prepaid rent	1,400	
Increase in accounts payable	14,000	
Increase in salaries payable	1,000	
Decrease in income taxes payable	(600)	4,600
Net cash flows from operating activities		$12,000

TRY IT! SE2, SE3, SE6, E2A, E3A, E4A, E8A, E2B, E3B, E4B, E8B

LO3 Step 2: Determining Cash Flows from Investing Activities

CASH FLOW

STUDY NOTE: *Investing activities involve long-term assets and short- and long-term investments. Inflows and outflows of cash are shown in the investing activities section of the statement of cash flows.*

Determining cash flows from investing activities is step 2 in preparing the statement of cash flows. In this step, accounts involving cash receipts and cash payments from investing activities are examined individually. The objective is to explain the change in each account balance from one period to the next.

Although investing activities relate mainly to the long-term assets shown on the balance sheet, they also include any short-term investments shown under current assets on the balance sheet and any investment gains and losses on the income statement. The balance sheets in Exhibit 5 show that Eureka had no short-term investments and that its long-term assets consisted of investments and plant assets. The income statement in Exhibit 4 shows that Eureka had a gain on the sale of investments and a loss on the sale of plant assets.

The following transactions pertain to Eureka's investing activities in 2014:

1. Purchased investments in the amount of $78,000.
2. Sold for $102,000 investments that cost $90,000.
3. Purchased plant assets in the amount of $120,000.
4. Sold for $5,000 plant assets that cost $10,000 and that had accumulated depreciation of $2,000.
5. Issued $100,000 of bonds at face value in a noncash exchange for plant assets.

In the sections that follow, we explain the effects of these transactions on Eureka's cash flows by analyzing their impact on the accounts related to investing activities.

Investments

Financial Statement Information Eureka's balance sheet (Exhibit 5) shows a $12,000 decrease in investments. To explain this decrease and its effects on the statement of cash flows, we will analyze the increases and decreases in Eureka's Investments account.

Purchase of Investments

Transaction 1 Purchased investments in the amount of $78,000.

Journal Entry

A = L + SE
+78,000
−78,000

	Dr.	Cr.
Investments	78,000	
Cash		78,000
Purchase of investments		

Cash Flow Analysis

Purchase of investments	($78,000)

Sale of Investments

Transaction 2 Sold for $102,000 investments that cost $90,000.

Journal Entry

A = L + SE
+102,000   +12,000
−90,000

	Dr.	Cr.
Cash	102,000	
Investments		90,000
Gain on Sale of Investments		12,000
Sale of Investments for a gain		

Cash Flow Analysis

Sale of investments	$102,000

STUDY NOTE: *The $102,000 price obtained, not the $12,000 gained, constitutes the cash flow.*

Note that the gain on the sale is included in the $102,000. This is the reason we excluded it in computing cash flows from operations. If it had not been excluded in that section, it would have been counted twice.

Reconciliation We have now explained the $12,000 decrease in the Investments account during 2014, as illustrated in the following T account:

Investments			
Dr.		**Cr.**	
Beg. Bal.	127,000	Sales	90,000
Purchases	78,000		
End. Bal.	**115,000**		

Purchases and sales are listed separately as cash outflows and inflows to give analysts a complete view of investing activities. However, some companies prefer to list them as a single net amount. If Eureka Corporation had short-term investments or marketable securities, the analysis of cash flows would be the same.

Plant Assets

Financial Statement Information Eureka's balance sheet shows the following:

- $210,000 increase in plant assets
- $35,000 increase in accumulated depreciation

Purchase of Plant Assets

Transaction 3 Purchased plant assets in the amount of $120,000.

Journal Entry

A = L + SE
+120,000
−120,000

	Dr.	Cr.
Plant Assets	120,000	
Cash		120,000

Cash Flow Analysis

Purchase of plant assets	($120,000)

Comment Cash outflows and cash inflows related to plant assets are listed separately, but companies sometimes combine them into a single net amount, called *capital expenditures*, when the cash inflows from sales are immaterial.

Sale of Plant Assets

Transaction 4 Sold for $5,000 plant assets that cost $10,000 and that had accumulated depreciation of $2,000.

Journal Entry

A = L + SE
+5,000 +3,000
+2,000
−10,000

	Dr.	Cr.
Cash	5,000	
Accumulated Depreciation	2,000	
Loss on Sale of Plant Assets	3,000	
Plant Assets		10,000
Sale of plant assets at a loss		

Cash Flow Analysis

Sale of plant assets	$5,000

STUDY NOTE: *The amount of a loss or gain on the sale of an asset is determined by the amount of cash received and does not represent a cash outflow or inflow.*

Note that this transaction results in a positive cash flow of $5,000, even though the plant assets were sold at a loss of $3,000. As noted in our analysis of operating activities, the loss on the sale of plant assets is added back to net income. This action avoids counting the loss in two sections of the statement of cash flows.

Issued Bonds in Exchange for Plant Assets

Transaction 5 Issued $100,000 of bonds at face value in a noncash exchange for plant assets.

Journal Entry

A = L + SE
+100,000 +100,000

	Dr.	Cr.
Plant Assets	100,000	
Bonds Payable		100,000
Issued bonds at face value for plant assets		

Cash Flow Analysis

Schedule of Noncash Investing and Financing Transactions	
Issue of bonds payable for plant assets	$100,000

Although this transaction does not involve an inflow or outflow of cash, it is a significant transaction involving both an investing activity (the purchase of plant assets) and a financing activity (the issue of bonds payable). Because one purpose of the statement of cash flows is to show important investing and financing activities, the transaction is *disclosed* at the bottom of the statement of cash flows or in a separate schedule.

Reconciliation We have now explained all the changes related to Eureka's Plant Assets account. The following T accounts summarize these changes:

Plant Assets

Dr.		Cr.	
Beg. Bal.	505,000	Sales	10,000
Cash Purchase	120,000		
Noncash Purchase	100,000		
End. Bal.	**715,000**		

Accumulated Depreciation

Dr.		Cr.	
Sale	2,000	Beg. Bal.	68,000
		Depreciation Expense	37,000
		End. Bal.	**103,000**

Had the balance sheet included specific plant asset accounts (e.g., Equipment and the related accumulated depreciation account) or other long-term asset accounts (e.g., Intangibles), the analysis would have been the same.

APPLY IT!

The following T accounts show Andre Company's plant assets and accumulated depreciation at the end of 2015:

Plant Assets

Dr.		Cr.	
Beg. Bal.	65,000	Disposals	23,000
Purchases	33,600		
End. Bal.	**75,600**		

Accumulated Depreciation

Dr.		Cr.	
Disposals	14,700	Beg. Bal.	34,500
		Depreciation	10,200
		End. Bal.	**30,000**

Andre's income statement shows a $4,400 gain on the sale of plant assets. Compute the amounts that should be shown as cash flows from investing activities and show how they should appear on Andre's 2015 statement of cash flows.

SOLUTION

Cash flows from investing activities:

Purchase of plant assets	$(33,600)
Sale of plant assets	12,700

The T accounts show total purchases of plant assets of $33,600, which is an outflow of cash, and the disposal of plant assets that cost $23,000 and that had accumulated depreciation of $14,700. The cash inflow from the disposal was as follows.

Plant assets	$23,000
Less accumulated depreciation	14,700
Book value	$ 8,300
Add gain on sale	4,400
Cash inflow from sale of plant assets	$12,700

Because the gain on the sale is included in the $12,700 in the investing activities section of the statement of cash flows, it should be deducted from net income in the operating activities section.

TRY IT! SE4, SE6, E5A, E6A, E8A, E5B, E6B, E8B

LO 4 Step 3: Determining Cash Flows from Financing Activities

Determining cash flows from financing activities is step 3 in preparing the statement of cash flows. It is very similar to determining cash flows from investing activities, but the accounts analyzed relate to short-term borrowings, long-term liabilities, and stockholders' equity. Because Eureka Corporation does not have short-term borrowings, we deal only with long-term liabilities and stockholders' equity accounts.

The following transactions pertain to Eureka's financing activities in 2014:

1. Issued $100,000 of bonds at face value in a noncash exchange for plant assets.
2. Repaid $50,000 of bonds at face value at maturity.
3. Issued 15,200 shares of $5 par value common stock for $175,000.
4. Paid cash dividends in the amount of $7,000.
5. Purchased treasury stock for $25,000.

Bonds Payable

Financial Statement Information Eureka's balance sheet (Exhibit 5) shows a $50,000 increase in Bonds Payable.

Issued Bonds

Transaction 1 Issued $100,000 of bonds at face value in a noncash exchange for plant assets. We have already analyzed Transaction 1 in connection with plant assets, but we also need to account for the change in the Bonds Payable account. As noted, this transaction is reported on the schedule of noncash investing and financing transactions.

Redeemed Bonds

Transaction 2 Repaid $50,000 of bonds at face value at maturity.

Journal Entry

A = L + SE
−50,000   −50,000

	Dr.	Cr.
Bonds Payable	50,000	
Cash		50,000
Repayment of bonds at face value at maturity		

Cash Flow Analysis

Repayment of bonds	($50,000)

Reconciliation The following T account explains the change in Bonds Payable:

Bonds Payable

Dr.		Cr.	
Repayment	50,000	Beg. Bal.	245,000
		Noncash Issue	100,000
		End. Bal.	**295,000**

If Eureka Corporation had any notes payable, the analysis would be the same.

Common Stock

Increase in Common Stock and Additional Paid-in Capital

Financial Statement Information Eureka's balance sheet (Exhibit 5) shows a $76,000 increase in common stock and a $99,000 increase in additional paid-in capital.

Transaction 3 Issued 15,200 shares of $5 par value common stock for $175,000.

Journal Entry

A	=	L	+	SE
+175,000				+76,000
				+99,000

	Dr.	Cr.
Cash	175,000	
Common Stock		76,000
Additional Paid-in Capital		99,000
Issued 15,200 shares of $5 par value common stock		

Cash Flow Analysis

Issuance of common stock	$175,000

Reconciliation The following analysis of this transaction is all that is needed to explain the changes in the two accounts during 2014:

	Common Stock			Additional Paid-in Capital		
Dr.		Cr.		Dr.		Cr.
	Beg. Bal.	200,000			Beg. Bal.	115,000
	Issue	76,000			Issue	99,000
	End. Bal.	**276,000**			**End. Bal.**	**214,000**

Retained Earnings

Increase in Retained Earnings

Financial Statement Information Eureka's balance sheet (Exhibit 5) shows a $9,000 increase in retained earnings.

Transaction 4 Paid cash dividends in the amount of $7,000.

Journal Entry

A	=	L	+	SE
−7,000				−7,000

	Dr.	Cr.
Retained Earnings	7,000	
Cash Dividends		7,000
To close the Cash Dividends account		

Cash Flow Analysis

Payment of dividends	($7,000)

Reconciliation Recall that dividends will reduce Retained Earnings and that net income appears in the operating activities section of the statement of cash flows. Thus, we have now explained all the changes related to Eureka's Retained Earnings account. This T account shows the change in the Retained Earnings account:

Retained Earnings			
Dr.		Cr.	
Cash Dividends	7,000	Beg. Bal.	132,000
		Net Income	16,000
		End. Bal.	**141,000**

Treasury Stock

Increase in Treasury Stock

Financial Statement Information Eureka's balance sheet (Exhibit 5) shows a $25,000 increase in treasury stock.

STUDY NOTE: Dividends paid, not dividends declared, appear on the statement of cash flows.

High-tech companies with large amounts of intangible assets can lose up to 80 percent of their value in times of financial stress. As a hedge against economic downturns, these companies need to build cash reserves and may therefore choose to hoard cash rather than pay dividends.

Patryk Kosmider/Shutterstock.com

Transaction 5 Purchased treasury stock for $25,000.

Journal Entry

A	=	L	+	SE
−25,000				−25,000

	Dr.	Cr.
Treasury Stock	25,000	
Cash		25,000
Purchased treasury stock		

STUDY NOTE: *The purchase of treasury stock qualifies as a financing activity, but it is also a cash outflow.*

Cash Flow Analysis

Purchase of treasury stock	($25,000)

Reconciliation The following T account explains the change in Treasury Stock:

Treasury Stock

Dr.		Cr.
Purchase	25,000	

Step 4: Preparing the Statement of Cash Flows

We have now analyzed all of Eureka Corporation's income statement items, explained all balance sheet changes, and taken all additional information into account. Exhibit 8 shows how these data are assembled in Eureka's statement of cash flows.

Exhibit 8
Statement of Cash Flows: Indirect Method

Eureka Corporation
Statement of Cash Flows
For the Year Ended December 31, 2014

Cash flows from operating activities:		
Net income		$ 16,000
Adjustments to reconcile net income to net cash flows from operating activities:		
Depreciation	$ 37,000	
Gain on sale of investments	(12,000)	
Loss on sale of plant assets	3,000	
Changes in current assets and current liabilities:		
Decrease in accounts receivable	8,000	
Increase in inventory	(34,000)	
Decrease in prepaid expenses	4,000	
Increase in accounts payable	7,000	
Increase in accrued liabilities	3,000	
Decrease in income taxes payable	(2,000)	14,000
Net cash flows from operating activities		$ 30,000
Cash flows from investing activities:		
Purchase of investments	$ (78,000)	
Sale of investments	102,000	
Purchase of plant assets	(120,000)	
Sale of plant assets	5,000	
Net cash flows from investing activities		(91,000)
Cash flows from financing activities:		
Repayment of bonds	$ (50,000)	
Issuance of common stock	175,000	
Payment of dividends	(7,000)	
Purchase of treasury stock	(25,000)	
Net cash flows from financing activities		93,000
Net increase in cash		$ 32,000
Cash at beginning of year		15,000
Cash at end of year		$ 47,000
Schedule of Noncash Investing and Financing Transactions		
Issue of bonds payable for plant assets		$100,000

Cash Flows and the Financial Statements

As shown in Exhibit 9, the statement of cash flows explains the changes in cash on the balance sheet and reconciles the change in Cash (reported on the Balance Sheet) from one period to the next.

Exhibit 9
Relationship of the Statement of Cash Flows to the Balance Sheet

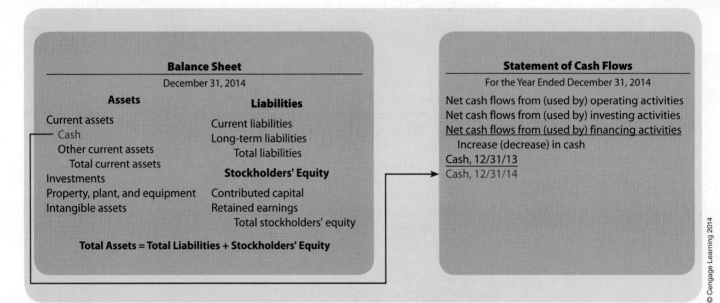

Balance Sheet
December 31, 2014

Assets	Liabilities
Current assets	Current liabilities
Cash	Long-term liabilities
Other current assets	Total liabilities
Total current assets	
Investments	**Stockholders' Equity**
Property, plant, and equipment	Contributed capital
Intangible assets	Retained earnings
	Total stockholders' equity

Total Assets = Total Liabilities + Stockholders' Equity

Statement of Cash Flows
For the Year Ended December 31, 2014

Net cash flows from (used by) operating activities
Net cash flows from (used by) investing activities
Net cash flows from (used by) financing activities
    Increase (decrease) in cash
Cash, 12/31/13
Cash, 12/31/14

© Cengage Learning 2014

APPLY IT!

During 2015, Brown Company issued $1,000,000 in long-term bonds at par, repaid $200,000 of notes payable at face value, issued notes payable of $40,000 for equipment, paid interest of $40,000, paid dividends of $25,000, and repurchased common stock in the amount of $50,000. Prepare the cash flows from financing activities section of the statement of cash flows.

SOLUTION

Cash flows from financing activities:	
Issuance of long-term bonds	$1,000,000
Repayment of notes payable	(200,000)
Payment of dividends	(25,000)
Purchase of treasury stock	(50,000)
Net cash flows from financing activities	$ 725,000

Note: Interest is an operating activity. The exchange of the notes payable for equipment is a noncash investing and financing transaction.

TRY IT! SE5, SE6, E7A, E8A, E7B, E8B

SECTION 3

BUSINESS APPLICATIONS

**BUSINESS
APPLICATIONS**

- Evaluate a company's cash-generating efficiency
  - Cash flow yield
  - Cash flows to sales
  - Cash flows to assets
  - Free cash flow
- Ethics

**RELEVANT
LEARNING OBJECTIVE**

LO 5 Analyze the statement of cash flows.

CASH FLOW **LO 5** Analyzing Cash Flows

An analysis of the statement of cash flows can reveal significant relationships. One area on which analysts focus is the cash inflows and outflows from operating activities, the first section on the statement of cash flows. Analysts use the information in this section to compute cash flow yield, cash flows to sales, cash flows to assets, and free cash flow.

Cash Flow Ratios

Cash flows from operating activities represent the cash generated from current or continuing operations. They are a measure of the ability to pay bills on time and to meet unexpected needs for cash, as well as how management spends the company's cash.

While the level of cash at the bottom of the statement of cash flows is certainly an important consideration, such information can be obtained from the balance sheet. The focal point of cash flow analysis is on cash inflows and outflows from operating activities. These cash flows are used in ratios that measure **cash-generating efficiency**, which is a company's ability to generate cash from its current or continuing operations. The ratios that analysts use to compute cash-generating efficiency are cash flow yield, cash flows to sales, and cash flows to assets.

In this section, we compute these ratios for **Amazon.com** in 2011 using data for net income and net cash flows from Exhibit 1 and the following information from Amazon.com's 2011 annual report (all dollar amounts are in millions):

	2011	2010
Net sales	$48,077	$34,204
Total assets	25,278	18,797

Cash Flow Yield **Cash flow yield** is the ratio of net cash flows from operating activities to net income. For **Amazon.com**, it is calculated as follows.

Business Perspective
Can a Company Have Too Much Cash?

Having a surplus of cash on hand can be a benefit or a risk. Many companies put their excess cash to good use by investing in productive assets, conducting research and development, paying off debt, buying back stock, or paying dividends. Of course, companies must also keep enough cash on hand for emergencies; but when companies like **ExxonMobil**, **Microsoft**, and **Cisco Systems** accumulated large amounts of cash before the market crash in 2008, some commentators argued that this was poor management. They pointed out that shareholders suffer when executives are too conservative and keep the money in low-paying money market accounts or make unwise acquisitions.[4] However, these companies and others, like **Ford** and **Google**, that had cash reserves not only survived the down years, but also were prospering by 2010.[5] For financial statement users, it is important to look closely at the components of the statement of cash flows.

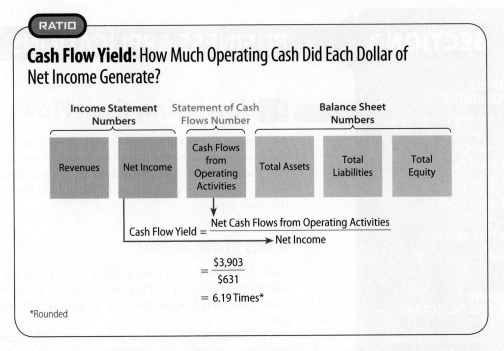

Cash Flow Yield: How Much Operating Cash Did Each Dollar of Net Income Generate?

$$\text{Cash Flow Yield} = \frac{\text{Net Cash Flows from Operating Activities}}{\text{Net Income}}$$

$$= \frac{\$3,903}{\$631}$$

$$= 6.19 \text{ Times*}$$

*Rounded

Cash flow yield is an important financial ratio because it shows whether a company is generating sufficient cash flow in relation to its net income or profitability. For most companies, the cash flow yield should exceed 1.0. Amazon.com's cash flow yield in 2011 was much better than that. With a cash flow yield of 6.19 times, Amazon.com was generating about $6.19 of cash for every dollar of net income.

The cash flow yield needs to be examined carefully. For instance, a firm with significant depreciable assets should have a cash flow yield greater than 1.0 because depreciation expense is added back to net income to arrive at cash flows from operating activities. If special items, such as discontinued operations, appear on the income statement and are material, income from continuing operations (from the income statement) should be used as the denominator. Also, an artificially high cash flow yield may result because a firm has very low net income, which is the denominator in the ratio.

Cash Flows to Sales **Cash flows to sales** is the ratio of net cash flows from operating activities to net sales. For **Amazon.com**, it is calculated as follows.

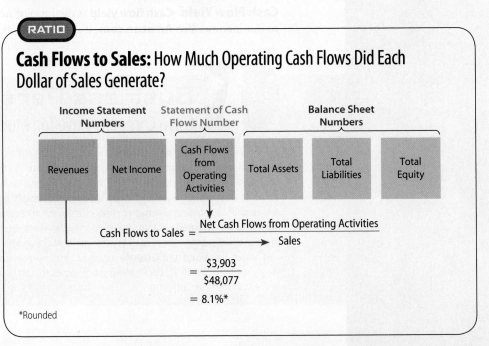

Cash Flows to Sales: How Much Operating Cash Flows Did Each Dollar of Sales Generate?

$$\text{Cash Flows to Sales} = \frac{\text{Net Cash Flows from Operating Activities}}{\text{Sales}}$$

$$= \frac{\$3,903}{\$48,077}$$

$$= 8.1\%*$$

*Rounded

Amazon.com generated positive cash flows to sales of 8.1 percent. Another way to state this result is that every dollar of sales generated 8.1 cents in cash.

Cash Flows to Assets Cash flows to assets is the ratio of net cash flows from operating activities to average total assets. **Amazon.com**'s ratio is calculated as follows.

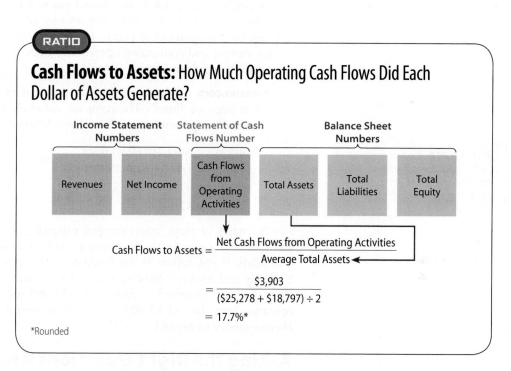

At 17.7 percent, Amazon.com's cash flows to assets ratio indicates that for every dollar of assets, the company generated almost 18 cents. This excellent result is higher than its cash flows to sales ratio because of its good asset turnover ratio:

$$\text{Asset Turnover} = \text{Sales} \div \text{Average Total Assets}$$
$$2.2 \text{ Times*} = \$48,077 \div \$22,038$$
$$\text{or}$$
$$\text{Asset Turnover} = \text{Cash Flows to Assets} \div \text{Cash Flows to Sales}$$
$$2.2 \text{ Times*} = 17.7\% \div 8.1\%$$

* Rounded

Cash flows to sales and cash flows to assets are closely related to the profitability measures of profit margin and return on assets. They exceed those measures by the amount of the cash flow yield ratio because cash flow yield is the ratio of net cash flows from operating activities to net income.

Free Cash Flow

As noted in an earlier chapter, **free cash flow** is the amount of cash that remains after deducting the funds a company must commit to continue operating at its planned level. Free cash flow is a very useful analytic tool. A study of 100 different measures showed it to be the best predictor of future increases in stock price.[6]

Free cash flow can be positive or negative:

- *Positive free cash flow* means that the company has met all of its planned cash commitments and has cash available to reduce debt or to expand.
- *Negative free cash flow* means that the company will have to sell investments, borrow money, or issue stock in the short term to continue at its planned level. If a company's free cash flow remains negative for several years, it may not be able to raise cash by issuing stocks or bonds. On the statement of cash flows, cash commitments for current and continuing operations, interest, and income taxes are incorporated in cash flows from current operations.

Amazon.com has a stated primary financial objective of "long-term sustainable growth in free cash flow."[7] The company definitely achieved this objective in 2011, as shown in the computation (in millions) that follows.

STUDY NOTE: *The computation for free cash flow sometimes uses net capital expenditures in place of purchases plus sales of plant assets.*

$$\frac{\text{Free Cash}}{\text{Flow}} = \frac{\text{Net Cash Flows from}}{\text{Operating Activities}} - \text{Dividends} - \frac{\text{Purchases of}}{\text{Plant Assets}} + \frac{\text{Sales of}}{\text{Plant Assets}}$$

$$= \$3,903 - \$0 - \$1,811 + \$0$$

$$= \$2,092$$

Purchases of plant assets (capital expenditures) and sales (dispositions) of plant assets, if any, appear in the investing activities section of the statement of cash flows. Dividends, if any, appear in the financing activities section. Amazon.com is a growing company and does not have material sales of plant assets and does not pay dividends. The company's positive free cash flow of $2,092 million was due primarily to its strong operating cash flow of $3,903 million. Consequently, the company does not have to borrow money to expand.

Asking the Right Questions About the Statement of Cash Flows

Most readers of financial statements are accustomed to looking at the "bottom line" to get an overview of a company's financial status. They look at total assets on the balance sheet and net income on the income statement. However, the statement of cash flows requires a different approach because changes in the components of the statement during the year are far more revealing.

In interpreting a statement of cash flows, it pays to know the right questions to ask. To illustrate, we will use **Amazon.com** as an example.

Cash Flows and Net Income *What are the primary reasons that Amazon.com's cash flows from operating activities differed from net income in 2011?*

For Amazon.com, the largest positive items in 2011 were accounts payable and depreciation. They are added to net income for different reasons. Accounts payable represents

Business Perspective
What Do You Mean, "Free Cash Flow"?

Because the statement of cash flows has been around for less than 25 years, no generally accepted analyses have yet been developed. For example, the term *free cash flow* is commonly used in the business press, but there is no agreement on its definition. An article in *Forbes* defines *free cash flow* as "cash available after paying out capital expenditures and dividends, but *before taxes and interest*" [emphasis added].[8] An article in *The Wall Street Journal* defines it as "operating income less maintenance-level capital expenditures."[9] The definition with which we are most in agreement is the one used in *BusinessWeek*: free cash flow is net cash flows from operating activities less net capital expenditures and dividends. This "measures truly discretionary funds—company money that an owner could pocket without harming the business."[10]

an increase in the amount owed to creditors, whereas depreciation represents a noncash expense that is deducted in arriving at net income. Amazon.com's two largest negative items were increases in inventories and amortization of unearned revenue. As a growing company, Amazon.com was managing its operating cycle by generating cash from creditors to pay for increases in inventories.

Investing Activities *What were Amazon.com's most important investing activities other than capital expenditures?*

Amazon.com was actively buying and selling investments. However, sales of marketable securities and other investments were not sufficient to offset the purchase of marketable securities and other investments and the purchase of various assets.

Financing Activities *How did Amazon.com manage its financing activities during 2011?*

Excess tax benefits from stock-based compensation and proceeds from long-term debt provided some funds to buy back treasury stock and pay off some long-term debt, but the inflows were less than the outflows. Because of its good cash flow from operations, Amazon.com did not need long-term financing.

Cash Flow Trends *What has been the trend of cash flows for Amazon.com?*

Because cash flows can vary from year to year, analysts should look at trends in cash flow measures over several years. For example, Amazon.com's management states:

> *Because of our model we are able to turn our inventory quickly and have a cash-generating operating cycle. On average our high inventory velocity means we generally collect from consumers before our payments to suppliers come due. Inventory turnover was 10, 11, and 12 for 2011, 2010, and 2009. We expect variability in inventory turnover over time since it is affected by several factors, including our product mix, the mix of sales by us and by other sellers, our continuing focus on in-stock inventory availability, our investment in new geographies and product lines, and the extent to which we choose to utilize outsource fulfillment providers. Accounts payable days were 74, 72, and 68 for 2011, 2010, and 2009. We expect some variability in accounts payable days over time since they are affected by several factors, including the mix of product sales, the mix of sales by other sellers, the mix of suppliers, seasonality, and changes in payment terms over time, including the effect of balancing pricing and timing of payment terms with suppliers.*[11]

Ethical Considerations in Analyzing the Statement of Cash Flows

Although cash inflows and outflows are not as subject to manipulation as earnings are, managers are acutely aware of users' emphasis on cash flows from operations as an important measure of performance. Thus, an incentive exists to overstate these cash flows.

In earlier chapters, we cited an egregious example of earnings management. As you may recall, by treating operating expenses of about $10 billion over several years as purchases of equipment, **WorldCom** reduced reported expenses and improved reported earnings. In addition, by classifying payments of operating expenses as investments on the statement of cash flows, it was able to show an improvement in cash flows from operations. The inclusion of the expenditures in the investing activities section did not draw special attention because the company normally had large capital expenditures.

Another way a company can show an apparent improvement in its performance is through lack of transparency, or lack of full disclosure, in its financial statements. For instance, securitization—the sale of batches of accounts receivable—is clearly a means of financing, and the proceeds from it should be shown in the financing activities section of the statement of cash flows. However, because the accounting standards are somewhat vague about where these proceeds should go, some companies net the proceeds against the accounts receivable in the operating activities section of the statement and bury the explanation in the notes to the financial statements. By doing so, they make collections of receivables look better than they actually were. It is not illegal to do this; but from an ethical standpoint, it obscures the company's true performance.

APPLY IT!

In 2015, Benson Corporation had year-end assets of $2,400,000, sales of $2,000,000, net income of $400,000, net cash flows from operating activities of $360,000, dividends of $100,000, purchases of plant assets of $200,000, and sales of plant assets of $40,000. In 2014, year-end assets were $2,200,000. Calculate cash flow yield, cash flows to sales, cash flows to assets, and free cash flow.

SOLUTION

$$\text{Cash Flow Yield} = \frac{\$360,000}{\$400,000} = 0.9 \text{ Times}$$

$$\text{Cash Flows to Sales} = \frac{\$360,000}{\$2,000,000} = 0.18, \text{ or } 18\%$$

$$\text{Cash Flows to Assets} = \frac{\$360,000}{(\$2,400,000 + \$2,200,000) \div 2} = 0.16, \text{ or } 16\% \text{ (rounded)}$$

$$\text{Free Cash Flow} = \$360,000 - \$100,000 - \$200,000 + \$40,000 = \$100,000$$

TRY IT! SE7, SE8, E9A, E9B

A Look Back At: Amazon.com, Inc.

Annette Shaff/Shutterstock.com

The beginning of this chapter focused on the extent of **Amazon.com**'s cash flow. Complete the following requirements to answer the questions posed at the beginning of the chapter.

Section 1: Concepts
How do relevance and classification apply to the statement of cash flows?

Section 2: Accounting Applications
How is the statement of cash flows prepared using the indirect method?

Section 3: Business Applications
Are Amazon.com's operations generating sufficient operating cash flows?

SOLUTION

Section 1: Concepts
The statement of cash flows is *relevant* to management, investors, and creditors for assessing the current and future liquidity of a company, its dividend policy, and its financing needs. Operating activities *classify* inflows and outflows from operating activities and include among other things cash inflows from the sales of goods and services, sale of trading securities, as well as interest and dividends on loans and investments while cash outflows include cash spent for wages, inventory, expenses, interest, taxes, and purchase of trading securities. Investing activities *classify* the acquisition and sale of short-term marketable securities, long-term investments, and property, plant, and equipment and the making and collecting of loans. Financing activities *classify* obtaining resources from stockholders and creditors and show proceeds from stock issues and from short- and long-term borrowings and deductions for repayment of loans, payment of dividends, and purchase of treasury stock. Finally, non-cash investment and financing activities are *disclosed* in a separate schedule.

Section 2: Accounting Applications

The indirect method of preparing the statement of cash flows begins with net income and derives cash flows from operations by adjusting for items that reconcile net income to cash flows from operations. These include expense items like depreciation that do not use cash in the current year, gains and losses, and changes in current assets and current liabilities.

Section 3: Business Applications

Amazon.com's operations are generating sufficient cash flows, as evidenced by its cash flow yield of 6.19 times in 2011. This cash flow yield is more than twice that of 2010 (3.03 times = $3,495 / $1,152).

Both years easily exceeded the 1.0 level normally considered the minimum acceptable cash flow yield. Although net income decreased from 2010 to 2011, net cash flows from operating activities grew by $408 million.

Free cash flow measures the sufficiency of cash flows in a different way, and as mentioned earlier in the chapter, it is a key financial objective of Amazon.com's management. The free cash flow in 2011 was $2,092, compared to $2,516 ($3,495 − $0 − $979 + $) in 2010. Although Amazon.com's free cash flow decreased by $424 million it still has sufficient free cash flow.

An examination of Amazon.com's statement of cash flows in Exhibit 1 shows how the company is investing its free cash flow. In addition to investing in long-term assets ($1,811 million in 2011 and $979 million in 2010), the company increased its investment in marketable securities because purchases exceeded sales each year. Thus, the company did not have to rely on borrowing money (because repayments exceeded proceeds from debt) or issuing stock to finance its growth. Although it did not pay a cash dividend, Amazon.com did repurchase common stock in the amount of $277 million in 2011. Finally, cash and cash equivalents increased from $3,444 million in 2010 to $3,777 million in 2011. One must conclude that Amazon.com is a very successful and growing company. It will be interesting to see if it can maintain its success.

Review Problem

Deliga Corporation is a distributor of accessories for cell phones, iPods, iPhones, and other small electronic devices. Its income statement for 2015 and comparative balance sheets for 2015 and 2014 follow.

			D	E
		Deliga Corporation		
		Income Statement		
		For the Year Ended December 31, 2015		
4	Net sales			$825,000
5	Cost of goods sold			460,000
6	Gross margin			$365,000
7	Operating expenses (including depreciation expense of $6,000			
8	on buildings and $11,550 on equipment and amortization			
9	expense of $2,400)			235,000
10	Operating income			$130,000
11	Other income:			
12	Interest expense		$(27,500)	
13	Dividend income		1,700	
14	Gain on sale of investments		6,250	
15	Loss on disposal of equipment		(1,150)	(20,700)
16	Income before income taxes			$109,300
17	Income taxes expense			26,100
18	Net income			$ 83,200

	A	B	C	D	E	F
1		\multicolumn{5}{c}{Deliga Corporation}				
2		Comparative Balance Sheets				
3		December 31, 2015 and 2014				
4						Increase or
5			2015	2014	Change	Decrease
6		**Assets**				
7	Cash		$ 52,925	$ 60,925	$ (8,000)	Decrease
8	Accounts receivable (net)		148,000	157,250	(9,250)	Decrease
9	Inventory		161,000	150,500	10,500	Increase
10	Prepaid expenses		3,900	2,900	1,000	Increase
11	Long-term investments		18,000	43,000	(25,000)	Decrease
12	Land		75,000	62,500	12,500	Increase
13	Buildings		231,000	231,000	—	—
14	Accumulated depreciation—buildings		(45,500)	(39,500)	(6,000)	Increase
15	Equipment		79,865	83,615	(3,750)	Decrease
16	Accumulated depreciation—equipment		(21,700)	(22,800)	1,100	Decrease
17	Intangible assets		9,600	12,000	(2,400)	Decrease
18	Total assets		$712,090	$741,390	$(29,300)	
19						
20	**Liabilities and Stockholders' Equity**					
21	Accounts payable		$ 66,875	$116,875	$(50,000)	Decrease
22	Notes payable (current)		37,850	72,850	(35,000)	Decrease
23	Accrued liabilities		2,500	—	2,500	Increase
24	Income taxes payable		10,000	—	10,000	Increase
25	Bonds payable		105,000	155,000	(50,000)	Decrease
26	Mortgage payable		165,000	175,000	(10,000)	Decrease
27	Common stock, $10 par value		200,000	170,000	30,000	Increase
28	Additional paid-in capital		45,000	25,000	20,000	Increase
29	Retained earnings		104,865	46,665	58,200	Increase
30	Treasury stock		(25,000)	(20,000)	(5,000)	Increase
31	Total liabilities and stockholders' equity		$712,090	$741,390	$(29,300)	

The company's records for 2015 provide this additional information:

a. Sold long-term investments that cost $35,000 for a gain of $6,250; made other long-term investments in the amount of $10,000.
b. Purchased five acres of land to build a parking lot for $12,500.
c. Sold equipment that cost $18,750 and that had accumulated depreciation of $12,650 at a loss of $1,150; purchased new equipment for $15,000.
d. Repaid notes payable in the amount of $50,000; borrowed $15,000 by signing new notes payable.
e. Converted $50,000 of bonds payable into 3,000 shares of common stock.
f. Reduced the Mortgage Payable account by $10,000.
g. Declared and paid cash dividends of $25,000.
h. Purchased treasury stock for $5,000.

1. Prepare Deluga's statement of cash flows for 2015.
2. Compute the company's cash flow yield, cash flows to sales, cash flows to assets, and free cash flow for 2015. (Round ratios to one decimal place.)

SOLUTION   1.

	A	B	C	D	E
1			**Deliga Corporation**		
2			**Statement of Cash Flows**		
3			**For the Year Ended December 31, 2015**		
4	Cash flows from operating activities:				
5	Net income				$83,200
6	Adjustments to reconcile net income to net cash flows				
7	from operating activities:				
8			Depreciation expense—buildings	$ 6,000	
9			Depreciation expense—equipment	11,550	
10			Amortization expense—intangible assets	2,400	
11			Gain on sale of investments	(6,250)	
12			Loss on disposal of equipment	1,150	
13			Changes in current assets and current liabilities:		
14			Decrease in accounts receivable	9,250	
15			Increase in inventory	(10,500)	
16			Increase in prepaid expenses	(1,000)	
17			Decrease in accounts payable	(50,000)	
18			Increase in accrued liabilities	2,500	
19			Increase in income taxes payable	10,000	(24,900)
20	Net cash flows from operating activities				$58,300
21	Cash flows from investing activities:				
22	Sale of long-term investments			$ 41,250[a]	
23	Purchase of long-term investments			(10,000)	
24	Purchase of land			(12,500)	
25	Sale of equipment			4,950[b]	
26	Purchase of equipment			(15,000)	
27	Net cash flows from investing activities				8,700
28	Cash flows from financing activities:				
29	Repayment of notes payable			$(50,000)	
30	Issuance of notes payable			15,000	
31	Reduction in mortgage			(10,000)	
32	Dividends paid			(25,000)	
33	Purchase of treasury stock			(5,000)	
34	Net cash flows from financing activities				(75,000)
35	Net (decrease) in cash				$ (8,000)
36	Cash at beginning of year				60,925
37	Cash at end of year				$52,925
38					
39			**Schedule of Noncash Investing and Financing Transactions**		
40	Conversion of bonds payable into common stock				$50,000
41					
42	[a]$35,000 + $6,250 (gain) = $41,250				
43	[b]$18,750 − $12,650 = $6,100 (book value) − $1,150 (loss) = $4,950				

2.

$$\text{Cash Flow Yield} = \frac{\$58,300}{\$83,200} = 0.7 \text{ Time*}$$

$$\text{Cash Flows to Sales} = \frac{\$58,300}{\$825,000} = 7.1\%^*$$

$$\text{Cash Flows to Assets} = \frac{\$58,300}{(\$712,090 + \$741,390) \div 2} = 8.0\%^*$$

$$\text{Free Cash Flow} = \$58,300 - \$25,000 - \$12,500 - \$15,000 + \$4,950 = \$10,750$$

*Rounded

Chapter Review

Describe the principal purposes and concepts underlying the statement of cash flows, and identify its components and format. **LO 1**

The statement of cash flows is relevant to investors and creditors by providing information about a company's cash receipts and cash payments during a period in order to assess the company's cash-generating ability. It is relevant to management to assess liquidity, determine dividend policy, and plan investing and financing activities. Investors and creditors use it to assess the company's cash-generating ability.

The statement of cash flows has three major classifications: (1) operating activities, which involve the cash effects of transactions and other events that enter into the determination of net income; (2) investing activities, which involve the acquisition and sale of marketable securities and long-term assets and the making and collecting of loans; and (3) financing activities, which involve obtaining resources from stockholders and creditors. Noncash investing and financing transactions are also important because they affect future cash flows.

Use the indirect method to determine cash flows from operating activities. **LO 2**

The indirect method adjusts net income for all items in the income statement that do not have cash flow effects (such as depreciation, amortization, and gains and losses on sales of assets) and for changes in assets and liabilities that affect operating cash flows. Generally, increases in current assets have a negative effect on cash flows, and decreases have a positive effect. Conversely, increases in current liabilities have a positive effect on cash flows, and decreases have a negative effect.

Determine cash flows from investing activities. **LO 3**

Investing activities involve the acquisition and sale of property, plant, and equipment and other long-term assets, including long-term investments. They also involve the acquisition and sale of short-term marketable securities, other than trading securities, and the making and collecting of loans. Cash flows from investing activities are determined by analyzing the cash flow effects of changes in each account related to investing activities. The effects of gains and losses reported on the income statement must also be considered.

Determine cash flows from financing activities. **LO 4**

Determining cash flows from financing activities is almost identical to determining cash flows from investing activities. The difference is that the accounts analyzed relate to short-term borrowings, long-term liabilities, and stockholders' equity. After the changes in the balance sheet accounts from one accounting period to the next have been explained, all the cash flow effects should have been identified, and the statement of cash flows can be prepared.

Analyze the statement of cash flows. **LO 5**

Analysts tend to focus on a firm's degree of liquidity, which is determined by cash inflows and outflows. The ratios used to measure a firm's ability to generate sufficient cash are cash flow yield, cash flows to sales, and cash flows to assets. Free cash flow—the cash that remains after deducting the funds a firm must commit to continue operating at its planned level—is another important measure of the adequacy of cash flow.

Key Terms and Ratios

cash 471 (LO1)
cash equivalents 471 (LO1)
direct method 474 (LO1)
financing activities 472 (LO1)
indirect method 475 (LO1)
investing activities 472 (LO1)

marketable securities 471 (LO1)
noncash investing and
  financing transactions 474 (LO1)
operating activities 472 (LO1)
statement of cash flows 471 (LO1)
trading securities 472 (LO1)

RATIOS
cash flow yield 491 (LO5)
cash flows to assets 493 (LO5)
cash flows to sales 492 (LO5)
cash-generating
  efficiency 491 (LO5)
free cash flow 493 (LO5)

Chapter Assignments

DISCUSSION QUESTIONS

LO 1 **DQ1.** Which statement is more useful—the income statement or the statement of cash flows?

LO 2 **DQ2.** If a company has positive earnings, can cash flows from operating activities ever be negative?

LO 2, 3 **DQ3.** Which adjustments to net income in the operating activities section of the statement of cash flows are directly related to cash flows in other sections?

LO 5 **DQ4.** How would you respond to someone who says that the most important item on the statement of cash flows is the change in the cash balance for the year?

LO 5 **DQ5. BUSINESS APPLICATION ▶** If a company's cash flow yield is less than 1.0, would its cash flows to sales and cash flows to assets be greater or less than profit margin and return on assets, respectively?

LO 5 **DQ6. BUSINESS APPLICATION ▶** In computing free cash flow, what is an argument for treating the purchases of treasury stock like dividend payments?

SHORT EXERCISES

LO 1 **Classification of Cash Flow Transactions**

SE1. CONCEPT ▶ The list that follows itemizes Alpha Pro Corporation's transactions. Identify each as (a) an operating activity, (b) an investing activity, (c) a financing activity, (d) a noncash transaction, or (e) none of the above.

1. Sold land.
2. Declared and paid a cash dividend.
3. Paid interest.
4. Issued common stock for plant assets.
5. Issued preferred stock.
6. Borrowed cash on a bank loan.

LO 2

Computing Cash Flows from Operating Activities: Indirect Method

SE2. Stewart Construction Corporation had a net income of $16,500 during 2014. In that year, the company had depreciation expense of $7,000. Accounts Receivable increased by $5,500, and Accounts Payable increased by $2,500. Those were the company's only current assets and current liabilities. Use the indirect method to determine net cash flows from operating activities.

LO 2

Computing Cash Flows from Operating Activities: Indirect Method

SE3. During 2014, Cupello Corporation had a net income of $144,000. Included on its income statement were depreciation expense of $16,000 and amortization expense of $1,800. During the year, Accounts Receivable decreased by $8,200, Inventories increased by $5,400, Prepaid Expenses decreased by $1,000, Accounts Payable decreased by $14,000, and Accrued Liabilities decreased by $1,700. Use the indirect method to determine net cash flows from operating activities.

LO 3

Cash Flows from Investing Activities and Noncash Transactions

SE4. During 2014, Fargo Company purchased land for $375,000. It paid $125,000 in cash and signed a $250,000 mortgage for the rest. The company also sold for $95,000 cash a building that originally cost $90,000, on which it had $70,000 of accumulated depreciation, making a gain of $75,000. Prepare the cash flows from investing activities section and the schedule of noncash investing and financing transactions of the statement of cash flows.

LO 4

Cash Flows from Financing Activities

SE5. During 2014, North Dakota Company issued $1,000,000 in long-term bonds at 96, repaid $150,000 of bonds at face value, paid interest of $80,000, and paid dividends of $50,000. Prepare the cash flows from the financing activities section of the statement of cash flows.

LO 1, 2, 3, 4

Identifying Components of the Statement of Cash Flows

SE6. CONCEPT ▶ Assuming the indirect method is used to prepare the statement of cash flows, tell whether each of the following items would be reported (a) in cash flows from operating activities, (b) in cash flows from investing activities, (c) in cash flows from financing activities, (d) in the schedule of noncash investing and financing transactions, or (e) not on the statement of cash flows at all:

1. Dividends paid
2. Cash receipts from sales
3. Decrease in accounts receivable
4. Sale of plant assets
5. Gain on sale of investments
6. Issue of stock for plant assets
7. Issue of common stock
8. Net income

LO 5

Cash-Generating Efficiency Ratios and Free Cash Flow

SE7. BUSINESS APPLICATION ▶ In 2014, Melvin Corporation had year-end assets of $1,100,000, sales of $1,580,000, net income of $180,000, net cash flows from operating activities of $360,000, purchases of plant assets of $240,000, and sales of plant assets of $40,000, and it paid dividends of $80,000. In 2013, year-end assets were $1,000,000. Calculate the cash-generating efficiency ratios of cash flow yield, cash flows to sales, and cash flows to assets. Also calculate free cash flow. (Round to the nearest tenth of a percent.)

LO 5

Cash-Generating Efficiency Ratios and Free Cash Flow

SE8. BUSINESS APPLICATION ▶ Examine the cash flow measures in requirement **2** of the Review Problem at the end of this chapter. Discuss the meaning of these ratios.

EXERCISES: SET A

LO 1   **Classification of Cash Flow Transactions**

E1A. CONCEPT ▶ VIP Corporation engaged in the transactions that follow. Identify each transaction as (a) an operating activity, (b) an investing activity, (c) a financing activity, (d) a noncash transaction, or (e) not on the statement of cash flows. Assume the indirect method is used. (*Hint:* More than one answer may apply.)

1. Paid interest.
2. Increased dividends receivable.
3. Declared and paid a cash dividend.
4. Purchased a long-term investment.
5. Increased accounts receivable.
6. Sold equipment at a loss.
7. Issued long-term bonds for plant assets.
8. Issued common stock.
9. Declared and issued a stock dividend.
10. Decreased wages payable.
11. Purchased a 60-day Treasury bill.
12. Repaid notes payable.
13. Purchased land.

LO 2   **Cash Flows from Operating Activities: Indirect Method**

E2A. The condensed single-step income statement for the year ended December 31, 2014, of Conti Chemical Company, a distributor of farm fertilizers and herbicides, follows.

Sales		$26,000,000
Less: Cost of goods sold	$15,200,000	
Operating expenses (including depreciation of $1,640,000)	7,600,000	
Income taxes expense	800,000	23,600,000
Net income		$ 2,400,000

Selected accounts from Conti Chemical's balance sheets for 2014 and 2013 follow.

	2014	2013
Accounts receivable	$4,800,000	$3,400,000
Inventory	1,680,000	2,040,000
Prepaid expenses	520,000	360,000
Accounts payable	1,920,000	1,440,000
Accrued liabilities	120,000	200,000
Income taxes payable	280,000	240,000

Prepare a schedule of cash flows from operating activities using the indirect method.

LO 2   **Computing Cash Flows from Operating Activities: Indirect Method**

E3A. During 2014, Ortega Corporation had net income of $82,000. Included on its income statement were depreciation expense of $4,600 and amortization expense of $600. During the year, Accounts Receivable increased by $6,800, Inventories decreased by $3,800, Prepaid Expenses decreased by $400, Accounts Payable increased by $10,000, and Accrued Liabilities decreased by $900. Determine net cash flows from operating activities using the indirect method.

LO 2   **Preparing a Schedule of Cash Flows from Operating Activities: Indirect Method**

E4A. For the year ended June 30, 2014, net income for Flake Corporation was $14,800. Depreciation expense was $4,000. During the year, Accounts Receivable increased by

(Continued)

$8,800, Inventories increased by $14,000, Prepaid Rent decreased by $2,800, Accounts Payable increased by $28,000, Salaries Payable increased by $2,000, and Income Taxes Payable decreased by $1,200. Use the indirect method to prepare a schedule of cash flows from operating activities.

LO 3 **Computing Cash Flows from Investing Activities: Investments**

E5A. Wilma Company's T account for long-term available-for-sale investments at the end of 2014 follows.

Investments

Dr.		Cr.	
Beg. Bal.	76,000	Sales of Investments	78,000
Purchases of Investments	116,000		
End. Bal.	**114,000**		

In addition, Wilma's income statement shows a loss on the sale of investments of $13,000. Compute the amounts to be shown as cash flows from investing activities, and show how they appear in the statement of cash flows.

LO 3 **Computing Cash Flows from Investing Activities: Plant Assets**

E6A. The T accounts for plant assets and accumulated depreciation for Street Company at the end of 2014 follow.

Plant Assets / Accumulated Depreciation

Dr.		Cr.		Dr.		Cr.	
Beg. Bal.	130,000	Disposals	46,000	Disposals	29,400	Beg. Bal.	69,000
Purchases	67,200					Depreciation	20,400
End. Bal.	**151,200**					**End. Bal.**	**60,000**

In addition, Street's income statement shows a gain on sale of plant assets of $8,800. Compute the amounts to be shown as cash flows from investing activities, and show how they appear on the statement of cash flows.

LO 4 **Determining Cash Flows from Financing Activities: Notes Payable**

E7A. All transactions involving Notes Payable and related accounts of Sally Company during 2014 follow.

	Dr.	Cr.
Cash	36,000	
Notes Payable		36,000
Bank loan		

	Dr.	Cr.
Patent	60,000	
Notes Payable		60,000
Purchase of patent by issuing note payable		

	Dr.	Cr.
Notes Payable	10,000	
Interest Expense	1,000	
Cash		11,000
Repayment of note payable at maturity		

Determine the amounts of the transactions affecting financing activities and show how they appear on the statement of cash flows for 2014.

LO **2, 3, 4**   **Preparing the Statement of Cash Flows: Indirect Method**

E8A. Keeper Corporation's income statement for the year ended June 30, 2014, and its comparative balance sheets for June 30, 2014 and 2013 follow.

Keeper Corporation
Income Statement
For the Year Ended June 30, 2014

Sales	$234,000
Cost of goods sold	156,000
Gross margin	$ 78,000
Operating expenses	45,000
Operating income	$ 33,000
Interest expense	2,800
Income before income taxes	$ 30,200
Income taxes expense	12,300
Net income	$ 17,900

Keeper Corporation
Comparative Balance Sheets
June 30, 2014 and 2013

	2014	2013
Assets		
Cash	$ 69,900	$ 12,500
Accounts receivable (net)	21,000	26,000
Inventory	43,400	48,400
Prepaid expenses	3,200	2,600
Furniture	55,000	60,000
Accumulated depreciation—furniture	(9,000)	(5,000)
Total assets	$183,500	$144,500
Liabilities and Stockholders' Equity		
Accounts payable	$ 13,000	$ 14,000
Income taxes payable	1,200	1,800
Notes payable (long-term)	37,000	35,000
Common stock, $10 par value	115,000	90,000
Retained earnings	17,300	3,700
Total liabilities and stockholders' equity	$183,500	$144,500

Keeper issued a $22,000 note payable for purchase of furniture; sold at carrying value furniture that cost $27,000 with accumulated depreciation of $15,300; recorded depreciation on the furniture for the year, $19,300; repaid a note in the amount of $20,000; issued $25,000 of common stock at par value; and paid dividends of $4,300. Prepare Keeper's statement of cash flows for the year 2014 using the indirect method.

LO **5**   **Cash-Generating Efficiency Ratios and Free Cash Flow**

E9A. BUSINESS APPLICATION ▶ In 2014, Andy's Corporation had year-end assets of $2,400,000, sales of $3,300,000, net income of $280,000, net cash flows from operating activities of $390,000, dividends of $120,000, purchases of plant assets of $500,000, and sales of plant assets of $90,000. In 2013, year-end assets were $2,100,000. Calculate free cash flow and the cash-generating efficiency ratios of cash flow yield, cash flows to sales, and cash flows to assets. (Round to one decimal point or the nearest tenth of a percent.)

EXERCISES: SET B

Visit the textbook companion website at www.cengagebrain.com to access Exercise Set B for this chapter.

PROBLEMS

LO 1   ## Classification of Cash Flow Transactions

P1. CONCEPT ▶ Analyze each transaction listed in the table that follows and place X's in the appropriate columns to indicate the transaction's classification and its effect on cash flows using the indirect method.

	Cash Flow Classification				Effect on Cash Flows		
Transaction	**Operating Activity**	**Investing Activity**	**Financing Activity**	**Noncash Transaction**	**Increase**	**Decrease**	**No Effect**
1. Paid a cash dividend.							
2. Decreased accounts receivable.							
3. Increased inventory.							
4. Incurred a net loss.							
5. Declared and issued a stock dividend.							
6. Retired long-term debt with cash.							
7. Sold available-for-sale securities at a loss.							
8. Issued stock for equipment.							
9. Decreased prepaid insurance.							
10. Purchased treasury stock with cash.							
11. Retired a fully depreciated truck (no gain or loss).							
12. Increased interest payable.							
13. Decreased dividends receivable on investment.							
14. Sold treasury stock.							
15. Increased income taxes payable.							
16. Transferred cash to money market account.							
17. Purchased land and building with a mortgage.							

LO 1, 5   ## Interpreting and Analyzing the Statement of Cash Flows

✔ 2: Free cash flow, 2013: ($183,114)
✔ 2: Free cash flow, 2014: $290,316

P2. The comparative statements of cash flows for Wung Corporation, a manufacturer of high-quality suits for men, follow. To expand its markets and familiarity with its brand, the company attempted a new strategic diversification in 2013 by acquiring a chain of retail men's stores in outlet malls. Its plan was to expand in malls around the country, but department stores viewed the action as infringing on their territory.

Wung Corporation
Statement of Cash Flows
For the Years Ended December 31, 2014 and 2013

(In thousands)	2014	2013
Cash flows from operating activities:		
Net income (loss)	$ (43,090)	$ 76,030
Adjustments to reconcile net income to net cash flows from operating activities:		
Depreciation	$ 70,438	$ 50,036
Loss on closure of retail outlets	70,000	
Changes in current assets and current liabilities:		
Decrease (increase) in accounts receivable	100,000	(89,606)
Decrease (increase) in inventory	120,814	(102,290)
Decrease (increase) in prepaid expenses	2,734	4,492
Increase (decrease) in accounts payable	61,158	2,532
Increase (decrease) in accrued liabilities	3,000	(5,576)
Increase (decrease) in income taxes payable	(16,600)	(12,562)
	$ 411,544	$(152,974)

Net cash flows from operating activities	$ 368,454	$ (76,944)
Cash flows from investing activities:		
Capital expenditures, net	$ (32,290)	$ (66,224)
Purchase of Retail Division, cash portion	—	(402,000)
Net cash flows from investing activities	$ (32,290)	$(468,224)
Cash flows from financing activities:		
Increase (decrease) in notes payable to banks	$ (247,000)	$ 456,800
Reduction in long-term debt	(18,476)	(21,622)
Payment of dividends	(45,848)	(39,946)
Purchase of treasury stock	—	(25,000)
Net cash flows from financing activities	$ (311,324)	$ 370,232
Net increase (decrease) in cash	$ 24,840	$(174,936)
Cash at beginning of year	32,064	207,000
Cash at end of year	$ 56,904	$ 32,064

Schedule of Noncash Investing and Financing Transactions

Issue of bonds payable for retail acquisition	$ 100,000

REQUIRED

Evaluate the success of the company's strategy by answering the questions that follow.

1. **ACCOUNTING CONNECTION** ▶ What are the primary reasons cash flows from operating activities differ from net income in 2013 and in 2014? What is the effect of the acquisition in 2013? What conclusions can you draw from the changes in 2014?

2. **BUSINESS APPLICATION** ▶ Compute free cash flow for both years. What was the total cost of the acquisition? Was the company able to finance expansion in 2013 by generating internal cash flow? What was the situation in 2013?

3. **ACCOUNTING CONNECTION** ▶ What are the most significant financing activities in 2013? How did the company finance the acquisition? Do you think this is a good strategy? What other issues might you question in financing activities?

4. **ACCOUNTING CONNECTION** ▶ Based on results in 2014, what actions was the company forced to take and what is your overall assessment of the company's diversification strategy?

LO **2, 3, 4, 5**

✔ 1: Net cash flows from operating activities: $23,400
✔ 1: Net cash flows from investing activities: ($7,200)
✔ 1: Net cash flows from financing activities: $51,000

Statement of Cash Flows: Indirect Method

P3. Chaplin Arts, Inc.'s comparative balance sheets for December 31, 2014 and 2013, follow.

Chaplin Arts, Inc.
Comparative Balance Sheets
December 31, 2014 and 2013

	2014	2013
Assets		
Cash	$ 94,560	$ 27,360
Accounts receivable (net)	102,430	75,430
Inventory	112,890	137,890
Prepaid expenses	—	20,000
Land	25,000	—
Building	137,000	—
Accumulated depreciation—building	(15,000)	—
Equipment	33,000	34,000
Accumulated depreciation—equipment	(14,500)	(24,000)
Patents	4,000	6,000
Total assets	$479,380	$276,680

(Continued)

Liabilities and Stockholders' Equity

Accounts payable	$ 10,750	$ 36,750
Notes payable (current)	10,000	—
Accrued liabilities	—	12,300
Mortgage payable	162,000	—
Common stock, $10 par value	180,000	150,000
Additional paid-in capital	57,200	37,200
Retained earnings	59,430	40,430
Total liabilities and stockholders' equity	$479,380	$276,680

The following additional information about Chaplin Arts's operations during 2013 is available: (a) net income, $28,000; (b) building and equipment depreciation expense amounts, $15,000 and $3,000, respectively; (c) equipment that cost $13,500 with accumulated depreciation of $12,500 sold at a gain of $5,300; (d) equipment purchases, $12,500; (e) patent amortization, $3,000; purchase of patent, $1,000; (f) funds borrowed by issuing notes payable, $25,000; notes payable repaid, $15,000; (g) land and building purchased for $162,000 by signing a mortgage for the total cost; (h) 1,500 shares of $20 par value common stock issued for a total of $50,000; and (i) paid cash dividends, $9,000.

REQUIRED

1. Using the indirect method, prepare a statement of cash flows for Chaplin Arts.
2. **ACCOUNTING CONNECTION** ▶ Why did Chaplin Arts have an increase in cash of $67,200 when it recorded net income of only $28,000? Discuss and interpret.
3. **BUSINESS APPLICATION** ▶ Compute and assess cash flow yield and free cash flow for 2014. (Round to one decimal place.) What is your assessment of Chaplin Arts' cash-generating ability?

LO **2, 3, 4, 5**

✔ 1: Net cash flows from operating activities: ($106,000)
✔ 1: Net cash flows from investing activities: $34,000
✔ 1: Net cash flows from financing activities: $24,000

Statement of Cash Flows: Indirect Method

P4. Ben Tools, Inc.'s comparative balance sheets for December 31, 2014 and 2013, follow.

Ben Tools, Inc.
Comparative Balance Sheets
December 31, 2014 and 2013

	2014	2013
Assets		
Cash	$ 257,600	$ 305,600
Accounts receivable (net)	738,800	758,800
Inventory	960,000	800,000
Prepaid expenses	14,800	26,800
Long-term investments	440,000	440,000
Land	361,200	321,200
Building	1,200,000	920,000
Accumulated depreciation—building	(240,000)	(160,000)
Equipment	480,000	480,000
Accumulated depreciation—equipment	(116,000)	(56,000)
Intangible assets	20,000	40,000
Total assets	$4,116,400	$3,876,400
Liabilities and Stockholders' Equity		
Accounts payable	$ 470,800	$ 660,800
Notes payable (current)	40,000	160,000
Accrued liabilities	10,800	20,800
Mortgage payable	1,080,000	800,000
Bonds payable	1,000,000	760,000
Common stock	1,300,000	1,300,000
Additional paid-in capital	80,000	80,000
Retained earnings	254,800	194,800
Treasury stock	(120,000)	(100,000)
Total liabilities and stockholders' equity	$4,116,400	$3,876,400

During 2014, the company had net income of $96,000 and building and equipment depreciation expenses of $80,000 and $60,000, respectively. It amortized intangible assets in the amount of $20,000; purchased investments for $116,000; sold investments for $150,000, on which it recorded a gain of $34,000; issued $240,000 of long-term bonds at face value; purchased land and a warehouse through a $320,000 mortgage; paid $40,000 to reduce the mortgage; borrowed $60,000 by issuing notes payable; repaid notes payable in the amount of $180,000; declared and paid cash dividends in the amount of $36,000; and purchased treasury stock in the amount of $20,000.

REQUIRED

1. Using the indirect method, prepare a statement of cash flows for Ben Tools.
2. **ACCOUNTING CONNECTION** ▶ Why did Ben Tools experience a decrease in cash in a year in which it had a net income of $96,000? Discuss and interpret.
3. **BUSINESS APPLICATION** ▶ Compute and assess cash flow yield and free cash flow for 2014. Why is each of these measures important in assessing cash-generating ability?

LO **2, 3, 4, 5**

SPREADSHEET

✔ 1: Net cash flows from operating
activities: $126,600
✔ 1: Net cash flows from investing
activities: ($25,800)
✔ 1: Net cash flows from financing
activities: $14,000

Statement of Cash Flows: Indirect Method

P5. Yong Company's income statement for the year ended December 31, 2014, and its comparative balance sheets as of December 31, 2014 and 2013, follow.

Yong Company
Income Statement
For the Year Ended December 31, 2014

Sales		$1,609,000
Cost of goods sold		1,127,800
Gross margin		$ 481,200
Operating expenses (including depreciation expense of $46,800)		449,400
Income from operations		$ 31,800
Other income (expenses):		
Gain on sale of furniture and fixtures	$ 7,000	
Interest expense	(23,200)	(16,200)
Income before income taxes		$ 15,600
Income taxes expense		4,600
Net income		$ 11,000

Yong Company
Comparative Balance Sheets
December 31, 2014 and 2013

	2014	2013
Assets		
Cash	$164,800	$ 50,000
Accounts receivable (net)	165,200	200,000
Merchandise inventory	350,000	450,000
Prepaid rent	2,000	3,000
Furniture and fixtures	148,000	144,000
Accumulated depreciation—furniture and fixtures	(42,000)	(24,000)
Total assets	$788,000	$823,000
Liabilities and Stockholders' Equity		
Accounts payable	$143,400	$200,400
Income taxes payable	1,400	4,400
Notes payable (long-term)	40,000	20,000
Bonds payable	100,000	200,000
Common stock, $20 par value	240,000	200,000
Additional paid-in capital	181,440	121,440
Retained earnings	81,760	76,760
Total liabilities and stockholders' equity	$788,000	$823,000

(Continued)

During 2014, the company engaged in these transactions:

a. Sold at a gain of $7,000 furniture and fixtures that cost $35,600, on which it had accumulated depreciation of $28,800.

b. Purchased furniture and fixtures in the amount of $39,600.

c. Paid a $20,000 note payable and borrowed $40,000 on a new note.

d. Converted bonds payable in the amount of $100,000 into 4,000 shares of common stock.

e. Declared and paid $6,000 in cash dividends.

REQUIRED

1. Using the indirect method, prepare a statement of cash flows for Yong. Include a supporting schedule of noncash investing transactions and financing transactions.

2. **ACCOUNTING CONNECTION** ▶ What are the primary reasons for Yong's large increase in cash from 2013 to 2014, despite its low net income?

3. **BUSINESS APPLICATION** ▶ Compute and assess cash flow yield and free cash flow for 2014. (Round to one decimal place.) Compare and contrast what these two performance measures tell you about Yong's cash-generating ability.

ALTERNATE PROBLEMS

LO 1   **Classification of Cash Flow Transactions**

P6. CONCEPT ▶ Analyze each transaction listed in the table that follows and place X's in the appropriate columns to indicate the transaction's classification and its effect on cash flows using the indirect method.

	Cash Flow Classification				Effect on Cash Flows		
Transaction	Operating Activity	Investing Activity	Financing Activity	Noncash Transaction	Increase	Decrease	No Effect
1. Increased accounts payable.							
2. Decreased inventory.							
3. Increased prepaid insurance.							
4. Earned a net income.							
5. Declared and paid a cash dividend.							
6. Issued stock for cash.							
7. Retired long-term debt by issuing stock.							
8. Purchased a long-term investment with cash.							
9. Sold trading securities at a gain.							
10. Sold a machine at a loss.							
11. Retired fully depreciated equipment.							
12. Decreased interest payable.							
13. Purchased available-for-sale securities (long-term).							
14. Decreased dividends receivable.							
15. Decreased accounts receivable.							
16. Converted bonds to common stock.							
17. Purchased 90-day Treasury bill.							

LO **2, 3, 4, 5**

RATIO

SPREADSHEET

✔ 1: Net cash flows from operating
activities: $548,000
✔ 1: Net cash flows from investing
activities: $6,000
✔ 1: Net cash flows from financing
activities: ($260,000)

Statement of Cash Flows: Indirect Method

P7. Reed Corporation's income statement for the year ended June 30, 2014, and its comparative balance sheets as of June 30, 2014 and 2013, follow.

Reed Corporation
Income Statement
For the Year Ended June 30, 2014

Sales		$8,081,800
Cost of goods sold		7,312,600
Gross margin		$ 769,200
Operating expenses (including depreciation expense of $120,000)		378,400
Income from operations		$ 390,800
Other income (expenses)		
Loss on sale of equipment	$ (8,000)	
Interest expense	(75,200)	(83,200)
Income before income taxes		$ 307,600
Income taxes expense		68,400
Net income		$ 239,200

Reed Corporation
Comparative Balance Sheets
June 30, 2014 and 2013

	2014	2013
Assets		
Cash	$ 334,000	$ 40,000
Accounts receivable (net)	200,000	240,000
Inventory	360,000	440,000
Prepaid expenses	1,200	2,000
Property, plant, and equipment	1,256,000	1,104,000
Accumulated depreciation—property, plant, and equipment	(366,000)	(280,000)
Total assets	$1,785,200	$1,546,000
Liabilities and Stockholders' Equity		
Accounts payable	$ 128,000	$ 84,000
Notes payable (due in 90 days)	60,000	160,000
Income taxes payable	52,000	36,000
Mortgage payable	720,000	560,000
Common stock, $5 par value	400,000	400,000
Retained earnings	425,200	306,000
Total liabilities and stockholders' equity	$1,785,200	$1,546,000

During 2014, the corporation sold at a loss of $8,000 equipment that cost $48,000, on which it had accumulated depreciation of $34,000. It also purchased land and a building for $200,000 through an increase of $200,000 in Mortgage Payable; made a $40,000 payment on the mortgage; repaid $160,000 in notes but borrowed an additional $60,000 through the issuance of a new note payable; and declared and paid a $120,000 cash dividend.

REQUIRED

1. Using the indirect method, prepare a statement of cash flows. Include a supporting schedule of noncash investing and financing transactions.
2. **ACCOUNTING CONNECTION** ▶ What are the primary reasons for Reed's large increase in cash from 2013 to 2014?
3. **BUSINESS APPLICATION** ▶ Compute and assess cash flow yield and free cash flow for 2014. (Round to one decimal place.) How would you assess the corporation's cash-generating ability?

LO **2, 3, 4, 5**

✔ 1: Net cash flows from operating
activities: $93,600
✔ 1: Net cash flows from investing
activities: ($28,800)
✔ 1: Net cash flows from financing
activities: $204,000

Statement of Cash Flows: Indirect Method

P8. Shah Fabrics, Inc.'s comparative balance sheets for December 31, 2014 and 2013, follow.

Shah Fabrics, Inc.
Comparative Balance Sheets
December 31, 2014 and 2013

	2014	2013
Assets		
Cash	$ 378,240	$ 109,440
Accounts receivable (net)	409,720	301,720
Inventory	451,560	551,560
Prepaid expenses	—	80,000
Land	100,000	—
Building	548,000	—
Accumulated depreciation—building	(60,000)	—
Equipment	132,000	136,000
Accumulated depreciation—equipment	(58,000)	(96,000)
Patents	16,000	24,000
Total assets	$1,917,520	$1,106,720
Liabilities and Stockholders' Equity		
Accounts payable	$ 43,000	$ 147,000
Notes payable (current)	40,000	—
Accrued liabilities	—	49,200
Mortgage payable	648,000	—
Common stock, $10 par value	720,000	600,000
Additional paid-in capital	228,800	148,800
Retained earnings	237,720	161,720
Total liabilities and stockholders' equity	$1,917,520	$1,106,720

Additional information about Shah Fabrics' operations during 2014 is as follows: (a) net income, $112,000; (b) building and equipment depreciation expense amounts, $60,000 and $12,000, respectively; (c) equipment that cost $54,000 with accumulated depreciation of $50,000 sold at a gain of $21,200; (d) equipment purchases, $50,000; (e) patent amortization, $12,000; purchase of patent, $4,000; (f) funds borrowed by issuing notes payable, $100,000; notes payable repaid, $60,000; (g) land and building purchased for $648,000 by signing a mortgage for the total cost; (h) 6,000 shares of $40 par value common stock issued for a total of $200,000; and (i) paid cash dividend, $36,000.

REQUIRED

1. Using the indirect method, prepare a statement of cash flows for Shah Fabrics.
2. **ACCOUNTING CONNECTION ▶** Why did Shah Fabrics have an increase in cash of $268,800 when it recorded net income of only $112,000? Discuss and interpret.
3. **BUSINESS APPLICATION ▶** Compute and assess cash flow yield and free cash flow for 2014. (Round to one decimal place.) What is your assessment of Shah Fabrics' cash-generating ability?

LO **2, 3, 4, 5**

✔ 1: Net cash flows from operating
activities: ($212,000)
✔ 1: Net cash flows from investing
activities: $68,000
✔ 1: Net cash flows from financing
activities: $48,000

Statement of Cash Flows: Indirect Method

P9. Kohl Ceramics, Inc.'s comparative balance sheets, for December 31, 2014 and 2013, follow.

Kohl Ceramics, Inc.
Comparative Balance Sheets
December 31, 2014 and 2013

	2014	2013
Assets		
Cash	$ 515,200	$ 611,200
Accounts receivable (net)	1,477,600	1,517,600
Inventory	1,920,000	1,600,000
Prepaid expenses	29,600	53,600
Long-term investments	880,000	880,000
Land	722,400	642,400
Building	2,400,000	1,840,000
Accumulated depreciation—building	(480,000)	(320,000)
Equipment	960,000	960,000
Accumulated depreciation—equipment	(232,000)	(112,000)
Intangible assets	40,000	80,000
Total assets	$8,232,800	$7,752,800
Liabilities and Stockholders' Equity		
Accounts payable	$ 941,600	$1,321,600
Notes payable (current)	80,000	320,000
Accrued liabilities	21,600	41,600
Mortgage payable	2,160,000	1,600,000
Bonds payable	2,000,000	1,520,000
Common stock	2,600,000	2,600,000
Additional paid-in capital	160,000	160,000
Retained earnings	509,600	389,600
Treasury stock	(240,000)	(200,000)
Total liabilities and stockholders' equity	$8,232,800	$7,752,800

During 2014, the company had net income of $192,000 and building and equipment depreciation expenses of $160,000 and $120,000, respectively. It amortized intangible assets in the amount of $40,000; purchased investments for $232,000; sold investments for $300,000, on which it recorded a gain of $68,000; issued $480,000 of long-term bonds at face value; purchased land and a warehouse through a $640,000 mortgage; paid $80,000 to reduce the mortgage; borrowed $120,000 by issuing notes payable; repaid notes payable in the amount of $360,000; declared and paid cash dividends in the amount of $72,000; and purchased treasury stock in the amount of $40,000.

REQUIRED

1. Using the indirect method, prepare a statement of cash flows for Kohl Ceramics.
2. **ACCOUNTING CONNECTION** ▶ Why did Kohl Ceramics experience a decrease in cash in a year in which it had a net income of $192,000? Discuss and interpret.
3. **BUSINESS APPLICATION** ▶ Compute and assess cash flow yield and free cash flow for 2014. Why is each of these measures important in assessing cash-generating ability?

LO **2, 3, 4, 5**

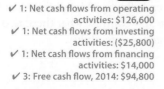

✔ 1: Net cash flows from operating
activities: $126,600
✔ 1: Net cash flows from investing
activities: ($25,800)
✔ 1: Net cash flows from financing
activities: $14,000
✔ 3: Free cash flow, 2014: $94,800

Statement of Cash Flows: Indirect Method

P10. William Corporation's income statement for the year ended December 31, 2014, and its comparative balance sheets as of December 31, 2014 and 2013, follow.

(Continued)

William Corporation
Income Statement
For the Year Ended December 31, 2014

Sales		$1,609,000
Cost of goods sold		1,127,800
Gross margin		$ 481,200
Operating expenses (including depreciation expense of $46,800)		449,400
Income from operations		$ 31,800
Other income (expenses)		
Gain on sale of furniture and fixtures	$ 7,000	
Interest expense	(23,200)	(16,200)
Income before income taxes		$ 15,600
Income taxes expense		4,600
Net income		$ 11,000

William Corporation
Comparative Balance Sheets
December 31, 2014 and 2013

	2014	2013
Assets		
Cash	$164,800	$ 50,000
Accounts receivable (net)	165,200	200,000
Merchandise inventory	350,000	450,000
Prepaid rent	2,000	3,000
Furniture and fixtures	148,000	144,000
Accumulated depreciation—furniture and fixtures	(42,000)	(24,000)
Total assets	$788,000	$823,000
Liabilities and Stockholders' Equity		
Accounts payable	$143,400	$200,400
Income taxes payable	1,400	4,400
Notes payable (long-term)	40,000	20,000
Bonds payable	100,000	200,000
Common stock, $20 par value	240,000	200,000
Additional paid-in capital	181,440	121,440
Retained earnings	81,760	76,760
Total liabilities and stockholders' equity	$788,000	$823,000

During 2014, William engaged in these transactions:

a. Sold at a gain of $7,000 furniture and fixtures that cost $35,600, on which it had accumulated depreciation of $28,800.

b. Purchased furniture and fixtures in the amount of $39,600.

c. Paid a $20,000 note payable and borrowed $40,000 on a new note.

d. Converted bonds payable in the amount of $100,000 into 4,000 shares of common stock.

e. Declared and paid $6,000 in cash dividends.

REQUIRED

1. Using the indirect method, prepare a statement of cash flows for William. Include a supporting schedule of noncash investing transactions and financing transactions.

2. **ACCOUNTING CONNECTION ▶** What are the primary reasons for William's large increase in cash from 2013 to 2014, despite its low net income?

3. **BUSINESS APPLICATION ▶** Compute and assess cash flow yield and free cash flow for 2014. (Round to one decimal place.) Compare and contrast what these two performance measures tell you about William's cash-generating ability.

CASES

LO **1, 2**   ## Conceptual Understanding: EBITDA and the Statement of Cash Flows

C1. When **Fleetwood Enterprises, Inc.**, a large producer of recreational vehicles and manufactured housing, warned that it might not be able to generate enough cash to satisfy debt requirements and could be in default of a loan agreement, its cash flow, defined in the financial press as "EBITDA" (earnings before interest, taxes, depreciation, and amortization), was a negative $2.7 million. The company would have had to generate $17.7 million in the next accounting period to comply with the loan terms.[12] To what section of the statement of cash flows does EBITDA most closely relate? Is EBITDA a good approximation for this section of the statement of cash flows? Explain your answer, which should include an identification of the major differences between EBITDA and the section of the statement of cash flows you chose.

LO **5**   ## Interpreting Financial Reports: Classic Case—Anatomy of a Disaster

C2. On October 16, 2001, Kenneth Lay, chairman and CEO of **Enron Corporation**, announced the company's earnings for the first nine months of 2001 as follows:

> *Our 26 percent increase in recurring earnings per diluted share shows the very strong results of our core wholesale and retail energy businesses and our natural gas pipelines. The continued excellent prospects in these businesses and Enron's leading market position make us very confident in our strong earnings outlook.*[13]

Less than six months later, the company filed for the biggest bankruptcy in U.S. history. Its stock dropped to less than $1 per share, and a major financial scandal was underway. Enron's statement of cash flows for the first nine months of 2001 and 2000 (restated to correct the previous accounting errors) follow. Assume you report to an investment analyst, who has asked you to analyze this statement for clues as to why the company went under.

Enron Corporation
Statement of Cash Flows
For the Nine Months Ended September 30, 2001 and 2000

(In millions)	2001	2000
Cash Flows from Operating Activities:		
Reconciliation of net income to net		
cash provided by operating activities:		
Net income	$ 225	$ 797
Cumulative effect of accounting changes, net of tax	(19)	—
Depreciation, depletion and amortization	746	617
Deferred income taxes	(134)	8
Gains on sales of non-trading assets	(49)	(135)
Investment losses	768	0
Changes in components of working capital:		
Receivables	987	(3,363)
Inventories	1	339
Payables	(1,764)	2,899
Other	464	(455)
Trading investments		
Net margin deposit activity	(2,349)	541
Other trading activities	173	(555)
Other, net	198	(566)
Net Cash Provided by (Used in) Operating Activities	$ (753)	$ 127

(Continued)

Cash Flows from Investing Activities:		
Capital expenditures	$(1,584)	$(1,539)
Equity investments	(1,172)	(858)
Proceeds from sales of non-trading investments	1,711	222
Acquisition of subsidiary stock	0	(485)
Business acquisitions, net of cash acquired	(82)	(773)
Other investing activities	(239)	(147)
Net Cash Used in Investing Activities	$(1,366)	$(3,580)
Cash Flows from Financing Activities:		
Issuance of long-term debt	$ 4,060	$ 2,725
Repayment of long-term debt	(3,903)	(579)
Net increase in short-term borrowings	2,365	1,694
Issuance of common stock	199	182
Net redemption of company-obligated preferred securities of subsidiaries	0	(95)
Dividends paid	(394)	(396)
Net (acquisition) disposition of treasury stock	(398)	354
Other financing activities	(49)	(12)
Net Cash Provided by Financing Activities	$ 1,880	$ 3,873
Increase (Decrease) in Cash and Cash Equivalents	$ (239)	$ 420
Cash and Cash Equivalents, Beginning of Period	1,240	333
Cash and Cash Equivalents, End of Period	$ 1,001	$ 753

1. **BUSINESS APPLICATION** ▶ For the two time periods shown, compute the cash-generating efficiency ratios of cash flow yield, cash flows to sales (Enron's revenues were $133,762 million in 2001 and $55,494 million in 2000), and cash flows to assets (use total assets of $61,783 million for 2001 and $64,926 million for 2000). Also compute free cash flows for the two years. (Round to one decimal place or the nearest tenth of a percent.)

2. Prepare a memorandum to the investment analyst that assesses Enron's cash generating efficiency in light of the chairman's remarks and that evaluates its available free cash flow, taking into account its financing activities. Identify significant changes in Enron's operating items and any special operating items that should be considered. Include your computations as an attachment.

LO 5 ## Ethical Dilemma: Ethics and Cash Flow Classifications

C3. BUSINESS APPLICATION ▶ Precise Metals, Inc., a fast-growing company that makes metals for equipment manufacturers, has an $800,000 line of credit at its bank. One section in the credit agreement says that the ratio of cash flows from operations to interest expense must exceed 3.0. If this ratio falls below 3.0, the company must reduce the balance outstanding on its line of credit to one-half the total line if the funds borrowed against the line of credit exceed one-half of the total line.

After the end of the fiscal year, the company's controller informs the president: "We will not meet the ratio requirements on our line of credit in 2010 because interest expense was $1.2 million and cash flows from operations were $3.2 million. Also, we have borrowed 100 percent of our line of credit. We do not have the cash to reduce the credit line by $400,000."

The president says, "This is a serious situation. To pay our ongoing bills, we need our bank to increase our line of credit, not decrease it. What can we do?" "Do you recall the $500,000 two-year note payable for equipment?" replied the controller. "It is now classified as 'Proceeds from Notes Payable' in cash flows provided from financing activities in the statement of cash flows. If we move it to cash flows from operations and call it 'Increase in Payables,' it would increase cash flows from operations to $3.7 million and put us over the limit." "Well, do it," ordered the president. "It surely doesn't make any difference where it is on the statement. It is an increase in both places. It would be much worse for our company in the long term if we failed to meet this ratio requirement."

What is your opinion of the controller and president's reasoning? Is the president's order ethical? Who benefits and who is harmed if the controller follows the president's order? What are management's alternatives? What would you do?

LO **1, 5**

Conceptual Understanding: Alternative Uses of Cash

C4. Perhaps because of hard times in their start-up years, companies in the high tech sector of American industry seem more prone than those in other sectors to building up cash reserves. For example, companies like **Cisco Systems**, **Intel**, **Dell**, and **Oracle** have amassed large cash balances.

Assume you work for a company in the high-tech industry that has built up a substantial amount of cash. The company is still growing through development of new products, has some debt, and has never paid a dividend or bought treasury stock. The company is doing better than most companies in the current financial crisis but the company's stock price is lagging. Outline at least four strategies for using the company's cash to improve the company's financial outlook.

LO **1**

Interpreting Financial Reports: Analysis of the Statement of Cash Flows

C5. Refer to the statement of cash flows in **CVS Corporation**'s 2011 annual report, which you can find using either the "Investor Relations" portion of its website (do a web search for CVS investor relations) or by going to www.sec.gov and, under the "Filings" tab, clicking on "Search for company filings."

1. Does CVS use the indirect method of reporting cash flows from operating activities? Other than net earnings, what are the most important factors affecting the company's cash flows from operating activities? Explain the trend of each of these factors.
2. Based on the cash flows from investing activities, in 2010 and 2011, would you say that CVS is a contracting or an expanding company? Explain.
3. Has CVS used external financing during 2010 and 2011? If so, where did it come from?

LO **1, 5**

RATIO

SPREADSHEET

Interpreting Financial Reports: Cash Flows Analysis

C6. BUSINESS APPLICATION ▶ Refer to the 2011 annual reports of **CVS Corporation** and **Southwest Airlines**, which you can find using either the "Investor Relations" portion of each company's website (do a web search for CVS and Southwest investor relations) or by going to www.sec.gov and, under the "Filings" tab, clicking on "Search for company filings." Calculate for 2011 and 2010 each company's cash flow yield, cash flows to sales, cash flows to assets, and free cash flow. (Round to one decimal place or to the nearest tenth of a percent.) At the end of 2009, Southwest's total assets were $14,269 million and CVS's total assets were $61,641 million.

Discuss and compare the trends of the cash-generating ability of CVS and Southwest. Comment on each company's change in cash and cash equivalents over the two-year period.

Continuing Case: Annual Report Project

RATIO

C7. Using the most recent annual report of the company you have chosen to study and that you have accessed online at the company's website, examine the statement of cash flows and accompanying notes of your company. Answer the following questions:

1. Does the company use the direct or indirect method for computing cash flows from operating activities? What effect does depreciation have on cash flows? Have receivables, inventories, and payables had positive or negative effects on cash flows from operating activities?
2. What are the most important investing activities for the company in the most recent year?
3. What are the most important financing activities for the company in the most recent year?
4. **BUSINESS APPLICATION** ▶ Calculate cash flow yield, cash flows to sales, cash flows to assets, and free cash flow for the most recent year.

To this point, the indirect method of preparing the statement of cash flows has been used. In this section, the direct method is presented.

Determining Cash Flows from Operating Activities

The principal difference between the indirect and the direct methods appears in the cash flows from operating activities section of the statement of cash flows.

■ The indirect method starts with net income from the income statement and converts it to net cash flows from operating activities by adding or subtracting items that do not affect net cash flows.

■ The direct method converts each item on the income statement to its cash equivalent, as illustrated in Exhibit 1. For instance, sales are converted to cash receipts from sales and purchases are converted to cash payments for purchases.

Exhibit 1
Direct Method of Determining Net Cash Flows from Operating Activities

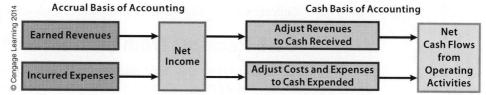

© Cengage Learning 2014

To illustrate how to determine cash flows from operating activities under the direct method, we will use Eureka Corporation. Eureka's schedule of cash flows from operating activities is presented in Exhibit 2.

Exhibit 2
Schedule of Cash Flows from Operating Activities: Direct Method

Eureka Corporation
Schedule of Cash Flows from Operating Activities
For the Year Ended December 31, 2014

Cash receipts from:		
Sales	$706,000	
Interest received	6,000	$712,000
Cash payments for:		
Purchases	$547,000	
Operating expenses	103,000	
Interest	23,000	
Income taxes	9,000	682,000
Net cash flows from operating activities		$ 30,000

© Cengage Learning 2014

Cash Receipts from Sales

Sales result in a positive cash flow for a company. Cash sales are direct cash inflows. Credit sales are not direct cash inflows because some receivables may be uncollectible. For example, you cannot assume that credit sales are automatically inflows of cash, because the collections of accounts receivable in any one accounting period are not likely to equal credit sales. Some receivables may be uncollectible, sales from a prior period may be collected in the current period, or sales from the current period may be collected in the next period.

▲ If accounts receivables *increase* from one accounting period to the next, cash receipts from sales will not be as great as sales.

▼ If accounts receivable *decrease* from one accounting period to the next, cash receipts from sales will exceed sales.

The relationships among sales, changes in the accounts receivable, and cash receipts from sales are reflected in the formula that follows.

$$\text{Sales} \begin{cases} + \text{ Decrease in Accounts Receivable} \\ \text{or} \\ - \text{ Increase in Accounts Receivable} \end{cases} = \begin{array}{c} \text{Cash Receipts} \\ \text{from Sales} \end{array}$$

Refer to the balance sheets and the income statement for Eureka Corporation in Exhibits 4 and 5 in Chapter 13. Note that sales were $698,000 in 2014 and that accounts receivable decreased by $8,000. Thus, cash received from sales is $706,000:

$$\$698{,}000 + \$8{,}000 = \$706{,}000$$

Collections were $8,000 more than sales recorded for the year.

Cash Receipts from Interest and Dividends

Although interest and dividends received are most closely associated with investment activity and are often called *investment income*, the FASB *classifies* the cash received from these items as operating activities. To simplify the examples in this text, it is assumed that interest income equals interest received and that dividend income equals dividends received. Thus, based on Exhibit 4 in Chapter 13, interest received by Eureka Corporation is assumed to equal $6,000, which is the amount of interest income.

Cash Payments for Purchases

The cost of goods sold (from the income statement) must be adjusted for changes in two balance sheet accounts to arrive at cash payments for purchases. First, the cost of goods sold must be adjusted for changes in inventory to arrive at net purchases. Then, net purchases must be adjusted for the change in accounts payable to arrive at cash payments for purchases.

▲ If inventory has *increased* from one accounting period to another, net purchases will be greater than the cost of goods sold because net purchases during the period have exceeded the dollar amount of the items sold during the period.

▼ If inventory has *decreased*, net purchases will be less than the cost of goods sold.

▲ If accounts payable have *increased*, cash payments for purchases will be less than net purchases.

▼ If accounts payable have *decreased*, cash payments for purchases will be greater than net purchases.

These relationships may be stated in equation form as follows.

$$\text{Cost of Goods Sold} \begin{cases} + \text{Increase in Inventory} \\ \text{or} \\ - \text{Decrease in Inventory} \end{cases} \begin{cases} + \text{Decrease in Accounts Payable} \\ \text{or} \\ - \text{Increase in Accounts Payable} \end{cases} = \text{Cash Payments for Purchases}$$

From Exhibits 4 and 5 in Chapter 13, cost of goods sold is $520,000, inventory increased by $34,000, and accounts payable increased by $7,000. Thus, cash payments for purchases for Eureka are computed as follows.

$$\$520,000 + \$34,000 - \$7,000 = \$547,000$$

Eureka purchased $34,000 more inventory than it sold and paid out $7,000 less in cash than it made in purchases. The net result is that cash payments for purchases exceeded the cost of goods sold by $27,000 ($547,000 − $520,000).

Cash Payments for Operating Expenses

Just as the cost of goods sold does not represent the amount of cash paid for purchases during an accounting period, operating expenses do not match the amount of cash paid to employees, suppliers, and others for goods and services. Three adjustments must be made to operating expenses to arrive at the cash outflows. The first adjustment is for changes in prepaid expenses, such as prepaid insurance or prepaid rent.

▲ If prepaid assets *increase* during the accounting period, more cash will have been paid out than appears on the income statement as expenses.

▼ If prepaid assets *decrease*, the expenses shown on the income statement will exceed the cash spent.

The second adjustment is for changes in liabilities resulting from accrued expenses, such as wages payable and payroll taxes payable.

▲ If accrued liabilities *increase* during the accounting period, operating expenses on the income statement will exceed the cash spent.

▼ If accrued liabilities *decrease*, operating expenses will fall short of cash spent.

The third adjustment is made because certain expenses do not require a current outlay of cash; those expenses must be subtracted from operating expense to arrive at cash payments for operating expenses. The most common expenses in this category are depreciation expense, amortization expense, and depletion expense. For example, in 2014, Eureka recorded depreciation expense of $37,000. No cash payment was made in this transaction. Therefore, to the extent that operating expenses include depreciation and similar items, an adjustment is needed to reduce operating expenses to the amount of cash expended.

The three adjustments to operating expenses are summarized in the equations that follow.

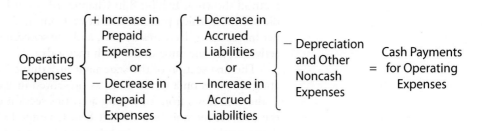

According to Exhibits 4 and 5 in Chapter 13, Eureka's operating expenses (including depreciation of $37,000) were $147,000, prepaid expenses decreased by $4,000, and accrued liabilities increased by $3,000. As a result, Eureka's cash payments for operating expenses are computed as follows.

$$\$147,000 - \$4,000 - \$3,000 - \$37,000 = \$103,000$$

If there are prepaid expenses and accrued liabilities that are *not* related to specific operating expenses, they are not included in these computations. One example is income taxes payable, which is the accrued liability related to income taxes expense. The cash payment for income taxes will be discussed shortly.

Cash Payments for Interest

The FASB classifies cash payments for interest as operating activities. For the sake of simplicity, all examples in this text assume that interest payments are equal to interest expense on the income statement. Thus, based on Exhibit 4 in Chapter 13, Eureka's interest payments are assumed to be $23,000 in 2014.

Cash Payments for Income Taxes

The amount of income taxes expense that appears on the income statement rarely equals the amount of income taxes actually paid during the year. To determine cash payments for income taxes, income taxes are adjusted by the change in Income Taxes Payable.

▲ If Income Taxes Payable *increased* during the accounting period, cash payments for taxes will be less than the expense shown on the income statement.

▼ If Income Taxes Payable *decreased*, cash payments for taxes will exceed income taxes on the income statement.

In other words, the following equation is applicable:

$$\text{Income Taxes} \begin{cases} + \text{Decrease in Income Taxes Payable} \\ \qquad\qquad \text{or} \\ - \text{Increase in Income Taxes Payable} \end{cases} = \begin{array}{l} \text{Cash Payments} \\ \text{for Income Taxes} \end{array}$$

In 2014, Eureka reported income taxes of $7,000 on its income statement and a decrease of $2,000 in Income Taxes Payable on its balance sheets (see Exhibits 4 and 5 in Chapter 13). As a result, cash payments for income taxes for Eureka during 2014 are calculated as follows.

$$\$7,000 + \$2,000 = \$9,000$$

Compiling the Statement of Cash Flows

Eureka's statement of cash flows under the direct method is presented in Exhibit 3. The only differences between that statement of cash flows and the one based on the indirect method shown in Exhibit 8 in Chapter 13 occur in the first and last sections. The middle sections, which present cash flows from investing activities and financing activities, net increases or decreases in cash, and the schedule of non-cash investing and financing activities, are the same under both methods.

The first section of the statement in Exhibit 3 shows the net cash flows from operating activities on a direct basis, as presented in Exhibit 2. The last section is the same as the cash flows from operating activities section of the statement of cash flows under the indirect method (see Exhibit 8 in Chapter 13). The FASB believes that when the direct method is used, a schedule must be provided that reconciles net income to net cash flows from operating activities. Thus, the statement of cash flows under the direct method includes a section that accommodates the main difference between it and the indirect method.

Exhibit 3
Statement of Cash
Flows: Direct Method

Eureka Corporation
Statement of Cash Flows
For the Year Ended December 31, 2014

Cash flows from operating activities:
Cash receipts from:

Sales	$ 706,000	
Interest received	6,000	$712,000
Cash payments for:		
Purchases	$ 547,000	
Operating expenses	103,000	
Interest	23,000	
Income taxes	9,000	682,000
Net cash flows from operating activities		$ 30,000
Cash flows from investing activities:		
Purchase of investments	$ (78,000)	
Sale of investments	102,000	
Purchase of plant assets	(120,000)	
Sale of plant assets	5,000	
Net cash flows from investing activities		(91,000)
Cash flows from financing activities:		
Repayment of bonds	$ (50,000)	
Issue of common stock	150,000	
Dividends paid	(7,000)	
Net cash flows from financing activities		93,000
Net increase in cash		$ 32,000
Cash at beginning of year		15,000
Cash at end of year		$ 47,000

Schedule of Noncash Investing and Financing Transactions

Issue of bonds payable for plant assets	$100,000

Reconciliation of Net Income to Net Cash Flows from Operating Activities

Net income		$ 16,000
Adjustments to reconcile net income to net cash flows from operating activities:		
Depreciation	$ 37,000	
Gain on sale of investments	(12,000)	
Loss on sale of plant assets	3,000	
Changes in current assets and current liabilities:		
Decrease in accounts receivable	8,000	
Increase in inventory	(34,000)	
Decrease in prepaid expenses	4,000	
Increase in accounts payable	7,000	
Increase in accrued liabilities	3,000	
Decrease in income taxes payable	(2,000)	14,000
Net cash flows from operating activities		$ 30,000
Cash flows from investing activities:		
Purchase of investments	$ (78,000)	
Sale of investments	102,000	
Purchase of plant assets	(120,000)	
Sale of plant assets	5,000	
Net cash flows from investing activities		(91,000)
Cash flows from financing activities:		
Repayment of bonds	$ (50,000)	
Issuance of common stock	175,000	
Payment of dividends	(7,000)	
Purchase of treasury stock	(25,000)	
Net cash flows from financing activities		93,000
Net increase in cash		$ 32,000
Cash at beginning of year		15,000
Cash at end of year		$ 47,000

Assignments

SHORT EXERCISES

SE1. Cash Receipts from Sales and Cash Payments for Purchases: Direct Method

During 2014, Nebraska Wheat Company, a maker of whole-grain products, had sales of $426,500. The ending balance of accounts receivable was $127,400 in 2013 and $96,200 in 2014. Also, during 2014, Nebraska Wheat had cost of goods sold of $294,200. The ending balance of inventory was $36,400 in 2013 and $44,800 in 2014. The ending balance of accounts payable was $28,100 in 2013 and $25,900 in 2014. Using the direct method, calculate cash receipts from sales and cash payments for purchases in 2014.

SE2. Cash Payments for Operating Expenses and Income Taxes: Direct Method

During 2014, Nebraska Wheat Company had operating expenses of $79,000 and income tax expense of $12,500. Depreciation expense of $20,000 for 2014 was included in operating expenses. The ending balance of prepaid expenses was $3,600 in 2013 and $2,300 in 2014. The ending balance of accrued liabilities (excluding income taxes payable) was $3,000 in 2013 and $2,000 in 2014. The ending balance of income taxes payable was $4,100 in 2013 and $3,500 in 2014. Calculate cash payments for operating expenses and income taxes in 2014 using the direct method.

EXERCISES

E1. Computing Cash Flows from Operating Activities: Direct Method

Vlieg Corporation engaged in the transactions that follow in 2014. Using the direct method, compute the various cash flows from operating activities as required.

a. During 2014, Vlieg had cash sales of $41,300 and sales on credit of $123,000. During the same year, accounts receivable decreased by $18,000. Determine the cash receipts from sales during 2014.

b. During 2014, Vlieg's cost of goods sold was $119,000. During the same year, merchandise inventory increased by $12,500 and accounts payable decreased by $4,300. Determine the cash payments for purchases during 2014.

c. During 2014, Vlieg had operating expenses of $45,000, including depreciation of $15,600. Also during 2014, related prepaid expenses decreased by $3,100 and relevant accrued liabilities increased by $1,200. Determine the cash payments for operating expenses to suppliers of goods and services during 2014.

d. Vlieg's income tax expense for 2014 was $4,300. Income taxes payable decreased by $230 that year. Determine the cash payments for income taxes during 2014.

E2. Preparing a Schedule of Cash Flows from Operating Activities: Direct Method

Vasquez Corporation's income statement follows.

Vasquez Corporation
Income Statement
For the Year Ended June 30, 2014

Sales		$122,000
Cost of goods sold		60,000
Gross margin		$ 62,000
Operating expenses:		
Salaries expense	$32,000	
Rent expense	16,800	
Depreciation expense	2,000	50,800
Income before income taxes		$ 11,200
Income taxes		2,400
Net income		$ 8,800

Additional information: (a) Accounts receivable increased by $4,400 during the year; (b) inventories increased by $7,000, and accounts payable increased by $14,000 during the year; (c) prepaid rent decreased by $1,400, while salaries payable increased by $1,000; and (d) income taxes payable decreased by $600 during the year.

Using the direct method, prepare a schedule of cash flows from operating activities.

PROBLEMS

P1. Cash Flows from Operating Activities: Direct Method

✔ Total operating activities: $47,600 inflows

Tanucci Clothing Store's income statement follows.

Tanucci Clothing Store
Income Statement
For the Year Ended June 30, 2014

Net sales		$4,900,000
Cost of goods sold:		
Beginning inventory	$1,240,000	
Net cost of purchases	3,040,000	
Goods available for sale	$4,280,000	
Ending inventory	1,400,000	
Cost of goods sold		2,880,000
Gross margin		$2,020,000
Operating expenses:		
Sales and administrative salaries expense	$1,112,000	
Other sales and administrative expenses	624,000	
Total operating expenses		1,736,000
Income before income taxes		$ 284,000
Income taxes		78,000
Net income		$ 206,000

Additional information: (a) other sales and administrative expenses include depreciation expense of $104,000 and amortization expense of $36,000; (b) accrued liabilities for salaries were $24,000 less than the previous year, and prepaid expenses were $40,000 more than the previous year; and (c) during the year accounts receivable (net) increased by $288,000, accounts payable increased by $228,000, and income taxes payable decreased by $14,400.

REQUIRED

Using the direct method, prepare a schedule of cash flows from operating activities.

P2. Statement of Cash Flows: Direct Method

✔ 1: Total operating activities: $548,000 inflows
✔ 1: Total financing activities: $260,000 outflows

Flanders Corporation's 2014 income statement and comparative balance sheet as of June 30, 2014 and 2013 follow.

Flanders Corporation
Income Statement
For the Year Ended June 30, 2014

Sales		$2,081,800
Cost of goods sold		1,312,600
Gross margin		$ 769,200
Operating expenses (including depreciation expense of $120,000)		378,400
Income from operations		$ 390,800
Other income (expenses):		
Loss on disposal of equipment	$ 8,000	
Interest expense	75,200	83,200
Income before income taxes		$ 307,600
Income taxes		68,400
Net income		$ 239,200

(Continued)

Flanders Corporation
Comparative Balance Sheets
For Years Ended June 30, 2014 and 2013

	2014	2013
Assets		
Cash	$ 334,000	$ 40,000
Accounts receivable (net)	200,000	240,000
Inventory	360,000	440,000
Prepaid expenses	1,200	2,000
Property, plant, and equipment	1,256,000	1,104,000
Accumulated depreciation—property, plant, and equipment	(366,000)	(280,000)
Total assets	$1,785,200	$1,546,000
Liabilities and Stockholders' Equity		
Accounts payable	$ 128,000	$ 84,000
Notes payable (due in 90 days)	60,000	160,000
Income taxes payable	52,000	36,000
Mortgage payable	720,000	560,000
Common stock, $5 par value	400,000	400,000
Retained earnings	425,200	306,000
Total liabilities and stockholders' equity	$ 1,785,200	$1,546,000

The following is additional information about 2014: (a) equipment that cost $48,000 with accumulated depreciation of $34,000 was sold at a loss of $8,000; (b) land and building were purchased in the amount of $200,000 through an increase of $200,000 in the mortgage payable; (c) a $40,000 payment was made on the mortgage; (d) the notes were repaid, but the company borrowed an additional $60,000 through the issuance of a new note payable; and (e) a $120,000 cash dividend was declared and paid.

REQUIRED

1. Use the direct method to prepare a statement of cash flows. Include a supporting schedule of noncash investing and financing transactions. Do not include a reconciliation of net income to net cash flows from operating activities.
2. What are the primary reasons for Flanders' large increase in cash from 2013 to 2014?
3. Compute and assess cash flow yield and free cash flow for 2014. (Round to one decimal place.)

P3. Statement of Cash Flows: Direct Method

Saudade Corporation's 2014 income statement and comparative balance sheet as of June 30, 2014 and 2013 follow.

✔ 1: Total operating activities: $638,400 inflows
✔ 1: Total financing activities: $303,000 outflows

Saudade Corporation
Income Statement
For the Year Ended June 30, 2014

Sales	$2,252,700
Cost of goods sold	1,451,200
Gross margin	$ 801,500
Operating expenses (including depreciation expense of $140,000)	397,300
Income from operations	$ 404,200
Other income (expenses):	
Loss on disposal of equipment	$ 7,500
Interest expense	74,800
	82,300
Income before income taxes	$ 321,900
Income taxes	69,200
Net income	$ 252,700

Saudade Corporation
Comparative Balance Sheets
For Years Ended June 30, 2014 and 2013

	2014	2013
Assets		
Cash	$ 393,900	$ 50,000
Accounts receivable (net)	180,000	250,000
Inventory	330,000	420,000
Prepaid expenses	1,400	2,300
Property, plant, and equipment	1,365,000	1,213,000
Accumulated depreciation—property, plant, and equipment	(404,000)	(297,000)
Total assets	$1,866,300	$1,638,300
Liabilities and Stockholders' Equity		
Accounts payable	$ 148,000	$ 85,000
Notes payable (due in 90 days)	75,000	150,000
Income taxes payable	53,300	39,000
Mortgage payable	740,000	587,000
Common stock, $5 par value	415,000	415,000
Retained earnings	435,000	362,300
Total liabilities and stockholders' equity	$1,866,300	$1,638,300

The following is additional information about 2014: (a) equipment that cost $49,000 with accumulated depreciation of $33,000 was sold at a loss of $7,500; (b) land and building were purchased in the amount of $201,000 through an increase of $201,000 in the mortgage payable; (c) a $48,000 payment was made on the mortgage; (d) the notes were repaid, but the company borrowed an additional $75,000 through the issuance of a new note payable; and (e) a $180,000 cash dividend was declared and paid.

REQUIRED

1. Use the direct method to prepare a statement of cash flows. Include a supporting schedule of noncash investing and financing transactions. Do not include a reconciliation of net income to net cash flows from operating activities.
2. What are the primary reasons for Saudade's large increase in cash from 2013 to 2014?
3. Compute and assess cash flow yield and free cash flow for 2014. (Round to one decimal place.)

CHAPTER 14

LEARNING OBJECTIVES

 LO1 Describe the concepts, standards of comparison, and sources of information used in measuring financial performance.

 LO2 Apply horizontal analysis, trend analysis, vertical analysis, and ratio analysis to financial statements.

 LO3 Apply financial ratio analysis in a comprehensive evaluation of a company's financial performance.

 LO4 Define *quality of earnings*, and identify the factors that affect quality of earnings and related management compensation issues.

FINANCIAL STATEMENT ANALYSIS

Business Insight
Starbucks Corporation

Formed in 1985, **Starbucks** is today a well-known specialty retailer. The company purchases, roasts, and sells whole coffee beans, along with a variety of freshly brewed coffees and other beverages and food items. It also produces and sells bottled coffee drinks and a line of premium ice creams.

Like many other companies, Starbucks uses financial performance measures, primarily earnings per share, in determining compensation for top management. Earnings per share and the six financial measures used in computing the most critical financial ratios appear in the company's Financial Highlights.[1] By linking compensation to financial performance, Starbucks provides its executives with incentive to improve the company's performance. Compensation and financial performance are thus linked to increasing shareholders' value.

STARBUCKS' FINANCIAL HIGHLIGHTS
(in millions, except earnings per share)

	2011	2010	2009
Net revenues	$11,700.4	$10,383.0	$9,774.6
Net earnings	1,245.7	948.3	390.8
Total assets	7,360.4	6,385.9	5,576.8
Total liabilities	2,973.1	2,703.6	2,531.1
Total equity	4,387.3	3,674.7	3,045.7
Cash flows from operating activities	1,612.4	1,704.9	1,389.0
Earnings per share—basic	$ 1.66	$ 1.27	$ 0.53

1. CONCEPT ▶ *What concepts underlie the standards that Starbucks can use to evaluate performance?*

2. ACCOUNTING APPLICATION ▶ *What analytical tools can Starbucks use to measure financial performance?*

3. BUSINESS APPLICATION ▶ *In what ways would having access to prior years' information aid this analysis? Why is earnings management important in your assessment?*

CONCEPTS
- ■ Relevance
- ■ Predictive value
- ■ Comparability
- ■ Timeliness

RELEVANT LEARNING OBJECTIVE

LO 1 Describe the concepts, standards of comparison, and sources of information used in measuring financial performance.

LO 1 Concepts Underlying Financial Performance Measurement

Financial statement analysis (or *financial performance measurement*) is used to show how items in a company's financial statements relate to the company's financial performance objectives. Users of accounting information interested in measuring a company's financial performance fall into two groups:

- ■ A company's top managers, who set and strive to achieve financial performance objectives; middle-level managers of business processes; and lower-level employees who own stock in the company
- ■ Creditors and investors, as well as customers who have cooperative agreements with the company

Both these groups of users want measures of financial performance that meet these underlying concepts:

- ■ **Relevance:** The measures need to make a difference in the analysis of a company's performance.
- ■ **Predictive value:** The users want measures that will help them make decisions about future actions.
- ■ **Comparability:** The users want measures that make useful comparison of one period of the company's performance with another and of the company's performance to other companies.
- ■ **Timeliness:** The users want measures that enable them to make decisions made in time to have the desired effects.

In the analysis of accounting information, managers, creditors, and investors want measures that relate to the following objectives:

- ■ **Profitability:** To continue operating, a company must earn a satisfactory net income. Management is responsible for monitoring and measuring net income, determining the causes of any deviations from financial performance plans, and correcting the deviations. Creditors and investors look at a company's past and present net income to identify trends and to judge potential earnings ability.
- ■ **Total Asset Management:** A company uses its assets to generate revenues. These assets are part of the cost of operating a business. To maximize net income, management must use all of the company's assets in a way that maximizes revenues while minimizing the investment in these assets.
- ■ **Liquidity:** A company must be able to pay its bills when they come due and meet unexpected needs for cash. Management must use cash, like other assets, to fund operations that generate maximum revenues. Creditors focus on liquidity because they expect to be paid what they are owed at the appropriate time.
- ■ **Financial Risk:** Management must use debt and stockholders' investments effectively without jeopardizing the company's future. Creditors and stockholders judge the risk involved in making a loan or an investment by looking at a company's past performance and current position. The more difficult it is to predict future profitability and liquidity, the greater the risk.
- ■ **Operating Asset Management:** Managing operating assets is much like managing total assets. Managers must use current assets and current liabilities in a way that supports revenue growth and minimizes investment.

Standards of Comparison

When analyzing financial statements, decision makers must judge whether the relationships they find in the statements are favorable or unfavorable. Three standards of comparison that they commonly use are rule-of-thumb measures, a company's past performance, and industry norms.

Rule-of-Thumb Measures Many financial analysts, investors, and lenders apply general standards, or *rule-of-thumb measures*, to key financial ratios. For example, the credit-rating firm of **Dun & Bradstreet** offers the following rules of thumb:

- **Current Ratio:** The higher the ratio, the more likely the company will be able to meet its liabilities. A ratio of 2 to 1 (2.0) or higher is desirable.
- **Current Liabilities to Net Worth Ratio (%):** Normally a business starts to have trouble when this relationship exceeds 80%.[2]

Past Performance Comparing financial measures or ratios of the same company over time is an improvement over using rule-of-thumb measures. Such a comparison gives the analyst some basis for judging whether the measure or ratio is getting better or worse. Thus, it may be helpful in showing future trends. However, such projections must be made with care. Trends reverse over time, and a company's needs may change. For example, even if a company improves its return on investment from 3 percent in one year to 4 percent the next year, the 4 percent return may not be adequate for the company's current needs. In addition, using a company's past performance as a standard of comparison is not helpful in judging its performance relative to that of other companies.

Industry Norms Using industry norms as a standard of comparison overcomes some of the limitations of comparing a company's measures over time. Industry norms show how a company compares with other companies in the same industry. For example, if companies in a particular industry have an average rate of return on investment of 8 percent, a 3 or 4 percent rate of return is probably not adequate. Using industry norms as standards has the following limitations:

- **Comparability:** Companies in the same industry may not be strictly comparable. For example, one company in the oil industry purchases oil products and markets them through service stations. The other, an international company, discovers, produces, refines, and markets its own oil products. Because of the disparity in their operations, these two companies cannot be directly compared.
- **Accounting differences:** Companies in the same industry with similar operations may not use the same accounting procedures. For example, they may use different methods of valuing inventories and of depreciating assets.
- **Diversity: Diversified companies** (or *conglomerates*) are large companies that have multiple segments and operate in more than one industry. They may not be comparable to any other company.

International Perspective
IFRS The Use and Evaluation of Performance Measures Must Change When Using IFRS

Financial statement users must carefully consider evaluations and comparisons of historical performance under IFRS for a variety of reasons. When a company switches from U.S. GAAP to IFRS, prior years' performance measures will not likely be comparable. In fact, 80 percent of companies surveyed in a research study of European companies reported higher net income for the same operations under IFRS than under U.S. GAAP. When this occurs, an IFRS profit margin will likely provide a more optimistic evaluation when compared with pre-IFRS results or with a U.S. GAAP- based competitor. Further, the definitions of assets, liabilities, and equity differ under IFRS. The combined effect is that debt to equity, return on equity, and return on assets ratios may not exhibit historical trends. Contracts and management compensation based on these IFRS measures also require a closer look.

The FASB provides a partial solution to the limitation posed by diversified companies. It requires a diversified company to report profit or loss, certain revenue and expense items, and assets for each of its segments. Segment information may be reported for operations in different industries or different geographical areas or for major customers.[3] Exhibit 1 shows how **Goodyear Tire & Rubber Company** reports data on sales, income, and assets for its tire products segments. These data allow the analyst to compute measures of profitability, such as profit margin, asset turnover, and return on assets, for each segment and to compare them with industry norms.

Exhibit 1
Selected Segment Information for Goodyear Tire & Rubber Company

(In millions)	2011	2010	2009
Sales:			
North American Tire	$ 9,859	$ 8,205	$ 6,977
Europe, Middle East and Africa Tire	8,040	6,407	5,801
Latin American Tire	2,472	2,158	1,814
Asia Pacific Tire	2,396	2,062	1,709
Net Sales	**$22,767**	**$18,832**	**$16,301**
Segment Operating Income:			
North American Tire	$ 276	$ 18	$ (305)
Europe, Middle East and Africa Tire	627	319	166
Latin American Tire	231	330	301
Asia Pacific Tire	234	250	210
Total Segment Operating Income	**$ 1,368**	**$ 917**	**$ 372**
Assets:			
North American Tire	$ 5,744	$ 5,243	$ 4,836
Europe, Middle East and Africa Tire	5,915	5,266	5,144
Latin American Tire	2,141	1,809	1,672
Asia Pacific Tire	2,482	2,150	1,548
Total Segment Assets	**$16,282**	**$14,468**	**$13,200**
Corporate	1,347	1,162	1,210
Total Assets	**$17,629**	**$15,630**	**$14,410**

Source: Goodyear Tire & Rubber Company, Form 10-K, For the Fiscal Year Ended December 31, 2011 (adapted).

Despite these limitations, if little information about a company's past performance is available, industry norms probably offer the best available standards for judging current performance—as long as they are used with care.

Sources of Information

The major sources of information about public corporations follow.

- **Reports published by a corporation**: A public corporation's annual report is an important source of financial information. Most public corporations also publish **interim financial statements** each quarter and sometimes each month. These reports, which present limited information in the form of condensed financial statements, are not subject to a full audit by an independent auditor. The financial community watches interim statements closely for early signs of change in a company's earnings trend.
- **Reports filed with the Securities and Exchange Commission (SEC):** Public corporations in the United States must file annual reports (**Form 10-K**), quarterly reports (**Form 10-Q**), and current reports (**Form 8-K**) with the SEC. If they have more than $10 million in assets and more than 500 shareholders, they must file these reports electronically at http://www.sec.gov/edgar/searchedgar/webusers .htm, where anyone can access them free of charge.

STUDY NOTE: *Publishers often redefine the content of the ratios that companies provide. While the general content is similar, variations occur. Be sure to ascertain and evaluate the information that a published source uses to calculate ratios.*

■ **Business periodicals and credit and investment advisory services:** Financial analysts must keep up with current events in the financial world. One leading source of financial news is *The Wall Street Journal*. It is the most complete financial newspaper in the United States and is published every business day. Credit and investment advisory services such as **Moody's Investors Service**, **Standard & Poor's**, and **Dun and Bradstreet** provide useful information, including details about a company's financial history, industry data, and credit ratings.

APPLY IT!

Identify each of the following as (a) an underlying concept, (b) an objective of financial statement analysis, (c) a standard for financial statement analysis, or (d) a source of information for financial statement analysis:

1. A company's past performance
2. Investment advisory services
3. Assessment of a company's future potential
4. Relevance
5. Industry norms
6. Annual report
7. Form 10-K
8. Timeliness

SOLUTION

1. c;   2. d;   3. b;   4. a;   5. c;   6. d;   7. d;   8. a

TRY IT! SE1, SE2, E1A, E1B

LO 2 Tools and Techniques of Financial Analysis

To gain insight into a company's financial performance, one must look beyond the individual numbers to the relationship between the numbers and their change from one period to another. The tools of financial analysis—horizontal analysis, trend analysis, vertical analysis, and ratio analysis—are intended to show these relationships and changes.

Horizontal Analysis

Comparative financial statements provide financial information for the current year and the previous year. To gain insight into year-to-year changes, analysts use **horizontal analysis**, in which changes from the previous year to the current year are computed in both dollar amounts and percentages. The percentage change relates the size of the change to the size of the dollar amounts involved. Note that it is important to ascertain the base amount used when a percentage describes an item. For example, inventory may be 50 percent of total current assets but only 10 percent of total assets.

Exhibits 2 and 3 present **Starbucks Corporation**'s comparative balance sheets and income statements and show both the dollar and percentage changes.

The percentage change is computed as follows.

$$\text{Percentage Change} = 100 \times \frac{\text{Comparative Year Amount} - \text{Base Year Amount}}{\text{Base Year Amount}}$$

The **base year** is the first year considered in any set of data. For example, when comparing data for 2010 and 2011, 2010 is the base year. As the balance sheets in Exhibit 2 show, between 2010 and 2011, Starbucks' total current assets increased by $1,038.5 million, from $2,756.4 million to $3,794.9 million, or by 37.7 percent, computed as follows.

$$\text{Percentage Change} = 100 \times \frac{\$1,038.5 \text{ million}}{\$2,756.4 \text{ million}} = 37.7\%$$

When examining such changes, it is important to consider the dollar amount of the change as well as the percentage change in each component. For example, the difference between the percentage increase in accounts receivable, net (27.7 percent) and total current assets (37.7 percent) is 10 percent. However, the dollar increase in total current assets is more than twelve times the dollar increase in accounts receivable ($1,038.5 million versus $83.8 million). Thus, even though the percentage changes differ by 10 percent, current assets require much more cash than accounts receivable.

Starbucks' balance sheets for 2010 and 2011 also show the following:

▲ Total assets *increased* by $974.5 million, or 15.3 percent.

▲ Shareholders' equity *increased* by $710.2 million, or 19.3 percent.

Starbucks' income statements in Exhibit 3 show the following:

▲ Net revenues *increased* by $993.0 million, or 9.3 percent.

▲ Gross margin *increased* by $502.3 million, or 8.0 percent.

This indicates that the cost of sales grew faster than net revenues. In fact, the cost of sales increased 11.0 percent compared with the 9.3 percent increase in net revenues.

In addition,

▲ Total operating expenses *increased* by $249 million, or 5.0 percent, which is lower than the 9.3 percent increase in net revenues.

▲ Operating income *increased* by $309.1 million, or 21.8 percent.

▲ Net income *increased* by $299.7 million, or 31.6 percent.

Exhibit 2
Comparative Balance Sheets with Horizontal Analysis

Starbucks Corporation
Consolidated Balance Sheets
For the Years Ended October 2, 2011 and October 3, 2010

(Dollar amounts in millions)	2011	2010	Increase (Decrease)	
			Amount*	Percentage*
Assets				
Current assets:				
Cash and cash equivalents	$1,148.1	$1,164.0	$(15.9)	(1.4)
Short-term investments—available-for-sale securities	855.0	236.5	618.5	261.5
Short-term investments—trading securities	47.6	49.2	(1.6)	(3.3)
Accounts receivable, net	386.5	302.7	83.8	27.7
Inventories	965.8	543.3	422.5	77.8
Prepaid and other current assets	161.5	156.5	5.0	3.2
Deferred income taxes, net	230.4	304.2	(73.8)	(24.3)
Total current assets	$3,794.9	$2,756.4	$1,038.5	37.7
Long-term investments – available-for-sale securities	107.0	191.8	(84.8)	(44.2)
Equity and cost investments	372.3	341.5	30.8	9.0
Property, plant, and equipment, net	2,355.0	2,416.5	(61.5)	(2.5)
Other assets	297.7	346.5	(48.8)	(14.1)
Other intangible assets	111.9	70.8	41.1	58.1
Goodwill	321.6	262.4	59.2	22.6
Total assets	$7,360.4	$6,385.9	$ 974.5	15.3
Liabilities and Shareholders' Equity				
Current liabilities:				
Accounts payable	540.0	282.6	257.4	91.1
Accrued compensation and related costs	364.4	400.0	(35.6)	(8.9)
Accrued occupancy costs	148.3	173.2	(24.9)	(14.4)
Accrued taxes	109.2	100.2	9.0	9.0
Insurance reserves	145.6	146.2	(0.6)	(0.4)
Other accrued liabilities	319.0	262.8	56.2	21.4
Deferred revenue	449.3	414.1	35.2	8.5
Total current liabilities	$2,075.8	$1,779.1	$ 296.7	16.7
Long-term debt	549.5	549.4	0.1	0.0
Other long-term liabilities	347.8	375.1	(27.3)	(7.3)
Total liabilities	2,973.1	2,703.6	269.5	10.0
Total shareholders' equity	4,384.9	3,674.7	710.2	19.3
Noncontrolling interests	2.4	7.6	(5.2)	(68.4)
Total equity	4,387.3	3,682.3	705.0	19.1
Total liabilities and shareholders' equity	$7,360.4	$6,385.9	$ 974.5	15.3

*Rounded
Source: Data from Starbucks Corporation, Form 10-K, For the Fiscal Year Ended October 2, 2011.

Exhibit 3
Comparative Income Statements with Horizontal Analysis

Starbucks Corporation
Consolidated Income Statements
For the Years Ended October 2, 2011 and October 3, 2010

(Dollar amounts in millions except per share amounts)	2011	2010	Increase (Decrease) Amount*	Percentage*
Net revenues	$11,700.4	$10,707.4	$993.0	9.3
Cost of sales, including occupancy costs	4,949.3	4,458.6	490.7	11.0
Gross margin	$ 6,751.1	$ 6,248.8	$502.3	8.0
Operating expenses				
Store operating expenses	$ 3,665.1	$ 3,551.4	$113.7	3.2
Other operating expenses	402.0	293.2	108.8	37.1
Depreciation and amortization expenses	523.3	510.4	12.9	2.5
General and administrative expenses	636.1	569.5	66.6	11.7
Restructuring charges	—	53.0	(53.0)	(100.0)
Total operating expenses	$ 5,226.5	$ 4,977.5	$249.0	5.0
Gain on sale of properties	30.2	—	30.2	—
Income from equity investees	173.7	148.1	25.6	17.3
Operating income	$ 1,728.5	$ 1,419.4	$309.1	21.8
Interest income and other, net	115.9	50.3	65.6	130.4
Interest expense	(33.3)	(32.7)	(0.6)	1.8
Income before taxes	$ 1,811.1	$ 1,437.0	$374.1	26.0
Income taxes	563.1	488.7	74.4	15.2
Net income	$ 1,248.0	$ 948.3	$299.7	31.6

*Rounded
Source: Data from Starbucks Corporation, Form 10-K, For the Fiscal Year Ended October 2, 2011.

The primary reason for the increases in operating income and net income is that operating expenses increased at a slower rate (5.0 percent) than net revenues (9.3 percent).

Trend Analysis

STUDY NOTE: *To reflect the general five-year economic cycle of the U.S. economy, trend analysis usually covers a five-year period.*

Trend analysis is a variation of horizontal analysis. With this tool, the analyst calculates percentage changes for several successive years instead of for just two years. Because of its long-term view, trend analysis can highlight basic changes in the nature of a business.

Exhibit 4 shows a trend analysis of **Starbucks'** five-year summary of net revenues and operating income.

Trend analysis uses an **index number** to show changes in related items over time. For an index number, the base year is set at 100 percent. Other years are measured in relation to that amount. For example, the 2011 index for Starbucks' net revenues is figured as follows (dollar amounts are in millions).

Exhibit 4
Trend Analysis

Starbucks Corporation Net Revenues and Operating Income Trend Analysis					
	2011	**2010**	**2009**	**2008**	**2007**
Dollar values (In millions)					
Net revenues	$11,700.4	$10,707.4	$9,774.6	$10,383.0	$9,411.5
Operating income	1,728.5	1,419.4	562.0	390.3	945.9
Trend analysis (In percentages)					
Net revenues	124.3	113.8	103.9	110.3	100.0
Operating income	182.7	150.1	59.4	41.3	100.0

Source: Data from Starbucks Corporation, Form 10-K, For the Fiscal Year Ended October 2, 2011.

$$\text{Index} = 100 \times \frac{\$11,700.4}{\$9,411.5} = 124.3\%$$

The trend analysis in Exhibit 4 shows the following:

▲ Net revenues *increased* over the five-year period.

▲ Overall, revenue *increased* 24.3 percent.

Net revenues grew faster than operating income in 2008 and 2009; however, operating income grew faster than net revenues in 2010 and 2011. Exhibit 5 illustrates these trends.

Exhibit 5
Graph of Trend Analysis
Shown in Exhibit 4

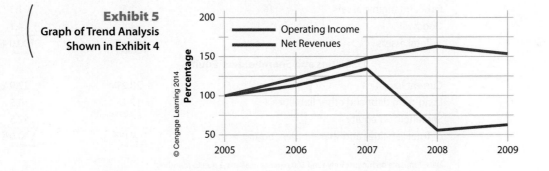

Vertical Analysis

Vertical analysis shows how the different components of a financial statement relate to a total figure in the statement. On the balance sheet, the figure would be total assets or total liabilities and stockholders' equity, and on the income statement, it would be net revenues or net sales. The analyst sets the total figure at 100 percent and computes each component's percentage of that total. The resulting financial statement, which is expressed entirely in percentages, is called a **common-size statement**. Common-size balance sheets and common-size income statements for **Starbucks** are shown in pie-chart form in Exhibits 6 and 8 and in financial statement form in Exhibits 7 and 9.

Exhibit 6

Common-Size Balance Sheets Presented Graphically

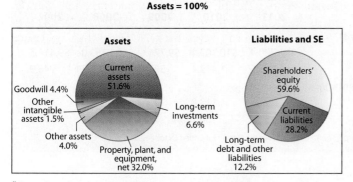

Rounding causes some additions not to total precisely.

Exhibit 7

Common-Size Balance Sheets

Starbucks Corporation Common-Size Balance Sheets October 2, 2011, and October 3, 2010		
	2011	**2010**
Assets		
Current assets	51.6%	43.2%
Long-term investments	6.6	8.3
Property, plant, and equipment, net	32.0	37.8
Other assets	4.0	5.4
Other intangible assets	1.5	1.1
Goodwill	4.4	4.1
Total assets	100.0%	100.0%
Liabilities and Shareholders' Equity		
Current liabilities	28.2%	27.9%
Long-term debt and other liabilities	12.2	14.5
Shareholders' equity	59.6	57.5
Total liabilities and shareholders' equity	100.0%	100.0%

Note: Amounts do not precisely total 100 percent in all cases due to rounding.
Source: Data from Starbucks Corporation, Form 10-K, For the Fiscal Year Ended October 2, 2011.

Vertical analysis and common-size statements are useful in comparing the importance of specific components in the operation of a business and in identifying important changes in the components from one year to the next. The main conclusions to be drawn from our analysis of Starbucks are the following:

■ Starbucks' assets consist largely of current assets and property, plant, and equipment.
■ Starbucks finances assets primarily through equity and current liabilities.
■ Starbucks has few long-term liabilities.

Looking at the pie charts in Exhibit 6 and the common-size balance sheets in Exhibit 7, you can see the following:

■ The composition of Starbucks' assets shifted from property, plant, and equipment (declined from 37.8% to 32.0%), long-term investments (from 8.3% to 6.6%), and other assets (from 5.4% to 4.0%) to current assets (from 43.2% to 51.6%).

■ The proportion of long-term debt and other liabilities decreased (from 14.5% to 12.2%) while current liabilities increased (from 27.9% to 28.2%) and shareholders' equity increased (from 57.5% to 59.6%).

The common-size income statements in Exhibit 9, illustrated as pie charts in Exhibit 8, show that Starbucks decreased its operating expenses from 2010 to 2011 by 1.9 percent of revenues (46.5% vs. 44.6%). In other words, revenues grew faster than operating expenses.

Exhibit 8
Common-Size Income
Statements Presented
Graphically

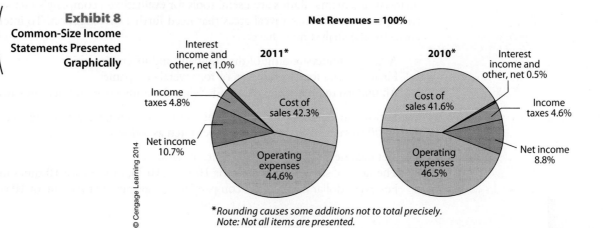

*Rounding causes some additions not to total precisely.
Note: Not all items are presented.*

© Cengage Learning 2014

Exhibit 9
Common-Size
Income Statements

Starbucks Corporation
Common-Size Income Statements
For the Years Ended October 2, 2011, and October 3, 2010

	2011	2010
Net revenues	100.0%	100.0%
Cost of sales, including occupancy costs	42.3	41.6
Gross margin	57.7%	58.4%
Operating expenses:		
Store operating expenses	31.3%	33.2%
Other operating expenses	3.4	2.7
Depreciation and amortization expenses	4.5	4.8
General and administrative expenses	5.4	5.3
Restructuring charges	—	0.5
Total operating expenses	44.6%	46.5%
Gain on sales of properties	0.3%	—%
Income from equity investees	1.5	1.4
Operating income	14.9%	13.3%
Interest income and other, net	1.0	0.5
Interest expense	(0.3)	(0.3)
Income before taxes	15.5%	13.4%
Income taxes	4.8	4.6
Net income	10.7%	8.9%

Note: Amounts do not precisely total 100 percent in all cases due to rounding.

Source: Data from Starbucks Corporation, Form 10-K, For the Fiscal Year Ended October 2, 2011.

Common-size statements are often used to make comparisons between companies. They allow an analyst to compare the operating and financing characteristics of two companies of different size in the same industry. For example, the analyst might want to compare Starbucks with other specialty retailers in terms of percentage of total assets financed by debt or in terms of operating expenses as a percentage of net revenues. Common-size statements would show those and other relationships. These statements can also be used to compare the characteristics of companies that report in different currencies.

Financial Ratio Analysis

Financial ratio analysis identifies key relationships between the components of the financial statements. Ratios are useful tools for evaluating a company's financial position and operations and may reveal areas that need further investigation. To interpret ratios correctly, the analyst must have:

- A general understanding of the company and its environment
- Financial data for several years or for several companies
- An understanding of the data underlying the numerator and denominator

Ratios can be expressed in several ways. For example, a ratio of net income of $100,000 to sales of $1,000,000 can be stated as follows.

- Net income is 1/10, or 10 percent, of sales.
- The ratio of sales to net income is 10 to 1 (10:1), or sales are 10 times net income.
- For every dollar of sales, the company has an average net income of 10 cents.

APPLY IT!

Using 2012 as the base year, prepare a trend analysis for the data that follow, and tell whether the results suggest a favorable or unfavorable trend. (Round to one decimal place.)

	2014	2013	2012
Net sales	$216,000	$152,000	$100,000
Accounts receivable (net)	40,000	29,000	20,000

SOLUTION

	2014	2013	2012
Net sales	216.0%	152.0%	100.0%
Accounts receivable (net)	200.0%	145.0%	100.0%

These results show favorable trends because the company is increasing sales at a faster pace than the amount of resources tied up in accounts receivable.

TRY IT! SE3, SE4, SE5, E2A, E3A, E4A, E2B, E3B, E4B

 ## LO3 Comprehensive Illustration of Financial Ratio Analysis

In this section, we perform a comprehensive financial ratio analysis of **Starbucks'** performance in 2010 and 2011. The following excerpt from the Management's Discussion and Analysis of Financial Condition section of Starbucks' 2011 annual report provides the context for our evaluation:

> *Starbucks results for fiscal 2011 reflect the strength and resiliency of our business model, the global power of our brand and the talent and dedication of our employees. Our business has performed well this year despite significant headwinds from commodity costs and a continuingly challenging consumer environment. Strong global comparable stores sales growth of 8% for the full year (US*

8% and International 5%) drove increased sales leverage and resulted in higher operating margins and net earnings. This helped mitigate the impact of higher commodity costs, which negatively impacted EPS by approximately $0.20 per share for the year, equivalent to approximately 220 basis points of operating margin. Most of the commodity pressure was related to coffee, with dairy, cocoa, sugar and fuel accounting for the rest. . . .

We are aggressively pursuing the profitable expansion opportunities that exist outside the US, including disciplined growth and scale in our more mature markets, and faster expansion in key emerging markets like China.

We will use the ratios introduced earlier in the text, as well as some commonly used supplemental financial ratios, to evaluate Starbucks' performance in relation to the five concepts: profitability, total asset management, liquidity, financial risk, and operating asset management. We will also evaluate Starbucks' market strength. The data that we use in computing all ratios are from Starbucks' Form 10-K, 2011, and Form 10-K, 2010. All dollar amounts shown in the computations are in millions.

Evaluating Profitability and Total Asset Management

Investors and creditors use profit margin to evaluate a company's ability to earn a satisfactory income (*profitability*). They use asset turnover to determine whether the company uses assets in a way that maximizes revenue (*total asset management*). These two ratios require only three numbers: revenue (or net revenue),* net income, and average total assets. Their combined effect is overall earning power—that is, return on assets.

Profit Margin **Profit margin** measures the net income produced by each dollar of sales. **Starbucks**' profit margins in 2011 and 2010 are computed as follows.

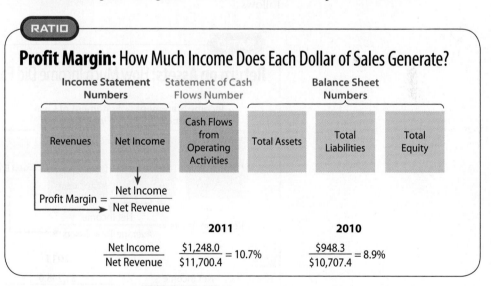

Starbucks' profit margin increased from 8.9 to 10.7 percent between 2011 and 2010 because as a percentage of revenue, operating expenses decreased, as shown in Exhibit 9.

Asset Turnover **Asset turnover** measures how efficiently assets are used to produce sales. **Starbucks**' asset turnover ratios in 2011 and 2010 are computed as follows.

---

* Starbucks refers to revenue as *net revenue*, and we use that term throughout our examples.

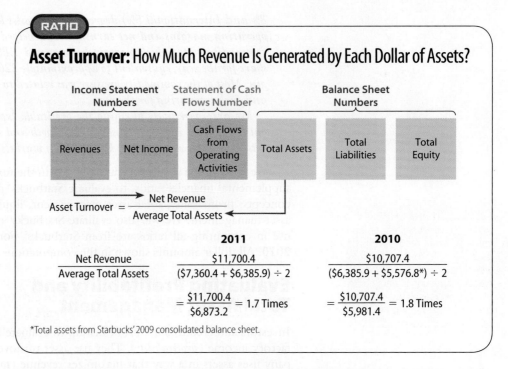

Asset Turnover: How Much Revenue Is Generated by Each Dollar of Assets?

$$\text{Asset Turnover} = \frac{\text{Net Revenue}}{\text{Average Total Assets}}$$

	2011	2010
$\dfrac{\text{Net Revenue}}{\text{Average Total Assets}}$	$\dfrac{\$11,700.4}{(\$7,360.4 + \$6,385.9) \div 2}$	$\dfrac{\$10,707.4}{(\$6,385.9 + \$5,576.8^*) \div 2}$
	$= \dfrac{\$11,700.4}{\$6,873.2} = 1.7 \text{ Times}$	$= \dfrac{\$10,707.4}{\$5,981.4} = 1.8 \text{ Times}$

*Total assets from Starbucks' 2009 consolidated balance sheet.

Starbucks' asset turnover decreased slightly to 1.7 times from 1.8 times because net sales increased slightly less in relation to average total assets.

Return on Assets **Return on assets** measures a company's overall earning power, or profitability. **Starbucks**' return on assets ratios in 2011 and 2010 are computed as follows.

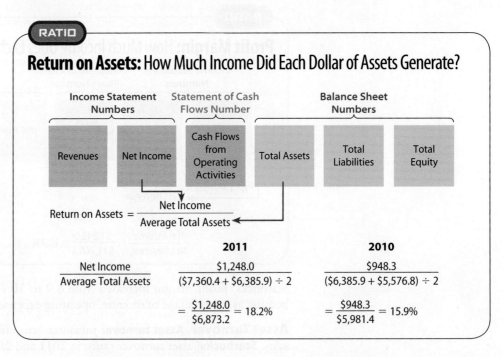

Return on Assets: How Much Income Did Each Dollar of Assets Generate?

$$\text{Return on Assets} = \frac{\text{Net Income}}{\text{Average Total Assets}}$$

	2011	2010
$\dfrac{\text{Net Income}}{\text{Average Total Assets}}$	$\dfrac{\$1,248.0}{(\$7,360.4 + \$6,385.9) \div 2}$	$\dfrac{\$948.3}{(\$6,385.9 + \$5,576.8) \div 2}$
	$= \dfrac{\$1,248.0}{\$6,873.2} = 18.2\%$	$= \dfrac{\$948.3}{\$5,981.4} = 15.9\%$

Starbucks' return on assets increased from 15.9 percent in 2010 to 18.2 percent in 2011 because net income increased more in relation to average total assets.

Profitability Ratio Relationships The relationships of the three financial ratios for profitability are as follows.

	Profit Margin		Asset Turnover		Return on Assets
	$\dfrac{\text{Net Income}}{\text{Net Sales}}$	$\times$	$\dfrac{\text{Net Sales}}{\text{Average Total Assets}}$	$=$	$\dfrac{\text{Net Income}}{\text{Average Total Assets}}$
2010	8.9%	$\times$	1.8	$=$	16.0%
2011	10.7%	$\times$	1.7	$=$	18.2%

Starbucks' return on assets increased in 2011 because of an increase in profit margin. Although Starbucks' profitability and total asset management ratios were relatively low, Starbucks is very good at generating cash from these returns on assets.

It is important to note that net income is sometimes not as useful in computing profitability ratios as it is for Starbucks. If a company has one-time items on its income statement, such as gains, or losses on the sale or disposal of discontinued operations, income from continuing operations may be a better measure of sustainable earnings than net income. Some analysts like to use earnings before interest and taxes (EBIT) for the earnings measure because it excludes the effects of the company's borrowings and the tax rates from the analysis. Whatever figure one uses for earnings, it is important to try to determine the effects of various components on future operations.

STUDY NOTE: *The analysis of both asset turnover and return on assets is improved if only productive assets are used in the calculations. For example, when investments in unfinished new plant construction or in nonoperating plants are removed from the asset base, the result is a better picture of the productivity of assets.*

Evaluating Liquidity

As mentioned, *liquidity* is a company's ability to pay bills when they are due and to meet unexpected needs for cash. Analysts compute cash flow yield, cash flows to sales, cash flows to assets, and free cash flow to evaluate a company's liquidity.

Cash Flow Yield **Cash flow yield** is the most important liquidity ratio because it measures a company's ability to generate operating cash flows in relation to net income. **Starbucks'** cash flow yields in 2011 and 2010 are computed as follows.

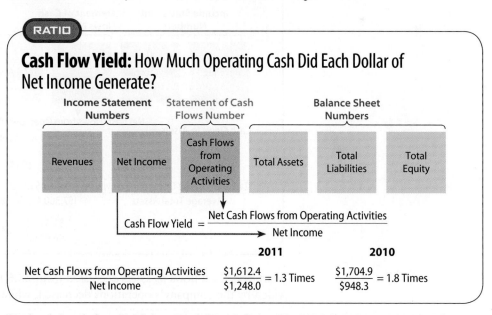

Starbucks' cash flow yield decreased from 1.8 times in 2010 to 1.3 times in 2011 because net cash flows from operating activities decreased while net income increased.

Cash Flows to Sales **Cash flows to sales** refers to the ability of sales to generate operating cash flows. **Starbucks'** cash flows to sales ratios in 2011 and 2010 are computed as follows.

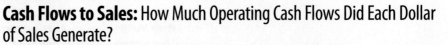

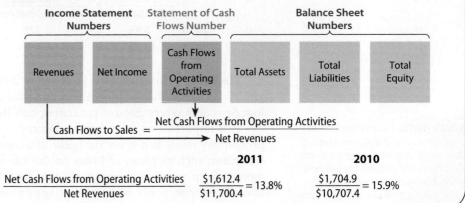

Starbucks' cash flows to sales decreased from 15.9 to 13.8 percent because the company's cash flows provided by its operations decreased while net revenues increased.

Cash Flows to Assets **Cash flows to assets** measures the ability of assets to generate operating cash flows. **Starbucks**' cash flows to assets ratios in 2011 and 2010 are computed as follows.

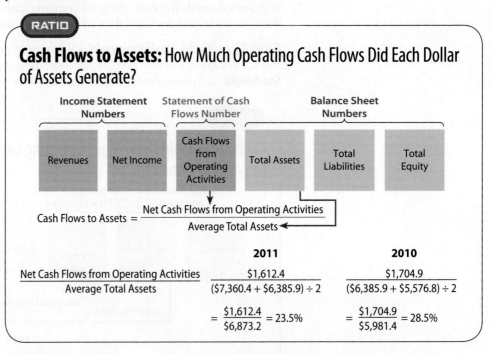

Starbucks' cash flows to assets decreased from 28.5 to 23.5 percent. The cash flows provided by the company's operations decreased, while the average total assets increased.

Free Cash Flow **Free cash flow** is a measure of the cash remaining after providing for commitments. **Starbucks**' free cash flows in 2010 and 2011 are computed as follows.

	2011	2010
Net Cash Flows from Operating Activities	$1,612.4 − $389.5 − $531.9	$1,704.9 − $171.0 − $440.7
− Dividends	= $691.0	= $1,093.2
− Net Capital Expenditures*		

*From the consolidated statements of cash flows.

Starbucks' free cash flow decreased. While the company's net capital expenditures (the difference between purchases and sales of plant assets) increased by $91.2 million ($531.9 − $440.7), the net cash provided by operating activities decreased by $92.5 million ($1,612.4 − $1,704.9). Another unfavorable factor in Starbucks' free cash flow is that the company paid dividends in the past two years. In sum, Starbucks is very proficient in turning its income into cash. It has very good cash flow returns and strong free cash flow.

Evaluating Financial Risk

Financial risk refers to a company's ability to survive in good times and bad. The aim of evaluating financial risk is to detect early signs that a company is headed for financial difficulty through its use of debt, or *financial leverage*, to finance part of the company. Many companies use financial leverage positively. They take advantage of the fact that interest paid on debt is tax-deductible, whereas dividends on stock are not. Because debt usually carries a fixed interest charge and the cost of financing can be limited, leverage can be used to advantage. If a company can earn a return on assets greater than the cost of interest, it increases the return to its stockholders. However, increasing amounts of debt in a company's capital structure can mean that the company is becoming more heavily leveraged. When this occurs, the company runs the risk of not earning a return on assets equal to the cost of financing the assets, thereby incurring a loss. This condition has a negative effect because it represents increasing legal obligations to pay interest periodically and the principal at maturity. Failure to make those payments can result in bankruptcy.

Declining profitability and liquidity ratios together with increased leverage are key indicators of possible failure. Ratios related to financial risk include debt to equity, return on equity, and interest coverage.

STUDY NOTE: *Because of innovative financing plans and other means of acquiring assets, lease payments and similar types of fixed obligations should be considered when evaluating financial risk.*

Debt to Equity Ratio The **debt to equity ratio** measures financial risk by showing the amount of assets provided by creditors in relation to the amount provided by stockholders. A higher ratio indicates more financial risk because it indicates the company is reling more heavily on debt financing. **Starbucks**' debt to equity ratios in 2010 and 2011 are computed as follows.

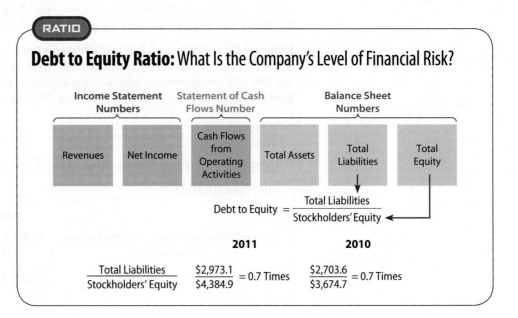

RATIO

Debt to Equity Ratio: What Is the Company's Level of Financial Risk?

Income Statement Numbers		Statement of Cash Flows Number	Balance Sheet Numbers		
Revenues	Net Income	Cash Flows from Operating Activities	Total Assets	Total Liabilities	Total Equity

$$\text{Debt to Equity} = \frac{\text{Total Liabilities}}{\text{Stockholders' Equity}}$$

	2011	2010
$\dfrac{\text{Total Liabilities}}{\text{Stockholders' Equity}}$	$\dfrac{\$2,973.1}{\$4,384.9} = 0.7 \text{ Times}$	$\dfrac{\$2,703.6}{\$3,674.7} = 0.7 \text{ Times}$

Starbucks' debt to equity ratio was stable at 0.7 times in both 2010 and 2011. Recall from Exhibit 2 that the company increased both its liabilities and its stockholders' equity from 2010 to 2011.

Return on Equity **Return on equity** measures the return to stockholders, or the profitability of stockholders' investments. **Starbucks**' return on equity ratios in 2010 and 2011 are computed as follows.

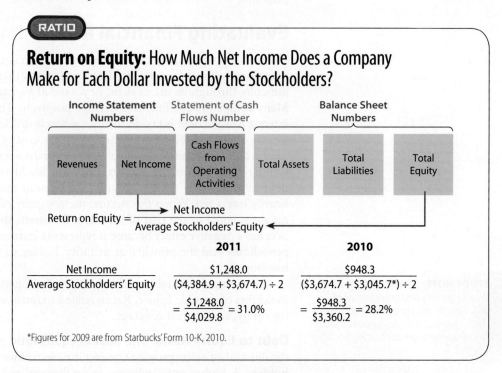

RATIO

Return on Equity: How Much Net Income Does a Company Make for Each Dollar Invested by the Stockholders?

	2011	2010
Net Income / Average Stockholders' Equity	$1,248.0 / ($4,384.9 + $3,674.7) ÷ 2	$948.3 / ($3,674.7 + $3,045.7*) ÷ 2
	$= \dfrac{\$1,248.0}{\$4,029.8} = 31.0\%$	$= \dfrac{\$948.3}{\$3,360.2} = 28.2\%$

*Figures for 2009 are from Starbucks' Form 10-K, 2010.

Starbucks' return on equity increased from 28.2 percent in 2010 to 31.0 percent in 2011. These are excellent returns compared to return on assets of 15.8 percent in 2010 and 18.1 percent in 2011. Note that both the overall profitability (return on assets) and the return to stockholders (return on equity) increased. The reason for this is that Starbucks' net income increased proportionally more than average stockholders' equity.

Interest Coverage The **interest coverage ratio** is a supplementary ratio that measures the degree of protection creditors have from default on interest payments. Analysts use this ratio to determine whether a company's interest payments are in peril. **Starbucks**' interest coverage ratios in 2010 and 2011 are computed as follows.

RATIO

Interest Coverage Ratio: How Many Times Did the Income Exceed Interest Expense?

	2011	2010
Income Before Income Taxes + Interest Expense / Interest Expense	$1,811.1 + $33.3 / $33.3	$1,437.0 + $32.7 / $32.7
	$= \dfrac{\$1,844.4}{\$33.3} = 55.4$ Times	$= \dfrac{\$1,469.7}{\$32.7} = 44.9$ Times

Starbucks' interest coverage increased from 44.9 times to 55.4 times, due to an increase in income before income taxes. Therefore, the interest coverage is at a very safe level.

Evaluating Operating Asset Management

Research has shown that successful companies carefully manage the operating assets and payables in the **operating cycle**.[4] As discussed in an earlier chapter, the operating cycle involves inventories, accounts receivable, and accounts payable. It spans the time it takes to purchase inventory, sell it, and collect for it. The **financing period**—the period between the time a supplier must be paid and the end of the operating cycle—defines how much additional financing the company must have to support its operations. Because additional debt increases a company's financial risk, it is important to keep the financing period at a manageable level.

The financial ratios that measure operating asset management include inventory turnover, days' inventory on hand, receivables turnover, days' sales uncollected, payables turnover, and days' payable. To determine the days in each component of the cash cycle, the turnover must first be computed by relating the average for each balance sheet account—inventory, accounts receivable, and accounts payable—to the respective income statement account for the period—cost of goods sold and net sales or revenues. The average number of days of each component is then determined by dividing the turnover into 365 days.

Inventory Turnover **Inventory turnover** measures the relative size of inventories. **Starbucks**' inventory turnover ratios in 2010 and 2011 are computed as follows.

Inventory Turnover: How Many Times Did the Company Sell Its Inventory During an Accounting Period?

	2011	**2010**
$\dfrac{\text{Cost of Goods Sold*}}{\text{Average Inventory}}$	$\dfrac{\$4,949.3}{(\$965.8 + \$543.3) \div 2}$	$\dfrac{\$4,458.6}{(\$543.3 + \$664.9**) \div 2}$
	$= \dfrac{\$4,949.3}{\$754.6} = 6.6 \text{ Times}$	$= \dfrac{\$4,458.6}{\$604.1} = 7.4 \text{ Times}$

*Starbucks refers to Cost of Goods Sold as Cost of Sales.
**Inventory from Starbucks' 2009 consolidated balance sheet.

Starbucks' inventory turnover decreased from 7.4 times in 2010 to 6.6 times in 2011 because the average inventory increased more in relation to the cost of goods sold.

Days' Inventory on Hand **Days' inventory on hand** measures the average number of days that it takes to sell inventory. **Starbucks**' days' inventory on hand ratios in 2010 and 2011 are computed as follows.

Days' Inventory on Hand: How Many Days Did It Take the Company to Sell Its Inventory?

	2011	**2010**
$\dfrac{\text{Days in Accounting Period}}{\text{Inventory Turnover}}$	$\dfrac{365 \text{ Days}}{6.6 \text{ Times}} = 55.3 \text{ Days}$	$\dfrac{365 \text{ Days}}{7.4 \text{ Times}} = 49.3 \text{ Days}$

Starbucks' days' inventory on hand increased from 49.3 days in 2010 to 55.3 days in 2011 due to the decrease in the inventory turnover.

Receivables Turnover **Receivables turnover** measures the relative size of accounts receivable and the effectiveness of credit policies. **Starbucks'** receivables turnover ratios in 2010 and 2011 are computed as follows.

> **RATIO**
>
> **Receivables Turnover:** How Many Times Did the Company Collect Its Accounts Receivable During an Accounting Period?
>
> | | **2011** | **2010** |
> |---|---|---|
> | $\dfrac{\text{Net Sales}}{\text{Average Accounts Receivable}}$ | $\dfrac{\$11,700.4}{(\$386.5 + \$302.7) \div 2}$ | $\dfrac{\$10,707.4}{(\$302.7 + \$271.0^*) \div 2}$ |
> | | $= \dfrac{\$11,700.4}{\$344.6} = 34.0 \text{ Times}$ | $= \dfrac{\$10,707.4}{\$286.9} = 37.3 \text{ Times}$ |
>
> *Accounts receivable from Starbucks' 2009 consolidated balance sheet.

Because most of Starbucks' sales are for cash or credit card, receivables are not a significant asset for Starbucks. Thus, its receivables turnover is very high. However, it declined slightly, from 37.3 times in 2010 to 34.0 times in 2011.

Days' Sales Uncollected **Days' sales uncollected** measures the average number of days it takes to collect receivables. **Starbucks'** days' sales uncollected ratios in 2010 and 2011 are computed as follows.

> **RATIO**
>
> **Days' Sales Uncollected:** How Many Days Does It Take to Collect Accounts Receivables?
>
> | | **2011** | **2010** |
> |---|---|---|
> | $\dfrac{\text{Days in Accounting Period}}{\text{Receivables Turnover}}$ | $\dfrac{365 \text{ Days}}{34.0 \text{ Times}} = 10.7 \text{ Days}$ | $\dfrac{365 \text{ Days}}{37.3 \text{ Times}} = 9.8 \text{ Days}$ |

Starbucks' high receivables turnover ratios resulted in an increase in days' sales uncollected from 9.8 days in 2010 to 10.7 days in 2011.

Payables Turnover **Payables turnover** measures the relative size of accounts payable and the credit terms extended to a company. **Starbucks'** payables turnover ratios in 2010 and 2011 are computed as follows.

> **RATIO**
>
> **Payables Turnover:** How Many Times Does a Company Pay Its Accounts Payable During an Accounting Period?
>
> | | **2011** | **2010** |
> |---|---|---|
> | $\dfrac{\text{Costs of Goods Sold} +/-\ \text{Change in Inventory}}{\text{Average Accounts Payable}}$ | $\dfrac{\$4,949.3 + \$422.5}{(\$540.0 + \$282.6) \div 2}$ | $\dfrac{\$4,458.6 - \$121.6}{(\$282.6 + \$267.1^*) \div 2}$ |
> | | $= \dfrac{\$5,371.8}{\$411.3} = 13.1 \text{ Times}$ | $= \dfrac{\$4,337.0}{\$274.9} = 15.8 \text{ Times}$ |
>
> *Accounts Payable from Starbucks' 2009 consolidated balance sheet.

Starbucks' payables turnover decreased from 15.8 times in 2010 to 13.1 times in 2011.

Days' Payable **Days' payable** measures the average number of days it takes to pay accounts payable. Starbucks' days' payable ratios in 2010 and 2011 are computed as follows.

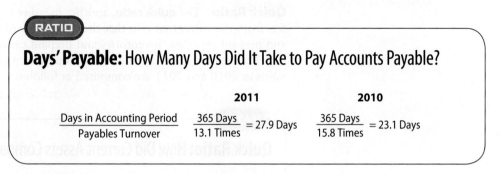

RATIO

Days' Payable: How Many Days Did It Take to Pay Accounts Payable?

	2011	**2010**
$\dfrac{\text{Days in Accounting Period}}{\text{Payables Turnover}}$	$\dfrac{365 \text{ Days}}{13.1 \text{ Times}} = 27.9 \text{ Days}$	$\dfrac{365 \text{ Days}}{15.8 \text{ Times}} = 23.1 \text{ Days}$

Strabucks' decrease in payables turnover resulted in an increase in days' payable from 23.1 days in 2010 to 27.9 days in 2011.

Financing Period We can now assess **Starbucks**' overall operating asset management by computing the financing period—the number of days of financing that must be provided. The financing period is computed by deducting the days' payable from the operating cycle (days' inventory on hand + days' sales uncollected). Starbucks' financing periods in 2010 and 2011 are computed as follows.

> **2011:** 55.3 Days + 10.7 Days – 27.9 Days = 38.1 Days
> **2010:** 49.3 Days + 9.8 Days – 23.1 Days = 36.0 Days

Since both days' inventory on hand and days' sales uncollected increased and days' payable increased, Starbucks had to provide 2.1 (38.1 – 36.0) more days of financing for its operating assets in 2011 than in 2010.

Supplemental Financial Ratios for Assessing Operating Asset Management and Liquidity

In evaluating operating asset management and liquidity, many analysts also consider two supplemental financial ratios: the current ratio and the quick ratio.

Current Ratio
The **current ratio** measures short-term debt-paying ability by comparing current assets with current liabilities. **Starbucks**' current ratios in 2010 and 2011 are computed as follows.

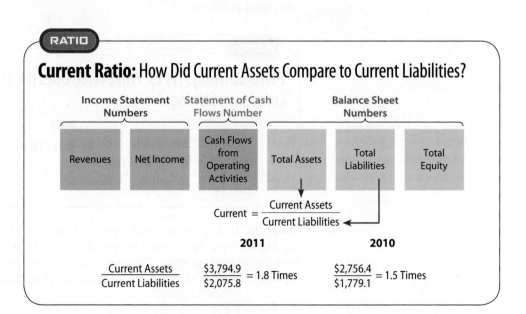

RATIO

Current Ratio: How Did Current Assets Compare to Current Liabilities?

Income Statement Numbers		Statement of Cash Flows Number	Balance Sheet Numbers		
Revenues	Net Income	Cash Flows from Operating Activities	Total Assets	Total Liabilities	Total Equity

$$\text{Current} = \frac{\text{Current Assets}}{\text{Current Liabilities}}$$

	2011	**2010**
$\dfrac{\text{Current Assets}}{\text{Current Liabilities}}$	$\dfrac{\$3,794.9}{\$2,075.8} = 1.8 \text{ Times}$	$\dfrac{\$2,756.4}{\$1,779.1} = 1.5 \text{ Times}$

Starbucks' current ratio was increased from 1.5 times in 2010 to 1.8 times in 2011. From 2010 to 2011, its current assets grew faster than its current liabilities.

Quick Ratio   The **quick ratio**, another measure of short-term debt-paying ability, differs from the current ratio in that the numerator of the quick ratio excludes inventories and prepaid expenses. Inventories and prepaid expenses take longer to convert to cash than the current assets included in the numerator of the quick ratio. **Starbucks'** quick ratios in 2010 and 2011 are computed as follows.

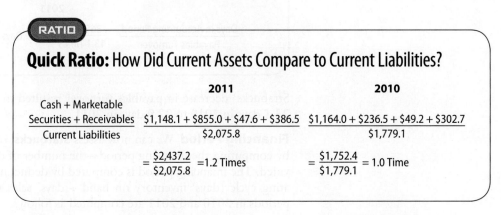

RATIO

Quick Ratio: How Did Current Assets Compare to Current Liabilities?

	2011	**2010**
Cash + Marketable Securities + Receivables / Current Liabilities	$\dfrac{\$1,148.1 + \$855.0 + \$47.6 + \$386.5}{\$2,075.8}$	$\dfrac{\$1,164.0 + \$236.5 + \$49.2 + \$302.7}{\$1,779.1}$
	$= \dfrac{\$2,437.2}{\$2,075.8} = 1.2\ \text{Times}$	$= \dfrac{\$1,752.4}{\$1,779.1} = 1.0\ \text{Time}$

Starbucks' quick ratio increased from 1.0 time in 2010 to 1.2 times in 2011.

Evaluating Market Strength with Financial Ratios

Market price is the price at which a company's stock is bought and sold. It indicates how investors view the potential return and risk connected with owning the stock. Market price by itself is not very informative, however, because companies have different numbers of shares outstanding, different earnings, and different dividend policies. Thus, market price must be related to earnings by considering the price/earnings (P/E) ratio and the dividend yield.

Price/Earnings (P/E)   **Price/earnings (P/E)**, which measures investors' confidence in a company, is the ratio of the market price per share to earnings per share. The P/E ratio is useful in comparing the earnings of different companies and the value of a company's shares in relation to values in the overall market. With a higher P/E ratio, the investor obtains less earnings per dollar invested. **Starbucks'** P/E ratios in 2010 and 2011 are computed as follows.

RATIO

Price/Earnings (P/E): What Value Does the Market Place on the Company's Earnings?

	2011	**2010**
Market Price per Share / Earnings per Share**	$\dfrac{\$37.86^*}{\$1.66} = 22.8\ \text{Times}$	$\dfrac{\$24.79^*}{\$1.27} = 19.5\ \text{Times}$

*Market price is the average for the fourth quarter reported in Starbucks' 2010 and 2011 annual reports.
**Earnings per share is Starbucks' basic EPS.

Starbucks' P/E ratio increased from 19.5 times in 2010 to 22.8 times in 2011 because the market value of its stock increased at a faster rate (from about $25 to about $38) than its earnings per share. The implication is that investors are confident that Starbucks' earnings will grow as fast in the future as it did in the past.

Dividend Yield **Dividend yield** measures a stock's current return to an investor in the form of dividends. **Starbucks'** dividend yields in 2010 and 2011 are computed as follows.

> **RATIO**
>
> ### Dividend Yield: What Is the Return from Dividends on Each Share of Stock?
>
> | | **2011** | **2010** |
> |---|---|---|
> | $\dfrac{\text{Dividends per Share}}{\text{Market Price per Share}}$ | $\dfrac{\$0.56}{\$37.86} = 1.5\%$ | $\dfrac{\$0.36}{\$24.79} = 1.5\%$ |

Starbucks's dividend yield was steady and rather low at 1.5 percent for both years 2010 and 2011. Because the dividend yield was rather low, we can conclude that those who invest in the company expect their return to come from increases in the stock's market value.

Financial Statement Analysis and Performance Assessment

The relationships of key financial ratios help the users of financial statements assess financial performance. These relationships are shown in Exhibit 10.

Exhibit 10
Relationships of Financial Ratios

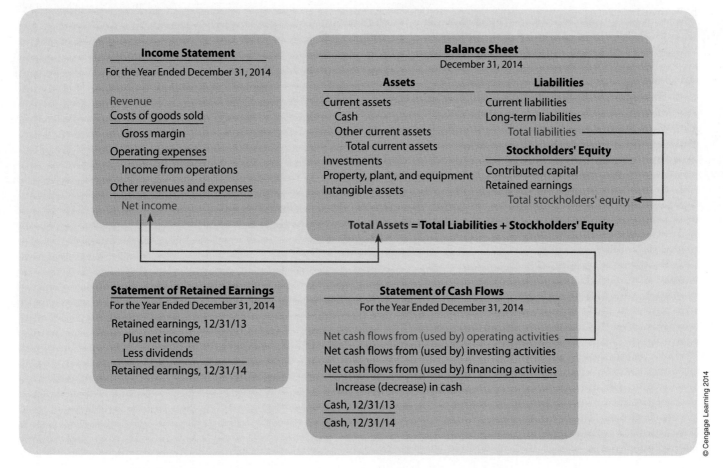

APPLY IT!

Kora's, a retail company, engaged in the transactions that follow. Opposite each transaction is a ratio and space to mark the effect of each transaction on the ratio. Show that you understand the effect of business activities on performance measures by placing an X in the appropriate column to show whether the transaction increased, decreased, or had no effect on the ratio.

Transaction	Ratio	Effect		
		Increase	**Decrease**	**None**
a. Accrued salaries.	Current ratio			
b. Purchased inventory.	Quick ratio			
c. Increased allowance for uncollectible accounts.	Receivables turnover			
d. Purchased inventory on credit.	Payables turnover			
e. Sold treasury stock.	Profit margin			
f. Borrowed cash by issuing bond payable.	Asset turnover			
g. Paid wages expense.	Return on assets			
h. Repaid bond payable.	Debt to equity ratio			
i. Accrued interest expense.	Interest coverage ratio			
j. Sold merchandise on account.	Return on equity			
k. Recorded depreciation expense.	Cash flow yield			
l. Sold equipment.	Free cash flow			

SOLUTION

Transaction	Ratio	Effect		
		Increase	**Decrease**	**None**
a. Accrued salaries.	Current ratio		X	
b. Purchased inventory.	Quick ratio		X	
c. Increased allowance for uncollectible accounts.	Receivables turnover	X		
d. Purchased inventory on credit.	Payables turnover		X	
e. Sold treasury stock.	Profit margin			X
f. Borrowed cash by issuing bond payable.	Asset turnover		X	
g. Paid wages expense.	Return on assets		X	
h. Repaid bond payable.	Debt to equity ratio	X		
i. Accrued interest expense.	Interest coverage ratio		X	
j. Sold merchandise on account.	Return on equity	X		
k. Recorded depreciation expense.	Cash flow yield	X		
l. Sold equipment.	Free cash flow	X		

TRY IT! SE6, SE7, SE8, SE9, SE10, E5A, E6A, E7A, E8A, E9A, E5B, E6B, E7B, E8B, E9B

BUSINESS APPLICATIONS

RELEVANT LEARNING OBJECTIVE

LO 4 Define *quality of earnings,* and identify the factors that affect quality of earnings and related management compensation issues.

LO 4 Evaluating Quality of Earnings

Net income (net earnings) is the measure most commonly used to evaluate a company's profitability. In fact, one survey indicated that the two important measures in evaluating common stocks were expected changes in earnings per share and return on assets.[5] Net income is a key component of both measures.

Because of the importance of net income, or the "bottom line," in measuring a company's prospects, there is significant interest in evaluating the quality of the net income. The **quality of earnings** refers to the substance of earnings and their sustainability into future periods. Quality of earnings is affected by the following:

- Accounting methods
- Accounting estimates
- One-time items

Accounting Methods

The accounting methods a firm uses affect its operating income. Generally accepted accounting methods include:

- Uncollectible receivables methods (percentage of net sales and aging of accounts receivable)
- Inventory methods (LIFO, FIFO, and average cost)
- Depreciation methods (accelerated, production, and straight-line)
- Revenue recognition methods

All these methods are designed to *match* revenues and expenses. However, the expenses are estimates, and the period or periods benefited cannot be demonstrated conclusively. In practice, it is hard to justify one method of estimation over another.

Different accounting methods have different effects on net income. Some methods are more conservative than others because they tend to produce a lower net income in the current period. For example, suppose that Rudy Company and Kanya Company have similar operations, but Rudy uses FIFO for inventory costing and the straight-line (SL) method for computing depreciation. Kanya uses LIFO for inventory costing and the double-declining-balance (DDB) method for computing depreciation. The income statements of the two companies might appear as shown in Exhibit 11.

Exhibit 11
Effects of Different Accounting Methods

	Rudy Company (FIFO and SL)	Kanya Company (LIFO and DDB)
Net sales	$462,500	$462,500
Cost of goods available for sale	$200,000	$200,000
Less ending inventory	30,000	25,000
Cost of goods sold	$170,000	$175,000
Gross margin	$292,500	$287,500
Less depreciation expense	$ 20,000	$ 40,000
Less other expenses	85,000	85,000
Total operating expenses	$105,000	$125,000
Income from continuing operations before income taxes	$187,500	$162,500

Impact of Different Accounting Methods on Income The income from continuing operations before income taxes for the firm that uses LIFO and DDB is lower because in periods of rising prices, the LIFO method produces a higher cost of goods sold. Also, in the early years of an asset's useful life, accelerated depreciation yields a higher depreciation expense. The result is lower operating income. However, future operating income should be higher.

CASH FLOW

Impact of Different Accounting Methods on Cash Flows Although the choice of accounting method does not affect cash flows except for possible differences in income taxes, the $25,000 difference in operating income stems solely from the choice of accounting methods. Estimates of the useful lives and residual values of plant assets could lead to an even greater difference. In practice, of course, differences in net income occur for many reasons; but the user of financial statements must be aware of the discrepancies that can occur as a result of the accounting methods used. In general, an accounting method or estimate that results in lower current earnings produces a better quality of operating income.

Impact of Different Accounting Methods on Financial Statements The latitude that companies have in their choice of accounting methods could cause problems in the interpretation of financial statements were it not for the conventions of *full disclosure* and *consistency*. As noted in an earlier chapter, **full disclosure** requires management to explain, in a note to the financial statements, the significant accounting policies used. For instance, in a note to its financial statements, **Starbucks** discloses that it uses the straight-line method for depreciation of property, plant, and equipment.[6] **Consistency** requires that the same accounting procedures be used from year to year. If a company changes its accounting procedure, it must explain the nature of the change and its monetary effect in a note to its statements.

Accounting Estimates

Users of financial statements also need to be aware of the impact that accounting estimates have on reported income. To comply with *accrual accounting* (the *matching rule*), accountants must assign revenues and expenses to the periods in which they occur. If they cannot establish a direct relationship between revenues and expenses, they systematically allocate the expenses among the periods that benefit from them. In doing so, they must make estimates and exercise judgment, based on realistic assumptions. However, there is latitude in making the estimate, and the final judgment will affect net income.

For example, when a company acquires an asset, the accountant must estimate the asset's useful life. Technological obsolescence could shorten the asset's expected useful life, and regular maintenance and repairs could lengthen it. Although the actual useful life cannot be known with certainty until some future date, the accountant's estimate of it affects both current and future operating income. Other areas that require accounting estimates include:

■ Residual value of assets
■ Uncollectible accounts receivable
■ Sales returns
■ Total units of production
■ Total recoverable units of natural resources
■ Amortization periods
■ Warranty claims
■ Environmental cleanup costs

The importance of accounting estimates depends on the industry in which a firm operates. For example, estimated uncollectible receivables for a credit card firm, such as **American Express**, or for a financial services firm, such as **Bank of America**, can have a material impact on earnings; but estimated useful life may be less important because depreciable assets represent a small percentage of the firm's total assets. **Starbucks** has few receivables, but it has major investments in depreciable assets. Thus, estimates of useful life and residual value are more important to Starbucks than an estimate of uncollectible accounts receivable. The company depreciates its equipment over 2 to 15 years and its buildings over 30 to 40 years.[7]

One-Time Items

If earnings increase because of one-time items, that portion of earnings will not be sustained in the future. In contrast, one-time decreases in earnings may not indicate that earnings will be poor in the future. Examples of one-time items include:

- Gains and losses
- Write-downs and restructurings
- Nonoperating items

Because management has choices in the content and positioning of these income statement components, there is a potential for managing earnings to achieve specific income targets. It is, therefore, critical for users of income statements to understand these factors and take them into consideration when evaluating a company's performance.

Exhibit 12 shows the components of a typical income statement. Net income or loss (the "bottom line" of the income statement) includes all revenues, expenses, gains, and losses over the period. When a company has both continuing and discontinued operations, the operating income section is called *income from continuing operations*. Income

Exhibit 12
Corporate Income Statement

	Dingo Corporation Income Statement For the Year Ended December 31, 2014		
Operating items before income taxes	Revenues		$ 1,850,000
	Costs and expenses		(1,100,000)
	Gain on sale of assets		300,000
	Write-downs of assets		(50,000)
	Restructurings		(150,000)
	Income from continuing operations before income taxes		$ 850,000
Income taxes	Income taxes expense		289,000
	Income from continuing operations		$ 561,000
Nonoperating items	Discontinued operations:		
	Income from operations of discontinued segment (net of taxes, $70,000)	$ 180,000	
	Loss on disposal of segment (net of taxes, $84,000)	(146,000)	34,000
	Net income		$ 595,000
Earnings per share information	Earnings per common share:		
	Income from continuing operations		$2.81
	Discontinued operations (net of taxes)		0.17
	Net income		$2.98

Business Perspective
Beware of the "Bottom Line!"

In the second quarter of 2007, **McDonald's** posted its second-ever loss: $711.7 million. Should this have been cause for concern? The answer is no because the loss resulted from a one-time noncash impairment (decline in value) of $1.6 billion related to investments in Latin America; the company was actually in a period of rapidly growing revenues and profits. In another example, **Campbell Soup** showed unrealistically positive results. Its income jumped by 31 percent due to a tax settlement and an accounting restatement. Without these items, its revenue and income would have been up less than 1 percent; soup sales—its main product—actually dropped by 6 percent. The lesson to be learned is to look beyond the "bottom line" to the components of the income statement when evaluating a company's performance.[8]

from continuing operations before income taxes may include gains or losses on the sale of assets, write-downs, and restructurings.

As you can see in Exhibit 12, the section of the income statement that follows income taxes may contain such nonoperating items as **discontinued operations**— segments that are no longer part of a company's operations—and gains (or losses) on the sale or disposal of these segments. Another item that may appear in this section is the write-off of goodwill when its value has been impaired. Earnings per share information appears at the bottom of the statement

Gains and Losses When a company sells or otherwise disposes of operating assets or marketable securities, a gain or loss generally results. Although these gains or losses appear in the operating section of the income statement, they usually represent one-time events. However, management often has some choice as to their timing. Thus, from an analyst's point of view, they should be ignored when considering operating income.

Write-Downs and Restructurings When management decides that an asset is no longer of value to the company, a write-down or restructuring occurs.

- A **write-down** (or *write-off*) is a reduction in the value of an asset below its carrying value on the balance sheet.
- A **restructuring** is the estimated cost of a change in a company's operations. It usually involves the closing of facilities and the laying off of personnel.

Both write-downs and restructurings reduce current operating income and boost future income by shifting future costs to the current period. They are often an indication of poor management decisions in the past, such as paying too much for the assets of another company or making operational changes that do not work out. Companies sometimes take all possible losses in the current year so that future years will be "clean" of these costs. Such "big baths," as they are called, commonly occur when a company is having a bad year. They also often occur in years when there is a change in management. The new management takes a "big bath" in the current year so it can show improved results in future years.

In a recent year, 34 percent of 500 large companies had write-downs of tangible assets, and 41 percent had restructurings. Another 19 percent had write-downs or charges related to intangible assets, often involving goodwill. In 2011, **Starbucks** did not have any restructuring costs, but in 2009 its restructuring costs were $332.4 million (compared with net income of only $390.8 million) in connection with the closing of a number of its stores.[9]

Nonoperating Items The nonoperating items that appear on the income statement include discontinued operations and gains or losses on the sale or disposal of these segments. These items can significantly affect net income. For example, in Exhibit 12, earnings per common share for income from continuing operations are $2.81; but when all the nonoperating items are taken into consideration, net income per share is $2.98. To

Business Perspective
Look Carefully at the Numbers

In recent years, companies have increasingly used pro forma statements—statements as they would appear without certain items—as a way of presenting a better picture of their operations than would be the case in reports prepared under GAAP. For example, in the first quarter of 2012, **GEO Group, Inc.**, reported pro forma net income of $18.8 million, even though its actual net income was $15.1 million. The higher pro forma figure came about by not deducting certain expenses which are required under GAAP. In addition, a common practice used by such companies as **Google**, **eBay**, and **Starbucks** is to provide in the notes to the financial statements income as it would be without the expense related to compensation for stock options.[10] Pro forma statements, which are unaudited, have come to mean whatever a company's management wants them to mean. As a result, the SEC issued rules that prohibit companies from giving more prominence to non-GAAP measures and from using terms that are similar to GAAP measures.[11] Nevertheless, companies still report pro forma results. Analysts should rely exclusively on financial statements that are prepared using GAAP and that are audited by an independent CPA.

make it easier to evaluate a company's ongoing operations, generally accepted accounting principles require that gains and losses from discontinued operations be reported separately on the income statement.

In Exhibit 12, the *disclosure* of discontinued operations has two parts:

- One part shows that after the decision to discontinue, the income from operations of the disposed segment was $180,000 (net of $70,000 taxes).
- The other part shows that the loss from the disposal of the segment was $146,000 (net of $84,000 tax savings). (The computation of the gains or losses involved in discontinued operations is covered in more advanced accounting courses.)

Management Compensation

Knowledge of performance measurement not only is important for evaluating a company, but also leads to an understanding of the criteria by which a board of directors evaluates and compensates management. Members of management are often paid based on the earnings of the company. As noted earlier, one intent of the Sarbanes-Oxley Act of 2002 was to strengthen the corporate governance of public corporations. Under this act, a public corporation's board of directors must establish a **compensation committee** made up of independent directors to determine how the company's top executives will be compensated. The company must file documents with the SEC, *disclosing* the components of compensation and the criteria used to remunerate top executives.

The components of **Starbucks**' compensation of executive officers are typical of those used by many companies. They include the following:

- Annual base salary
- Annual incentive bonuses
- Long-term incentive compensation (stock option awards)[12]

Incentive bonuses are based on financial performance measures that the compensation committee identifies as important to the company's long-term success, especially in terms of increasing the value of shareholders' investments in the company. Many companies tie incentive bonuses to measures such as growth in revenues and return on assets or return on equity. Starbucks bases 50 percent of its incentive bonus on an "adjusted consolidated operating income or adjusted business unit operating income," 30 percent on "adjusted earnings per share target approved by the compensation committee," and 20 percent on the executive's "specific individual performance goals."[13]

Stock option awards are usually based on how well the company is achieving its long-term strategic goals. In 2011, Starbucks' CEO received a base salary of $1,382,692 and a non-equity incentive plan compensation of $2,982,000. He also received a stock option awards of $11,479,494.[14]

From one vantage point, earnings per share is a "bottom-line" number that encompasses all the other performance measures. However, using a single performance measure as the basis for determining compensation has the potential of leading to practices that are not in the best interests of a company or its stockholders. For instance, management could boost earnings per share by reducing the number of shares outstanding (the denominator in the earnings per share equation) while not improving earnings. It could accomplish this by using cash to repurchase shares of the company's stock (treasury stock), rather than investing the cash in more profitable operations.

APPLY IT! ➤

The following data apply to Kawa, Inc.: net sales, $180,000; cost of goods sold, $87,500; loss from discontinued operations (net of income tax benefit of $17,500), $50,000; loss on disposal of discontinued operations (net of income tax benefit of $4,000), $12,500; operating expenses, $32,500; income taxes expense on continuing operations, $18,000. Prepare the company's income statement for the year ended December 31, 2014. (*Note*: Ignore earnings per share information.)

SOLUTION

Kawa, Inc.
Income Statement
For the Year Ended December 31, 2014

Net sales		$180,000
Cost of goods sold		87,500
Gross margin		$ 92,500
Operating expenses		32,500
Income from continuing operations before income taxes		$ 60,000
Income taxes expense		18,000
Income from continuing operations		$ 42,000
Discontinued operations		
Loss from discontinued operations (net of income tax benefit of $17,500)	$(50,000)	
Loss on disposal of discontinued operations (net of income tax benefit of $4,000)	(12,500)	(62,500)
Net loss		$ (20,500)

TRY IT! SE11, SE12, E10A, E11A, E12A, E10B, E11B, E12B

A Look Back At: Starbucks Corporation

AP Photo/Ted S. Warren

Starbucks Corporation

The beginning of this chapter focused on **Starbucks Corporation**. Complete the following requirements in order to answer the questions posed at the beginning of the chapter.

Section 1: Concepts
What concepts underlie the standards that Starbucks can use to evaluate performance?

Section 2: Accounting Applications
What analytical tools can Starbucks use to measure financial performance?

Section 3: Business Applications
In what ways would having access to prior years' information aid this analysis? Why is earnings management important in your assessment?

SOLUTION

Section 1: Concepts

Rule-of-thumb measures, a company's past performance, and industry norms are standards companies can use to assess financial performance. Rule-of-thumb measures are weak because they often lack *relevance*. A company's past performance is more reliable and it can be used for measuring the improvement (or lack thereof) in a particular ratio, but can be lacking in *predictive value* and *timeliness* because past performance is not a guarantee of future performance and a company's past performance is not helpful in judging its performance relative to the performance of other companies. Finally, Starbucks can use industry norms to *compare* financial performance, though it's important to note that firms even in the same industry are not always *comparable* because of having different accounting procedures and diversity issues.

Section 2: Accounting Applications

Ratio analysis may be used to measure profitability, total asset management, liquidity, financial risk, and operating asset management. Users of Starbucks' financial statements may employ such techniques as horizontal or trend analysis, vertical analysis, and ratio analysis.

Section 3: Business Applications

Prior years' information would be helpful in two ways. First, turnover, return, and cash flows to assets ratios could be based on average amounts. Second, a trend analysis could be performed for each company. Earnings management is important because it can be used to make a company look as if it is performing better than it is in reality

Review Problem

Comparative Analysis of Two Companies

Debra Wright is considering investing in a fast-food restaurant chain. She has narrowed her choice to Slim Burger or Tasty Steak. The 2014 income statements and balance sheets of the two companies follow.

	A	B	C	D	E
1			Income Statements		
2			For the Year Ended December 31, 2014		
3			(in thousands, except per share amounts)		
4				Fast Burger	Tasty Steak
5	Net sales			$53,000	$86,000
6	Costs and expenses:				
7		Cost of goods sold		$37,000	$61,000
8		Selling expenses		7,000	10,000
9		Administrative expenses		4,000	5,000
10		Total costs and expenses		$48,000	$76,000
11	Income from operations			$ 5,000	$10,000
12	Interest expense			1,400	3,200
13	Income before income taxes			$ 3,600	$ 6,800
14	Income taxes expense			1,800	3,400
15	Net income			$ 1,800	$ 3,400
16	Earnings per share			$ 1.80	$ 1.13
17					

A B	C	D	E
	Balance Sheets		
	December 31, 2014		
	(in thousands)		
		Fast Burger	**Tasty Steak**
	Assets		
Cash		$ 2,000	$ 4,500
Accounts receivable (net)		2,000	6,500
Inventory		2,000	5,000
Property, plant, and equipment (net)		20,000	35,000
Other assets		4,000	5,000
Total assets		$30,000	$56,000
	Liabilities and Stockholders' Equity		
Accounts payable		$ 2,500	$ 3,000
Notes payable		1,500	4,000
Bonds payable		10,000	30,000
Common stock, $1 par value		1,000	3,000
Additional paid-in capital		9,000	9,000
Retained earnings		6,000	7,000
Total liabilities and stockholders' equity		$30,000	$56,000

The following information pertaining to 2014 is also available to Debra:

- Fast Burger's statement of cash flows shows that it had net cash flows from operations of $2,200,000. Tasty Steak's statement of cash flows shows that its net cash flows from operations were $3,000,000.
- Net capital expenditures were $2,100,000 for Fast Burger and $1,800,000 for Tasty Steak.
- Fast Burger paid dividends of $500,000, and Tasty Steak paid dividends of $600,000.
- The market prices of the stocks of Fast Burger and Tasty Steak were $30 and $20, respectively.
- Debra does not have financial information pertaining to prior years. Thus, she used year-end amounts, rather than average amounts.

Perform a comprehensive ratio analysis of both Fast Burger and Tasty Steak using the steps that follow. Assume that all notes payable of the two companies are current liabilities and that all their bonds payable are long-term liabilities. Show dollar amounts in thousands, use end-of-year balances for averages, assume no change in inventory, and round all ratios and percentages to one decimal place.

1. Prepare an analysis of profitability and total asset management.
2. Prepare an analysis of liquidity.
3. Prepare an analysis of financial risk.
4. Prepare an analysis of operating asset management.
5. Prepare an analysis of market strength.
6. In each analysis, indicate which company apparently had the more favorable ratio. (Consider differences of 0.1 or less to be neutral.)

SOLUTION   1.

Ratio Name	Fast Burger	Tasty Steak	6. Company with More Favorable Ratio
Profit margin	$\dfrac{\$1,800}{\$53,000} = 3.4\%$	$\dfrac{\$3,400}{\$86,000} = 4.0\%$	Tasty Steak
Asset turnover	$\dfrac{\$53,000}{\$30,000} = 1.8$ Times	$\dfrac{\$86,000}{\$56,000} = 1.5$ Times	Fast Burger
Return on assets	$\dfrac{\$1,800}{\$30,000} = 6.0\%$	$\dfrac{\$3,400}{\$56,000} = 6.1\%$	Tasty Steak

2.

Ratio Name	Fast Burger	Tasty Steak	6. Company with More Favorable Ratio
Cash flow yield	$\dfrac{\$2,200}{\$1,800} = 1.2$ Times	$\dfrac{\$3,000}{\$3,400} = 0.9$ Time	Fast Burger
Cash flows to sales	$\dfrac{\$2,200}{\$53,000} = 4.2\%$	$\dfrac{\$3,000}{\$86,000} = 3.5\%$	Fast Burger
Cash flows to assets	$\dfrac{\$2,200}{\$30,000} = 7.3\%$	$\dfrac{\$3,000}{\$56,000} = 5.4\%$	Fast Burger
Free cash flow	$\$2,200 - \$500 - \$2,100$ $= (\$400)$	$\$3,000 - \$600 - \$1,800$ $= \$600$	Tasty Steak

3.

Ratio Name	Fast Burger	Tasty Steak	6. Company with More Favorable Ratio
Debt to equity ratio	$\dfrac{\$2,500 + \$1,500 + \$10,000}{\$1,000 + \$9,000 + \$6,000}$ $\dfrac{\$14,000}{\$16,000} = 0.9$ Time	$\dfrac{\$3,000 + \$4,000 + \$30,000}{\$3,000 + \$9,000 + \$7,000}$ $\dfrac{\$37,000}{\$19,000} = 1.9$ Times	Fast Burger
Return on equity	$\dfrac{\$1,800}{\$1,000 + \$9,000 + \$6,000}$ $\dfrac{\$1,800}{\$16,000} = 11.3\%$	$\dfrac{\$3,400}{\$3,000 + \$9,000 + \$7,000}$ $\dfrac{\$3,400}{\$19,000} = 17.9\%$	Tasty Steak
Interest coverage ratio	$\dfrac{\$3,600 + \$1,400}{\$1,400}$ $\dfrac{\$5,000}{\$1,400} = 3.6$ Times	$\dfrac{\$6,800 + \$3,200}{\$3,200}$ $\dfrac{\$10,000}{\$3,200} = 3.1$ Times	Fast Burger

4.

Ratio Name	Fast Burger	Tasty Steak	6. Company with More Favorable Ratio
Inventory turnover	$\dfrac{\$37,000}{\$2,000} = 18.5$ Times	$\dfrac{\$61,000}{\$5,000} = 12.2$ Times	Fast Burger
Days' inventory on hand	$\dfrac{365 \text{ Days}}{18.5 \text{ Times}} = 19.7$ Days	$\dfrac{365 \text{ Days}}{12.2 \text{ Times}} = 29.9$ Days	Fast Burger
Receivable turnover	$\dfrac{\$53,000}{\$2,000} = 26.5$ Times	$\dfrac{\$86,000}{\$6,500} = 13.2$ Times	Fast Burger
Day's sales uncollected	$\dfrac{365 \text{ Days}}{26.5 \text{ Times}} = 13.8$ Days	$\dfrac{365 \text{ Days}}{13.2 \text{ Times}} = 27.7$ Days	Fast Burger
Payables turnover	$\dfrac{\$37,000}{\$2,500} = 14.8$ Times	$\dfrac{\$61,000}{\$3,000} = 20.3$ Times	Tasty Steak
Days' payable	$\dfrac{365 \text{ Days}}{14.8 \text{ Times}} = 24.7$ Days	$\dfrac{365 \text{ Days}}{20.3 \text{ Times}} = 18.0$ Days	Fast Burger

Financing period

Fast Burger: 19.7 Days + 13.8 Days − 24.7 Days = 8.8 Days
Tasty Steak: 29.9 Days + 27.7 Days − 18.0 Days = 39.6 Days

Fast Burger's financing period of only 8.8 days is more favorable.

	Fast Burger	Tasty Steak	
Current ratio	$\dfrac{\$2,000 + \$2,000 + \$2,000}{\$2,500 + \$1,500}$ $\dfrac{\$6,000}{\$4,000} = 1.5$ Times	$\dfrac{\$4,500 + \$6,500 + \$5,000}{\$3,000 + \$4,000}$ $\dfrac{\$16,000}{\$7,000} = 2.3$ Times	Tasty Steak
Quick ratio	$\dfrac{\$2,000 + \$2,000}{\$2,500 + \$1,500}$ $\dfrac{\$4,000}{\$4,000} = 1.0$ Time	$\dfrac{\$4,500 + \$6,500}{\$3,000 + \$4,000}$ $\dfrac{\$11,000}{\$7,000} = 1.6$ Times	Tasty Steak

Note: This analysis indicates the company with the apparently more favorable ratio.

5.

Ratio Name	Fast Burger	Tasty Steak	6. Company with More Favorable Ratio
Price/earnings ratio	$\dfrac{\$30}{\$1.80} = 16.7$ Times	$\dfrac{\$20}{\$1.13} = 17.7$ Times	Tasty Steak
Dividend yield	$\dfrac{\$500,000 \div 1,000,000}{\$30}$ $= \dfrac{\$0.50}{\$30} = 1.7\%$	$\dfrac{\$600,000 \div 3,000,000}{\$20}$ $= \dfrac{\$0.20}{\$20} = 1.0\%$	Fast Burger

Chapter Review

Describe the concepts, standards of comparison, and sources of information used in measuring financial performance. **LO 1**

Important to measuring financial performance are the concepts of relevance, predictive value, comparability, and timeliness, which underlie the objectives of profitability, total asset management, liquidity, financial risk, and operating asset management. Creditors and investors use financial performance measurement to judge a company's past performance and current position, as well as its future potential and the risk associated with it. Creditors use the information from their analyses to make reliable loans that will be repaid with interest. Investors use the information to make investments that will provide a return that is worth the risk.

Three standards of comparison commonly used in evaluating financial performance are rule-of-thumb measures, a company's past performance, and industry norms. Rule-of-thumb measures are weak because of a lack of evidence that they can be widely applied and that they have predictive value. A company's past performance can offer a guideline for measuring improvement, but it is not helpful in judging performance relative to the performance of other companies. Although the use of industry norms overcomes this last problem, firms are not always comparable, even in the same industry.

The main sources of information about public corporations are annual reports and interim financial statements, reports filed with the SEC, business periodicals, and credit and investment advisory services.

Apply horizontal analysis, trend analysis, vertical analysis, and ratio analysis to financial statements. **LO 2**

Horizontal analysis involves the computation of changes in both dollar amounts and percentages from year to year.

Trend analysis calculates percentage changes for several years. The analyst computes the changes by setting a base year equal to 100 and calculating the results for subsequent years as percentages of the base year.

Vertical analysis uses percentages to show the relationship of the component parts of a financial statement to a total figure in the statement. The resulting financial statements, which are expressed entirely in percentages, are called common-size statements.

Financial ratio analysis identifies key relationships between the components of the financial statements. To interpret ratios correctly, the analyst must have a general understanding of the company and its environment, financial data for several years or for several companies, and an understanding of the data underlying the numerators and denominators.

Apply financial ratio analysis in a comprehensive evaluation of a company's financial performance. **LO 3**

A comprehensive ratio analysis includes the evaluation of a company's profitability, total asset management, liquidity, financial risk, operating asset management, and market strength.

Define *quality of earnings*, and identify the factors that affect quality of earnings and related management compensation issues. **LO 4**

The quality of earnings refers to the substance of earnings and their sustainability into future accounting periods. The quality of a company's earnings may be affected by the accounting methods and estimates it uses and by one-time items that it reports on its income statement. One-time items include gains and losses, write-downs and restructurings, and nonoperating items.

When a company has both continuing and discontinued operations, the operating income section of its income statement is called income from continuing operations. Income from continuing operations before income taxes is affected by choices of accounting methods and estimates and may contain gains and losses on the sale of assets, write-downs, and restructurings. The lower part of the income statement may contain such nonoperating items as discontinued operations. Earnings per share information appears at the bottom of the statement.

In public corporations, a committee made up of independent directors appointed by the board of directors determines the compensation of top executives. Although earnings per share can be regarded as a "bottom-line" number that encompasses all the other performance measures, using it as the sole basis for determining executive compensation may lead to management practices that are not in the best interests of the company or its stockholders.

Key Terms and Ratios

base year 534 (LO2)
common-size statement 537 (LO2)
compensation committee 557 (LO4)
consistency 554 (LO4)
discontinued operations 556 (LO4)
diversified companies 531 (LO1)
financial ratio analysis 540 (LO2)
financial statement analysis 530 (LO1)
financing period 547 (LO3)
Form 8-K 532 (LO1)
Form 10-K 532 (LO1)
Form 10-Q 532 (LO1)
full disclosure 554 (LO4)
horizontal analysis 534 (LO2)
index number 536 (LO2)

interim financial statements 532 (LO1)
operating cycle 547 (LO3)
quality of earnings 553 (LO4)
restructuring 556 (LO4)
trend analysis 536 (LO2)
vertical analysis 537 (LO2)
write-down 556 (LO4)

RATIOS

asset turnover 541 (LO3)
cash flow yield 543 (LO3)
cash flows to assets 544 (LO3)
cash flows to sales 543 (LO3)
current ratio 549 (LO3)
days' inventory on hand 547 (LO3)

days' payable 549 (LO3)
days' sales uncollected 548 (LO3)
debt to equity ratio 545 (LO3)
dividend yield 551 (LO3)
free cash flow 544 (LO3)
interest coverage ratio 546 (LO3)
inventory turnover 547 (LO3)
payables turnover 548 (LO3)
price/earnings (P/E) 550 (LO3)
profit margin 541 (LO3)
quick ratio 550 (LO3)
receivables turnover 548 (LO3)
return on assets 542 (LO3)
return on equity 546 (LO3)

Chapter Assignments

DISCUSSION QUESTIONS

LO 1   **DQ1.** How are past performance and industry norms useful in evaluating a company's performance? What are their limitations?

LO 2   **DQ2.** In a five-year trend analysis, why do the dollar values remain the same for their respective years while the percentages usually change when a new five-year period is chosen?

LO 3   **DQ3.** Why does a decrease in receivables turnover create the need for cash from operating activities?

LO 3   **DQ4.** Why would ratios that include one balance sheet account and one income statement account, such as receivables turnover or return on assets, be questionable if they came from quarterly or other interim financial reports?

CASH FLOW LO 3 **DQ5.** What is a limitation of free cash flow in comparing one company to another?

LO 4 **DQ6. BUSINESS APPLICATION ▶** In what way is selling an investment for a gain potentially a negative in evaluating quality of earnings?

LO 4 **DQ7. BUSINESS APPLICATION ▶** Is it unethical for new management to take an extra large write-off (a "big bath") in order to reduce future costs? Why or why not?

LO 4 **DQ8. BUSINESS APPLICATION ▶** Why is it useful to disclose discontinued operations separately on the income statement?

LO 4 **DQ9. BUSINESS APPLICATION ▶** Why is it essential that management compensation, including bonuses, be linked to financial goals and strategies that achieve shareholder value?

LO 4 **DQ10. BUSINESS APPLICATION ▶** What is one way a company can improve its earnings per share without improving its earnings or net income?

SHORT EXERCISES

LO 1 **Objectives and Standards of Financial Performance Evaluation**

SE1. CONCEPT ▶ Indicate whether each of the following items is (a) an underlying concept, (b) an objective or (c) a standard of comparison of financial statement analysis:

1. Industry norms
2. Assessment of a company's past performance
3. Comparability
4. The company's past performance
5. Assessment of future potential and related risk
6. Predictive value

LO 1 **Sources of Information**

SE2. For each piece of information in the list that follows, indicate whether the best source would be (a) reports published by the company, (b) SEC reports, (c) business periodicals, or (d) credit and investment advisory services.

1. Current market value of a company's stock
2. Management's analysis of the past year's operations
3. Objective assessment of a company's financial performance
4. Most complete body of financial disclosures
5. Current events affecting the company

LO 2 **Trend Analysis**

SE3. ACCOUNTING CONNECTION ▶ Using 2012 as the base year, prepare a trend analysis for the data that follow, and tell whether the results suggest a favorable or unfavorable trend. (Round to one decimal place.)

	2014	2013	2012
Net sales	$316,000	$272,000	$224,000
Accounts receivable (net)	86,000	64,000	42,000

LO 2 **Horizontal Analysis**

SE4. ACCOUNTING CONNECTION ▶ Vision, Inc.'s comparative income statements follow. Compute the amount and percentage changes for the income statements, and comment on the changes from 2013 to 2014. (Round the percentage changes to one decimal place.)

(Continued)

Vision, Inc.
Comparative Income Statements
For the Years Ended December 31, 2014 and 2013

	2014	2013
Net sales	$360,000	$290,000
Cost of goods sold	224,000	176,000
Gross margin	$136,000	$114,000
Operating expenses	80,000	60,000
Operating income	$ 56,000	$ 54,000
Interest expense	14,000	10,000
Income before income taxes	$ 42,000	$ 44,000
Income taxes expense	14,000	16,000
Net income	$ 28,000	$ 28,000
Earnings per share	$ 2.80	$ 2.80

LO 2 **Vertical Analysis**

SE5. ACCOUNTING CONNECTION ▶ Vision, Inc.'s comparative balance sheets follow. Prepare common-size statements, and comment on the changes from 2013 to 2014. (Round to one decimal place.)

Vision, Inc.
Comparative Balance Sheets
December 31, 2014 and 2013

	2014	2013
Assets		
Current assets	$ 48,000	$ 40,000
Property, plant, and equipment (net)	260,000	200,000
Total assets	$308,000	$240,000
Liabilities and Stockholders' Equity		
Current liabilities	$ 36,000	$ 44,000
Long-term liabilities	180,000	120,000
Stockholders' equity	92,000	76,000
Total liabilities and stockholders' equity	$308,000	$240,000

LO 3 **Operating Asset Management Analysis**

SE6. ACCOUNTING CONNECTION ▶ Using the information for Vision, Inc., in **SE4** and **SE5**, compute the current ratio, quick ratio, receivables turnover, days' sales uncollected, inventory turnover, days' inventory on hand, payables turnover, days' payable, and financing period for 2013 and 2014. Inventories were $8,000 in 2012, $10,000 in 2013, and $14,000 in 2014. Accounts receivable were $12,000 in 2012, $16,000 in 2013, and $20,000 in 2014. Accounts payable were $18,000 in 2012, $20,000 in 2013, and $24,000 in 2014. The company had no marketable securities or prepaid assets. Comment on the results. (Round to one decimal place.)

LO 3 **Profitability and Total Asset Management Analysis**

SE7. ACCOUNTING CONNECTION ▶ Using the information for Vision, Inc., in **SE4** and **SE5**, compute the profit margin, asset turnover, and return on assets for 2013 and 2014. In 2012, total assets were $200,000. Comment on the results. (Round to one decimal place.)

LO 3 **Financial Risk Analysis**

SE8. ACCOUNTING CONNECTION ▶ Using the information for Vision, Inc., in **SE4** and **SE5**, compute the debt to equity ratio, return on equity, and the interest coverage ratio for 2013 and 2014. In 2012 total stockholders' equity was $60,000. Comment on the results. (Round to one decimal place.)

LO 3

Liquidity Analysis

SE9. ACCOUNTING CONNECTION ▶ Using the information for Vision, Inc., in **SE4**, **SE5**, and **SE7**, compute the cash flow yield, cash flows to sales, cash flows to assets, and free cash flow for 2013 and 2014. Net cash flows from operating activities were $42,000 in 2013 and $32,000 in 2014. Net capital expenditures were $60,000 in 2013 and $80,000 in 2014. Cash dividends were $12,000 in both years. Comment on the results. (Round to one decimal place.)

LO 3

Market Strength Analysis

SE10. ACCOUNTING CONNECTION ▶ Using the information for Vision, Inc., in **SE4**, **SE5**, and **SE9**, compute the price/earnings (P/E) ratio and dividend yield for 2013 and 2014. The company had 10,000 shares of common stock outstanding in both years. The price of Vision's common stock was $60 in 2013 and $40 in 2014. Comment on the results. (Round to one decimal place.)

LO 4

Quality of Earnings

SE11. BUSINESS APPLICATION ▶ Each of the items that follow is a quality of earnings issue. Indicate whether the item is (a) an accounting method, (b) an accounting estimate, or (c) a nonoperating item. For any item for which the answer is (a) or (b), indicate which alternative is usually the more conservative choice.

1. LIFO versus FIFO
2. Extraordinary loss
3. 10-year useful life versus 15-year useful life
4. Straight-line versus accelerated method
5. Discontinued operations
6. Immediate write-off versus amortization
7. Increase versus decrease in percentage of uncollectible accounts

LO 4

Corporate Income Statement

SE12. BUSINESS APPLICATION ▶ Assume that Karib Corporation's chief financial officer gave you the following information: net sales, $720,000; cost of goods sold, $350,000; loss from discontinued operations (net of income tax benefit of $70,000), $200,000; loss on disposal of discontinued operations (net of income tax benefit of $16,000), $50,000; operating expenses, $130,000; income taxes expense on continuing operations, $100,000. Prepare the company's income statement for the year ended June 30, 2014. (Ignore earnings per share information.)

EXERCISES: SET A

LO 1

Issues in Financial Performance Evaluation: Objectives, Standards, Sources of Information, and Executive Compensation

E1A. CONCEPT ▶ Identify each of the following as (a) an underlying concept, (b) an objective of financial statement analysis, (c) a standard for financial statement analysis, (d) a source of information for financial statement analysis, or (e) an executive compensation issue:

1. Past ratios of the company
2. Linking performance to shareholder value
3. Average ratios of other companies in the same industry
4. Assessment of the future potential of an investment
5. Timeliness
6. Interim financial statements
7. SEC Form 10-K
8. Assessment of risk
9. Comparability
10. A company's annual report

LO 2   **Trend Analysis**

E2A. ACCOUNTING CONNECTION ▶ Using 2010 as the base year, prepare a trend analysis of the data that follow, and tell whether the situation shown by the trends is favorable or unfavorable. (Round to one decimal place.)

	2014	2013	2012	2011	2010
Net sales	$51,040	$47,960	$48,400	$45,760	$44,000
Cost of goods sold	34,440	30,800	31,080	29,400	28,000
General and administrative expenses	10,560	10,368	10,176	9,792	9,600
Operating income	6,040	6,792	7,144	6,568	6,400

LO 2   **Horizontal Analysis**

E3A. ACCOUNTING CONNECTION ▶ Compute the amount and percentage changes for Rivera Company's comparative balance sheets, and comment on the changes from 2013 to 2014. (Round the percentage changes to one decimal place.)

Rivera Company
Comparative Balance Sheets
December 31, 2014 and 2013

	2014	2013
Assets		
Current assets	$ 37,200	$ 25,600
Property, plant, and equipment (net)	218,928	194,400
Total assets	$256,128	$220,000
Liabilities and Stockholders' Equity		
Current liabilities	$ 22,400	$ 6,400
Long-term liabilities	70,000	80,000
Stockholders' equity	163,728	133,600
Total liabilities and stockholders' equity	$256,128	$220,000

LO 2   **Vertical Analysis**

E4A. ACCOUNTING CONNECTION ▶ Express Rivera Company's partial comparative income statements as common-size statements, and comment on the changes from 2013 to 2014.

Rivera Company
Partial Comparative Income Statements
For the Years Ended December 31, 2014 and 2013

	2014	2013
Net sales	$424,000	$368,000
Cost of goods sold	254,400	239,200
Gross margin	$169,600	$128,800
Selling expenses	$106,000	$ 73,600
General expenses	50,880	36,800
Total operating expenses	$156,880	$110,400
Operating income	$ 12,720	$ 18,400

LO 3   **Operating Asset Management Analysis**

E5A. ACCOUNTING CONNECTION ▶ Partial comparative balance sheet and income statement information for Posad Company follows.

	2014	2013
Cash	$ 13,600	$ 10,400
Marketable securities	7,200	17,200
Accounts receivable (net)	44,800	35,600
Inventory	54,400	49,600
Total current assets	$120,000	$112,800
Accounts payable	$ 40,000	$ 28,200
Net sales	$322,560	$220,720
Cost of goods sold	217,600	203,360
Gross margin	$104,960	$ 17,360

In 2012, the year-end balances for Accounts Receivable and Inventory were $32,400 and $51,200, respectively. Accounts Payable was $30,600 in 2012 and is the only current liability. Compute the current ratio, quick ratio, receivables turnover, days' sales uncollected, inventory turnover, days' inventory on hand, payables turnover, days' payable for each year, and financing period. (Round to one decimal place.) Comment on the change in the company's liquidity position, including its operating cycle and required days of financing from 2013 to 2014.

LO 3

Turnover Analysis

E6A. ACCOUNTING CONNECTION ▶ Designer Suits Rental has been in business for four years. Because the company has recently had a cash flow problem, management wonders whether there is a problem with receivables or inventories. Selected figures from the company's financial statements (in thousands) follow.

	2014	2013	2012	2011
Net sales	$144.0	$112.0	$96.0	$80.0
Cost of goods sold	90.0	72.0	60.0	48.0
Accounts receivable (net)	24.0	20.0	16.0	12.0
Merchandise inventory	28.0	22.0	16.0	10.0
Accounts payable	13.0	10.0	8.0	5.0

Compute the receivables turnover, inventory turnover, and payables turnover for each of the four years, and comment on the results relative to the cash flow problem that the firm has been experiencing. Merchandise inventory was $11,000, accounts receivable were $11,000, and accounts payable were $4,000 in 2010. (Round to one decimal place.)

LO 3

Profitability and Total Asset Management Analysis

E7A. ACCOUNTING CONNECTION ▶ Elm Company had total assets of $640,000 in 2012, $680,000 in 2013, and $760,000 in 2014. In 2013, Elm had net income of $77,112 on revenues of $1,224,000. In 2014, it had net income of $98,952 on revenues of $1,596,000. Compute the profit margin, asset turnover, and return on assets for 2013 and 2014. Comment on the apparent cause of the increase or decrease in profitability. (Round to one decimal place.)

LO 3

Financial Risk and Market Strength Ratios

E8A. ACCOUNTING CONNECTION ▶ An investor is considering investing in the long-term bonds and common stock of Companies A and B. Both firms operate in the same industry. Both also pay a dividend per share of $8 and have a yield of 10 percent on their long-term bonds. Other data for the two firms follow.

(Continued)

	Company A	Company B
Total assets	$4,800,000	$2,160,000
Total liabilities	2,160,000	1,188,000
Prior year stockholders' equity	2,120,000	750,000
Income before income taxes	576,000	259,200
Interest expense	194,400	106,920
Net income	136,800	74,800
Earnings per share	6.40	10.00
Market price of common stock	80.00	95.00

Compute the debt to equity ratio, return on equity ratio, interest coverage ratio, and price/earnings (P/E) ratio, as well as the dividend yield, and comment on the results. (Round to one decimal place.)

LO 3

Liquidity Analysis

E9A. Using the data from the financial statements of Stanford, Inc., that follow, compute the company's cash flow yield, cash flows to sales, cash flows to assets, and free cash flow. (Round to one decimal place.)

Net sales	$3,200,000
Net income	352,000
Net cash flows from operating activities	456,000
Total assets, beginning of year	2,890,000
Total assets, end of year	3,120,000
Cash dividends	120,000
Net capital expenditures	298,000

LO 4

Effect of Alternative Accounting Methods

E10A. BUSINESS APPLICATION ▶ At the end of its first year of operations, a company calculated its ending merchandise inventory according to three different accounting methods, as follows: FIFO, $47,500; average-cost, $45,000; LIFO, $43,000. If the company used the average-cost method, its net income for the year would be $17,000.

1. Determine net income if the company used the FIFO method.
2. Determine net income if the company used the LIFO method.
3. Which method is more conservative?
4. **CONCEPT ▶** Will the consistency convention be violated if the company chooses to use the LIFO method? Why or why not?
5. **CONCEPT ▶** Does the full-disclosure convention require disclosure of the inventory method used in the financial statements?

LO 4

Corporate Income Statement

E11A. BUSINESS APPLICATION ▶ Assume that Stream Toy Corporation's chief financial officer gave you the following information: net sales, $3,800,000; cost of goods sold, $2,100,000; extraordinary gain (net of income taxes of $7,000), $25,000; loss from discontinued operations (net of income tax benefit of $60,000), $100,000; loss on disposal of discontinued operations (net of income tax benefit of $26,000), $70,000; selling expenses, $100,000; administrative expenses, $80,000; income taxes expense on continuing operations, $600,000. Prepare the company's income statement for the year ended June 30, 2014. (Ignore earnings per share information.)

LO 4 **Corporate Income Statement**

E12A. BUSINESS APPLICATION ▶ Components of Van Corporation's income statement for the year ended December 31, 2014 follow. Recast the income statement in multi-step form, including allocating income taxes to appropriate items (assume a 30 percent income tax rate) and showing earnings per share figures (200,000 shares outstanding). (Round earnings per share figures to the nearest cent.)

Sales	$1,110,000
Cost of goods sold	(550,000)
Operating expenses	(225,000)
Restructuring	(110,000)
Total income taxes expense for period	(179,100)
Income from discontinued operations	160,000
Gain on disposal of discontinued operations	140,000
Extraordinary gain	72,000
Net income	$ 417,900
Earnings per share	$ 2.09

EXERCISES: SET B

Visit the textbook companion website at www.cengagebrain.com to access Exercise Set B for this chapter.

PROBLEMS

LO 2 **Horizontal and Vertical Analysis**

✔ 1: Net income: 34.9% increase
✔ 1: Total assets: 3.6% increase
✔ 2: 2014 Net income: 4.2%

P1. Obras Corporation's condensed comparative income statements and comparative balance sheets for 2014 and 2013 follow.

Obras Corporation
Comparative Income Statements
For the Years Ended December 31, 2014 and 2013

	2014	2013
Net sales	$3,276,800	$3,146,400
Cost of goods sold	2,088,800	2,008,400
Gross margin	$1,188,000	$1,138,000
Operating expenses:		
Selling expenses	$ 476,800	$ 518,000
Administrative expenses	447,200	423,200
Total operating expenses	$ 924,000	$ 941,200
Income from operations	$ 264,000	$ 196,800
Interest expense	65,600	39,200
Income before income taxes	$ 198,400	$ 157,600
Income taxes expense	62,400	56,800
Net income	$ 136,000	$ 100,800
Earnings per share	$ 3.40	$ 2.52

(Continued)

Obras Corporation
Comparative Balance Sheets
December 31, 2014 and 2013

	2014	2013
Assets		
Cash	$ 81,200	$ 40,800
Accounts receivable (net)	235,600	229,200
Inventory	574,800	594,800
Property, plant, and equipment (net)	750,000	720,000
Total assets	$1,641,600	$1,584,800
Liabilities and Stockholders' Equity		
Accounts payable	$ 267,600	$ 477,200
Notes payable (short-term)	200,000	400,000
Bonds payable	400,000	—
Common stock, $10 par value	400,000	400,000
Retained earnings	374,000	307,600
Total liabilities and stockholders' equity	$1,641,600	$1,584,800

REQUIRED

1. Prepare schedules showing the amount and percentage changes from 2013 to 2014 for the comparative income statements and the balance sheets. (Round to one decimal place.)

2. Prepare common-size income statements and balance sheets for 2013 and 2014. (Round to one decimal place.)

3. **ACCOUNTING CONNECTION ▶** Comment on the results in requirements **1** and **2** by identifying favorable and unfavorable changes in the components and composition of the statements.

LO 3   **Effects of Transactions on Ratios**

RATIO

P2. Davis Corporation, a clothing retailer, engaged in the transactions that follow. Opposite each transaction is a ratio and space to mark the effect of each transaction on the ratio.

			Effect	
Transaction	**Ratio**	**Increase**	**Decrease**	**None**
a. Issued common stock for cash.	Asset turnover	____	____	____
b. Declared cash dividend.	Current ratio	____	____	____
c. Sold treasury stock.	Return on equity	____	____	____
d. Borrowed cash by issuing note payable.	Debt to equity ratio	____	____	____
e. Paid salaries expense.	Inventory turnover	____	____	____
f. Purchased merchandise for cash.	Current ratio	____	____	____
g. Sold equipment for cash.	Receivables turnover	____	____	____
h. Sold merchandise on account.	Quick ratio	____	____	____
i. Paid current portion of long-term debt.	Return on assets	____	____	____
j. Gave sales discount.	Profit margin	____	____	____
k. Purchased marketable securities for cash.	Quick ratio	____	____	____
l. Declared 5% stock dividend.	Current ratio	____	____	____
m. Purchased a building.	Free cash flow	____	____	____

REQUIRED

ACCOUNTING CONNECTION ▶ Show that you understand the effect of business activities on performance measures by placing an *X* in the appropriate column to show whether the transaction increased, decreased, or had no effect on the indicated ratio.

✔ 1a: 2014 Current ratio: 1.5 times
✔ 1e: 2014 Inventory turnover: 3.9 times
✔ 2c: 2014 Return on assets: 5.0%
✔ 3b: 2014 Return on equity: 8.2%
✔ 4a: 2014 Cash flow yield: 1.7 times
✔ 5b: 2014 Dividend yield: 1.3%

LO 3

Comprehensive Ratio Analysis

P3. Tuxedo Corporation's condensed comparative income statements and balance sheets follow. All figures are given in thousands of dollars, except earnings per share.

Tuxedo Corporation
Comparative Income Statements
For the Years Ended December 31, 2014 and 2013

	2014	2013
Net sales	$800,400	$742,600
Cost of goods sold	454,100	396,200
Gross margin	$346,300	$346,400
Operating expenses:		
Selling expenses	$130,100	$104,600
Administrative expenses	140,300	115,500
Total operating expenses	$270,400	$220,100
Income from operations	$ 75,900	$126,300
Interest expense	25,000	20,000
Income before income taxes	$ 50,900	$106,300
Income taxes expense	14,000	35,000
Net income	$ 36,900	$ 71,300
Earnings per share	$ 2.46	$ 4.76

Tuxedo Corporation
Comparative Balance Sheets
December 31, 2014 and 2013

	2014	2013
Assets		
Cash	$ 31,100	$ 27,200
Accounts receivable (net)	72,500	42,700
Inventory	122,600	107,800
Property, plant, and equipment (net)	577,700	507,500
Total assets	$803,900	$685,200
Liabilities and Stockholders' Equity		
Accounts payable	$104,700	$ 72,300
Notes payable (short-term)	50,000	50,000
Bonds payable	200,000	110,000
Common stock, $10 par value	300,000	300,000
Retained earnings	149,200	152,900
Total liabilities and stockholders' equity	$803,900	$685,200

Additional data for Tuxedo in 2014 and 2013 follow.

	2014	2013
Net cash flows from operating activities	$64,000	$99,000
Net capital expenditures	$119,000	$38,000
Dividends paid	$31,400	$35,000
Number of common shares	30,000	30,000
Market price per share	$80	$120

Balances of selected accounts at the end of 2012 were accounts receivable (net), $52,700; inventory, $99,400; accounts payable, $64,800; total assets, $647,800; and stockholders' equity, $376,600. All of the bonds payable were long-term liabilities.

(Continued)

REQUIRED

Perform the following analyses. (Round to one decimal place.)

1. Prepare an operating asset management analysis by calculating for each year the (a) current ratio, (b) quick ratio, (c) receivables turnover, (d) days' sales uncollected, (e) inventory turnover, (f) days' inventory on hand, (g) payables turnover, (h) days' payable, and (i) financing period.

2. Prepare a profitability and total asset management analysis by calculating for each year the (a) profit margin, (b) asset turnover, and (c) return on assets.

3. Prepare a financial risk analysis by calculating for each year the (a) debt to equity ratio, (b) return on equity, and (c) interest coverage ratio.

4. Prepare a liquidity analysis by calculating for each year the (a) cash flow yield, (b) cash flows to sales, (c) cash flows to assets, and (d) free cash flow.

5. Prepare an analysis of market strength by calculating for each year the (a) price/earnings (P/E) ratio and (b) dividend yield.

6. **ACCOUNTING CONNECTION** ▶ After making the calculations, indicate whether each ratio improved or deteriorated from 2013 to 2014 (use *F* for favorable and *U* for unfavorable and consider changes of 0.1 or less to be neutral).

LO 3

Comprehensive Ratio Analysis of Two Companies

P4. Mel Filbert is considering an investment in the common stock of a chain of retail department stores. She has narrowed her choice to two retail companies, Single Corporation and Design Corporation, whose income statements and balance sheets follow.

✔ 1b: Single quick ratio: 1.5 times
✔ 1g: Single payables turnover: 17.9 times
✔ 2b: Single asset turnover: 2.5 times
✔ 3a: Single debt to equity ratio: 1.0 time
✔ 4b: Single cash flow to sales: 2.2%
✔ 5a: Single price/earnings ratio: 13.9 times

Income Statements

	Single	Design
Net sales	$12,560,000	$25,210,000
Costs and expenses:		
Cost of goods sold	$ 6,142,000	$14,834,000
Selling expenses	4,822,600	7,108,200
Administrative expenses	986,000	2,434,000
Total costs and expenses	$11,950,600	$24,376,200
Income from operations	$ 609,400	$ 833,800
Interest expense	194,000	228,000
Income before income taxes	$ 415,400	$ 605,800
Income taxes expense	200,000	300,000
Net income	$ 215,400	$ 305,800
Earnings per share	$ 4.31	$ 10.19

Balance Sheets

	Single	Design
Assets		
Cash	$ 80,000	$ 192,400
Marketable securities (at cost)	203,400	84,600
Accounts receivable (net)	552,800	985,400
Inventory	629,800	1,253,400
Prepaid expenses	54,400	114,000
Property, plant, and equipment (net)	2,913,600	6,552,000
Intangibles and other assets	553,200	144,800
Total assets	$4,987,200	$9,326,600

Liabilities and Stockholders' Equity		
Accounts payable	$ 344,000	$ 572,600
Notes payable	150,000	400,000
Income taxes payable	50,200	73,400
Bonds payable	2,000,000	2,000,000
Common stock, $20 par value	1,000,000	600,000
Additional paid-in capital	609,800	3,568,600
Retained earnings	833,200	2,112,000
Total liabilities and stockholders' equity	$4,987,200	$9,326,600

During the year, Single paid a total of $50,000 in dividends. The market price per share of its stock is currently $60. In comparison, Design paid a total of $114,000 in dividends, and the current market price of its stock is $76 per share. Single had net cash flows from operations of $271,500 and net capital expenditures of $625,000. Design had net cash flows from operations of $492,500 and net capital expenditures of $1,050,000. Information for prior years is not readily available. Assume that all notes payable are current liabilities and all bonds payable are long-term liabilities and that there is no change in inventory.

REQUIRED

Conduct a comprehensive ratio analysis for each company, using the available informa-tion. Compare the results. (Round to one decimal place, and consider changes of 0.1 or less to be indeterminate.)

1. Prepare an operating asset management analysis by calculating for each company the (a) current ratio, (b) quick ratio, (c) receivables turnover, (d) days' sales uncol-lected, (e) inventory turnover, (f) days' inventory on hand, (g) payables turnover, (h) days' payable, and (i) financing period.
2. Prepare a profitability and total asset management analysis by calculating for each company the (a) profit margin, (b) asset turnover, and (c) return on assets.
3. Prepare a financial risk analysis by calculating for each company the (a) debt to equity ratio, (b) return on equity, and (c) interest coverage ratio.
4. Prepare a liquidity analysis by calculating for each company the (a) cash flow yield, (b) cash flows to sales, (c) cash flows to assets, and (d) free cash flow.
5. Prepare an analysis of market strength by calculating for each company the (a) price/earnings (P/E) ratio and (b) dividend yield.
6. **ACCOUNTING CONNECTION ▶** Compare the two companies by inserting the ratio calculations from 1 through 5 in a table with the following column headings: Ratio Name, Single, Design, and Company with More Favorable Ratio. Indicate in the last column which company had the more favorable ratio in each case.
7. **BUSINESS APPLICATION ▶** How could the analysis be improved if information about these companies' prior years were available?

LO 4

RATIO

SPREADSHEET

✔ 1: Net income using FIFO and straight line: $190,800
✔ 1: Net income using LIFO and double-declining-balance: $93,200

Effect of Alternative Accounting Methods

P5. BUSINESS APPLICATION ▶ Furlong Corporation began operations in 2014. At the beginning of the year, the company purchased plant assets of $900,000, with an esti-mated useful life of 10 years and no residual value. During the year, the company had net sales of $1,300,000, salaries expense of $200,000, and other expenses of $80,000, excluding depreciation. In addition, Furlong purchased inventory as follows.

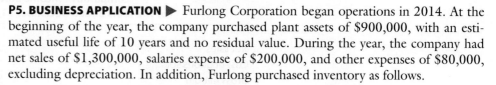

Jan. 15	400 units at $400	$160,000
Mar. 20	200 units at $408	81,600
June 15	800 units at $416	332,800
Sept. 18	600 units at $412	247,200
Dec. 9	300 units at $420	126,000
Total	2,300 units	$947,600

At the end of the year, a physical inventory disclosed 500 units still on hand. Furlong's managers know they have a choice of accounting methods, but they are unsure how those

(Continued)

methods will affect net income. They have heard of the FIFO and LIFO inventory methods and the straight-line and double-declining-balance depreciation methods.

REQUIRED

1. Prepare two income statements for Furlong, one using the FIFO and straight-line methods and the other using the LIFO and double-declining-balance methods. Ignore income taxes.
2. Prepare a schedule accounting for the difference in the two net income figures obtained in requirement **1**.
3. What effect does the choice of accounting method have on Furlong's inventory turnover? What conclusions can you draw? Use the year-end balance to compute the ratio. (Round to one decimal place.)
4. How does the choice of accounting methods affect Furlong's return on assets? Assume the company's only assets are cash of $80,000, inventory, and plant assets. Use year-end balances to compute the ratios. Is your evaluation of Furlong's profitability affected by the choice of accounting methods?

LO 4

Corporate Income Statement

✔ 1: Net income: $145,000

P6. BUSINESS APPLICATION ▶ Information concerning Krall Corporation's operations during 2014 follows.

a. Administrative expenses, $90,000
b. Cost of goods sold, $420,000
c. Extraordinary loss from an earthquake (net of taxes, $36,000), $60,000
d. Sales (net), $900,000
e. Selling expenses, $80,000
f. Income taxes expense applicable to continuing operations, $105,000

REQUIRED

1. Prepare the corporation's income statement for the year ended December 31, 2014 (ignore earnings per share data).
2. Which item in Krall's income statement affects the company's quality of earnings? Why does it have an effect on quality of earnings?

ALTERNATE PROBLEMS

LO 2

Horizontal and Vertical Analysis

P7. Rylander Corporation's condensed comparative income statements and balance sheets for 2014 and 2013 follow.

✔ 1: Net income, 34.9% increase
✔ 1: Total assets, 3.6% increase
✔ 2: 2014 Net income: 4.2%

Rylander Corporation
Comparative Income Statements
For the Years Ended December 31, 2014 and 2013

	2014	2013
Net sales	$6,553,600	$6,292,800
Cost of goods sold	4,177,600	4,016,800
Gross margin	$2,376,000	$2,276,000
Operating expenses:		
Selling expenses	$ 953,600	$1,036,000
Administrative expenses	894,400	846,400
Total operating expenses	$1,848,000	$1,882,400
Income from operations	$ 528,000	$ 393,600
Interest expense	131,200	78,400
Income before income taxes	$ 396,800	$ 315,200
Income taxes expense	124,800	113,600
Net income	$ 272,000	$ 201,600
Earnings per share	$ 3.40	$ 2.52

Rylander Corporation
Comparative Balance Sheets
December 31, 2014 and 2013

	2014	2013
Assets		
Cash	$ 162,400	$ 81,600
Accounts receivable (net)	471,200	458,400
Inventory	1,149,600	1,189,600
Property, plant, and equipment (net)	1,500,000	1,440,000
Total assets	$3,283,200	$3,169,600
Liabilities and Stockholders' Equity		
Accounts payable	$ 535,200	$ 954,400
Notes payable (short-term)	400,000	800,000
Bonds payable	800,000	—
Common stock, $10 par value	800,000	800,000
Retained earnings	748,000	615,200
Total liabilities and stockholders' equity	$3,283,200	$3,169,600

REQUIRED

1. Prepare schedules showing the amount and percentage changes from 2013 to 2014 for the comparative income statements and the balance sheets. (Round to one decimal place.)
2. Prepare common-size income statements and balance sheets for 2013 and 2014. (Round to one decimal place.)
3. **ACCOUNTING CONNECTION ▶** Comment on the results in requirements **1** and **2** by identifying favorable and unfavorable changes in the components and composition of the statements.

LO **3**

RATIO

Effects of Transactions on Ratios

P8. Koz Corporation engaged in the transactions that follow. Opposite each transaction is a ratio and space to indicate the effect of each transaction on the ratio.

		Effect		
Transaction	**Ratio**	**Increase**	**Decrease**	**None**
a. Sold merchandise on account.	Current ratio	___	___	___
b. Sold merchandise on account.	Inventory turnover	___	___	___
c. Collected on accounts receivable.	Quick ratio	___	___	___
d. Wrote off an uncollectible account.	Receivables turnover	___	___	___
e. Paid on accounts payable.	Current ratio	___	___	___
f. Declared cash dividend.	Return on equity	___	___	___
g. Incurred advertising expense.	Profit margin	___	___	___
h. Issued stock dividend.	Debt to equity ratio	___	___	___
i. Issued bonds payable.	Asset turnover	___	___	___
j. Accrued interest expense.	Current ratio	___	___	___
k. Paid previously declared cash dividend.	Dividend yield	___	___	___
l. Purchased treasury stock.	Return on assets	___	___	___
m. Recorded depreciation expense.	Cash flow yield	___	___	___

REQUIRED

ACCOUNTING CONNECTION ▶ Show that you understand the effect of business activities on performance measures by placing an *X* in the appropriate column to show whether the transaction increased, decreased, or had no effect on the indicated ratio.

Comprehensive Ratio Analysis

P9. Data for Obras Corporation in 2014 and 2013 follow. These data should be used in conjunction with the data in **P1**.

	2014	2013
Net cash flows from operating activities	$(196,000)	$144,000
Net capital expenditures	$40,000	$65,000
Dividends paid	$44,000	$34,400
Number of common shares	40,000	40,000
Market price per share	$36	$60

Selected balances at the end of 2012 were accounts receivable (net), $206,800; inventory, $547,200; total assets, $1,465,600; accounts payable, $386,600; and stockholders' equity, $641,200. All of Obras's notes payable were current liabilities; all its bonds payable were long-term liabilities.

REQUIRED

Perform a comprehensive ratio analysis following the steps outlined below. (Round to one decimal place.)

1. Prepare a operating asset management analysis by calculating for each year the (a) current ratio, (b) quick ratio, (c) receivables turnover, (d) days' sales uncollected, (e) inventory turnover, (f) days' inventory on hand, (g) payables turnover, (h) days' payable, and (i) financing period.
2. Prepare a profitability and total asset management analysis by calculating for each year the (a) profit margin, (b) asset turnover, and (c) return on assets.
3. Prepare a financial risk analysis by calculating for each year the (a) debt to equity ratio, (b) return on equity, and (c) interest coverage ratio.
4. Prepare a liquidity analysis by calculating for each year the (a) cash flow yield, (b) cash flows to sales, (c) cash flows to assets, and (d) free cash flow.
5. Prepare a market strength analysis by calculating for each year the (a) price/earnings (P/E) ratio and (b) dividend yield.
6. **ACCOUNTING CONNECTION ▶** After making the calculations, indicate whether each ratio improved or deteriorated from 2013 to 2014 (use *F* for favorable and *U* for unfavorable and consider changes of 0.1 or less to be neutral).

Comprehensive Ratio Analysis of Two Companies

P10. Lucy Lee is considering an investment in the common stock of a chain of retail department stores. She has narrowed her choice to two retail companies, Lucent Corporation and Ranbaxy Corporation, whose income statements and balance sheets follow.

Income Statements

	Lucent	Ranbaxy
Net sales	$50,240,000	$100,840,000
Costs and expenses:		
Cost of goods sold	$24,568,000	$ 59,336,000
Selling expenses	19,290,400	28,432,800
Administrative expenses	3,944,000	9,736,000
Total costs and expenses	$47,802,400	$ 97,504,800
Income from operations	$ 2,437,600	$ 3,335,200
Interest expense	776,000	912,000
Income before income taxes	$ 1,661,600	$ 2,423,200
Income taxes expense	800,000	1,200,000
Net income	$ 861,600	$ 1,223,200
Earnings per share	$ 8.62	$ 20.38

Balance Sheets

	Lucent	Ranbaxy
Assets		
Cash	$ 320,000	$ 769,600
Marketable securities (at cost)	813,600	338,400
Accounts receivable (net)	2,211,200	3,941,600
Inventory	2,519,200	5,013,600
Prepaid expenses	217,600	456,000
Property, plant, and equipment (net)	11,654,400	26,208,000
Intangibles and other assets	2,212,800	579,200
Total assets	$19,948,800	$37,306,400
Liabilities and Stockholders' Equity		
Accounts payable	$ 1,376,000	$ 2,290,400
Notes payable	600,000	1,600,000
Income taxes payable	200,800	293,600
Bonds payable	8,000,000	8,000,000
Common stock, $20 par value	4,000,000	2,400,000
Additional paid-in capital	2,439,200	14,274,400
Retained earnings	3,332,800	8,448,000
Total liabilities and stockholders' equity	$19,948,800	$37,306,400

During the year, Lucent paid a total of $200,000 in dividends. The market price per share of its stock is currently $120. In comparison, Ranbaxy paid a total of $456,000 in dividends, and the current market price of its stock is $152 per share. Lucent had net cash flows from operations of $1,086,000 and net capital expenditures of $2,500,000. Ranbaxy had net cash flows from operations of $1,970,000 and net capital expenditures of $4,200,000. Information for prior years is not readily available. Assume that all notes payable are current liabilities and all bonds payable are long-term liabilities and that there is no change in inventory.

REQUIRED

Conduct a comprehensive ratio analysis for each company, following the steps below. Compare the results. (Round to one decimal place, and consider changes of 0.1 or less to be indeterminate.)

1. Prepare an operating asset management analysis by calculating for each company the (a) current ratio, (b) quick ratio, (c) receivables turnover, (d) days' sales uncollected, (e) inventory turnover, (f) days' inventory on hand, (g) payables turnover, (h) days' payable, and (i) financing period.
2. Prepare a profitability and total asset management analysis by calculating for each company the (a) profit margin, (b) asset turnover, and (c) return on assets.
3. Prepare a financial risk analysis by calculating for each company the (a) debt to equity ratio, (b) return on equity, and (c) interest coverage ratio.
4. Prepare a liquidity analysis by calculating for each company the (a) cash flow yield, (b) cash flows to sales, (c) cash flows to assets, and (d) free cash flow.
5. Prepare an analysis of market strength by calculating for each company the (a) price/earnings (P/E) ratio and (b) dividend yield.
6. **ACCOUNTING CONNECTION ▶** Compare the two companies by inserting the ratio calculations from 1 through 5 in a table with the following column headings: Ratio Name, Lucent, Ranbaxy, and Company with More Favorable Ratio. Indicate in the last column which company had the more favorable ratio in each case.
7. **BUSINESS APPLICATION ▶** How could the analysis be improved if information about these companies' prior years were available?

LO **4**

✔ 1: Net income using FIFO and
straight line: $381,600
✔ 1: Net income using LIFO and
double-declining-balance: $186,400

Effect of Alternative Accounting Methods

P11. BUSINESS APPLICATION ▶ Minnows Corporation began operations in 2014. At the beginning of the year, the company purchased plant assets of $1,800,000, with an estimated useful life of 10 years and no residual value. During the year, the company had net sales of $2,600,000, salaries expense of $400,000, and other expenses of $160,000, excluding depreciation. In addition, Minnows purchased inventory as follows.

Jan. 15	800 units at $400	$ 320,000
Mar. 20	400 units at $408	163,200
June 15	1,600 units at $416	665,600
Sept. 18	1,200 units at $412	494,400
Dec. 9	600 units at $420	252,000
Total	4,600 units	$1,895,200

At the end of the year, a physical inventory disclosed 1,000 units still on hand. Minnows's managers know they have a choice of accounting methods, but they are unsure how those methods will affect net income. They have heard of the FIFO and LIFO inventory methods and the straight-line and double-declining-balance depreciation methods.

REQUIRED

1. Prepare two income statements for Minnows, one using the FIFO and straight-line methods and the other using the LIFO and double-declining-balance methods. Ignore income taxes.
2. Prepare a schedule accounting for the difference in the two net income figures obtained in requirement **1**.
3. What effect does the choice of accounting method have on Minnows's inventory turnover? What conclusions can you draw? Use the year-end balance to compute the ratio. (Round to one decimal place.)
4. How does the choice of accounting methods affect Minnows's return on assets? Assume the company's only assets are cash of $160,000, inventory, and plant assets. Use year-end balances to compute the ratios. Is your evaluation of Minnows's profitability affected by the choice of accounting methods? (Round to one decimal place.)

LO **4**

✔ 1: Net income: $176,000

Corporate Income Statement

P12. BUSINESS APPLICATION ▶ Income statement information for Linz Corporation in 2014 follows.

a. Administrative expenses, $220,000
b. Cost of goods sold, $880,000
c. Extraordinary loss from a storm (net of taxes, $20,000), $40,000
d. Income taxes expense, continuing operations, $84,000
e. Net sales, $1,780,000
f. Selling expenses, $380,000

REQUIRED

1. Prepare Linz's income statement for 2014 (ignore earnings per share data).
2. Which item in Linz's income statement affects the company's quality of earnings? Why does it have this effect?

CASES

Conceptual Understanding: Standards for Financial Performance Evaluation

C1. In 2005, in a dramatic move, **Standard & Poor's Ratings Group**, the large financial company that evaluates the riskiness of companies' debt, downgraded its rating of **General Motors** and **Ford Motor Co.** debt to "junk" bond status because of concerns about the companies' profitability and cash flows. Despite aggressive cost cutting, both companies still face substantial future liabilities for health care and pension obligations. They are losing money or barely breaking even on auto operations that concentrate on slow-selling SUVs. High gas prices and competition force them to sell the cars at a discount. What standards do you think Standard & Poor's would use to evaluate General Motors' progress? What performance measures would Standard & Poor's most likely use in making its evaluation? Was Standard & Poor's right in light of future events?

Interpreting Financial Reports: Using Segment Information

C2. Refer to Exhibit 1, which shows the segment information of **Goodyear Tire & Rubber Company**. In what business segments does Goodyear operate? What is the relative size of its business segments in terms of sales and income in the most recent year shown? Which segment is most profitable in terms of return on assets? Which segment is largest, and which segment is most profitable in terms of return on assets? (Round to one decimal place.)

Interpreting Financial Reports: Effect of a One-Time Item on a Loan Decision

C3. Apple a Day, Inc., and Unforgettable Edibles, Inc., are food catering businesses that operate in the same metropolitan area. Their customers include *Fortune* 500 companies, regional firms, and individuals. The two firms reported similar profit margins for the current year, and both base bonuses for managers on the achievement of a target profit margin and return on equity. Each firm has submitted a loan request to you, a loan officer for City National Bank. They have provided you with the following information:

	Apple a Day	Unforgettable Edibles
Net sales	$625,348	$717,900
Cost of goods sold	225,125	287,080
Gross margin	$400,223	$430,820
Operating expenses	281,300	371,565
Operating income	$118,923	$ 59,255
Gain on sale of real estate	—	81,923
Interest expense	(9,333)	(15,338)
Income before income taxes	$109,590	$125,840
Income taxes expense	25,990	29,525
Net income	$ 83,600	$ 96,315
Average stockholders' equity	$312,700	$390,560

1. Perform a vertical analysis and prepare a common-size income statement for each firm. Compute profit margin and return on equity. (Round to one decimal place.)
2. Discuss these results, the bonus plan for management, and loan considerations. Identify the company that is the better loan risk.

Interpreting Financial Reports: Comprehensive Ratio Analysis

C4. Refer to **CVS Corporation**'s 2011 annual report, which you can find using either the "Investor Relations" portion of its website (do a web search for CVS investor relations) or by going to www.sec.gov and, under the "Filings" tab, clicking on "Search for company filings." Using data from that report, conduct a comprehensive

(Continued)

ratio analysis that compares the company's performance in 2011 and 2010. Show all your computations. (Round to one decimal place.) After each group of ratios, comment on the performance of CVS. Prepare and comment on the following categories of ratios:

- Operating asset management analysis: current ratio, quick ratio, receivables turnover, days' sales uncollected, inventory turnover, days' inventory on hand, payables turnover, days' payable, and financing period (Accounts Receivable, Inventories, and Accounts Payable were [in millions] $5,457, $10,343, and $3,560, respectively, in 2009.)
- Profitability and total asset management analysis: profit margin, asset turnover, and return on assets (Total assets were [in millions] $61,641 in 2009.)
- Financial risk analysis: debt to equity ratio, return on equity, and interest coverage ratio (Total total shareholders' equity was [in millions] $35,768 in 2009.)
- Liquidity analysis: cash flow yield, cash flows to sales, cash flows to assets, and free cash flow
- Market strength analysis: price/earnings (P/E) ratio and dividend yield

LO 3

Interpreting Financial Reports: Comparison of Key Financial Performance Measures

C5. Refer to the 2011 annual reports for **CVS Corporation** and **Southwest Airlines Co.**, which you can find using either the "Investor Relations" portion of each company's website (do a web search for CVS and Southwest investor relations) or by going to www. sec.gov and, under the "Filings" tab, clicking on "Search for company filings." Prepare a table for the following key financial performance measures for the two most recent years for both companies. (Round to one decimal place.) Use your computations in **C4** or perform those analyses if you have not done so. Total assets for Southwest in 2009 were $14,269 million.

- Profitability and total asset management: profit margin, asset turnover, return on assets
- Financial risk: debt to equity ratio
- Liquidity: cash flow yield, free cash flow

Evaluate and comment on the relative performance of the two companies with respect to each of the above categories.

LO 4

Conceptual Understanding: Classic Quality of Earnings Case

C6. BUSINESS APPLICATION ▶ On January 19, 1988, **IBM** reported greatly increased earnings for the fourth quarter of 1987. Despite this reported gain in earnings, the price of IBM's stock on the New York Stock Exchange declined by $6 per share to $111.75. In sympathy with this move, most other technology stocks also declined.[15] IBM's fourth-quarter net earnings rose from $1.39 billion, or $2.28 a share, to $2.08 billion, or $3.47 a share, an increase of 49.6 percent and 52.2 percent over the same period a year earlier. Management declared that these results demonstrated the effectiveness of IBM's efforts to become more competitive and that, despite the economic uncertainties of 1988, the company was planning for growth. The apparent cause of the stock price decline was that the huge increase in income could be traced to nonrecurring gains. Investment analysts pointed out that IBM's high earnings stemmed primarily from such factors as a lower tax rate. Despite most analysts' expectations of a tax rate between 40 and 42 percent, IBM's was a low 36.4 percent, down from the previous year's 45.3 percent. Analysts were also disappointed in IBM's revenue growth. Revenues within the United States were down, and much of the company's growth in revenues came through favorable currency translations, increases that might not be repeated. In fact, some estimates of IBM's fourth-quarter earnings attributed $0.50 per share to currency translations and another $0.25 to tax-rate changes. Other factors contributing to IBM's rise in earnings were one-time transactions, such as the sale of **Intel Corporation** stock and bond redemptions, along with a corporate stock buyback program that reduced the amount of stock outstanding in the fourth quarter by 7.4 million shares. The analysts were concerned about the quality of IBM's earnings. Identify four quality of earnings issues reported in the case and the analysts' concern about each. In percentage terms, what is the impact of the currency changes on fourth quarter earnings? (Round to one decimal place.)

(*Optional*) Comment on management's assessment of IBM's performance.

Continuing Case: Annual Report Project

C7. Using the most recent annual report of the company you have chosen to study and that you have accessed online at the company's website, examine the financial statements and accompanying notes of your company. Conduct a comprehensive financial analysis for the past two years, as follows. (Round to one decimal place.)

- Operating asset management analysis: current ratio, quick ratio, receivables turnover, days' sales uncollected, inventory turnover, days' inventory on hand, payables turnover, days' payable, and financing period
- Profitability and total asset management analysis: profit margin, asset turnover, and return on assets
- Financial risk analysis: debt to equity ratio, return on equity, and interest coverage ratio
- Liquidity analysis: cash flow yield, cash flows to sales, cash flows to assets, and free cash flow
- Market strength analysis: price/earnings (P/E) ratio and dividend yield

APPENDIX A

The Time Value of Money

The **time value of money** is the concept that cash flows of equal dollar amounts separated by an interval of time have different present values because of the effect of compound interest. The notions of interest, present value, present value of an ordinary annuity, and annuity due are all related to the time value of money.

Interest

Interest is the cost associated with the use of money for a specific period of time.

Simple Interest

Measure **Simple interest** is the interest cost for one or more periods when the amount on which the interest is computed stays the same from period to period.

Example If you accept an 8 percent, $30,000 note due in 90 days, how much will you receive in total when the note comes due?

$$\text{Interest Expense} = \text{Principal} \times \text{Rate} \times \text{Time}$$
$$= \$30,000 \times 8/100 \times 90/360$$
$$= \underline{\underline{\$600}}$$

The total that you will receive is computed as follows.

$$\text{Total} = \text{Principal} + \text{Interest}$$
$$= \$30,000 + \$600$$
$$= \underline{\underline{\$30,600}}$$

Compound Interest

Measure **Compound interest** is the interest cost for two or more periods when the amount on which interest is computed includes all interest paid in previous periods.

Example You make a deposit of $5,000 in a savings account that pays 6 percent interest. You expect to leave the principal and accumulated interest in the account for three years. What will be your account balance at the end of the three years? Assuming that the interest is paid at the end of the year, that the interest is added to the principal at that time, and that this total in turn earns interest, the amount at the end of three years is computed as follows.

(1) Year	(2) Principal Amount at Beginning of Year	(3) Annual Amount of Interest (Col. 2 × 0.06)	(4) Accumulated Amount at End of Year (Col. 2 + Col. 3)
1	$5,000.00	$300.00	$5,300.00
2	5,300.00	318.00	5,618.00
3	5,618.00	337.08	5,955.08

At the end of three years, you will have $5,955.08 in your savings account.

Present Value

Present Value

Measure **Present value** is the amount that must be invested today at a given rate of compound interest to produce a given value at a future date.

Example Home State Bank needs $1,000 one year from now. How much should it invest today to achieve that goal if the interest rate is 5 percent?

$$\text{Present Value} \times (1.0 + \text{Interest Rate}) = \text{Future Value}$$
$$\text{Present Value} \times 1.05 = \$1,000.00$$
$$\text{Present Value} = \$1,000.00 \div 1.05$$
$$= \$952.38^*$$

*Rounded

Thus, to achieve a future value of $1,000.00, a present value of $952.38 must be invested. Interest of 5 percent on $952.38 for one year equals $47.62, and the two amounts added together equal $1,000.00.

Present Value of a Single Sum Due in the Future

Measure Present value that must be invested today at a given rate of compound interest to produce a given value at a date multiple time periods in the future.

Example Home State Bank wants to be sure of having $4,000 at the end of three years. How much must the company invest today in a 5 percent savings account to achieve that goal?

Manual Computation By adapting the preceding equation, the present value of $4,000 at compound interest of 5 percent for three years in the future may be computed as follows.

Year	Amount at End of Year	÷	1.0 + Interest Rate	=	Present Value at Beginning of Year
3	$4,000.00	÷	1.05	=	$3,809.52
2	3,809.52	÷	1.05	=	3,628.11
1	3,628.11	÷	1.05	=	3,455.34

Home State Bank must invest a present value of $3,455.34 to achieve a future value of $4,000 in three years.

Table Computation Table 1 is used to compute the value today of a single amount of cash to be received sometime in the future. To use Table 1, you must first know (1) the time period in years until funds will be received, (2) the stated annual rate of interest, and (3) the dollar amount to be received at the end of the time period.

In Table 1, look down the 5 percent column, finding the row for period 3. The factor there is 0.864. Multiplied by $1, this factor gives the present value of $1 to be received three years from now at 5 percent interest. For Home State Bank, the present value would be solved as follows.

$$\text{Present Value} = \text{Future Value} \times \text{Present Value Factor}$$
$$= \$4,000 \times 0.864$$
$$= \$3,456$$

Except for a rounding difference of $0.66, this gives the same result as the previous calculation.

The factor values for Table 1 are:

$$\text{PV Factor} = (1 + r)^{-n}$$

Where r is the rate of interest and n is the number of time periods.

Present Value of an Ordinary Annuity

Measure When we calculate the present value of equal amounts equally spaced over a period of time, we are computing the present value of an ordinary annuity. An **ordinary annuity** is a series of equal payments or receipts that will begin one time period from the current date.

Example Home State Bank has sold a piece of property and is to receive $15,000 in three equal annual cash payments of $5,000, beginning one year from today. What is the present value of this sale, assuming a current interest rate of 5 percent?

Manual Computation This present value can be determined by calculating a separate present value for each of the three payments (using Table 1) and summing the results, as follows.

Future Cash Receipts (Annuity)						
Year 1	Year 2	Year 3		Present Value Factor at 5 Percent (from Table 1)		Present Value
$5,000			×	0.952	=	$ 4,760
	$5,000		×	0.907	=	4,535
		$5,000	×	0.864	=	4,320
Total present value						$13,615

The present value of this sale is $13,615. Thus, there is an implied interest cost (given the 5 percent rate) of $1,385 associated with the payment plan that allows the purchaser to pay in three installments.

Table Computation Table 2 is used to compute the present value of a *series* of *equal* annual cash flows. Using Table 2, look down the 5 percent column, finding the row for period 3. The factor there is 2.723. That factor, when multiplied by $1, gives the present value of a series of three $1 payments, spaced one year apart, at compound interest of 5 percent. For Home State Bank, the present value would be solved as follows.

$$\text{Present Value} = \text{Periodic Payment} \times \text{Present Value Factor}$$
$$= \$5,000 \times 2.723$$
$$= \underline{\$13,615}$$

This result is the same as the one computed earlier.

The factor values for Table 2 are:

$$\text{PV Factor} = \frac{1 - (1 + r)^{-n}}{r}$$

Where r is the rate of interest and n is the number of time periods.

To summarize, if Home State Bank is willing to accept a 5 percent rate of return, management will be equally satisfied to receive a single cash payment of $13,615 today or three equal annual cash payments of $5,000 spread over the next three years.

Present Value of an Annuity Due

Measure An **annuity due** is a series of equal cash flows for N time periods, but the first payment occurs immediately. The present value of the first payment equals the face value of the cash flow; Table 2 then is used to measure the present value of N − 1 remaining cash flows.

Table Computation Home State Bank will make 20 lease payments; each payment of $10,000 is due on January 1, beginning in 2014. Determine the present value on January 1, 2014, assuming an interest rate of 8 percent.

$$\text{Present Value} = \text{Immediate Payment} + \text{Present Value of 19 Subsequent Payments at 8\%}$$
$$= \$10,000 + (\$10,000 \times 9.604)$$
$$= \underline{\$106,040}$$

APPLY IT!

For each of the following situations, identify the correct factor(s) to use from Table 1 or 2. Then use the factor(s) to compute the appropriate present value.

1. Annual net cash inflows of $35,000 for five years, discounted at 16 percent
2. An amount of $25,000 to be received at the end of ten years, discounted at 12 percent
3. The amount of $28,000 to be received at the end of two years, and $15,000 to be received at the end of years 4, 5, and 6, discounted at 10 percent.
4. The amount of 10 payments of $5,000 due on January 1, beginning immediately in 2014. Assume an interest rate of 10 percent.

SOLUTION

1. From Table 2, use factor 3.274, as follows.

    $35,000 × 3.274 = $114,590 present value

TABLE 1
Present Value of $1 to Be Received at the End of a Given Number of Time Periods

Periods	1%	2%	3%	4%	5%	6%	7%	8%	9%	10%	12%
1	0.990	0.980	0.971	0.962	0.952	0.943	0.935	0.926	0.917	0.909	0.893
2	0.980	0.961	0.943	0.925	0.907	0.890	0.873	0.857	0.842	0.826	0.797
3	0.971	0.942	0.915	0.889	0.864	0.840	0.816	0.794	0.772	0.751	0.712
4	0.961	0.924	0.888	0.855	0.823	0.792	0.763	0.735	0.708	0.683	0.636
5	0.951	0.906	0.883	0.822	0.784	0.747	0.713	0.681	0.650	0.621	0.567
6	0.942	0.888	0.837	0.790	0.746	0.705	0.666	0.630	0.596	0.564	0.507
7	0.933	0.871	0.813	0.760	0.711	0.665	0.623	0.583	0.547	0.513	0.452
8	0.923	0.853	0.789	0.731	0.677	0.627	0.582	0.540	0.502	0.467	0.404
9	0.914	0.837	0.766	0.703	0.645	0.592	0.544	0.500	0.460	0.424	0.361
10	0.905	0.820	0.744	0.676	0.614	0.558	0.508	0.463	0.422	0.386	0.322
11	0.896	0.804	0.722	0.650	0.585	0.527	0.475	0.429	0.388	0.350	0.287
12	0.887	0.788	0.701	0.625	0.557	0.497	0.444	0.397	0.356	0.319	0.257
13	0.879	0.773	0.681	0.601	0.530	0.469	0.415	0.368	0.326	0.290	0.229
14	0.870	0.758	0.661	0.577	0.505	0.442	0.388	0.340	0.299	0.263	0.205
15	0.861	0.743	0.642	0.555	0.481	0.417	0.362	0.315	0.275	0.239	0.183
16	0.853	0.728	0.623	0.534	0.458	0.394	0.339	0.292	0.252	0.218	0.163
17	0.844	0.714	0.605	0.513	0.436	0.371	0.317	0.270	0.231	0.198	0.146
18	0.836	0.700	0.587	0.494	0.416	0.350	0.296	0.250	0.212	0.180	0.130
19	0.828	0.686	0.570	0.475	0.396	0.331	0.277	0.232	0.194	0.164	0.116
20	0.820	0.673	0.554	0.456	0.377	0.312	0.258	0.215	0.178	0.149	0.104
21	0.811	0.660	0.538	0.439	0.359	0.294	0.242	0.199	0.164	0.135	0.093
22	0.803	0.647	0.522	0.422	0.342	0.278	0.226	0.184	0.150	0.123	0.083
23	0.795	0.634	0.507	0.406	0.326	0.262	0.211	0.170	0.138	0.112	0.074
24	0.788	0.622	0.492	0.390	0.310	0.247	0.197	0.158	0.126	0.102	0.066
25	0.780	0.610	0.478	0.375	0.295	0.233	0.184	0.146	0.116	0.092	0.059
26	0.772	0.598	0.464	0.361	0.281	0.220	0.172	0.135	0.106	0.084	0.053
27	0.764	0.586	0.450	0.347	0.268	0.207	0.161	0.125	0.098	0.076	0.047
28	0.757	0.574	0.437	0.333	0.255	0.196	0.150	0.116	0.090	0.069	0.042
29	0.749	0.563	0.424	0.321	0.243	0.185	0.141	0.107	0.082	0.063	0.037
30	0.742	0.552	0.412	0.308	0.231	0.174	0.131	0.099	0.075	0.057	0.033
40	0.672	0.453	0.307	0.208	0.142	0.097	0.067	0.046	0.032	0.022	0.011
50	0.608	0.372	0.228	0.141	0.087	0.054	0.034	0.021	0.013	0.009	0.003

2. From Table 1, use factor 0.322, as follows.

$25,000 × 0.322 = $8,050 present value

3. From Table 1, use the factors indicated in the table below.

Amount to Be Received	×	Present Value Factor	=	Present Value
$28,000	×	0.826	=	$23,128
15,000	×	0.683	=	10,245
15,000	×	0.621	=	9,315
15,000	×	0.564	=	8,460
Total				$51,148

4. From Table 2, use factor 5.759 as follows.

$5,000 + ($5,000 × 5.759) = $33,795

TABLE 1

Present Value of $1 to Be Received at the End of a Given Number of Time Periods (*Continued*)

14%	15%	16%	18%	20%	25%	30%	35%	40%	45%	50%	Periods
0.877	0.870	0.862	0.847	0.833	0.800	0.769	0.741	0.714	0.690	0.667	1
0.769	0.756	0.743	0.718	0.694	0.640	0.592	0.549	0.510	0.476	0.444	2
0.675	0.658	0.641	0.609	0.579	0.512	0.455	0.406	0.364	0.328	0.296	3
0.592	0.572	0.552	0.516	0.482	0.410	0.350	0.301	0.260	0.226	0.198	4
0.519	0.497	0.476	0.437	0.402	0.328	0.269	0.223	0.186	0.156	0.132	5
0.456	0.432	0.410	0.370	0.335	0.262	0.207	0.165	0.133	0.108	0.088	6
0.400	0.376	0.354	0.314	0.279	0.210	0.159	0.122	0.095	0.074	0.059	7
0.351	0.327	0.305	0.266	0.233	0.168	0.123	0.091	0.068	0.051	0.039	8
0.308	0.284	0.263	0.225	0.194	0.134	0.094	0.067	0.048	0.035	0.026	9
0.270	0.247	0.227	0.191	0.162	0.107	0.073	0.050	0.035	0.024	0.017	10
0.237	0.215	0.195	0.162	0.135	0.086	0.056	0.037	0.025	0.017	0.012	11
0.208	0.187	0.168	0.137	0.112	0.069	0.043	0.027	0.018	0.012	0.008	12
0.182	0.163	0.145	0.116	0.093	0.055	0.033	0.020	0.013	0.008	0.005	13
0.160	0.141	0.125	0.099	0.078	0.044	0.025	0.015	0.009	0.006	0.003	14
0.140	0.123	0.108	0.084	0.065	0.035	0.020	0.011	0.006	0.004	0.002	15
0.123	0.107	0.093	0.071	0.054	0.028	0.015	0.008	0.005	0.003	0.002	16
0.108	0.093	0.080	0.060	0.045	0.023	0.012	0.006	0.003	0.002	0.001	17
0.095	0.081	0.069	0.051	0.038	0.018	0.009	0.005	0.002	0.001	0.001	18
0.083	0.070	0.060	0.043	0.031	0.014	0.007	0.003	0.002	0.001		19
0.073	0.061	0.051	0.037	0.026	0.012	0.005	0.002	0.001	0.001		20
0.064	0.053	0.044	0.031	0.022	0.009	0.004	0.002	0.001			21
0.056	0.046	0.038	0.026	0.018	0.007	0.003	0.001	0.001			22
0.049	0.040	0.033	0.022	0.015	0.006	0.002	0.001				23
0.043	0.035	0.028	0.019	0.013	0.005	0.002	0.001				24
0.038	0.030	0.024	0.016	0.010	0.004	0.001	0.001				25
0.033	0.026	0.021	0.014	0.009	0.003	0.001					26
0.029	0.023	0.018	0.011	0.007	0.002	0.001					27
0.026	0.020	0.016	0.010	0.006	0.002	0.001					28
0.022	0.017	0.014	0.008	0.005	0.002						29
0.020	0.015	0.012	0.007	0.004	0.001						30
0.005	0.004	0.003	0.001	0.001							40
0.001	0.001	0.001									50

TABLE 2

Present Value of $1 Received Each Period for a Given Number of Time Periods

Periods	1%	2%	3%	4%	5%	6%	7%	8%	9%	10%	12%
1	0.990	0.980	0.971	0.962	0.952	0.943	0.935	0.926	0.917	0.909	0.893
2	1.970	1.942	1.913	1.886	1.859	1.833	1.808	1.783	1.759	1.736	1.690
3	2.941	2.884	2.829	2.775	2.723	2.673	2.624	2.577	2.531	2.487	2.402
4	3.902	3.808	3.717	3.630	3.546	3.465	3.387	3.312	3.240	3.170	3.037
5	4.853	4.713	4.580	4.452	4.329	4.212	4.100	3.993	3.890	3.791	3.605
6	5.795	5.601	5.417	5.242	5.076	4.917	4.767	4.623	4.486	4.355	4.111
7	6.728	6.472	6.230	6.002	5.786	5.582	5.389	5.206	5.033	4.868	4.564
8	7.652	7.325	7.020	6.733	6.463	6.210	5.971	5.747	5.535	5.335	4.968
9	8.566	8.162	7.786	7.435	7.108	6.802	6.515	6.247	5.995	5.759	5.328
10	9.471	8.983	8.530	8.111	7.722	7.360	7.024	6.710	6.418	6.145	5.650
11	10.368	9.787	9.253	8.760	8.306	7.887	7.499	7.139	6.805	6.495	5.938
12	11.255	10.575	9.954	9.385	8.863	8.384	7.943	7.536	7.161	6.814	6.194
13	12.134	11.348	10.635	9.986	9.394	8.853	8.358	7.904	7.487	7.103	6.424
14	13.004	12.106	11.296	10.563	9.899	9.295	8.745	8.244	7.786	7.367	6.628
15	13.865	12.849	11.938	11.118	10.380	9.712	9.108	8.559	8.061	7.606	6.811
16	14.718	13.578	12.561	11.652	10.838	10.106	9.447	8.851	8.313	7.824	6.974
17	15.562	14.292	13.166	12.166	11.274	10.477	9.763	9.122	8.544	8.022	7.120
18	16.398	14.992	13.754	12.659	11.690	10.828	10.059	9.372	8.756	8.201	7.250
19	17.226	15.678	14.324	13.134	12.085	11.158	10.336	9.604	8.950	8.365	7.366
20	18.046	16.351	14.878	13.590	12.462	11.470	10.594	9.818	9.129	8.514	7.469
21	18.857	17.011	15.415	14.029	12.821	11.764	10.836	10.017	9.292	8.649	7.562
22	19.660	17.658	15.937	14.451	13.163	12.042	11.061	10.201	9.442	8.772	7.645
23	20.456	18.292	16.444	14.857	13.489	12.303	11.272	10.371	9.580	8.883	7.718
24	21.243	18.914	16.936	15.247	13.799	12.550	11.469	10.529	9.707	8.985	7.784
25	22.023	19.523	17.413	15.622	14.094	12.783	11.654	10.675	9.823	9.077	7.843
26	22.795	20.121	17.877	15.983	14.375	13.003	11.826	10.810	9.929	9.161	7.896
27	23.560	20.707	18.327	16.330	14.643	13.211	11.987	10.935	10.027	9.237	7.943
28	24.316	21.281	18.764	16.663	14.898	13.406	12.137	11.051	10.116	9.307	7.984
29	25.066	21.844	19.189	16.984	15.141	13.591	12.278	11.158	10.198	9.370	8.022
30	25.808	22.396	19.600	17.292	15.373	13.765	12.409	11.258	10.274	9.427	8.055
40	32.835	27.355	23.115	19.793	17.159	15.046	13.332	11.925	10.757	9.779	8.244
50	39.196	31.424	25.730	21.482	18.256	15.762	13.801	12.234	10.962	9.915	8.305

TABLE 2

Present Value of $1 Received Each Period for a Given Number of Time Periods (*Continued*)

14%	15%	16%	18%	20%	25%	30%	35%	40%	45%	50%	Periods
0.877	0.870	0.862	0.847	0.833	0.800	0.769	0.741	0.714	0.690	0.667	1
1.647	1.626	1.605	1.566	1.528	1.440	1.361	1.289	1.224	1.165	1.111	2
2.322	2.283	2.246	2.174	2.106	1.952	1.816	1.696	1.589	1.493	1.407	3
2.914	2.855	2.798	2.690	2.589	2.362	2.166	1.997	1.849	1.720	1.605	4
3.433	3.352	3.274	3.127	2.991	2.689	2.436	2.220	2.035	1.876	1.737	5
3.889	3.784	3.685	3.498	3.326	2.951	2.643	2.385	2.168	1.983	1.824	6
4.288	4.160	4.039	3.812	3.605	3.161	2.802	2.508	2.263	2.057	1.883	7
4.639	4.487	4.344	4.078	3.837	3.329	2.925	2.598	2.331	2.109	1.922	8
4.946	4.772	4.607	4.303	4.031	3.463	3.019	2.665	2.379	2.144	1.948	9
5.216	5.019	4.833	4.494	4.192	3.571	3.092	2.715	2.414	2.168	1.965	10
5.453	5.234	5.029	4.656	4.327	3.656	3.147	2.752	2.438	2.185	1.977	11
5.660	5.421	5.197	4.793	4.439	3.725	3.190	2.779	2.456	2.197	1.985	12
5.842	5.583	5.342	4.910	4.533	3.780	3.223	2.799	2.469	2.204	1.990	13
6.002	5.724	5.468	5.008	4.611	3.824	3.249	2.814	2.478	2.210	1.993	14
6.142	5.847	5.575	5.092	4.675	3.859	3.268	2.825	2.484	2.214	1.995	15
6.265	5.954	5.669	5.162	4.730	3.887	3.283	2.834	2.489	2.216	1.997	16
6.373	6.047	5.749	5.222	4.775	3.910	3.295	2.840	2.492	2.218	1.998	17
6.467	6.128	5.818	5.273	4.812	3.928	3.304	2.844	2.494	2.219	1.999	18
6.550	6.198	5.877	5.316	4.844	3.942	3.311	2.848	2.496	2.220	1.999	19
6.623	6.259	5.929	5.353	4.870	3.954	3.316	2.850	2.497	2.221	1.999	20
6.687	6.312	5.973	5.384	4.891	3.963	3.320	2.852	2.498	2.221	2.000	21
6.743	6.359	6.011	5.410	4.909	3.970	3.323	2.853	2.498	2.222	2.000	22
6.792	6.399	6.044	5.432	4.925	3.976	3.325	2.854	2.499	2.222	2.000	23
6.835	6.434	6.073	5.451	4.973	3.981	3.327	2.855	2.499	2.222	2.000	24
6.873	6.464	6.097	5.467	4.948	3.985	3.329	2.856	2.499	2.222	2.000	25
6.906	6.491	6.118	5.480	4.956	3.988	3.330	2.856	2.500	2.222	2.000	26
6.935	6.514	6.136	5.492	4.964	3.990	3.331	2.856	2.500	2.222	2.000	27
6.961	6.534	6.152	5.502	4.970	3.992	3.331	2.857	2.500	2.222	2.000	28
6.983	6.551	6.166	5.510	4.975	3.994	3.332	2.857	2.500	2.222	2.000	29
7.003	6.566	6.177	5.517	4.979	3.995	3.332	2.857	2.500	2.222	2.000	30
7.105	6.642	6.234	5.548	4.997	3.999	3.333	2.857	2.500	2.222	2.000	40
7.133	6.661	6.246	5.554	4.999	4.000	3.333	2.857	2.500	2.222	2.000	50

ENDNOTES

Chapter 1

1 http://imanet.org/about_ethics_statement.asp.
2 Based on Andrew Ross Sorkin, "Albertsons Nears Deal, Yet Again, To Sell Itself," *The New York Times*, January 23, 2006.
3 Based on Karen Lundebaard, "Bumpy Ride," *The Wall Street Journal*, May 21, 2001.
4 Based on Curtis C. Verschoor, "Economic Crime Results from Unethical Culture," *Strategic Finance*, March 2009.
5 *Statement No. 1A* (New York: Institute of Management Accountants, 1982).

Chapter 4

1 Adapted from "Just In Time, Toyota Production System & Lean Manufacturing," http://www.strategosinc.com/just_in_time.htm.

Chapter 6

1 Based on Omar Aguilar, "How Strategic Performance Management Is Helping Companies Create Business Value," *Strategic Finance*, January 2003.
2 Jeremy Hope and Robin Frase, "Who Needs Budgets?" *Harvard Business Review*, February 2003.

Chapter 7

1 EVA is a registered trademark of the consulting firm Stern Stewart & Company.

Chapter 8

1 www.irobot.com

Chapter 9

1 Based on Alan Fuhrman, "Your e-Banking Future," *Strategic Finance*, April 2002.

Chapter 11

1 Based on Christopher Lawton, "Anheuser-Busch Rolls Out the Price Jump," *The Wall Street Journal*, October 23, 2002.

Chapter 12

1 www.nist.gov/baldrige
2 www.iso.org

Chapter 13

1 Data from Amazon.com, Inc., Form 10-K, For the Fiscal Year Ended December 31, 2011.
2 Based on American Institute of Certified Public Accountants, *Accounting Trends & Techniques* (New York: AICPA, 2011).

3 Based on Martin Peers and Robin Sidel, "WorldCom Causes Analysts to Evaluate EBITDA's Role," *The Wall Street Journal*, July 15, 2002.
4 Based on Ian McDonald, "Companies Are Rolling in Cash. Too Bad," *The Wall Street Journal*, August 20, 2006; Justin Lahart, "U.S. Firms Build Up Record Cash Piles," *The Wall Street Journal*, June 11, 2010.
5 Based on Lulu Chang, "Companies Hoarding Cash," *CNBC*, July 19, 2010.
6 Based on "Free Cash Flow Standouts," *Upside Newsletter*, October 3, 2005.
7 Amazon.com, *Form 10-K*, For the Fiscal Year Ended December 31, 2011.
8 Gary Slutsker, "Look at the Birdie and Say: 'Cash Flow'," *Forbes*, October 25, 1993.
9 Jonathan Clements, "Yacktman Fund Is Bloodied but Unbowed," *The Wall Street Journal*, November 8, 1993.
10 Jeffery Laderman, "Earnings, Schmearnings—Look at the Cash," *BusinessWeek*, July 24, 1989.
11 Amazon.com, *Form 10-K*, For the Fiscal Year Ended December 31, 2011.
12 Data from Fleetwood Enterprises, Inc., *10Q*, July 29, 2001.
13 Enron Corporation, *Press Release*, October 16, 2001.

Chapter 14

1 Data from Starbucks Corporation, Form 10-K, For the Fiscal Year Ended October 2, 2011.
2 Based on "Fourteen Key Business Ratios," *dnb.com*, 2012.
3 Based on *Statement of Financial Accounting Standards No. 131*, "Segment Disclosures" (Norwalk, Conn.: Financial Accounting Standards Board, 1997).
4 Based on Belverd E. Needles, Jr., Anton Shigaev, Marian Powers, and Mark L. Frigo, "Strategy and Integrated Financial Ratio Performance Measures: A Longitudinal Multi-Country Study of High Performance Companies," in *Studies in Financial and Managerial Accounting*, vol. 20, edited by Marc Epstein and Jean-Francois Manzoni (London: JAI Elsevier Science Ltd., 2010), pp. 211–252.
5 Based on Belverd E. Needles, Jr., Marian Powers, and Mark L. Frigo, "Performance Measurement and Executive Compensation: Practices of High Performance Companies," in *Studies in Financial and Managerial Accounting*, vol. 18, edited by Marc Epstein and Jean-Francois Manzoni (London: JAI Elsevier Science Ltd., 2008).
6 Based on Starbucks Corporation, Form 10-K, For the Fiscal Year Ended October 2, 2011.
7 Ibid.
8 Based on "After Charge for Licensing, McDonald's Posts a Record Loss," *The New York Times*, July 25, 2007; Christina Cheddar Berk, "Campbell's Profit Jumps 31 Percent," *The Wall Street Journal*, November 22, 2005.
9 Based on American Institute of Certified Public Accountants, *Accounting Trends & Techniques* (New York: AICPA, 2011); Starbucks Corporation, Form 10-K, For the Fiscal Year Ended October 2, 2011; Starbucks Corporation, Form 10-K, For the Fiscal Year Ended September 27, 2009.
10 Based on Jonathan Weil, "Pro Forma in Earnings Reports?... As If," *The Wall Street Journal*, April 24, 2003.
11 Based on David Henry, "The Numbers Game," *BusinessWeek*, May 14, 2001.
12 Starbucks Corporation, *Proxy Statement*, 2011.
13 Ibid.
14 Ibid.
15 Based on "Technology Firms Post Strong Earnings but Stock Prices Decline Sharply," *The Wall Street Journal*, January 21, 1988; Donald R. Seace, "Industrials Plunge 57.2 Points—Technology Stocks' Woes Cited," *The Wall Street Journal*, January 21, 1988.

GLOSSARY

A

Accounting rate-of-return method A method of evaluating capital investments designed to measure the estimated performance of a potential capital project. It is calculated by dividing the project's average annual net income by the average cost of the investment. (p. 374)

Activity base The activity for which relationships are established. Also called *denominator activity* or *cost driver*. (p. 166)

Activity-based costing (ABC) A method of assigning costs that calculates a more accurate product cost than traditional methods by categorizing all indirect costs by activity, tracing the indirect costs to those activities, and assigning those costs to products using a cost driver related to the cause of the cost. (pp. 59, 127)

Activity-based management (ABM) An approach to managing an organization that identifies all major operating activities, determines the resources consumed by each activity and the cause of the resource usage, categorizes the activities as either adding value to a product or service or not adding value, and seeks to reduce or eliminate non-value-adding activities. (p. 127)

Actual costing method A method of cost measurement that uses the actual costs of direct materials, direct labor, and overhead to calculate a product or service unit cost. (p. 17)

Appraisal costs The costs of activities that measure, evaluate, or audit products, processes, or services to ensure their conformance to quality standards and performance requirements. (p. 440)

Asset turnover A measure of profitability that shows how efficiently assets are used to produce sales; calculated as Net Revenue ÷ Average Total Assets. (pp. 257, 541)

Auction-based pricing Occurs when sellers post what they have for sale, ask for price bids, and accept the buyer's offer to purchase at a certain price; also occurs when buyers post what they want, ask for prices, and accept a seller's offer to sell at a certain price. (p. 398)

Average costing method A process costing method that assigns an average cost to all products made during an accounting period. (p. 88)

Avoidable costs Costs that can be eliminated by dropping a segment. (p. 338)

B

Backflush costing A product costing approach in which all product costs are first accumulated in the Cost of Goods Sold account and at the end of the period are "flushed back," or worked backward, into the appropriate inventory accounts. (p. 135)

Balanced scorecard A framework that links the perspectives of an organization's four basic stakeholder groups—financial (investors), learning and growth (employees), internal business processes, and customers—with the organization's mission and vision, performance measures, strategic and tactical plans, and resources. (p. 260)

Base year In financial analysis, the first year to be considered in any set of data. (p. 534)

Batch-level activities Activities performed each time a batch of goods is produced. (p. 128)

Benchmarking A technique for determining a company's competitive advantage by comparing its performance with that of its closest competitors. (pp. 262, 436)

Benchmarks Measures of the best practices in an industry. (p. 262)

Bill of activities A list of activities and related costs that is used to compute the costs assigned to activities and the product unit cost. (p. 129)

Breakeven point The point at which total revenues equal total costs. (p. 173)

Budget(s) Plan of action based on forecasted transactions, activities, and events; includes a forecasted income statement, statement of cash flows, and balance sheet. (pp. 20, 200)

Budget committee A committee made up of top management that has overall responsibility for budget implementation. (p. 220)

Budgeted balance sheet A statement that projects an organization's financial position at the end of an accounting period. (p. 216)

Budgeted income statement A projection of an organization's net income for an accounting period based on the revenues and expenses estimated for that accounting period. (p. 212)

Budgeting The process of identifying, gathering, summarizing, and communicating financial and nonfinancial information about an organization's future activities. (p. 200)

Business plan A comprehensive statement of how a company will achieve its strategic, tactical, and operating objectives. (p. 20)

C

Capital expenditures budget A detailed plan outlining the anticipated amount and timing of capital outlays for long-term assets during an accounting period. (p. 213)

Capital investment analysis The process of making decisions about capital investments. It includes identifying the need for a capital investment, analyzing courses of action to meet that need, preparing reports for managers, choosing the best alternative, and dividing funds among competing needs. Also called *capital budgeting*. (p. 366)

Capital investment decisions Management decisions about when and how much to spend on capital facilities and other long-term projects. (p. 366)

Carrying value The unexpired portion of an asset's cost. Also called *book value*. (p. 369)

Cash budget A projection of the cash that an organization will receive and the cash that it will pay out during an accounting period. (p. 213)

Cash flow yield A measure of a company's ability to generate operating cash flows in relation to net income; calculated as Net Cash Flows from Operating Activities ÷ Net Income. (p. 543)

Cash flows to assets A measure of the ability of assets to generate operating cash flows; calculated as Net Cash Flows from Operating Activities ÷ Average Total Assets. (p. 544)

Cash flows to sales A measure of the ability of sales to generate operating cash flows; calculated as Net Cash Flows from Operating Activities ÷ Net Sales. (p. 543)

Committed costs The costs of design, development, engineering, testing, and production that are engineered into a product or service at the design stage of development. (p. 405)

Common-size statement A financial statement in which the components are expressed as percentages of a total figure in the statement. (p. 537)

Compensation committee A committee of independent directors appointed by a public

corporation's board of directors to determine how top executives will be compensated. (p. 557)

Computer-aided design (CAD) A computer-based engineering system with a built-in program to identify poorly designed parts or manufacturing processes, which means that engineers can correct these problems before production begins. (p. 442)

Computer-integrated manufacturing (CIM) systems The use of computers to coordinate the production and its support operations. (p. 443)

Consistency The convention requiring that once a company has adopted an accounting procedure, it must use it from one period to the next unless a note to the financial statements informs users of a change in procedure. (p. 554)

Continuous budget A rolling 12-month budget that summarizes budgets for the next 12 months. Each month managers prepare a budget for that month, 12 months hence. (p. 220)

Continuous improvement The management concept that one should never be satisfied with what is, but should instead constantly seek improved efficiency and lower cost through better methods, products, services, processes, or resources. (p. 138)

Contribution margin (CM) The amount that remains after all variable costs are subtracted from sales. (p. 171)

Contribution margin income statement An income statement that is formatted to emphasize cost behavior rather than organizational functions (sometimes referred to as a variable costing income statement). (p. 171)

Controllable costs and revenues Costs and revenues that are the result of a manager's actions, influence, or decisions. (p. 249)

Conversion costs The costs of converting direct materials into a finished product; the sum of direct labor costs and overhead costs. Also called *processing costs*. (pp. 6, 89, 136)

Core competency The activity that a company does best and that gives it an advantage over its competitors. (p. 124)

Cost allocation The process of assigning a collection of indirect costs to a specific cost object using an allocation base known as a cost driver. (p. 55)

Cost behavior The way costs respond to changes in volume or activity. (p. 164)

Cost center A responsibility center whose manager is accountable only for controllable costs that have well-defined relationships between the center's resources and certain products or services. (p. 250)

Cost driver An activity base that causes a cost pool to increase in amount as the cost driver increases in volume. (p. 552)

Cost hierarchy A framework for classifying activities according to the level at which their costs are incurred. (p. 128)

Cost object The destination of an assigned, or allocated, cost. (p. 55)

Cost of capital The minimum desired rate of return on an investment, such as assets invested in an investment center. (p. 259)

Cost of goods manufactured The cost of all units completed and moved to Finished Goods Inventory during an accounting period. (p. 720)

Cost of goods manufactured budget A detailed plan that summarizes the estimated costs of production during an accounting period. (p. 918)

Cost of goods sold The amount a merchandiser paid for the merchandise it sold during an accounting period or the cost to a manufacturer of making the products it sold during an accounting period. Also called *cost of sales* or *cost of revenue*. (p. 12)

Cost-plus contracts Job contracts that require the customer to pay all costs incurred in performing the job plus a predetermined amount of profit. (p. 53)

Cost-plus transfer price A price based on either the full cost or the variable costs incurred by the producing division plus an agreed-on profit percentage. (p. 408)

Cost pool The collection of overhead costs assigned to a cost object. (p. 55)

Cost savings The decrease in operating costs that will result from the proposed capital investments. (p. 369)

Cost-volume-profit (CVP) analysis An examination of the cost behavior patterns that underlie the relationships among cost, volume of output, and profit. (p. 173)

Costs of conformance The costs of good quality that are incurred to ensure the successful development of a product or service. (p. 440)

Costs of nonconformance The costs of poor quality that are incurred to correct defects in a product or service. (p. 440)

Costs of quality Both the costs of achieving quality and the costs of poor quality in the manufacture of a product or the delivery of a service. (pp. 138, 440)

Current ratio A measure of liquidity, or short-term debt-paying ability; calculated as Current Assets ÷ Current Liabilities. (p. 549)

D

Days' inventory on hand A measure that shows the average number of days taken to sell inventory; calculated as Days in Accounting Period ÷ Inventory Turnover. (p. 547)

Days' payable A measure that shows the average number of days a company takes to pay its accounts payable; calculated as Days in Accounting Period ÷ Payables Turnover. (p. 549)

Days' sales uncollected A measure that shows the number of days, on average, that a company must wait to receive payment for credit sales; calculated as Days in Accounting Period ÷ Receivables Turnover. (p. 548)

Debt to equity ratio A measure of profitability that shows the proportion of a company's assets that is financed by creditors and the proportion financed by the stockholders; calculated as Total Liabilities ÷ Total Stockholders' Equity. (p. 545)

Decentralized organization A business that is organized into divisions or operating segments with a separate manager assigned to each segment. (p. 408)

Delivery cycle time The time between the acceptance of an order and the final delivery of the product or service to the customer. (p. 443)

Delivery time The time between the completion of a product and its receipt by the customer. (p. 443)

Deming Prize A prize created by the Japanese Union of Scientists and Engineers that honors individuals or groups who have contributed to the development and dissemination of total quality control. (p. 437)

Differential cost A cost that changes among alternatives. Also called an *incremental cost*. (p. 332)

Direct costs Costs that can be conveniently and economically traced to a cost object. (p. 4)

Direct labor budget A detailed plan that estimates the direct labor hours needed during an accounting period and the associated costs. (p. 208)

Direct labor costs The costs of the labor needed to make a product or perform a service that can be conveniently and economically traced to specific units of the product or service. (p. 5)

Direct labor efficiency variance The difference between the standard direct labor hours allowed for good units produced and the actual direct labor hours worked multiplied by the standard direct labor rate. Also called *direct labor quantity* or *usage variance*. (p. 299)

Direct labor rate standard The hourly direct labor rate that is expected to prevail during the next accounting period for each function or job classification. (p. 292)

Direct labor rate variance The difference between the standard direct labor rate and the actual direct labor rate multiplied by the actual direct labor hours worked. Also called *direct labor spending variance*. (p. 299)

Direct labor time standard The expected labor time required for each department, machine, or process to complete the production of one unit or one batch of output. (p. 292)

Direct materials costs The costs of the materials used in making a product that can be conveniently and economically traced to specific units of the product. (p. 5)

Direct materials price standard A careful estimate of the cost of a specific direct material in the next accounting period. (p. 291)

Direct materials price variance The difference between the standard price and the actual price per unit multiplied by the actual quantity purchased. Also called *direct materials spending* or *rate variance*. (p. 296)

Direct materials purchases budget A detailed plan that identifies the quantity of purchases required to meet budgeted production and inventory needs and the costs associated with those purchases. (p. 206)

Direct materials quantity standard An estimate of the amount of direct materials, including scrap and waste, that will be used in an accounting period. (p. 291)

Direct materials quantity variance The difference between the standard quantity allowed and the actual quantity used multiplied by the standard price. Also called *direct materials efficiency* or *usage variance.* (p. 296)

Discontinued operations Segments that are no longer part of a company's operations. (p. 556)

Discretionary cost center A responsibility center whose manager is accountable for costs only and in which the relationship between resources and the products or services produced is not well defined. (p. 958)

Diversified companies Companies that operate in more than one industry. Also called *conglomerates.* (p. 541)

Dividend yield A measure of a stock's current return to an investor in the form of dividends; calculated as Dividends per Share ÷ Market Price per Share. (p. 551)

E

Economic value added (EVA) The shareholder wealth created by an investment center; calculated as After-Tax Operating Income − [Cost of Capital in Dollars × (Total Assets − Current Liabilities)]. (p. 259)

EFQM Excellence Award An annual award presented by the European Foundation for Quality Management to businesses and organizations operating in Europe that excel in quality management. (p. 437)

Engineering method A method that separates costs into their fixed and variable components by performing a step-by-step analysis of the tasks, costs, and processes involved in completing an activity or product. (p. 171)

Enterprise resource planning (ERP) system A database system that combines the management of all major business activities with support activities to form one easy-to-access, centralized data warehouse. (p. 449)

Equivalent production A measure that applies a percentage-of-completion factor to partially completed units to compute the equivalent number of whole units produced during a period for each type of input. Also called *equivalent units.* (p. 89)

External failure costs The costs incurred to correct mistakes discovered by customers after the delivery of a defective product or service. (p. 440)

F

Facility-level activities Activities performed to support a facility's general manufacturing process. (p. 128)

Financial budgets Budget projections of the financial results for an accounting period. (p. 200)

Financial ratio analysis A technique of financial performance evaluation that identifies key relationships between components of the financial statements. (p. 540)

Financial statement analysis An evaluation method that shows how items in a company's financial statements relate to the company's financial performance objectives. Also called *financial performance measurement.* (p. 530)

Financing period The amount of time from the purchase of inventory until it is sold and payment is collected, less the amount of time creditors give the company to pay for the inventory. (p. 547)

Finished Goods Inventory account An inventory account that shows the costs assigned to all completed products that have not been sold. (p. 10)

First-in, first-out (FIFO) costing method A process costing method in which the cost flow follows the actual flow of production so that the costs assigned to the first products processed are the first costs transferred out when those products flow to the next process, department, or work cell. (p. 87)

Fixed cost(s) A cost that remains constant within a defined range of activity or time period. (pp. 6, 166)

Fixed cost formula A horizontal line in the relevant range, $Y = b$, where Y is total fixed cost and b is the fixed cost in the relevant range. (p. 166)

Fixed overhead budget variance The difference between budgeted and actual fixed overhead costs. Also called *budgeted fixed overhead variance.* (p. 306)

Fixed overhead volume variance The difference between budgeted fixed overhead costs and the overhead costs that are applied to production using the standard fixed overhead rate. (p. 306)

Flexible budget A summary of expected costs for a range of activity levels. Also called a *variable budget.* (p. 253)

Flexible budget formula An equation that determines the expected, or budgeted, cost for any level of output; calculated as (Variable Cost per Unit × Number of Units Produced) + Budgeted Fixed Costs. (p. 253)

Form 8-K Current reports filed by U.S. public corporations with the Securities and Exchange Commission. (p. 532)

Form 10-K An annual report filed by U.S. public corporations with the Securities and Exchange Commission. (p. 532)

Form 10-Q A quarterly report filed by U.S. public corporations with the Securities and Exchange Commission. (p. 532)

Free cash flow The amount of cash that remains after deducting the funds a company must commit to continue operating at its planned level; calculated as Net Cash Flows from Operating Activities − Dividends − Purchases of Plant Assets + Sales of Plant Assets. (p. 544)

Full disclosure The convention requiring that a company's financial statements and the accompanying notes present all information relevant to the users' understanding of the statements. Also called *transparency*. (p. 554)

Full product cost A cost that includes not only the costs of direct materials and direct labor but also the costs of all production and nonproduction activities required to satisfy the customer. (p. 124)

G

Goal/vision The overriding objective of a business to increase the value of the stakeholders' interest in the business. (p. 19)

Gross margin pricing method Emphasizes the use of income statement information to determine a selling price; also called the *income statement method*. (p. 399)

H

High-low method A three-step approach to separating a mixed cost into its variable and fixed components. (p. 170)

Horizontal analysis A technique for analyzing financial statements in which changes from the previous year to the current year are computed in both dollar amounts and percentages. (p. 534)

I

Incremental analysis A technique used in decision analysis that compares alternatives by focusing on the differences in their projected revenues and costs. Also called *differential analysis*. (p. 332)

Incremental revenue Total revenue if product/service is sold at split-off point minus total revenue if product/service is sold after further processing. (p. 343)

Incurred costs The actual costs incurred in making a product. (p. 405)

Index number In trend analysis, a number that shows changes in related items over time and that is calculated by setting the base year equal to 100 percent. (p. 536)

Indirect costs Costs that cannot be conveniently or economically traced to a cost object. (p. 4)

Indirect labor costs The costs of labor for production-related activities that cannot be conveniently or economically traced to a unit of the product or service. (p. 5)

Indirect materials costs The costs of materials that cannot be conveniently and economically traced to a unit of the product or service. (p. 5)

Indirect method The procedure for converting the income statement from an accrual basis to a cash basis by adjusting net income for items that do not affect cash flows, including depreciation, amortization, depletion, gains, losses, and changes in current assets and current liabilities. (p. 475)

Inspection time The time spent looking for product flaws or reworking defective units. (p. 133)

Interest coverage ratio A measure of the degree of protection a company has from default on interest payments; calculated as (Income Before Income Taxes + Interest Expense) ÷ Interest Expense. (p. 546)

Interim financial statements Financial statements issued for a period of less than one year, usually a quarter or a month. (p. 532)

Internal failure costs The costs incurred to correct mistakes found by the company when defects are discovered before a product or service is delivered to a customer. (p. 440)

Inventory turnover A ratio indicating the number of times a company's average inventory is sold during an accounting period; calculated as Cost of Goods Sold ÷ Average Inventory. (p. 547)

Investment center A responsibility center whose manager is accountable for profit generation and who can also make significant decisions about the resources the center uses. (p. 250)

ISO 9000 Guidelines created by the International Organization for Standardization (ISO) that cover the design, development, production, final inspection and testing, installation, and servicing of products, processes, and services. (p. 438)

ISO 14000 Guidelines created by the International Organization for Standardization (ISO) that provide a management framework to minimize the harmful environmental effects of business activities and continually improve environmental performance. (p. 439)

ISO 26000 Guidelines created by the International Organization for Standardization (ISO) that provide social responsibility guidance. (p. 439)

ISO 31000 Guidelines created by the International Organization for Standardization (ISO) that outline risk management principles and guidelines. (p. 439)

J

Job order A customer order for a specific number of specially designed, made-to-order products. (p. 46)

Job order cost card A document on which all costs incurred in the production of a particular job order are recorded; part of the subsidiary ledger for the Work in Process Inventory account. (p. 46)

Job order costing system A product costing system that traces the costs of direct materials, direct labor, and overhead to a specific batch of products or a specific job order; used by companies that make unique or special-order products. (p. 46)

Joint costs The common costs shared by two or more products before they are split off. Also called *common costs*. (p. 343)

Joint products Two or more products made from a common material or process that cannot be identified as separate products or services during some or all of the production process. (p. 343)

Just-in-time (JIT) operating philosophy A system that requires that all resources—materials, personnel, and facilities—be acquired and used only as needed; it focuses on eliminating or reducing waste in the production of products and services. (p. 131)

K

Kaizen Suggestions from employees for improvements to the production process. (pp. 133, 436)

L

Lean operation An operating philosophy that requires that all resources—materials, personnel, and facilities—be acquired and used only as needed to create value for customers; its objective is to reduce costs by eliminating waste. (p. 131)

M

Make-or-buy decisions Decisions about whether to make a part internally or buy it from an external supplier. (p. 335)

Malcolm Baldrige National Quality Award An award created by the U.S. Congress that recognizes U.S. organizations for their achievements in quality and business performance. (p. 438)

Management information systems (MIS) The interconnected subsystems that provide the information needed to run a business. (p. 449)

Managerial accounting The process of generating and communicating accounting information about operating, investing, and financing activities for internal use by managers. (p. 2)

Manufacturing cost flow The flow of manufacturing costs (direct materials, direct labor, and overhead) through the Materials Inventory, Work in Process Inventory, and Finished Goods Inventory accounts into the Cost of Goods Sold account. (p. 10)

Margin of safety The number of sales units or amount of sales dollars by which actual sales can fall below planned sales without resulting in a loss. (p. 173)

Marginal cost The change in total cost caused by a one-unit change in output. (p. 397)

Marginal revenue The change in total revenue caused by a one-unit change in output. (p. 397)

Market transfer price Based on the price that could be charged if a segment could buy from or sell to an external party; also called *external market price*. (p. 408)

Master budget A set of operating budgets and a set of financial budgets that detail an organization's financial plans for a specific accounting period. (p. 200)

Materials Inventory account An inventory account that shows the balance of the cost of unused materials. (p. 10)

Minimum rate of return The rate of return that must be exceeded to ensure profitability. Also called the *hurdle rate*. (p. 367)

Mission statement A description of the fundamental way in which a company will achieve the goal of increasing stakeholders' value. (p. 20)

Mixed cost formula A linear equation, $Y = a(X) + b$, where

Y is total mixed cost, a is the variable rate per unit, X is the units produced, and b is the fixed cost for the period. (p. 167)

Mixed costs Costs that have both variable and fixed components. (p. 167)

Moving time The time spent moving a product from one operation or department to another. (p. 133)

N

Negotiated transfer price A price arrived at through bargaining between the managers of the buying and selling divisions or segments. (p. 408)

Net cash inflows The balance of increases in projected cash receipts over increases in projected cash payments resulting from a capital investment. (p. 369)

Net present value method A method of evaluating capital investments in which all future cash flows for each proposed project are discounted to their present values and the amount of the initial investment is subtracted from their sum. The projects with the highest positive net present value—the amount that exceeds the initial investment—are selected for implementation. (p. 371)

Non-value-adding activity An activity that adds cost to a product or service but does not increase its market value. (p. 126)

Non-value-adding cost The cost of an activity that adds cost to a product or service but does not increase its market value. (p. 7)

Normal capacity The average annual level of operating capacity needed to meet expected sales demand. (p. 166)

Normal costing method A method of cost measurement that combines the actual direct costs of materials and labor with estimated overhead costs to determine a product or service unit cost. (p. 18)

O

Operating budgets Budget plans used in daily operations. (p. 200)

Operating capacity The upper limit of an organization's productive output capability, given its existing resources. (p. 165)

Operating cycle The time it takes to sell products and collect payment for them. (p. 547)

Operating objectives Short-term goals that outline expectations for the performance of day-to-day operations. (p. 20)

Operations costing system A product costing system that combines parts of job order costing and process costing to create a hybrid system designed specifically for an organization's production process. (p. 46)

Opportunity costs The benefits that are forfeited or lost when one alternative is chosen over another. (p. 334)

Organization chart A visual representation of an organization's hierarchy of responsibility for the purposes of management control. (p. 251)

Outsourcing The use of other companies to perform a process or service in the value chain that is not among an organization's core competencies. (pp. 124, 335)

Overapplied overhead costs The amount by which overhead costs applied using the predetermined overhead rate exceed the actual overhead costs for the accounting period. (p. 56)

Overhead budget A detailed plan of anticipated manufacturing costs, other than direct materials and direct labor costs, that must be incurred to meet budgeted production needs. (p. 208)

Overhead costs Production-related costs that cannot be practically or conveniently traced to an end product or service. Also called *factory overhead, factory burden, manufacturing overhead, service overhead,* or *indirect production costs.* (p. 5)

P

Participative budgeting A process in which personnel at all levels of an organization actively engage in making decisions about a budget. (p. 219)

Payables turnover The number of times, on average, that a company pays its accounts payable in an accounting period; calculated as (Cost of Goods Sold +/− Change in Merchandise Inventory) ÷ Average Accounts Payable (p. 548)

Payback period method A method of evaluating capital investments that bases the decision to invest in a capital project on the minimum length of time it will take to get back the amount of the initial investment in cash. The payback period is calculated by dividing the cost of investment by the annual net cash inflows. (p. 373)

Performance-based pay The linking of employee compensation to the achievement of measurable business targets. (p. 264)

Performance management and evaluation system A set of procedures that account for and report on both financial and nonfinancial performance so that a company can identify how well it is doing, where it is going, and what improvements will make it more profitable. (p. 248)

Performance measurement The use of quantitative tools to gauge an organization's performance in relation to a specific goal or an expected outcome. (p. 248)

Performance measures Quantitative tools that gauge and compare an organization's performance in relation to a specific goal or an expected outcome. (p. 248)

Period costs The costs of resources used during an accounting period that are not assigned to products or services. Also called *noninventoriable costs*

or *selling, administrative, and general expenses.* (p. 5)

Practical capacity Theoretical capacity reduced by normal and expected work stoppages. Also called *engineering capacity.* (p. 166)

Predetermined overhead rate The rate calculated before an accounting period begins by dividing the cost pool of total estimated overhead costs by the total estimated cost driver for that pool. (p. 56)

Prevention costs The costs associated with the prevention of defects and failures in products and services. (p. 440)

Price/earnings (P/E) ratio A measure of confidence in a company's future; calculated as Market Price per Share ÷ Earnings per Share. (p. 550)

Primary processes Components of the value chain that add value to a product or service. (p. 124)

Prime costs The primary costs of production; the sum of direct materials costs and direct labor costs. (p. 6)

Pro forma financial statements Financial statements that show projections rather than actual results and that are often used to communicate business plans to external parties. (p. 201)

Process cost report A report that managers use to track and analyze costs in a process costing system. (pp. 46, 87)

Process costing system A product costing system that traces the costs of direct materials, direct labor, and overhead to processes, departments, or work cells and then assigns the costs to the products manufactured by those processes, departments, or work cells; used by companies that produce large amounts of similar products or liquid products or that have long, continuous production runs of identical products. (pp. 46, 86)

Process mapping A method of using a visual diagram to indicate process inputs, outputs, constraints, and flows to help managers to identify unnecessary efforts and inefficiencies in a business process. (p. 437)

Process value analysis (PVA) A technique that analyzes business processes by relating activities to the events that prompt those activities and to the resources that the activities consume. (p. 125)

Processing time The actual amount of time spent working on a product. (p. 133)

Product costing system A set of procedures that is used to account for an organization's product costs and to provide timely and accurate unit cost information for pricing, cost planning and control, inventory valuation, and financial statement preparation. (p. 46)

Product costs The costs assigned to inventory, which include the costs of direct materials, direct labor, and overhead. Also called *inventoriable costs*. (p. 5)

Product-level activities Activities performed to support a particular product line. (p. 128)

Product unit cost The cost of manufacturing a single unit of a product, computed either by dividing the total cost of direct materials, direct labor, and overhead by the total number of units produced, or by determining the cost per unit for each element of the product cost and summing those per unit costs. (p. 5)

Production budget A detailed plan showing the number of units that a company must produce to meet budgeted sales and inventory needs. (p. 205)

Production cycle time The time it takes to make a product. (p. 443)

Profit center A responsibility center whose manager is accountable for both revenue and costs and for the resulting operating income. (p. 250)

Profit margin A measure of profitability that shows the percentage of each sales dollar that results in net income; calculated as Net Income ÷ Net Revenues (or Net Sales). (pp. 257, 541)

Pull-through production A production system in which a customer's order triggers the purchase of materials and the scheduling of production for the required products. (p. 132)

Purchase-order lead time The time it takes a company to take and process an order and organize so that production can begin. (p. 443)

Push-through production A production system in which products are manufactured in long production runs and stored in anticipation of customers' orders. (p. 132)

Q

Quality The result of an operating environment in which a product or service meets or conforms to a customer's specifications the first time it is produced or delivered. (p. 436)

Quality of earnings The substance of earnings and their sustainability into future periods. (p. 553)

Queue time The time a product spends waiting to be worked on once it enters a new operation or department. (p. 133)

Quick ratio A measure of short-term debt-paying ability; calculated as (Cash + Marketable Securities + Receivables) ÷ Current Liabilities. (p. 550)

R

Receivables turnover A ratio for measuring the average number of times receivables are turned into cash during an accounting period; calculated as Net Sales ÷ Average Accounts Receivable. (p. 548)

Regression analysis A mathematical approach to separating a mixed cost into its variable and fixed components. (p. 171)

Relevant range The span of activity in which a company expects to operate. (p. 166)

Residual income (RI) The operating income that an investment center earns above a minimum desired return on invested assets; calculated as Investment Center's Operating Income − (Desired ROI × Assets Invested). (p. 258)

Responsibility accounting An information system that classifies data according to areas of responsibility and reports each area's activities by including only the categories that the assigned manager can control. (p. 248)

Responsibility center An organizational unit whose manager has been assigned the responsibility of managing a portion of the organization's resources. The five types of responsibility centers are a cost center, discretionary cost center, revenue center, profit center, and investment center. (p. 248)

Restructuring The estimated cost of a change in a company's operations, usually involving the closing of facilities and the laying off of personnel. (p. 556)

Return on assets A measure of profitability that shows how efficiently a company uses its assets to produce income; calculated as Net Income ÷ Average Total Assets. (p. 542)

Return on assets pricing method Focuses on earning a specified rate of return on the assets employed in the operation; also called the *balance sheet method*. (p. 400)

Return on equity A measure of how much income is earned on each dollar invested by the company's owners/stockholders; calculated as Net Income ÷ Average Stockholders' Equity. (p. 546)

Return on investment (ROI) A traditional performance measure that takes into account both operating income and the assets invested to produce that income; calculated as Operating Income ÷ Assets Invested. (p. 256)

Return on quality (ROQ)   The result that occurs when the marginal revenues possible from a higher-quality good or service exceed the marginal costs of providing that higher quality. (p. 436)

Revenue center   A responsibility center whose manager is accountable primarily for revenue and whose success is based on its ability to generate revenue. (p. 250)

S

Sales budget   A detailed plan, expressed in both units and dollars, that identifies the product (or service) sales expected during an accounting period. (p. 204)

Sales forecast   A projection of the estimated sales in units based on an analysis of external and internal factors. (p. 205)

Sales mix   The proportion of each product's unit sales relative to the company's total unit sales. (p. 176)

Sales mix decision   A decision to select the alternative that maximizes the contribution margin per constrained resource. (p. 340)

Scatter diagram   A chart of plotted points that helps determine whether a linear relationship exists between a cost item and its related activity measure. (p. 169)

Segment margin   A segment's sales revenue minus its direct costs (direct variable costs and direct fixed costs traceable to the segment). (p. 338)

Sell-or-process-further decision   A decision about whether to sell a joint product at the split-off point or sell it after further processing. (p. 343)

Selling and administrative expenses budget   A detailed plan of operating expenses, other than those related to production, that are needed to support sales and overall operations during an accounting period. (p. 209)

Service unit cost   The cost to perform one service. (p. 5)

Short-run decision analysis   The systematic examination of any decision whose effects will have the greatest impact within the next year. (p. 332)

Six Sigma   A level of quality by which customers would perceive a company's products and services as perfect. (p. 436)

Software as a service (SaaS)   A database system that utilizes the Internet, social media, and mobile technologies to manage all business activities on demand. (p. 449)

Special order decisions   Decisions about whether to accept or reject special orders at prices below the normal market prices. (p. 336)

Split-off point   A specific point in the production process at which two or more joint products become separate and identifiable. At that point, a company may choose to sell the product as is or process it into another form for sale to a different market. (p. 343)

Standard costing   A method of cost control with three components: a standard, or predetermined, performance level; a measure of actual performance; and a measure of the difference, or variance, between standard and actual performance. (p. 290)

Standard costing method   A method of cost measurement that uses the estimated or standard costs of direct materials, direct labor, and overhead to calculate a product or service unit cost. (p. 18)

Standard costs   Realistic estimates of costs based on analyses of both past and projected operating costs and conditions. (p. 290)

Standard direct labor cost   The standard wage for direct labor multiplied by the standard hours of direct labor. (p. 292)

Standard direct materials cost   The standard price for direct materials multiplied by the standard quantity for direct materials. (p. 291)

Standard fixed overhead rate   Total budgeted fixed overhead costs divided by an expression of capacity, usually normal capacity in terms of standard direct labor hours or units. (p. 292)

Standard overhead cost   The sum of the estimates of variable and fixed overhead costs in the next accounting period. (p. 292)

Standard variable overhead rate   Total budgeted variable overhead costs divided by an expression of capacity, such as the expected number of standard machine hours or standard direct labor hours. (p. 292)

Statement of cost of goods manufactured   A formal statement summarizing the flow of all manufacturing costs incurred during an accounting period. (p. 15)

Static budgets   Budgets that are prepared once a year and do not change during the annual budget period. (p. 219)

Step cost   A cost that remains constant in a relevant range of activity and increases/decreases in a stairstep-like manner when activity is outside the relevant range. (p. 166)

Storage time   The time a product spends in materials storage, work in process inventory, or finished goods inventory. (p. 133)

Strategic objectives   Broad, long-term goals that determine the fundamental nature and direction of a business and that serve as a guide for decision making. (p. 20)

Strategic planning   The process by which management establishes an organization's long-term goals. (p. 218)

Sunk cost   A cost that was incurred because of a previous decision and that cannot be recovered through the current decision. (p. 333)

Supply chain The path that leads from the suppliers of the materials from which a product is made to the final consumer. Also called the *supply network*. (pp. 20, 124)

Support services Components of the value chain that facilitate the primary processes but do not add value to a product or service. (p. 124)

T

Tactical objectives Mid-term goals that position an organization to achieve its long-term strategies. (p. 20)

Target costing A pricing method designed to enhance a company's ability to compete, especially in markets for new and emerging products; calculated as Target Price – Desired Profit. (p. 404)

Theoretical capacity The maximum productive output for a given period in which all machinery and equipment are operating at optimum speed, without interruption. Also called *ideal capacity*. (p. 166)

Theory of constraints (TOC) A management theory that contends that limiting factors, or bottlenecks, occur during the production of any product or service, but that once managers identify such a constraint, they can focus their attention and resources on it and achieve significant improvements. (p. 135)

Throughput time The time it takes to move a product through the entire production process. (p. 133)

Time and materials pricing A pricing method used by service companies by which they use two computations: one for direct labor and one for materials and parts; also called parts and labor pricing. (p. 402)

Total direct labor cost variance The difference between the standard direct labor cost for good units produced and actual direct labor costs. (p. 299)

Total direct materials cost variance The difference between the standard cost and actual cost of direct materials. Also called *good units produced*. (p. 296)

Total fixed overhead cost variance The difference between actual fixed overhead costs and the standard fixed overhead costs that are applied to good units produced using the standard fixed overhead rate. (p. 304)

Total manufacturing costs The total costs of direct materials, direct labor, and overhead incurred and transferred to Work in Process Inventory account during an accounting period. Also called *current manufacturing costs*. (p. 11)

Total overhead cost variance The difference between actual overhead costs and standard overhead costs applied. (p. 302)

Total quality management (TQM) A management tool that requires that all parts of a business work together to build quality into the business's product or service. (pp. 138, 436)

Total variable overhead cost variance The difference between actual variable overhead costs and the standard variable overhead costs that are applied to good units produced using the standard variable overhead rate. (p. 303)

Transfer price The price at which goods and services are charged and exchanged between a company's divisions or segments. (p. 408)

Trend analysis A variation of horizontal analysis in which percentage changes are calculated for several successive years instead of for two years. (p. 536)

U

Underapplied overhead costs The amount by which actual overhead costs exceed the overhead costs applied using the predetermined overhead rate for the accounting period. (p. 57)

Unit-level activities Activities performed each time a unit is produced. (p. 128)

V

Value-adding activity An activity that adds value to a product or service as perceived by the customer. (p. 126)

Value-adding cost The cost of an activity that increases the market value of a product or service. (p. 7)

Value-based systems An accounting system that provides better customer-related, activity-based information than does the traditional cost-based system. (p. 124)

Value chain A sequence of activities, or primary processes, that add value to a product or service; also includes support services that facilitate these activities. (p. 124)

Variable cost(s) A cost that changes in direct proportion to a change in productive output (or some other measure of volume). (pp. 6, 164)

Variable cost formula A straight line equation, $Y = a(X)$, where Y is total variable cost, a is the variable rate per unit, and X is the units produced. (p. 165)

Variable costing A method of preparing profit center performance reports that classifies a manager's controllable costs as either fixed or variable and produces a variable costing income statement. (p. 254)

Variable overhead efficiency variance The difference between the standard direct labor hours allowed for good units produced and the actual hours worked multiplied by the standard variable overhead rate per hour. (p. 304)

Variable overhead spending variance The difference between actual variable overhead costs and the standard variable overhead rate multiplied by the actual hours used. Also called the *variable overhead rate variance*. (p. 304)

Variance   The difference between a standard cost and an actual cost. (p. 290)

Variance analysis   The process of computing the differences between standard costs and actual costs and identifying the causes of those differences. (p. 291)

Vertical analysis   A technique for analyzing financial statements that uses percentages to show how the different components of a statement relate to a total figure in the statement. (p. 537)

W

Work cell   An autonomous production line that can perform all required operations efficiently and continuously. (p. 132)

Work in Process Inventory account   An inventory account used to record the manufacturing costs incurred and assigned to partially completed units of product. (p. 10)

Write-down   A reduction in the value of an asset below its carrying value on the balance sheet. Also called a *write-off*. (p. 556)

Z

Zero-based budgeting   Budgets that are prepared anew each period. All budget items must be justified; nothing is taken for granted. (p. 220)

COMPANY NAME INDEX

SUBJECT INDEX